Publications of the
Carnegie Endowment for International Peace
Division of Economics and History

ECONOMIC AND SOCIAL HISTORY OF THE WORLD WAR

British Series

JAMES T. SHOTWELL, Ph.D., LL.D.

GENERAL EDITOR

With the Collaboration of the

BRITISH EDITORIAL BOARD

Sir William H. Beveridge, K.C.B., M.A., B.C.L. (*Chairman*)
F. W. Hirst, Esq.
Thomas Jones, M.A., LL.D.
J. M. Keynes, C.B., M.A.
Professor W. R. Scott, D.Phil., Litt.D., LL.D., F.B.A.
Professor J. T. Shotwell (*ex officio*)

DICTIONARY OF
OFFICIAL WAR-TIME
ORGANIZATIONS

BY

N. B. DEARLE, M.A., D.Sc.

Formerly Fellow of All Souls College
Oxford

LONDON : HUMPHREY MILFORD
OXFORD UNIVERSITY PRESS
NEW HAVEN : YALE UNIVERSITY PRESS
1928

Printed in Great Britain

EDITOR'S PREFACE

In the autumn of 1914, when the scientific study of the effects of war upon modern life passed suddenly from theory to history, the Division of Economics and History of the Carnegie Endowment for International Peace proposed to adjust the programme of its researches to the new and altered problems which the War presented. The existing programme, which had been prepared as the result of a conference of economists held at Berne in 1911, and which dealt with the facts then at hand, had just begun to show the quality of its contributions; but for many reasons it could no longer be followed out. A plan was therefore drawn up at the request of the Director of the Division, in which it was proposed, by means of an historical survey, to attempt to measure the economic cost of the War and the displacement which it was causing in the processes of civilization. Such an ' Economic and Social History of the World War ', it was felt, if undertaken by men of judicial temper and adequate training, might ultimately, by reason of its scientific obligations to truth, furnish data for the forming of sound public opinion, and thus contribute fundamentally towards the aims of an institution dedicated to the cause of international peace.

The need for such an analysis, conceived and executed in the spirit of historical research, was increasingly obvious as the War developed, releasing complex forces of national life not only for the vast process of destruction but also for the stimulation of new capacities for production. This new economic activity, which under normal conditions of peace might have been a gain to society, and the surprising capacity exhibited by the belligerent nations for enduring long and increasing loss—often while presenting the outward semblance of new prosperity—made necessary a reconsideration of the whole field of war economics. A double obligation was therefore placed upon the Division of Economics and History. It was obliged to concentrate its work upon the problem thus presented, and to study it as a whole; in other words, to apply to it the tests and disciplines of history. Just as the War itself was a single event, though penetrating by seemingly unconnected ways to the remotest parts of the world, so the analysis of it must be developed according to a plan at once all-embracing and yet adjustable to the practical limits of the available data.

During the actual progress of the War, however, the execution of this plan for a scientific and objective study of war economics proved impossible in any large and authoritative way. Incidental studies and surveys of portions of the field could be made and were made under the direction of the Division, but it was impossible to undertake a general history for obvious reasons. In the first place, an authoritative statement of the resources of belligerents bore directly on the conduct of armies in the field. The result was to remove as far as possible from scrutiny those data of the economic life of the countries at war which would ordinarily, in time of peace, be readily available for investigation. In addition to this difficulty of consulting documents, collaborators competent to deal with them were for the most part called into national service in the belligerent countries and so were unavailable for research. The plan for a war history was therefore postponed until conditions should arise which would make possible not only access to essential documents but also the co-operation of economists, historians, and men of affairs in the nations chiefly concerned, whose joint work would not be misunderstood either in purpose or in content.

Upon the termination of the War the Endowment once more took up the original plan, and it was found with but slight modification to be applicable to the situation. Work was begun in the summer and autumn of 1919. In the first place a final conference of the Advisory Board of Economists of the

Division of Economics and History was held in Paris, which limited itself to planning a series of short preliminary surveys of special fields. Since, however, the purely preliminary character of such studies was further emphasized by the fact that they were directed more especially towards those problems which were then fronting Europe as questions of urgency, it was considered best not to treat them as part of the general survey but rather as of contemporary value in the period of war settlement. It was clear that not only could no general programme be laid down *a priori* by this conference as a whole, but that a new and more highly specialized research organization than that already existing would be needed to undertake the Economic and Social History of the War, one based more upon national grounds in the first instance and less upon purely international co-operation. Until the facts of national history could be ascertained, it would be impossible to proceed with comparative analysis ; and the different national histories were themselves of almost baffling intricacy and variety. Consequently the former European Committee of Research was dissolved, and in its place it was decided to erect an Editorial Board in each of the larger countries and to nominate special editors in the smaller ones, who should concentrate, for the present at least, upon their own economic and social war history.

The nomination of these boards by the General Editor was the first step taken in every country where the work has begun. And if any justification was needed for the plan of the Endowment, it at once may be found in the lists of those, distinguished in scholarship or in public affairs, who have accepted the responsibility of editorship. This responsibility is by no means light, involving, as it does, the adaptation of the general editorial plan to the varying demands of national circumstances or methods of work ; and the measure of success attained is due to the generous and earnest co-operation of those in charge in each country.

Once the editorial organization was established there could be little doubt as to the first step which should be taken in each

1569·60

instance toward the actual preparation of the history. Without documents there can be no history. The essential records of the War, local as well as central, have therefore to be preserved and to be made available for research in so far as is compatible with public interest. But this archival task is a very great one, belonging of right to the governments and other owners of historical sources and not to the historian or economist who proposes to use them. It is an obligation of ownership ; for all such documents are public trust. The collaborators on this section of the war history, therefore, working within their own field as researchers, could only survey the situation as they found it and report their findings in the form of guides or manuals ; and perhaps, by stimulating a comparison of methods, help to further the adoption of those found to be most practical. In every country, therefore, this was the point of departure for actual work ; although special monographs have not been written in every instance.

This first stage of the work upon the war history, dealing with little more than the externals of archives, seemed for a while to exhaust the possibilities of research. And had the plan of the history been limited to research based upon official documents little more could have been done, for once documents have been labelled ' secret' few government officials can be found with sufficient courage or initiative to break open the seal. Thus vast masses of source material essential for the historian were effectively placed beyond his reach, although much of it was quite harmless from any point of view. While war conditions thus continued to hamper research, and were likely to do so for many years to come, some alternative had to be found.

Fortunately such an alternative was at hand in the narrative, amply supported by documentary evidence, of those who had played some part in the conduct of affairs during the War, or who, as close observers in privileged positions, were able to record from first- or at least second-hand knowledge the economic history of different phases of the Great War, and of its effect upon society.

Thus a series of monographs was planned consisting for the most part of unofficial yet authoritative statements, descriptive or historical, which may best be described as about half-way between memoirs and blue-books. These monographs make up the main body of the work assigned so far. They are not limited to contemporary, war-time studies ; for the economic history of the war must deal with a longer period than that of the actual fighting. It must cover the years of ' deflation ' as well, at least sufficiently to secure some fairer measure of the economic displacement than is possible in purely contemporary judgements.

With this phase of the work the editorial problems assumed a new aspect. The series of monographs had to be planned primarily with regard to the availability of contributors, rather than of source material as in the case of most histories ; for the contributors themselves controlled the sources. This in turn involved a new attitude towards those two ideals which historians have sought to emphasize, consistency and objectivity. In order to bring out the chief contribution of each writer it was impossible to keep within narrowly logical outlines ; facts would have to be repeated in different settings and seen from different angles, and sections included which do not lie within the strict limits of history ; and absolute objectivity could not be obtained in every part. Under the stress of controversy or apology, partial views would here and there find their expression. But these views are in some instances an intrinsic part of the history itself, contemporary measurements of facts as significant as the facts with which they deal. Moreover, the work as a whole is planned to furnish its own corrective ; and where it does not, others will.

In addition to this monographic treatment of source material, a number of studies by specialists is already in preparation, dealing with technical or limited subjects, historical or statistical. These monographs also partake to some extent of the nature of first-hand material, registering as they do the data of history close enough to the source to permit verification in ways impossible later. But they also belong to that constructive process by which history passes from analysis to synthesis. The process is a long and difficult one, however, and work upon it has only just begun. To quote an apt characterization, in the first stages of a history like this one is only ' picking cotton '. The tangled threads of events have still to be woven into the pattern of history ; and for this creative and constructive work different plans and organizations may be needed.

In a work which is the product of so complex and varied co-operation as this, it is impossible to indicate in any but a most general way the apportionment of responsibility of editors and authors for the contents of the different monographs. For the plan of the History as a whole and its effective execution the General Editor is responsible ; but the arrangement of the detailed programmes of study has been largely the work of the different Editorial Boards and divisional Editors, who have also read the manuscripts prepared under their direction. The acceptance of a monograph in this series, however, does not commit the editors to the opinions or conclusions of the authors. Like other editors, they are asked to vouch for the scientific merit, the appropriateness and usefulness of the volumes admitted to the series ; but the authors are naturally free to make their individual contributions in their own way. In like manner the publication of the monographs does not commit the Endowment to agreement with any specific conclusions which may be expressed therein. The responsibility of the Endowment is to History itself—an obligation not to avoid but to secure and preserve variant narratives and points of view, in so far as they are essential for the understanding of the War as a whole.

J. T. S.

AUTHOR'S PREFACE

This book seeks to set out in a concise form, suitable for reference by those interested, the main facts about the various organizations officially established in Great Britain and Ireland in connexion with the Great War. What was aimed at was to give briefly their origin (method and time of appointment), their objects and purposes, their composition (i.e. departments, bodies, and interests represented), and, where possible, the dates of their dissolution, together with a reference to sources of information which would enable those who wished to follow up the matter further. The contents cover not only special branches or sections of Government Departments, but Commissions, Committees, and similar bodies. The extent of the material available made some limits necessary, and the chief of them may be shortly indicated.

First, the term 'official' was regarded as implying a connexion, direct or indirect, with the Central Government. It thus covered organizations established by it or in co-operation with it, including bodies set up locally for such purposes, either by existing Local Authorities or otherwise. It did not, however, include normally specifically local bodies established in entire independence of the Central Authorities, unless, as with certain Allotment Committees, they definitely illustrated particular features of the organization. Similarly, non-official organizations were not included, except in a few special cases.

Secondly, the period of the war was taken to cover post-war reconstruction. A rough time-limit was set with the end of the year 1922, but organizations established subsequently were included, if their connexion with the war was sufficiently clear. It also proved difficult, especially during the war, to decide whether particular bodies were or were not set up as a result of it. In the actual war period and the immediate sequel, therefore, the benefit of the doubt was given liberally; but after 1920 the test for admission was far stricter.

A third question arose in regard to international organizations. These were included when Great Britain was represented in them and affected by them. This, however, would have involved a very great addition to the mass of information, if extended to post-war international organizations, notably those of the League of Nations. Consequently the signing of the Peace Treaties was made a rough dividing line for their inclusion.

The subject-matter is arranged under sections for the different Government Departments, which are placed in alphabetical order, additional sections being included for the Cabinet, Parliament, and the Privy Council. The subject-matter in each section is also arranged alphabetically. Where more than one Department was concerned, the entry was put under the Department chiefly affected, the connexion with others being indicated by cross-references. To save space, a number of abbreviations have been adopted, a list of which is given on pp. xv–xvii below.

In conclusion I desire to thank most warmly those who have contributed assistance and advice in the preparation of this book. In particular, I would refer to Sir William Beveridge, K.C.B., Director of the London School of Economics and Political Science, who suggested not only the undertaking of the work, but the main lines on which it should proceed. I am also indebted to him for much valuable assistance in various directions. Among others from whom I received valuable help and advice were Professor W. G. S. Adams, Dr. Hubert Hall, Mr. B. M. Headicar and the staff of the British Library of Political Science, and the officials of the Newspaper Room of the British Museum. For all such help, I owe a deep debt of gratitude.

N. B. D.

June 1928.

CONTENTS

Contents

ABBREVIATIONS

So far as the available information allows, each entry in the Dictionary attempts to deal briefly with a number of subjects which are denoted by the abbreviations set out immediately below:

App. = Appointed, Appointment.
Obj. = Object.
Repr. = Representing.
Ref. = Reference.
Diss. = Dissolution.

In addition, a number of names and titles of Government Departments, Journals or Newspapers, and certain public and other bodies are indicated by the following list of abbreviations, which is arranged in alphabetical order of these abbreviations:

A.A.C.	Aeronautics Advisory Committee.
A.B.	2nd Air Board, established Dec. 1916.
A.C.	Army Council.
A.C.(S)	Advisory Committee to the Committee and Department of Scientific and Industrial Research.
Adm.	Admiralty.
A.E.U.	Amalgamated Engineering Union.
A.M.	Air Ministry.
A.S.E.	Amalgamated Society of Engineers.
B.A.	Board of Agriculture (becoming Ministry Dec. 1919, *see* M.A.).
B.A.(Sc.)	Scottish Board of Agriculture.
B.E.	Board of Education.
B.M.A.	British Medical Association.
B.T.	Board of Trade (heading—Trade, Board of).
C.C.B.	Cotton Control Board.
Cd.	Command Papers, series to 1918 inclusive (presented to the House of Commons by the Command of his Majesty).
C.E.	Chancellor of the Exchequer.
C.M.D.	Coal Mines Department.
Cmd.	Command Papers, series from 1919 inclusive (as with Cd.).
C.O.	Colonial Office.
Col.	Column.
Cole.	G. D. H. Cole, Trade Unionism and Munitions, in the Carnegie Endowment's Social and Industrial History of the World War British Series.
C.S.	Chief Secretary to the Lord Lieutenant of Ireland.
C.S.C.	Civil Service Commission.
D.A.T.I.	Department of Agriculture and Technical Instruction, Ireland.
D.C.	Development Commission.
E.E.	Employment (formerly Labour) Exchanges.
E.P.D.	Excess Profits Duty.
F.B.I.	Federation of British Industries.
F.B.(Sc.)	Fishery Board (Scotland).
F.C.	Food Controller.

F.C.C.(s)	Local Food Control Committee(s).
F.O.	Foreign Office.
F.P.D.	Food Production Department (Board of Agriculture).
G.B.	Great Britain.
G.I.	Government of India.
Hall.	Dr. Hubert Hall, Litt.D., F.S.A., British Archives and the History of the World War, in the Carnegie Endowments Social and Industrial History of the World War, British Series.
H.C.	House of Commons.[1]
H.L.	House of Lords.
H.M.F.	His Majesty's Forces.
H.M.S.O.	Stationery Office unnumbered publications.
H.M.W.C.	Health of Munition Workers Committee.
I.C.S.	Indian Civil Service.
I.F.S.	Irish Free State.
In.O.	India Office.
I.O.	Irish Office.
J.B.A.	Journal of the Board (Ministry) of Agriculture.
J.I.C.(s)	Joint Industrial Council(s).
L.A.(s)	Local Authoritie(s).
L.C.B.	Liquor Control Board (Central Control Board, Liquor Traffic).
L.C.C.	London County Council.
L.E.A.(s)	Local Education Authoritie(s).
L.E.C.(s)	Local Employment (formerly Advisory) Committee(s) (Ministry of Labour).
L.G.	Labour Gazette (monthly) (Ministry of Labour ; formerly Board of Trade).
L.G.B.	Local Government Board.
L.G.B.(Sc.)	Local Government Board (Scotland).
L.G.B.(I.)	Local Government Board (Ireland).
L.L.	Lord Lieutenant of Ireland.
L.Y.B.	Labour Year Book.
M.A.	Ministry of Agriculture (since Dec. 1919)
M.B.	Ministry of Blockade.
M.F.	Ministry of Food.
M.H.	Ministry of Health.
M.I.	Ministry of Information.
M.L.	Ministry of Labour.
M.M.	Ministry of Munitions.
M.N.S.	Ministry, Department, of National Service.
M.Pen.	Ministry of Pensions.
M.R.	Ministry of Reconstruction.
M.R.C.	Medical Research Committee, (later) Council.
M.S.	Ministry of Shipping.
M.S.A.(s)[2]	Military Service Act(s).
M.T.	Ministry of Transport.
M.W.A.(s)[2]	Munitions of War Act(s).

[1] H.C. No. (with date) refers to papers in the annual series of Accounts and Papers 'ordered to be printed by the House of Commons'.

[2] A date after one of these abbreviations refers to the Act of a particular year.

N.F.J.	National Food Journal (Ministry of Food).
N.H.I.C.	National Health Insurance Commission or Joint Committee. Where a single National Commission is intended the abbreviations Eng. (England), Sc. (Scotland), I. (Ireland), and W. (Wales) are added.
N.M.B.	National Maritime Board.
N.P.L.	National Physical Laboratory.
N.R.F.	National Relief Fund.
N.U.R.	National Union of Railwaymen.
N.U.T.	National Union of Teachers.
Orton.	W. A. Orton, Labour in Transition.
O.S.C.	Overseas Settlement Committee, (later) Department.
O.T.D.	Overseas Trade Department.
O.W.	Office of Works (heading—Works, Office of).
P.C.	Privy Council.
P.M.	Prime Minister.
P.O.	Post Office.
q.v.	Quo vide, i.e. see (reference).
R.A.C.	Advisory Council to Ministry of Reconstruction.
R.A.F.	Royal Air Force.
R.A.M.C.	Royal Army Medical Corps.
R.C.	Reconstruction Committee.
R.E.C.	Railway Executive Committee.
R.F.C.	Royal Flying Corps.
S.B.H.	Scottish Board of Health.
S.C.	Statutory Committee on War Pensions.
S.C.P.	Standing Committee on Prices (Profiteering Acts).
S.C.T.	Standing Committee on Trusts (Profiteering Acts).
Sec.	Secretary.
S.E.D.	Scottish Education Department (and prior to Nov. 1918 Committee of Council for Education in Scotland).
S.I.R.	Dept. (formerly Committee) for Scientific and Industrial Research.
S.O.	Scottish Office.
S.S.	Secretary of State for Scotland.
T.	Times.
Tre.	Treasury.
T.U.(s)	Trade Union(s).
T.U.C.	Trade Union Congress.
U.I.	Unemployment Insurance.
U.K.	United Kingdom.
U.S.A.	United States of America.
W.A.E.C.(s)	War Agricultural Executive (County) Committee(s).
W.C.B.	Wool Textile Production Board of Control.
W.E.A.	Workers' Educational Association.
W.M.V.	War Munition Volunteers.
W.O.	War Office.
W.P.C.(s)	Local War Pension Committee(s).
W.T.D.	War Trade Department.
W.W.A.C.(s)	Women's War Agricultural (County) Committee(s).

ADMIRALTY, THE

ABBREVIATION

Adm. = Admiralty.

ACCELERATION OF CLAIMS.—*See* Claims.

ACCOUNTING, ADMIRALTY, EXPERT COMMITTEE.—*App.* by Adm. in 1921 or 1922. *Obj.* To investigate Adm.'s system of accounting. *Repr.* Tre., experts. *Ref.* H.C., Nos. 39, &c., 1922, p. xxxix. *See also* Financial Control below.

ADMIRALTY, BOARD OF, MAINTENANCE COMMITTEE.—*App.* during reorganization of work of Board in 1917. *Obj.* To deal with questions of personnel, production, finance, &c., to meet needs of Operations Committee (*see* next entry), subject to final responsibility of full Board. *Repr.* Members of Board of Admiralty responsible for these matters. *Ref.* Cd. 9005. *Presumably Permanent.*

ADMIRALTY, BOARD OF, OPERATIONS COMMITTEE.—*App.* as with Maintenance Committee (preceding entry). *Obj.* To deal with naval strategy and organization and equipment of the Navy as a fighting force. *Repr.* The Board, Naval Staff. *Ref.* Cd. 9005. *Presumably Permanent.*

AIRCRAFT, ADMIRALTY EXPENDITURE IN AMERICA.—In H.C., Nos. 83, &c., 1919, p. xv, reference is made to two Committees of Inquiry into Admiralty purchases of aeronautical supplies from an American firm. Details are not given.

ANTI-SUBMARINE SCIENTIFIC RESEARCH COMMITTEES.—*App.* by Adm. in Manchester, Glasgow, and London in 1918. *Obj.* To organize co-operation of scientific and engineering talent in anti-submarine campaign, and carry out researches for which naval establishments are not available. *Repr.* Scientists, engineers, manufacturers. *Ref.* Cmd. 325, p. 46. *Diss.* Close of War.

ANTI-SUBMARINE SELECTION COMMITTEE.—*App.* by Adm. in 1918. *Obj.* To make preliminary selection of officers and men for training in use of special anti-submarine apparatus. *Repr.* Practical naval officers, sound experts, psychologists. *Ref.* Cmd. 325, p. 47. *Diss.* Close of War (or earlier).

AIR BOARD : AIR, JOINT, COMMITTEE.—*See* A.M., W.O.

AIR JOINT WAR COMMITTEE.—*See* W.O.

ARC WELDING.—*See* Welding.

AVIATION, BRITISH COMMISSION.—*See* M.M.

CLAIMS, ACCELERATION, COMMITTEE.—*App.* by Adm., with consent of Tre., in 1915 or 1916. *Obj.* To assist in settling claims of Admiralty contractors regarding extra costs of acceleration of work. *Repr.* Adm., Parliament (members experienced in such work). *Ref.* H.C., No. 123, 1917, p. vii.

COASTING TRADE, ADMIRALTY, COMMITTEE.—*App.* prior to June 1917. Full details not available. *See* Cd. 8741, p. 2.

CONTRABAND COMMITTEE.—Joint Appointment.—*See* F.O.

CONTRACTS.—*See* Adm.

DEMOBILIZATION.—*See* M.L., Tre.

EXPENDITURE EMERGENCY INTER-DEPARTMENTAL COMMITTEE.—Joint Appointment.—*See* Tre.

FINANCE COMMITTEE, ADMIRALTY.—*See* H.C., Nos. 83, &c., 1919, p. vii, which refers to this as constituted in 1892, and reconstituted with extended powers in 1919, to ensure continuous financial criticism.

FINANCIAL CONTROL, ADMIRALTY, COMMITTEE OF INQUIRY. —*App.* by Adm. in 1920, following recommendation of Public Accounts Committee, in 1919. *Obj.* To investigate provision for financial control at Adm., with special reference to accounting. *Repr.* Official and expert. *Ref.* H.C., Nos. 54, &c., 1920, p. xii. *Diss.* Apparently in 1921.
(This is also described as special Committee for inquiring into Adm. system of accounting.)

FISHERMEN AND FISHING VESSELS DEMOBILIZATION COMMITTEE.—*App.* jointly by Adm. and Fishery Departments in 1918. *Obj.* To organize demobilization as affecting fishing industry. *Repr.* Adm., Fishery Departments. *Ref.* Cmd. 231, p. xiv. *Diss.* After Demobilization.

FISHERMEN, PURCHASE OF ADMIRALTY TRAWLERS AND DRIFTERS, SUB-COMMITTEE.—*App.* by Reconstruction Admiralty Committee (q.v.) during 1918. *Obj.* To prepare scheme to assist fishermen to purchase. *Repr.* The Committee and presumably fishing interests. *Ref.* Cmd. 833, p. xvii.

GRATUITY, MERCHANT SHIPS.—*See* M.S.

INSTITUTES.—*See* W.O.

INVENTIONS AND RESEARCH BOARD, ADMIRALTY.—*App.* by Adm., apparently early in the War. *Obj.* To promote and develop inventions and research in connexion with naval war. *Repr.* Adm. ; various experts. *Ref.* Cd. 9005, p. 62.
The Board had a Central Committee. In 1918 a well-known engineer was appointed as Director of Experiments and Research to supervise executive arrangements, and Local Committees, composed largely of scientists, and Experimental Stations were established in various places.

IRON ORE IMPORTS CONTROL, CENTRAL COMMITTEE.—*App.* presumably by Adm., before April 1916. *Obj.* To control chartering of vessels, and apportion and direct tonnage, for iron-ore imports. *Repr.* Official and expert. *Ref.* T., April 5, 1916, p. 14.
(N.B. The actual origin of this Committee is not stated in the reference and the appointing body may have been B.T. and not Adm.)

JERRAM COMMITTEE.—*See* Naval Pay.

LABOUR EMBARGOES.—*See* M.M.

MAINTENANCE COMMITTEE.—*See* Admiralty, Board of.

MARINE ENGINEER CORPS, ROYAL.—*App.* and organized by Adm. in 1918. *Obj., Repr.* To form mobile body in shipbuilding and other work, consisting of men unfit for military service. *Ref.* Cmd. 325, p. 54. *Diss.* Presumably at end of War.

MERCANTILE MARINE.—*See* B.T.

MERCHANT SHIPS.—*See* Royal Dockyards.

MINES INFORMATION COMMITTEE.—*App.* by Adm. at request of Allied Governments, late in 1918. *Obj.* To promulgate internationally information regarding dangerous areas and safe routes at sea. *Repr.* Not stated. *Ref.* Cmd. 325, p. 49.

NAVAL, ALLIED, COMMISSION.—*App.* by Allied Governments, Nov. 1918. *Obj.* To supervise carrying out of naval conditions of Armistice. *Repr.* Allied Governments and Admiralties. *Ref.* Cmd. 325, p. 41.

NAVAL, ALLIED, COUNCIL.—*App.* by chief Allied Governments, Dec. 1917. *Obj.* To co-ordinate conduct of naval war and development of scientific operations in connexion with it. *Repr.* Admiralties and Naval Staffs of countries concerned. *Ref.* Cd. 9005, p. 38 ; Cmd. 325, p. 54.

NAVAL LIAISON, INTER-ALLIED, COMMITTEE.—*App.* by Allied Governments about end of 1917. *Obj.* To provide liaison between Military Staff of Supreme War Council (*see* Cabinet) and the Naval Council (above). *Repr.* Military and naval officers of Allies. *Ref.* Cmd. 325, p. 22.

NAVAL PAY COMMITTEE (JERRAM COMMITTEE).—*App.* by Adm., Jan. 1919. *Obj.* To investigate existing rates of pay, allowances, &c., of ranks (other than officers) in Royal Navy and Marines, and make recommendations. *Repr.* Naval officers, with advisory assessors representing the men. *Ref.* Cmd. 149. *Diss.* Mar. 1919.

NAVAL PAY COMMITTEE, OFFICERS SUB-COMMITTEE.—*App.* by Adm. as Sub-Committee of Naval Pay Committee, early in 1919. *Obj.* To investigate pay, allowances, &c. of officers (including reserve officers) of Royal Navy and Marines and make recommendations. *Repr.* Naval officers. *Ref.* Cmd. 270. *Diss.* May 1919.

NAVAL PAY COMMITTEE, OFFICERS ON HALF-PAY SUB-COM-MITTEE.—*Obj.* To deal with officers on half-pay. *Otherwise* as preceding entry.

NAVAL PAY.—*See also* Cabinet *under* Army and Navy Pay.

NAVAL PRIZE, HIGH COURT TRIBUNAL.—*App.* under Naval Prize Act, 1918, in Aug. 1918, with provision for filling of vacancies by the Crown. *Obj.* To decide questions connected with Naval Prize Fund established under the Act. *Repr.* Lords of Appeal, Public Services, The Navy. *Ref.* P.G.A., 1918.

NAVAL SUPPLY DEPOTS SAFETY COMMITTEE.—*App.* by Adm. in or before 1921. *Obj.* To investigate and advise on safety of depots. *Repr.* Adm. H.O. and others. *Ref.* Cmd. 1632, p. 2.

NAVAL WELFARE ADVISORY COMMITTEE.—*App.* by Adm. by Oct. 1919. *Obj.* To consider and make recommendations on conditions of

Lower Deck. *Repr.* Not stated, but presumably included representatives of the men. *Ref.* T., 15th Oct. 1919, p. 9.

NAVY AND AIR FORCE.—*See* Cabinet.

OBSOLETE WARSHIPS, SALE CONTRACTS, COMMITTEE.—*App.* by Adm. in 1921. *Obj.* To investigate operation of contracts for sale of warships for immediate breaking-up in dockyard towns. *Repr.* Adm. *Ref.* H.C., No. 33, 1923, p. 163. *Diss.* Nov. 1921.

OPERATIONS COMMITTEE.—*See* Admiralty, Board of.

ORDER IN COUNCIL OF MARCH, 1915.—Joint Committee. *See* F.O.

OXYGEN SUPPLIES ALLOCATION COMMITTEE.—*App.* by Adm. prior to Aug. 1917, and W.O. representatives subsequently added. *Obj.* To organize distribution of available supplies. *Repr.* Adm., W.O. (later) and others. *Ref.* Cd. 9144, p. 24.

PORT AND TRANSIT.—*See* M.S.

PRESS BUREAU.—Separate department under instructions of Adm. and W.O. *See* W.O.

PRESS CENSORSHIP COMMITTEE.—Joint appointment. *See* W.O.

PROCURATOR-GENERAL.—*See* Tre.

RECONSTRUCTION, ADMIRALTY, COMMITTEE.—*App.* by Adm. early in 1918. *Obj.* To deal with demobilization, resettlement, and other post-war questions affecting Adm. *Repr.* Adm., other Government Departments affected, naval officers. *Ref.* Cmd. 325, p. 53. *Diss.* Not before 1920.

(Various Sub-Committees were appointed to deal with particular problems.)

ROYAL DOCKYARDS, UTILIZATION FOR CONSTRUCTION OF MERCHANT SHIPS.—This subject was reported on by the Contracts Departmental (Colwyn) Committee (Cmd. 581). *See* Tre.

SHALE INDUSTRY, SCOTLAND, COMMITTEES.—*See* M.M.

SHIPBUILDING ADVISORY COMMITTEE.—*App.* by Adm. about June 1917, as Adm. Committee, a similar Committee (*see* T., 24th Nov. 1917, p. 6) having previously been attached to Lloyds. *Obj.* To advise generally on expediting mercantile shipbuilding, and carry out certain duties in placing and following up contracts. *Repr.* Shipbuilders and repairers, marine engineers. *Ref.* B.T.J., 29th Nov. 1917. *Diss.* Absorbed in Shipbuilding Council (*see* below), Nov. 1917.

SHIPBUILDING, AUXILIARY DEPARTMENT.—Established by Adm. in 1917 to organize work for destruction of submarines. *See* T., 24th Nov. 1917, p. 6.

SHIPBUILDING COUNCIL.—*App.* by Adm., Nov. 1917. *Obj.* To advise generally, and in particular as to means of increasing and expediting both naval and mercantile shipbuilding and repairs. *Repr.* Adm., the Navy, shipbuilding and marine engineering firms (including members of Shipbuilding Advisory Committee). *Ref.* B.T.J., 29th Nov. 1917.

SHIPBUILDING DEPARTMENT.—*App.* by War Cabinet, May 1917, under a Controller of the Navy. *Obj.* To co-ordinate claims of Adm. and mercantile marine on shipbuilding capacity of country, and secure largest possible output of mercantile tonnage, responsibility being transferred from M.S. *Repr.* Official and expert. *Ref.* Cd. 9005, p. 110.

(The Department had three branches—Dockyards and Shipbuilding (Navy Requirements), Armament Production, and Auxiliary Shipbuilding (including provision of all mercantile tonnage). There was also a special staff dealing with output and development of suggestions for expediting specifications and output.)

SHIPBUILDING, EXPEDITING, DISTRICT COMMITTEES.—*App.* by Adm., Mar. 1917, in chief shipbuilding centres. *Obj.* To assist in carrying out Adm. scheme for expediting and increasing naval and merchant shipbuilding. *Repr.* Adm. (Shipyard Labour Department), shipbuilders, &c. *Ref.* T., 26th Mar. 1917, p. 5.

SHIPPING CONTROL COMMITTEE.—*See* M.S.

SHIP REPAIRS, NEGOTIATING COMMITTEE.—*See* M.S.

SHIPS, DIVERSION IN WAR TIME, COMMITTEE.—*App.* by Adm., apparently early in the War. *Obj.* To control distribution of diverted ships to most suitable ports for discharge. *Repr.* Adm. and presumably shipping interests. *Ref.* Cd. 8469.

SHIPS, MERCHANT.—*See* Royal Dockyards.

SHIPS, RATES FOR REQUISITIONING, COMMITTEE.—*App.* presumably by Adm. early in the War. *Obj.* To fix rates of payment (subsequently called Blue Book rates) for requisitioned ships. *Repr.* Leading shipowners. *Ref.* H.C., No. 136, 1920, p. iii.

SHIPYARD LABOUR ADVISORY COMMITTEE.—*App.* by Adm., Feb. 1917. *Obj.* To advise and co-operate with the Shipyard Labour Department (*see* next entry) in organizing supplies of labour for naval and merchant shipbuilding. *Repr.* Engineering and Shipbuilding Employers' Federations and T.U.'s. *Ref.* B.T.J., 8th Feb. 1917.

SHIPYARD LABOUR DEPARTMENT.—*App.* by Adm. under a Director of Shipyard Labour, Jan. 1917. *Obj.* To organize uniform national policy for utilizing available labour for naval and merchant shipbuilding, exercising powers hitherto held by M.M. over establishments concerned. *Repr.* Official and expert. *Ref.* B.T.J., 18th Jan. 1917. *Diss.* Winter of 1918–19.

SHIPYARD TIME-KEEPING COMMITTEES.—*App.* by Shipyard Trade Unions in certain districts, under agreements with Adm. and employers in 1916 or later. *Obj.* To deal with cases of persistent bad time-keeping. *Repr.* Shipyard T.U.'s. *Ref.* H.C., No. 181, 1917.

STEEL ROLLING.—*See* M.M.

STOCKTAKING, ARMAMENT SUPPLY DEPOTS (ROYAL NAVY), COMMITTEE.—*App.* by Adm. in 1920. *Obj.* To investigate results of stocktaking and exercise Adm.'s powers of writing off deficiencies. *Repr.* Adm. and others. *Ref.* H.C., No. 56, 1921, p. 163. *Diss.* Before end 1921.

SUPPLY DEPOTS, ADMIRALTY, COMMITTEE.—*App.* by Adm. in 1920. *Obj.* To investigate and advise upon the protection and safety of armament supply depots. *Repr.* Adm., H.O. (Explosives Department) and others. *Ref.* Cmd. 1324, p. 2 ; 1632, p. 2. *Diss.* Probably 1921.

TRAMP OWNERS COMMITTEE.—*App.* by owners of tramp steamers, about Sept. 1914. *Obj.* To negotiate with Adm. for rates for requisitioned tramp steamers. *Repr.* Tramp owners. *Ref.* H.C., No. 245, 1919, p. 3. *Diss.* Not clear whether continued or not after conclusion of agreement.

TRANSPORT ARBITRATION BOARD, ADMIRALTY.—*App.* by Royal Warrant on 3rd Aug. 1914. *Obj.* To deal with disputed claims over vessels requisitioned by Adm., and, after the War, in respect of vessels under Indemnity Act, 1920. *Repr.* Government nominees, ship and cargo owners, underwriters, marine insurance, marine engineers, seamen. *Ref.* B.T.J., 20th Aug. 1914 ; P.G.A., 1920. *Diss.* Continued after Aug. 1920 by Indemnity Act.

TRAWLER OWNERS REPRESENTATIVE COMMITTEE.—*App.* by the trawler owners during 1916. *Obj.* To negotiate with Adm. and put in force agreements for hire, valuation, and compensation for loss of trawlers. *Repr.* Trawler owners. *Ref.* Cmd. 585, p. 25. *Diss.* After Armistice apparently.

WELDING COMMITTEE.—*App.* by Adm. in 1918. *Obj.* To investigate questions of welding in ship-construction. *Repr.* Not stated. *Ref.* Cmd. 340, p. 61.

AGRICULTURE AND FISHERIES, ENGLAND AND WALES, AND (SUBSEQUENTLY) MINISTRY OF

The *Board of Agriculture and Fisheries* was in existence at the outbreak of the War. It became a Ministry by the Ministry of Agriculture and Fisheries Act, of 23rd Dec. 1919 (9 & 10 Geo. V, c. 91). *See* Public General Acts, 1919.

The *Food Production Department* was established by the Board in Jan. 1917 under a Director-General, four Assistant Directors-General and Assistant Secretary. Its *objects* were to organize labour supply (including women's labour), sowings, supply and distribution of tractors and machinery, use of fertilizers and feeding stuffs, increased production of eggs and cheese, and cultivation of unused land, and to act as clearing house for, and supervise generally, the work of War Agricultural (County) Committees (q.v.). It *represented* mainly the permanent staff of the Board, with assistance of expert agriculturalists. Its main divisions or branches were for Labour, Local Organization, Mechanical Cultivation (*see* below), Supplies, Technical, Women, and Secretarial. *Reference*, J.B.A., Feb. and Mar. 1917. With the decrease in its functions after the war its work was gradually *reabsorbed* into general organization of the Board, and it finally came to an end in March 1920.

ABBREVIATIONS

B.A.	Board of Agriculture and Fisheries to Dec. 1919.
M.A.	Ministry of Agriculture and Fisheries from Jan. 1920.
F.P.D.	Food Production Department.
W.A.E.C.(s)	War Agricultural Executive (County) Committee(s).
W.W.A.C.(s)	Women's War Agricultural (County) Committee(s).
J.B.A.	Journal of Board (Ministry) of Agriculture.

AGRICULTURAL ADMINISTRATIVE COUNCIL.—*App.* by M.A. in 1920 under the Ministry of Agriculture and Fisheries Act, 1919. *Obj.* To advise M.A. on all administrative matters. *Repr.* Official Departmental Body. *Ref.* J.B.A., Jan. 1921 (Report of Lord Lee's speech). *Permanent Body.*

AGRICULTURAL ADVISORY COMMITTEE.—*See* Food, Home Production, Advisory Committee. (This latter was the original title, which was subsequently changed to the Agricultural Advisory Committee.)

AGRICULTURAL ADVISORY COMMITTEE (ENGLAND AND WALES).—*App.* by M.A. under the Ministry of Agriculture and Fisheries Act, 1919, in Dec. 1920. *Obj.* To advise M.A. on all matters in regard to exercise of their powers over agriculture. *Repr.* Agricultural Councils (England and Wales), County Agricultural Committees, landowners, tenant farmers, Labour, Scotland (for certain purposes). *Ref.* P.G.A., 1919.

AGRICULTURAL ADVISORY COUNCIL, CENTRAL.—*App.* jointly by B.A., B.A.(Sc.), D.A.T.I., and F.C., July 1918. *Obj.* To amalgamate the separate Advisory Committees of the Departments, and to carry out their duties jointly. *Repr.* B.A., B.A.(Sc.), D.A.T.I., F.C., and various agricultural organizations. *Ref.* J.B.A., Aug. 1918. *Diss.* Presumably on

constitution of Agriculture, Councils of, England and Wales (q.v.), in Dec. 1919 under the Ministry of Agriculture and Fisheries Act, 1919.
(*See also* Feeding Stuffs, for Feeding Stuffs Sub-Committee.)

AGRICULTURAL COLLEGES, LOSSES DUE TO THE WAR.—*See* B.E. under Universities, Losses.

AGRICULTURAL COMMISSIONERS (MINIMUM PRICES).—*App.* jointly by M.A., B.A.(Sc.), B.T., and Tre., Jan. 1921, under the Agriculture Act, 1920. *Obj.* To fix minimum prices under the Act. *Repr.* The Four Departments. *Ref.* P.G.A., 1920 ; J.B.A., Feb. 1921. *Diss.* 1st Oct. 1921 under Corn Production Acts (Repeal) Act, 1921.

AGRICULTURAL COMMITTEE OF THE CABINET.—*Ref.* without details, Cmd. 1810, p. 2.

AGRICULTURAL COMMITTEES OF COUNTY BOROUGH COUNCILS, AND LONDON COUNTY COUNCIL.—*App., Obj., Ref.* as with Committees of County Councils (*see* next entry), except that establishment permissive and not compulsory. *Ref.* P.G.A., 1919.

AGRICULTURAL COMMITTEES (STATUTORY) OF COUNTY COUNCILS.—*App.* by County Councils, with approval of M.A., under Ministry of Agriculture and Fisheries Act during 1920. *Obj.* To act as authorities for all agricultural matters in their counties and co-ordinate existing Committees dealing with agriculture within their counties under a single supervision. *Repr.* Two-thirds chosen by the County Council, including usually nominees of county agricultural organizations and allotment-holders. *Ref.* P.G.A., 1919, and J.B.A., Nov. 1920. *Permanent Bodies.*
(For Sub-Committees, *see under* Horticulture, War Agricultural Executive Committees, and Women.)

AGRICULTURAL CONSULTATIVE COMMITTEE ON HOME-GROWN FOODSTUFFS.—*App.* by B.A., Aug. 1914. *Obj.* To review position and secure best use of home-grown food-supplies. *Repr.* Farmers and other agriculturalists, experts. *Ref.* J.B.A., Aug. 1914. *Diss.* Jan. 1917.

AGRICULTURAL COSTINGS COMMITTEE.—Joint appointment, *see* M.F.

AGRICULTURAL EDUCATION ASSOCIATION COMMITTEES.—*App.* by the Association, July 1918. *Obj.* To survey and report upon various branches of agricultural education. *Repr.* The Association. *Ref.* J.B.A. June 1919. *Diss.* Apparently May 1919 (reports published).

AGRICULTURAL EXECUTIVE COUNTY BOROUGH SUB-COMMITTEES.—*App.* by County Committees (*see* next entry) and the County Borough Councils for boroughs surrounded wholly or partly by the County area, from June 1919. *Obj.* To administer within the boroughs the powers referred to in the next entry, subject to the approval of County Committees. *Repr.* County Committees ; County Borough Councils. *Ref.* J.B.A., Feb. 1919.

AGRICULTURAL EXECUTIVE COUNTY COMMITTEES.—*App.* by B.A. and County Councils from June 1919. *Obj.* To administer as agents of the Board various powers under the D.O.R.A. regulations and Corn Production Act, 1918, superseding the War Agricultural Executive Committees, and subsequently entrusted with training of disabled men. *Repr.* B.A., County Councils, Labour, Women. *Ref.* J.B.A., Feb. 1919.

AGRICULTURAL EXECUTIVE COUNTY COMMITTEES, THRESH-ING SUB-COMMITTEES.—*App.* by main Committees at instance of B.A., replacing Sub-Committees of previous War Committees now dissolved, after June 1919. *Obj.* To arrange threshing operations and rates of payment with local threshing proprietors for season of 1919–20. *Repr.* Former Committees reconstituted. *Ref.* J.B.A., Sept. 1919.

(For other Sub-Committees, *see under* Horticulture, War Agriculture, &c.)

AGRICULTURAL EXECUTIVE DISTRICT COMMITTEES.—*App.* by County Executive Committees from June 1919. *Obj.* To assist the main Committees locally in carrying out their functions. *Repr.* As with District Committees of War Agricultural Executive Committees and largely composed of their members. *Ref.* J.B.A., June 1919.

(For appointment of District Executive Officers, see Cmd. 325, p. 236.)

AGRICULTURAL IMPLEMENTS AND MACHINERY COMMITTEE (PROFITEERING ACTS).—*See* B.T.

AGRICULTURAL MACHINERY ADVISORY COMMITTEE.—Joint appointment with M.M. and M.F., *see* M.M.

AGRICULTURAL MACHINERY AND IMPLEMENTS DEPARTMENTAL COMMITTEE.—*App.* by B.A., May 1919. *Obj.* To arrange for testing, adaptation, and improvement of inventions, machinery, and new devices, and advise generally on developments of agricultural machinery. *Repr.* B.A., agriculture, engineering, and scientific experts, agricultural research. *Ref.* Cmd. 506. *Diss.* About end of 1919.

AGRICULTURAL MACHINERY TESTS, ADVISORY COMMITTEE.—*App.* by M.A. in autumn of 1920, apparently on recommendation of Departmental Committee. *Obj.* To advise M.A. on conditions, &c., for admission to tests. *Repr.* Agricultural engineers, farmers, landowners, workpeople, agricultural scientists, and experts. *Ref.* J.B.A. Dec. 1921.

AGRICULTURAL POLICY, WALES, SUB-COMMITTEE OF THE WELSH AGRICULTURAL COUNCIL.—*App.* by the Council Nov. 1921. *Obj.* To draft suggestions for an agricultural policy for Wales. *Repr.* Much as with the Council. *Ref.* J.B.A., July 1922. *Diss.* Draft report presented, May 1922.

AGRICULTURAL PRODUCE.—*See* Produce.

AGRICULTURAL RELIEF OF ALLIES COMMITTEE.—*App.* by the Royal Agricultural Society in 1915. *Obj.* To organize and co-ordinate help to farmers in allied countries to resume cultivation of holdings. *Repr.* Agriculture generally, including Central Chamber of Agriculture, County Agricultural Associations, National Farmers' Union, Breeding Societies, agriculturalists of Dominions. *Ref.* J.B.A., June 1920, pp. 251–2.

For Scottish Committee, *see* Board of Agriculture (Scotland) under Belgian Relief. A Sub-Committee was also established in Canada which supplied small tools, p. 253.

AGRICULTURAL SUB-COMMITTEES of the Local Advisory (Employment) Committees of Ministry of Labour.—*See* War Agricultural Executive Committees, Labour Sub-Committees.

AGRICULTURAL TRIBUNAL OF INVESTIGATION.—*App.* by P.M., Dec. 1922. *Obj.* To report upon methods adopted abroad to promote food production and employment on the land, and to advise on means of securing similar results in G.B. *Repr.* Experts in Economics and Political Science, with Agricultural Assessor. *Ref.* Cmd. 2145. *Diss.* May 1924.

AGRICULTURE AND FISHERIES BOARD AND ROYAL AGRI-CULTURAL SOCIETY JOINT COMMITTEE.—*App.* apparently between March 1916 and June 1917. Other details lacking. *See* Cd. 8741, p. 2.

AGRICULTURE, CONDITIONS, TRIBUNAL.—*See* Cab.

AGRICULTURE, COUNCIL OF, ENGLAND.—*App.* under Ministry of Agriculture and Fisheries Act, 1919, in 1920. *Obj.* To assist M.A. meeting at least twice yearly for public discussion of questions affecting agriculture and rural industries. *Repr.* M.A., County and County Borough Agricultural Committees, Agricultural Wages Board, owners, tenant farmers, agricultural labour, women, horticulturalists, agricultural education. *Ref.* P.G.A. 1919. *Permanent Body.*

AGRICULTURE, COUNCIL OF, WALES.—*App., Obj.* as with Council for England. *Repr.* As with England, except for omission of horticulturalists, and inclusion of University of Wales to represent agricultural education. *Ref.* P.G.A. 1919. *Permanent Body.*
  (Under the Act the two Councils may agree to act together.)

AGRICULTURE ORGANIZING COMMITTEE.—*App.* (formed) by leading men interested in agriculture, Dec. 1916. *Obj.* To develop proposals to organize agriculture to increase food production and overcome difficulties of immediate future. *Repr.* Prominent landowners and public men connected with agriculture. *Ref.* T., 4th Dec. 1916, p. 6.

AGRICULTURE, ROYAL COMMISSION.—*App.* by Royal Warrant of 15th July 1919. *Obj.* To inquire into economic prospects of British Agriculture, with special reference to prices, costs, wages, and hours. *Repr.* Agriculturists and Labour (equal numbers), agricultural education, research and statistics, banking, chartered accountants, legal profession. *Ref.* Cmd. 473. *Diss.* During 1920.
  (*See also under* Machinery.)

ALLOTMENTS ADVISORY COMMITTEE.—*App.* by M.A., Dec. 1922. *Obj.* To advise M.A. in matters affecting allotments in England and Wales. *Repr.* M.A., L.A.'s (urban and rural), Parliamentary Allotments Committee, Agricultural Organization Society, landholders, allotment holders. *Ref.* T., 12th Dec. 1922.

ALLOTMENTS COMMITTEES, LOCAL.—*App.* by some L.A.'s in 1916 (late) or 1917 under Cultivation of Lands Order. *Obj.* To put Order in operation, secure land, organize allotments, &c. *Repr.* L.A.'s (in some cases), allotment holders, horticulturalists, &c. *Ref.* J.B.A. April and June 1917. *Diss.* Some may still exist for general allotment purposes.
  (*See also* Croydon Vacant Lands Cultivation Committee.)

ALLOTMENTS CULTIVATION IN CUMBERLAND AND WESTMOR-LAND COMMITTEE.—*App.* by L.A.'s, and interests concerned in these counties, Aug.–Sept. 1914. *Obj.* To promote and assist cultivation of allotments to increase food supply. *Repr.* L.A., landowners, farmers, horticulturalists, manufacturers. *Ref.* J.B.A., Sept. 1914.

ALLOTMENTS DEPARTMENT, AGRICULTURAL ORGANIZATION SOCIETY, PROVISIONAL COMMITTEE ON CO-OPERATION WITH ALLOTMENT HOLDERS.—*App.* by the Society, early 1917. *Obj.* To prepare scheme for a department to supply co-operatively needs of allotment holders. *Repr.* The Society, Allotment Holders' Associations. *Ref.* J.B.A., Mar. 1918.

(N.B. The Society was undergoing considerable reorganization in 1917, largely in connexion with war needs.)

ALLOTMENTS, DEPARTMENTAL COMMITTEE.—*App.* by M.A. and S.S. jointly, about July 1921. *Obj.* To investigate provision of allotments by L.A.'s and to make recommendations to obtain adequate provision and security of tenure. *Repr.* M.A., L.A.'s (including Scotland), Agricultural Organization Society, Allotments Holders' Societies. *Ref.* J.B.A. Sept. 1921.

ALLOTMENTS, LOCAL ASSOCIATIONS' COMMITTEES.—*App.* by Associations of allotment holders and others, often with official encouragement, during and since the War. *Obj.* To organize Associations' work of purchasing and developing allotments. *Repr.* Local allotment holders. *Ref.* J.B.A. July, Nov. 1917, Feb. 1922. *Diss.* Some apparently permanent.

ALLOTMENTS OF TENANTS ON SERVICE MANAGEMENT COMMITTEES.—*App.* in some areas from about Mar. 1916, sometimes at least by L.A.'s. *Obj.* To manage allotments of tenants during absence on military service. *Repr.* L.A.'s allotment holders and their families. *Ref.* J.B.A., April 1916. *Diss.* Presumably after return of tenants.

ARMY CATTLE COMMITTEE. *App.* by B.A. in first half of 1917. *Obj.* To arrange purchases of cattle in U.K. for feeding the Army from Sept.–Dec. 1917. *Ref.* J.B.A., Mar. 1920 (p. 1256), H.M.S.O., 1918. *Diss.* The Committee's active duties terminated about end of 1917, but its second report was not published till 1919.

BASIC SLAG COMMITTEE.—*App.* by M.A. July, 1920, as *permanent Committee. Obj.* To consider development, improvement, and extended use of basic slag. *Repr.* M.A., steel-makers, slag-grinders, agricultural consumers. *Ref.* J.B.A., Sept. 1921.

(N.B. The appointment was due to changes in basic slag caused by considerable substitution during War of basic open hearth for Bessemer process in steel manufacturing.)

BASKET-MAKING COMMITTEE.—Assisted by F.P.D. *See* M.Pen.

BEES, HONEY, STUDY OF HABITS, COMMITTEE.—*App.* by B.A. July 1918. *Obj.* To investigate habits and epidemic diseases of bees, to secure improvements in bee-keeping. *Repr.* B.A., Universities, agricultural and other research, bee-keepers. *Ref.* J.B.A., Aug. 1918.

BEE-KEEPING COUNTY COMMITTEES.—*App.* in many counties by Horticultural Sub-Committees of W.A.E.C.'s at request of F.P.D., from Nov. 1918. *Obj.* To carry out schemes for rationing of candy and bee-food and for local registration and restocking of bees. *Repr.* Horticultural Sub-Committees, bee-keeping interests. *Ref.* J.B.A., Dec. 1918. *Diss.*

Originally intended to continue for some time, but may have ceased to exist early in 1921.

BELGIAN RELIEF (AGRICULTURAL), SCOTTISH COMMITTEE.— *See* B.A.(Sc.)

BOTANIC SOCIETY.—*See* Royal Botanic Society.

BOTANY, NATIONAL INSTITUTE OF AGRICULTURAL, COUNCIL. —*App.* as *permanent body* by the Institute (established 1915) and Agricultural and Milling Associations, at instigation of B.A., in 1918.   *Obj.* To supervise generally the Institute's work in co-operation with the Institute of Plant Breeding, in improving and increasing national seed supply.   *Repr.* B.A., The Institute, Royal Agricultural Society, associations in seed trade, farmers, millers, agricultural merchants.   *Ref.* J.B.A., July 1918, Feb. 1922.

   (N.B. Three Committees of the Council exercise general supervision over the main sections of its work—the Crop Improvement Branch, the Official Seed Testing Station, direct control over which was delegated to the Institute by M.A. after passing of the Seeds Act 1920, and the Potato Testing Station.)

BOVINE TUBERCULOSIS.—*See* Milk.

CANNING COMMITTEE (BOARD OF AGRICULTURE).—Mentioned in Cmd. 905, p. 75.   No details.

CATTLE, BRITISH, UTILIZATION COMMITTEE.—*App.* some time prior to June 1917, apparently a B.A. Committee.   No other details. *See* Cd. 8741, p. 3.

CATTLE, IMPORTATION, ROYAL COMMISSION.—*App.* by Royal Warrant, 11th May 1921.   *Obj.* To inquire generally into effects and desirability of importation of cattle for purposes other than immediate slaughter and as means of restoring British herds after war losses.   *Repr.* Five eminent public men, connected with Industry, Civil Service, Legal Profession, the Universities, Chartered Accountants.   *Ref.* J.B.A., June, 1921.   *Diss.* Oct. 1921.   *See also under* Embargo.

CENSUS OF AGRICULTURAL LABOUR, COMMITTEE OF SCRUTINY.—*See* W.O.

COMMERCIAL BRANCH (BOARD OF AGRICULTURE).—*App.* temporarily by B.A., in or before Dec. 1918, by amalgamation of existing sections of B.A.   *Obj.* To take charge of measures of commercial reconstruction in connexion with agriculture.   *Repr.* The sections concerned, *Ref.* J.B.A., Dec. 1918.

COMPULSORY TILLAGE APPEAL TRIBUNAL.—*App.* by B.A. late in 1918 under the Corn Production Act, 1917.   *Obj.* To hear objections by farmers against compulsory tillage order.   *Repr.* Agricultural experts nominated by B.A.   *Ref.* P.G.A., 1917.   Cmd. 929, pp. 77–8.

   (Similar bodies were apparently appointed in Scotland and Ireland, with corresponding composition and duties.)

CONCILIATION.—*See under* Wages.

CO-OPERATION.—*See* Village Clubs Association.

COST OF LIVING.—*See under* Financial Results of Farming.

CREDIT, AGRICULTURAL, COMMITTEE.—*App.* by M.A. as Sub-Committee of Agricultural Committee of Cabinet, Oct. 1922. *Obj.* To investigate existing credit facilities for agriculturalists in G.B. and make recommendations. *Repr.* M.A., B.A. (Sc.), persons with expert knowledge. *Ref.* Cmd. 1810. *Diss.* Jan. 1923.

CREDIT FACILITIES FOR FARMERS, SUB-COMMITTEE OF THE AGRICULTURAL ADVISORY COMMITTEE.—*App.* by the Committee, at request of the Agricultural Council for England, Nov. 1921. *Obj.* To consider possibility of reviving pre-war schemes for providing credits for farmers. *Repr.* The Agricultural Council and the Advisory Committee, bankers, estate agents. *Ref.* J.B.A., Jan., June 1922. *Diss.* Reported Mar. 1922.

CROP IMPROVEMENT.—*See under* Botany, National Institute of Agricultural.

CROYDON, VACANT LANDS CULTIVATION COMMITTEE.—*App.* early in the war by local effort, with branches later at Purley and Wallington. *Obj.* To secure cultivation of vacant lands and undertake inspection, letting, &c., through a Gardens' Sub-Committee. *Repr.* Landholders, horticulturalists, solicitors, local residents generally. *Ref.* J.B.A., Jan. 1915. *Diss. See under* Allotments.

DAIRY, DAIRYING.—*See* Milk.

DRAINAGE.—*See* Land Drainage.

EDUCATION, AGRICULTURAL, SUB-COMMITTEES OF AGRICULTURAL (COUNTY COUNCIL) COMMITTEES.—Formation would take place in cases where agricultural education is transferred from Education to Agricultural Committees, in which case the former should be suitably represented on the Sub-Committee. *See* J.B.A., Feb. 1920.

EGG COLLECTION FOR WOUNDED, NATIONAL, COMMITTEE.— *Obj.* To secure adequate supplies of new-laid eggs for wounded in hospital. *Ref.* J.B.A., Oct. 1915. Other details lacking.

ELECTRO-CULTURE COMMITTEE.—*App.* by B.A., Jan. 1918. *Obj.* To advise on all electrical questions affecting electro-culture, especially on apparatus and electrical measurements. *Repr.* B.A. (sec.), Royal Society, Institute of Civil and Electrical Engineering. *Ref.* J.B.A., Feb. 1918.

EMBARGO ON CANADIAN CATTLE, SCIENTIFIC COMMITTEE.— *App.* by M.A. in 1920. *Obj.* To investigate question of disease in connexion with removal of embargo. *Repr.* Scientists. *Ref.* J.B.A., Feb. 1920.

EMBARGO.—*See also* Cabinet, Cattle.

EX-SERVICE MEN.—*See* Land Settlement.

FARM PRODUCE FOR HIS MAJESTY'S FORCES, COUNTY COMMITTEES.—*App.* by B.A. in consultation with W.O. for counties and groups of counties in Oct. 1914. *Obj.* To secure satisfactory working of arrangements for supply of farm produce for the Forces. *Repr.* Leading tenant farmers in the districts concerned, nominated by chief Agricultural Societies and Associations. *Ref.* J.B.A., Oct., Nov. 1914.

FARM PRODUCE FOR H.M. FORCES, ORGANIZING COMMITTEE— *App.* by B.A., in consultation with W.O., late in 1914. *Obj.* To facilitate purchase of farm produce for the Forces direct from the farmers. *Repr.* B.A., W.O., Chambers of Agriculture, Agricultural Societies, Farmers' Associations, Farmers' Central Trading Board. *Ref.* J.B.A., Oct., Nov. 1914.

FARM PRODUCE, LOSS BY FIRE, JOINT COMMITTEE.—*App.* jointly by B.A. and F.C., in 1917 or spring of 1918. *Obj.* To investigate problem and means of avoiding loss. *Repr.* Not stated. *Ref.* J.B.A., July 1918.

FARM SETTLEMENT TRADING ACCOUNTS SUB-COMMITTEES.— *App.* by Land Settlement Department, of B.A., in spring of 1920. *Obj.* To report on methods of valuing assets for trading accounts of farm settlements of ex-service men. *Repr.* Agricultural and other experts. *Ref.* Cmd. 1184, pp. 31–3. *Diss.* May 1920.

FARM WORKERS' BRANCH, BOARD OF AGRICULTURE.—*App.* by the Board, Mar. 1919, the existing Labour Branch of Food Production Department, which dealt with supply of labour for agriculture, being merged into it. *Obj.* To deal with all matters affecting agricultural labour, not covered by Wages Board (conciliation, profit-sharing, international arrangements, &c.). *Repr.* Official and expert. *Ref.* T., 7th Mar. 1919, p. 7.

FEEDING-STUFFS COMMITTEE.—Largely representing B.A., B.A.(Sc.) and D.A.T.I., but appointed by M.M. *See* M.M.

FEEDING-STUFFS SUB-COMMITTEE, CENTRAL AGRICULTURAL ADVISORY COUNCIL.—*App.* by the Council in late summer or autumn of 1918. *Obj.* To consider questions arising in regard to feeding-stuffs. *Repr.* As with the Council. *Ref.* J.B.A., Jan. 1919.

FERTILIZERS, ALLOCATION, JOINT COMMITTEE. *App.* jointly by B.A., B.A.(Sc.), and D.A.T.I., May 1918. *Obj.* To allocate available supplies equitably between England and Wales, Scotland and Ireland. *Repr.* The three Departments. *Ref.* Cmd. 185, p. lii.

FERTILIZERS, CENTRAL DEPARTMENTAL COMMITTEES.— *See* M.M.

FERTILIZERS COMMITTEE.—*App.* May 1915 and terminated Jan. 1917. *See* Hall, p. 361; Cd. 8741, p. 5. Other details lacking.

FERTILIZERS, COUNTY ADVISORY COMMITTEES OF MER-CHANTS.—*App.* by National Association of Corn and Agricultural Merchants, with approval of F.P.D., about May 1918. *Obj.* To advise, &c., on working of scheme for distributing fertilizers to farmers. *Repr.* Merchants (covered by the Association), Agricultural Co-operative Societies. *Ref.* J.B.A., June 1918.

FERTILIZERS, DEPARTMENTAL COMMITTEE.—*App.* by B.A., Nov. 1915. *Obj.* To organize adequate supplies for farmers. *Repr.* B.A., B.A.(Sc.), D.A.T.I., Adm., B.T., M.M., W.O. *Ref.* J.B.A., Nov. 1915.

(*See also under* Potash below, and B.T., under Sulphuric Acid and Fertilizers.)

FINANCE, STANDING COMMITTEE. *App.* by F.P.D., Nov. 1917. *Obj.* To examine and revise expenditure of F.P.D., *Repr.* Presumably official with financial experts. *Ref.* H.C., No. 151, 1917–18, p. 28.

FINANCIAL RESULTS OF FARMING, COMMITTEE OF AGRICULTURAL WAGES BOARD.—*App.* by the Board, Mar. 1918. *Obj.* To inquire into financial results of farming and market-gardening and cost of living of rural workers. *Repr.* The Board (employers, workmen, and appointed members), agricultural research, economists, statisticians. *Ref.* Cmd. 76. *Diss.* Mar. 1919.

FISH CANNING.—*See* Fish, Technical Committees.

FISH (CURED) COMMITTEE.—Originally appointed by B.A., but transferred. *See* M.F.

FISHERY, PORT, COMMITTEES.—*App.* by B.A., in co-operation with Adm., in 1917. *Obj.* To advise and assist in organizing scheme for protection of steam trawlers, and form the connecting link between naval authorities and the fishing industry. *Repr.* Local fishing industry. *Ref.* Cmd. 585, p. 16. *Diss.* Presumably on or after close of War.

FISH FOOD AND MOTOR LOAN COMMITTEE.—*App.* by B.A. originally as Fish Food Committee, Mar. 1917, and reconstituted with fuller title, April 1917, on reconstruction of Motor Loan Committee (q. v.), as Joint Committee with M.F. *Obj.* To assist conservation and distribution of fish, increase production by installation of motor engines in fishing-boats and other means, prevent waste, and encourage substitution of fish for other foods. *Repr.* Parliament, B.A., D.A.T.I., M.F., Adm., D.C. *Ref.* Cmd. 585, pp. xix–xx, 64–74 ; B.T.J., 29th Mar. 1917. *Diss.* Part of functions taken over by Fish Section of M.F., but Committee continued operations till after Armistice, not finally coming to an end till June 1922.

FISH FREEZING.—*See* Fish, Technical, Committees.

FISH, FRESHWATER, COMMITTEE.—*App.* by B.A. Mar. 1917. *Obj.* To consider possibilities of, and examine scheme for increasing home food supplies from, freshwater fish and eels. *Repr.* Parliament, Thames Conservancy, Salmon and Trout Fisheries' Associations, Angling Societies and Journals, piscatorial research, owners of fishing rights. *Ref.* J.B.A., Mar. or April 1917 ; Cmd. 497, p. 8. *Diss.* Mar. 1919.

FISHING INDUSTRY, MAN POWER, JOINT (DISTRICT) COMMITTEES OF INQUIRY.—*App.* by B.A., in consultation with Adm., in summer of 1918, for various coastal districts. *Obj.* To investigate fishing personnel and general conditions in their districts. *Repr.* B.A., Adm. (including naval surgeon), local experts. *Ref.* Cmd. 585, p. 33. *Diss.* At Armistice.

FISH, NORWEGIAN PURCHASE COMMITTEE.—B.A., represented. *See* B.T.

FISH, TECHNICAL, COMMITTEES.—*App.* by B.A., during the War. *Obj.* To consider and advise upon various technical subjects (e. g. fish canning, fish freezing). *Repr.* Members of the industry. *Ref.* Cmd. 585, p. xiii.

FLAX CONTROL BOARD.—*See* W.O.

FLAX FACTORIES COSTINGS COMMITTEES.—*App.* by B.A., in 1918 or early 1919. *Obj.* To develop costings' scheme for factories

controlled by Flax Production Branch. *Repr.* Experts (accountants, &c.).
Ref. H.C., No. 116, 1920, p. 34. *Diss.* Probably early in 1919.

FLAX, GOVERNMENT FACTORIES, DISPOSAL COMMITTEE.—
App. by Flax Production Branch of B.A. in autumn of 1919. *Obj.* To
consider proposals for purchase and arrange terms of sale. *Repr.* B.A.
(Flax Production Branch), Tre., Flax Control Board, Disposals Board.
Ref. Cmd. 1208, p. 17. *Diss.* 1920 or early 1921.

FLAX PRODUCTION BRANCH, BOARD OF AGRICULTURE.—*App.*
as temporary branch by B.A., Oct.–Dec. 1917, at instance of Flax Control
Board. *Obj.* To organize increased production of flax in England and
Wales and deal with crop. *Repr.* Departmental, with expert help. *Ref.*
J.B.A., Jan. 1918 ; Cmd. 216. *Diss.* June 1920.

FLAX PRODUCTION COMMITTEE.—*App.* by B.A., Jan. 1918. *Obj.*
To assist in carrying out measures for increasing production in England
and Wales. *Repr.* B.A., flax growers, farmers, dealers, flax users. *Ref.*
J.B.A., Jan. 1918.

FLAX PRODUCTION SCHEME EXAMINATION COMMITTEE.—*App.*
by Flax Control Board. *See* W.O.

FLAX PRODUCTION, YEOVIL LOCAL COMMITTEE. *App.* locally
in 1914 or 1915. *Obj.* To supervise experiments in flax growing. *Repr.*
Local interests. *Ref.* Cmd. 1208, p. 4.

(Other Local Committees are referred to in Cmd. 216, p. 19, but no
details are given.)

**FODDER SHORTAGE AND INCREASED FOOD SUPPLIES, JOINT
COMMITTEE.—**Inter-Departmental Committee. *See* M.F.

FOOD, HOME PRODUCTION, ADVISORY COMMITTEE.—*App.* by
B.A., in Jan. 1917, becoming subsequently the Agricultural Advisory
Committee. *Obj.* To advise on policy, and on means of immediately
increasing home output and securing permanent increase in British ·
agriculture after the War. *Repr.* B.A., D.C., Farmers' Associations,
Small Holdings Movement, general agricultural interests, agricultural
research. *Ref.* J.B.A., Feb. 1917 ; Cd. 9005, p. 158. *Diss.* July 1918,
apparently absorbed into Agricultural Advisory Council (q. v.).

**FOOD PRODUCTION COMMITTEES OF AGRICULTURAL AND
HORTICULTURAL COLLEGES.—***App.* by the Colleges, at request of
B.A., from Mar. 1917, sometimes in co-operation with L.A.'s. *Obj.* To
assist small cultivators to develop vegetable gardening and provide
instruction. *Repr.* The Colleges ; L.A.'s (where concerned); expert
gardeners. *Ref.* J.B.A., April 1917.

**FOOD PRODUCTION COMMITTEES OF LOCAL AUTHORITIES
(INCLUDING PARISH COUNCILS).—***App.* by L.A.'s, at instigation of
B.A., where not already in existence, from Mar. 1917. *Obj.* To secure
full cultivation of vacant lands and private gardens in district, and supply
expert advice. *Repr.* L.A.'s, local residents. *Ref.* J.B.A., April 1917.

(N.B. As B.A. aimed at establishing a Committee or Society for Food
Production in every village and suburban district, these Committees,
therefore, were formed mainly where no War Food Society (q. v.) already
existed.)

FOOD PRODUCTION DEPARTMENT.—*See* Heading to Section.

FOOD PRODUCTION IN ENGLAND AND WALES, DEPARTMENTAL COMMITTEE.—*App.* by B.A., June 1915 (distinct from Agricultural Consultative Committee), and often known as Committee on Home Production of Food. *Obj.* To report on steps to maintain and increase home production of food. *Repr.* Parliament, B.A., agriculture, business experts. *Ref.* Cd. 8048, 8095 (reports). *Diss.* Oct. 1915.

FOOD PRODUCTION SOCIETIES.—*See* War Food Societies.

FOOD SUPPLY OF THE UNITED KINGDOM, COMMITTEE OF ROYAL SOCIETY.—*See* B.T.

FOOT AND MOUTH DISEASE, DEPARTMENTAL COMMITTEE.— *App.* by M.A. about April 1922. *Obj.* To inquire into causes of recent outbreak, and suggest alterations in methods of dealing with it. *Repr.* B.A., agriculturalists. *Ref.* J.B.A., May 1922.

FRUIT DRYING CENTRES.—*App.* by F.P.D. in chief producing districts of the country from July 1917. *Obj.* To secure economy and avoid waste by providing for pulping and drying surplus food and vegetables for winter use. *Repr.* Official and expert. *Ref.* T., 13th Aug. 1917, p. 3. (*See also under* Vegetables.)

GARDENERS, PANEL OF PATRIOTIC.—*App.* jointly by F.P.D. and Royal Horticultural Society early in 1917. *Obj.* To provide expert instruction and advice to allotment holders and Food Production Societies. *Repr.* Expert gardeners (who volunteered to assist). *Ref.* J.B.A., April 1917.

GOATS' MILK.—*See* Milk.

GOVERNMENT STORES, USE AFTER THE WAR, COMMITTEE.— *App.* by B.A., June 1918. *Obj.* To consider best means of utilizing available stores for agriculture and horticulture after the War and of sale to farmers, &c. *Repr.* Landowners, agriculturists, agricultural experts, scientists. *Ref.* J.B.A., July 1918.

GRAIN SUPPLIES COMMITTEE.—*App.* by B.A., Sept. 1915. *Obj.* To take measures necessary to secure provision of emergency reserves of wheat. *Repr.* Not stated. *Ref.* Cd. 8741, Cmd. 1544, pp. 1, 20. *Diss.* Oct. 1916, on establishment of Wheat Commission (*see* M.F.).

HARVEST, CENTRAL COMMITTEE, TEMPORARY ADVISORY COMMITTEES.—*See* M.N.S.

HAY : ALLOTMENT, COUNTY, COMMITTEES ; REQUISITIONING AREA COMMITTEES.—*See* W.O.

HOME FOOD CULTURE SOCIETY (CUMBERLAND AND WESTMORLAND).—Apparently the same as Allotments Cultivation (Cumberland and Westmorland) Committee (q. v.).

HOME PRODUCTION OF FOOD.—*See* Food, and Agricultural Advisory Council on Home-Grown Foodstuffs.

HONEY BEES.—*See* Bees.

C

HOP INDUSTRY CONTROL COMMITTEE.—*App.* by B.A., Oct. 1917, brought subsequently under M.F., and retransferred to M.A., Mar. 1921. *Obj.* To control the industry under war restrictions of brewing, take over stocks except brewers' stocks, and, after Armistice, secure restoration of pre-War acreage under hops. *Repr.* B.A. growers, merchants, factors, brewers, agricultural research. *Ref.* J.B.A., Oct. 1917, Feb. 1922. *Control continued till Aug. 1925.*

HOPS COMMITTEE OF MANAGEMENT.—*App.* by B.A., Aug. 1917. *Obj.* To take over, under Government scheme, 1917 crop and purchase at prices covering cost of production. *Repr.* B.A., hop growers and other interests concerned. *Ref.* B.T.J., 9th Aug. 1917. *Diss.* Apparently absorbed into Hop Control Committee (preceding entry), Oct. 1917.

HORSE BREEDING COMMITTEE (NO. 1).—*See* Horses, Supply, below.

HORSE BREEDING COMMITTEE (NO. 2).—*App.* by B.A., May 1917. *Obj.* To advise on distribution of surplus Army mares after the War and formation of staff to supervise light horse breeding. *Repr.* B.A., W.O., Office of Woods and Forests, landowners. *Ref.* Cd. 8916, p. 25. *Diss.* Oct. 1917.

HORSES, SUPPLY FOR MILITARY PURPOSES, COMMITTEE (HORSE BREEDING COMMITTEE (NO. 1)).—*App.* by B.A., after consultation with Advisory Council on Light Horse Breeding, Aug. 1915. *Obj.* To secure supply of suitable horses for military use. *Repr.* B.A., W.O. horse breeders, agriculturalists, Agricultural and Hunters' Societies. *Ref.* Cd. 8134. *Diss.* Oct. 1915.

HORSES, UTILIZATION AND FEEDING COMMITTEE.—Co-operation in appointment. *See* B.T.

HORTICULTURAL ADVISORY COMMITTEE OF GROWERS AND DISTRIBUTORS, (LATER) COUNCIL.—*App.* originally as Committee, by B.A. about April 1918, and reconstituted as a Council on a representative basis with smaller membership in 1921. *Obj.* To advise on distribution of produce and organization of trades created by the War, and on promotion of market-gardening, fruit-growing, and horticulture generally. *Repr.* B.A., Trade Associations, Royal Horticultural Society ; and after reconstitution, Agricultural T.U.'s, Allotment Holders' Societies. *Ref.* J.B.A., May 1918, July 1921. *Apparently Permanent.*

HORTICULTURAL COUNTY COMMITTEES, SUB-COMMITTEES.— *App.* by County Councils from April 1919, at instance of B.A., as *Permanent Committees*, replacing Sub-Committees of W.A.E.C.'s. *Obj.* To foster commercial and domestic fruit and vegetable cultivation and develop horticultural instruction. *Repr.* County Councils, with special reference to their work as L.E.A.'s. *Ref.* J.B.A., April 1918.

HORTICULTURAL (COUNTY) SUB-COMMITTEES OF WAR AGRI-CULTURAL EXECUTIVE COMMITTEES.—*App.* in some cases in 1917 by W.A.E.C.'s or independent local action, and made general from April 1918, at instance of F.P.D. *Obj.* To develop production and livestock rearing by allotment holders and small cultivators and organize marketing of surplus produce. *Repr.* L.A.'s, and L.E.A.'s, Womens' War Agricultural Committees. *Ref.* J.B.A., April 1918. *Diss.* June–Sept. 1919.

HORTICULTURAL (COUNTY) SUB-COMMITTEES, EXECUTIVE MARKETING COMMITTEES.—*App.* by Sub-Committees, at instance of F.P.D., from April 1918. *Obj.* To organize schemes for marketing surplus produce of allotment holders and small cultivators. *Repr.* Horticultural Sub-Committees. *Ref.* J.B.A., April 1918. *Diss.* By end June 1919.

HORTICULTURAL FOOD PRODUCTION, DISTRICT AND BOROUGH COMMITTEES.—*App.* from April 1918, where not already in existence, at instance of F.P.D., by Horticultural Sub-Committees of W.A.E.C.'s for each borough, urban or rural district in their counties. *Obj.* To work locally under supervision of Horticultural Sub-Committees. *Repr.* Local interests. *Ref.* J.B.A., May 1918. *Diss.* End June 1919.

HORTICULTURAL FOOD PRODUCTION, VILLAGE COMMITTEES. —*App.* from April 1918, where not already in existence, by District and Borough Committees at instance of F.P.D. *Obj., Repr., Diss.* As with District, &c., Committees. *Ref.* J.B.A., April 1918.

HORTICULTURE, CHAMBER OF.—*App.* Nov. 1918 by those interested, apparently as result of war developments. *See* J.B.A., Dec. 1918.

HOSTEL SUB-COMMITTEE OF THE HERTFORDSHIRE WOMEN'S WAR AGRICULTURAL COUNCIL.—*App.* by the Council in June 1916. *Obj.* To manage hostel established for residence and training of girls for work on farms and place them in suitable situations when trained. *Repr.* The Council. *Ref.* J.B.A., Dec. 1916.

INDIAN WHEAT COMMITTEE.—*App.* by B.A., by arrangement with Cabinet Committee on Food Supplies (q. v.), Mar. 1915. *Obj.* To prepare scheme for regulation of shipments of Indian Wheat, and later reappointed (May 1915) to supervise its working. *Repr.* Cabinet, B.A., In. O., Tre., I.C.S., wheat importers. *Ref.* J.B.A., May 1915, Cd. 9090. *Diss.* Oct. 1916, superseded by Wheat Commission (*see* M.F.).

INDIAN WHEAT, CONSULTATIVE COMMITTEE OF AGENTS.— *App.* by Indian Wheat Committee, April or May 1915. *Obj.* To hold day to day consultation regarding sales of Indian wheat. *Repr.* Agent firms. *Ref.* J.B.A., May 1915. *Diss.* Presumably terminated, or taken over by Wheat Commission, Oct. 1916.

INTELLIGENCE DEPARTMENT, MINISTRY OF AGRICULTURE.— *App.* by M.A., about end 1919. *See* J.B.A., Feb. 1920.

JOINT COMMITTEE, BOARD OF AGRICULTURE AND ROYAL AGRICULTURAL SOCIETY.—*App.* May 1917 and came to an end Dec. 1917. *Ref.* Cd. 8741, without details.

JOINT COMMITTEE.—*See* Official Committee, Orders Committee.

LABOUR SUPPLY, COUNTY COMMITTEES.—*App.* locally at suggestion of B.A., in April and May 1915. *Obj.* To investigate and deal with shortages of agricultural labour. *Repr.* General agricultural interests. *Ref.* J.B.A., May 1915. *Diss.* Apparently absorbed in War Agricultural (County) Committees in autumn of 1915.

LABOUR.—*See also under* W.A.E.C.'s.

LADIES' COUNTY WAR SUB-COMMITTEE, WILTSHIRE.—*App.* before June 1916. *Obj.* Presumably to secure supplies of upper and middle class women for work in agriculture. *Repr.* Not stated. *Ref.* J.B.A., June 1916, p. 270.

LAND DRAINAGE COMMITTEES, AREA AND COUNTY.—*App.* as required under the Land Drainage Act, 1918, from Jan. 1919 onwards, by County and County Borough Councils, and B.A., for counties or areas (combinations of counties). *Obj.* To secure proper exercise of power by existing authorities and carry out schemes of drainage in small areas. *Repr.* County Councils, County Borough Councils (if any), B.A. *Ref.* P.G.A., 1917, J.B.A., Jan. 1919, Cmd. 325, p. 325. *Permanent Bodies* subsequently made into Sub-Committees of County Agricultural Committees under Ministry of Agriculture and Fisheries Act, 1919.

(N.B. The Land Drainage Act was largely due to need of increased food production created by the War.)

LAND SETTLEMENT COMMITTEE (WINFREY COMMITTEE).— *App.* by B.A., after June 1916. *Obj.* To report upon provision for land settlement of ex-service men, including situation on demobilization, and upon questions of tithe rent charge and glebe and charity land. *Repr.* Parliament, B.A., landowners, agriculturalists. *Ref.* Cd. 8916. *Diss.* Not before 1918.

LAND SETTLEMENT FOR SOLDIERS AND SAILORS COMMITTEE (VERNEY COMMITTEE).—*App.* by B.A., July 1915. *Obj.* To report upon steps for promotion of land settlement of ex-service men after the War. *Repr.* Parliament B.A., W.O., D.C., L.A.'s, agricultural interests, Legal Profession, Labour. *Ref.* Cd. 8182, 8277. *Diss.* June 1916.

LAND SETTLEMENT OF SERVICE MEN, INTERVIEWING (LOCAL) SUB-COMMITTEES.—*App.* by L.A.'s, on recommendation of B.A., from Mar. 1919. *Obj.* To interview ex-service applicants for land in their districts. *Repr.* L.A.'s concerned. *Ref.* J.B.A., Mar. 1919.

LAND SETTLEMENT.—*See also* Pembrey Farm Settlement.

LINLITHGOW COMMITTEE.—*See* Produce, Agricultural.

LIVESTOCK AND MEAT PRODUCTION, DEPARTMENTAL COMMITTEE.—*App.* by B.A., Jan 1918. *Obj.* To consider statistical returns of number of livestock and home production of meat. *Repr.* B.A., B.A.(Sc.), D.A.T.I., B.T., M.F., statistical experts. *Ref.* J.B.A., Sept. 1919; Cmd. 62. *Diss.* Aug. 1919.

LIVESTOCK COMMITTEES, WOMEN'S INSTITUTES.—*App.* by some Institutes in 1918. *Obj.* To organize communal keeping of pigs by members. *Repr.* Members of Institutes. *Ref.* J.B.A., June 1918.

LOSS OF FARM PRODUCE BY FIRE.—*See* Farm Produce.

MACHINERY AND IMPLEMENT SECTION, FOOD PRODUCTION DEPARTMENT.—*App.* by F.P.D., Feb. 1917, and reorganized as Mechanical Cultivation Division, Oct. 1917. *Obj.* To deal with purchase, supply, and working of agricultural tractors and machinery. *Repr.* Mainly Departmental, apparently with expert assistance. *Ref.* J.B.A., Mar., Oct. 1917. *Diss. See* Heading to Section.

(*See also under* Agricultural and War Agricultural.)

MARKETING, EXECUTIVE COMMITTEES.—*See* Horticultural Sub-Committees.

MARKETING SOCIETIES (CO-OPERATIVE).—*App.* in some districts by Marketing Executive Committees or Horticultural Sub-Committees under control of the former. *Obj.* To carry on co-operative marketing of produce of allotments and small cultivators. *Repr.* Allotment holders and small cultivators in district. *Ref.* J.B.A., June 1918.

MECHANICAL CULTIVATION.—*See under* Machinery above.

MILITARY SERVICE (LOCAL AND APPEAL) TRIBUNALS, AGRICULTURAL REPRESENTATIVES.—*App.* directly by B.A. to Appeal Tribunals, and on nomination of War Agricultural (County) Committees to Local Tribunals, Jan.–Mar. 1916. *Obj.* To represent B.A. before Tribunals, and, later, deal with substitution cases. *Consisting of*: Prominent agriculturalists. *Ref.* J.B.A., April, Dec. 1916. *Diss.* At or after Armistice.

MILK DEPOTS, COUNTRY.—*App.* in certain districts on recommendation of Committee on Production and Distribution of Milk (*see* below) from Dec. 1917. *Obj.* To prevent loss of milk through souring, provide adequate cooling arrangements, and utilize available supplies to best advantage. *Repr.* Not stated. *Ref.* Cd. 8886, p. 7.
 (N.B. Some Depots had been established earlier in Scotland.)

MILK PRICES ADVISORY COMMITTEES (DISTRICT).—*See* M.F.

MILK PRICES, BIRMINGHAM.—*See* L.G.B.

MILK PRODUCTION AND DISTRIBUTION COMMITTEE.—*App.* by B.A., with concurrence of F.C., April 1917. *Obj.* To consider milk trade combinations and general problems of production and distribution. *Repr.* Parliament, B.A., B.A.(Sc.), D.A.T.I., M.F., L.G.B., Consumers Council (added on formation), agriculturalists, labour. *Ref.* Cd. 8606 ; Cmd. 483. *Diss.* End 1919.

MILK PRODUCTION AND DISTRIBUTION, AGRICULTURAL SUB-COMMITTEE.—*App.* by main Committee in 1917. *Obj.* To investigate agricultural problems specially affecting milk production. *Repr.* B.A., M.F., F.P.D., L.G.B., L.G.B.(Sc.), agriculture, agricultural research. *Ref.* Cmd. 315, p. 5. *Diss.* June 1919.

MILK PRODUCTION AND DISTRIBUTION, BOVINE TUBERCULOSIS SUB-COMMITTEE.—*App.* by main Committee in 1918. *Obj.* To consider methods of establishing accredited herd system without unduly restricting milk production. *Repr.* B.A., F.P.D., L.G.B., L.G.B.(Sc.), agriculture. *Ref.* Cmd. 484, pp. 30–1. *Diss.* June 1919.

MILK PRODUCTION AND DISTRIBUTION, DAIRY EDUCATION SUB-COMMITTEE.—*App.* by main Committee in autumn of 1918. *Obj.* To report on existing deficiencies of education and future requirements of industry. *Repr.* B.A., F.P.D., M.F., agriculture, agricultural research, Agricultural Colleges, women. *Ref.* Cmd. 483, p. 50. *Diss.* Jan. 1919.

MILK PRODUCTION AND DISTRIBUTION, DAIRY FARMS' LABOUR SUB-COMMITTEE.—*App.* by main Committee in autumn of 1918. *Obj.* To suggest means of meeting shortage of labour and attracting workers. *Repr.* B.A., F.P.D., M.F., L.G.B., agriculture, labour, women. *Ref.* Cmd. 483, p. 39. *Diss.* May 1919.

MILK PRODUCTION AND DISTRIBUTION, DAIRYING SUB-COMMITTEE.—*App.* by main Committee in 1917 or 1918. *Obj.* To investigate economics of dairying. *Repr.* B.A., F.P.D., M.F., agriculture, agricultural research. *Ref.* Cmd. 315, p. 5. *Diss.* June 1919 or earlier.

MILK PRODUCTION AND DISTRIBUTION, FINANCE AND ECONOMICS SUB-COMMITTEE. —*App.* by main Committee, apparently in 1918. *Obj.* To investigate financial and economic problems of milk production. *Repr.* Not stated. *Ref.* Cmd. 315, pp. 14–16. *Diss.* About June 1919.

MILK PRODUCTION AND DISTRIBUTION, GOATS' MILK SUB-COMMITTEE.—*App.* by main Committee in 1918. *Obj.* To report upon keeping of goats for milk production. *Repr.* Main Committee and presumably experts. *Ref.* J.B.A., Jan. 1919. *Diss.* Aug. 1918.

MILK PRODUCTION AND DISTRIBUTION, HANDLING SUB-COMMITTEE.—*App.* by main Committee in 1918. *Obj.* To consider steps for ensuring delivery of milk in wholesome condition and preventing waste. *Repr.* B.A., F.P.D., M.F., L.G.B., L.G.B.(Sc.), M.M., agriculture, labour, women. *Ref.* Cmd. 483, p. 31. *Diss.* June 1919.

MILK PRODUCTION AND DISTRIBUTION, PASTEURIZATION SUB-COMMITTEE.—*App.* by main Committee in 1918. *Obj.* To investigate preservation of milk by pasteurization. *Repr.* Not stated. *Ref.* Cmd. 315, p. 8 and App. C. *Diss.* June 1919 or earlier.

MILK PRODUCTION AND DISTRIBUTION, VARIATION IN PRICES, SUB-COMMITTEE.—*App.* by main Committee, Oct. 1918. *Obj.* To consider possible variations in producers' prices in different districts. *Repr.* Not stated. *Ref.* Cmd. 233, p. 3. *Diss.* In or after Nov. 1918.

MILK PRODUCTION AND DISTRIBUTION, WHOLESALE TRADE SUB-COMMITTEE.—*App.* by main Committee, by arrangement with M.F., Mar. 1918. *Obj.* To advise on steps for immediate control of wholesale distribution and establishment of milk depots. *Repr.* M.F., B.A., F.P.D., B.A.(Sc.), L.G.B., L.G.B.(Sc.), M.M., M.R., agriculture, co-operators, consumers, women, accountants. *Ref.* Cd. 9095 ; Cmd. 315, p. 6. *Diss.* May 1918.

MILK PRODUCTION AND DISTRIBUTION, WINTER PRICES SUB-COMMITTEE.—*App.* by main Committee, May 1918. *Obj.* To advise on fixing of winter prices. *Repr.* M.F., B.A., F.P.D., M.Pen., agriculture, agricultural research, labour, women. *Ref.* Cmd. 315, p. 7. *Diss.* Oct. 1918.

MILK.—*See also* M.F.

MOTOR LOAN COMMITTEE.—*App.* by B.A., in consultation with D.C., Feb. 1917. *Obj.* To develop productivity of fishing fleet by installation of motor engines. *Repr.* B.A., Adm., D.C. *Ref.* Cmd. 585, pp. 58–64. *Diss.* Enlarged and reconstituted as Fish Food and Motor Loan Committee (q. v).

NITRATE OF SODA EXECUTIVE.—*See* M.M.

NITROGEN PRODUCTS COMMITTEE.—*See* M.M.

OFFICERS.—*See* Training in Agriculture, and in B.E. section.

OFFICIAL COMMITTEE, JOINT, OF BOARD OF AGRICULTURE AND MINISTRY OF FOOD.—*App.* jointly by B.A., and F.C., during 1918. *Obj.* To co-ordinate the work of B.A. and M.F. *Repr.* B.A., M.F. *Ref.* J.B.A., Sept., Oct. 1918. *Diss.* June 1919.

OFFICIAL SEED TESTING STATION.—*See* Seed Testing.

OILS AND FATS, CONSULTATIVE COMMITTEE.—*App.* by arrangement with B.A. *See* M.M.

ORDERS COMMITTEE, JOINT, OF BOARD OF AGRICULTURE AND MINISTRY OF FOOD.—*App.* jointly by B.A., and F.C., about Dec. 1917. *Obj.* To organize circulation of information to farmers regarding Government Orders. *Repr.* B.A., M.F. *Ref.* J.B.A., Feb. 1918. *Diss.* After Armistice.

PASTEURIZATION.—*See* Milk.

PEMBREY FARM SETTLEMENT ADVISORY COMMITTEE.—*App.* by B.A., in 1917. *Obj.* To advise on suitable properties for settlement for ex-service men in Wales. *Repr.* Welsh M.P.'s; Welsh Agricultural Council. *Ref.* Cmd. 851, p. 2. *Diss.* About Nov. 1917. (This Committee chose Pembrey Site out of several alternatives.)

PEMBREY FARM SETTLEMENT COMMITTEE.—*App.* by B.A., May 1920. *Obj.* To inquire into the working of the colony (ex-service men) and suggest modifications. *Repr.* B.A., agriculturalists, experts. *Ref.* Cmd. 851. *Diss.* June 1920.

PIG AND POTATO CLUBS, COMMITTEE OF GLOUCESTERSHIRE COUNTY SCHEME.—*App.* locally under this scheme at instigation of F.P.D., in spring of 1917. *Obj.* To organize scheme for developing pig-rearing and potato culture through Pig and Potato Clubs. *Repr.* The Clubs, &c. *Ref.* J.B.A., Nov. 1921.

PIG BREEDING COMMITTEE.—*App.* by Pig Breeders' Societies, Feb. 1918. *Obj.* To consult with B.A. on preparation of scheme for maintaining and stimulating pig production. *Repr.* Pig Breeders' Associations and Societies. *Ref.* T., 22nd Feb. 1918, p. 7. *Diss.* Apparently later in 1918.

PIG CLUB, MAISEMORE, COMMITTEE.—*App.* locally through influence of Rural League, prior to Feb. 1918. *Obj.* To maintain pig-keeping in villages and secure co-operative purchase of feeding stuffs. *Repr.* Local pig keepers and other residents. *Ref.* J.B.A., Feb. 1918.

PIGKEEPING ADVISORY COMMITTEE.—*App.* by B.A., Mar. 1918. *Obj.* To advise on measures for extension of pigkeeping. *Repr.* B.A., pig breeders, &c. *Ref.* J.B.A., Mar. 1918.

PIG PRODUCTION SECTION.—*App.* by F.P.D., May 1918. *Obj.* To promote and deal with problems of pig production. *Repr.* Official and expert. *Ref.* Hall, p. 363. *Diss.* Jan. 1919.

PIT TIMBER.—*See* H.O.

POTASH AND PHOSPHATES DISTRIBUTION COMMITTEE.—*App.* by F.P.D., apparently in late summer of 1917. *Obj.* To organize distribution of supplies to farmers, and deal with complaints. *Repr.* Not stated. *Ref.* J.B.A., Sept. 1917. (*See also* M.F. *under* Phosphates.)

POTASH DISTRIBUTION COMMITTEE.—M.A. represented. *See* B.T.

POTASH, PRODUCTION FROM BRITISH FELSPAR, SUB-COM-MITTEE OF FERTILIZERS COMMITTEE.—*App.* by Fertilizers' Committee about middle of 1916. *Obj.* To conduct experiments into possibility of producing potash from British felspar. *Repr.* B.A., Geological Survey, and the supervisor of certain previous experiments on felspar (a civil engineer). *Ref.* J.B.A., Feb. 1917.

POTATO CLUBS.—*General establishment* promoted (one or two earlier instances) by Agricultural Organization Society in spring of 1917. *Obj.* To combine residents of villages or districts to grow potatoes for own consumption. *Repr.* Inhabitants of village or district concerned with small Committee, where necessary, to supervise labour. *Ref.* J.B.A., April 1917.

POTATO CONFERENCE, INTERNATIONAL, JOINT COMMITTEE OF MINISTRY OF AGRICULTURE AND ROYAL HORTICULTURAL SOCIETY.—*App.* jointly by M.A. and Society in summer of 1921. *Obj.* To make the necessary arrangements for the Conference (held Nov. 1921). *Repr.* M.A., B.A.(Sc.), D.A.T.I., Royal Horticultural and National Potato Societies, National Institute of Agricultural Botany. *Ref.* J.B.A., July, 1921. *Diss.* Nov. 1921.

POTATOES, GROWERS' PRICES, 1918 AND 1919, COMMISSIONS.—*See* M.F.

POTATO TESTING STATION.—*See under* Botany, National Institute of Agricultural.

POULTRY ADVISORY COMMITTEE.—*App.* by B.A., June 1917. *Obj.* To advise on reorganization of industry to meet war conditions. *Repr.* B.A., B.A.(Sc.), M.F., Poultry Societies and Clubs, Poultry Co-operators, Poultry Research. *Ref.* J.B.A., July 1917. *Diss.* July 1920.

POULTRY BRANCH, BOARD OF AGRICULTURE.—*Ref.* in J.B.A., Dec. 1919.

PRESERVATION OF FOOD AND VEGETABLES, COMMITTEE.—*Ref.* in J.B.A., May 1917. *See* Vegetable Drying and Fruit Preserving Committee, which is apparently the same Committee.

PRICES.—*See* Milk, and next entry.

PRODUCE, AGRICULTURAL, DISTRIBUTION AND PRICES (LIN-LITHGOW) COMMITTEE.—*App.* by M.A., Dec. 1922. *Obj.* To consider methods and costs of selling of agricultural, &c. produce in G.B., and means of diminishing disparity between prices paid to producers and charged to consumers. *Repr.* Parliament, M.A. agriculture, agricultural research, business men and other experts, women. *Ref.* H.M.S.O., 1924 (collected reports): Cmd. 1854, 1892, 1927, 1921, and H.M.S.O., 1923, separate reports. *Diss.* Nov. 1923.

QUARTERING COMMITTEES, LOCAL.—*See* J.B.A., July 1918, p. 469. These Committees were apparently responsible for finding quarters for agricultural workers, including prisoners of war gangs.

RABBIT, NATIONAL UTILITY, ASSOCIATION.—*App.* at instance of F.P.D., in May 1918. *Obj.* To provide quick increase in supply of pedigree breeding stock, through central breeding station in London, and organize local Rabbit Clubs in affiliation with Association. *Repr.* Leading rabbit breeders and keepers. *Ref.* J.B.A., July 1918, p. 462.

RENTS.—*See* W.A.E.C.'s.

REORGANIZATION, OFFICE COMMITTEE.—*App.* by B.A. in 1917. *Obj.* To consider reorganization of work with a view to economy. *Repr.* Not stated. *Ref.* H.C., No. 132, 1918, p. 29.

ROYAL AGRICULTURAL SOCIETY.—*See* Joint Committee, War Emergency Committee.

ROYAL SOCIETY.—*See* Food Supply.

RURAL BRANCH, MINISTRY OF AGRICULTURE.—*App.* by M.A., about Jan. 1920. *Obj.* To render permanent war work of stimulating small cultivation, and carry out propaganda and organization for stimulating rural industries. *Repr.* Official and expert. *Ref.* J.B.A., Feb. 1920.

SAVING THE FOOD OF THE NATION.—Reference is made to educational campaign for this purpose in J.B.A., Sept. 1915.

SEED POTATOES, DEPARTMENTAL COMMITTEE.—*App.* by B.A. in 1916. *Obj.* To secure preservation of sufficient potatoes of 1916 crop for seed. *Repr.* Not stated. *Ref.* Hansard (H.C.), 14th Dec. 1916, Vol. 88, Col. 865. *Diss.* In 1917.

SEEDS ADVISORY COMMITTEE.—*App.* by F.P.D., June 1917. *Obj.* To advise in regard to supply, &c. of seeds (other than cereal seeds). *Repr.* Not stated. *Ref.* Cd. 9005 ; Hall, p. 363.

SEEDS, CEREAL, ADVISORY COMMITTEE.—*App.* by F.P.D., June 1917. *Obj.* To advise in regard to supply, &c. of cereal seeds. *Repr.* Not stated. *Ref.* Cd. 9005 : Hall, p. 361.

SEEDS.—*See also* Seed Potatoes.

SEED TESTING STATION, OFFICIAL.—*App.* by B.A., Nov. 1917, its establishment, decided on before war, being apparently accelerated by war conditions. *Obj.* To provide adequate British tests for seeds and secure supplies of high germinative capacity. *Repr.* Part of organization of B.A., control over it being delegated in 1920 to Committee of Council of National Institute of Agricultural Botany (*see* above). *Ref.* J.B.A., Sept. 1918, Feb. 1922. *Permanent.*

SEED WHEAT PURCHASING, LOCAL COMMITTEES.—*App.* by National British and Irish Corn Trades Associations, on behalf of F.P.D., June 1917. *Obj.* To purchase and inspect sufficient supplies for 1917–18 sowings and fix prices. *Repr.* Agricultural interests (including traders). *Ref.* J.B.A., July 1917, p. 469.

SETTLEMENT ON THE LAND.—*See* Land Settlement.

SETTLEMENT, EMPIRE.—*See* C.O., Empire Settlement Committee, which paid some attention to land settlement at home.

SHAW (WILTS).—*See* Women's Training.

SHELLFISH.—*See* L.G.B.

SMALL HOLDINGS (COLONIES) ACT, 1918, SPECIAL COMMITTEES OF COUNTY COUNCILS.—*App.* suggested by B.A. to County Councils, where existing Small Holdings and Allotments Committees not suitable for purpose. *Obj.* To acquire land for Small Holdings Colonies for ex-service men. *Repr.* The Councils and others. *Ref.* J.B.A., Oct. 1918.

SOLDIERS' CLUBS ASSOCIATION, SUB-COMMITTEE ON CO-OPERATION.—*See* Village Clubs Association, Sub-Committee on Co-operation.

SOLDIERS, RELEASE FOR AGRICULTURAL WORK, AGRICULTURAL REPRESENTATIVES.—*App.* by War Agricultural (County) Committees, June 1916, to act with the Military Representatives and the Labour Exchanges. *Obj.* To deal with release of soldiers for work in their counties. *Repr.* The Committees. *Ref.* J.B.A., June 1916.

SPECIAL INQUIRIES BRANCH, BOARD OF AGRICULTURE.—*App.* by B.A., Aug. 1914. *Obj.* To deal with matters of home supplies and to collect information on agricultural questions. *Repr.* Officers of B.A. in various districts in touch with local business correspondents, Agricultural Colleges, Provincial Councils of Agriculture. *Ref.* J.B.A., Sept. 1914.

STAFF COMMITTEE, FOOD PRODUCTION DEPARTMENT.—*App.* by F.P.D., in 1917. *Obj.* To scrutinize and advise upon proposed increases in staff. *Repr.* Chief administrative, financial and accounting officers of F.P.D. *Ref.* H.C., No. 151, 1917–18, p. 23.

STAFFS, SPECIAL INVESTIGATION COMMITTEE.—*See* Cabinet.

STEAM CULTIVATION AND THRESHING ADVISORY COMMITTEE.—*App.* by M.A., Feb. 1920, as *Standing Committee*. *Obj.* To advise M.A. on all questions of steam cultivation and threshing. *Repr.* M.A. (presumably), agriculturalists, threshing firms. *Ref.* J.B.A., Mar. 1920.
 (*See also* War Agricultural Executive Committees, and Threshing.)

SULPHATE OF AMMONIA DISTRIBUTION COMMITTEE.—*See* M.F.

SULPHURIC ACID AND FERTILIZERS.—*See* M.M.

TECHNICAL COMMITTEE, FOOD PRODUCTION DEPARTMENT.—*App.* by F.P.D. early in 1917. *Obj.* To advise upon technical matters including war time difficulties. *Repr.* F.P.D., and agricultural experts. *Ref.* J.B.A., Mar. 1917.

TEST MEETING FOR WOMEN FARM WORKERS IN MIDLAND COUNTIES, MANAGEMENT COMMITTEE.—*App.* by F.P.D. in co-operation with Lord Mayor of Birmingham, Sept. 1917. *Obj.* To carry out, with Women's Branch of F.P.D., practical examination of women with three to twelve months' farm experience, as part of general scheme of training and placing on land. *Repr.* B.A., Agricultural Societies, farmers, women. *Ref.* J.B.A., Sept. 1917. *Diss.* Oct. 1917 (after meeting).
 (Similar meetings were held subsequently in other districts, e. g. at Rhuddlan and Warrington).

THRESHING ADVISORY COMMITTEE.—*App.* by B.A. in summer of 1918, and reconstituted Aug.–Sept. 1919, for 1918–19 and 1919–20 seasons. *Obj.* To advise on organization and payment of threshing operations and decide unsettled local disputes. *Repr.* B.A., and interests concerned. *Ref.* J.B.A., Sept. 1918. *Diss.* Feb. 1920, on appointment of Advisory Committee on Steam Cultivation and Threshing (q. v.).

THRESHING.—*See also under* Agricultural Executive Committees, and War Agricultural Executive (County) Committees.

TILLAGE.—*See* Compulsory Tillage.

TIMBER, HOME GROWN, ADVISORY (INTER-DEPARTMENTAL) COMMITTEE.—*App.* by B.A., Nov. 1915. *Obj.* To organize more efficient use of, and where necessary to purchase and distribute, native timber. *Repr.* B.A., B.A.(Sc.), D.A.T.I., other timber purchasing departments. *Ref.* J.B.A., Jan. 1916. *Diss.* Mar. 1917, work having been taken over by Timber Supplies Department (*see* W.O.).

TIMBER, PIT, CENTRAL COMMITTEE.—*See* H.O., *under* Pit Timber.

TITHE RENT CHARGE ACT 1918, PAYMENTS, DEPARTMENTAL COMMITTEE.—*App.* by M.A. in 1921. *Obj.* To recommend values for calculation of commutation under the Act. *Repr.* Departmental. *Ref.* J.B.A., Dec. 1921. *Diss.* Before end of 1921 (apparently).

(The war did not directly cause this appointment but seems to have rendered a settlement of the question more urgent.)

TOY INDUSTRY SUB-COMMITTEE OF WOMEN'S INSTITUTES' EXECUTIVE COMMITTEE.—*App.* in spring of 1918 by Executive Committee. *Obj.* To organize toy-making in villages through the Institutes. *Repr.* The Executive Committee. *Ref.* J.B.A., Oct. 1918.

TRAINING IN AGRICULTURE, OFFICERS' COMMITTEE.—*App.* by B.A., Dec. 1918. *Obj.* To recommend awards of agricultural scholarships under scheme for higher agricultural training to officers and men of like standing and to advise and assist generally in the execution of the Scheme for training them in agriculture. *Repr.* Parliament, B.A. agriculturalists, with special Welsh representation, experts in agricultural education. *Ref.* J.B.A., Jan. 1919 ; T., 28th Dec. 1918, p. 3. (*See also* B.E. Officers.)

TRAINING, WOMEN.—*See under* Women.

UNEMPLOYMENT INSURANCE IN AGRICULTURE.—*App.* by Agricultural Wages Board, Dec. 1920. *Obj.* To report how far Unemployment Insurance Acts can be beneficially applied to agriculture. *Repr.* The Board. *Ref.* Cmd. 1344. *Diss.* April 1921.

VACANT LANDS CULTIVATION SOCIETIES.—*App.* in various districts mostly under Land Cultivation Order by L.A.'s during 1917 or later, but sometimes earlier by private action. *Obj.* To secure and manage allotments and sometimes supply of manures, implements, &c. *Repr.* L.A.'s (where concerned), farmers, horticulturalists, allotment holders. *Ref.* J.B.A., Mar. 1918.

VEGETABLE DRYING AND FRUIT PRESERVING COMMITTEE.— *App.* by B.A., with grant from D.C., Sept. 1914. *Obj.* To supervise working of factories erected to test possibility of establishing these industries on a commercial scale, the experiment being developed out of scheme of Central Committee for Women's Employment for providing for unemployed women. *Repr.* B.A., D.C. agricultural experts. *Ref.* Cd. 8066, pp. 4, 102–3.

VENISON COMMITTEE.—*See* M.F.

VERNEY COMMITTEE.—*See* Land Settlement.

VILLAGE CLUBS ASSOCIATION COMMITTEE.—*App.* by Association, which was established in 1918 by agriculturalists and others interested, with assistance of B.A. *Obj.* To promote establishment of village clubs. *Repr.* The interests represented in the Association. *Ref.* J.B.A., Sept. 1918. (The Association was largely the result of war developments and intended to be permanent.)

VILLAGE CLUBS ASSOCIATION, AND NATIONAL FEDERATION OF WOMEN'S INSTITUTES, JOINT STANDING COMMITTEE.—*App.* by the two bodies, with assistance of B.A., and D.C., in autumn of 1919. *Obj.* To adopt measures to ensure co-operation between them and prevent overlapping. *Repr.* The two Associations (equally). *Ref.* J.B.A., Dec. 1918. *Intended to be Permanent.*

VILLAGE CLUBS ASSOCIATION SUB-COMMITTEE ON CO-OPERA-TION.—*App.* by the Association, Sept. 1919. *Obj.* To promote a scheme of co-operation with the Soldiers' Clubs Association, and the Federation of Women's Clubs, who appointed similar sub-Committees. *Repr.* The Association. *Ref.* J.B.A., Sept. 1918. *Apparently Permanent.*

WAGES, AGRICULTURAL, DISTRICT COMMITTEES.—*App.* for counties or combinations of counties (thirty-nine Committees in all) by Wages Board and B.A., under Corn Production Act, 1917, between Jan. and May 1918. *Obj.* To recommend suitable district rates to the Wages Board. *Repr.* Employers and workpeople (equal numbers), appointed members. *Ref.* P.G.A., 1917, J.B.A., Oct. 1917. *Diss.* Oct. 1921—*see* Wages, Agricultural, Joint Local Conciliation Committees.

WAGES, AGRICULTURAL, JOINT LOCAL CONCILIATION COM-MITTEES.—*App.* under the Corn Production Acts (Repeal) Act 1921, from Oct. 1921, by employers' and workpeoples' associations in various districts, to replace the District Wages Committees, the employers' and workpeoples' representatives on which acted as Interim Conciliation Com-mittees, pending appointment of permanent Committees. *Obj.* To agree upon district rates of wages. *Repr.* Employers and workpeople in the district in agriculture. *Ref.* P.G.A., 1921.

WAGES AND CONDITIONS OF EMPLOYMENT IN AGRICULTURE, INVESTIGATORS.—*App.* by B.A., Oct. 1917. *Obj.* To collect informa-tion for use of Agricultural Wages Board. *Repr.* Skilled investigators. *Ref.* Cmd. 24. *Diss.* Oct. 1918.

WAGES BOARD, AGRICULTURAL.—*App.* by B.A., Nov. 1917, under Corn Production Act, 1917. *Obj.* To fix minimum wages (including allowances) for workpeople in agriculture. *Repr.* Employers, workpeople (equal numbers), and appointed members (including B.A., agricultural research, smallholders, Trade Board experts). *Ref.* P.G.A., 1917 ; J.B.A., Oct. 1917. *Diss.* 1st Oct. 1921, along with which Committees of the Board, not previously terminated, came to an end.

WAGES BOARD, AGRICULTURAL, ADMINISTRATION COMMITTEE.—*App.* by Wages Board about end of 1917. *Obj.* To exercise general administrative powers of Board. *Repr.* As with Wages Board. *Ref.* J.B.A., Sept. 1920. *Diss.* 1st Oct. 1921.

WAGES BOARD, AGRICULTURAL, ALLOWANCES COMMITTEE.—*App.* by Wages Board, Dec. 1917. *Obj.* To consider basis for determining value of allowances in fixing wages. *Repr.* Wages Board. *Ref.* J.B.A., Feb. 1918. *Diss.* Mar. 1918.

WAGES BOARD, AGRICULTURAL, AREAS COMMITTEE.—*App.* by Wages Board, Dec. 1917. *Obj.* To report in detail upon areas and membership of District Wage Committees. *Repr.* Wages Board. *Ref.* J.B.A., Dec. 1917. *Diss.* 20th Dec. 1917 (suggested areas adopted by Wages Board).

WAGES BOARD, AGRICULTURAL, COTTAGE RENTS COMMITTEE.—*App.* by Wages Board, Dec. 1917. *Obj.* To consider the basis for assessing value of rent of cottages in fixing wages. *Repr.* Wages Board. *Ref.* J.B.A., Jan. 1918.

WAGES BOARD, AGRICULTURAL, MINIMUM RATES FOR HAY AND CORN HARVEST, COMMITTEE.—*App.* by Wages Board about April 1918. *Obj.* To report upon principles for fixing such rates. *Repr.* Wages Board. *Ref.* L.G., May 1918.

WAGES BOARD, AGRICULTURAL, SELECTION COMMITTEE.—*App.* by Wages Board, Dec. 1917. *Obj.* To select representative members (employers and workmen) for District Wage Committees from names suggested. *Repr.* Employers' and workpeoples' representatives on Wages Board. *Ref.* J.B.A., Jan. 1918.

WAGES BOARD, AGRICULTURAL, WOMEN'S AND GIRLS' WAGES COMMITTEE.—*App.* by Wages Board, about April 1918. *Obj.* To consider recommendations from District Wages Committees as to principles for fixing minimum rates for women and girls. *Repr.* Wages Board. *Ref.* L.G., May 1918.

WAGES BOARD.—*See also* Financial Results of Farming.

WAR AGRICULTURAL COUNTY COMMITTEES.—*App.* by County Councils from about Oct. 1915 and in certain cases earlier, and reorganized in autumn of 1916. *Obj.* To organize supply of agricultural labour, promote measures for increasing food-supply, act as link between farmers and B.A., and exercise locally certain war powers of B.A. *Repr.* County Councils, Agricultural Associations, landowners, farmers, labour. *Ref.* J.B.A., Oct. 1915, Jan. 1917. *Diss.* Practically superseded by W.A.E.C.'s early in 1917 (q. v.).

WAR AGRICULTURAL DISTRICT COMMISSIONERS.—*See* Cd. 9005 for appointment by F.P.D. as ex-officio members of W.A.E.C.'s (*see* below) and act as link between them and F.P.D.

WAR AGRICULTURAL DISTRICT SUB-COMMITTEES.—*App.* by or through County Committees, from about end of 1915, for rural districts and urban districts with agricultural populations, and brought under

W.A.E.C.'s early in 1917. *Obj.* To advise and assist County Committees in their districts and form link between them and agriculturalists. *Repr.* Local landowners, farmers, labourers, &c. *Ref.* J.B.A., Oct. 1915, June 1917; Cd. 9005, p. 157. *Diss.* Presumably absorbed into organization under Agricultural Committees (Statutory), May 1919.

WAR AGRICULTURAL EXECUTIVE (COUNTY) COMMITTEES.— *App.* by War Agricultural County Committees, which they practically superseded, at instigation of B.A., Jan. 1917,[1] and reorganized, May 1918. *Obj.* To perform functions of the County Committees, and, with exceptions, to exercise locally special war powers of B.A., *Repr.* The County Committees, with additional members appointed by B.A. *Ref.* J.B.A., Jan. 1917, July 1918 ; Cd. 9005, p. 157. *Diss.* 31st May 1919, being replaced by Agricultural Committees (Statutory) under the Corn Production Act (*see* above). A Federation of War Agricultural Executive (County) Committees is mentioned on p. 339 of J.B.A., June 1917.

WAR AGRICULTURAL EXECUTIVE (COUNTY) COMMITTEES, CULTIVATION SUB-COMMITTEES.—*App.* by W.A.E.C.'s, at instance of F.P.D., from May 1918, on general reorganization of the Committees taking over then or later duties from various other Sub-Committees. *Obj.* To control horse and tractor schemes, survey and supervise farming and recommend Cultivation Orders. *Repr.* W.A.E.C.'s. *Ref.* J.B.A., July 1918. *Diss.* Duties reduced in 1919, with closing down of Horse and Tractor Scheme, and Sub-Committees transferred in June, with modified functions, to new Agricultural Committees (Statutory) (*see* above).

WAR AGRICULTURAL EXECUTIVE (COUNTY) COMMITTEES : JOINT SUB-COMMITTEES WITH COUNTY BOROUGH COUNCILS.— *App.* jointly by the two bodies at instance of B.A., in 1917, in cases where their areas were contiguous. *Obj.* To secure more efficient cultivation of agricultural lands in borough areas. *Repr.* The Committees and Councils. *Ref.* J.B.A., Dec. 1917. *Diss.* Apparently at end of May 1919.

WAR AGRICULTURAL EXECUTIVE (COUNTY) COMMITTEES : LABOUR SUB-COMMITTEES.—*App.* by W.A.E.C.'s at request of F.P.D., May 1917, and reconstituted later to act under W.A.E.C.'s as Agricultural Sub-Committees of the Local Advisory (Employment) Committees of M.L. *Obj.* To deal generally with supply of labour, including women, and, up to May 1918, horses ; and from Jan. 1919 to advise on demobilization of agriculturalists. *Repr.* W.A.E.C.'s and Women's War Agricultural Committees and, on reconstitution, containing equal representation of employers and workpeople on Local Advisory Committees. *Ref.* J.B.A., June 1917, Feb. 1919. *Diss.* On 31st May 1919 as such, but continued under the new Agricultural Committees (Statutory) (*see* above), certain duties being transferred to Cultivation Sub-Committees.

WAR AGRICULTURAL EXECUTIVE (COUNTY) COMMITTEES ; MACHINERY SUB-COMMITTEES.—*App.* by W.A.E.C.'s at request of F.P.D. in first half of 1917. *Obj.* To organize use of tractors, steam tackle, and other agricultural machinery. *Repr.* B.A. ; W.A.E.C.'s. *Ref.* J.B.A.,

---

[1] Individual County Committees appear to have appointed Executive Committees earlier, but their general organization seems to date from Jan. 1917.

June 1917. *Diss.* May 1918 (duties taken over by Cultivation Sub-Committees).

WAR AGRICULTURAL EXECUTIVE (COUNTY) COMMITTEES ; SOLDIER LABOUR SUB-COMMITTEES.—*App.* in many counties prior to May 1917, by War Agricultural (County) Committees or W.A.E.C.'s. *Obj.* To distribute available supplies of soldier labour. *Repr.* The appointing Committees. *Ref.* J.B.A., June 1917. *Diss.* Absorbed into Labour Sub-Committees (*see* above) from May 1917.

WAR AGRICULTURAL EXECUTIVE (COUNTY) COMMITTEES ; SUPPLIES SUB-COMMITTEES.—*App.* by W.A.E.C.'s at request of F.P.D., from May 1917. *Obj.* To organize supplies of fertilizers, seeds, and other agricultural requirements. *Repr.* W.A.E.C.'s, dealers, merchants, Agricultural Co-operative Trading Societies. *Ref.* J.B.A., June 1917. *Diss.* Certain duties transferred to Cultivation Sub-Committees, May 1918 ; but continued for other work and apparently as Sub-Committees of Agricultural Committees (Statutory) (*see* above).

WAR AGRICULTURAL EXECUTIVE (COUNTY) COMMITTEES ; THRESHING SUB-COMMITTEES.—*App.* by W.A.E.C.'s, at instance of F.P.D., mostly from April 1918, though apparently schemes were in operation earlier in certain counties. *Obj.* To organize threshing and secure best use of machinery for threshing 1918 crop. *Repr.* W.A.E.C.'s and their Machinery Sub-Committees ; threshing trade. *Ref.* J.B.A. April 1918.

WAR AGRICULTURAL MACHINERY SUB-COMMITTEES (DISTRICT).—*App.* by District Sub-Committees at instance of Mechanical Cultivation Branch of F.P.D., from Oct. 1917. *Obj.* To increase local interest in scheme of machinery distribution, &c. and secure more effective supervision. *Repr.* Apparently as with District Sub-Committees. *Ref.* J.B.A., Oct. 1917. *Diss.* Presumably as with W.A.E.C.'s (*see* above).

WAR AGRICULTURAL PARISH CORRESPONDENTS OF DISTRICT SUB-COMMITTEES.—*App.* by District Sub-Committees at request of F.P.D., from May 1917. *Obj.* To act as correspondents of the Sub-Committees in each parish. *Repr.* Persons experienced in agriculture. *Ref.* J.B.A., June 1917. *Diss.* Presumably as with W.A.E.C.'s (*see* above).

WAR AGRICULTURAL PARISH SUB-COMMITTEES.—*App.* in many counties for individual parishes, mainly in 1917. *Obj.* To keep the W.A.E.C.'s in touch with each parish. *Repr.* Local landowners, farmers, labourers. *Ref.* Cd. 9005, pp. 157–8. *Diss.* Presumably as with W.A.E.C.'s (*see* above).

WARBLE FLY PEST, SCIENTIFIC COMMITTEE.—*App.* by M.A. in or before Mar. 1921. *Obj.* To conduct experiments for discovery of remedies. *Repr.* Scientists. *Ref.* J.B.A., April 1921, pp. 92–3.

WARBLE FLY PEST, SCIENTIFIC SUB-COMMITTEE.—*See* W.O.

WAR EMERGENCY COMMITTEE, ROYAL AGRICULTURAL SOCIETY.—*App.* by the Society, presumably early in the War. *Obj.* To advise Government Departments concerned, focus agricultural opinion, assist agriculturalists in dealing with grievances and difficulties and to consider proposals for dealing with land and effects of Government regulations. *Repr.* The Society and others. *Ref.* T., 9th Feb. 1917 ; J.B.A., June, 1920.

WAR FOOD SOCIETIES, BOROUGH AND URBAN.—*App.* through L.A.'s or Local War Savings Associations, at instigation of B.A., mostly from about Dec. 1915 (a few earlier). *Obj.* To increase local food production and economize consumption. *Repr.* L.A.'s ; local residents. *Ref.* J.B.A., Dec. 1915.

WAR FOOD SOCIETIES, VILLAGE.—*App.* in villages, with Parish Councils as L.A.'s concerned. Otherwise as with Borough Societies.
　(N.B. These Societies were sometimes called Food Production Societies.)

WHEAT, INDIAN.—*See* Indian Wheat.

WHEAT SUPPLIES ROYAL COMMISSION.—*See* M.F.

WINFREY COMMITTEE.—*See* Land Settlement.

WOMEN'S CLUBS FEDERATION, SUB-COMMITTEE ON CO-OPERATION.—*See under* Village Clubs Association.

WOMEN'S EMPLOYMENT COMMITTEE.—*See* M.R.

WOMEN'S EMPLOYMENT IN AGRICULTURE IN ENGLAND AND WALES SUB-COMMITTEE.—Transferred to B.A., Mar. 1919. *See* M.R.

WOMEN'S FARM LABOUR COMMITTEES (COUNTY AND DISTRICT).—*See* W.W.A.C.'s and Women's War Agricultural District Committees.

WOMEN'S INSTITUTES, NATIONAL FEDERATION, EXECUTIVE COMMITTEE.—*App.* by Conferences of Women's Institutes, the Agricultural Organization Society, and F.P.D. (Women's Branch), about end 1917. *Obj.* To develop Women's Institutes, in co-operation with Women's Branch of F.P.D. *Repr.* F.P.D. (Women's Branch) ; B.E. ; Agricultural Organization Society ; Women's Institutes ; National Federation of Women Workers. *Ref.* J.B.A., Jan. 1918. *Presumably Permanent.*

WOMEN'S INSTITUTES, NATIONAL FEDERATION, HANDICRAFTS SUB-COMMITTEE.—*App.* by the Federation, prior to June 1920. *Obj.* To promote development of handicraft by Institutes. *Repr.* The Federation. *Ref.* J.B.A., June 1920. *Presumably Permanent.*

WOMEN'S INSTITUTES, VILLAGE.—*App.* by Parish Councils, War Savings Associations, &c. from Sept. 1915, at instance of B.A., who aimed at substituting them for War Food Societies (*see* above), where few men were available. *Obj.* To improve conditions of village life for women and promote local production and economy of food. *Repr.* Women in villages. *Ref.* J.B.A., Jan. 1917, Oct. 1918. *Intended to be Permanent.*

WOMEN'S LABOUR DEPARTMENT, BOARD OF AGRICULTURE.—*App.* by B.A., Jan. 1917, becoming eventually Women's Branch of F.P.D. *Obj.* To organize supply and stimulate recruiting of women's labour, improve conditions of agricultural employment for town-bred women, and act as clearing house for Women's Farm Labour Committees. *Repr.* Departmental, with representation of agricultural interests and women. *Ref.* J.B.A., Feb. 1917. *Diss.* April 1919.

WOMEN'S LAND ARMY.—*App.* by B.A. through W.W.A.C.'s., in co-operation with M.L. and M.N.S. in spring of 1917. *Obj., Repr.* To be composed of women for training and employment on the land. *Ref.* J.B.A., Oct. 1917. *Diss.* Disbandment completed by 30th Nov. 1919.

(N.B. J.B.A., April 1920, p. 1161, refers to County Committees in charge of Women's Land Army, but does not state whether these are W.W.A.C.'s, or special Committees.)

WOMEN'S MISSION TO FRANCE (BERKSHIRE).—*App.* by Berkshire Women's Farm Labour Committee, Feb. 1916. *Obj.* To investigate war work of French women in agriculture. *Repr.* B.T., The Committee, women in families of farmers, smallholders, clerks, University College, Reading. *Ref.* J.B.A., June 1916. *Diss.* Presumably later in 1916.

WOMEN'S NATIONAL LAND SERVICE CORPS.—*App.* in 1916, possibly at instance of B.A., and by voluntary effort, receiving Government grant. *Obj.* To conduct national appeal for women for agriculture and generally assist Women's Farm Labour Committees (*see* W.W.A.C.'s), subsequently acting as agents for B.A. for supply of seasonal workers and of instructors for Women's Land Army (q. v.). *Repr.* Prominent men and women, especially those interested in agriculture and women's problems. *Ref.* J.B.A., Mar. 1916, Oct. 1918. *Diss.* Apparently absorbed into organization of Women's Land Army in autumn of 1917.

WOMEN'S SELECTION COMMITTEES (IRELAND).—To select Irish women for agricultural work in England. *See* M.L.

WOMEN'S SUB-COMMITTEES OF THE AGRICULTURAL COMMITTEES (STATUTORY) OF COUNTY COUNCILS.—*App.* by the Committees from 1st June 1919, to replace W.W.A.C.'s. *Obj.* To deal with training, employment, and organization of women on the land. *Repr.* Composed of members of W.W.A.C.'s. *Ref.* J.B.A., June 1919. *Intended to be Permanent.*

WOMEN'S TRAINING SCHOOL (AT SHAW, WILTS.) FOR FARM WORKERS COMMITTEE—This was a private Committee formed locally in 1916, to start, control, and manage a training school for women. *See* J.B.A., Dec. 1916.

WOMEN'S WAGES.—*See under* Wages Board, Agricultural, and Women's War Agricultural (County) Wages Committees.

WOMEN'S WAR AGRICULTURAL (COUNTY) COMMITTEES.—*App.* from Oct. 1915 (occasionally earlier) by War Agricultural (County) Committees, at request of B.A., being known at first as Women's Farm Labour Committees, and reorganized in autumn of 1916, in co-operation with women organizers of E.E's. *Obj.* To recruit women for, and deal with their employment in, agriculture. *Repr.* War Agricultural Committees, agricultural interests, women, labour, the members in some counties being elected later by the District Committees. *Ref.* J.B.A., Mar. 1916. *Diss.* Absorbed into Women's Sub-Committees of Agricultural Committees (Statutory) of County Councils (q. v.), from 1st June 1919.

WOMEN'S WAR AGRICULTURAL (COUNTY) FINANCE COMMITTEES.—*App.* in each county by the W.W.A.C., at instance of B.A., Mar. or April 1917. *Obj.* To arrange disbursement of Government funds allotted to W.W.A.C.'s. *Repr.* W.W.A.C.'s. *Ref.* J.B.A., May 1917. *Diss.* Presumably as with War Agricultural Committees (q. v.).

WOMEN'S WAR AGRICULTURAL (COUNTY) INSTRUCTION AND DEPOT COMMITTEES.—*Obj.* To arrange for instruction and placing of women and provide depots for unemployed land workers. *Otherwise* as with Finance Committees.

WOMEN'S WAR AGRICULTURAL (COUNTY) SELECTION AND ALLOCATION COMMITTEES.—*Obj.* To select women for training and allocate to various districts, and supervise conditions of work. *Otherwise* as with Finance Committees. *See also* T., 16th Mar. 1917, p. 3.

(These Committees appointed District Committees, to act under them for the various districts in their counties and see to the detailed training of the women. *Ref.* J.B.A., May 1917.)

WOMEN'S WAR AGRICULTURAL (COUNTY) WAGES COMMITTEES. —*Obj.* To fix fair rates for different classes of work. *Repr.* W.W.A.C.'s and on similar basis, with additional representatives of W.A.E.C.'s. *Otherwise* as with Finance Committees. *See also* T., 16th Mar. 1917, p. 3.

For Hostel Committee, *see under* Hostels.

WOMEN'S WAR AGRICULTURAL (DISTRICT) COMMITTEES.— *App.* by W.W.A.C.'s, at instance of B.A., or in some cases by Village Registrars, for various districts from Oct. 1915, but occasionally earlier (e. g. Cornwall had Committee in every village by Oct. 1915) and called at first Women's Farm Labour Committees. *Obj.* As with W.W.A.C.'s. *Repr.* Much as with W.W.A.C.'s. *Ref.* J.B.A., Mar. 1916, Oct. 1918. *Diss.* As with W.W.A.C.'s.

WOMEN'S WAR AGRICULTURAL DISTRICT SELECTION AND ALLOCATION COMMITTEES, AND EMPLOYMENT EXCHANGES, JOINT COMMITTEES.—*App.* by Committees and E.E's. concerned, at instance of B.A., about May 1917. *Obj.* To interview and adjudicate upon recruits for the Land Army. *Repr.* Committees and E.E.'s concerned. *Ref.* J.B.A., Oct. 1918. *Diss.* As with W.W.A.C.'s.

WOMEN'S WAR AGRICULTURAL DISTRICT COMMITTEES VILLAGE OR PARISH REGISTRARS.—*Ref.* J.B.A., Nov. 1916, Aug. 1918. They acted as agents of the District Committees and generally assisted in their villages.

AGRICULTURE, SCOTLAND, BOARD OF

ABBREVIATIONS
B.A.(Sc.) = Board of Agriculture, Scotland.
S.S.   = Secretary for Scotland.

AGRICULTURAL ADVISORY COMMITTEE.—*App.* jointly by Scottish Council of Agriculture and B.A.(Sc.) in autumn of 1920. *Obj.* To act as advisory body on agricultural problems. *Repr.* The Council and, through B.A.(Sc.), farmers, smallholders, and farm labourers. *Ref.* Cmd. 1306, p. xii. *Intended to be Permanent.*

AGRICULTURAL COSTINGS COMMITTEE.—Joint Appointment. *See* M.F. A Scottish Sub-Committee was appointed by the main body on which the Scottish Council of Agriculture were represented later. *See* Cmd. 1692, p. 12.

AGRICULTURAL DISTRICT COMMITTEES.—*App.* by B.A.(Sc.) to carry out recommendation of the Food Production Committee (*see* B.A.) late in 1915, thirty-one committees being established by the close of the year covering practically all Scotland. *Obj.* To organize and develop locally home production of food for war purposes. *Repr.* District Committees of County Councils, Secondary Education Committees, Agricultural Societies, Farmers' and Farm Servants' Unions, Agricultural Colleges. *Ref.* Cmd. 8282, pp. xxxiv–v. *Diss.* These bodies, like similar War Agricultural County Committees in England, to which they corresponded, appear to have been practically superseded by the Agricultural Executive District Committees (q. v.).

AGRICULTURAL EXECUTIVE COUNTY COMMITTEES.—*See* next entry.

AGRICULTURAL EXECUTIVE DISTRICT COMMITTEES, SCOTLAND.—*App.* by District Committees (*see* above) at request of B.A.(Sc.) in 1917, for each Local Government district and county, reorganized in 1919, becoming Statutory Agricultural Committees at beginning of 1921. *Obj.* To exercise executive powers to secure increased cultivation and harvests and (later) functions under Corn Production Acts and various statutory powers. *Repr.* District Committees, and (after reorganization) various agricultural societies and farm labourers. *Ref.* Cd. 8624, p. xxx ; Cmd. 773, p. lxvi, 1692, pp. 9, 12–14. *Permanent,* but powers subsequently curtailed.

AGRICULTURAL LABOUR, SELECTION FOR RELEASE, SCOTLAND, COMMITTEE.—Joint Appointment. *See* M.N.S.

AGRICULTURAL WAGES.—*See* Wages.

AGRICULTURE, SCOTTISH COUNCIL OF.—*App.* by S.S. early in 1920. *Obj.* To discuss and advise upon matters brought before it by B.A.(Sc.) or by its own members. *Repr.* Agricultural Executive District Committees, with members nominated by B.A.(Sc.) representing general agricultural interests. *Ref.* Cmd. 773, p. lxvi ; Cmd. 1306, p. xii. *Intended to be Permanent.*

(Committees were appointed by the Council from time to time. *See*, for instance, Cmd. 1692, p. 12.)

ALLOTMENTS DEPARTMENTAL COMMITTEE.—*See* B.A.

BELGIAN RELIEF, SCOTTISH COMMITTEE.—*App.* by Highland and Agricultural Society in Scotland during War. *Obj.* To assist Belgian farmers to resume cultivation of holdings as opportunity offered. *Repr.* Scottish agriculturalists. *Ref.* J.B.A., June 1920, p. 253. Details incomplete.

COMPULSORY TILLAGE APPEAL TRIBUNALS.—*See* B.A.

EMERGENCY ADVISORY COMMITTEE, SCOTLAND.—Referred to on p. xlv, of Cmd. 185, as Committee of B.A.(Sc.). Details lacking.

ELECTORAL BODIES FOR AGRICULTURAL EXECUTIVE COMMITTEES.—*App.* by certain bodies at instance of B.A.(Sc.) after reorganization of Committees in 1919. *Obj.* To elect most of the members of Committees. *Repr.* County Councils, Scottish Chamber of Agriculture, Highlands and Agricultural Society, National Farmers' Union, &c. *Ref.* Cmd. 773, p. lxii.

FERTILIZERS, CENTRAL DEPARTMENTAL COMMITTEE.—*See* M.M.

FERTILIZERS DEPARTMENTAL COMMITTEE.—Close co-operation by B.A.(Sc.) with this. *See* B.A.

FERTILIZERS JOINT ALLOCATION COMMITTEE.—*See* B.A.

FISHERIES, FISH.—*See* F.B.(Sc.).

FOOD PRODUCTION, SCOTLAND, ADVISORY COMMITTEE.—*App.* by B.A.(Sc.) Jan. 1917. *Obj.* To advise B.A.(Sc.) generally on policy and means of immediately increasing output of food and permanently developing Scottish Agriculture. *Repr.* B.A.(Sc.), agricultural interests. *Ref.* Cd. 9005, p. 158.

FOOD PRODUCTION IN SCOTLAND, COMMITTEE.—*App.* by S.S., June 1915. *Obj.* To report on steps necessary to maintain and increase home production of food, on assumption of war continuing beyond harvest of 1916. *Repr.* Parliament, B.A.(Sc.), agricultural and business experts. *Ref.* B.T.J., July 1915.

GAME AND HEATHER BURNING (SCOTLAND) COMMITTEE.—*App.* by S.S., Nov. 1919. *Obj.* To consider, relatively to war restrictions, measures for protecting permanent pastures from damage by game and for regulating heather burning. *Repr.* Parliament (Scottish members), B.A.(Sc.) (sec.), Scottish landowners, legal profession, scientists, Royal Society of Edinburgh. *Ref.* Cmd. 1401. *Diss.* July 1921.

GOAT KEEPING ADVISORY COUNCIL.—*App.* by B.A.(Sc.), about Aug. 1919. *Obj.* To assist in developing goat keeping and meeting increased demands for goats of milking strains. *Repr.* Leading Scottish goat keepers. *Ref.* Cmd. 773, p. xlix. Probably *Permanent.*

GRAZING OF DEER FORESTS (WASON) COMMITTEE.—*App.* by B.A.(Sc.) in 1916 or earlier. *Obj.* To consider utilization of deer forests for grazing cattle and sheep. *Repr.* Not stated. *Ref.* Cd. 9069, p. xliv. *Diss.* Probably later in 1916.

HERRINGS.—*See* F.B.(Sc.).

HILL PASTURES, IMPROVEMENT COMMITTEES.—*App.* by B.A.(Sc.) in 1918, one for S.E. counties and one for S.W. district, owing to scarcity of meat. *Obj.* To assist scheme for improving hill pastures and increasing supplies of stock and meat. *Repr.* Not stated. *Ref.* Cmd. 773, p. lix. *Diss.* Probably before end of 1919.

LAND USED AS DEER FORESTS, SCOTLAND, COMMITTEE.—*App.* by S.S., Nov. 1919. *Obj.* To report on agricultural or productive use of lands used as deer forests. *Repr.* B.A.(Sc.), Scottish landowners and others. *Ref.* Cmd. 1636. *Diss.* Nov. 1921.

MILK DEPOTS, COUNTRY.—*See* B.A.

PLANT TESTING STATION AND STANDING COMMITTEE.—*App.* advocated before War, but made more urgent and possibly expedited by it. For details, *see* Cmd. 1692, pp. 70–2.

POTASH FROM WOODLANDS AND UNDERGROWTH COMMITTEE. —*App.* by B.A.(Sc.) late in 1914. *Obj.* To carry out experiments in obtaining potash from ash of woodland clearings and undergrowth. *Repr.* Interests concerned, scientific experts. *Ref.* Cd. 7899, p. lxxvi.

POTATO CROPS' INSPECTION AND CERTIFICATION SCHEME, PANEL OF REFEREES.—*App.* by B.A.(Sc.), in 1919 or early 1920. *Obj.* To adjudicate doubtful cases and re-examine crops under Board's scheme for inspection and certification of potato crops. *Repr.* Potato merchants. *Ref.* Cmd. 1306, p. xc. Apparently *Permanent.*

SMALLHOLDINGS OFFICIAL BUREAU.—*App.* by B.A.(Sc.) with consent of S.S., in 1918. *Obj.* To bring proposed schemes to knowledge of ex-service men, &c. *Repr.* Official and expert. *Ref.* Cmd. 185, pp. ix, x. Probably *Permanent.*

TIMBER, HOME GROWN, INTER-DEPARTMENTAL COMMITTEE. —*See* B.A.

TRANSPORT, INLAND, SCOTLAND, STANDING CONFERENCE.— *See* S.O.

WAGES, AGRICULTURAL, SCOTLAND, CENTRAL COMMITTEE.— *App., Obj., Repr.* much as with Wages Board, Agricultural, for England and Wales (*see* B.A.), but appointment not completed till June 1918, after election of District Committees (*see* next entry), the representatives being members of these Committees, with the exception of appointed members and women. *Ref.* Cd. 9005, p. 103. *Diss.* As with English Wages Board.

WAGES, AGRICULTURAL, SCOTLAND, DISTRICT COMMITTEES.— *App.* Jan.–April 1918. Otherwise as with England and Wales (*see* B.A.). Sub-Committees were established in certain cases. *Ref.* Cd. 9005, p. 103 ; Cmd. 185, p. lxiv. *Diss.* As with English Committees.

WAGES, AGRICULTURAL, SCOTLAND, LOCAL JOINT CONCILIA-TION COMMITTEES.—As with similar Committees in England. *See* B.A.

WASON COMMITTEE.—*See* Grazing of Deer Forests.

WHITLEY COUNCIL, DEPARTMENTAL.—*App.* by B.A.(Sc.), April 1920. *Obj.* Joint discussion of matters affecting staff of B.A.(Sc.). *Repr.* Higher officials and general staff of B.A. *Ref.* Cmd. 1306, p. ix. *Permanent Body.*

WOMEN'S AGRICULTURAL DISTRICT COMMITTEES, SCOTLAND.
—*App.* jointly by B.A.(Sc.) with M.L. for Agricultural Executive Committee
districts in 1917, to be worked in connexion with M.L.   *Obj.* To ascertain
needs of farmers and supply of women available, and provide workers for
farms in connexion with training scheme.   *Repr.* Persons interested in
agriculture.   *Ref.* Cd. 9069, p. iii.

WOMEN'S EMPLOYMENT IN AGRICULTURE.— *See* M.R.

**WOMEN'S RURAL INSTITUTES (SCOTLAND) ADVISORY COM-
MITTEE.**—*App.* by the organization of the Institutes in 1917.   *Obj.* To
advise generally on organization.   *Repr.* Not stated.   *Ref.* Cmd. 185, pp. xi,
xii.   Possibly *Permanent.*

**WOMEN'S TRAINING FOR AGRICULTURE (SCOTLAND) JOINT
INTER-DEPARTMENTAL COMMITTEE.**—*App.* by B.A.(Sc.), M.L., and
M.N.S. early in 1917.   *Obj.* To organize scheme for training inexperienced
women for agriculture and forestry.   *Repr.* B.A.(Sc.), M.L., M.N.S.   *Ref.*
Cd. 9069, p. liii.   *Diss.* Apparently late in 1917.

AGRICULTURE AND TECHNICAL INSTRUCTION, IRELAND, DEPARTMENT OF

ABBREVIATION

D.A.T.I. = Department of Agriculture and Technical Instruction, Ireland.

AGRICULTURE COSTINGS COMMITTEE.—*See* M.F.

AGRICULTURE COUNTY COMMITTEES, COUNCIL.—These bodies were established in Ireland under the Agriculture and Technical Instruction (Ireland) Act, 1899. They undertook much of the administrative work in Irish agriculture in connexion with the War.

AGRICULTURAL WAGES BOARD, IRELAND.—*See* Wages.

COMPULSORY TILLAGE APPEAL TRIBUNAL.—*See* B.A., and report of D.A.T.I. for 1919–20, p. 81.

DAIRYING IN IRELAND, DECLINE OF, DEPARTMENTAL COMMITTEE.—*App.* by D.A.T.I., Sept. 1919. *Obj.* To report upon causes of decline and make recommendations for improving supplies of milk products. *Repr.* Irish agriculturalists, Irish Agricultural Organization Society, Irish Land and Labour Association, T.U.'s. *Ref.* Cmd. 808. *Diss.* May 1920.

DIVERSION OF TRAFFIC COMMITTEE.—*App.* by D.A.T.I., at conference with Carrier Companies, June 1920. *Obj.* To discuss with Companies detailed arrangement for diversion of perishable goods to different routes to avoid delays in traffic, due to labour troubles, &c. *Repr.* D.A.T.I., Carrier Companies and others. *Ref.* D.A.T.I. Report for 1919–20, p. 111.

EX-OFFICERS' HIGHER EDUCATION, ASSESSMENT COMMITTEE.—*App.* by D.A.T.I. early in 1919. *Obj.* To assist in administering scheme of higher and agricultural education for ex-officers and men of like education and to interview applicants. *Repr.* D.A.T.I., M.L. (Irish Department), Agricultural and Veterinary Colleges, Royal College of Science (Dublin). *Ref.* Cmd. 929, p. 23.
  (This is presumably the Committee for the Higher Technical Education and Agricultural Training of Ex-Service Men referred to in the report of D.A.T.I. for 1919–20, p. 89.

FERTILIZERS, CENTRAL DEPARTMENTAL COMMITTEE.—*See* M.M.

FERTILIZERS JOINT ALLOCATION COMMITTEE.—Joint appointment. *See* B.A.

FISHERMEN, DEMOBILIZATION.—*See* Adm.

FISHERY HARBOURS.—*See* D.C.

FISHERY.—*See also* H.O. *under* Coal Supplies, Fishery Sub-Committee.

FISHING VESSELS, IRISH, WAR RISKS INSURANCE COMMITTEE.—*App.* by D.A.T.I. with approval of Tre., Dec. 1917. *Obj.* To undertake insurance of Irish fishing vessels against war risks. *Repr.* D.A.T.I., Tre., experts. *Ref.* Cmd. 106, p. 107. *Diss.* May 1919.

FISH, IRISH, COMMITTEE.—*App.* by D.A.T.I. early in 1917. *Obj.* To advise and assist D.A.T.I. in increasing supplies of coarse fish. *Repr.*

Parliament, D.A.T.I., Department of Woods and Forest, riparian owners. *Ref.* Cmd. 44, p. 15.

FLAX SCUTCHING AND DISPOSAL OF TOW, DEPARTMENTAL COMMITTEE.—*App.* by D.A.T.I., Dec. 1917. *Obj.* To inquire into charges for scutching of flax and disposal of tow. *Repr.* D.A.T.I., farmers, scutch-mill owners. *Ref.* Cd. 9029. *Diss.* Mar. 1918.

FLAX SCUTCHING AND DISPOSAL OF TOW, DEPARTMENTAL COMMITTEE (NO. 2).—*App.* by D.A.T.I., Sept. 1918. *Obj.* To inquire into the charges for scutching flax and tow, with special reference to Scutch-mills (Ireland) Order, 1918, and the award to workers of 27th Aug. 1918 under M.W.A.'s, and recommend charges to be fixed. *Repr.* D.A.T.I., farmers, scutch-mill owners. *Ref.* Cd. 9196. *Diss.* Oct. 1918.

FOOD PRODUCTION IN IRELAND, ADVISORY COMMITTEE.—*App.* by D.A.T.I., Jan. 1917. *Obj.* To advise D.A.T.I. on policy and means of immediately increasing home output of food and securing permanent increase in Irish agriculture. *Repr.* D.A.T.I., agricultural interests, agricultural research. *Ref.* Cd. 9005, p. 158.

FOOD PRODUCTION IN IRELAND, DEPARTMENTAL COMMITTEE.—*App.* by D.A.T.I., June 1915. *Obj.* To report on steps necessary to maintain and increase home production of food. *Repr.* Parliament, D.A.T.I., L.A.'s, Irish Agricultural Organization Society, agricultural, business, and economic, experts. *Ref.* Cd. 8046. *Diss.* Aug. 1915.

FORESTRY, IRISH CONSULTATIVE COMMITTEE.—*See* D.C.

HARBOURS, STANDING INTER-DEPARTMENTAL CONFERENCE. —*See* M.T.

INSURANCE, WAR RISKS.—*See* Fishing Vessels, Irish.

MOTOR TRACTOR SECTION.—*App.* by D.A.T.I., Mar. 1917. *Obj.* To promote greatest possible use of tractors in food production campaign. *Repr.* Official and expert. *Ref.* Cd. 9016.

PEAT, IRISH, COMMITTEE.—*See* S.I.R.

PIG-BREEDING INDUSTRY, IRISH, DEPARTMENTAL COMMITTEE.—*App.* by D.A.T.I., Oct. 1914. *Obj.* To report upon present state of the industry, with special reference to recent decrease in pigs in Ireland. *Repr.* D.A.T.I., pig breeders. *Ref.* Cd. 7890. *Diss.* April 1915.

PUBLICITY SECTION.—*App.* by D.A.T.I., early in 1917. *Obj.* To circulate information as to need for increased food production and as to regulations and administrative measures taken. *Repr.* Official and expert. *Ref.* Cd. 9016, p. 88.

TILLAGE.—*See* Compulsory Tillage.

TIMBER, HOME-GROWN, INTER-DEPARTMENTAL COMMITTEE. —*See* B.A.

WAGES BOARD, WAGES DISTRICT COMMITTEES, AGRICULTURAL.—Generally much as with Board and Committees for England and Wales (*see* B.A.). The Board held first meeting in Sept. 1917. *See also* Cmd. 106, p. 14.

WOOL PURCHASE, IRELAND, ADVISORY COMMITTEE.—*See* W.O.

AIR BOARD AND (LATER) MINISTRY, THE,

INCLUDING THE AERONAUTICS ADVISORY COMMITTEE

The first *Air Board*, established by the Cabinet in May 1916 (*see under* War Office), was a joint Advisory Body to the War Office and the Admiralty. The existence of a separate Department for the Air commenced with the establishment of the *Second Air Board* in December 1916 under a President and Parliamentary Secretary by the New Ministries and Secretaries Act, 1916 (6 & 7 Geo. V, c. 68), to secure and maintain an adequate supply of aircraft and to be responsible for principles of design, and allocation of supplies between military and naval services. The organization of actual manufacture was transferred to the Ministry of Munitions, who were represented on the Board. This Board contained representatives of Parliament, the Admiralty, War Office, and Ministry of Munitions and various experts.

By the summer of 1917, the possibility of a surplus of aircraft over immediate requirements rendered further measures necessary to secure its most efficient utilization, and especially the provision of an Air War Staff for the Board. Consequently, by the Air Force (Constitution) Act of Nov. 1917, the *Air Ministry* replaced the Air Board, and an Air Council was constituted on 2nd Jan. 1918, on similar lines to the Army Council. The Air Council included representatives of the Admiralty, War Office, and Ministry of Munitions. This body was entrusted with the duties of organizing a definite Air Force, the necessary powers being gradually transferred from the Admiralty and the War Office. The Air Minister received the status of a Secretary of State. The Ministry was established as a *Permanent Department*. The Aeronautics Advisory Committee, established 1909, reported direct to the Prime Minister, until establishment of the Ministry, when it reported to the Air Council. In Nov. 1919, the Meteorological Office (pre-war body) was transferred to the Ministry, the Meteorological Committee being reconstituted (*see* Cmd. 800, p. 7). *References*. Public General Acts, 1916, 1917–18 ; Cd. 9005, pp. 57–63.

ABBREVIATIONS

A.M. = Air Ministry.
A.B. = Second Air Board.
A.A.C. = Aeronautics Advisory Committee.
N.P.L. = National Physical Laboratory.
R.A.F. = Royal Air Force.
R.F.C. = Royal Flying Corps.

ACCIDENTS INVESTIGATION COMMITTEE.—*App.* by A.M., Jan. 1918. *Obj.* To advise Accident Department of A.M. on accidents and investigations concerning them. *Repr.* A.A.C. and other experts. *Ref.* Cd. 9145, pp. 12–13 ; Cmd. 448, pp. 23–4. Possibly *Permanent*.

ADHESIVES.—*See* S.I.R.

AERIAL OPERATIONS COMMITTEE.—*See* Cabinet *under* Priorities, War, Committee.

AERODROME CONSTRUCTION.—*See* Tre.

AERODYNAMICS.—*See* next entry.

AERONAUTICAL RESEARCH COMMITTEE.—*App.* by A.M., on recommendation of Education and Research, Aeronautical, Committee (q. v.), in 1920. *Obj.* To take over, with extended powers, the functions of the A.A.C. *Repr.* Presumably, as with A.A.C., A.M., Royal Society, scientists, engineers, &c. *Ref.* Cmd. 1120, pp. 4, 5. *Permanent Body.* (The Committee was to act with appropriate Sub-Committees.)

AERONAUTICS ADVISORY TECHNICAL SUB-COMMITTEES.—*App.* by A.A.C. during the War, the Sub-Committees, though they partly arose from the normal work of the A.A.C., being actually appointed as a result of the War. *Obj.* To advise on special matters connected with various technical and engineering problems of aviation. *Repr.* A.M., A.A.C., Army, Navy, N.P.L., Royal Aircraft Establishments, Aeronautical Inspection Department, experts. *Ref.* Cd. 8629, p. 7 ; Cmd. 488, pp. 6, 11, 16, 18, 19, 20 ; Cmd. 1458, pp. 4, 5. Apparently *Permanent Bodies.*

The following Sub-Committees were appointed : Aerodynamics (1917 or 1918), Aeronautics (1916 or 1917), Airships and Kite Balloons (Aug. 1917), Engine, Internal Combustion Problems (Feb. 1917), Light Alloys (about Dec. 1917), Meteorology (Aug. 1918), Materials and Chemistry (1919 or earlier), Research, Co-ordination of Theory and Practice (1918), Scale Effects (1917). Certain other Sub-Committees are dealt with below.

AIR CONFERENCE.—*Held* at Guildhall, London, 12th–14th Oct. 1920. *Obj.* General discussion of problems of military and civilian aviation. *Repr.* A.M., R.A.F., Royal Society and various aeronautical and constructive societies, manufacturers, scientists. *Ref.* Cmd. 1157. The Conference passed a resolution in favour of holding Annual Conferences, and a Second Conference was held, Feb. 1922 (*see* Cmd. 1619).

AIR-SCREW DESIGN COMMITTEE.—*App.* by A.M. early in 1918. *Obj.* To investigate questions of air-screw design. *Repr.* N.P.L., experts. *Ref.* Cd. 9145, p. 8. *Diss.* Possibly replaced in 1919 by panel of Aerodynamics Sub-Committee (*see under* Aeronautics Advisory Technical Sub-Committees.)

AIRSHIPS.—*See under* Aeronautics Advisory.

AIR TRANSPORT SUB-COMMITTEE.—*App.* by Aeronautical Research Committee, in 1922 or 1923. *Obj.* To consider scientific and technical problems of Imperial Air Mail routes and act as co-ordinating body between Research Committee and Civil Aviation Department. *Repr.* These two bodies, Research Directorate, Royal Society, scientists. *Ref.* Aeronautical Research Committee's Report for 1922–3 (H.M.S.O., 1923). *Still in existence,* end 1923.

AIR.—*See also* Imperial Air Communications below, Cabinet, and W.O.

ALLOYS RESEARCH COMMITTEE.—A private Committee appointed by the Institute of Mechanical Engineers co-operating with Light Alloys Sub-Committee (*see under* Aeronautics Advisory Technical Sub-Committees). *Ref.* Cmd. 488, p. 18.

ALUMINIUM CORROSION.—*See* S.I.R.

AMERICAN AVIATION MISSION.—*App.* by U.S.A. Government in winter of 1918–19. *Obj.* To investigate military and civil uses of aviation in England, France, and Italy. *Repr.* U.S.A. War Departments and manufacturers. *Ref.* Cmd. 384. *Diss.* July–Aug. 1919.

AVIATION, BRITISH COMMISSION IN PARIS.—*Obj.* To make contracts for aeroplanes and engines. *See* H.C. Nos. 83 etc., 1919, p. xv. For Aviation, *see also* Cabinet.

BALLOONS.—*See* Kite Balloons.

CHEMISTRY.—*See under* Aeronautics Advisory.

CIVIL AERIAL TRANSPORT COMMITTEE.—*App.* by B.A., April 1917. *Obj.* To report upon possible post-war development of civil and commercial aviation and post-war uses of surplus aircraft and personnel of R.A.F. *Repr.* Parliament, prominent public men, various Government Departments, Meteorological Office, Dominions and Indian Governments, Aircraft and Aero-engine Manufacturers, Labour, aircraft experts. *Ref.* Cd. 8916. *Diss.* Report signed May, issued Dec., 1918.

(N.B. The Committee divided the inquiry between five Sub-Committees on Business Questions relating to Manufacture, Labour, Law and Policy, Research and Education, Technical Questions. *See* Cd. 9005, p. 64.)

CIVIL AVIATION ADVISORY COMMITTEE AND (LATER) BOARD. —*App.* by A.M., Feb.–May 1919. *Obj.* To advise the Civil Aviation Department (q. v.) on policy and methods of assisting civil aviation. *Repr.* A.M., W.O., manufacturers, insurance, flying and scientific experts. *Ref.* Cmd. 449, 770. *Diss.* Replaced in 1922 by permanent Civil Aviation Advisory Board with similar reference and wider representation (*see* Cmd. 1739).

CIVIL AVIATION DEPARTMENT.—*App.* by the Government through A.M., Feb. 1919. *Obj.* To develop civilian aviation, including transition from war to peace flying. *Repr.* Official and expert. *Ref.* Cmd. 418, p. 2. *Permanent Department.*

COMMISSIONS BOARD (R.F.C.).—*App.* to select candidates for commissions in R.F.C. *Ref.* Cd. 8825, p. 80. Other details not given.

COMPETITIONS COMMITTEE.—*App.* by A.M., possibly in conjunction with aircraft industry, late in 1919. *Obj.* To draw up rules for competitions, with object of furthering safety and comfort of air travel. *Repr.* A.M. and aircraft industry, with expert assistance. *Ref.* Cmd. 800, p. 12. *Diss.* Early 1920.

CONTRACTS FOR CLOTHING, COURT OF INQUIRY.—*App.* by Air Council, Aug. 1919. *Obj.* To investigate various allegations as to contracts for Women's Royal Air Force. *Repr.* A.M., R.A.F., Women's Royal Air Force. *Ref.* Cmd. 347. *Diss.* Aug. 1919. *See also* Tre.

DESIGN.—*See* Air-screw Design, and Aeronautics Advisory.

EDUCATION AND RESEARCH, AERONAUTICS, COMMITTEE.— *App.* by A.M., Oct. 1918, with revision of reference in 1919. *Obj.* To report upon organization of aeronautical education and research after the war and (later) upon decisions of Government in these matters. *Repr.*

A.M., S.I.R., N.P.L., Imperial College of Science, Science Museum, aircraft manufacturers, scientists. *Ref.* Cmd. 554. *Diss.* Dec. 1919.

EDUCATION, ARMY, IMPERIAL.—*See* W.O.

EDUCATION.—*See also under* Civil Aerial Transport Committee.

ELECTRIFICATION.—*See* Kite Balloons.

ENGINE.—*See* Aeronautics Advisory.

FIRE PREVENTION SUB-COMMITTEE.—*App.* by A.A.C. in 1919. *Obj.* To consider measures to minimize risks of fire on aircraft. *Repr.* A.M., A.A.C., R.A.F., Royal Society, scientists. *Ref.* Cmd. 1120, pp. 4, 13.

IMPERIAL AIR COMMUNICATIONS COMMITTEE.—*App.* by special Conference of Premiers of the Empire prior to Imperial Conference of June–Aug. 1921. *Obj.* To report upon cost of providing imperial service of airships and aeroplanes. *Repr.* A.M., C.O., In.O., Tre., Governments of Dominions. *Ref.* Cmd. 1474, pp. 45–55. *Diss.* July, 1921.

INFORMATION AFFECTING INSURANCE COMMITTEE.—*App.* by Conference held at A.M. with representatives of aviation and insurance, Jan. 1921. *Obj.* To consider procedure and responsibility for collecting and disseminating information. *Repr.* A.M. Society of Aircraft Constructors, Lloyds. *Ref.* Cmd. 1342, p. 12.

INSTITUTES.—*See* W.O.

INTER-ALLIED AERONAUTICAL COMMISSION OF CONTROL.—*See* Cmd. 1073, pp. 19, 20. *App.* by Allied Powers jointly, in 1919 or 1920, to carry out aircraft provisions of Peace Treaties. Other details lacking.

INTERNATIONAL COMMISSION ON AERIAL NAVIGATION.—*App.* in 1922 by Governments concerned in International Air Convention arranged by Peace Conference. *Obj.* To secure the carrying out of the Convention. *Repr.* The Governments concerned. *Ref.* P.G.A., 1920; Cmd. 1559, p. 5. *Permanent Body.*

INTERNATIONAL RADIO COMMUNICATION TECHNICAL COMMITTEE.—*App.* by chief Allied Governments between Mar. and Sept. 1921. *Obj.* To deal with technical problems in connexion with International Radio Convention. *Repr.* Technical experts of countries represented. *Ref.* Cmd. 1559, p. 11.

INTERNATIONAL RADIO CONVENTION, GOVERNMENT DEPARTMENTAL COMMITTEE.—*App.* apparently by Committee of Imperial Defence in 1919. *Obj.* To prepare British scheme for such a Convention. *Repr.* Presumably Government Departments concerned, and possibly others. *Ref.* Cmd. 800, p. 6. *Diss.* During 1920.

INTERNATIONAL SUB-COMMISSION ON AERIAL NAVIGATION.—*App.* by Peace Conference in 1919. *Obj.* To draw up scheme for International Convention for the Regulation of International Aerial Navigation. *Repr.* Allied and Associated States. *Ref.* H.C., No. 266, 1919. *Diss.* Reported during 1919.

INVENTIONS, AIR, COMMITTEE.—*App.* by A.B., Aug. 1917. *Obj.* To examine all inventions relating to heavier-than-air craft and develop and operate suitable ones. *Repr.* A.B., A.A.C., Adm., W.O., R.A.F., M.M., N.P.L., scientific experts. *Ref.* Cd. 9145, pp. 11, 12 ; Cmd. 488, p. 23.

KITE BALLOONS, ELECTRIFICATION, COMMITTEE.—*App.* by A.A.C. in 1919. *Obj.* To report upon means of protecting kite balloons from damage caused by atmospheric electrical discharges. *Repr.* A.M., A.A.C., R.A.F., Royal Society, scientists. *Ref.* Cmd. 1120, p. 4.

KITE BALLOONS.—*See also* Aeronautics Advisory Technical Sub-Committees.

LOAD FACTORS SUB-COMMITTEE.—*App.* by A.A.C., at request of A.M., Oct. 1919. *Obj.* To prepare rules for load factors of civil aircraft and grant of certificates of air worthiness. *Repr.* A.M., A.A.C., Royal Aeronautical Society, Society of British Aircraft Constructors. *Ref.* Cmd. 1120, pp. 4, 11.

MEDICAL ADMINISTRATION COMMITTEE.—*App.* by A.B., after establishment of separate medical air service, in 1917. *Obj.* To advise on administration of service. *Repr.* A.B., M.R.C., medical and other experts. *Ref.* Cd. 8981, p. 63. *Diss.* 1918 or 1919.

MEDICAL (CIVIL AVIATION), INTER-ALLIED, SUB-COMMITTEE.— *App.* in 1921 to annual Anglo-Franco-Belgian Conferences on Civil Aviation by Governments concerned. *Obj.* To investigate fatigue and other medical problems, as affecting civil pilots. *Repr.* Medical experts of the three Countries. *Ref.* Cmd. 1559, p. 14. Presumably more or less *Permanent.*

MEDICAL INVESTIGATION, AIR, COMMITTEE.—*App.* by A.B., in consultation with M.R.C., in 1917. *Obj.* To advise generally on medical aspects of aeronautics, co-ordinate investigations, and circulate information. *Repr.* A.B., M.R.C., W.O., medical experts, scientific research, with correspondents in France. *Ref.* Cd. 8981, pp. 62, 77.

(N.B. A Medical Research Committee, referred to in Cd. 9005, p. 63, as appointed to investigate physiological and similar problems of flying at high altitudes and disabilities specially affecting flying men, may be the same body.)

MEDICAL SERVICES, AIR, ADVISORY COMMITTEE.—*App.* by A.B. in 1917. *Obj.* To advise upon best medical organization for war service. *Repr.* A.B., M.R.C., medical and other experts. *Ref.* Cd. 8981, p. 62.

METEOROLOGY.—*See* Heading to Section and Aeronautics Advisory Technical Sub-Committees.

MUSICAL, AIR FORCE, DIRECTORATE.—*App.* by A.M. in 1918. *Obj.* To provide music for R.A.F., and establish and administer School of Music for training musicians. *Repr.* Musicians. *Ref.* Cmd. 325, p. 100. *School intended to be permanent.*

NAVIGATIONAL INSTRUMENTS COMMITTEE.—*App.* by A.M. in 1920 or 1921. *Obj.* To report generally upon subject with view to issue of directions by A.M. *Repr.* A.M., aircraft industries, insurance. *Ref.* Cmd. 1559, p. 6. *Diss.* 1921.

ORGANIZATION, AIR, COMMITTEE.—*App.* by War Cabinet, Aug. 1917. *Obj.* To work out a scheme to give effect to Cabinet's decision to establish

A.M. *Repr.* War Cabinet, A.B., Adm., Tre., W.O. *Ref.* Cd. 9005, p. 59. *Diss.* By Nov. 1917.

OXYGEN SUPPLY FOR FLYING MEN, INVESTIGATION COMMITTEE.—*App.* by A.B. in 1917. *Obj.* To study supply of oxygen to flying men. *Repr.* Medical and other experts. *Ref.* Cd. 8825, p. 79.

RESEARCH.—*See* Aeronautical Advisory Technical Sub-Committees, Civil Aerial Transport, Education, Medical Investigation.

STAFFS INVESTIGATION COMMITTEE.—*App.* by A.M. in 1919. *Obj.* To report on reductions of staff and redistribution of duties. *Repr.* Chief Departments of A.M. *Ref.* H.C., No. 168, 1919, p. 6.

STORES ACCOUNTS (AIR MINISTRY) COMMITTEE.—*App.* apparently by A.M. in 1920. *Obj.* To prepare improved system of store accounts for A.M. *Repr.* Not stated. *Ref.* H.C., No. 321, 1920, p. xiv.

TECHNICAL.—*See* Aeronautics Advisory, and Civil Aerial Transport.

BLOCKADE, MINISTRY OF

The Ministry was established in the first part of 1916, taking over various functions from other Departments, notably the Foreign Office, under a Minister of Blockade. It was organized into five Departments for (i) Enemy Supplies Restriction, (ii) War Trade (*see* separate heading), (iii) Foreign Trade, (iv) Finance, and (v) War Trade Statistical, which are dealt with below. The Ministry appears to have come to an end in 1919.

ABBREVIATION
M.B. = Ministry of Blockade.

BLOCKADE MINISTRY COMMITTEE.—*App.* prior to Sept. 1917. *Ref.* Cd. 8741, p. 3. No details.

CEMENT EXPORTS COMMITTEE.—*App.* by M.B., Nov. 1917. *Obj.* To inquire into desirability of permitting exports of cement to Holland to be resumed. *Repr.* Parliament, W.O., merchants. *Ref.* Cd. 9023. *Diss.* Mar. 1918.

ENEMY SUPPLIES RESTRICTION DEPARTMENT.—*App.* by M.B., June 1916. *Obj.* To deal with diversion from enemy countries of supplies not touched by the Naval Blockade and administer agreements for purchase of fish and agricultural products. *Repr.* Official and expert. *Ref.* Cd. 9220, p. 15.

FINANCE DEPARTMENT.—*App.* by M.B. in 1916. *Obj.* To prevent transaction of enemy business through this country. *Repr.* Official and expert. *Ref.* Cd. 9005 ; H.C., No. 132, 1918, p. 44.

FOREIGN TRADE DEPARTMENT.—*App.* by M.B. in 1916. *Obj.* Chiefly to prepare and administer Black List of enemy firms in neutral countries. *Repr.* Official and expert. *Ref.* No. 132, 1918, p. 44.

INTELLIGENCE.—*See* W.T.D.

STATISTICAL, WAR TRADE, DEPARTMENT.—*App.* in May 1915, and transferred to M.B. in 1916. *Obj.* To collect and report on information regarding foreign trade of Holland and Scandinavia for purposes of blockade and rationing agreements. *Repr.* Official and expert. *Ref.* Cd. 9220, p. 14 ; H.C. No. 132, 1918, p. 44.

THE CABINET, AND THE GOVERNMENT
GENERALLY, INCLUDING THE LAW OFFICERS

(N.B. This Section includes many Inter-Allied Bodies, Royal Commissions and bodies appointed by or at instance of Imperial War Conference and Committee of Imperial Defence. Bodies, however, which are clearly attached to particular Government Departments are dealt with in the sections dealing with those Departments, even when their immediate appointment was made by the Prime Minister or Cabinet. Bodies originating in the Privy Council are dealt with under that heading.)

Important modifications were made in the pre-war Cabinet System during the War. In the winter of 1914–15, a small War Committee of the Cabinet was established (*see* below), though the final responsibility remained with the full Cabinet. In December 1916, on Mr. Lloyd George's accession to the Premiership, the War Cabinet was established, meeting for the first time on the 9th December. It consisted of five members of the Government, who did not, with one exception, have charge of administrative departments. A representative of the Overseas Dominions (General Smuts) attended its meetings, when in the country, from June 1917. The War Cabinet initiated policy and co-ordinated the activities of Government Departments. For this purpose, Ministers, Departmental Officials, and certain experts attended meetings of the War Cabinet, when their particular Departments were under discussion. The War Cabinet was assisted by a Secretariat, ' built up on the nucleus of the secretariat of the Committee of Imperial Defence ', and the Prime Minister was assisted by a smaller secretariat. *References*, Cd. 9005, Cmd. 325 (War Cabinet Reports for 1917 and 1918). The Imperial War Cabinet is dealt with below.

(N.B. During the existence of the War Cabinet, a reference to the Cabinet, without qualification, means the general body of ministers who normally form the Cabinet.)

ACCOMMODATION, WAR CABINET, COMMITTEE.—Reference in Cmd. 62, p. 3. No details. *See also* O.W.

AERIAL OPERATIONS COMMITTEE.—*See* Priorities, War, Committee.

AGRICULTURAL, AGRICULTURE.—*See* B.A., M.R.

AIR COMMUNICATIONS COMMITTEE OF IMPERIAL ECONOMIC CONFERENCE.—*App.* by Conference, Oct. 1919. *Obj.* To discuss Burney scheme of air communications with view to imperial co-operation for interchange of information on air matters. *Repr.* A.M., Tre., C.O., Dominions, I.F.S., India. *Ref.* Cmd. 2009, pp. 363–5. *Diss.* Nov. 1923.

AIRCRAFT.—*See under* Oxygen Research.

AIR, JOINT WAR COMMITTEE.—*App.* by Cabinet. *See* W.O.

ALIENS, CERTIFICATES OF NATURALIZATION REVISION COMMITTEE.—*See* H.O.

ALIENS IN GOVERNMENT OFFICES COMMITTEE.—*App.* by P.M., Aug. 1918. *Obj.* To examine cases for continuance in Government employment on national grounds of aliens, not of Allied parentage. *Repr.* Parliament, Legal Profession. *Ref.* Cmd. 195. *Diss.* Feb. 1919.

ALLOCATION.—*See under* Priorities, War.

AMERICAN BOARD.—*App.* by War Cabinet during 1917. *Obj.* To consider British requirements for purchases in America, along with Inter-Allied Executives, and determine allocation and priority of finance and transport between Government Departments (referring disputed points to War Cabinet) and pass on requirements to Inter-Allied Council on War Purchases and Finance. *Repr.* War Cabinet, F.O., M.S., Tre., and Departments requiring supplies. *Ref.* Cd. 9005, p. 173.

(N.B. Similar organizations were established in France and Italy.)

AMERICAN EXCHANGES, ANGLO-FRENCH MISSION.—*App.* jointly by British and French Governments, about Aug. 1915. *Obj.* To visit America and promote arrangements for stabilizing exchanges. *Repr.* British and French Governments, Tre., bankers. *Ref.* B.T.J., 9th Sept. 1915. *Diss.* Presumably later in 1915.

ANTI-SUBMARINE COMMITTEES OF EXPERTS.—*App.* by War Cabinet, in 1917 or 1918, in Manchester, Glasgow, and London. *Obj.* To co-ordinate scientific and engineering talent for anti-submarine campaign. *Repr.* Leading scientists, engineers, and manufacturers. *Ref.* Cmd. 325, p. 46. *Diss.* At or after close of War.

APPORTIONMENT, PERMANENT INTERNATIONAL COMMITTEE, WITH INTER-ALLIED COMMISSION.—*App.* internationally and by Allies at Berne before American entry to War and joined by America, Nov. or Dec. 1917. *Obj.* Apparently to settle questions of apportionment between Allies and Neutrals. *Repr.* International and Inter-allied. *Ref.* T., 6th Dec. 1917, p. 8.

ARMY AND NAVY PAY COMMITTEE.—*App.* by War Cabinet in 1918. *Obj.* To investigate questions of pay and allowances in Army on behalf of War Cabinet. *Repr.* War Cabinet and presumably others. *Ref.* Cmd. 325, p. 5.

AVIATION AND TANKS, INTER-ALLIED TECHNICAL COMMITTEES.—*App.* under military representatives of Supreme War Council about beginning of 1918. *Obj.* To secure interchange of views, and act as technical advisers to Supreme Council. *Repr.* Technical experts. *Ref.* Cmd. 325, p. 22.

AWARDS TO INVENTORS, INVESTIGATING COMMITTEE.—*App.* by the Commission (*see* next entry), at suggestion of Tre., in 1919. *Obj.* To carry out preliminary examination of doubtful cases to avoid waste of time. *Repr.* The Commission. *Ref.* Cmd. 1112, p. 6. *Diss. See* next entry.

AWARDS TO INVENTORS, ROYAL COMMISSION.—*App.* by Royal Warrant, Mar. 1919, and powers extended by Warrant of Oct. 1919. *Obj.* To hear and adjudicate upon disputed claims in respect of inventions utilized for war purposes. *Repr.* Parliament, Tre., Patents Office, Legal

Profession, banking, scientists, employers (engineering and chemical), labour. *Ref.* Cmd. 1112, 1782. *Diss.* Second Report issued Nov. 1922, but work apparently not completed.

BELGIAN AND NORTHERN FRANCE INVADED PROVINCES COMMITTEE.—A committee which was carrying out work of provisioning these provinces and similar measures is referred to in T., 6th Dec. 1917, p. 8. Other details are lacking.

BELGIAN (INDUSTRIAL AND AGRICULTURAL) RECONSTRUCTION, INTER-ALLIED COMMISSION.—*App.* by Allied Governments in 1918. *Obj.* To organize reconstruction of reoccupied areas of Belgium. *Repr.* Chief Allied Governments. *Ref.* Cmd. 325, p. 27.

BELGIAN RECONSTRUCTION, BRITISH COMMISSION.—*App.* by the Government, April 1919. *Obj.* To give assistance to reconstruction of Belgian industries. *Repr.* Prominent public man and two commercial secretaries of Legation at Brussels with staff of technical experts. *Ref.* B.T.J., 1st May 1919, p. 563; T., 17th Sept. 1919, p. 14. *Diss.* Sept. 1919.

BELGIAN RELIEF COMMITTEE.—*See* Cmd. 325, p. 169.

BELGIAN TRADE COMMITTEE.—Joint Committee of B.T. and F.O. appointed apparently by Government.—*See* B.T.

BLOCKADE.—*See under* Paris International Conference.

BRITISH EMPIRE STATISTICAL CONFERENCE.—*Arranged* to meet in London, Jan. 1920, and worked through Committees and Sub-Committees. *Obj.* To discuss co-ordination of official statistics throughout British Empire. *Repr.* Government statistical officers in States of British Empire. *Ref.* Cmd. 648. *Diss.* Feb. 1920.

BRITISH NATIONALITY, LAW OF, COMMITTEE.—*App.* by Imperial Conference, Oct.–Nov. 1923. *Obj.* To investigate various questions of Law of British Nationality. *Repr.* H.O., Dominions, &c. *Ref.* Cmd. 1989, pp. 21–2. *Diss.* Nov. 1923.

BRITISH TRADE CORPORATION.—*App.* by Royal Charter of April 1917, with provision for remaining British in character and free from foreign control. *Obj.* To give financial assistance to British traders and manufacturers, especially in overseas trade, and in circumstances unsuited to normal banking operations. *Repr.* Directors were prominent men in industry, business, and banking. *Ref.* B.T.J., 17th May 1917. *Permanent.*

(The work has included organization of Bureau of Trade Information, *see* T., 18th June 1917, p. 2.)

BRYCE COMMITTEE.—*See* German Outrages.

CHARTERING, NEUTRAL SHIPPING, INTER-ALLY COMMITTEE, AND (LATER) CHARTERING EXECUTIVE.—*App.* as Committee by British, French, and Italian Governments, April 1916, becoming Chartering Executive Dec. 1916, with powers in full operation by Mar. 1917. *Obj.* Under the Committee, to secure neutral tonnage for Allies at favourable rates, whilst Executive had wide powers of chartering neutral and other shipping for the various Governments and their nationals. *Repr.* The three Governments, Commission Internationale de Ravitaillement. *Ref.* Cd. 9005; T., 14th Mar. 1917, p. 3.

CIVIL INDUSTRIES COMMITTEE.—*See* M.M., under Priorities, War.

CIVIL SERVICE, APPLICATION OF WHITLEY REPORT, ETC.—*See* M.L.

CIVIL SERVICE, CONCILIATION.—*See* Conciliation.

CLASSICS IN EDUCATION COMMITTEE.—*App.* by P.M., Nov. 1919. *Obj.* To investigate and advise on position of classics in educational system. *Repr.* H. L., Universities, Public and other Secondary Schools, teachers, and educational experts, British and Royal Societies, women. *Ref.* H.M.S.O., 1921. *Diss.* June 1921.

COAL AND COKE.—*See also under* Programmes Committees.

COAL INDUSTRY (SANKEY) COMMISSION.—*App.* by the Government under Coal Industry Commission Act, Feb. 1919. *Obj.* To inquire into position and conditions of the industry. *Repr.* Judges, mining employers, and T.U.'s, employers and workpeople in other industries, with expert assessors. *Ref.* L.G. Mar. 1919 ; Cmd. 360. *Diss.* June 1919.

COAL TRADE CO-ORDINATION COMMITTEE.—*App.* by Government in summer of 1916. *Obj.* To co-ordinate work of Committees dealing with the industry. *Repr.* The Committees, through their Chairmen. *Ref.* Cd 8697, p. 170. *Diss.* By Feb. 1917.

COMMERCIAL AND INDUSTRIAL POLICY AFTER THE WAR, COMMITTEE.—*App.* by Cabinet, July 1916. *Obj.* To consider post-war policy with special reference to Paris Resolutions (*see* Economic Conference) the position of essential industries, &c. *Repr.* Parliament, S.I.R., Industry, Agriculture, general business and commercial interests, Labour. *Ref.* Cd. 9032–5. *Diss.* Dec. 1917.

COMMISSION INTERNATIONALE D'ACHATS DE BOIS.—*App.* jointly by British, French, and Italian Governments early in 1916 and subsequently joined by other Allies. *Obj.* Joint purchase of timber for Governments concerned. *Repr.* The various Governments, Timber Supplies Department (*see* B.T.). *Ref.* B.T.J., 7th Mar. 1918.

COMMISSION INTERNATIONALE DE RAVITAILLEMENT.—*App.* jointly by British and French Governments, Aug. 1914, and subsequently joined by other Allies. *Obj.* To organize joint purchase of munitions, equipment, and food for Governments concerned, and eventually all allies, and prevent competition in the same markets. *Repr.* The Governments concerned, the British representation including Committee of Imperial Defence, chief Government Departments, and military, naval, and commercial experts. *Ref.* B.T.J., 26th Nov. 1914, 16th May 1918.

COMMISSION INTERNATIONALE DE RAVITAILLEMENT, BRITISH EXECUTIVE STAFF.—*App.* as part of organization of Commission, Aug. 1914, and attached for general administrative purposes to F.O. *Obj.* To handle information obtained through the Commission's work, carry out general official work, inquiries, &c. *Repr.* Civil Servants, with Director from B.T., business men, military experts. *Ref.* B.T.J., 16th May 1918.

COMMISSION INTERNATIONALE DE RAVITAILLEMENT, RUSSIAN COMMITTEE.—*App.* by Cabinet, in 1914 or 1915. *Obj.* To deal with Russian needs and supplies under the Commission and later those of Rumania (*see also* Rumanian Supplies) and advise Commission upon Russian questions, where Cabinet sanction needed. *Repr.* As with Commission with special representation of Russia and Rumania. *Ref.* Cd. 9005. *Diss.* In abeyance by end of 1917.

COMMISSION INTERNATIONALE DE RAVITAILLEMENT, RUSSIAN LIQUIDATION COMMITTEE.—*App.* by Allied Governments, under the Commission in 1917, after military breakdown of Russia. *Obj.* To utilize speedily for other purposes supplies intended for Russia. *Repr.* Allied Governments. *Ref.* Cmd. 325, p. 26; H.C., No. 116, 1920, p. 38. *Diss.* Apparently not before 1920.

COMPENSATION.—*See* Defence of the Realm Losses, and War Compensation.

CONCILIATION AND ARBITRATION BOARD (GOVERNMENT EMPLOYEES)—*App.* by War Cabinet, Feb. 1917. *Obj.* To settle questions of remuneration of non-manual Government employees. *Repr.* Parliament Employers, Labour, assisted by official and employees' representatives. *Ref.* Cd. 9017.

CONSCIENTIOUS OBJECTORS.—*See* B.T.

COTTON, EGYPTIAN, CONTROL ADVISORY BOARD.—*App.* jointly by British and Egyptian Governments, Mar. 1918. *Obj.* To assist the Commission (*see* next entry) to carry out scheme of purchase and control. *Repr.* Export houses, cotton growers, banks. *Ref.* B.T.J., 21st Mar. 1918.

COTTON, EGYPTIAN, CONTROL COMMISSION.—*App.* jointly by British and Egyptian Governments, Mar. 1918. *Obj.* To carry out from Aug. 1918, on behalf of British Government, purchase and control of Egyptian cotton crops. *Repr.* British and Egyptian Governments. *Ref.* B.T.J., 21st Mar. 1918.

COTTON INQUIRY TRIBUNAL.—*App.* by P.M., Sept. 1918. *Obj.* To inquire into matters arising out of recent dispute in cotton industry. *Repr.* Public men with business and administrative experience. *Ref.* T., 28th Sept. 1918, p. 3. *Diss.* Later in 1918.

COTTON.—*See also under* Programmes Committees.

COUNTY COURTS, LORD CHANCELLOR'S COMMITTEE.—*App.* by Lord Chancellor, *Dec.* 1916. *Obj.* To report on existing County Courts' organization. *Repr.* County Court Judges, Legal Profession. *Ref.* Cmd. 431. *Diss.* 1918 or 1919.

COUNTY COURT STAFFS, LORD CHANCELLOR'S COMMITTEE.— *App.* by Lord Chancellor, July 1919. *Obj.* To inquire into conditions of employment and remuneration of County Court Staffs. *Repr.* Parliament, Tre., Judges, Legal Profession. *Ref.* Cmd. 1049. *Diss.* July 1920.

CREWE HOUSE COMMITTEE.—*App.* by the Government. *See* M.I.

DARDANELLES, SPECIAL COMMISSION.—*App.* by Special Commissions (Dardanelles and Mesopotamia) Act, 1916 of 17th Aug. 1916, which named the Commissioners. *Obj.* To inquire into origin, inception and conduct of, and responsibility for, operations in Dardanelles and

Gallipoli. *Repr.* Parliament, the Dominions, Naval and Military Authorities, Judges, Legal Profession. *Ref.* P.G.A., 1916, c. 34 ; Cd. 8490. *Diss.* Dec. 1917.

DEBT FUNDING DELEGATION TO U.S.A.—*App.* by Cabinet in autumn of 1922. *Obj.* To visit U.S.A. and discuss arrangements for funding British Debt. *Repr.* Government and Financial Experts. *Ref.* T., 29th Sept. 1922, p. 16. *Diss.* The arrangement for funding was reached in 1923.

DECIMAL COINAGE, ROYAL COMMISSION.—*App.* by Royal Warrant, Aug. 1918. *Obj.* To consider introduction of a decimal system of coinage. *Repr.* Parliament, Tre., The Mint., Government Actuary, G.I., Banking ; Manufacture, Commerce, Insurance, Economists, Labour, and other prominent public men. *Ref.* Cmd. 628. *Diss.* Feb. 1920.

DEFENCE AND POLICE.—*See* Irish Convention.

DEFENCE OF THE REALM (LICENSED TRADE CLAIMS) ROYAL COMMISSION.—*App.* by Royal Warrant, 2nd Aug. 1915. *Obj.* To adjudicate on Liquor Trade claims for compensation in respect of exercise of Government powers under D.O.R.A. *Repr.* Legal Profession, chartered accountants, business men. *Ref.* Cmd. 1265. *Diss.* Mar. 1921.

DEFENCE OF THE REALM (LOSSES) ROYAL COMMISSION.—*App.* by Royal Warrant 31st Mar. 1915 and reconstituted with extended powers 18th Dec. 1918 (*see* Cmd. 404, p. 5). *Obj.* To consider claims for compensation for losses to property or business owing to state interference for Defence of the Realm, and subsequently deal with claims under Indemnity Act, 1920. *Repr.* Parliament, agriculture, industry, Legal Profession. *Ref.* Cmd. 8359 ; P.G.A., 1920, c. 48. *Diss.* Aug. 1920, functions taken over by War Compensation Court (q. v.).

DEMOBILIZATION, MILITARY, COMMITTEE OF THE BRITISH EMPIRE.—*App.* by War Cabinet, July 1918, by resolution of Imperial War Conference. *Obj.* To co-ordinate demobilization plans and procedure of various Imperial Governments. *Repr.* W.O., In.O., M.S., Military Authorities of Dominions and Colonies. *Ref.* Cd. 9177, p. 7 ; B.T.J., 1st Aug. 1918. *Diss.* At or before close of demobilization.

DEMOBILIZATION SECTION, WAR CABINET.—*App.* by War Cabinet, Dec. 1918, under Sir E. Geddes. *Obj.* To co-ordinate work of Government Departments dealing with demobilization. *Repr.* War Cabinet, official and expert. *Ref.* Cmd. 325, p. 279. *Diss.* During 1919.

DEMOBILIZATION, WAR CABINET, COMMITTEE.—*App.* by War Cabinet, 30th Oct. 1918, sometimes known as Smuts Committee. *Obj.* To supervise and control demobilization and resettlement. *Repr.* War Cabinet (Gen. Smuts, Chairman). *Ref.* Cmd. 325, p. 5. *Diss.* Dec. 1918 on establishment of Demobilization Section.

DEMOBILIZATION.—*See also* M.L.

DISPOSALS.—*See* M.M.

DOUBLE INCOME TAX.—*See* Income Tax.

DYE INDUSTRY DEVELOPMENT, CABINET COMMITTEE.—*App.* by the Government in first half of War. *Obj.* To consider means for establishing and securing British dye-making industry. *Repr.* The Cabinet. *Ref.* B.T.J., 23rd May 1918, p. 627. *Diss.* Apparently prior to Dec. 1916.

EASTERN, WAR CABINET, COMMITTEE.—*App.* by War Cabinet, Mar. 1918, absorbing two previous Committees for Middle East and Persia. *Obj.* To deal with ' the multifarious questions that arise between the Eastern shores of the Mediterranean and the frontiers of India '. *Repr.* War Cabinet the Dominions, Imperial General Staff, F.O., In.O., *Ref.* Cmd. 325, p. 4. *Diss.* Part of its work taken over by Peace Conference in 1919, but it continued as Departmental Committee of F.O.

EAST, MIDDLE, COMMITTEE.—*See* preceding entry.

ECONOMIC CONFERENCE, ALLIED.—*App.* by Allied Governments and held at Paris, 14th–17th June 1916. *Obj.* To concert joint measures to secure economic conditions against enemy powers, during and after the War. *Repr.* The Allied Governments. *Ref.* Cd. 8271.

(N.B. A preliminary Conference was held at Paris in Mar. 1916, which settled the mandate for the June Conference.)

ECONOMIC DEFENCE AND DEVELOPMENT, CABINET COMMITTEE.—*App.* by War Cabinet during 1918. *Obj.* To deal at discretion with economic questions, only referring larger ones, requiring sanction, to War Cabinet. *Repr.* Ministers of Departments largely concerned with economic questions. *Ref.* Cmd. 325, p. 4.

ECONOMY CABINET COMMITTEE.—*App.* by Cabinet in 1919 to secure departmental economies. *See* T., 21st Oct. 1919, p. 13.

ELECTORAL SYSTEMS.—*See* Irish Convention.

EMERGENCY LEGISLATION, CONTINUANCE, COMMITTEE.—*App.* by War Cabinet on recommendation of M.R., Dec. 1918. *Obj.* To continue work of Select Committee on Termination of the War (*see* Parliament), in dealing with war emergency legislation. *Repr.* Cabinet, Government Departments concerned. *Ref.* Cd. 9231, Cmd. 325, p. 301.

(*See also* M.R. *under* Period of the War.)

EXCHANGES, INTER-IMPERIAL, COMMITTEE.—*App.* by Imperial Economic Conference, Oct. 1923. *Obj.* To consider and suggest remedies for Exchange difficulties between different parts of the Empire. *Repr.* (mainly expert) B.T., C.O., Tre., the Dominions, I.F.S., India, Protectorates, &c. (through C.O.), Banking. *Ref.* Cmd. 2009, pp. 456, 477–8. *Diss.* Nov. 1923.

EXPENDITURE.—*See* W.O.

FERTILIZERS.—A number of Central Committees were established in London in 1917 for dealing centrally with the supply of fertilizers and representing the departments concerned, including a general Fertilizers Committee and Committees for particular fertilizers, e. g. Phosphates and Potash, Sulphate of Ammonia (*see* M.F.). *Ref.* Cd. 9069, pp. xxxvii–ix, xlviii.

FINANCIAL ASSISTANCE IN IMPERIAL DEVELOPMENT COMMITTEE.—*App.* by Imperial Economic Conference, Oct. 1923. *Obj.* To investigate problem of financial co-operation in development, including

British Government's scheme for assistance towards acceleration of work on orders placed in U.K. *Repr.* British and Imperial Governments. *Ref.* Cmd. 2009, p. 13. *Diss.* Nov. 1923.

FLAX, HEMP, AND JUTE.—*See under* Programmes Committees, and Tre.

FOOD, CABINET COMMITTEE.—*App.* by Cabinet in early summer of 1916. *Obj.* To make special investigation of food supplies and prices. *Repr.* Cabinet. *Ref.* T., 13th June 1916, p. 3. *Diss.* Later in 1916.

FOOD COMMITTEE OF ALLIES.—*App.* in or before 1916. *Obj.* To deal with food questions affecting allies jointly. *Repr.* Chief Allied Governments. *Ref.* (without full details) T., 27th Nov. 1916, p. 9.

FOOD, INTER-ALLIED.—*See* M.F.

FOOD SUPPLIES, CABINET COMMITTEE.—*App.* by Cabinet early in the War. *Obj.* To consider arrangements for conserving and regulating food supplies. *Repr.* Cabinet. *Ref.* Cd. 7763, p. 35. *Diss.* Not clear, possibly not till establishment of Food Control, possibly after a short period.

FOREST AUTHORITY, INTERIM.—*App.* by War Cabinet, Oct. 1918, on recommendation of Sub-Committee of Ministers. *Obj.* To make preliminary arrangements for development of forestry in U.K. *Repr.* Cabinet, B.A., landowners, agriculture. *Ref.* J.B.A., Nov. 1918, p. 928. *Diss.* During 1919, replaced by Forestry Commission.

(According to H.C., No. 128, 1921, p. 46, this body began as informal Committee brought together by Chairman of Forestry Committee of M.R.)

FORESTRY COMMISSION.—*App.* by Cabinet in latter part of 1919 under Forestry Act, 1919. *Obj.* To act as permanent central forestry authority replacing Forestry Branch of B.A. *Repr.* Interim Forestry Authority, Forestry Sub-Committee, landowners, forestry experts, with special representatives for Scotland, Wales, and Ireland. *Ref.* J.B.A., Jan. 1920 ; P.G.A., 1919. *Permanent Body.*

FORESTRY CONSULTATIVE COMMITTEES (FOUR).—*App.* by Order-in-Council under Forestry Act, 1919, for England, Scotland, Ireland, and Wales, Mar. 1920. *Obj.* To advise and assist Forestry Commission (q. v.) in exercise of duties and powers. *Repr.* Parliament, B.A., B.A.(Sc.), D.A.T.I., experts in forestry and woodland industries, L.A.'s interested in forestry, Afforestation Societies, woodland owners, Labour. *Ref.* P.G.A., 1919 ; Cmd. 929, pp. 8, 9 ; H.C. No. 128, 1926, pp. 54–60. *Permanent Bodies.*

(The Committees appoint Sub-Committees, where necessary, e. g. to carry out a Census of Woodlands.—*See* H.C., No. 108, 1922, p. 37.)

FORESTRY EDUCATION, IMPERIAL, INTER-DEPARTMENTAL COMMITTEE.—*App.* jointly by Departments concerned, Oct. 1920. *Obj.* To prepare scheme for Central Institution for training Forestry Officers, as proposed by British Empire Forestry Conference. *Repr.* Parliament, Forestry Commission, C.O., In.O., the Dominions, Royal Society. *Ref.* Cmd. 1166. *Diss.* Feb. 1921.

(N.B. The British Empire Forestry Conference, held July 1920, appointed various Committees to investigate and report to the Conference on various Forestry problems.)

FORESTRY, EMPIRE, ASSOCIATION.—Incorporated under Royal Charter, prior to Sept. 1921, for promotion of forestry within the Empire. *See* H.C., No. 108, 1922, p. 9.

FORESTRY, SUB-COMMITTEE OF MINISTERS.—*App.* by War Cabinet in early summer of 1918. *Obj.* To consider afforestation in light of proposals of Forestry Sub-Committee of R.C. *Repr.* War Cabinet and Ministers. *Ref.* J.B.A., Aug. 1918, p. 518. *Diss.* July–Aug. 1918.

GAS TRACTION COMMITTEE.—*App.* by the Government, Nov. 1917. *Obj.* To consider substitution of gas power for petrol, especially on motor vehicles, and question of Government encouragement. *Repr.* (largely technical experts) Petroleum Executive, Petrol Control Board, Government Departments concerned, L.A.'s (Urban), Metropolitan Police, gas producers, motor manufacturers, motor users. *Ref.* B.T.J., 6th Dec. 1917. *Diss.* By 1921, probably earlier.

GAS TRACTION EXPERIMENTAL SUB-COMMITTEE.—*App.* by Gas Traction Committee, June 1918. *Obj.* To carry out experiments and tests in gas traction, as recommended in Interim Report of main Committee. *Repr.* Petroleum Executive, experts in gas, petrol, motor traction, and engineering. *Ref.* B.T.J., 13th June 1918.

GERMAN OUTRAGES INQUIRY COMMITTEE (BRYCE COMMITTEE).—*App.* by P.M., Dec. 1914. *Obj.* To report on evidence of alleged German outrages and breaches of the laws of war. *Repr.* Parliament, Legal Profession, historical, constitutional, and other research, other prominent public men. *Ref.* Cd. 7894–5. *Diss.* Spring, 1915.

GERMAN WAR TRIALS, BRITISH MISSION.—*App.* by the Government, April or May 1921. *Obj.* To attend and follow proceedings at trial of German War Criminals at Leipzig. *Repr.* Law Officers, Procurator General's Department, Legal Profession. *Ref.* Cmd. 1450, p. 7. *Diss.* Later in 1921.

GERMAN WAR TRIALS, INTER-ALLIED COMMISSION.—*App.* by Allied Governments, Feb. 1920. *Obj.* To examine and report on German Government's proposals to try accused persons at Leipzig. *Repr.* Allied Governments. *Ref.* Cmd. 1450, p. 4. *Diss.* About April 1920.

GOVERNMENT EXPENDITURE BUSINESS COMMITTEE.—*App.* by the Government, Jan. 1918. *Obj.* To inquire into expenditure of war and other Government Departments. *Repr.* Prominent business men. *Ref.* T., 15th Jan. 1918, p. 6.

GOVERNMENT LABOUR COMMITTEES.—*See* Labour.

GOVERNMENT MACHINERY FOR DEALING WITH TRADE AND COMMERCE COMMITTEE.—*App.* by the War Cabinet in 1918. *Obj.* To report upon existing arrangements and proposals for improving them. *Repr.* The Government, L.G.B., Legal Profession, business men. *Ref.* Cmd. 319. *Diss.* July 1919.

GRAVES.—*See* W.O.

GREEK ARMY, INTER-ALLIED COMMISSION.—*App.* by chief Allied Governments in 1917, to sit at Athens. *Obj.* To report on progress of

Greek mobilization. *Repr.* The Governments concerned. *Ref.* Cmd. 325, p. 26. *Diss.* At or after close of War.

GREEK SUPPLIES, INTER-ALLIED COMMITTEE.—*App.* about end 1917. Other details much as with Rumanian Supplies, Inter-Allied, Committee (*see* below).

HEALTH, INTERNATIONAL ORGANIZATION, INFORMAL CON-FERENCE.—*Held* in London at invitation of British Government, Mar. 1919, to prepare outline scheme of organization for establishment after formation of League of Nations. *Ref.* Cmd. 923, p. 77, which also (pp. 77–9) describes establishment of Health Organization under the League.

HEALTH, POLISH TYPHUS COMMISSION.—*App.* by Council of League of Nations, May 1920. *Obj.* To organize measures recommended by Health Conferences appointed by the League and held at M.H., Mar. 1920, and secure dispatch of supplies. *Repr.* The League of Nations. *Ref.* Cmd. 923, p. 80.

HEMP.—*See under* Programmes Committees.

HERRINGS, CURED, ADVISORY COMMITTEE.—*See* F.B.(Sc.).

HIDES.—*See under* Programmes Committees.

HOME AFFAIRS, CABINET COMMITTEE.—*App.* by War Cabinet, June 1918. *Obj.* To deal with questions of internal policy, requiring Departmental co-operation or reference to War Cabinet. *Repr.* Ministers of Departments mainly affected. *Ref.* Cmd. 325, p. 4.

HOME TRADE DISTRICT TRANSPORT COMMITTEES.—Established to carry out Cabinet Policy. *See* B.T.

HONOURS, ROYAL COMMISSION.—*App.* by Royal Warrant, Sept. 1922. *Obj.* To advise on future procedure for assisting P.M. in recommending grant of honours. *Repr.* Parliament, including prominent business men, Legal Profession, and Labour. *Ref.* Cmd. 1789. *Diss.* Dec. 1922.

HOUSING, CABINET COMMITTEE.—*App.* by Cabinet, Nov. 1919. *Obj.* To devise new means of dealing with difficulties of housing problem. *Repr.* The Cabinet. *Ref.* T., 18th Nov. 1919, p. 12.

(A similar Committee was appointed after the General Election of 1922 to inquire into position with view to Government legislature in 1923. *See* T., 12th Dec. 1922.)

HOUSING, IRISH.—*See* Irish Convention.

HOUSING OF THE INDUSTRIAL POPULATION OF SCOTLAND, ROYAL COMMISSION.—*App.* by Royal Warrant in 1912. *Obj.* To survey industrial housing conditions in Scotland, the Commission eventually dealing with special housing problems due to the War. *Repr.* Parliament (Scottish Members), L.G.B.(Sc.), L.A.'s(Sc.), representative Scottish men and women, including medical profession. *Ref.* Cd. 8131. *Diss.* Sept. 1917.

IMPERIAL COMMUNICATIONS, CABINET COMMITTEE.—*App.* by the Cabinet prior to Sept. 1920. *Ref.* (without details) Cmd. 905, p. 25.

IMPERIAL CONFERENCE, 1923; IMPERIAL ECONOMIC CONFERENCE, 1923.—For details, *see* Cmd. 1987–8, 2009, and for Committees appointed, Air Communications, British Nationality, Exchanges, Financial Assistance, Overseas Settlement, Treaties.

IMPERIAL ECONOMIC COMMITTEE.—*App.* after Imperial Economic Conference, Nov. 1923. *Obj.* To advise upon economic and commercial matters other than shipping, referred to them by any Imperial Government and form advisory body on questions arising out of the Conference. *Repr.* British Government, the Dominions, India, Crown Colonies, and Protectorates. *Ref.* Cmd. 2009, pp. 570–8. *Standing Body.*

IMPERIAL INVESTIGATION BOARD COMMITTEE.—*App.* by Imperial War Conference, 11th July 1918. *Obj.* To frame scheme for Imperial Investigation Board to deal with ocean freight rates within the Empire. *Repr.* Governments represented at Conference. *Ref.* B.T.J., 18th July 1918.

IMPERIAL MINERAL RESOURCES BUREAU, GOVERNING BODY. —*App.* by Royal Charter, about Aug. 1918. *Obj.* To collect information, and advise, upon development of mineral resources of Empire and coordinate work of existing agencies. *Repr.* British, Dominions, and Indian, Governments, Imperial Institute, Institutes of Metals, Mining, and Metallurgy, Mining Engineers. *Ref.* B.T.J., 1st Aug. 1918. *Permanent Body. See also* P.C.

IMPERIAL PREFERENCE, METHODS AND MACHINERY, COMMITTEE.—*App.* by P.M., Aug. 1917. *Obj.* To consider best methods and machinery for giving effect to resolutions of Imperial War Conference, for development of imperial resources and for Imperial Preference. *Repr.* Government Departments concerned. *Ref.* B.T.J., 23rd Aug. 1917.

IMPERIAL RESEARCH COMMITTEE.—*App.* (constituted) by prominent public men about Oct. 1916. *Obj.* To advocate conservation and development of Imperial resources and establishment of Imperial Development Board. *Repr.* Public men of all parties. *Ref.* T., 29th Jan. 1917, p. 7.

IMPERIAL TRADE INVESTIGATION BOARD.—*App.* by Cabinet in 1919. *Obj.* To devise scheme for increasing trade and improving communication within the Empire. *Repr.* Governments of U.K., Dominions, and India ; commercial interests. *Ref.* T., 18th Aug. 1919.

IMPERIAL WAR CABINET.—*App.* at Imperial War Conference, Mar.–May 1917, the Conference dividing into two bodies, the Imperial War Cabinet and Conference. *Obj.* To deliberate on conduct of war and larger issues of Imperial policy. *Repr.* War Cabinet, Governments of Dominions, G.I., Crown Colonies and Protectorates (through C.O.). *Ref.* Cd. 9005.

IMPERIAL WAR CONFERENCE, 1917.—*App.* on invitation of P.M. Dec. 1916, meeting in London, Mar. 1917 (*see* preceding entry), retaining separate duties after establishment of Imperial War Cabinet. *Obj.* To discuss non-war and minor war problems of Imperial interest. *Repr.* British, Dominions, and Indian Governments, Crown Colonies and Protectorates (through C.O.). *Ref.* Cd. 9005. *Diss.* May 1917.

IMPERIAL WAR CONFERENCE, 1918.—*App.* on invitation of P.M. meeting in London, June 1918. *Obj.* To discuss various war and post-war problems of Imperial interest. *Repr.* As with 1917 Conference. *Ref.* Cd. 9177. *Diss.* July 1918.

IMPERIAL WAR MUSEUM.—*App.* by War Cabinet, Mar. 1917, as National, and subsequently Imperial, War Museum, its organization being connected with W.O. and O.W. *Obj.* To form museum of the War, guard war records and trophies, and collect materials for history of the War. *Repr.* Official and expert. *Ref.* Hall, pp. 103–4.

IMPERIAL WAR MUSEUM, GENERAL COMMITTEE.—*App.* by War Cabinet, Mar. 1917. *Obj.* To organize the Museum. *Repr.* War Cabinet, Adm., W.O., M.M., experts. *Ref.* Cd. 9061. *Permanent Body.*
(The Committee established the following Sub-Committees : Admiralty, Air Services, Art, Dominions, Library, Loan Exhibitions, Munitions, Religious Work, War Office, and Women's Work, a Medical Section, and a Local War Museums Association.)

IMPORT RESTRICTIONS COMMITTEE.—*App.* by the Government, Dec. 1916. *Obj.* To report on further restriction of imports. *Repr.* The Government and experts. *Ref.* Cd. 9005, p. 124. *Diss.* Feb. 1917, with the suggested scheme coming into operation in March, but reassembled later in the year to prepare extended scheme.

IMPORTS.—*See under* Maritime Transport Council.

INCOME-TAX, ROYAL COMMISSION.—*App.* by Royal Warrant, April 1919. *Obj.* To investigate the Income-Tax and Super-Tax systems and suggest alterations. *Repr.* Parliament, P.C., Tre., Inland Revenue Department, bankers, manufacturers, actuaries and accountants, Legal Profession, economists, Labour, women. *Ref.* Cmd. 615. *Diss.* Mar. 1920.
The Commission (*see* Cmd. 615, pp. 168–71) appointed a Committee of members to confer with Dominions' representatives on practical arrangements to remedy hardships of Double Income-Tax within the Empire.

INDUSTRIAL CONFERENCE, NATIONAL.—*App.* by the Government, Feb. 1919 (first meeting 27th Feb.). *Obj.* To consider the industrial situation, with special reference to labour unrest. *Repr.* Employers' and Workpeople's Associations and Federations, J.I.C.'s Trade Boards, and other interested bodies (e. g. T.U.C., F.B.I.). *Ref.* L.G. Mar. 1919. *Diss.* April 1919.

INDUSTRIAL CONFERENCE, NATIONAL, PROVISIONAL JOINT COMMITTEE.—*App.* by Conference, 27th Feb. 1919. *Obj.* To report to Conference on causes and methods of dealing with unrest, with special reference to wages, conditions of labour, unemployment, and co-operation between employers and employed. *Repr.* Employers and workpeople in equal numbers, including women, with Government Chairman (the Miners', Railway, and Transport Unions, and the A.S.E., took no part in forming Committee). *Ref.* Cmd. 139, 501. *Diss.* Reported, 4th April 1919, but by resolution of Conference remained in being, pending carrying out of recommendations agreed to by Conference, eventually resigning, July 1921 (*see* L.G., Aug. 1921, p. 395), as position ' rendered futile any further efforts to secure legislative effect to their joint recommendations '.

INDUSTRIAL CONFERENCE, PROVISIONAL JOINT COMMITTEE, SUB-COMMITTEE NO. 1.—*App.* by Provisional Joint Committee, Mar. 1919. *Obj.* To recommend methods of industrial negotiation, including establishment of permanent Industrial Council to advise the Government, and of dealing with war advances and regulating wages. *Repr.* Employers and workpeople in equal numbers. *Ref.* Cmd. 139, 501. *Diss.* Mar. 1919.

INDUSTRIAL CONFERENCE, PROVISIONAL JOINT COMMITTEE, SUB-COMMITTEES NOS. 2 and 3.—*App.* as with Sub-Committee No. 1. *Obj.* To make recommendations regarding legal minimum wage and maximum working hours (No. 2) : to consider unemployment and recommend steps for its prevention and for maintenance of unemployed, in present emergency and permanently (No. 3). *Other details* as with Sub-Committee No. 1.

INDUSTRIAL UNREST, COMMISSION OF INQUIRY.—*App.* by P.M. June 1917. *Obj.* To report upon industrial unrest and make recommendations at the earliest possible moment. (G.B. was divided into eight divisions, a separate body of Commissioners dealing with each.) *Repr.* Employers and workpeople, with neutral Chairmen. *Ref.* Cd. 8662–9, 8696. *Diss.* July 1917.

INFORMATION ADVISORY COMMITTEE.—*App.* by the Government. *See* M.I.

INSANITY AND CRIME COMMITTEE.—*App.* by Lord Chancellor, July 1922. *Obj.* To report upon changes in law, practice, and procedure in criminal trials, where plea of insanity raised, a problem rendered more urgent by the War. *Repr.* Parliament, H.O., Judges, and Lawyers. *Ref.* Cmd. 2005. *Diss.* Nov. 1923.

IRISH CONVENTION.—*App.* by P.M. in summer of 1917 (first meeting, 25th July). *Obj.* To attempt to secure an agreed constitution for future Government of Ireland. *Repr.* Prominent Irishmen of all creeds and parties. *Ref.* Cd. 9019. *Diss.* April 1918.

The Convention appointed the following Committees :—Selection of Chairman (25th July), Preliminary Procedure (26th July), Grand Committee, to settle general procedure in consultation with Chairman and exercise powers conferred by the Convention (9th Aug.), a Sub-Committee of this being appointed (14th Aug.) to advise the Secretariat on publications. *See also* following entries.

IRISH CONVENTION, COMMITTEE ON HOUSING.—*App.* by the Convention, Feb. 1918. *Obj.* To consider best method of Government assistance to urban housing in Ireland. *Repr.* The Convention. *Ref.* Cd. 9019, App. II, XVI. *Diss.* April 1918.

IRISH CONVENTION, DELEGATION TO CONFER WITH THE CABINET.—*App.* by the Convention Jan. 1918, on suggestion of P.M. *Obj.* To confer with Cabinet to avoid financial deadlock over control of Customs. *Repr.* The Convention. *Ref.* Cd. 9019, App. II. *Diss.* Feb. 1918.

IRISH CONVENTION, SUB-COMMITTEE ON DEFENCE AND POLICE.—*App.* by Grand Committee, Nov. 1917. *Obj.* To consider delegation of powers of local defence to Irish Government and future of

Royal Irish Constabulary and Dublin Police Force. *Repr.* The Convention. *Ref.* Cd. 9019, App. II, XV. *Diss.* Feb. 1918.

IRISH CONVENTION, SUB-COMMITTEE ON ELECTORAL SYSTEMS AND AREAS.—*App.* by Grand Committee, Nov. 1917. *Obj.* To deal with questions of franchise and elections under an Irish Parliament. *Repr.* The Convention. *Ref.* Cd. 9019, App. II, V. *Diss.* Dec. 1917.

IRISH CONVENTION, SUB-COMMITTEE ON LAND PURCHASE.— *App.* by Grand Committee, Nov. 1917. *Obj.* To inquire into problems of land purchase in Ireland. *Repr.* The Convention. *Ref.* Cd. 9019, App. II, IX. *Diss.* Jan. 1918.

IRISH CONVENTION SUB-COMMITTEE OF NINE.—*App.* by Grand Committee, Oct. 1917. *Obj.* To sit privately to arrange basis for agreement as to Irish Constitution. *Repr.* The Convention. *Ref.* Cd. 9019, App. II, IV. *Diss.* Nov. 1917.

IRISH CONVENTION : SUB-COMMITTEE ON POWERS OF IRISH PARLIAMENT.—*App.* by Grand Committee, Nov. 1917. *Obj.* To consider powers of Irish Parliament to amend its own constitution. *Repr.* The Convention. *Ref.* Cd. 9019, App. II. *Diss.* Dec. 1917.

IRISH REBELLION, CASES OF MR. SHEEHY SKEFFINGTON AND OTHERS, ROYAL COMMISSION.—*App.* by Royal Warrant, Aug. 1916. *Obj.* To inquire into arrest and execution of Messrs. Skeffington, Dickson, and McIntyre. *Repr.* English and Irish Bar., Irish Judges. *Ref.* Cd. 8376. *Diss.* Sept. 1916.

IRISH REBELLION, ROYAL COMMISSION.—*App.* by Royal Warrant, May 1916. *Obj.* To inquire into causes of Irish Rebellion and responsibility of civil and military authorities. *Repr.* Imperial Administration, Civil Service, Judges. *Ref.* Cd. 8279. *Diss.* June 1916.

IRISH REBELLION (VICTIMS) COMMITTEE.—*App.* in 1916. *Ref.* Cd. 8741, p. 6. Details lacking.

JUTE.—*See under* Programmes Committees.

LABOUR CONSULTATIVE COMMITTEE OF GOVERNMENT DEPARTMENTS.—*App.* by War Cabinet, Nov. 1917. *Obj.* To advise War Cabinet Committee (*see* next entry) in work of co-ordinating departmental labour settlements. *Repr.* Government Departments chiefly concerned. *Ref.* T., 30th Nov. 1917, p. 9.

LABOUR EMBARGOES.—*See* M.M.

LABOUR, WAR CABINET, COMMITTEE.—*App.* by War Cabinet, Nov. 1917, and transferred to M.L. early 1918. *Obj.* To lay down general policy for settlement of industrial disputes, including 12½ per cent. War bonus, and co-ordinate work of Government Departments dealing with labour questions. *Repr.* War Cabinet, M.L., M.M., M.N.S., and Departments concerned in particular questions. *Ref.* L.G., Dec. 1917 ; T., 30th Nov. 1917, p. 9.

LABOUR.—*See under* Priorities, War.

LAND FOR SAILORS AND SOLDIERS SETTLEMENTS, CABINET COMMITTEE.—*App.* by War Cabinet, about June 1918. *Obj.* To consider and approve proposals of B.A., and M.R., for acquisition and administration of land for settlements. *Repr.* War Cabinet. *Ref.* Cd. 9231, p. 25. *Diss.* Autumn of 1918.

LAND SETTLEMENT, CABINET COMMITTEE.—*App.* by Cabinet, Aug. 1919. *Obj.* To investigate question of land settlement with special reference to cost of existing schemes. *Repr.* Cabinet. *Ref.* Cmd. 1306, p. xix. *Diss.* Early 1920.

LAND SETTLEMENT, EX-SERVICE MEN, CENTRAL EXECUTIVE COMMITTEE.—Appointment recommended by Section IV, R.A.C. (*see* M.R.) for dealing generally with allocation, training, and settlement. *See* Cmd. 325, p. 310.

LAND SETTLEMENT, IRELAND.—*See under* Irish Convention.

LEATHER AND HIDES, INTER-ALLIED EXECUTIVE.—Appointment suggested in Nov. 1918 after Armistice, but abandoned owing to opposition. *See* Cmd. 788, p. 18.

LEATHER.—*See also under* Programmes Committees, and W.O.

LEGAL PROCEDURE, BRITISH AND FOREIGN, COMMITTEE.— *App.* by Lord Chancellor, April 1918. *Obj.* To consider improvements in conduct of legal proceedings, and enforcement of judgements, between British subjects and foreigners. *Repr.* Judges, Legal Profession, manufacturers, merchants. *Ref.* Cmd. 251. *Diss.* May 1919.

LICENCED TRADE CLAIMS (DEFENCE OF THE REALM) ROYAL COMMISSION.—*See* Defence of the Realm.

LOCAL GOVERNMENT, ROYAL COMMISSION.—*App.* by Royal Warrant, Feb. 1923. *Obj.* To investigate effects of procedure for extending or creating county boroughs or other L.A.'s, and relations of L.A.'s generally. *Repr.* Parliament, prominent public men. *Ref.* Cmd. 1944, p. 58.

LOCAL WAR MUSEUMS.—*See* Imperial War Museum.

LONDON GOVERNMENT, ROYAL COMMISSION.—*App.* by Royal Warrant, Oct. 1921. *Obj.* To report upon reorganization of London government, and surrounding areas. *Repr.* H.C., M.H., L.A.'s, manufacturers, business men, Legal Profession, Labour. *Ref.* Cmd. 1830. *Diss.* Mar. 1923.

MAN POWER, CABINET COMMITTEE.—*App.* by War Cabinet, Dec. 1917. *Obj.* To investigate position before final decision taken by War Cabinet on man-power policy. *Repr.* Cabinet (a small committee). *Ref.* T., 8th Dec., p. 9, 12th, p. 9, 1917. *Diss.* Probably by end of year.

MAN POWER COMMITTEE.—*App.* by Government, Dec. 1917. *Obj.* To overhaul use of man power by various departments, lay down principles as to use, and investigate cases of wasteful employment. *Repr.* Adm., W.O., M.M., M.N.S. *Ref.* T., 14th Dec. 1917, p. 9.

MAN POWER DISTRIBUTION BOARD.—*App.* by the Cabinet, Sept. 1916. *Obj.* To survey supplies of labour, advise on most economical methods of use and secure fair allocation to, and proper co-ordination among, Government Departments affected. *Repr.* Cabinet, Parliament, L.G.B., Labour. *Ref.* Cd. 9005, p. 83; Cole, p. 130. *Diss.* Jan. 1917, work taken over by M.N.S.

MARITIME TRANSPORT COUNCIL, ALLIED.—*App.* by chief Allied Governments, early in 1918. *Obj.* To advise on transport questions and adjust import programmes to available tonnage. *Repr.* Governments of U.K., U.S.A., France, Italy. *Ref.* Cmd. 325, pp. 22–4.
  (The Committee had National Sections for each of the four Nations, co-ordinated by a main Executive Committee (Executive of the Council), and Sub-Committees on Imports and Tonnage.)

MEDICAL SERVICES.—*See* M.N.S.

MERCHANTS COMMITTEE.—*App.* by London Chamber of Commerce in 1917. *Obj.* To report on Government control of trade. *Repr.* Various types of merchants. *Ref.* T., 24th July 1917, p. 12. *Diss.* July or Aug. 1917.

MESOPOTAMIA COMMISSION.—*App.* Aug. 1916, by Special Commissions (Dardanelles and Mesopotamia) Act, which named the Commissioners. *Obj.* To investigate origin, conduct, and responsibility for operations in Mesopotamia. *Repr.* Parliament, Naval and Military Authorities, and other public men. *Ref.* P.G.A., 1916 ; Cd. 8610. *Diss.* May 1917.

MILITARY SERVICE ACTS, 1916, LABOUR ADVISORY COMMITTEE. —*App.* by Government, Jan. 1916, apparently at instance of Parliamentary Labour Party. *Obj.* To deal with cases of alleged victimization of workmen under the Acts and prevent industrial conscription. *Repr.* Labour M.P.'s. *Ref.* L.Y.B., 1919, p. 7.

MILITARY SERVICE, REVIEW OF EXCEPTIONS, ACT ADVISORY COMMITTEE.—*App.* referred to in T., of 9th May 1917, p. 3, with object of advising generally in regard to the Act.

MILK, REGULATIVE AND ADMINISTRATIVE POWERS, COMMITTEE.—*App.* by Cabinet in 1918 or 1919. *Obj.* To arrange scheme for extended control of production and distribution of milk. *Repr.* Not stated. *Ref.* Cmd. 824, p. xxxvii. *Diss.* Apparently before June 1919.

MINEFIELDS.—*See* Adm.

MISSIONS, BRITISH WAR.—*See* Russia, and F.O. *under* United States.

MIXED ARBITRAL TRIBUNALS.—*App.* jointly by British and German and presumably other enemy Governments, in 1920 under the Peace Treaties. *Obj.* To decide disputed claims in respect of obligations under economic clauses of Treaties. *Repr.* British and German, &c. Governments. *Ref.* Clearing Office (Germany) 2nd Annual Report, p. 2 (H.M.S.O., 1922). *Still in existence* end 1922.

MODERN LANGUAGES COMMITTEE.—*App.* by P.M., Aug. 1916. *Obj.* To investigate position of modern languages in British education, and means of promoting study. *Repr.* Parliament, B.E., S.E.D., F.O., Civil Service Commission, Diplomatic Service, L.E.A.'s, Universities, Public Schools, teachers (men and women), W.E.A., women, business men. *Ref.* Cd. 9036 ; T., 11th Oct. 1916, p. 3. *Diss.* April 1918.

MUNITIONS CABINET COMMITTEE.—*App.* by P.M., Feb. 1915. *Obj.* To investigate, supervise, and organize munitions production. *Repr.* The Cabinet, Adm., W.O., Tre., B.T. *Ref.* Cd. 9005, p. 68 ; T., 14th April 915, p. 9. *Diss.* Staff absorbed into M.M., May–June 1915. For other Munitions Committees, *see* M.M.

NATIONAL AND IMPERIAL DEFENCE SUB-COMMITTEE.—*App.* by P.M. as Sub-Committee of Committee of Imperial Defence, Mar. 1923. *Obj.* To inquire into co-operation of Navy, Army, and Air Force for defence and establishment of co-ordinating authority. *Repr.* The Government, Committee of Imperial Defence. *Ref.* Cmd. 2029. *Diss.* Nov. 1923.

NATURAL SCIENCE COMMITTEE.—*App.* by P.M., Aug. 1916. *Obj.* To investigate position of Natural Science in British education, and means of promoting study. *Repr.* Parliament, B.E., B.A., Imperial College of Science, L.E.A.'s, Medical Profession, Public Schools, teachers, women, industry, scientists, educational experts. *Ref.* Cmd. 9011 ; T., 11th Oct. 1916, p. 9. *Diss.* Feb. 1918.

NATIONAL REGISTER.—*See* L.G.B.

NAVAL, ALLIED, COMMISSION, COUNCIL.—*See* Adm.

NAVAL AND MILITARY DEPENDENTS.—*See* N.H.I.C.

NAVAL PAY, CABINET COMMITTEE.—*App.* by Cabinet in or after June 1919. *Obj.* To review increases recommended by Adm. Committee and Sub-Committees (*see* Adm.) *Repr.* Cabinet. *Ref.* H.C., No. 87, 1923, p. iii. *Diss.* During 1919.

NAVY AND AIR FORCE RELATIONS, SUB-COMMITTEE.—*App.* by National and Imperial Defence Sub-Committee (*see* above) apparently in or after Mar. 1923. *Obi.* To investigate existing relations and suggest improvements. *Repr.* Parliament, Cabinet, industrial experts. *Ref.* Cmd. 1938, 2029. *Diss.* July 1923.

NECESSITOUS AREAS IN EUROPE.—*See* M.F.

NITRATE OF SODA EXECUTIVE.—*See* M.M.

OILS.—*See* C.O., M.F., M.M.

OVERSEAS SETTLEMENT, IMPERIAL COMMITTEE OF IMPERIAL ECONOMIC CONFERENCE.—*App.* by Conference, Oct. 1923. *Obj.* To consider problems of settlement within the Empire. *Repr.* The Government, Parliament, C.O., O.T.D., O.S.C., I.F.S., The Dominions, Crown Colonies and Protectorates (through C.O.). *Ref.* Cmd. 2009, p. 136. *Diss.* Nov. 1923.
   See also State-Aided Settlement below.

OXYGEN RESEARCH CLEARING HOUSE COMMITTEE.—*App.* by a Conference of Departments interested, under the War Priorities Committee, July 1918 and transferred to S.I.R., Jan. 1919. *Obj.* To co-ordinate investigations by different Departments, and, after transfer, to supervise much of former work of War Departments. *Repr.* All Departments interested. *Ref.* Cd. 9144, p. 24. Apparently *Permanent.*
   (By Aug. 1920 this Committee had established Sub-Committees for Aircraft and for Economic, Industrial, and Medical Uses of Oxygen.)

OXYGEN TECHNICAL PRODUCTION COMMITTEE.—*App. Repr. Ref.* as with Oxygen Research Clearing House Committee (*see* above). *Obj.* To deal with technical problems connected with increased production of oxygen. Apparently *Permanent.*

PALESTINE, ZIONIST COMMISSION.—*App.* by Zionist organization with authority of Government early in 1918. *Obj.* To investigate present position of Jewish colonies in Palestine. *Repr.* Zionist organization. *Ref.* T., 12th Feb. 1918, p. 8.

PAPER.—*See under* Programmes Committees.

PARIS INTERNATIONAL CONFERENCE, TECHNICAL COMMITTEES.—This Conference summoned, Dec. 1917, to promote co-ordination of civil and military efforts, established technical Committees to deal with main problems, such as Armaments and Aviation, Finance, Maritime Transport, and Supplies. A Blockade Section was to rearrange the convention with Switzerland regarding the blockade. It was arranged that definite Inter-Allied Committees and organizations were to be set up for these purposes, the representation thus being on inter-allied basis. These Committees were thus the nucleus of important inter-allied organizations (*see* e.g. Maritime Transport Council). *Ref.* T., 6th Dec. 1917, p. 8.

PARLIAMENT, IRISH.—*See* Irish Convention.

PENSIONS, PRE-WAR, COMMITTEE.—*App.* by Government in 1917. *Obj.* To report upon new scale of pre-war service pensions to meet increased cost of living. *Repr.* Adm., M.Pen., Tre., W.O. *Ref.* T., 14th Feb. 1918, p. 7. *Diss.* In or before Feb. 1918.

PENSIONS, WIDOWS AND ORPHANS, WAR CABINET COMMITTEE. —*App.* by War Cabinet, Mar. 1918. *Obj.* To report on proposals for new Royal Warrant to raise scales. *Repr.* War Cabinet. *Ref.* T., 21st Mar. 1918, p. 7.

PENSIONS.—*See also* M.Pen. under Royal Warrant and Standing Joint Committee.

'PERIOD OF THE WAR' INTERPRETATION COMMITTEE.— *See* M.R.

PERSIA COMMITTEE.—*See* Eastern War Cabinet Committee.

PETROLEUM INTER-ALLIED, ORGANIZATION.—*App.* by Inter-Allied Conference at Paris, May 1918. *Obj.* To deal with petroleum problems of Allies in connexion with the War. *Repr.* U.K., U.S.A., France, Italy. *Ref.* T., 25th May 1918, p. 7.

PETROLEUM.—*See also* Programmes Committees, and M.M.

POOR PERSONS RULES COMMITTEE.—*App.* by Lord Chancellor in 1919. *Obj.* To report upon administration of Poor Persons' Rules and means for securing efficiency. *Repr.* Parliament, Judges, Legal Profession. *Ref.* Cmd. 430. *Diss.* Oct. 1919.

PORTS CONGESTION COMMITTEE.—*App.* by P.M. by Nov. 1915. *Obj.* To investigate causes of congestion, regulate and co-ordinate work, and instruct executive bodies concerned. *Repr.* Adm., W.O., B.T., the Port Authorities, shipping interests, railways, underwriters, merchants. *Ref.* B.T.J., 11th Nov. 1915. For Ports, *see also* M.S.

POTASH COMPANY, BRITISH.—*App.* jointly by the Government and three British firms specially concerned in experimenting in potash production, in 1917 or 1918. *Obj.* To produce potash from blast furnace dust. *Repr.* (on Board of Directors) Government and firms concerned. *Ref.* B.T.J., 5th Sept. 1918.

PRESS.—*See* W.O.

PRE-WAR PRACTICES.—*See* Restoration of Pre-War Practices.

PRIORITIES JOINT BOARD.—*See* next entry.

PRIORITIES, WAR, COMMITTEE.—*App.* by War Cabinet as Aerial Operations Committee, Sept. 1917, to deal with priority for Air Force, and quickly reconstituted as general Priorities Committee, and sometimes called Priorities Joint Board. *Obj.* To settle all questions of priority regarding whole munitions programme. *Repr.* Members of Government specially concerned. *Ref.* B.T.J., 17th Jan. 1918; Cmd. 325, pp. 1, 2. *Diss.* Jan. 1919.

PRIORITIES, WAR, COMMITTEE, ADVISORY COMMITTEE.—*App.* by main Committee in autumn of 1917. *Obj.* To investigate needs of certain non-essential industries with a view to their satisfaction without sacrificing more essential interests. *Repr.* B.T., prominent industrial and business men. *Ref.* B.T.J., 17th Jan. 1918. *Diss.* By Jan. 1919.
    (This appears to be the Industries Sub-Committee referred to in B.T.J., 31st Oct. 1918, p. 556.)

PRIORITIES, WAR, COMMITTEE; ALLOCATION SUB-COM-MITTEES.—*App.* by main Committee in autumn of 1917. *Obj.* To investigate supplies and requirements of specific materials, and allocate supplies according to main Committee's policy. *Repr.* Various consuming Departments. *Ref.* B.T.J., 17th Jan. 1918. *Diss.* By Jan. 1919.

PRIORITIES, WAR, COMMITTEE; GENERAL SERVICES SUB-COMMITTEE.—*App.* by main Committee in autumn of 1917. *Obj.* To consider requirements of Public Utility Services, and formulate demands to main Committee for allocation of supplies. *Repr.* L.G.B., B.T., Adm., A.M., W.O., civil engineers. *Ref.* B.T.J., 17th Jan. 1918. *Diss.* By Jan. 1919.

PRIORITIES, WAR, COMMITTEE: PERMANENT LABOUR SUB-COMMITTEE.—*App.* by main Committee in autumn of 1917. *Obj.* To co-ordinate departmental methods of dealing with dilution, release for military service and other labour matters. *Repr.* Government Departments concerned, possibly others. *Ref.* Cmd. 325, p. 2. *Diss.* By Jan. 1919.

PRIORITIES, WAR, COMMITTEE, WORKS' CONSTRUCTION COM-MITTEE.—*App.* by main Committee, Jan. 1918. *Obj.* To settle priority for all large extension of works, especially for labour. *Repr.* Not stated. *Ref.* H.C., No. 132, 1918, p. 8; B.T.J., 17th Jan. 1918. *Diss.* By Jan. 1919.

PRIORITIES, WAR, LOCAL COMMITTEES.—*Ref.* without details, B.T.J., 5th Sept. 1918, p. 319.

PRIORITY, POST-WAR, CABINET COMMITTEE.—*App.* by War Cabinet in 1918. *Obj.* To determine broad outlines of post-war policy, and control centrally various departmental controls after the Armistice. *Repr.* War Cabinet, B.T., M.L., M.M., M.R., M.S. *Ref.* Cd. 9231, p. 13 ; B.T.J., 7th Nov. 1918, p. 580. *See also* M.R.

PRIORITY, POST-WAR, STANDING COUNCIL.—*App.* by War Cabinet, in 1918. *Obj.* To consult trade organizations concerned, and advise and assist Cabinet Committee. *Repr.* Government Departments affected, industry, commerce, Labour. *Ref.* Cd. 9231, p. 13.

PRISONERS OF WAR, BRITISH, TREATMENT BY THE ENEMY, GOVERNMENT COMMITTEE.—*App.* by the Government prior to April 1916. *Obj.* To inquire into allegations respecting enemy treatment of prisoners of war. *Repr.* Judges, Legal Profession. *Ref.* Cd. 8224, 8351, 8998. *Diss.* 1918 or later.

PRISONERS, EXCHANGE OF, DELEGATION.—*App.* by the Government, June 1918. *Obj.* To meet German delegation in conference over direct exchange of British and German prisoners. *Repr.* Government Prisoners of War Organizations. *Ref.* T., 4th June 1918, p. 7.

PRIZE CLAIMS COMMITTEE.—*App.* by the Government apparently with head-quarters at B.T., Nov. 1914. *Obj.* To consider claims of third parties against Prize Court awards and suggest means of meeting them out of prize funds. *Repr.* Government, Adm., F.O., Tre., Colonial Interests, Legal Profession. *Ref.* B.T.J., 3rd and 17th Dec. 1914.

PROBATE REGISTRIES, DISTRICT, COMMITTEE.—*App.* jointly by Lord Chancellor, and President of Probate, Divorce, and Admiralty Division, July 1922. *Obj.* To inquire into alteration of functions, organization and terms of employment in interests of economy and efficiency. *Repr.* Judges, Barristers, and others. *Ref.* Cmd. 1968. *Diss.* July 1923.

PRODUCTION.—*See* B.T.

PROGRAMMES COMMITTEES, INTER-ALLIED.—*App.* by Allied Governments at suggestion of Allied Maritime Transport Council in summer of 1918 for various commodities. *Obj.* To frame co-ordinated import programmes for all Allies, and control purchase and distribution of supplies. *Repr.* The appointing Governments. *Ref.* Cmd. 325, p. 23.

Separate Committees were formed for Coal and Coke ; Cotton ; Flax and Hemp and Jute ; Hides and Leather ; Paper ; Petroleum ; Timber ; Tin ; Tobacco ; Wool (q. v.).

PROVISIONAL GOVERNMENT OF IRELAND, CABINET COMMITTEE.—*App.* under Treaty with Ireland of Dec. 1921. *Ref.* (without details) 1st Report of Irish Distress Committee, App. III (H.M.S.O., 1922).

PUBLIC ASSISTANCE ADMINISTRATION, CO-ORDINATION, INTER-DEPARTMENTAL COMMITTEE.—*App.* by P.M., Feb. 1923. *Obj.* To examine means of co-ordinating arrangements for grant of public assistance (including Insurance Schemes) on account of sickness, destitution and unemployment. *Repr.* H.C., M.L., M.H., M.Pen., S.B.H. *Ref.* Cmd. 2011. *Diss.* Dec. 1923.

PUBLIC TRUSTEE OFFICE, ORGANIZATION COMMITTEE.—*App.* by Lord Chancellor, April 1919. *Obj.* To report generally on organization of the office. *Repr.* Tre., Legal Profession, accountancy, business men. *Ref.* Cmd. 421. *Diss.* Oct. 1919.

PUBLIC UTILITY SERVICES.—*See* Priorities, War, Committee, General Services.

PURCHASE AND FINANCE, WAR, INTER-ALLIED COUNCIL.—*App.*

jointly by chief European Allied Governments at request of U.S.A., April 1917, to sit in London. *Obj.* To co-ordinate purchases of Allies, especially from U.S.A., and determine priority for materials and finance. *Repr.* The appointing Governments. *Ref.* Cd. 9005, pp. 19, 169.

QUININE, INTER-ALLIED, COMMITTEE.—*App.* by Allied Governments, about July 1918. *Obj.* To secure jointly for Allies Dutch supplies of cinchona bark. *Repr.* Chief Allied Governments. *Ref.* Cmd. 499. *Diss.* Agreement secured with Dutch manufacturers, Sept. 1918, lasting till Sept. 1919.

RAILWAY RECRUITING APPEAL COMMITTEE.—*App.* by the Government Sept. 1917. *Obj.* To deal with cases of alleged victimization of Trade Unionists in matters of recruiting, after reference to General Manager of Company concerned. *Repr.* Legal Profession, Employers, Labour. *Ref.* L.Y.B., 1919, p. 143.

RAW MATERIALS, COMMITTEE OF MINISTERS.—*App.* by War Cabinet, after the Imperial War Conference, July or Aug. 1918. *Obj.* To take action on inter-imperial and inter-allied problems of acquisition and distribution of materials. *Repr.* Cabinet. *Ref.* Cd. 9231, p. 12.

RAW MATERIALS, ESSENTIAL, INTER-IMPERIAL COMMITTEE.— *App.* by various Imperial Governments, under resolution of Imperial War Conference of 28th June 1918. *Obj.* To consider methods to be adopted within the Empire to secure for Imperial and Allied use supplies of raw materials essential for reconstruction. *Repr.* Governments represented at the Conference. *Ref.* B.T.J., 14th July 1918. *Diss.* July 1918.

RECRUITING, SPECIAL CABINET COMMITTEE.—*App.* by the Cabinet, Feb. 1916. *Obj.* To review questions of starred trades and certified occupations in light of working of Derby Scheme and Military Service Act, 1916. *Repr.* Cabinet. *Ref.* T., 3rd Feb. 1916, p. 5. *Diss.* Later in 1916.

RELIEF.—*See* Supply and Relief ; Unemployment ; and L.G.B.

RENT RESTRICTIONS ACT INQUIRY COMMITTEE.—*See* M.H.

REPARATIONS GRANTS (COMPENSATION FOR SUFFERING AND DAMAGE BY ENEMY ACTION) ROYAL COMMISSION.—*App.* by Royal Warrant, Aug. 1921. *Obj.* To consider cases of moral claims by British Nationals to grant from funds provided for this purpose from Reparations receipts. *Repr.* Legal Profession (Lords of Appeal), surveyors. *Ref.* Cmd. 1798. *Still sitting* end 1922.

RESEARCH CO-ORDINATION, GOVERNMENT, COMMITTEE.—*App.* by the Government shortly after the Armistice. *Obj.* To consider co-ordination of research required by Government Departments. *Repr.* The Cabinet and others. *Ref.* Cmd. 1471, p. 16. *Diss.* By beginning of 1920.

RESERVED OCCUPATIONS.—*See* B.T.

RESTORATION OF PRE-WAR PRACTICES JOINT COMMITTEE.— *App.* by the Government, Nov. 1918. *Obj.* To prepare agreed proposals for carrying out Government pledges for restoration of pre-war T.U. practices. *Repr.* Employers and T.U.'s, the Committee conferring when necessary with M.L. *Ref.* L.G., Feb. 1919, p. 46. *See also* M.M., M.R.

RETAIL PROFITS, CABINET COMMITTEE.—*App.* by the Cabinet, July 1917. *Obj.* To lay down principles of policy for classes (retail traders and stock raisers) not yet subject to control. *Repr.* The Cabinet. *Ref.* T., 8th Aug. 1917.

RUMANIAN SUPPLIES, INTER-ALLIED COMMITTEE.—*App.* jointly by Allied Governments at Jassy late in 1917, taking over much work from Russian Committee of Commission Internationale de Ravitaillement. *Obj.* To co-ordinate demands and supplies of materials for Rumania, working through the Commission. *Repr.* Allied Governments, the Commission. *Ref.* Cd. 9005.

(A similar Committee was established for Greece (q.v.) a little later.)

RUSSIA, BRITISH WAR MISSION.—*App.* by War Cabinet early in 1917. *Obj.* To visit Russia to promote co-operation in various directions in prosecution of war. *Repr.* War Cabinet, W.O., Finance. *Ref.* Cd. 9005, p. 16. *Diss.* Returned Mar. 1917.

RUSSIAN, RUSSIAN LIQUIDATION, COMMITTEES.—*See under* Commission Internationale de Ravitaillement.

RUSSIAN TRADE AGREEMENT.—Inter-Departmental Committee, which drew up draft for trade agreement with Russia in 1920, referred to in T., 6th Oct. 1920, p. 16.

ST. DAVIDS' COMMITTEE.—*See* Unemployment Grants.

SALVAGE.—*See* W.O.

SANITARY.—*See* L.G.B.

SERBIAN ARMY, INTER-ALLIED COMMISSION.—*App.* by chief Allied Governments in 1917, to sit at Salonica. *Obj.* To secure adequate co-operation of British and French Governments in supplying Serbian Army. *Repr.* The Governments concerned. *Ref.* Cmd. 325, p. 26. *Diss.* At or after close of War.

SHIPBUILDING, NATIONAL JOINT COMMITTEE.—*See* M.L.

SHIPPING CONTROL, INTERNATIONAL COMMITTEE.—*App.* originally by Cabinet. *See* M.S. For Shipping *see also* B.T.

SHIPPING, IMPERIAL INVESTIGATION COMMITTEE.—*App.* by P.M., June 1920, under Resolution 11 of Imperial War Conference of 26th July 1918. *Obj.* To investigate complaints as to the freights, facilities, and conditions of inter-imperial trade, survey facilities for inter-imperial maritime transport, suggest improvements, and prepare scheme for permanent organization. *Repr.* Parliament, C.O., B.T., In.O., Dominion Governments, persons experienced in shipping and commerce. *Ref.* Cmd. 1872, which gives good account of appointment and operations of Committee. *Still sitting* end 1922.

(The Committee appointed Sub-Committees as required and held special Conferences of interests concerned in subjects of investigation. It also encouraged formation of Associations of Shippers in negotiating with shipowners in regard to rebates.)

SIR JOHN JACKSON, LTD., ROYAL COMMISSION.—*App.* by Royal Warrant, Nov. 1916. *Obj.* To investigate charges against the firm and arrangements with W.O. for erection of huts. *Repr.* Legal Profession, surveyors, business men. *Ref.* Cd. 8518. *Diss.* Mar. 1917.

SKEFFINGTON, MR. SHEEHY.—*See* Irish Rebellion.

SMUTS COMMITTEE.—*See under* Demobilization.

SOCIAL AND ECONOMIC CONSULTATIVE COMMITTEE.—*App.* by the Government, Oct. 1916. *Obj.* To act as centre of information for Government on such matters. *Repr.* Experienced social workers and others. *Ref.* T., 5th Oct. 1916.

SOCIÉTÉ SUISSE DE SURVEILLANCE ÉCONOMIQUE.—*App.* by agreement between British, French, Italian, and Swiss Governments in autumn of 1915. *Obj.* To supervise Swiss imports from or through allied countries, to ensure that neither imports, nor goods manufactured from them, reached enemy countries. *Repr.* Not stated. *Ref.* B.T.J., 9th May 1918.

STAFFS, GOVERNMENT DEPARTMENTS, SPECIAL INVESTIGA-TION COMMITTEE.—*App.* by Finance Committee of Cabinet about July 1920, acting through Panels which dealt with each Department separately. *Obj.* To investigate staffing and methods of various Departments, and report upon possible economies. *Repr.* Parliament, business men, Civil Service (other than particular Departments under consideration). *Ref.* Cmd. 1069. *Diss.* From Aug. 1920.

STAFFS, TEMPORARY, GOVERNMENT DEPARTMENTS, SPECIAL COMMITTEE.—*App.* by Sir A. Geddes, who had been entrusted by the Cabinet with the work, in spring of 1919. *Obj.* To investigate best means of expediting dispersal of temporary staffs. *Repr.* Presumably largely business men. *Ref.* T., 6th May 1919, p. 12.

STATE-AIDED SETTLEMENT, IMPERIAL, SUB-COMMITTEE OF CONFERENCE OF PRIME MINISTERS.—*App.* by Conference, July 1921. *Obj.* To report on state-aided empire settlement and migration. *Repr.* C.O., Imperial Premiers. *Ref.* Cmd. 1580, pp. 3–4. *Diss.* Aug. 1921, proposals being adopted by Conference and put in force by O.S.C.
See also Overseas Settlement above.

STATISTICAL, BRITISH EMPIRE CONFERENCE.—*See* British Empire.

STORE CATTLE, IMPORTATION, ROYAL COMMISSION.—*App.* by Order-in-Council, May 1921. *Obj.* To inquire into importation of store cattle, with special reference to food supplies and dangers of cattle disease. *Repr.* Parliament, Civil Service, Legal Profession, Accountancy, Zoological Research. *Ref.* Cmd. 1139. *Diss.* Aug. 1921.

SUPPLIES, INTERNATIONAL COMMISSION.—*See* Commission Internationale de Ravitaillement.

SUPPLY AND RELIEF, SUPREME (ALLIED) COUNCIL.—*App.* by four chief Allied Powers not later than Nov. 1918. *Obj.* To provide necessities for liberated Allied territories, newly-formed friendly states, and eventually enemy countries, and co-ordinate allied and neutral supplies.

Repr. Governments concerned. *Ref.* Cmd. 325, p. 34 ; B.T.J., 16th Jan. 1919, p. 71.

SUPREME COURT FEES COMMITTEE.—*App.* by Lord Chancellor in 1920 or 1921. *Obj.* To consider scales of fees in light of modern conditions. *Repr.* Supreme Court, Barristers, Solicitors. *Ref.* Cmd. 1565. *Diss.* Nov. 1921.

SUPREME ECONOMIC COUNCIL.—*App.* by Allied and Associated Governments in winter of 1918–19, with separate departments for various powers, including British Department appointed by the British Government. *Obj.* To advise, assist, and collect information generally, on economic matters and problems of peace negotiations, putting into operation economic conditions of peace, and general economic reconstruction. *Repr.* The Governments concerned, mainly through various experts. *Ref.* Monthly Bulletin of Statistics of British Department of Council and subsequently of League of Nations, July 1919, June 1921. *Diss.* About April 1921.

SUPREME WAR COUNCIL.—*App.* by Governments of U.K., France, and Italy, at Rapallo, Nov. 1917, and subsequently adhered to by that of U.S.A. *Obj.* To co-ordinate allied military policies and secure single strategic plan. *Repr.* The four Governments (in each case by P.M., and one other Minister) with assistance of permanent military staff, the Council meeting monthly at Versailles. *Ref.* Cmd. 9005, p. 15. *Diss.* After close of War.

SWITZERLAND.—*See* Société Suisse and *under* Paris International Conference.

TANKS.—*See* Aviation and Tanks.

TIMBER ALLOCATION COMMITTEE.—One of Allocation Sub-Committees of War Priorities Committee (q. v.). *See also* Cmd. 325, p. 206.

TIMBER.—*See* Commission International d'Achats de Bois, and *under* Programmes Committees, and W.O.

TIN, ALLIED CENTRAL BUYING EXECUTIVE.—*App.* jointly by Allied Governments, Aug. 1918. *Obj.* To organize purchase of tin for allied requirements. *Repr.* Chief Allied Governments. *Ref.* Cmd. 325, p. 224.

TIN.—*See also under* Programmes Committees.

TOBACCO.—*See under* Programmes Committees.

TONNAGE.—*See under* Maritime Transport Council.

TRADE AND POLICY.—*See under* Unemployment.

TRADE, INTER-ALLIED, COMMITTEES.—*App.* jointly by Allied Governments prior to June 1918 at Christiania, Stockholm, &c. *Obj.* To supervise generally the special restrictions on allied trade with Scandinavia and Finland. *Repr.* The Governments concerned. *Ref.* B.T.J., 27th June, 5th Sept. 1918, 6th Mar. 1919.

TRADE RELATIONS WITHIN THE EMPIRE, COMMITTEE.—*App.* by War Cabinet in 1917 or 1918. *Obj.* To consider generally questions of post-war trade between different parts of the Empire. *Repr.* Not Stated. *Ref.* Cd. 9231, p. 12.

TRANSPORT CO-ORDINATION.—*See* M.S.

TRANSPORT, MARITIME.—*See* Maritime Transport.

TREATIES, INTER-IMPERIAL RELATIONS, COMMITTEE.—*App.* by Imperial Conference, Oct.–Nov. 1923. *Obj.* To investigate question of imperial relations in regard to negotiations, &c. of treaties. *Repr.* The Government, C.O., I.F.S., the Dominions, India. *Ref.* Cmd. 1987, p. 13. *Diss.* Nov. 1923.

UNEMPLOYMENT, ADVANCES TO BOARDS OF GUARDIANS, COMMITTEE.—*App.* by the Government late in 1921, presumably co-operating with M.H. *Obj.* To recommend advances out of funds for relief of unemployment, where guardians unable otherwise to raise loans. *Repr.* M.H., S.B.H., experts. *Ref.* Cmd. 1697, pp. 203–4, 264. *Still sitting* end 1922.

UNEMPLOYMENT, CABINET, COMMITTEE.—*App.* by Coalition Government, in 1921, and reappointed Nov. 1922. *Obj.* To advise Cabinet on general measures for remedying unemployment. *Repr.* Cabinet. *Ref.* L.G. Sept. 1923, p. 316. *Still in existence* end 1922.

UNEMPLOYMENT, CABINET, COMMITTEES.—T., 9th Aug. 1922, pp. 8, 13, mentions the appointment of two Committees to deal with subject in preparation for winter emergency. The Trade and Policy Committee dealt generally with the situation, appointing a Sub-committee to examine conditions of trade all over the world. The other Committee dealt with Methods of Relief.

UNEMPLOYMENT GRANTS COMMITTEE.—*App.* by the Government, Dec. 1920, and known as St. Davids' Committee. *Obj.* To administer grants for assisting L.A.'s, and, from autumn of 1923, Public Utility Societies, in carrying out schemes of relief work. *Repr.* Parliament, public men with industrial and business experience. *Ref.* L.G., 1920, pp. 9, 61, 570, Cmd. 1697, pp. 212–13 (a good account).

UNIVERSITIES, OXFORD AND CAMBRIDGE, ROYAL COMMIS-SION.—*App.* by Royal Warrant, Nov. 1919, to sit in three separate Committees, for Oxford, Cambridge, and Estates Management. *Obj.* To consider applications by the Universities for state financial assistance, and inquire into financial resources, administration, and general government of Universities and their Colleges and make recommendations. *Repr.* Parliament, P.C., Tre., Civil Service, Oxford, Cambridge, London and Provincial Universities, including Women's Colleges, Public Schools, Royal Society, Educational Experts, Legal and Medical Professions, Labour, W.E.A. *Ref.* Cmd. 1588.

WAR AIMS, PROPAGANDA.—Government appointments. *See* M.I.

WAR COMMITTEE OF THE CABINET.—*App.* by the Cabinet in winter of 1914–15. *Obj.* To deal expeditiously with administration of the War, subject to final responsibility of whole Cabinet. *Repr.* Ministers chiefly concerned. *Ref.* Cd. 9005, p. vii.

WAR COMPENSATION COURT.—*App.* by Royal Warrant of 8th Sept. 1920, under Indemnity Act, 1920, taking over functions and members of Defence of the Realm Losses Royal Commission (*see* above). *Obj.* Much as with Commission. *Repr.* Judges Legal Profession. *Ref.* P.G.A., 1920 ; Cmd. 1044, p. 3 ; 2nd Report of Court (H.M.S.O., 1923). Apparently *still sitting* end 1922.

WAR EMERGENCY LEGISLATION, CONTINUANCE COMMITTEE. *See* Emergency Legislation.

WAR MUSEUM.—*See* Imperial War Museum.

WAR TRADE ADVISORY COMMITTEE.—*App.* by the Government in or before May 1916. *Obj.* To advise on restrictions of enemy trade, co-ordinate administration of W.T.D., Contraband Committee and Enemy Exports Committee, and advise Cabinet on questions of policy connected with their work. *Repr.* W.T.D. and the two Committees concerned, Adm., W.O., B.A., B.T., C.O., F.O., In.O., M.M., Law Officers of the Crown, Committee of Imperial Defence, War Trade Intelligence Department. *Ref.* T., 24th May 1916, p. 5.

WHEAT, EXECUTIVE, COMMISSION, &c.—*See* M.F.

WIRELESS TELEGRAPHY COMMISSION.—*See* C.O.

WOMEN IN INDUSTRY, WAR CABINET COMMITTEE.—*App.* by War Cabinet, Sept. 1918. *Obj.* To investigate relations between women's and men's wages. *Repr.* Legal Profession, M.R., and other Government Departments, experts in Industrial Conciliation, women, Medical Profession. *Ref.* Cmd. 135. *Diss.* April 1919.

WOOL PROGRAMMES COMMITTEE.—*App.* by Allied Maritime Transport Council (*see under* Programmes) in 1918. *Obj.* To collect information necessary for international rationing of wool and for securing sufficient for military needs. *Repr.* Council and chief Allied Governments. *Ref.* Cmd. 325, p. 213.

COLONIAL OFFICE

AGRICULTURAL DEPARTMENTS, COLONIAL COMMITTEE.—*App.* by C.O. in 1919 or early 1920. *Obj.* To consider their staffing, salaries, and recruitment. *Repr.* C.O., West Indian Agriculture, Botanical Experts, Empire Cotton Growing Committee. *Ref.* Cmd. 730. *Diss.* May 1920.

AGRICULTURAL SUB-COMMITTEE, EMPIRE SETTLEMENT COMMITTEE.—*App.* by main Committee, April 1917. *Obj.* To consider inducements to ex-service men to remain in U.K. in agriculture and industry, in relation to those offered for settlement in the Dominions. *Repr.* Main Committee. *Ref.* Cd. 8672. *Diss.* July 1917.

ANGLO-PERUVIAN COMMITTEE.—*App.* at Lima at end of 1920, presumably by C.O. in co-operation with Peruvian authorities. *Obj.* To look after interests and supervise repatriation of British emigrants to Peru, and assist those unable to find employment. *Repr.* English and Peruvians jointly. *Ref.* Cmd. 1580, p. 20. *Diss.* About end 1921.

BRITISH SOUTH AFRICA COMPANY CLAIMS COMMISSION.—*App.* by C.O. July 1919. *Obj.* To report upon sums due to the Company in respect of administration of Southern Rhodesia, including war expenditure. *Repr.* H.L., Tre., Legal Profession, accountants. *Ref.* Cmd. 1129. *Diss.* Jan. 1921.

CANADIAN COUNCIL OF IMMIGRATION OF WOMEN.—*App.* by Canadian Immigration and Colonization Department in 1920 or early 1921. *Obj.* To organize work connected with wage-earning employment of immigrant women and welfare of unaccompanied women. *Repr.* Canadian Provincial Governments and National Women's Associations. *Ref.* Cmd. 1134, p. 5. Presumably *Permanent.*

COLONIAL BLUE BOOKS COMMITTEE.—*App.* by C.O. in or before 1917. *Obj.* To consider suitability of, and improvement in, existing blue books. *Repr.* C.O., B.T., Crown Agents for the Colonies, F.B.I. *Ref.* Cd. 8916, p. 13.

COLONIAL ECONOMIC DEVELOPMENT COMMITTEE.—*App.* by C.O., Dec. 1919. *Obj.* To promote economic development of colonies and protectorates, by inquiries and recommendations regarding possible developments, examination of particular schemes, &c. *Repr.* Parliament, C.O., Crown Agents for the Colonies, experienced Colonial Administrators, bankers, and business men, civil engineers. *Ref.* T., 13th Dec., 1919, p. 14.

COLONIAL RESEARCH COMMITTEE.—*App.* by C.O., Mar. or April 1919. *Obj.* To administer grants for assisting researches in smaller colonies and protectorates, with special reference to post-war development of Imperial resources. *Repr.* Parliament, C.O., S.I.R. *Ref.* Cmd. 1144. *To continue for some years.*

COLONIAL RESEARCH COMMITTEE (1920).—*App.* by C.O., Nov. 1920. *Obj.* To report on means for securing co-operation of British Universities in research for prevention of disease and for development of resources in Colonies and Protectorates. *Repr.* Parliament, C.O., and (mainly) scientists. *Ref.* B.T.J., 25th Nov. 1920.

COTTAGES FOR EX-SERVICE MEN IN IRELAND TRUST.—*App.* as body corporate under Irish Free State (Consequential Provisions) Act, 1920, sec. 3, about end of 1922. *Obj.* To organize provision of cottages for ex-service men in Ireland. *Repr.* Governments of G.B. (through C.O.), I.F.S. and Northern Ireland. *Ref.* P.G.A., 1922. *Permanent Body.*

DISABLED OFFICERS EMPLOYMENT COMMITTEE.—*See* In.O.

DOMINIONS WAR CONTINGENTS COMMITTEE.—*App.* by C.O. *Obj.* To assist Contingents Committees in chief Dominions and act as *liaison* for them with Government Departments. *Repr.* Parliament, C.O., Tre., W.O., Dominions, business men. *Ref.* T., 25th Aug., 1914.

EDIBLE AND OIL PRODUCING NUTS AND SEEDS COMMITTEE.— *App.* by C.O. June 1915. *Obj.* To report upon prospects of West African trade in these products and provision for industries dependent on them. *Repr.* C.O., B.A., B.T., Gold Coast and Nigerian Governments, Imperial Institute, Chambers of Commerce, Bank of British West Africa, traders, margarine manufacturers. *Ref.* Cd. 8247. *Diss.* May 1916.

EMIGRANTS, EMIGRATION.—*See under* Overseas Settlement.

EMPIRE SETTLEMENT COMMITTEE.—*App.* by C.O. Feb. 1917, first sitting in April. *Obj.* To report upon provision for ex-service emigrants, prepare suitable information as to openings, and advise on distribution among troops, and establishment of Central Emigration Authority, the Committee being divided into two, a General Purposes Sub-Committee for Empire Settlement and an Agricultural Sub-Committee (*see* above) for agricultural settlement at home. *Repr.* Parliament, Government Departments chiefly concerned, the Dominions (including State) Governments, British South Africa Company, industry, agriculture, Labour, experts in land settlement. *Ref.* Cd. 8672. *Diss.* July 1917.

EMPIRE SETTLEMENT, STATE-AIDED, CONFERENCE.—*Held* at C.O. Jan.–Feb. 1921. *Obj.* To advise upon means of carrying out Government proposals for permanent policy of state-aided imperial settlement. *Repr.* C.O., M.L., Tre., O.S.C., Governments of Canada, Australia, and New Zealand. *Ref.* Cmd. 1474, pp. 59–62. *Diss.* Feb. 1921.

EX-SERVICE MEN.—*See* Cottages, Empire Settlement.

FALKLAND ISLES, RESEARCH AND DEVELOPMENT, INTER-DEPARTMENTAL COMMITTEE.—*App.* by C.O. in 1917. *Obj.* To advise on means of reviving the whaling industry of the Isles after the War, and of development and research. *Repr.* C.O., Adm., B.A., S.I.R., British Museum. *Ref.* Cmd. 657. *Diss.* Aug. 1919.

FUEL OIL HOME PRODUCTION COMMITTEE.—*See* M.M.

IMPERIAL PREFERENCE COMMITTEE.—*See* Cabinet.

IRISH DISTRESS AND (LATER) GRANTS COMMITTEE.—*App.* by the Government, May 1922, and working in connexion with C.O. *Obj.* To investigate applications for assistance from Irish refugees and authorize grants, negotiate with Provisional Government for return to homes, and (later) make advances to persons with claims against British or Irish Governments. *Repr.* Parliament, Cabinet, Provisional Government of Ireland Committee, Tre., Crown Solicitor for Ireland *Ref.* Report H.M.S.O., 1922, Cmd. 2032. *Still sitting* end 1922.

MEDICAL SERVICES, COLONIAL, DEPARTMENTAL COMMITTEE.— *App.* by C.O., Nov. 1919. *Obj.* To consider generally position of medical services under C.O. *Repr.* C.O., Colonial Administration, Medical Profession. *Ref.* Cmd. 939. *Diss.* July 1920.

MISSIONS IN INDIA COMMITTEE.—Joint appointment. *See* In.O.

NUTS.—*See* Edible and Oil-Producing Nuts, &c.

OIL SUPPLIES COMMITTEE.—*App.* by C.O. on behalf of Cabinet in summer of 1918. *Obj.* To inquire and advise as to policy for securing supplies for naval, military, and industrial purposes. *Repr.* H.L., A.C.(S.) and others. *Ref.* Cd. 9144, p. 23.

OIL.—*See also under* Edible and Oil Producing Nuts, &c., and M.M.

OVERSEAS, EMPLOYMENT BRANCH, SETTLEMENT SELECTION COMMITTEES.—Co-operation with O.S.C. *See* M.L.

OVERSEAS EMPLOYMENT INTER-DEPARTMENTAL COMMITTEE. —*App.* jointly by O.S.C., M.L. and other Departments in summer of 1919. *Obj.* To direct and co-ordinate work of overseas employment. *Repr.* O.S.C., In.O., M.L., O.T.D. *Ref.* Cmd. 573, p. 11.

OVERSEAS SETTLEMENT COMMITTEE AND (LATER) DEPARTMENT.—*App.* by C.O., Dec. 1918, in place of voluntary Committee of Emigrants Information Office, and at first known as the Government Emigration Committee, its staff forming a sub-department of C.O. *Obj.* To create organization to deal with post-war problems of overseas settlement within the Empire. *Repr.* Parliament, C.O., B.A., B.T., M.H., M.L., W.O., the Press, Women. *Ref.* Cmd. 573. The Committee eventually became the Overseas Settlement Department of the C.O.

OVERSEAS SETTLEMENT DELEGATION TO AUSTRALIA AND NEW ZEALAND.—*App.* by O.S.C. Mar. 1923, at invitation of Governments of these Dominions. *Obj.* To visit these Dominions and investigate fully possibilities of settlement. *Repr.* Parliament, C.O., O.S.C., The Army, Labour. *Ref.* Cmd. 2132, 2167. *Diss.* Returned Nov. 1923, reports published in spring of 1924.

OVERSEAS SETTLEMENT, GENERAL ADVISORY COMMITTEE.— *App.* by O.S.C. in 1920. *Obj.* To advise in all matters of overseas settlement. *Repr.* O.S.C. *Ref.* Cmd. 573, p. 3.

OVERSEAS SETTLEMENT IMPERIAL COMMITTEE.—*See* Cabinet.

OVERSEAS SETTLEMENT JOINT COMMITTEE.—*App.* jointly by O.S.C. and N.R.F., July 1918. *Obj.* To administer jointly grant from N.R.F. *Repr.* O.S.C., N.R.F. *Ref.* Cmd. 573, p. 12.

OVERSEAS SETTLEMENT.—*See also under* Women.

PRIZES, OVERSEAS, DISPOSAL COMMITTEE.—Joint Appointment. *See* Tre.

PALESTINE DISTURBANCES.—*App.* by High Commissioner for Palestine, May 1921. *Obj.* To report upon recent disturbances in Jaffa district. *Repr.* Palestine Administrative and Judicial Services. *Ref.* Cmd. 1540. *Diss.* Aug. 1921.

PALESTINE GOVERNMENT COMMITTEE, COMMISSIONS, ETC.— An account of these as part of the new system of government in Palestine is given in Cmd. 1499.

RUBBER SITUATION IN BRITISH COLONIES AND PROTECTO-RATES COMMITTEE.—*App.* by C.O., in 1921 or early 1922. *Obj.* To investigate existing rubber situation in the Empire and advise remedial measures. *Repr.* C.O. Governments of Ceylon and Malay States, rubber planters, colonial merchants, and other business men. *Ref.* Cmd. 1678, 1756.

   (The subject had previously been investigated for the Government of the Straits Settlements and Federated Malay States, who had appointed the Duncan Committee (reported Jan. 1921) and various Commissions to investigate the rubber and general trade depression and the extension of credit facilities (Cmd. 1678, p. 3). The Rubber Situation Committee suggested, in connexion with a proposed scheme, the appointment of an Advisory Committee to C.O. of official and non-official members, and Local Committees of the rubber industry appointed by the Governments of the Dependencies concerned to supervise the application of the scheme (*see* Cmd. 1756, pp. 5, 6.)

RUBBER.—*See also* W.O.

SEEDS.—*See* Edible and Oil-Producing Nuts, &c.

SOUTH AFRICA, 1820 MEMORIAL, CENTRAL AND BRANCH COMMITTEES.—*App.* in South Africa, in 1920, at instigation of 1820 Settlers Memorial Association. *Obj.* To attempt to ' repeat events of 1820 by encouraging and training agricultural settlers to replace those who fell in the War '. *Repr.* South African Government, farmers, and others. *Ref.* Cmd. 1580, pp. 19, 20.

STEPHENSON COMMITTEE.—*See* Rubber Situation Committee above.

TECHNICAL INFORMATION BUREAU, IMPERIAL INSTITUTE.— *App.* as permanent branch of the Scientific and Technical Research Department of the Institute, by C.O., Oct. 1914, the need for the Bureau having been rendered more urgent by the War. *Obj.* To deal with inquiries about new products and materials in the Empire and little-known processes and machinery. *Repr.* Not stated. *Ref.* B.T.J., 22nd Oct. 1914. *Permanent.*

VETERINARY DEPARTMENTS IN COLONIES AND PROTECTO-RATES COMMITTEE.—*App.* by C.O. in 1919 or 1920. *Obj.* To inquire into their staffing, salaries, and recruiting. *Repr.* C.O., B.A., Veterinary Colleges. *Ref.* Cmd. 922. *Diss.* Aug. 1920.

WEST INDIAN SHIPPING COMMITTEE.—*App.* by C.O., Sept. 1918. *Obj.* To report upon after-war position of shipping as affecting British West Indian trade and inter-colonial communications, and measures for maintaining communications. *Repr.* Parliament, Adm., B.T., M.S., O.T.D., P.O., Crown Agents for the Colonies, West Indian Committee, steamship lines. *Ref.* Cmd. 372. *Diss.* Aug. 1919.

WEST INDIES, TROPICAL AGRICULTURAL COLLEGE COMMITTEE.—*App.* by C.O., Aug. 1919. *Obj.* To consider desirability of establishing a college. *Repr.* Parliament, C.O., B.T., West Indian Government, West Indian Committee, Empire Cotton Growing Association, West Indian landowners, botanical and other experts. *Ref.* Cmd. 562. *Diss.* Oct. 1919.

WIRELESS TELEGRAPHY COMMISSION.—*App.* by Cabinet, Dec. 1920. *Obj.* To decide upon most suitable plant for scheme of Imperial wireless communications (*see* next entry), and choose sites for stations, &c. *Repr.* Parliament, C.O., scientists, electrical engineers. *Ref.* Cmd. 1572. *Diss.* Dec. 1921.

WIRELESS TELEGRAPHY, IMPERIAL, COMMITTEE.—*App.* by C.O., Nov. 1919. *Obj.* To prepare completed scheme of Imperial wireless communications. *Repr.* Parliament, Adm., P.O., N.P.L., Electricity Commissioners, engineering experts, scientists. *Ref.* Cmd. 777. *Diss.* May 1920.

WOMEN, BRITISH, SOCIETY FOR OVERSEAS SETTLEMENT.—*See under* Women's Emigration Societies.

WOMEN'S EMIGRATION ADVISORY COMMITTEE.—*App.* by O.S.C. in summer of 1919. *Obj.* To secure for O.S.C. advice of women's Emigration Societies. *Repr.* Societies interested in women's emigration. *Ref.* Cmd. 573, p. 7.

WOMEN'S EMIGRATION, OPENINGS IN THE EMPIRE, MISSIONS (THREE).—*App.* by O.S.C. with consent of Tre. in 1919. *Obj.* To visit Canada, Australia, and New Zealand with reference to openings for women. *Repr.* Representative women. *Ref.* Cmd. 403, 573 (pp. 6, 7), 745, 933. *Diss.* Sept. 1919, June and August 1920.

WOMEN'S EMIGRATION SOCIETIES' JOINT COUNCIL. This—a pre-war body—had acted as selection board for women emigrants. During 1919, in consultation with the O.S.C., it was extended and reorganized as the 'Society for the Overseas Settlement of British Women', and, after inquiry by a small Commission of representative men and women, a further reorganization was carried out to include representatives of organized labour and the chief women's organizations (*see* Cmd. 573, pp. 7, 8).

DEVELOPMENT COMMISSION

ABBREVIATION

D.C. = Development Commission.

AGRICULTURAL RESEARCH ADVISORY COMMITTEE.—*App.* by D.C. in 1917 or 1918. *Obj.* To report on ' special research ' grants and other matters. *Repr.* D.C., B.A., B.A.(Sc.), D.A.T.I., Royal Society, scientific research. *Ref.* H.C., No. 118, 1918, p. 2. *Permanent Committee*, replacing Agricultural Research Advisory Board of B.A.

FISHERIES RESEARCH ADVISORY COMMITTEE.—*App.* by D.C., April 1919, the appointment being largely due to war-time development of food research. *Obj.* To report on character and scope of research for fisheries of U.K. and prepare preliminary scheme, with provision for co-ordination with Food Investigation Board of S.I.R. *Repr.* D.C., S.I.R., M.R.C., Universities' Grants Committee, Royal Society, scientists, fishing industry. *Ref.* H.C., No. 230, 1920, pp. 202–10. Reappointed as *Permanent Committee*, Mar. 1920.

Later in 1920 the Committee appointed Sub-Committees on Marine Fish Hatching and Shellfish Development; Freshwater (including Salmon) Fisheries; and Education.

FISHERMEN, INSHORE, WAR DETERIORATION OF VESSELS, INTER-DEPARTMENTAL CONFERENCE.—*Held* at instance of D.C. during 1919. *Obj.* To consider means of restoring fishing fleets to pre-war conditions. *Repr.* Government Departments concerned. *Ref.* H.C., No. 230, 1920, p. 223. *Diss.* Close of Conference.

FISHERY HARBOURS STANDING INTER-DEPARTMENTAL CON-FERENCE.—*App.* jointly by D.C. and other Government Departments concerned in 1919 (late) or 1920. *Obj.* To secure co-ordination in exercising powers of D.C. over fishery harbours. *Repr.* Government Departments concerned. *Ref.* H.C., No. 230, 1920, p. 231. *Permanent.*

FISH FOOD AND MOTOR LOAN COMMITTEE.—Consulted in appointment. *See* B.A.

HUMAN NUTRITION.—*See* N.H.I.C.

RECLAMATION AND LAND DRAINAGE JOINT COMMISSIONERS. *App.* jointly by D.C. and B.A., B.A.(Sc.), and D.A.T.I., Dec. 1918, for England and Wales, Scotland, and Ireland respectively. *Obj.* To administer grant for this purpose to provide work for demobilized men. *Repr.* D.C. and the Department of Agriculture concerned in each case. *Ref.* H.C., No. 214, 1919, p. 2.

RED CROSS SOCIETY AND ORDER OF ST. JOHN JOINT FINANCE COMMITTEE.—Voluntary body which assisted Rural Industries Scheme (*see* below) with grant for establishing ex-service men in rural industries. *See* D.C. Report 1921–2, pp. 10, 11 (H.M.S.O., 1922).

RURAL INDUSTRIES INTELLIGENCE BUREAU, COMMITTEE OF. —*App.* by D.C. in autumn of 1921. *Obj.* To advise generally on principles and procedure in establishing Bureau and subsequently to control generally its work in distributing advice and information on revival of rural industries. *Repr.* Trustees of the Bureau, various Government Departments, Labour, Ex-Service Men, Agricultural and other Research, Women's Institutes, and other Associations interested. *Ref.* D.C., Report for 1921–2, pp. 8–11. *Permanent Body.*

The Trustees of the Bureau, appointed by the B.A., represented Parliament, agriculture, business and ex-service men. A Central Trading Society was established in connexion with the Bureau.

VEGETABLES DRYING COMMITTEE.—*See* B.A.

EDUCATION (ENGLAND AND WALES), BOARD OF

The Board was established in 1899 by the Board of Education Act (62 & 63 Vict., c. 33) replacing the Committee of Council on Education. A few temporary organizations were added to the Board during and after the War.

ABBREVIATIONS

B.E. = Board of Education for England and Wales.
L.E.A.'s = Local Education Authority(ies).
N.U.T. = National Union of Teachers.
W.E.A. = Workers Educational Association.

ADULT EDUCATION COMMITTEE.—*App.* by B.E., April 1921 (for a previous Committee, *see* M.R.). *Obj.* To promote provision of liberal education for adults and co-ordination of existing organizations for the purpose. *Repr.* The Universities : Voluntary Organizations for Adult Education. *Ref.* Cmd. 1718, p. 9. Apparently a *Standing Committee.*

AGRICULTURAL TRAINING.—*See under* Officers.

BUILDINGS, EDUCATIONAL, FOR MILITARY USE, COMMITTEE.
—*App.* by B.E., Jan. 1915. *Obj.* To confer with L.E.A.'s in certain areas, as to use of educational buildings as hospitals. *Repr.* Parliament, B.E., Inspectors of Schools. *Ref.* Cd. 8274, p. 14. *Diss.* Apparently before end of 1915.

BURNHAM COMMITTEE.—*See* Salaries for Teachers in Elementary Schools.

CANAL BOAT CHILDREN.—*See* L.G.B.

CANTEEN, CENTRAL SCHOOLS, COMMITTEES.—*App.* early in War at instigation of B.E. in districts where not in existence. *Obj.* To organize schemes for feeding school children, as result of distress due to the War. *Repr.* L.E.A.'s and local Relief of Distress Committees (*see* L.G.B.). *Ref.* Cd. 7730.
(N.B. It is possible that in big centres District Committees were established under the Central Committees.)

CONTINUATION SCHOOLS BUILDING COMMITTEE.—*App.* by B.E. in 1918. *Obj.* To advise on buildings required for compulsory continuation schools under Education (Fisher) Act of 1918. *Repr.* Official and expert. *Ref.* T., 3rd Feb. 1919, p. 7 ; B.E. Circular, 1086. *Diss.* Feb. 1919.

EDUCATION, ARMY, IMPERIAL.—*See* W.O.

ENGINEERING EDUCATION REPRESENTATIVE COMMITTEE.—
App. by Conference of bodies interested, held at instance of B.E., Oct. 1917. *Obj.* To establish central organization to co-ordinate and improve engineering education. *Repr.* B.E., other Government Departments concerned, Dominions' High Commissioners, Universities, Public Schools, engineering employers. *Ref.* Cd. 9045, pp. 82–4.

ENGLISH (LANGUAGE AND LITERATURE) COMMITTEE.—*App.* by B.E., May 1919. *Obj.* To inquire into position of English studies in education system, and means of promoting them. *Repr.* Universities, L.E.A.'s, teachers, men of letters, Legal Profession, educationists, journalists, women. *Ref.* Cmd. 1718, p. 9 ; T., 5th May 1919, p. 9. *Diss.* April 1921.

EX-SERVICE MEN, TRAINING AS TEACHERS, STANDING AD-VISORY COMMITTEE.—*App.* by B.E. late in 1918. *Obj.* To advise on applications of ex-service men for training as teachers in elementary schools, without passing necessary examinations. *Repr.* L.E.A.'s, Training Colleges, teachers. *Ref.* Cmd. 165, p. 56 ; 325, p. 297.

FREE PLACES.—*See* Scholarships.

HEALTH SERVICE, JOINT LOCAL COMMITTEES.—*App.* jointly by L.E.A.'s and Local Sanitary Authorities from 1918. *Obj.* To ensure con-tinuous co-operation in health work. *Repr.* The authorities concerned. *Ref.* Cmd. 420, p. 37. Apparently *Permanent.*

HIGHER EDUCATION, ADVISORY CONSULTATIVE COMMITTEES OF BUSINESS MEN.—*App.* by Education Committee of L.C.C., on recommendation of Higher Education Sub-Committee for Banking, Chemical Industry, and Engineering, in 1917. *Obj.* To advise L.C.C. in regard to schemes of higher education in relation to their industries. *Repr.* Business men in the trades concerned. *Ref.* T., 12th July 1917, p. 3.

HIGHER EDUCATION.—*See also* Salaries.

HORSE CHESTNUTS.—*See* M.F.

JUVENILE EDUCATION IN RELATION TO EMPLOYMENT AFTER THE WAR, DEPARTMENTAL COMMITTEE.—*App.* by B.E., April 1916. *Obj.* To consider post-war provision for children and young persons, with special reference to war conditions. *Repr.* B.E., B.A., B.T., H.O., Employers, Labour, women, schoolmasters, experts in juvenile problems. *Ref.* Cd. 8374, 8512. *Diss.* Mar. 1917.

JUVENILE ORGANIZATION, CENTRAL STANDING AND LOCAL COMMITTEES.—Transferred to B.E., Oct. 1919. *See* H.O.

JUVENILE UNEMPLOYMENT CENTRES ADVISORY COMMITTEE. —*App.* by B.E. about Dec. 1918. *Obj.* To assist L.E.A.'s in organizing these centres. *Repr.* B.E., other Government Departments concerned, L.E.A.'s, Juvenile Organizations. *Ref.* Cmd. 722, p. 53. *Diss.* About middle of 1919.

JUVENILE WAR WORKERS, EDUCATION GRANT, CENTRAL COMMITTEE.—*App.* by B.E. and S.E.D. in 1919. *Obj.* To administer training grant from N.R.F. *Repr.* B.E., N.R.F. and others. *Ref.* Cmd. 356, p. 7.

MODERN LANGUAGES COMMITTEE.—*See* Cabinet.

NATURAL SCIENCE COMMITTEE.—*See* Cabinet.

OFFICERS' AGRICULTURAL TRAINING SCHEME, SUB-COM-MITTEES.—*App.* by Agricultural Education Committees of County Councils early in 1919. *Obj.* To carry out scheme for training officers and men of like standing for the land (except for the grant of scholarships) and later organize training of disabled ex-officers for the land. *Repr.* County Council and others. *Ref.* J.B.A., Jan. 1919.

OFFICERS' UNIVERSITY AND TECHNICAL TRAINING.—*See* M.L.

PHYSICAL EDUCATION ADVISORY COMMITTEE.—*App.* by B.E. in 1918. *Obj.* To report on changes in syllabus of training. *Repr.* Largely expert. *Ref.* Cmd. 420, p. 158. *Diss.* Early 1919.

SALARIES FOR TEACHERS IN ELEMENTARY SCHOOLS, CONSTITUENT COMMITTEE.—*App.* jointly by L.E.A.'s and Teachers' Organizations at instance of B.E. about July 1919. *Obj.* To work out scheme for joint organization to deal with salaries. *Repr.* L.E.A.'s, N.U.T. *Ref.* Cmd. 443, Appendix. *Diss.* Sept. 1919.

SALARIES FOR TEACHERS IN ELEMENTARY SCHOOLS, DEPARTMENTAL COMMITTEES.—*App.* by B.E., Dec. 1917. *Obj.* To report upon principles which should determine scale of salaries. *Repr.* B.E., L.E.A.'s, teachers, school managers, Legal Profession. *Ref.* Cd. 8939. *Diss.* Dec. 1917.

SALARIES FOR TEACHERS IN ELEMENTARY SCHOOLS, STANDING COMMITTEE (BURNHAM COMMITTEE).—*App.* jointly by L.E.A.'s and N.U.T. as result of Constituent Committee's work, Sept. 1919. *Obj.* To secure solution of salary problem on national basis. *Repr.* L.E.A.'s, N.U.T. *Ref.* Cmd. 443. Standing Committee.

SALARIES FOR TEACHERS IN SECONDARY AND TECHNICAL SCHOOLS AND INSTITUTIONS FOR HIGHER EDUCATION, DEPARTMENTAL COMMITTEE.—*App.* by B.E. in latter part of 1917. *Obj.*, *Repr.* as with Departmental Committee for Elementary Schools. *Ref.* Cd. 9140. *Diss.* July 1918.

SALARIES FOR TEACHERS IN SECONDARY SCHOOLS, IN TECHNICAL SCHOOLS, SCHOOLS OF ART, ETC., STANDING COMMITTEES.—Such Committees were appointed in May 1920, for Secondary, and in Dec. 1920 for Technical, &c., Schools, with similar object and representation to Committee for Elementary Schools (*see* earlier entry). *See* Cmd. 1412, pp. 2, 3 ; 1451, p. 1 ; 1718, pp. 7, 8.

SCHOLARSHIPS AND FREE PLACES, DEPARTMENTAL COMMITTEE.—*App.* by B.E., Oct. 1919. *Obj.* To report upon present position and future arrangements. *Repr.* Parliament, B.E., L.E.A.'s, Teachers, Labour. *Ref.* Cmd. 968. *Diss.* July 1920.

SCHOLARSHIPS, INDUSTRIAL AND COMMERCIAL, IN HIGHER EDUCATION, SUB-COMMITTEE OF CONSULTATIVE COMMITTEE ON SCHOLARSHIPS FOR HIGHER EDUCATION.—*App.* by main Committee (pre-war) in late summer of 1915, largely for post-war needs. *Obj.* To deal with problem of scholarships as affecting industry, agriculture, and commerce. *Repr.* The main Committee. *Ref.* Cd. 8291. *Diss.* By May 1916.

SEA SERVICE, NATIONAL SCHEME OF TRAINING, COMMITTEE.—*App.* by B.E. in 1918. *Obj.* To prepare draft scheme, calculated to maintain supply of British seamen. *Repr.* B.E., Adm., B.T., L.E.A.'s, Mercantile Marine, Shipowners, Medical Profession, Clergy, Training Ships. *Ref.* Cmd. 408. *Diss.* July 1919.

SECONDARY EDUCATION IN WALES, DEPARTMENTAL COMMITTEE.—*App.* by Welsh Department of B.E., July 1919. *Obj.* To consider and advise upon organization and consolidation. *Repr.* Parliament, B.E., L.E.A.'s (Wales), Universities, teachers, Clergy, women. *Ref.* Cmd. 967. *Diss.* Sept. 1920.

A Conference, summoned jointly by the Central Welsh Board (under B.E.) and the Federation of Welsh Education Authorities in July 1921, appointed a Committee to investigate the practical difficulties of applying the Departmental Committee's proposals. *See* Cmd. 1639, p. 13.

SECONDARY EDUCATION.—*See also under* Salaries.

SOCIAL STUDIES.—*See* H.O.

TEACHERS.—*See* Ex-Service, Salaries.

TECHNICAL OPTICS COMMITTEE.—*App.* by Imperial College of Science in 1916. *Obj.* To manage for the College part of new Department of Technical Optics whose establishment was accelerated by the War, and advise L.C.C. as to the elementary optical work at Northampton Institute. *Repr.* The College, Adm., M.M., W.O., S.I.R., employers and workpeople in the industry. *Ref.* Cd. 8594, p. 70. *Permanent Body.*

THEATRICAL CHILDREN LICENCES COMMITTEE.—*App.* by B.E., Jan. 1919. *Obj.* To advise on revision of rules in reference to Education Act, 1918. *Repr.* B.E., Police Magistrates, theatrical and similar interests, women. *Ref.* Cmd. 484. *Diss.* July 1919.

UNIVERSITIES, LOSSES DUE TO THE WAR, INQUIRY.—The Advisory Committee (pre-war) of B.E. on University Grants undertook the inquiry in autumn of 1914, and subsequently other inquiries, at request of B.E. and S.E.D. *Obj.* To inquire into losses due to the War of grant-receiving Universities and Colleges in G.B. and of English Agricultural Colleges. *Repr.* The Advisory Committee. *Ref.* Cd. 7934, p. 6. *Diss.* Inquiry completed in winter of 1914–15.

UNIVERSITY EDUCATION IN WALES, ROYAL COMMISSION.—*App.* by Royal Warrant, April 1916. *Obj.* To investigate work of University of Wales and relations with other post-secondary education in Wales, and to report on desirable changes. *Repr.* Parliament, B.E., D.C., Royal Society, Universities, Women's Education. *Ref.* Cd. 8500, 8991. *Diss.* Feb. 1918.

UNIVERSITIES STANDING COMMITTEE.—*App.* by Bureau of the Universities of the Empire, May 1918. *Obj.* To promote co-operation among the Universities of U.K. *Repr.* Heads of various Universities. *Ref.* Cmd. 165, p. 66.

UNIVERSITY GRANTS (STANDING) COMMITTEE.—*See* Tre.

EDUCATION IN IRELAND

COMMISSIONERS OF NATIONAL EDUCATION, AND INTERMEDIATE EDUCATION BOARD

DUBLIN UNIVERSITY ROYAL COMMISSION.—*App.* by Royal Warrant, Mar. 1920. *Obj.* To consider University's application for State financial assistance and inquire into financial resources, administration and constitution. *Repr.* Universities of Oxford, Cambridge and Dublin, Royal Society. *Ref.* Cmd. 1078. *Diss.* Nov. 1920.

EDUCATION, IRISH, COMMITTEE.—*App.* by C.S., May 1919. *Obj.* To frame educational measures for the whole of Ireland, with safeguarding of religious views of the inhabitants. *Repr.* Commissioners of National Education and Intermediate Education Board, D.A.T.I., B.E., S.E.D. *Ref.* T., 10th May 1919, p. 12.

GRANTS.—*See under* Intermediate and Primary Education.

INTERMEDIATE EDUCATION, IRELAND, VICE-REGAL COMMITTEE.—*App.* by L.L., Aug. 1918. *Obj.* To report upon improvements in teachers' remuneration and conditions of service and distribution of grants. *Repr.* Commissioners of National Education (Ireland), Intermediate Education Board, D.A.T.I., Tre., Judges, Universities, Teachers, Clergy. *Ref.* Cmd. 66. *Diss.* Mar. 1919.

PRIMARY EDUCATION (IRELAND) VICE-REGAL COMMITTEE.—*App.* by L.L., Aug. 1918. *Obj.* To report upon the position, salaries and pensions of teachers and distribution of grants. *Repr.* Commissioners of National Education (Ireland), Tre., Universities, Teachers, Clergy. *Ref.* Cmd. 60. *Diss.* Feb. 1919.

TEACHERS' SALARIES, IRELAND, GOVERNMENT COMMITTEE.—*App.* by the Government in 1918. *Obj.* To investigate financial position and salaries of Irish teachers. *Repr.* Commissioners of National Education (Ireland) and others. *Ref.* Cmd. 299, pp. 5, 7.

TRAINING COLLEGES AND UNIVERSITIES (IRELAND) RELATIONS COMMITTEE.—*App.* by Commissioners of National Education (Ireland) in first half of 1919. *Obj.* To consider relations between Teachers' Training Colleges and Universities. *Repr.* The Commissioners and others. *Ref.* Cmd. 299, p. 7. *Diss.* After June 1919.

UNIVERSITY GRANTS COMMITTEE.—*See* Tre.

EDUCATION IN SCOTLAND

The Committee of Council for Education in Scotland became the *Scottish Education Department* in Nov. 1918 by Education (Scotland) Act, 1918 (8 & 9 Geo. V, c. 48).

ABBREVIATION

S.E.D. = Scottish Education Department (previously Committee of Council for Education in Scotland).

ADVISORY COUNCIL.—*App.* by Order-in-Council, under Education (Scotland) Act, 1918, Nov. 1918. *Obj.* To advise S.E.D. on educational matters. *Repr.* Bodies interested in education, to extent of at least two-thirds of members. *Ref.* P.G.A., 1918. *Permanent.*

ADVISORY COUNCILS, LOCAL.—*App.* by all L.E.A.'s in Scotland as required by Education (Scotland) Act, 1918, from Dec. 1918. *Obj.* To advise L.E.A.'s on educational matters in their area. *Repr.* Bodies interested in education. *Ref.* P.G.A., 1918. *Permanent.*

ADVISORY SUB-COMMITTEES TO ADVISORY COUNCIL were appointed during 1920 to deal with problems of organization and classification of schools under the Act of 1920 (*see* Cmd. 1266, p. 12).

EX-SERVICE STUDENTS SELECTION FOR HIGHER EDUCATION, ADVISORY COMMITTEE.—*App.* by Officers' University and Training (Scotland) Committee (*see* M.L.) at request of S.E.D. about end of 1918, subsequently dividing into Sub-Committees, which sat concurrently at Edinburgh and Glasgow. *Obj.* To advise S.E.D. in selection of officers for training. *Repr.* Scottish Universities and Institutions for Higher Education. *Ref.* Cmd. 782, p. 19.

JUVENILE WAR WORKERS, EDUCATION GRANT, SCOTTISH COMMITTEE.—*App.* by S.E.D. in 1919. Other details as with English Committee. *See* B.E.

SALARIES.—*See below under* Teachers.

SCHOOL MANAGEMENT COMMITTEES.—*App.* as required by Education (Scotland) Act, 1918, by each L.E.A. under schemes approved by S.E.D. for schools and groups of schools and in certain cases for particular towns or parishes. *Obj.* To manage schools or groups of schools within the area of the authority. *Repr.* L.E.A.'s, parents, teachers, religious bodies, in certain cases local residents. *Ref.* P.G.A., 1918.

TEACHERS (SCOTLAND), REMUNERATION, DEPARTMENTAL COMMITTEE.—*App.* by S.E.D., July 1917. *Obj.* To advise upon suitable scales of salaries and disposal of grant in aid of salaries. *Repr.* Parliament, S.E.D., L.E.A.'s, school managers, teachers. *Ref.* Cd. 9091, pp. 7, 8; H.M.S.O., 1917. *Diss.* Nov. 1917.

UNIVERSITIES, LOSSES DUE TO THE WAR, INQUIRY.—*See* B.E.

UNIVERSITY GRANTS COMMITTEE.—*See* Tre.

FISHERY BOARD, SCOTLAND

ABBREVIATIONS

F.B.(Sc.) = Fishery Board, Scotland.

FISHERIES, FRESHWATER, SCOTTISH COMMITTEE.—*App.* by S.S., April 1917. *Obj.* To consider means of securing additional freshwater fish for home consumption. *Repr.* S.O., F.B.(Sc.), riparian owners. *Ref.* Cd. 9018, p. x. *Diss.* In 1917.

FISHERIES, SEA, SCOTTISH COMMITTEE.—An alternative name for Fish Food, Scotland, Committee. *See below.*

FISHERMEN DEMOBILIZATION.—*See* Adm.

FISHERY.—*See also* B.T., under Coal Supplies, Strikes, Fishery Sub-Committees.

FISHERY HARBOURS.—*See* D.C.

FISH FOOD, SCOTLAND, COMMITTEE.—*App.* by F.B.(Sc.) about April 1917. *Obj.* To assist in conservation and distribution of fish, in increasing production and preventing waste. *Repr.* S.O., F.B.(Sc.), B.A.(Sc.). *Ref.* Cmd. 585, p. 64. *Diss.* Probably in 1920.

FISHING TRADE, WAR EMERGENCY (SCOTLAND) COMMITTEE.—*App.* by F.B., Aug. or Sept. 1914. *Obj.* To deal with war emergency. *Repr.* F.B.(Sc.)., fishing interests. *Ref.* Cmd. 231, pp. xi, xii.

FISH TRANSPORT FACILITIES COMMITTEE.—*See* M.T.

HARBOURS, STANDING CONFERENCE.—*See* M.T.

HERRINGS, CURED, GUARANTEE SCHEME ADMINISTRATIVE COMMITTEE.—*App.* by F.B.(Sc.), Sept. 1919. *Obj.* To administer the Government guarantee to the industry for autumn 1919 season. *Repr.* Scottish Fishing Industry. *Ref.* Cmd. 833, p. xi. *Diss.* Close of season.

HERRINGS, CURED, GUARANTEE SCHEME, ADVISORY COMMITTEE.—*App.* by the Government about June 1919. *Obj.* To prepare scheme for consideration of Government for guarantee to herring fishers for autumn season of 1919. *Repr.* Not stated. *Ref.* Cmd. 833, p. vii. *Diss.* About Sept. 1919.

TRANSPORT, INLAND, SCOTLAND, STANDING CONFERENCE.—Joint appointment. *See* S.O.

WHALING INDUSTRY, SCOTLAND, COMMITTEE—*App.* by F.B.(Sc.) about Dec. 1918. *Obj.* To inquire into general position of industry and demand for making war-time prohibition of whaling permanent. *Repr.* F.B.(Sc.). *Ref.* Cmd. 833, p. xvi. *Diss.* Dec. 1919.

FOOD, MINISTRY OF

The Ministry of Food was established on 22nd Dec. 1916 by the New Ministries and Secretaries Act, 1916 (6 & 7 Geo. V, c. 63), under a Food Controller and Parliamentary Secretary. The *Object* was to economize and maintain the supply of food during the war by regulating supply and consumption and encouraging production. *The Duration* was for the War and twelve months after, or any shorter period fixed by H.M. in Council, but this was extended to 16th Sept. 1922, with modified powers, by the Ministry of Food Continuation Act, 1920 (10 & 11 Geo. V, c. 47), subject to earlier termination by Order-in-Council. *Reference.* Public General Acts, 1916, 1920.

ABBREVIATIONS

F.C. = Food Controller.
M.F. = Ministry of Food.
F.C.C.(s) = Food Control Committee(s).
N.F.J. = National Food Journal.

ACCOUNTANTS.—*See* District Supervising.

AFRICA MERCHANTS ADVISORY COMMITTEE.—Existence, without details, referred to in T., 19th Jan. 1917, p. 29.

AGRICULTURAL ADVISORY COMMITTEE TO THE MINISTRY OF FOOD. *App.* by F.C., about Mar. 1918, by arrangement with the chief agricultural bodies. *Obj.* To advise M.F. on questions of policy of control, and on prices, production and distribution of food. *Repr.* M.F., B.A., B.A.(Sc.), D.A.T.I., Chambers of Agriculture, Farmers' Union, Agricultural Societies. *Ref.* N.F.J., 8th May 1918. *Diss.* Absorbed into Agricultural Advisory Council (q.v.), July 1918.

AGRICULTURAL ADVISORY COUNCIL, CENTRAL.—*App.* jointly by F.C. and B.A., July 1918, to amalgamate the Advisory Committees of the two Departments. *Obj.* As with Advisory Committee (*see* previous entry) but covering both Departments. *Repr.* M.F., B.A., chief agricultural organizations of U.K. *Ref.* N.F.J., 24th July 1918.

For Feeding Stuffs Sub-Committee, *see* B.A.

AGRICULTURAL COSTINGS COMMITTEE.—*App.* by M.F., B.A., B.A.(Sc.), and D.A.T.I., jointly, Dec. 1918. *Obj.* To obtain adequate information of costs and results of farming. *Repr.* The four Departments, Central Agricultural Advisory Council, Irish Agriculture, Consumer's Council, Agricultural Colleges. *Ref.* Cmd. 1028. *Diss.* April 1921 (publication of Final Report on Milk).

AGRICULTURAL MACHINERY ADVISORY COMMITTEE.—*See* B.A.

AMERICAN SPECIAL FOOD MISSION.—*App.* by American Food Controller (Mr. Hoover), about Nov. 1917. *Obj.* To visit U.K. and European Allies, to survey food situation and collect data for propaganda in U.S.A. *Repr.* American Food Control, Chambers of Commerce and other prominent citizens. *Ref.* T., 8th Dec. 1917, p. 8.

AGRICULTURAL REPRESENTATIVE COMMITTEE.—*App.* by leading agricultural bodies about Feb. 1918. *Obj.* To negotiate with F.C.

on various disputed matters. *Repr.* Farmers' Union, Chambers of Agriculture, Royal Agricultural Society. *Ref.* T., 16th Mar. 1918, pp. 6, 7. *Diss.* Mar. 1918, on constitution of Agricultural Advisory Committee (q.v.).

ALLOCATION (MARKETS) COMMITTEES.—*App.* by F.C., late in second half of 1917, for each market district. *Obj.* Allocation of cattle to butchers. *Repr.* Auctioneers, butchers, consumers. *Ref.* Information privately communicated. *Diss.* On or before termination of Meat Control, July 1920.

BACON ADVISORY COMMITTEE.—*App.* by F.C. in second half of 1917. *Obj.* To advise on allocation and control of bacon. *Repr.* M.F., importers, wholesalers, retailers. *Ref.* Information privately communicated.

BACON RETAILERS' COMMITTEE.—*App.* by F.C. in second half of 1917. *Obj.* To advise M.F. in questions connected with retail bacon trade. *Repr.* Retail traders. *Ref.* Information privately communicated.

BACON WHOLESALERS' COMMITTEE.—As with Retailers' Committee (q.v.), but for wholesale trade.

BACON WHOLESALERS' (AREA) COMMITTEES.—*App.* under M.F. in 1917 or 1918. *Obj.* To regulate distribution of controlled bacon in their areas. *Repr.* Wholesale traders in each area. *Ref.* N.F.J., 25th Dec. 1918.

BEANS COMMITTEE.—*App.* by M.F., or interests affected, Aug. 1917. *Obj.* To examine claims of those affected by requisitioning of beans and peas and take up matters with M.F. *Repr.* Merchants concerned. *Ref.* T., 20th Oct. 1917, p. 10.

BREAD COMMITTEE (ROYAL COMMISSION ON WHEAT SUPPLIES).—*App.* by the Commission in second half of 1917. *Obj.* To control use of flour in bread baking, &c. *Repr.* Business interests concerned. *Ref.* Information privately communicated.

BREAD, SALE BY WEIGHT, INTER-DEPARTMENTAL COMMITTEE.—*App.* by M.F. in 1920 or 1921. *Obj.* To report on sale of bread by weight and provisions of Bread Acts in light of experience of administration of M.F. *Repr.* Parliament, M.F., B.T., M.H., L.A.'s, Medical Profession, Labour. *Ref.* Cmd. 1400. *Diss.* June 1921.

BREAD SUBSIDY COMMITTEE.—*App.* by M.F. in 1918. *Obj.* To investigate working of Bread Subsidy and suggest improvements. *Repr.* Not stated. *Ref.* H.C., No. 142, 1919, pp. 5, 6. *Diss.* By April 1919.

BREWING ECONOMIES COMMITTEE.—*App.* by F.C., at suggestion of B.T., April–May 1918. *Obj.* To formulate a scheme for economies in transport and fuel in brewing and distribution of beer. *Repr.* Interests concerned. *Ref.* B.T.J., 16th May 1922.

BREWING TRADES, APPEALS BOARD.—*App.*, *Repr.*, *Ref.* as with Brewing Trades Area Committees (q.v.). *Obj.* To adjudicate on cases not settled by Area Committees, with final appeal to M.F.

BREWING TRADES, AREA COMMITTEES.—*App.* by F.C. in conjunction with Brewers and Licensed Victuallers' Societies, Feb. 1917. *Obj.* To settle local disputes within these trades. *Repr.* Brewers, licensed victuallers (equal numbers). *Ref.* N.F.J., 12th Mar. 1919.

BUTCHERS' COMMITTEES, LOCAL.—*App.* by Local F.C.C.'s, Feb. 1918. *Obj.* To secure co-operation in purchase and allocation of meat. *Repr.* Local butchers. *Ref.* N.F.J., 13th Feb. 1918.

BUTTER AND CHEESE CONTROL ADVISORY COMMITTEE.—*App.* by F.C., Sept. 1917, for butter, and apparently later for cheese. *Obj.* To advise generally on control and distribution of supplies. *Repr.* M.F., D.A.T.I., farmers, importers, traders, dealers, Co-operative Societies, Irish creameries. *Ref.* T., 26th Sept. 1917, p. 3. *Diss.* On or before 31st Jan. 1920.

(About the same time a Butter Department of M.F. was established.)

BUTTER AND CHEESE IMPORTS COMMITTEE.—*App.* by F.C., Nov. 1917. *Obj.* To organize imports (including Irish imports) and distribution of butter and cheese. *Repr.* Traders, Co-operative Wholesale Society, M.F. (sec.). *Ref.* N.F.J., 22nd May 1918.

BUTTER, IRISH, EXPORTS COMMITTEE.—*App.* by M.F. in 1917 or 1918 and extended to cheese, Nov. 1918. *Obj.* To carry out orders regulating export of butter and, later, cheese from Ireland. *Repr.* Official and expert. *Ref.* T., 10th Nov. 1918.

CAERPHILLY CHEESE COMMITTEE.—*App.* by F.C., June 1918. *Obj.* To control distribution of Caerphilly cheese. *Repr.* M.F., producers, dealers, traders. *Ref.* N.F.J., 10th July 1918. *Diss.* May 1919.

CANADA.—*See* Wheat Export.

CANDLES.—*See* Soap.

CARTRIDGE ADVISORY COMMITTEE.—*App.* by F.C. about Sept. 1917. *Obj.* To limit quantity, fix prices and arrange distribution of sporting cartridges. *Repr.* Sporting gun and ammunition trade, landowners. *Ref.* N.F.J., 12th Feb. 1919. *Diss.* By 27th Feb. 1919.

CATERING TRADES ADVISORY COMMITTEE.—*App.* by Caterers' Associations, June 1918. *Obj.* To act as *liaison* between M.F. and individual caterers. *Repr.* Various Caterers' Associations. *Ref.* N.F.J., 12th June 1918.

CATTLE AND MEAT CONTROL, CENTRAL ADVISORY COMMITTEE.—*App.* by F.C. in or after June 1917. *Obj.* To advise on, and assist in organizing, control of cattle and meat. *Repr.* M.F., B.A., B.A.(Sc.), D.A.T.I., Consumers Council, farmers, butchers, meat traders. *Ref.* N.F.J., 22nd May 1918. *Diss.* By June 1920.

CATTLE CAKES.—*See* Corn.

CATTLE GRADING CENTRAL COMMITTEE.—*App.* by F.C., Sept. 1919. *Obj.* To deal with complaints of grading of cattle (*see* Market Grading). *Repr.* M.F., farmers, butchers. *Ref.* N.F.J., 10th Sept. 1919.

CATTLE (IRISH) VALUATION COMMITTEE.—*App.* by F.C., June 1917, at eight ports of entry. *Obj.* To value cattle and sheep on arrival from Ireland. *Repr.* M.F., D.A.T.I., British and Irish farmers. *Ref.* N.F.J., 10th July 1918.

CATTLE PURCHASE, ARMY, LOCAL AUCTIONEERS' COMMITTEES. —*App.* by F.C. or W.O. in 1917, under Army Cattle Purchase Scheme.

Obj. To organize work of live-stock auctioneers and cattle salesmen. *Repr.* All licensed live-stock auctioneers and cattle salesmen required to join Local Committees. *Ref.* J.B.A., Jan. 1918.

CATTLE PURCHASING COMMITTEE, SCOTLAND.—*App.* by Auctioneers Societies, apparently at request of F.C., Aug. 1917. *Obj.* To purchase cattle for Army in next few months. *Repr.* Auctioneers. *Ref.* J.B.A., Sept. 1917.

CATTLE SUPPLY COMMITTEES.—*App.* in all market districts by local organizations of agriculturalists, by arrangement with M.F., from Mar. 1918. *Obj.* To be responsible for getting sufficient cattle for slaughter. *Repr.* Local agriculturalists. *Ref.* T., 16th Mar. 1918, p. 7.

CATTLE.—*See also* Allocation ; Market Grading ; Requisition.

CENTRAL FOOD CLEARING HOUSE.—*App.* by F.C., Jan. 1918. *Obj.* To act generally as clearing house of information and work out food quota for various districts. *Repr.* Official and expert. *Ref.* T., 26th Jan. 1918.

CEREALS (HOME) COMMITTEE.—*App.* as Committee of Wheat Supplies Royal Commission in second half of 1917. *Obj.* To exercise control of home-grown cereals, including use in brewing. *Repr.* M.F., farmers, dealers, brewers. *Ref.* Information privately communicated.

CEREALS (MISCELLANEOUS) COMMITTEE.—*App.*, *Ref.* as with Cereals (Home) Committee (q.v.). *Obj.* To control rice, beans, peas, oatmeal, &c. *Repr.* M.F., farmers, importers, dealers. *Diss.* Apparently absorbed in other Committees of Royal Commission by end of 1917.

CEREALS, OILS AND FATS FOR COTTON TEXTILE INDUSTRIES, MANCHESTER CHAMBER OF COMMERCE COMMITTEE.—*App.* through the Chamber of Commerce, at request of F.C., about Mar. 1918. *Obj.* To control and regulate distribution of supplies of cereals, oils and fats for these industries. *Repr.* Various branches of these industries. *Ref.* B.T.J., 12th Sept. 1918. *Diss.* Absorbed into Cotton Textile Industries Association for Oils and Fats (*see* Oils and Fats), Sept. 1918.

CHEESE.—*See* Butter and Cheese, Caerphilly Cheese.

COCOA ADVISORY COMMITTEE.—*App.* by F.C. in second half of 1917. *Obj.* To advise on control of cocoa. *Repr.* M.F., importers, traders, dealers, manufacturers. *Ref.* Information privately given. *Diss.* By May 1919.

COCOA GRADING COMMITTEES, LONDON AND LIVERPOOL.— *App.* by F.C., Mar. 1918. *Obj.* To grade imports of raw cocoa and fix fair values for sale, on basis of M.F. prices for top grades. *Repr.* Cocoa brokers in London and Liverpool. *Ref.* B.T.J., 28th Mar. 1918, p. 387. *Diss.* By May 1919.

COFFEE ADVISORY COMMITTEE.—*App.* by F.C. in second half of 1917. *Obj.* To advise on control of coffee. *Repr.* M.F., importers, traders, dealers, preparers. *Ref.* Information privately communicated. *Diss.* By May 1919.

COLD STORAGE ALLOCATION COMMITTEE.—*App.* by F.C., before July 1918. *Obj.* To allocate foodstuffs between different cold storages. *Repr.* M.F., W.O. *Ref.* N.F.J., 10th July 1918.

CONSUMERS' COUNCIL.—*App.* by F.C., Jan. 1918. *Obj.* To act as advisory body, representing general consumers, on food control. *Repr.* T.U.'s, Co-operative Societies, Women's Industrial Organizations, other Labour organizations, unorganized consumers. *Ref.* N.F.J., 23rd Jan., 13th Feb. 1918.

CONSUMERS' COUNCIL, FOOD CONTROL SUB-COMMITTEE.—*See* Food Control.

CONSUMERS' COUNCIL, SUB-COMMITTEE ON REFORMS.—*App.* by the Council early in Jan. 1919. *Obj.* To report to the Council upon continuance in peace time of war food controls. *Repr.* Consumers' Council. *Ref.* T., 3rd Feb. 1919, p. 7 ; N.F.J., 12th Feb. 1919. *Diss.* Feb. 1919 (reported).

CONSUMERS' COUNCILS, LOCAL.—*App.* by Local F.C.C.'s during 1918. *Obj., Repr.* Similar to Consumers' Council. *Ref.* N.F.J., 13th Mar. 1918 and subsequent issues.

CORN AND AGRICULTURAL MERCHANTS, NATIONAL ASSOCIA-TION OF, PROVINCIAL AREA COMMITTEES.—*App.* by the Association, about Sept. 1919. *Obj.* To deal with grant of licences to dealers in cattle-cakes and meals under Order of 15th Sept. 1919. *Repr.* Interests covered by Association. *Ref.* J.B.A., Sept. 1919.

COSTINGS DEPARTMENT.—*App.* by the late Lord Rhondda, June 1917, being his first important action as F.C., with representatives in various areas. *Obj.* To ascertain profits of food manufacturers and dealers with a view to fixing fair prices and profits. *Repr.* Official and expert, the local representatives being leading firms of accountants. *Ref.* Cd. 9005, p. 181.

CROPS (1917), GRAIN AND POTATOES, ADVISORY COMMITTEE.— *App.* by F.C., June 1917. *Obj.* To advise on marketing and distribution of 1917 crops. *Repr.* M.F., farmers, traders, dealers, agricultural scientists. *Ref.* J.B.A., June 1917. *Diss.* After 1917 harvest.

CRUSHERS AND REFINERS ADVISORY COMMITTEE.—Referred to in B.T.J., 28th Aug. 1919, p. 294, as fixing maximum prices of home manufactured cakes and meals. Other details lacking.

DECONTROL.—*See* Food, Reduction in Prices.

DISTRICT SUPERVISING ACCOUNTANTS.—*App.* by M.F. in honorary capacity in various districts, July–Aug. 1917. *Obj.* To supervise investigations of costs of food production and distribution in districts. *Repr.* Prominent Chartered Accountants. *Ref.* T., 15th Aug. 1917, p. 3.

DOGS INTER-DEPARTMENTAL COMMITTEE.—*App.* by, or in connexion with, M.F., in spring of 1918. *Obj.* To consider allowance of meals for dog biscuits, and further limitations of dogs in the country. *Repr.* The Departments concerned. *Ref.* T., 1st May 1918, p. 7.

DOMESTIC SERVICE ADVISORY COMMITTEE.—*App.* by F.C. before Dec. 1917. *Obj.* To advise on questions of domestic service, and train staffs for communal kitchens. *Repr.* Not stated. *Ref.* N.F.J., 26th Dec. 1917.

DRIED FRUITS ADVISORY COMMITTEE.—*App.* by F.C., in second half of 1917. *Obj.* To advise on control of dried fruits. *Repr.* M.F., importers, preparers, dealers. *Ref.* Information privately communicated. *Diss.* By May 1919.

EDIBLE OILS.—*See* Margarine, Oils.

FAIR PRICES COUNCILS.—*App.* by M.F. from Apr. 1920, for various foods, such as jam (April), fish (May), fruit and vegetables (July). *Obj.* In cases where fixed maximum prices were impossible owing to price conditions, to keep M.F. and public fully informed as to price movements and market conditions and enable fair prices to be secured. *Repr.* M.F. and all branches (productive and distributive) of trades concerned. *Ref.* B.T.J., 1920, 29th April, p. 597–8, 3rd June, p. 754, 22nd July, p. 87.

FARMERS' SELECTION COMMITTEES.—*App.* by F.C., in co-operation with Royal Agricultural Society, Chambers of Agriculture and Farmers' Union, Mar. 1918, for each local market. *Obj.* To arrange supply of local market from local produce. *Repr.* Farmers and Market Authorities. *Ref.* N.F.J., 10th April 1918.

FATS.—*See* Meat and Fats, Oils.

FEEDING STUFFS ADVISORY COMMITTEE, CENTRAL.—*App.* by F.C., Nov. 1917. *Obj.* To control allocation and distribution of feeding stuffs. *Repr.* M.F., B.A., B.A. (Sc.), D.A.T.I., traders, farmers. *Ref.* N.F.J., 12th Dec. 1917. *Diss.* Apparently absorbed into Allocation Committee (*see* next entry) in autumn of 1918.

FEEDING STUFFS, ALLOCATION COMMITTEE OF FEEDING STUFFS BOARD.—*App.* by F.C., Sept. 1918. *Obj.* To control allocation and distribution of feeding stuffs, working under the Board, in conjunction with Official Committee, Joint (*see* below) of B.A. and M.F. *Repr.* M.F., B.A., trades concerned. *Ref.* N.F.J., 9th Oct. 1918. *Diss.* By Mar. 1919.

FEEDING STUFFS, AREA COMMITTEES.—*App.* by F.C., but mainly nominated by Feeding Stuffs County Committees in autumn of 1918. *Obj.* To regulate distribution of local produce. *Repr.* Farmers, dealers, millers, brewers, Co-operators. *Ref.* N.F.J., 23rd Oct. 1918. *Diss.* By Mar. 1919.

FEEDING STUFFS BOARD, MINISTRY OF FOOD.—*App.* by F.C., Sept. 1918. *Obj.* To administer generally control of feeding stuffs. *Repr.* Not stated. *Ref.* N.F.J., 9th Oct. 1918. *Diss.* By Mar. 1919 apparently.

FEEDING STUFFS, COUNTY COMMITTEES.—*App.* by F.C. in most counties, in autumn of 1918. *Obj.* To advise local representatives of M.F. on control of feeding stuffs and questions of licensing and registration. *Repr.* Farmers, dealers, millers, brewers, Co-operators. *Ref.* N.F.J., 23rd Oct. 1918. *Diss.* By Mar. 1919.

(These Committees seem to have developed out of, and superseded, the 35 Provincial Committees (q.v.) established Nov. 1917.)

FEEDING STUFFS, PORT COMMITTEES.—*App.* by F.C., Nov. 1917, for London, Bristol, Hull, Liverpool and Scotland. *Obj.* To allocate feeding stuffs passing through the port. *Repr.* Importers, millers, traders, with additional members appointed by F.C. *Ref.* N.F.J., 12th Dec. 1919 *Diss.* By Mar. 1919.

FEEDING STUFFS PROVINCIAL COMMITTEES.—*App.* by F.C. about Nov. 1917. *Obj.* To allocate supplies locally. *Repr.* M.F., dealers, farmers, with additional members appointed by F.C. *Ref.* N.F.J., 12th Dec. 1917. *Diss.* Autumn of 1918 (*see* County Committees).

FEEDING STUFFS.—*See also* B.A. under Feeding Stuffs.

FERTILIZERS, ADVISORY COMMITTEE.—*App.* by F.C., Jan. or Feb. 1917. *Obj.* To advise on measures to increase supply and control of output and distribution. *Repr.* Departments concerned ; manufacturers of basic slag, sulphate of ammonia and super-phosphate. *Ref.* J.B.A., Feb. 1917.

(In addition to Committees mentioned elsewhere, there may have been Committees for Basic Slag, Blast Furnace Dust and Waste Carbonate of Lime.)

FERTILIZERS CONTROL COMMITTEE.—*App.* by F.C., Jan. 1917. *Obj.* To prepare scheme for increasing supplies, and controlling output and distribution, of fertilizers in U.K. *Repr.* M.F., B.A., B.A.(Sc.), Tre., B.T., Geological Survey, agriculture, agricultural and chemical research. *Ref.* J.B.A., Feb. 1917 ; B.T.J., 18th Jan. 1917.

FERTILIZERS.—*See also* Sulphate of Ammonia.

FINANCE BOARD, JOINT, MINISTRY OF FOOD.—*App.* by F.C., Sept. 1918. *Obj.* To co-ordinate finances of Royal Commissions on Wheat and Sugar with rest of M.F. *Repr.* M.F., the Commissions. *Ref.* N.F.J., Sept. 1918.

FINANCE COMMITTEE, WHEAT SUPPLIES ROYAL COMMISSION. —*App.* by the Commission in 1916 or 1917. *Obj.* To deal with financial problems of wheat control. *Repr.* The Commission. *Ref.* Information privately communicated.

FISH, CURED, COMMITTEE.—*App.* originally by B.A. (q.v.) are transferred to M.F., May 1917. *Obj.* To deal with control of cured fish, and attempt to secure increased imports and increased use as food. *Repr.* M.F., B.A., B.A.(Sc.), D.A.T.I., the Navy, trawler owners. *Ref.* Cmd. 585, p. 66. *Diss.* Absorbed into Fish Section of M.F. in autumn of 1917.

FISH DISTRIBUTION COMMITTEE.—*App.* in 1918, appointing body not stated. *Obj.* To consider problems of fish distribution. *Repr.* Fishery Departments and others. *Ref.* Cmd. 231, p. xiv.

FISH FOOD.—*See* B.A.

FISH, PRESERVED (IMPORT RESTRICTION).—*See* B.T.

FLOUR MILLS CONTROL COMMITTEE.—*App.* as Committee of Wheat Supplies Royal Commission, April 1917. *Obj.* To control and regulate prices, mixtures and distribution of wheat and flour, and frame financial scheme for control. *Repr.* M.F., millers, farmers, dealers. *Ref.* N.F.J., 13th Feb. 1918. *Diss.* On termination of control.

(N.B. This Committee had Finance, Grain Grading, and Technical, Sub-Committees, in charge of its various functions.)

FODDER SHORTAGE, JOINT INTER-DEPARTMENTAL COMMITTEE.—*App.* by M.F. and B.A., Jan. 1918. *Obj.* To stimulate increased production by farmers and make suggestions for this. *Repr.* M.F., B.A., F.P.D. *Ref.* N.F.J., 23rd Jan. 1918.

FOOD, CHEMISTRY OF.—*See* S.I.R.

FOOD COMMITTEE OF REPRESENTATIVES, INTER-ALLIED.—
App. by Inter-Allied Food Council (q.v.), Aug. 1918. *Obj.* To act as
executive body of Council, and as sole liaison between Food Executive and
Inter-Allied Maritime Transport Council, Finance Council, and Scientific
Commission. *Repr.* The four Food Ministries and the Councils and the
Commission. *Ref.* N.F.J., 28th Aug. 1918. *Diss.* Absorbed into Food
Section of Supreme Economic Council (q.v.), Feb. 1919.

FOOD CONTROL COMMITTEE FOR IRELAND.—*App.* on recom-
mendation of Chief Secretary for Ireland, about Sept. 1917. *Obj.* To advise
F.C. on maintenance and distribution of supplies, and enforcement or
modifications of Orders. *Repr.* Various Irish Departments, farmers,
merchants, dealers, Medical Profession, consumers. *Ref.* N.F.J., 12th
Sept. 1917.

FOOD CONTROL COMMITTEES, JOINT.—These were Committees
appointed by more than one L.A., for whose formation licence was given
in F.C. Order of Aug. 1917. Composition, &c. as with local F.C.C.'s (q.v.).

FOOD CONTROL COMMITTEES, LOCAL, ENGLAND AND WALES.—
App. generally by Borough, Urban and Rural District Councils under Order
of Aug. 1917, certain other committees, which were appointed earlier, being
brought under the Order. *Obj.* Local administration of food distribution
and control, conduct of economy campaigns and (later) requisitioning of
foodstuffs. *Repr.* Not more than twelve persons (not necessarily members
of the Council), including representatives of Labour, Women, and Co-
operative Societies, the number of private food traders being limited.
Ref. N.F.J., 12th Sept. 1917 ; F.C.'s Order of 22nd Aug. 1917.

In Nov. 1918, membership was raised to 16, with at least 2 women and
2 or 3 representatives of Labour, in districts with over 20,000 inhabitants.
If a food trader was a member, there must also, if available, be one representative of Co-operative Societies. *See* T., 8th Nov. 1918, p. 3.

FOOD CONTROL COMMITTEES, LOCAL, IRELAND.—*App.* by
County Borough Councils in the boroughs, the rest of Ireland being under
the Food Control Committee, Ireland (q.v.). *Obj., Repr.* As in England
(q.v.). *Ref.* N.F.J., 12th Sept. 1917.

FOOD CONTROL COMMITTEES, LOCAL, SCOTLAND.—*App.* by
Town Councils in larger boroughs, and by Joint Committees of County and
smaller Borough Councils elsewhere. *Obj., Repr., Ref.* As in England (q.v.).

FOOD CONTROL SUB-COMMITTEE OF CONSUMERS' COUNCIL.—
Referred to in N.F.J., 12th Feb. ; B.T.J., 6th Feb. 1919.

FOOD COUNCIL, MINISTRY OF FOOD.—*App.* by F.C., Sept. 1918.
Obj. To consider general questions of policy. *Repr.* Parliamentary and
official heads of M.F. *Ref.* N.F.J., 9th Oct. 1918.

FOOD COUNCIL, INTER-ALLIED.—*App.* by Allied Food Controller's
Conference in London, at suggestion of American Food Controller, July
1918. *Obj.* Co-ordination and supervision of food programmes and elimination of competition in purchase, transport, &c., and to act as channel of
communications between various inter-allied food executives and the

Inter-Allied Maritime Transport and Financial Councils. *Repr*. Food Controllers of U.K., U.S.A., France, Italy. *Ref*. N.F.J., 14th and 28th Aug. 1918 ; T., 20th Aug. 1918, p. 4. *Diss*. Absorbed in Food Section of Supreme Economic Council, Feb. 1919.

FOOD EXECUTIVE, INTER-ALLIED.—*See* preceding entry.

FOOD DIVISIONS.—G.B., for purposes of Food Control, was apportioned in 1917 into sixteen Food Divisions, consisting of Counties or groups of Counties, each under a Commissioner and Assistant Commissioner. *See* Cd. 9005, p. 178.

FOOD ECONOMY COMMITTEES, LOCAL.—*App*. jointly by M.F., B.A., and L.E.A.'s in autumn of 1917, through F.C.C.'s. *Obj*. To conduct local food economy campaigns in their districts and control and supervise public kitchens, &c., in co-operation with Food Economy Commissioners appointed to organize the work. *Repr*. Important local organizations, including L.E.A.'s, T.U.'s, Friendly Societies, Religious Bodies, War Savings Committees, &c. *Ref*. T., 6th Oct. 1917, p. 6.

FOOD ECONOMY DEPARTMENT.—Established at M.F. about Mar. 1917, to organize centrally campaign for food economies and work of the Local Committees concerned. *See* T., 27th Mar. 1917, p. 9.

FOOD ECONOMY, PARLIAMENTARY COMMITTEE.—*See* Parliament.

FOOD NEEDS OF GERMANY AND AUSTRIA, INTER-ALLIED COMMISSION.—*App*. by Allied Governments, Jan. 1919, G.B. being represented by F.C. *Obj*. To investigate food situation in Germany and Austria. *Repr*. Governments of U.K., U.S.A., France, Italy. *Ref*. N.F.J., 22nd Jan. 1919. *Diss*. Absorbed into Food Section (q.v.) of Supreme Economic Council, Feb. 1919.

FOOD, REDUCTION IN PRICES, COMMITTEE.—*App*. by F.C., Feb. 1919. *Obj*. To assist in expediting decontrol and consider reduction of food prices. *Repr*. M.F., B.A., B.T., Consumers' Council. *Ref*. N.F.J., 26th Feb. 1919.

FOOD SECTION, SUPREME ECONOMIC COUNCIL.—This section carried out under the Council (*see* Cabinet) the work of dealing with food problems. There are references to it in N.F.J. of various dates.

FOOD SURVEY BOARD.—*App*. by F.C., April 1918. *Obj*. To survey national food consumption, correlate public service and civilian consumption, and adjust diets and distribution of food to physical needs of population. *Repr*. M.F., other Government Departments concerned, hospitals, eating-house keepers. *Ref*. N.F.J., 8th May 1918.

FOOD (WAR) COMMITTEE OF THE ROYAL SOCIETY.—*App*. by the Society in 1917 (or possibly earlier). *Obj*. To advise M.F. on food problems. *Repr*. The Society, L.G.B. and others. *Ref*. Cd. 9157, p. 15 ; Cmd. 413, p. 137.

FORAGE, ALLIES', COMMITTEE.—Details lacking. *See* Oats Control Committee.

FREIGHTS (WHEAT) COMMITTEE.—*App.*, as Committee of the Wheat Supplies Royal Commission, in 1917. *Obj.* To deal with all questions of wheat freights. *Repr.* Business interests concerned. *Ref.* Information privately communicated.

FUEL.—*See under* Brewing Economies.

GENERAL PURPOSES COMMITTEE (WHEAT COMMISSION).—*App.* by the Wheat Supplies Royal Commission, in 1916 or 1917. *Obj.* To deal with general questions affecting Commission. *Repr.* Business interests represented on Commission. *Ref.* Information privately communicated.

GRADING.—*See* Cattle, Market Grading.

GRAIN DISTRIBUTION COMMITTEE.—*App.* by M.F., May 1917. *Obj.* To advise on marketing and distribution of 1917 grain and potato crops. *Repr.* Parliament, M.F., B.A.(Sc.), Wheat Commission, land-owners, agriculturalists, grain trade, land agents, agricultural research. *Ref.* T., 1917.

GRAIN GRADING.—*See under* Flour Mills.

GROCERS' (RETAIL) COMMITTEE.—*App.* by F.C. apparently in 1918. *Obj.* To advise M.F. in control, rationing, &c., as affecting retail grocers. *Repr.* Not stated. *Ref.* N.F.J., 9th Oct. 1918.

GROSVENOR HOUSE COMMITTEE.—*See* Milk Production and Distribution Advisory Committee.

HARVESTING OF HORSE CHESTNUTS.—*See* Horse Chestnuts.

HOME SUPPLIES BOARD, MINISTRY OF FOOD.—*App.* by F.C., Sept. 1918. *Obj.* To consider questions affecting control, production and distribution of home supplies. *Repr.* M.F. (Secretariat and Supply Divisions affected), Wheat Commission. *Ref.* N.F.J., 9th Oct. 1918.

HOP INDUSTRY CONTROL COMMITTEE.—*See* B.A.

HORSE CHESTNUTS, HARVESTING, SCHOOL COMMITTEES.— *App.* by Governing Bodies, Managers and Teachers, after request of F.C. and M.M. to B.E., Aug. 1917. *Obj.* To organize collection of horse chestnuts as substitute for grain for industrial use. *Repr.* Governing Bodies, Teachers &c., and local residents. *Ref.* J.B.A., Sept. 1917.

HORSES, UTILIZATION AND FEEDING, COMMITTEE.—*See* B.T.

HOSPITALS ADVISORY COMMITTEE.—*App.* by F.C., April 1918. *Obj.* To draw up ration scheme for, and advise generally in regard to, hospitals. *Repr.* Hospitals, Medical Profession. *Ref.* N.F.J., 8th May 1918.

HOTEL MEALS COMMITTEE.—*App.* by London Hotel and Restaurant proprietors, in course of discussion with B.T. and military authorities, in Nov. 1916. *Obj.* To work out general scheme of economies in consumption of food in hotels and restaurants, including checks on spending by members of army and navy. *Repr.* London hotel and restaurant proprietors. *Ref.* T., 29th Nov. 1916, p. 5 ; 7th Mar. 1917, p. 3.

IMPORTS BOARD, MINISTRY OF FOOD.—*App.* by F.C., Sept. 1918. *Obj.* To deal with adjustment of import programme, allocation of tonnage and authorization of purchases. *Repr.* M.F. (Secretariat and Supply Divisions concerned). *Ref.* N.F.J., 9th Oct. 1918.

JAM PRICES ADVISORY COMMITTEE.—*App.* by F.C. in second half of 1919. *Obj.* To advise as to control of jam. *Repr.* Fruit growers, manufacturers, dealers. *Ref.* Hansard (H.C.), 29th Oct. 1919.

KITCHENS' BRANCH.—*See* next entry.

KITCHENS, CENTRAL, COMMITTEE.—*App.* by F.C., April 1917. *Obj.* To organize model National Kitchen and (later) promote establishment of communal kitchens. *Repr.* M.F., Labour, consumers' generally, food experts. *Ref.* N.F.J., 28th Aug. 1918, p. 660. *Diss.* Apparently absorbed later into Kitchens' Branch of M.F., when established.

KITCHENS (NATIONAL) COMMITTEE, KINGSTON.—*App.* by Kingston and District Council of Social Welfare in 1917 or 1918. *Obj.* To establish National Kitchen in district. *Repr.* Local religious and social societies. *Ref.* N.F.J., 14th Aug. 1918.
(Inserted to illustrate local effort in this direction.)

LANDED GRAIN, LOCAL COMMITTEES.—*App.* by Royal Commission on Wheat Supplies, presumably in 1917. *See* N.F.J., 25th Sept. 1918. Details lacking.

LINOLEUM TRADE ADVISORY COMMITTEE.—*App.* by F.C. in second half of 1917. *Obj.* To advise as to control of production of linoleum and supply of materials to the trade. *Repr.* M.F., manufacturers, dealers. *Repr.* Information privately communicated.

LINSEED OIL DISTRIBUTION COMMITTEE.—*App.* by United Kingdom Linseed Oil Consumers' Association, before July 1918. *Obj.* To allocate supplies of oil to consuming trades. *Ref.* Hansard (H.C.), 31st July 1918, Vol. 109, Col. 415.

LIVESTOCK AND MEAT SUPPLIES, CENTRAL ADVISORY COMMITTEE.—*App.* by F.C. late in 1917 and sometimes called Central Advisory Committee on Meat and Livestock. *Obj.* To advise generally on control of livestock. *Repr.* Dealers, farmers, butchers. *Repr.* Hansard (H.C.), 16th Jan. 1918, Vol. 101, Col. 282. *Diss.* Still in existence Aug. 1919.

LIVESTOCK, AREA ADVISORY COMMITTEES.—*App.* by F.C. late in 1917. *Obj.* To organize distribution of meat supplies locally. *Repr.* Farmers, dealers, butchers, auctioneers, and possibly M.F. *Repr.* Hansard (H.C.), 16th Jan. 1918, Vol. 101, Col. 282.

LIVESTOCK AREAS.—The Ministry divided the country late in 1917 into nineteen areas, each under presidency of Livestock Commissioner, which were divided into market districts. The object was to secure for each area its fair share of cattle for its population, and prevent undue depletion of herds in producing districts. *See* Cd. 9005, p. 179.

LIVESTOCK, IRISH, VALUATION COMMITTEES.—*App.* by F.C., June 1918, commencing to function in July. *Obj.* To value fat cattle and sheep at ports of importation from Ireland, prior to purchase by Food Control. *Repr.* M.F., Irish interests, British butchers. *Ref.* B.T.J., 4th July 1918.

LIVESTOCK (SCOTLAND) CENTRAL ADVISORY COMMITTEE.— *App.* &c., much as with Livestock and Meat Supplies Central Advisory Committee (q.v.).

LIVESTOCK.—*See also* Meat and Livestock.

LONDON.—*See* Vegetable, Wholesale Food Markets.

MARGARINE AND EDIBLE OILS ADVISORY COMMITTEE.—*App.* by F.C. in second half of 1917. *Obj.* To advise as to control of margarine and edible oils. *Repr.* Manufacturers, dealers, traders. *Repr.* Information privately communicated.

MARGARINE CLEARING HOUSE.—Self-supporting body, co-operating with M.F. *See* Cd. 9220, p. 9.

MARGARINE CONTROL COMMITTEE.—*App.* by F.C. in second half of 1917. *Obj.* To arrange scheme of control as recommended by Advisory Committee. *Repr.* M.F., manufacturers, traders, dealers. *Repr.* Information privately communicated.

MARKET DISTRICTS, LIVESTOCK.—*See* Allocation, Livestock.

MARKET GRADING COMMITTEES.—*App.* by F.C., in co-operation with local organizations, Dec. 1917, for each local market. *Obj.* To carry out grading and valuation of cattle and sheep brought to the market. *Repr.* Farmers, butchers, auctioneers (acting for M.F.). *Ref.* N.F.J., 9th Jan. 1918, 10th Sept. 1919. (Also called Valuation Committees.)

MEAT DISTRIBUTION COMMITTEE, LONDON.—Details lacking. Probably appointed 1917 or early 1918.

MEAT DISTRIBUTION COMMITTEE, NATIONAL.—*App.* by F.C. before June 1918. *Obj.* To organize distribution of controlled meat (home and imported). *Repr.* M.F., importers, distributers, wholesalers. *Ref.* N.F.J., 12th June 1918. *Diss.* In or before July 1920.

MEAT AND FATS EXECUTIVE, INTER-ALLIED.—*App.* jointly by British, French and Italian Governments, in autumn of 1917. *Obj.* To organize joint purchases of meat and fats for all European Allies. *Repr.* Governments concerned. *Ref.* Cd. 9005, pp. 171–2.

MEAT AND LIVESTOCK EXECUTIVE BOARD, MINISTRY OF FOOD.—*App.* by F.C. before June 1918. *Obj.* To carry out general control of home and imported meat. *Repr.* M.F., agricultural interests, meat traders, auctioneers, &c. *Ref.* N.F.J., 12th June 1918.

MEAT, IMPORTED, PANEL OF RETAILERS.—Four retailers appointed after deputation of London retail butchers to M.F., to decide if certain imported meat is suitable for public consumption. *See* T., 29th April 1919, p. 2.

MEAT PRODUCTS LTD., NATIONAL.—Self-supporting body, co-operating with M.F. *See* Cd. 9220, p. 9.

MEAT WHOLESALE SUPPLY ASSOCIATIONS.—*App.* by Meat Traders' Associations, at request of M.F., in winter of 1917–18. *Obj.* To assist M.F., in control of meat and organization of distribution (*see also under* Smithfield). *Repr.* Wholesale traders, all wholesale meat salesmen selling on commission being compelled to join an Association. *Ref.* N.F.J., 26th Mar. 1918 ; J.B.A., Jan. 1918.

MEAT.—*See also* Cattle and Meat ; Smithfield Market ; and under Live-stock.

MERCANTILE MARINE RATIONING COMMITTEE.—*App.* by repre-sentatives of officers and men of mercantile marine after conference with F.C., Mar. 1918. *Obj.* To prepare detailed scheme for voluntary reduction of the meat ration during the war. *Repr.* B.T., shipowners, officers and men. *Ref.* T., 5th April 1918.

MILK, CENTRAL ADVISORY COMMITTEE.—*App.* by F.C. by Sept. 1918. *Obj.* To advise as to policy in control of milk and fixing of milk prices. *Repr.* M.F., B.A., dairy farmers, wholesale and retail traders, consumers. *Ref.* N.F.J., 9th Oct. 1918.

MILK, CLEARING HOUSE FOR GREATER LONDON, COMMITTEE. —*App.* by F.C., Oct.–Nov. 1918. *Obj.* To advise as to distribution in winter of 1918–19. *Repr.* Wholesalers, retailers, Co-operative Societies. *Repr.* N.F.J., 11th Dec. 1918. *Diss.* About end of 1918.

MILK COMBINE INQUIRY SUB-COMMITTEE.—*App.* by M.F., Mar. 1918. *Obj.* To inquire into control of collection, utilization and distribution of milk sold wholesale. *Repr.* M.F., B.A., B.A.(Sc.), L.G.B., M.M., Con-sumers' Council, agriculture, Labour, women. *Ref.* T., Mar. 1918.

MILK CONTROL BOARD.—*App.* by M.F. to control and regulate distribution of milk, probably about summer of 1918. Other details lack-ing. *See* B.T.J., June 1918, p. 322 and Cmd. 413, p. 136.

MILK, FUTURE CONTROL, INTER-DEPARTMENTAL CON-FERENCE.—*App.* by Departments concerned, Feb. 1919. *Obj.* To con-sider future of milk control. *Repr.* M.F., B.A., B.A.(Sc.), D.A.T.I., L.G.B. *Repr.* Hansard (H.C.), 20th Feb. 1919, Vol. 112, Col. 1125.

MILK, POWERS OF MINISTRY OF FOOD, INTER-DEPARTMENTAL COMMITTEE.—*App.* by M.F., B.A., L.G.B., and S.O., June 1919. *Obj.* To decide legal and administrative methods required for exercise of powers of control retained by M.F. *Repr.* The appointing Departments. *Repr.* Hansard (H.C.), 2nd July 1919, Vol. 117, Cols. 986–9.

MILK PRICES ADVISORY COMMITTEES.—*App.* by F.C., possibly in co-operation with B.A., in various districts, April 1918. *Obj.* To in-vestigate local costs of production of milk for fixing summer prices for 1918. *Repr.* M.F., Local F.C.C.'s, War Agricultural Committees. *Ref.* N.F.J., 12th June 1918. *Diss.* Presumably later in 1918.

MILK PRICES, INVESTIGATION COMMITTEE.—*App.* by a Con-ference of delegates of Local F.C.C.'s at M.F., 3rd Nov. 1919. *Obj.* To investigate prices of milk, with reference to those fixed for winter of 1919–20. *Repr.* Local F.C.C.'s. *Ref.* N.F.J., 10th Dec. 1919 ; T., 14th Nov. 1919, p. 9. *Diss.* Dec. 1919.

MILK PRICES, TRAVELLING COMMISSION.—*App.* by F.C., Jan. 1919. *Obj.* To investigate production costs for fixing prices after April 1919, and consider variations in different areas. *Repr.* M.F., B.A., B.A.(Sc.), Agricultural Advisory Committee, Consumer's Council, Agricultural Re-search. *Ref.* Cmd. 205, 233. *Diss.* May 1919.

MILK PRICES.—*See also* L.G.B.

MILK PRODUCERS' ASSOCIATED COUNCIL.—Mentioned without details on p. 19 of Final Report (Cd. 483) of Milk Production and Distribution Committee of B.A.

MILK, PRODUCTION AND DISTRIBUTION, ADVISORY COMMITTEE.—*App.* by F.C., April 1917, and often called Grosvenor House Committee. *Obj.* To report upon Food Orders affecting milk and difficulties of fixing maximum prices, and advise as to future Orders. *Repr.* M.F., agricultural and trading interests concerned. *Ref.* J.B.A., July 1917. *Diss.* May 1917.

MILK, PRODUCTION AND DISTRIBUTION, COMMITTEE AND SUB-COMMITTEES.—*See* B.A.

NECESSITOUS AREAS IN EUROPE, SUPPLY AND RELIEF, SUPREME INTER-ALLIED COUNCIL.—*App.* by Allied Governments, Jan. 1918. *Obj.* To organize relief and co-ordinate food, finance and shipping for the purpose. *Repr.* Governments of U.K. (including F.C.), U.S.A., France, Italy. *Ref.* N.F.J., 9th Jan. 1918. *Diss.* Absorbed into Food Section of Supreme Economic Council, Feb.–Mar. 1919.

NECESSITOUS AREAS IN GERMANY AND AUSTRIA.—*See* Food Needs.

NORWICH MUNICIPAL MILK SCHEME SUB-COMMITTEE OF LOCAL FOOD CONTROL COMMITTEE.—Proposal to constitute Public Health Committee of City of Norwich as Sub-Committee to carry out scheme for Municipal Milk Supply. *See* N.F.J., 9th Jan. 1918. Other details lacking.

OATS CONTROL COMMITTEE.—*App.* by F.C. in first half of 1917. *Obj.* To carry out purchase and control of imports for U.K. and Allies and undertake duties previously performed by Forage, Allies', Committee. *Repr.* Parliament, B.T., W.O., Wheat Commission, Commission Internationale de Ravitaillement, Allied Governments, Railways, traders, importers. *Ref.* Cd. 8447, p. 27 ; T., 21st Mar. 1917, p. 9.

OFFICIAL COMMITTEE, JOINT, OF MINISTRY OF FOOD AND BOARD OF AGRICULTURE.—*App.* jointly by F.C. and B.A., before July 1918. *Obj.* To co-ordinate generally work of the two Departments. *Repr.* Official staffs of two Departments. *Ref.* N.F.J., 9th Oct. 1918 ; J.B.A., Oct. 1918. *Diss.* Mar. 1919.

OILS AND FATS, CONSULTATIVE COMMITTEE.—*See* M.M.

OILS AND FATS DEPARTMENT.—*App.* by M.F. in 1917 or very early in 1918. *Obj.* To carry out general administration in connexion with these products. *Repr.* Official and expert. *Ref.* N.F.J., 13th Mar. 1918.

OILS AND FATS, PROVISIONAL GENERAL COMMITTEE OF THE COTTON TEXTILE INDUSTRIES ASSOCIATION.—*App.* by the Association, with approval of F.C., Sept. 1918. *Obj.* To control distribution of vegetable oils and animal fats required in textile trades. *Repr.* English, Scottish and Irish sections of textile industry. *Ref.* N.F.J., 9th Oct. 1918.

OILS AND FATS.—*See* Cereals ; and M.M., S.I.R.

OILS AND OIL-SEEDS, VEGETABLE, INTER-ALLIED EXECUTIVE. —*App.* jointly by various Allied Governments about end of 1917. *Obj.* To organize joint purchase of these products on behalf of Allies. *Repr.* The Governments concerned. *Ref.* Cd. 9005, p. 171.

OIL-SEED EXECUTIVE, INTER-ALLIED.—*App.* by British, French and Italian Governments, about end of 1917. *Obj.* To organize joint purchase, and allocate supplies, of oils, oil-seeds and fats for European Allies. *Repr.* The appointing Governments. *Ref.* Cd. 9005, p. 172.

OIL-SEEDS (MERCHANTS AND BROKERS) ADVISORY COMMITTEE.—*App.* by F.C. in second half of 1917. *Obj.* To deal generally with control of oil-seeds. *Repr.* Merchants, brokers. *Ref.* Information privately communicated.

OIL-SEEDS' PRODUCTS ASSOCIATION LTD., UNITED KINGDOM. —*App.* by the industry, at instigation of M.F., in 1918. *Obj.* To form self-governing body through which control of the industry could be carried out. *Repr.* Crushers, refiners. *Ref.* N.F.J., 11th Sept. 1918, p. 7.

OIL-SEEDS SUPPLY COMMITTEES.—*App.* by Oils and Fats Department of M.F., Feb. 1918, for areas of distribution (London, Bristol, Hull, Liverpool, Scotland). *Obj.* To organize supply and distribution of oil-seeds and edible oils under the Department. *Repr.* M.F. (presumably), dealers, traders. *Ref.* N.F.J., 13th Mar. 1918. *Diss.* Apparently April 1919.

ORDERS, COMMITTEE, JOINT.—*App.* by F.C. and B.A. about Dec. 1917. *Obj.* To organize distribution of information to farmers in regard to Government Orders. *Repr.* M.F., B.A. *Ref.* J.B.A., Feb. 1918.

ORDERS COMMITTEE, MINISTRY OF FOOD.—*App.* by F.C. in the second half of 1917. *Obj.* To supervise drafting of Food Orders. *Repr.* Departmental. *Ref.* Information privately communicated.

PACKERS' COMMITTEE.—An American body, charged with allotting Allied requirements among packing houses after notification by Purchase, Co-ordination, Division. *See* Cd. 9005, p. 171.

PAINT AND VARNISH TRADE ADVISORY COMMITTEE.—*App.* by F.C. in second half of 1917. *Obj.* To deal with control of materials used by these trades. *Repr.* Manufacturers, traders, dealers. *Ref.* Information privately communicated.

PHOSPHATES AND POTASH DISTRIBUTION COMMITTEE.—*App.* presumably by M.F. as with other Fertilizers' Committees (but possibly by B.A.), in 1917. *Obj.* To deal with general control and distribution of these products. *Repr.* Departments concerned and manufacturers, possibly others. *Ref.* Cd. 9069, p. xxxviii. (*See* B.A. *under* Potash.)

PIGS, SALE FOR SLAUGHTER, COMMITTEE.—*App.* by F.C., before Aug. 1918. *Obj.* To organize sale of pigs for slaughter under Area Livestock Commissioners of M.F. *Repr.* Not stated. *Ref.* Hansard (H.C.), 8th Aug. 1918, Vol. 109, Col. 1692. *Diss.* End of 1918 (Pigs (Sales) Order revoked).

POTATOES ADVISORY COMMITTEE, IRELAND.—*App.* by F.C. in 1917 or early 1918. *Obj.* To encourage increased production in Ireland and dispose of surplus. *Repr.* Not stated. *Ref.* Hansard (H.C.), 18th Mar. 1918, Vol. 104, Col. 630–1. *Diss.* Early in 1919.

POTATOES CONTROL COMMITTEES.—*App.* by F.C., Aug. 1918, in deficit zones which required to import potatoes, Potatoes, Zonal, Committees (q.v.) dealing with surplus areas. *Obj.* To control loading of potatoes, deal with disputes, and arrange import of potatoes into areas. *Repr.* M.F., dealers, growers. *Ref.* N.F.J., 28th Aug. 1918. *Diss.* Early in 1919.

POTATOES, DAMAGE TO PITS, COMMITTEES.—*App.* by F.C., at request of East Anglian farmers, May 1919. *Obj.* To assess damage to potato pits in area. *Repr.* M.F., potato growers. *Ref.* Hansard (H.C.), 21st May 1919.

POTATOES, DISTRIBUTION, COMMITTEE.—*App.* by M.F. in 1917 or early 1918. *Obj.* To advise as to distribution of supplies. *Repr.* M.F., growers, distributors. *Ref.* N.F.J., 26th June 1918. *Diss.* June 1918 (apparently).

POTATOES DISTRIBUTION COMMITTEES FOR AREAS IN DEFICIT ZONES.—*App.* by F.C., Sept. 1918, for large areas in deficit zones. *Obj.* To undertake importing functions of Potato Control Committees (q.v.) for their areas. *Repr.* Presumably as with Control Committees. *Ref.* N.F.J., 28th June 1918. *Diss.* Early in 1919.

POTATOES, GROWERS' PRICES, COMMISSION.—*App.* by F.C. and B.A., July 1918. *Obj.* To fix prices for 1919 potato crop after full inquiry in different areas. *Repr.* H.C., M.F., B.A. *Ref.* Hansard (H.C.), 8th Aug. 1918, Vol. 109, Col. 1694. *Diss.* Nov. 1918. (Similar Committee appointed in 1919.)

POTATOES, IRISH IMPORTS INTO SOUTH WALES AND SOUTH WESTERN COUNTIES, ADVISORY COMMITTEE.—*App.* by F.C. in 1917 for South Wales, and extended later to South Western Counties. *Obj.* To allocate distribution of potatoes in these areas, and control import of Irish potatoes under licence. *Repr.* Growers, dealers, importers and possibly M.F. *Ref.* N.F.J., 27th Feb. 1918.

POTATOES, SCOTTISH ALLOCATION AUTHORITY.—*App.* by F.C., Nov. 1918. *Obj.* To perform functions of Control and Zonal Committees (q.v.) for Scotland, controlling loading, import and export of potatoes, and dealing with disputes. *Repr.* M.F., dealers, growers. *Ref.* Potatoes (Scottish Central Allocation Authority) Order (of F.C.), 5th Nov. 1918.

POTATOES (SEED) COUNTY MARKETING SOCIETIES.—*App.* through M.F., apparently in 1918. *Obj.* To assist in collecting, marketing and distributing seed potatoes left to them by M.F. for 1918–19 season. *Repr.* Producers, dealers, &c. *Ref.* N.F.J., 25th Dec. 1918. *Diss.* End of sowing season of 1918–19.

POTATOES ZONAL COMMITTEES.—*App.* by F.C., Aug. 1918, in surplus zones, which were able to export potatoes, corresponding to Control Committees (q.v.) in deficit zones. *Obj.* To control loading of potatoes and export to other areas and deal with disputes and complaints. *Repr.* M.F., dealers. *Ref.* N.F.J., 28th Aug. 1917.

POTATO PURCHASING COMMITTEES, LOCAL AND DISTRICT.— *App.* by F.C., apparently in second half of 1917. *Obj.* To purchase adequate supplies where local production inadequate. *Repr.* Not stated. *Ref.* Hansard (H.C.), 18th Mar. 1918, Vol. 104, Col. 631–2. *Diss.* Apparently merged in Potato Control Committees (q.v.).

POULTRY SUB-COMMITTEES OF COUNTY FEEDING STUFFS COMMITTEES.—*App.* by F.C., on nomination of poultry keepers, June 1918. *Obj.* To carry out locally, under supervision of M.F. and B.A., scheme of rationing feeding-stuffs for poultry. *Repr.* Poultry keepers. *Ref.* N.F.J., 12th June 1918, and subsequent issues.

PRICES, WHOLESALE, ADVISORY COMMITTEE.—*App.* by F.C. in second half of 1917. *Obj.* To deal with certain questions of wholesale prices. *Repr.* Not stated. *Ref.* Information privately communicated.

PRICES.—*See also* Fair Prices, Food, Reduction in Prices.

PROVISIONS' EXPORT COMMITTEE, ALLIED.—*App.* by British, French and Italian Governments to sit in New York, about April 1917. *Obj.* To act as sole agency for puchase from U.S.A. of foodstuffs, other than wheat and cereals, for all European Allies, under instruction of Meat and Fats Executive (q.v.). *Repr.* The three Governments. *Ref.* Cd. 9005, p. 171.

PURCHASE, CO-ORDINATION, DIVISION.—This was an American body, dealing with requirements of European Allies, as received from Provisions' Export Commission. *See* Cd. 9005, p. 171.

PURCHASING (WHEAT) COMMITTEE.—*App.* as Committee of Wheat Supplies, Royal Commission, during 1917. *Obj.* To purchase all cereals, pulses and flour for importation. *Repr.* Merchants, importers, dealers. *Ref.* Information privately communicated.

RABBITS AND GAME ADVISORY COMMITTEE.—*App.* by F.C., Nov.–Dec. 1917. *Obj.* To increase supplies of rabbits and game in markets, and to advise as to control. *Repr.* M.F., B.A., Health Services, landowners, farmers. *Ref.* N.F.J., 26th Dec. 1917.

RATIONING CENTRAL CLASSIFICATION COMMITTEE.—*App.* by F.C., Mar. 1918. *Obj.* To decide disputed questions from Local F.C.C.'s as to scheme for supplementary rations. *Repr.* Government Departments concerned, Labour, Women. *Ref.* N.F.J., 27th Mar. 1918.

RATIONING CENTRAL CLEARING HOUSE.—*App.* by M.F., about beginning of 1918, to detect frauds, and prevent duplication of issue of tickets, in connexion with sugar and, later, other rationed foods. *See* Cd. 9005, p. 179.

RATIONING CONSULTATIVE COMMITTEE.—*App.* by F.C., June 1917. *Obj.* To consider questions of policy in regard to compulsory rationing, and other references from Rationing Departments. *Repr.* Not stated. *Ref.* Cd. 8741, p. 9; F.C. Order, No. 201, 1917.

RATIONING SCHEME COMMITTEE.—*App.* by F.C., June 1917. *Obj.* To draw up scheme of rationing on basis of findings of Rationing Consultative Committee. *Repr.* Not stated. *Ref.* Information privately communicated.

RATIONING.—*See also* Mercantile Marine.

REFORMS.—*See under* Consumers' Council.

REQUISITION, LOCAL SELECTION COMMITTEES.—*App*. by F.C. in second half of 1917. *Obj*. To select cattle for requisitioning in their district. *Repr*. Farmers of district. *Ref*. Information privately communicated.

SCHOOL COMMITTEES.—*See* Horse Chestnuts.

SEED CRUSHERS AND REFINERS TRADE ADVISORY COMMITTEE.—*App*. by F.C. in second half of 1917. *Obj*. To deal with matters affecting supplies to these trades. *Repr*. Business interests involved. *Ref*. Information privately communicated.

SEED WHEAT, 1917, SUPPLIES COMMITTEE.—*App*. by F.C. in latter part of 1917. *Obj*. To select suitable crops of wheat for cleaning and distribution by M.F. as seed. *Repr*. Scientific experts in agriculture. *Ref*. B.T.J., 1st Nov. 1917.

SELF-SUPPLIERS ADVISORY COMMITTEE.—*App*. by F.C., Feb. 1918. *Obj*. To consider question of increased rations of meat and fats to self-suppliers (i.e. persons producing for own consumption). *Repr*. M.F., F.P.D., B.A.(Sc.), Rabbits and Game, and Venison, Committees, Consumers' Council. *Ref*. N.F.J., Mar. 1918. *Diss*. Mar. 1918.

SELLING (WHEAT) COMMITTEE.—*App*. as Committee of Wheat Supplies Royal Commission, in latter half of 1917. *Obj*. To deal with all sales of cereals, flour and pulses in U.K. *Repr*. M.F., business interests involved. *Ref*. Information privately communicated.

SHIPOWNERS' PROVISION POOL COMMITTEE.—*App*. by Shipowners, Dec. 1917. *Obj*. To organize and administer pool of food stores for merchant ships trading between England and places abroad. *Repr*. Merchant shipowners. *Ref*. T., 2nd July 1918. *Diss*. July 1918, work taken over by M.F.

SMITHFIELD MARKET BOARD OF CONTROL.—*App*. by F.C. in spring of 1918. *Obj*. To secure efficient working of rationing scheme in the market, and act as temporary governing body. *Repr*. M.F., Meat Traders, Labour. *Ref*. N.F.J., 8th May 1918.

SOAP AND CANDLES ADVISORY COMMITTEE.—*App*. by F.C. in second half of 1917. *Obj*. To advise upon distribution of materials and fixing of prices. *Repr*. Soap and candle trades. *Ref*. N.F.J., 14th July 1918. *Diss*. Merged into Council of newly-formed Soapmakers Federation, June 1918.

SPIRITS TRADE ADVISORY COMMITTEE.—Details not available, but duties included dealings with M.F. in regard to prices of spirits. The Committee did not come to an end till after 3rd July 1919. *See* B.T.J. of this date, p. 35.

STORAGE (WHEAT) COMMITTEE.—*App*. as Committee of Wheat Supplies Royal Commission, in 1917. *Obj*. To deal with all questions of storage of wheat. *Repr*. Not stated. *Ref*. Information privately communicated.

SUGAR, CANE, GRADING COMMITTEE.—*App.* by Sugar Commission or M.F., during the War. *Obj.* To organize grading of imported sugar. *Repr.* Official and expert. *Ref.* B.T.J., 17th Apr. 1919, p. 537; N.F.J., 14th May 1919.

SUGAR COMMITTEE, INTERNATIONAL.—*App.* by the American Food Controller, after consultation with Sugar Commission, about Sept. 1917. *Obj.* To purchase supplies of Cuban and American sugar for Allies. *Repr.* U.S.A. Government, Sugar Commission, and Allied Governments not represented by the Commission. *Ref.* B.T.J., 25th Oct. 1917.

SUGAR DISTRIBUTION BOARD.—*See* H.C., No. 113, 1919, p. 6. It was appointed by M.F., with same chairman as Sugar Commission, and its work was practically completed by July 1919. Other details are lacking.

SUGAR DISTRIBUTION COMMITTEE.—*App.* by F.C., Mar. 1917. *Obj.* To consider existing system of distribution and suggest improvements. *Repr.* Parliament, M.F. (sec.), sugar importers, wholesale and retail traders including grocers and multiple shops, Co-operative Congress, Chambers of Commerce. *Ref.* B.T.J., 29th Mar.; T., 26th Mar., p. 10, 1917.

SUGAR, DISTRIBUTION DURING RAILWAY STRIKE, TRADE COMMITTEE.—*App.* by F.C. about 27th Sept. 1919. *Obj.* To deal with transport of sugar for distribution. *Repr.* Sugar refining and distributing trades. *Ref.* N.F.J., 15th Oct. 1919. *Diss.* Oct. 1919.

SUGAR SUPPLIES, ROYAL COMMISSION.—*App.* by Royal Warrant, Aug. 1914, and, though it was not merged into M.F., the two organizations were combined in 1917. *Obj.* To carry out purchase, sale, distribution and general control of sugar, the Commission undertaking similar work for France early in 1916, and later for other Allies. *Repr.* The Government, M.F. (when formed), importers, traders, Labour. *Ref.* Cd. 8728, 8978. *Diss.* The Final Report was issued April 1921, but the formal winding up of Commission had still to be completed.

SUGAR SUPPLIES, ROYAL COMMISSION.—Staffs, Special Investigation Committee. *See* Cabinet.

SULPHATE OF AMMONIA DISTRIBUTION ADVISORY COMMITTEE.—*App.* by F.C., Jan. or Feb. 1917. *Obj.* To advise on production and distribution of sulphate of ammonia, and regulate scheme for distribution to farmers. *Repr.* Manufacturers of sulphate of ammonia, including L.A.'s, Gas and Oil Companies, &c. *Ref.* J.B.A., Feb. 1917; Cd. 9069, p. xxxviii. *Diss.* May 1921.

TEA ADVISORY COMMITTEE.—*App.* by F.C., Mar. 1917. *Obj.* To recommend regulations for wholesale and retail trades to avoid formal control. *Repr.* M.F., traders (wholesale and retail). *Ref.* N.F.J., 22nd May 1918.

TEA CONTROL COMMITTEE.—*App.* by F.C., Mar. 1917. *Obj.* To prepare regulations for the trade as recommended by Advisory Committee. *Repr.* M.F. Blenders, Wholesalers, Retailers, Packet Firms. *Ref.* N.F.J., 22nd May 1918.

VEGETABLE MARKETS COMMITTEE, LONDON.—*App.* by F.C., Mar. 1918. *Obj.* To report upon fruit and vegetable markets in Metropolitan Police Area and advise as to relieving congestion. *Repr.* M.F., F.P.D., Market Authorities, Railways, Traders, Co-operators. *Ref.* N.F.J., 27th Mar. 1918.

VEGETABLE SUPPLIES, SELECT COMMITTEE OF GOVERNMENT FACTORS.—*App.* by F.C. in second half of 1917. *Obj.* To advise on measures for dealing with vegetable supplies. *Repr.* Factors acting on behalf of the Government. *Ref.* Information privately communicated.

VENISON COMMITTEE.—*App.* in July 1916, apparently by B.A., and taken over by M.F. in winter of 1917–18. *Obj.* To increase kill of deer to supplement meat supplies. *Repr.* M.F., B.A., landowners, traders. *Ref.* N.F.J., 28th Nov. 1917.

WEST AFRICAN ADVISORY COMMITTEE.—*App.* by M.F. in second half of 1917. *Obj.* To prepare scheme of distribution of West African products in connexion with control of oil cake. *Repr.* West African merchants. *Ref.* Information privately communicated.

WHEAT CONSERVATION COMMITTEE.—*See* L.G.B.

WHEAT EXECUTIVE, INTER-ALLIED.—*App.* by British, French and Italian Governments, Dec. 1916, as development of existing joint purchase scheme, and subsequently connected with M.F. *Obj.* To purchase and allocate wheat, flour, and (subsequently) other cereals for the three countries. *Repr.* The three Governments. *Ref.* Cd. 9005,

WHEAT EXPORT COMPANY, NEW YORK.—*App.* by Royal Commission on Wheat Supplies, apparently early in 1917, a similar Company being established in Canada. *Obj.* To act as sole agency for purchase of wheat in U.S.A., for all European Allies under instructions of Wheat Executive. *Repr.* Firms of grain merchants who were members of the Commission. *Ref.* H.C., No. 151, 1917, p. viii.

WHEAT SUPPLIES, ROYAL COMMISSION.—*App.* by Royal Warrant, Oct. 1916, and reappointed with extended reference, April 1917, its organization being eventually combined with that of M.F. *Obj.* To maintain wheat supplies and to purchase, sell and control wheat on behalf of the Government. *Repr.* Trade and other interests involved, selected for expert knowledge and administrative skill. *Ref.* Cmd. 1544. *Diss.* In course of liquidation by May 1921.

WHEAT SUPPLIES ROYAL COMMISSION, COMMITTEE OF CHAIR-MEN.—*App.* by the Commission, in co-operation with F.C., in second half of 1917. *Obj.* To co-ordinate work of various Committees of the Commission. *Repr.* Chairmen of these Committees. *Ref.* Information privately communicated.

WHEAT SUPPLIES ROYAL COMMISSION.—*See also* Cereals, Finance, Flour Mills, Freights, General Purposes, Storage.

WHOLESALE FOOD MARKETS, LONDON, DEPARTMENTAL COM-MITTEE.—*App.* by F.C., Oct. 1919. *Obj.* To inquire into efficiency of markets and their effect on prices. *Repr.* M.F., Consumers' Council, L.A.'s Railways, Agriculture, Labour. *Ref.* Cmd. 634, 1341. *Diss.* Mar. 1921.

FOREIGN OFFICE

ABBREVIATION

F.O. = Foreign Office.

ALIENS AFTER THE WAR.—*See* M.R.

ARAB BUREAU.—*App.* by F.O. in 1917 or early 1918, with head-quarters at Cairo. *Obj.* To collect and correlate intelligence from Arab countries engaged in the War. *Repr.* Not stated. *Ref.* H.C., No. 231, 1920, p. vi. *Diss.* During 1919.

ARCHANGEL SUB-COMMITTEE.—*See under* Russia Committee.

BELGIAN TRADE COMMITTEE.—Joint appointment. *See* B.T.

BRITISH COMMUNITIES ABROAD, FOREIGN OFFICE COM-MITTEE.—*App.* by F.O. in 1919 or early 1920. *Obj.* To report on fostering solidarity among British Communities abroad and propagating British ideals abroad. *Repr.* Parliament, F.O., O.T.D., and Civil Service generally, Diplomatic and Consular Service, commercial men, economic experts, persons with knowledge of East. *Ref.* Cmd. 672; B.T.J., 6th May 1920. *Diss.* Mar. 1920.

ATHENS RELIEF COMMITTEE.—*App.* locally, with assistance from British Legation in Athens, in 1915. *Obj.* To administer relief in Athens. *Repr.* Local residents. *Ref.* H.C., No. 7, 1923, p. xxii. *Diss.* 1919.

CHOLERA PREVENTION.—*See under* Pilgrimage Quarantine.

COMMERCIAL ATTACHÉ AND CONSULAR SERVICE COMMITTEE. —*App.* by F.O. in first half of 1917. *Obj.* To consider enlargement and improvement of service. *Repr.* F.O., B.T., Tre., Chambers of Commerce, F.B.I. *Ref.* Cd. 8715. *Diss.* Aug. 1917.

COMMERCIAL INTELLIGENCE, IMPERIAL, COMMITTEE.—*Ref.* without details, T., 11th Nov. 1916, p. 6.

COMMERCIAL INTELLIGENCE ORGANIZATION COMMITTEE.— *App.* jointly by F.O. and B.T., Jan. 1917. *Obj.* To consider best form of organization of foreign trade and reorganization of existing system of providing commercial intelligence, with special reference to post-war con-ditions. *Repr.* F.O., B.T., Chambers of Commerce, F.B.I., Railways. *Ref.* Cd. 8715, p. 3. *Diss.* April 1917.

COMMERCIAL INTELLIGENCE.—*See also* Foreign Trade, Promotion.

COMMISSION INTERNATIONALE DE RAVITAILLEMENT, BRIT-ISH EXECUTIVE STAFF.—Attached for executive purposes to F.O. *See* Cabinet.

CONSULAR SERVICE, RECRUITING COMMITTEE.—*App.* jointly by F.O., and B.T. in 1918. *Obj.* To consider the methods of recruiting for consular service with special reference to ex-officers. *Repr.* Appointing Departments and others. *Ref.* Cmd. 325, p. 220.

CONTRABAND COMMITTEE.—*App.* by the Government, Mar. 1915, on establishment of Blockade of Germany, to sit at F.O. *Obj.* To scrutinize imports intended for neutrals, adjacent to enemy countries, for detention of those intended for the latter. *Repr.* F.O., Adm., B.T., Legal Profession. *Ref.* Cd. 8145, 8469. *Diss.* Transferred to O.T.D. in 1917.

(An administrative Contraband Department was also established in 1917 or earlier. *See* Cd. 9220, pp. 13–14.)

EASTERN AFFAIRS DEPARTMENTAL COMMITTEE.—A continuation of the Eastern War Cabinet Committee. *See under* Cabinet.

EGYPT, NEW LEGISLATION, ADVISORY COMMITTEE.—*App.* by F.O., Nov. 1917. *Obj.* To consider drafts of new legislation for Egypt. *Repr.* F.O., Law Officers of the Crown, Legal Profession. *Ref.* Cd. 9220.

ENEMY DEBTS COMMITTEE.—*App.* by F.O. in 1916 or 1917. *Obj.* To consider arrangements for business and financial transactions with enemies, interrupted by outbreak of war. *Repr.* H.C., F.O., Bank of England commerce, industry, accountancy, Legal Profession. *Ref.* Cd. 8916.

ENEMY EXPORTS COMMITTEE.—*App.* by the Government, Mar. 1915, on establishment of Blockade of Germany, sitting at F.O. *Obj.* To investigate cargoes of west-bound neutral ships with view to stop enemy goods. *Repr.* F.O., Adm., B.T. *Ref.* Cd. 8469.

FINANCE SECTION, FOREIGN OFFICE.—*App.* by F.O., May 1916, incorporating in it Finance Section of Foreign Trade Department (q.v.). *Obj.* To deal with financial matters connected with the Blockade, and prevent financial transactions with enemies. *Repr.* F.O., Foreign Trade Department, Experts in Foreign Credits and Exchange. *Ref.* B.T.J., 25th May 1916.

FOREIGN CLAIMS OFFICE.—*App.* by F.O. prior to Sept. 1817. *Ref.* without details, Cd. 8741, p. 6.

FOREIGN TRADE DEPARTMENT.—*App.* about beginning of 1916, as new department, the Trading with the Enemy Department of H.O. being merged into it. *Obj.* To carry out the Trading with the Enemy (Extension of Powers) Act, 1915, prevent trading with enemies in neutral countries, and to continue work of H.O. against trading with the enemy. *Repr.* Mainly official, largely previous H.O. staff, with assistance of business men. *Ref.* B.T.J., 6th Jan. 1916. *Diss.* Transferred to O.T.D. in 1917.

FOREIGN TRADE, PROMOTION, DEPARTMENTAL COMMITTEE. —*App.* by F.O., apparently in 1916. *Obj.* To consider improvement in Government machinery for promoting foreign trade. *Repr.* F.O., including Legal Advisers, Diplomatic Service. *Ref.* Cd. 8715. *Diss.* Aug. 1916.

HAMADAN BOARD OF CONTROL.—*See* Russia Committee.

INFORMATION DEPARTMENT, FOREIGN OFFICE.—*App.* by F.O. prior to Sept. 1917. *Ref.* without details, Cd. 8741, p. 6.

MISSIONS, BRITISH, SPECIAL.—*App.* by F.O:, from time to time for various war and post-war purposes in various countries. For full list *see* H.C., No. 10, 1922, pp. 414–15. References are also made on pp. xxi–xxiii and pp. xlviii–xlix, to particular missions.

MISSIONS, BRITISH WAR.—*See* United States and Cabinet *under* Russia.

MISSIONS IN INDIA.—Joint Appointment. *See* In.O.

NEUTRALS DETENTION (CLAIMS TO COMPENSATION) COMMITTEE.—*App.* apparently by F.O., prior to Sept. 1917. *Obj.* To deal with claims of neutrals to compensation for losses caused by detention. *Repr.* Not stated. *Ref.* Cd. 8741, p. 8. *See also* Ships, Neutral.

ORDER-IN-COUNCIL OF MARCH 1915, COMMITTEE.—*See* Ships (Neutral) Detention Committee, below.

PASSPORT OFFICE.—*See* W.O.

PILGRIMAGE QUARANTINE INTER-DEPARTMENTAL COMMITTEE.—*App.* by F.O., after consultation with L.G.B., early in 1919. *Obj.* To advise on measures to prevent spread of cholera from resumption of Pilgrimages to Mecca, with references to post-war conditions in Russia. *Repr.* F.O., L.G.B., Indian and Egyptian Health Services. *Ref.* Cmd. 978, pp. 89, 369. Still in existence, June 1921.

PRISONERS OF WAR DEPARTMENT.—*App.* under F.O. *Ref.* without details, Cd. 9220, p. 13. *See also* W.O.

REGISTRIES, FOREIGN OFFICE, COMMITTEE.—*App.* by F.O. in autumn of 1918. *Obj.* To report on reorganization of departmental system of registration. *Repr.* F.O., Tre., experts. *Ref.* Cd. 9220, p. 14.

RUSSIA, INFORMATION COMMITTEE.—*App.* by F.O., May 1920. *Obj.* To inquire into imprisonment, &c. of British subjects and political and economic conditions of Russia. *Repr.* Parliament, Legal Profession, Labour, with assistance from Diplomatic Service. *Ref.* Cmd. 1041, 1240. *Diss.* Feb. 1921.

RUSSIA INTER-DEPARTMENTAL COMMITTEE.—*App.* jointly by F.O., Tre., and W.O., prior to 1917. *Obj.* To advise on questions of policy affecting expenditure in or for Russia. *Repr.* F.O., M.B., Tre., W.O., financial experts. *Ref.* H.C. 1920, Nos. 54 &c., p. 392, No. 116, pp. 26–7.

   This Committee appointed various subsidiary bodies, e.g. Archangel Sub-Committee, dealing with purchase of stores, &c. (*see* No. 116, p. 25), and Hamadan Board of Control (*see* No. 116, pp. 26–7), appointed in 1917, to supervise finance, &c. of Russian Units operating against Bolsheviks in Persia).

SHIPS, NEUTRAL, DETENTION COMMITTEE.—*App.* by F.O., Adm., and B.T., Mar. 1916, and sometimes called the Order-in-Council of Mar. 1915 Committee. *Obj.* To report whether there are avoidable delays in bringing neutral ships and cargoes into British ports under Blockade Order of Mar. 1915. *Repr.* Parliament, shipowners, Legal Profession. *Ref.* Cd. 8469. *Diss.* Feb. 1917. *See also* Neutrals.

TREATIES WITH ENEMY COUNTRIES REVISION COMMITTEE.— *App.* by F.O. prior to Sept. 1917. *Ref.* without details, Cd. 8741, p. 11.

UNITED STATES, BRITISH WAR MISSION.—*App.* first as Special Mission under the Foreign Secretary, April 1917, in connexion with entry of U.S.A. into the War, and subsequently as Permanent Mission. *Obj.* To discuss with U.S.A. best means of organizing their activities in the War, and to supervise and co-ordinate activities affecting G.B. *Repr.* The Government, various experts. *Ref.* Cd. 9005, pp. 16–17.

   (The Mission was accompanied by a Labour Delegation to discuss with U.S.A. authorities the War labour problems in the light of British experience.)

HEALTH INSURANCE, NATIONAL COMMISSIONS AND JOINT COMMITTEE

Under the National Insurance Act, 1911, separate Commissions were established for England, Wales, Scotland, and Ireland, with a Joint Committee for common purposes. Excluding the Medical Research Committee (*see* below), by which they were assisted, the work of the Commissions was absorbed into the Ministry of Health and the Scottish Board of Health from July 1919, under Acts of that year. By an Order-in-Council of 25th Mar. 1920, under the Ministry of Health Act, 1919, the Medical Research Committee became the Medical Research Council under a Special Committee of the Privy Council for Medical Research.

ABBREVIATIONS

B.M.A. = British Medical Association.
N.H.I.C. = National Health Insurance Commissions or Joint Committee. Where a single National Commission is intended the abbreviations Eng. (England), Sc. (Scotland), I. (Ireland), and W. (Wales) are added.
M.R.C. = Medical Research Committee and (later) Council.
R.A.M.C. = Royal Army Medical Corps.

ACCESSORY FOOD FACTORS (VITAMINES) COMMITTEE.—*App.* jointly by M.R.C., and Lister Institute of Preventive Medicine in 1917. *Obj.* To consider best means of co-ordinating inquiries. *Repr.* M.R.C., Lister Institute, scientific research, women, with correspondents abroad. *Ref.* Cd. 8981, pp. 69, 77.

ANŒROTIC BACTERIA AND INFECTIONS COMMITTEE.—*App.* by M.R.C., Mar. 1917. *Obj.* To co-ordinate inquiries into anœrotic organisms, with special reference to wound infections. *Repr.* M.R.C., R.A.M.C., Medical Profession, scientific research, with correspondents in France. *Ref.* Cd. 8981, p. 76. *Diss.* Early in 1920.

ANTHROPOMETIC METHODS AND STANDARDS.—*App.* by M.R.C. about May 1920. *Obj.* To advise on methods and standards to be adopted in investigations. *Repr.* Army; R.A.F.; medical and scientific experts. *Ref.* Cmd. 1088, pp. 40, 98.

APPROVED SOCIETIES, ADMINISTRATION ALLOWANCE AND JOINT ENLISTMENT COMMITTEES.—*See* L.G.B.

BUILDINGS, COOLING, &c.—*See* S.I.R.

CEREBRO-SPINAL FEVER, BACTERIOLOGICAL STUDIES, SPECIAL ADVISORY COMMITTEE.—*App.* by M.R.C. in spring of 1915. *Obj.* To investigate the disease with special reference to the prevailing epidemic. *Repr.* Medical experts. *Ref.* Cd. 8423. *Diss.* Report on epidemic published early in 1916.

CHILD LIFE (ANTE-NATAL AND POST-NATAL) COMMITTEES.—*App.* by M.R.C. early in 1919, working in two sections at London and Edinburgh. *Obj.* To investigate questions of health of mothers and children, largely through inquiries at Maternity and Child Welfare Centres. *Repr.* Medical experts. *Ref.* Cmd. 412, pp. 57, 89, Cmd. 978, p. 114.

(This investigation was probably facilitated by the developments of

Maternity and Child Welfare Work during, and in part as a result of, the War.)

CINCHONA DERIVATIVES AND MALARIA COMMITTEE.—*App.* by M.R.C. about May 1920. *Obj.* To investigate medical and economic questions connected with use of derivatives. *Repr.* Medical experts, including Indian Medical Service. *Ref.* Cmd. 1088, pp. 18, 97.

DEFICIENCY DISEASES IN VIENNA, MISSION OF INVESTIGA-TION.—*App.* by Accessory Food Factors Committee (*see* above), Oct. 1919. *Obj.* To study the diseases on the spot. *Repr.* Lady doctors. *Ref.* Cmd. 1088, pp. 66–7. *Diss.* June 1920.

DRUG ACCOUNTS, SCOTLAND, COMMITTEE.—*App.* as combination of Insurance Committees under N.H.I.C.(Sc.) early in 1915. *Obj.* To price and report upon drugs, periodically revising tariff. *Repr.* N.H.I.C.(Sc.) Local Insurance Committees. *Ref.* Cmd. 827, pp. 10–11, 38. Probably permanent as Committee was intended partly to deal with war problem and partly with general considerations (*see* Cmd. 1235, p. 14).

DRUG TARIFF DEPARTMENTAL COMMITTEE.—*App.* by N.H.I.C., Feb. 1915. *Obj.* To report upon existing drug tariff, and advisability of revision, with due account of war conditions. *Repr.* N.H.I.C., Tre., B.M.A., Pharmaceutical Society, Institute of Chemistry. *Ref.* Cd. 8062. *Diss.* Sept. 1915.

DRUGS, ECONOMY, PRICES.—*See* H.O.

GOVERNMENT OF IRELAND ACT, APPLICATION TO HEALTH INSURANCE, COMMITTEE.—*App.* by N.H.I.C., Oct. 1921. *Obj.* To report on steps necessary to carry out the Act in respect of Health Insurance. *Repr.* Government Actuary, M.H., N.H.I.C., N.H.I.C.(I), M.L. *Ref.* Cmd. 1575. *Diss.* 1921.

HEALTH AND UNEMPLOYMENT INSURANCE INTER-DEPART-MENTAL COMMITTEE.—*See* M.L.

HUMAN NUTRITION RESEARCH BOARD, PROVISIONAL COM-MITTEE.—*App.* jointly by M.R.C., D.C., and S.I.R., in 1919. *Obj.* To survey inquiries under scheme for developing work of Food (War) Com-mittee of Royal Society. *Repr.* M.R.C., B.A., B.T., D.C., S.I.R., Royal Society, scientific exports. *Ref.* Cmd. 412, p. 54.

INDUSTRIAL FATIGUE RESEARCH BOARD.—*App.* jointly by M.R.C., and S.I.R. under administration of former, in first half of 1918, after consultation with H.O. and M.L., consisting of small Central Com-mittee, and panel of representative men and women in various industries. *Obj.* To investigate relations of hours of labour and conditions and methods of employment to industrial fatigue, as affecting health and efficiency of workers. *Repr.* H.O., M.M., M.R.C., S.I.R., physiologists, with assessors representing employers and workpeople in various industries. *Ref.* Cmd. 9144, p. 31. *Permanent Body.*

INFLUENZA, EMERGENCY RESEARCH COMMITTEE.—*App.* by M.R.C., in co-operation with M.H. and W.O., in spring of 1920. *Obj.* To organize investigations in view of possible epidemic. *Repr.* M.R.C., M.H., W.O., London research workers. *Ref.* Cmd. 1088, p. 49. *Diss.* later in 1920.

MEDICAL SUPPLIES FOR WAR PURPOSES, SPECIAL COMMITTEE OF ROYAL SOCIETY.—*App.* by the Society, apparently early in the War, in co-operation with N.H.I.C. *Obj.* To advise and assist generally in technical problems of manufacture of sufficient drugs, medicines, and medical appliances for war needs. *Repr.* The Society, experts. *Ref.* Cd. 8890, p. 40.

MEDICAL WAR CENTRAL COMMITTEE (ENGLAND AND WALES).— *App.* by Annual Representative Meeting of B.M.A., in co-operation with N.H.I.C. and W.O., July 1915. *Obj.* To deal with all medical matters arising out of the war and (later) reconstruction, to organize profession for war service, being recognized from May 1916 by A.C. as authority to deal with claims of doctors (other than conscientious objectors) for exemption from military service. *Repr.* Medical Profession; N.H.I.C. *Ref.* Cd. 8890, pp. 34–5, Cd. 9005, p. 189.

MEDICAL WAR (IRELAND), MEDICAL SERVICES (SCOTLAND), EMERGENCY COMMITTEES.—*App.*, *Obj.*, *Repr.* as with Central Committee (England). *Ref.* Cd. 9005, p. 189 ; Reconstruction Pamphlets, No. 12.

MEDICAL WAR COMMITTEES, LOCAL.—*App.* in various districts under Central Committees (*see* above) from July 1915. *Obj.* To assist Central Committees in their districts, and provide information. *Repr.* Medical Profession in their districts. *Ref.* Cmd. 8890, pp. 34–5.

MUNITIONS AND HUT BUILDING.—Special machinery for medical treatment of large bodies of workpeople at Gretna and other new factories, of Belgian munition workers, and of men engaged on hut building, was set up from time to time by N.H.I.C. *See* Cd. 9005, p. 190.

NAVAL AND MILITARY DEPENDANTS (MEDICAL TREATMENT) COMMITTEE.—*App.* by the Government, Sept. 1914, and associated with N.H.I.C. *Obj.* To organize and administer scheme for free medical attendance, and medicines and appliances at cost price, to dependants of men with Forces who could not afford to pay for treatment. *Repr.* The Government, N.H.I.C., N.R.F., B.M.A., Pharmaceutical Society. *Ref.* Cd. 8890, pp. 38–9. *Diss.* Aug. 1916, on formation of Statutory Committee on War Pensions.

(N.B. The Local work was done by the Local Representative Committees set up by the Committee on the Prevention and Relief of Distress, *see* L.G.B.)

NERVE INJURIES COMMITTEE.—*App.* by M.R.C. in 1918 or 1919. *Obj.* To investigate problems arising out of injuries to the nervous system. *Repr.* Medical experts, with specialists for specific classes of injury. *Ref.* Cmd. 412, pp. 62, 63, 89.

NOVOCAIN SUB-COMMITTEE OF THE ROYAL SOCIETY.—*App.* by the Society at request of N.H.I.C., in 1915. *Obj.* To organize in scientific institutions the manufacture of intermediate products of novocain to secure adequate supplies for war needs. *Repr.* The Society, &c. *Ref.* Cmd. 183, p. 7.

(Similar co-operation by the Society was secured in regard to other drugs, but special Committees do not appear to have been appointed.)

OXYGEN, CLINICAL USES COMMITTEE.—*App.* by M.R.C. about May 1920. *Obj.* To promote investigation of medicinal uses of Oxygen. *Repr.* M.R.C., medical experts. *Ref.* Cmd. 1088, pp. 71, 97.

OXYGEN.—*See also* S.I.R., *under* Oxygen Research Committee.

PATHOLOGICAL METHODS, SPECIAL COMMITTEE.—*App.* by M.R.C. in 1917. *Obj.* To report upon standardization of routine pathological methods. *Repr.* M.R.C., Medical Departments of Adm., W.O., L.G.B., pathological research, with co-opted experts for particular problems. *Ref.* Cd. 8981, p. 75.

(The Committee appointed a Sub-Committee to study the media used, *see* Cmd. 412, p. 71.)

PHTHISIS, OCCUPATIONAL INCIDENCE, COMMITTEE.—*App.* by M.R.C. in or before 1917. *Obj.* To investigate incidence of phthisis in particular occupations and suggest schemes of research. *Repr.* Parliament, M.R.C., H.O., Royal Society, medical and scientific research. *Ref.* Cd. 8981, p. 75.

RELIEF OF DISTRESS (WELSH INSURANCE COMMISSION) INTELLIGENCE BUREAU.—*App.* by N.H.I.C. (W.). *See* L.G.B.

RHEUMATISM AND ALLIED DISEASES COMMITTEE.—*App.* to co-operate with similar Committee of M.H. (q.v.).

RYAN COMMITTEE.—*See* Soldiers' Contributions.

SALVARSAN COMMITTEE.—*App.* by M.R.C. in 1917. *Obj.* To investigate manufacture, testing, &c. of salvarsan and salvarsan substitutes. *Repr.* M.R.C., L.G.B., Adm., W.O., scientists, experts. *Ref.* Cd. 8981, pp. 65–6, 76.

SHELL SHOCK.—*See* W.O.

SOLDIERS' CONTRIBUTIONS (RYAN) COMMITTEE.—Apparently dealt with problem of dealing with contributions to National Health Insurance from the men joining the forces during the War. *See* Cmd. 78, pp. 34–5.

SOLDIERS' HEART DISEASES ADVISORY COMMITTEE.—*See* W.O.

SURGICAL SHOCK SPECIAL INVESTIGATION COMMITTEE.—*App.* by M.R.C. in summer of 1917. *Obj.* To co-ordinate inquiries into surgical shock and allied conditions, and correlate laboratory and clinical observations, work being co-ordinated with that of similar Committee of American Physiologists. *Repr.* M.R.C., Royal Society, Physiologists, Medical Profession, Army Medical Service. *Ref.* Cd. 8825, p. 78. *Diss.* Suspended from July 1919.

TUBERCULOSIS INDUSTRIAL SUB-COMMITTEE.—*App.* by M.R.C., in 1920 or earlier. M.H. represented on it. Details lacking. *See* Cmd. 1397, pp. 105, 154.

VITAMINES.—*See* Accessory Food Factors.

HEALTH, MINISTRY OF, SCOTTISH BOARD OF

See under Local Government Board (England and Wales), Local Government Board (Scotland).

HOME OFFICE

ABBREVIATION

H.O. = Home Office.

ABSENTEEISM.—*See* Coal Mines.

ACETYLENE COMMITTEE.—*App.* by H.O., Nov. 1916. *Obj.* To consider amendment of existing regulations for filling, &c. of cylinders of dissolved acetylene. *Repr.* H.O., Adm., N.P.L., engineering, gas, and other experts. *Ref.* B.T.J., 9th Nov. 1916.

ADOPTION.—*See* Child Adoption.

ADVISORY PANELS.—*See* S.I.R.

AIR RAID SHELTERS COMMITTEE.—*App.* by H.O. in winter of 1916–17 or earlier. *Obj.* To assist Commissioner of Police to secure sufficient accommodation for shelters in London. *Repr.* ' A Committee of Experts '. *Ref.* Cd. 9005, p. 55.

ALIENS AFTER THE WAR.—*See* M.R.

ALIENS, ALLIED NATIONALITY, ENLISTMENT COMMITTEE.— The object is conveyed by title. The Committee came to an end before Sept. 1917. Details lacking. *See* Cd. 8741, p. 2.

ALIENS AND NATIONALITY COMMITTEE.—*App.* by H.O. in or after Aug. 1918, under the British Nationality and Status of Aliens Act, 1918. *Obj.* Originally to inquire into cases under the Act before orders issued revoking certificates of Naturalization, and later dealt with conditions under which aliens should be permitted to enter the country. *Repr.* Legal Profession, H.O., M.H. (when health questions considered) and others. *Ref.* Cmd. 1397, p. 143 ; P.G.A., 1918. *Diss.* Apparently on passing of Aliens (Restriction) Amendment Act, late in 1919.

(The Dominions Governments were empowered to appoint similar committees, and some appear to have done so : *see* Cmd. 1397, p. 21.)

ALIENS, DEPORTATION, ADVISORY COMMITTEE.—*App.* by H.O. early in 1920, under Aliens Restriction (Amendment) Act, 1919. *Obj.* To advise H.O. on grant of licences to remain in U.K. to enemy aliens liable to deportation. *Repr.* Parliament, and other persons chosen by H.O. *Ref.* P.G.A., 1919.

ALIENS, DESTITUTE, COMMITTEE.—*App.* by H.O., in 1914. *Obj.* To advise on provision for destitute aliens. *Repr.* H.O., L.G.B., and others. *Ref.* Cd. 7763.

ALIENS, ENEMY, ADVISORY COMMITTEE.—*App.* by H.O. prior to June 1915. *Obj.* To advise on internment and repatriation of enemy aliens. *Repr.* Parliament, Judges, Legal Profession, Army, Labour. *Ref.* Cd. 8430, p. 28. *Diss.* Replaced by Aliens, Enemy, Revision of Internment Exemptions Advisory Committee in July 1919, the new Committee being the same as before, with the addition of one member.

ALIENS, ENEMY, REVISION OF INTERNMENT EXEMPTIONS ADVISORY COMMITTEE.—*App.* by H.O., July 1918, replacing Aliens, Enemy, Advisory Committee (*see* above). *Obj.* To review exemptions from internment and advise on each case. *Repr.* Parliament, Judges, Legal Profession, The Army, Labour. *Ref.* T., 23rd July 1918, p. 6. *Diss.* Not later than July 1918.

ALIENS IN GOVERNMENT OFFICES COMMITTEE.—*App.* by H.O., July 1918. *Obj.* To decide on exceptions from new rule limiting employment in Government offices to children of natural-born subjects of Britain or Allies. *Repr.* Judges and public men unconnected with Civil Service. *Ref.* T., 26th July 1918, p. 6.

ALIENS IN PROHIBITED AREAS COMMISSIONERS.—*App.* by H.O., June 1916. *Obj.* To review permits to reside in prohibited areas and to advise on cancellations. *Repr.* H.C., Civil Service. *Ref.* Cd. 8419. *Diss.* Oct. 1916.

ALIENS REPATRIATION COMMITTEE.—*App.* by H.O., May 1919. *Obj.* To decide appeals by interned enemy aliens against compulsory repatriation. *Repr.* Parliament, Legal Profession. *Ref.* Cmd. 383. *Diss.* Oct. 1919.

ALIENS RESTRICTIONS COMMITTEE.—*App.* prior to Mar. 1916. Cd. 8256 makes it H.O. Committee, but secretary (Cd. 8741, p. 2) was attached to Committee of Imperial Defence. Other details lacking.

ALIENS RESTRICTIONS REGULATIONS ADVISORY COMMITTEE. —Details lacking, but presumably largely legal. Appointed before June 1917. *See* Cd. 8741, p. 2.

ALIENS.—*See also* Certificates of Naturalization and N.H.I.C.

ANTHRAX DISINFECTION COMMITTEE.—*App.* by H.O., Feb. 1919. *Obj.* To erect and work trial disinfecting station, report on construction and working of such stations, and advise generally on disinfection. *Repr.* Parliament, H.O., Factory Inspectorate, L.G.B., and various interests concerned, including Labour. *Ref.* L.G., Feb. 1919, p. 76.

ANTHRAX.—*See also under* Horsehair.

BREATHING APPARATUS IN COAL MINES COMMITTEE.—*See* S.I.R.

CERTIFICATES OF NATURALIZATION (REVOCATION) COMMITTEE.—*App.* by H.O. or the Government in 1918. *Obj.* To report on revocation of certificates granted to enemy aliens by reason of their actions during the War. *Repr.* Parliament, Judges, Legal Profession. *Ref.* Cd. 1569 ; T., 8th Oct. 1918, p. 5.

CHILD ADOPTION COMMITTEE.—*App.* by H.O., Aug. 1920. *Obj.* To consider problems of legal provision for adoption of children. *Repr.* Parliament, Legal Profession, educationists, experts in juvenile problems, Labour, women. *Ref.* Cmd. 1254. *Diss.* Feb. 1921.

CIVILIAN INTERNMENT CAMPS COMMITTEE.—*App.* by H.O. prior to June 1917, probably early in the War. Other details lacking. *See* Cd. 8741, p. 3.

CLERICAL AND COMMERCIAL EMPLOYMENTS COMMITTEE.— *App.* by H.O., Oct. 1915. *Obj.* To consider means (including employment of women) of replacing enlisted men in these occupations. *Repr.* Parliament, H.O., W.O., professional and business men, Labour, women. *Ref.* Cd. 8110. *Diss.* Nov. 1915.

CLERICAL AND COMMERCIAL EMPLOYMENTS, SUPPLY AND TRAINING OF WOMEN, LOCAL COMMITTEES.—*App.* in a few important towns by local initiative prior to Nov. 1915, and establishment elsewhere by L.E.A.'s suggested subsequently by main Committee. *Obj.* To organize supply and training of women for these employments. *Repr.* L.E.A.'s ; local business men. *Ref.* Cd. 8110.

COAL MINES ABSENTEEISM COMMITTEES.—*App.* in some cases by local initiative from 1915, and later, especially after Dec. 1916, at instigation of Coal Mining Organization Committee (q.v.), usually by mine-owners and miners jointly, but sometimes by miners alone. They consisted of (*a*) Pit Committees (individual pits), (*b*) Colliery Group Committees, and (*c*) District Committees. Sometimes only one type of Committee was established in a district and at others two only. *Obj.* To watch and deal with absenteeism, and bad time-keeping at the collieries concerned, and take disciplinary measures. *Repr.* Usually mine-owners and miners, sometimes miners only. *Ref.* Cd. 8345, p. 5.

COAL MINES, TIMEKEEPING.—*See* Coal Mines, Absenteeism.

COAL MINING ORGANIZATION DEPARTMENTAL COMMITTEE.— *App.* by H.O., Feb. 1915. *Obj.* To investigate means of promoting necessary production of coal, and assist generally in stimulating output. *Repr.* H.O., mine-owners and miners. *Ref.* Cd. 7939 ; L.G., June 1915. *Diss.* Feb. or Mar. 1917, on establishment of Coal Control (*see* B.T.).

COCAINE AND OPIUM PERMITS COMMITTEE.—*App.* by H.O. prior to Sept. 1917. Other details lacking. *See* Cd. 8741, p. 3.

COCAINE IN DENTISTRY.—*App.* by H.O., Nov. 1916. *Obj.* To report upon regulation of use of cocaine in dentistry. *Repr.* Parliament, Judges, physiological research. *Ref.* Cd. 8489. *Diss.* Feb. 1917.

COLLIERY RECRUITING, ALLOTMENT, JOINT COMMITTEES.— *App.* by the industry in some areas in first half of 1918. *Obj.* To allot quota of recruits required between different mines. *Repr.* Mine-owners, miners. *Ref.* Cmd. 339, p. 34. *Diss.* At or before close of War.

COLLIERY RECRUITING APPEAL COURTS.—*App.* in 1916 or 1917 in various areas by or through H.O., and transferred later to M.N.S. *Obj.* To hear appeals from Local Courts in their areas. *Repr.* H.O., mine-owners, miners. *Ref.* Cd. 9120, p. 51.

COLLIERY RECRUITING, BALLOTING COMMITTEES.—*App.* at individual mines in first half of 1918. *Obj.* To conduct ballots to secure recruits required from the mine. *Repr.* Workmen in the mine. *Ref.* Cmd. 339, p. 34. *Diss.* At or before close of War.

COLLIERY RECRUITING, CENTRAL COURT.—*App.* by H.O., Feb. 1916, and transferred to M.N.S. early in 1917. *Obj.* To deal with appeals from decisions of Colliery Recruiting, Local and Appeal, Courts (q.v.)

and issue instructions for their guidance. *Repr.* H.O., W.O., mine-owners, miners. *Ref.* Cd. 8345, p. 4.

COLLIERY RECRUITING LOCAL COURTS.—*App.* by H.O. in various colliery districts, in co-operation with the industry, early in 1916 and transferred to M.N.S. early in 1917. *Obj.* To deal with questions of enlistment of coal miners under M.S.A.'s. *Repr.* H.O., mine-owners, miners. *Ref.* Cd. 8345, p. 4.

COLLIERY TRAVELLING MEDICAL BOARDS.—*App.* locally Jan. 1917 through H.O. *Obj.* To assist Colliery Recruiting Courts (q.v.) in dealing with enlistment of miners. *Repr.* Medical men. *Ref.* Cd. 9120, p. 5.

COMPENSATION.—*See* Workmen's Compensation.

CONSCIENTIOUS OBJECTORS EMPLOYMENT COMMITTEE.—*App.* by H.O., June 1916. *Obj.* To arrange for suitable employment of men exempted from military service on condition of obtaining work of national importance. *Repr.* Parliament, Civil Servants. *Ref.* Cd. 8697, pp. 21–2 ; H.C. No. 69, 1922, p. 34.

CORNISH MINES RECRUITING COURT.—*App.* in 1917 or earlier for Cornish Tin Mines. *Obj.* To deal with questions of recruiting from tin mines. *Repr.* as with Colliery Recruiting Courts (q.v.). *Ref.* Cd. 9120, p. 66.

DESBOROUGH COMMITTEE.—*See* Police Service.

DESTRUCTION OF DOCUMENTS.—*See* M.M.

DISABLED SOLDIERS AND SAILORS.—*See* Workmen's Compensation.

DRUGS, ECONOMY, COMMITTEE.—*App.* by H.O., at suggestion of N.H.I.C., in winter of 1914–15. *Obj.* To advise medical profession on use and economy of drugs. *Repr.* N.H.I.C., medical profession. *Ref.* Cmd. 183, pp. 4, 5.

DRUGS, PRICES, COMMITTEE.—*App.* by H.O., or N.H.I.C., probably in winter of 1914–15. *Obj.* To advise in regard to current prices of drugs, with special reference to artificial inflation. *Repr.* Wholesale and retail drug trade. *Ref.* Cmd. 183, p. 5.

DRUGS.—*See also* N.H.I.C.

ENEMY BANKS.—*See* Tre.

FACTORY STAFF COMMITTEE.—Referred to without details in Cmd. 1403, pp. 9, 10, where the subject of re-organization of the Factory Inspectorate is dealt with.

FIRE BRIGADES, CO-ORDINATION, COMMITTEE.—*App.* by H.O. in winter of 1916–17 or earlier. *Obj.* To prepare and apparently supervise scheme for co-ordinating work of London fire brigades in air raids. *Repr.* The various Fire Brigades. *Ref.* Cd. 9005, p. 55. *Diss.* Not earlier than autumn of 1917.

FIRE BRIGADES (PAY, &c.) COMMITTEE.—*App.* by H.O., Dec. 1919. *Obj.* To report upon pay, hours and conditions of professional fire brigades in G.B. *Repr.* Parliament, H.O. (sec.), London Fire Brigade, Magistrates, Labour. *Ref.* Cmd. 710. *Diss.* May 1920.

FIRE PREVENTION COMMITTEE.—*App.* by H.O., Mar. 1916. *Obj.* To experiment on value of dry powder extinguishers compared with water or other appliances, in extinguishing fires caused by bombs. *Repr.* H.O., N.P.L., London Fire Brigade. *Ref.* Cd. 8250. *Diss.* April 1916.

HORSEHAIR DISINFECTION DEPARTMENTAL COMMITTEE.—*App.* by H.O., Jan. 1921, the pre-war Committee on Anthrax in Wool being re-appointed, with additions, for this purpose. *Obj.* To report upon practicability of applying to horsehair methods used in disinfecting wool. *Repr.* Parliament, H.O., horsehair manufacturers, Labour, Medical Profession, medical research. *Ref.* Cmd. 1365. *Diss.* April 1921.

HOURS OF LABOUR, MUNITIONS, COMMITTEE.—*See* M.M.

INFORMATION, HOME OFFICE, BUREAU.—*See* M.I.

INTERNMENT CAMPS.—*See* Civilian Internment Camps.

IRON MINERS, LIABILITY TO PHTHISIS COMMITTEE.—*App.* by H.O. and Coal Controller in 1918. *Obj.* To investigate tendency of iron ore dust to produce phthisis. *Repr.* H.O., Medical Profession, mine-owners, miners. *Ref.* Cmd. 339, p. 39. *Diss.* Not earlier than 1919.

JUVENILE ORGANIZATIONS CENTRAL STANDING COMMITTEE.—*App.* by H.O., Dec. 1916, and transferred to B.E., Oct. 1919. *Obj.* To bring together various workers in dealing with increased juvenile delinquency and co-ordinate and extend work of voluntary organizations for recreation and social interests of juveniles. *Repr.* H.O., B.E., chief Voluntary Organizations concerned. *Ref.* Cmd. 722, pp. 45. *Permanent.*

JUVENILE ORGANIZATIONS LOCAL COMMITTEES.—*App.* locally from Dec. 1916, often at instance of Central Committee, and brought under B.E., Oct. 1919. *Obj.* To secure local development and co-ordination of the work. *Repr.* L.E.A.'s, teachers, various Organizations. *Ref.* Cmd. 722, pp. 4, 5. *Permanent.*

MINERS, MINES.—*See* N.H.I.C., H.O.

MOTOR DRIVERS, PARTIALLY DISABLED, LICENSING COMMITTEE.—*App.* by H.O., Jan. 1916. *Obj.* To report upon granting and conditions of licences to partially disabled men to drive public motor vehicles in London. *Repr.* W.O., Metropolitan Police, medical profession, Bus Companies, motorists, Labour. *Ref.* Cd. 8314. *Diss.* July 1916.

MOTOR DRIVERS, PARTIALLY DISABLED, REVIEWING COMMITTEE. *App.* by H.O., Dec. 1918. *Obj.* To review and report upon decisions of previous Committee (q.v.). *Repr.* As with previous Committee and Municipal Tramways and Ex-Service Societies. *Ref.* Cmd. 312. *Diss.* July 1919.

MUNITIONS MANUFACTURE IN FRANCE, MISSION OF INQUIRY. *App.* by H.O., Oct. 1915. *Obj.* To investigate French methods of manufacture. *Repr.* H.O. (Explosives' Inspectorate). *Ref.* Cd. 8272. *Diss.* Oct. 1915.

NATURALIZATION.—*See* Certificates of Naturalization.

OPIUM.—*See under* Cocaine.

PASSENGER TRAFFIC BETWEEN UNITED KINGDOM AND HOLLAND, &c. COMMITTEE.—*App.* by H.O., presumably early in the War. *Obj.* To advise on conditions for permitting travel to and from Holland, &c. and generally advise on control of passenger traffic with the Continent. *Repr.* Not stated. *Ref.* Cd. 8741, p. 8 ; Hall, British Archives, p. 74.

PASSENGER TRAFFIC OFFICE.—This was established by H.O., to control passenger traffic with the Continent. *Ref.* Hall, p. 74 (*see* preceding entry).

PERMIT OFFICE.—*App.* by H.O. early in War. *Obj.* To administer issue of permits to enter the country, and certain special restrictions on persons desiring to go abroad. *Repr.* Official. *Ref.* Cd. 8741, p. 8. *Apparently still in existence at end of 1922.*

PIT COMMITTEES.—*See* Coal Mines, Absenteeism.

PIT TIMBER, HOME-GROWN, CENTRAL JOINT COMMITTEE.—*App.* jointly by H.O., B.A., and B.T., April 1916. *Obj.* To secure adequate supplies of home-grown pit timber, and organize work of local Pitwood Committees (q.v.). *Repr.* The three Departments, and the Coal Mining Organization (q.v.) and Home-grown Timber (*see* B.A.) Committees. *Ref.* Cd. 8345, p. 8 ; B.T.J., 31st Jan. 1918.

PITWOOD ALLOCATION COMMITTEE, WALES.—*App.* locally with official consent, replacing previous Local Committees, May 1917. *Obj.* To deal with whole supply of area. *Repr.* H.O., Adm., B.T., coal-owners, pitwood importers. *Ref.* Cd. 9120, p. 53.

PITWOOD ASSOCIATIONS.—Were formed mostly in 1917 by coal-owners of various districts to organize their own supplies of pitwood (*see* Cd. 9120), and in some cases considerably relieved the Committees.

PITWOOD, HOME-GROWN, DISTRICT COMMITTEES.—*App.* by, or at instance of, H.O. in 1917. *Obj.* To stimulate use of home-grown pit-wood. *Repr.* Presumably as with Local Committees. *Ref.* Cd. 9120, p. 28.

PITWOOD, HOME-GROWN, LOCAL COMMITTEES.—*App.* at instance of H.O., June 1916, for each coal-field or sometimes larger districts and subsequently utilized by C.M.D. (*see* B.T.). *Obj.* To deal locally with supply of home-grown pit timber. *Repr.* H.O., Home-grown Timber Committee (*see* B.A.), transport authorities, coal and wood owners, experts. *Ref.* Cd. 8345, p. 8. *Diss.* Mostly by end of 1918.

POLICE, EMPLOYMENT OF WOMEN, COMMITTEE.—*App.* by H.O., Feb. 1920. *Obj.* To report upon value and future conditions of women police. *Repr.* Parliament, H.O., W.O., Local Justices, Legal Profession, Women, Labour. *Ref.* Cmd. 877. *Diss.* July 1920.

POLICE FEDERATION.—*App.* in 1919 under Police Act, 1919. *Obj.* To enable members of Police Force in England and Wales to negotiate generally with the authorities respecting their welfare and efficiency. *Repr.* To cover all the Forces below rank of superintendent, acting through Branch Boards and Central Conferences and Committees. *Ref.* P.G.A. 1919. *Permanent.*

POLICE FORCE, COST OF LIVING BONUS, COMMITTEE.—*App.* by H.O. in 1920. *Obj.* To report upon arrangements for grant of bonus. *Repr.* Not stated. *Ref.* L.G., Dec. 1920, p. 663. *Diss.* Sept. 1920.

POLICE, METROPOLITAN, MEDICAL SERVICES COMMITTEE.— *App.* by H.O., April 1919. *Obj.* To report on the organization. *Repr.* Parliament, Metropolitan Police, medical and surgical experts. *Ref.* T., 12th April 1919, p. 9.

POLICE SERVICE COMMITTEE.—*App.* jointly by H.O. and S.O. about July 1923. *Obj.* To report upon readjustment of conditions, in light working of Desborough Committee's Report and fall in cost of living. *Repr.* Parliament, L.A.'s, Labour. *Ref.* L.G., Aug. 1923, p. 311.

POLICE SERVICE OF ENGLAND, WALES AND SCOTLAND COMMITTEE (DESBOROUGH COMMITTEE).—*App.* by H.O., March 1919. *Obj.* To consider changes desirable in pay, conditions and method of recruiting, of Police Forces. *Repr.* Parliament, L.A.'s, Labour. *Ref.* Cmd. 253, 574. *Diss.* End 1919.

PRESS CENSORSHIP.—*App.* by the Government under the H.O. at outbreak of War. *Obj.* To deal with Press Censorship, so far as not covered by the military censorship. *Repr.* Official and expert. *Ref.* Hall, p. 74. *Diss.* After close of War. For Press *see also* W.O.

PRISON OFFICERS' PAY COMMITTEE.—*App.* by H.O., Feb. 1923. *Obj.* To consider changes in remuneration and conditions of officers of prisons, &c. *Repr.* Parliament, H.O., Labour and others. *Ref.* Cmd. 1959. *Diss.* July, 1923.

RECRUITING.—*See* Colliery Recruiting, Cornish Mines.

REPRESENTATION.—*See* Parliament.

SAFETY CONFERENCE.—*App.* (organized) jointly by H.O. and British Industrial Safety First Association in London, Sept. 1919. *Obj.* To discuss generally questions of industrial safety. *Repr.* H.O., the Association, manufacturers and others. *Ref.* Cmd. 1403, p. 18.

SAFETY, WORKS' COMMITTEES.—*App.* during the War in individual works at instance of H.O., and known later as Safety First Committees. *Obj.* To secure co-operation of management and workpeople in preventing accidents. *Repr.* Employers, workpeople. *Ref.* Cmd. 340, pp. iv, 16. *Intended to be Permanent.*

(Similar Committees had been appointed in certain cases prior to the War ; but progress was stimulated by the War, with considerable further development afterwards (*see* Cmd. 941, p. 16), and the British Industrial Safety First Association, formed in 1918, in which H.O. and other Government Departments were represented (*see* Cmd. 340, p. xv), was one result of the movement.)

SHALE INDUSTRY, MINES COMMITTEES.—*See* M.M.

SHIPYARD, TONNAGE OUTPUT, COMMITTEES.—*App.* in various shipyards during War at instance of H.O. and M.M. *Obj.* To secure co-operation of management and workpeople in increasing output. *Repr.* Management, workpeople. *Ref.* Cmd. 340, p. 26.

SHOPS COMMITTEE.—*App.* by H.O., Mar. 1915, *Obj.* To consider best conditions for securing enlistment and employment of men on national work, without unduly interfering with retail trades. *Repr.* Parliament, H.O., B.T., distributive traders, manufacturers, Labour, women. *Ref.* Cd. 8113. *Diss.* Oct. 1915.

(The Committee were assisted by a Sub-Committee of Shopkeepers, and other Sub-Committees discussed matters with employers in the chief distributive trades in Liverpool.)

SILVERTOWN EXPLOSION COMMITTEE.—*App.* by H.O., Jan. 1917. *Obj.* To inquire into explosion, resulting in serious loss of life, at chemical works in Silvertown. *Repr.* H.O. and others. *Ref.* T., 24th Jan. 1917, p. 9. *Diss.* Later in 1917.

SOCIAL STUDIES, JOINT UNIVERSITIES COUNCIL.—*App.* by a number of Universities, June 1918. *Obj.* To prepare schemes of theoretical and practical study for social workers and continuation school teachers. *Repr.* The Universities. *Ref.* Cmd. 340, p. 47. Apparently *Permanent* (*see* Cmd. 1403, p. 81).

SOCIAL WORKERS, TRAINING UNIVERSITY COMMITTEE.—*App.* jointly, at instigation of H.O., in 1917 by Universities and others. *Obj.* To investigate principles of training social workers. *Repr.* Universities, B.E., L.E.A.'s, H.O. *Ref.* Cmd. 340, p. 46. *Diss.* About the end of 1917.

SPECIAL CONSTABULARY, METROPOLITAN, DISCIPLINE BOARD. —*App.* by Head-quarters Organization of Constabulary in 1914. *Obj.* To investigate and advise upon disciplinary cases. *Repr.* Legal Profession and others. *Ref.* Cmd. 536, p. 3. *Diss.* At or after Armistice or somewhat later.

STATE MANAGEMENT DISTRICTS CENTRAL COUNCIL.—*App.* jointly by H.O. and S.O. in 1921. *Obj.* To advise the two Departments, on central administration of liquor traffic in districts under direct state control, taken over from L.C.B. *Repr.* H.O., S.O., former members of L.C.B., Brewers, Caterers, &c. *Ref.* H.C. No. 20 (Session 2), 1922. *Still in existence end 1922.*

SUBSTITUTION, LOCAL, COMMITTEES.—*App.* by H.O. from Sept. 1916. *Obj.* To carry out locally Government Substitution Scheme to secure unfit and over-age men or women to release fit men for military service. *Repr.* The Government, Military Authorities, Employers, Labour. *Ref.* Cole, pp. 178–9 ; L.Y.B., 1919, p. 36. *Diss.* Apparently replaced by, or absorbed into, Committees and general organizations of M.N.S. (q.v.).

SUBSTITUTION, TRADE CONFERENCES.—*App.* from time to time in non-munitions trades at instigation of H.O., from about June, 1915. *Obj.* To negotiate agreements for substitution of women for enlisted men in those trades. *Repr.* H.O., employers, T.U.'s. *Ref.* Cd. 8276.

SUBSTITUTION, WALSALL LEATHER EQUIPMENT TRADES COMMITTEE.—*App.* in 1915 by Conference of Employers. *Obj.* To consider provision and training of women substitutes. *Repr.* H.O., employers, T.U.'s. *Ref.* Cd. 8276.

(A former Leather Preparation School was re-opened by the Employers' Association, and put under the charge of a Joint School Committee.)

SUMMER TIME COMMITTEE.—*App.* by H.O., Sept. 1916. *Obj.* To inquire into social and economic effects of, and report generally upon, Summer Time Act. *Repr.* Parliament, H.O., agriculture, employers, Labour, women. *Ref.* Cd. 8487. *Diss.* Feb. 1917.

TIMBER.—*See* Pit Timber, Pitwood.

TIME COMMITTEE.—*App.* by H.O., Sept. 1919. *Obj.* To report on adoption in U.K. for public purposes of ' 24 ' method of expressing time. *Repr.* Parliament, H.O., Adm., B.T., Railways, business men, Labour. *Ref.* T., 26th Sept. 1919, p. 10. *Diss.* Apparently early 1920.

TRADING WITH THE ENEMY DEPARTMENT.—Merged into Foreign Trade Department, in 1916. *See* F.O.

TWO-SHIFT SYSTEM DEPARTMENTAL COMMITTEE.—*App.* by H.O., Aug. 1920. *Obj.* To report upon amendment of Factory Acts to permit employment of women and young persons on this system and suggest suitable arrangements. *Repr.* Parliament, H.O., M.L., Employers, T.U.'s (including Women's Unions), Legal Profession, Lady Doctors. *Ref.* Cmd. 1037. *Diss.* Nov. 1920.

WAR CHARITIES COMMITTEE.—*App.* by H.O., April 1916. *Obj.* To consider representations made regarding War charities and advise on control and supervision in public interest. *Repr.* Parliament, H.O., L.G.B., L.G.B.(Sc.), experts in charitable work, Labour, women. *Ref.* Cd. 8287. *Diss.* June 1916.

(The Charities (Control) Committee (next entry) appears to have resulted from the report, which also recommended establishment of representative Committees to organize individual charities.)

WAR CHARITIES (CONTROL) COMMITTEE.—*App.* by H.O. in 1916. *Obj.* To exercise, under Charity Commissioners, control over War charities recommended by War Charities Committee (q.v.). *Repr.* As with War Charities Committee. *Ref.* Cd. 8741.

WELFARE AND WELFARE WORKERS COMMITTEE.—*App.* by Second Representative Conference organized by H.O. on Training of Welfare Supervisors, July 1920 (first Conference June 1917). *Obj.* To report on such training and on welfare work generally. *Repr.* The Conference (which included representatives of H.O., Universities, Welfare Workers' Associations, Employers, Labour). *Ref.* Cmd. 1403, p. 84 ; H.M.S.O., 1920. *Diss.* Before end of 1920.

WELFARE WORKERS TRAINING SUB-COMMITTEE.—*App.* by Joint University Council for Social Studies (*see under* Social Workers above) late in 1920. *Obj.* To investigate training of welfare workers. *Repr.* As with the Council. *Ref.* Cmd. 1403, p. 84. *Diss.* Not before 1921.

WOMEN POLICE.—*See* Police, Employment of Women.

WOMEN'S EMPLOYMENT.—Joint appointment. *See* B.T., *under* Women's War Employment (Industrial) Central Committee.

WORKMEN'S COMPENSATION DEPARTMENTAL COMMITTEE.— *App.* by H.O., May 1919. *Obj.* To inquire into working of Compensation and question of State System of Accident Insurance. *Repr.* Parliament,

H.O., Tre., N.H.I.C., Actuaries, Legal and Medical Professions, Labour. *Ref.* Cmd. 816. *Diss.* July 1920.

WORKMEN'S COMPENSATION, DISABLED SOLDIERS AND SAILORS, INTER-DEPARTMENTAL COMMITTEE.—*App.* by H.O., at suggestion of M.L. and M.Pen., Mar. 1918. *Obj.* To report upon special provision for disabled men in respect of Workmen's Compensation. *Repr.* Parliament, H.O., M.L., M.Pen., Tre., Insurance Companies. *Ref.* Cmd. 49. *Diss.* April 1918.

INDIA OFFICE AND GOVERNMENT OF INDIA

ABBREVIATIONS

In.O. = India Office.
G.I. = Government of India.
I.C.S. = Indian Civil Service.

ARMY IN INDIA COMMITTEE.—*App.* by In.O., Nov. 1919. *Obj.* To report upon administration and organization with special reference to post-war conditions. *Repr.* Parliament, I.C.S., Military Officers in India, prominent Indians. *Ref.* Cmd. 943.

BENGAL DETENUS COMMITTEE.—*App.* by Government of Bengal in 1918. *Obj.* To report on the behaviour of detenus and internees as affecting safety and defence of India. *Repr.* British Judge of Indian High Court, prominent Indians. *Ref.* Cd. 9198. *Diss.* Aug. 1918.

COTTON CONTRACTS AT BOMBAY COMMITTEE.—*App.* by Government of Bombay, about June 1918. *Obj.* To establish Clearing House on Liverpool model and license brokers. *Repr.* Cotton merchants, &c. *Ref.* B.T.J., 11th July 1918.

COTTON, INDIAN, COMMITTEE.—*App.* by G.I., Sept. 1917. *Obj.* To consider results of attempts to introduce long-stapled cotton into India, and possibilities of future developments, and make detailed study of local conditions. *Repr.* G.I., British Cotton Growing Association, millowners, Indian agriculture, agricultural research, professional engineers. *Ref.* Cmd. 523, p. 36.

CURRENCY.—*See* Exchange and Currency.

DISABLED OFFICERS EMPLOYMENT COMMITTEE.—*App.* jointly by In.O. and C.O. in latter half of 1917. *Obj.* To assist disabled officers wanting employment in India, Burma, Malay States, and Eastern Colonies. *Repr.* The two Departments. *Ref.* Cd. 8916, p. 20.

EXCHANGE AND CURRENCY, INDIAN, COMMITTEE.—*App.* by In.O., May 1919. *Obj.* To examine effects of War on Indian exchange and currency and report on future policy. *Repr.* G.I., Tre., banking, finance and commerce (English and Indian), prominent Indians. *Ref.* Cmd. 527. *Diss.* Dec. 1919.

FISCAL, INDIAN, COMMISSION.—*App.* by G.I., Oct. 1921. *Obj.* To report generally on fiscal policy of G.I., including Imperial Preference. *Repr.* In.O., Government of Bombay, I.C.S., Indian Judges, British, Indian and Burmese business men, economists, prominent Indians. *Ref.* Cmd. 1794. *Diss.* July 1922.

(The subject had been much discussed for some time, *see* pp. 1–5 of Cmd. 1794.)

FORESTRY EDUCATION.—*See* Cabinet.

GOVERNMENT SYSTEM, INDIAN, INQUIRY COMMITTEE.—*App.* by G.I., Sept. 1919. *Obj.* To examine generally allocation and conduct of business, and recruiting, of civil departments in India. *Repr.* Home and Indian Civil Service, Anglo-Indians, Indian Judges. *Ref.* T., 12th Sept. 1919.

GRAVES, INDIAN.—*See* W.O.

HIDES, BUYING, INDIA COMMITTEE.—*App.* by G.I. in or before 1917. *Obj.* To buy hides in India for British Government. *Repr.* Buying agents in Calcutta. *Ref.* T., 6th Dec. 1917, p. 13.

HOME ADMINISTRATION, INDIA, COMMITTEE.—*App.* by In.O., Mar. 1919. *Obj.* To report upon organization of India Office and relations of Secretary of State to Government of India and generally on questions of Indian home administration. *Repr.* Government, Parliament, In.O., C.O., Council of India (including native members), Indian Princes, public men with administrative or Indian experience, Labour. *Ref.* Cmd. 207. *Diss.* June 1919.

HUNTER COMMITTEE.—*See* Punjab, &c., Disturbances.

INDIAN MUNITIONS BOARD.—*App.* by G.I. in or before 1915. *Obj.* To organize Indian resources for the armies in the East, and develop generally Indian manufacturing power, and brought under M.M. and apparently re-organized later to organize general output of war material in India and deal with questions of priority. *Repr.* Manufacturers and others. *Ref.* Cd. 9005, pp. 78, 154. *Diss.* After Dec. 1919.

INDUSTRIAL DEVELOPMENT COMMISSION, INDIA.—*App.* by G.I., May 1916. *Obj.* To report upon possibilities of further industrial development, including employment of Indian capital, and methods of Government assistance. *Repr.* G.I., Chambers of Commerce, Indian firms and English firms in India, other public men (English and Indian). *Ref.* Cmd. 51. *Diss.* During 1918.

LIQUOR SHOPS LOCAL ADVISORY COMMITTEES.—*App.* by provincial or municipal authorities in India, presumably under orders of Central Government, during War. *Obj.* To advise on numbers and location of liquor shops in their areas. *Repr.* Included official and non-official members. *Ref.* Cmd. 1535.

   (These Committees appear to have originated during the War, the earliest appointments being in the year 1914–15.)

MEDICAL SERVICES, INDIAN, COMMITTEE.—*App.* by G.I., April 1919. *Obj.* To report on re-organization of services, both civil and military. *Repr.* G.I., In.O., I.C.S., Indian Army. *Diss.* April 1919.

MISSIONS IN INDIA (ALIENS), INTER-DEPARTMENTAL CONFERENCE.—*App.* jointly by In.O., F.O., and C.O., in 1917. *Obj.* To consider conditions under which aliens may conduct missionary or educational work after the War. *Repr.* The three Departments. *Ref.* Cd. 8916.

OVERSEAS EMPLOYMENT COMMITTEE.—Joint Appointment, *see* C.O.

PRESS ACTS, INDIA, COMMITTEE.—*App.* by G.I., Mar. 1921. *Obj.* To report upon retention, &c. of Acts restricting press in India to prevent sedition. *Repr.* G.I. prominent Indians (non-official). *Ref.* Cmd. 1489. *Diss.* Later in 1921.

PUBLIC WORKS COMMITTEE.—*App.* by G.I., Dec. 1916. *Obj.* To consider modernization of Indian Public Works Department. *Repr.* I.C.S., The Department, L.G.B., L.C.C. *Ref.* B.T.J., 21st Dec. 1916.

PUNJAB, &c. DISTURBANCES COMMITTEE (HUNTER COM-MITTEE).—*App.* by G.I., Oct. 1919. *Obj.* To investigate recent disturbances in Punjab, Delhi, and Bombay and measures taken to deal with them. *Repr.* Judges (English and Indian), G.I., Indian Army, prominent Indians (Legislative Council and Legal Profession). *Ref.* Cmd. 681. *Diss.* Mar. 1920.

RAILWAYS, INDIAN, COMMITTEE.—*App.* by In.O., Nov. 1920. *Obj.* To investigate administration and working of Indian Railways. *Repr.* G.I., Indian and English Railways, Indian Commerce, British commercial interests in India, Banking, general Indian interests. *Ref.* Cmd. 1512. *Diss.* Aug. 1921.

RETRENCHMENT, INDIAN, COMMITTEE.—*App.* by G.I. in or before 1922. *Obj.* To recommend reductions in expenditure of G.I., in light of financial position. *Repr.* Prominent Englishmen (business men, &c.) and Indians. *Ref.* Report of Committee for 1922–3 (H.M.S.O., 1923).

RUBBER RESEARCH.—*See* S.I.R.

SEDITION COMMITTEE.—*App.* By G.I., Dec. 1917. *Obj.* To investigate criminal conspiracies connected with revolutionary risings in India, and advise as to legislation. *Repr.* G.I., British and Indian Judges, I.C.S. *Ref.* Cd. 9190. *Diss.* April 1918.

STORES, INDIAN, COMMITTEE.—*App.* by Indian Munitions Board, Dec. 1919. *Obj.* To devise scheme for purchase of stores in India. *Repr.* In.O., Indian Railway Board, Indian Army, Railways and Public Works, Business Men and Experts, British and Indian. *Ref.* B.T.J., 22nd Jan. 1920, pp. 114–15.

TRADE, INDIAN, COMMISSION.—*App.* by G.I. early in the War, and revived, after falling into abeyance, on more permanent basis, July 1917. *Obj.* To assist in finding markets in U.K. and elsewhere for Indian products to make good war losses of markets, help export trade generally and organize purchase of machinery abroad. *Repr.* G.I., I.C.S., business men, &c. *Ref.* T., 25th July 1917, p. 11.

INFORMATION, DEPARTMENT AND (LATER) MINISTRY OF

The Department of Information was formed in Feb. 1917 to provide a more complete organization for supplying information on the causes of, and necessary organization for, the War, and to co-ordinate and extend the work of existing departments, being responsible partly to the Prime Minister and partly to the Foreign Office. *The Ministry* was established under Lord Beaverbrook in March, 1918. It was responsible for the publicity work in the Dominions and in Allied and Neutral Countries, and worked in close touch with the Committees (*see* below) dealing with publicity in Great Britain (National War Arms Committee) and in enemy countries (Crewe House Committee). The Ministry also undertook the organization of hospitality and entertainment for American troops in Great Britain. The Ministry was brought to a close at the end of 1918, its remaining functions being transferred to other Departments, chiefly the Foreign Office (News Department). *See* Cmd. 325, pp. 34–6.

ABBREVIATION
M.I.=Department and Ministry of Information.

AMERICAN TROOPS, LOCAL HOSPITALITY SUB-COMMITTEES.— *App.* in the chief towns of U.K., at instance of M.I., in 1918. *Obj.* To organize locally hospitality and entertainment for American troops in this country. *Repr.* Local public men, &c. *Ref.* Cmd. 325, p. 36.

BRITISH WAR MISSION.—*App.* by M.I. in spring of 1917. *Obj.* To visit U.S.A. for propaganda purposes connected with their participation in the War. *Repr.* Prominent public men. *Ref.* H.C. No. 116, 1920, p. 46.

COMMERCIAL PROPAGANDA, BUREAU OF INFORMATION, MADRID.—*App.* by M.I., May 1918. *Obj.* To assist commercial propaganda in Spain. *Repr.* Not stated. *Ref.* H.C. No. 231, 1920, p. xi. *Diss.* Nov. 1918.

CREWE HOUSE COMMITTEE.—*App.* by the Government under the Chairmanship of Lord Northcliffe in 1917 or earlier, and subsequently worked in close connexion with M.I. *Obj.* To organize work of publicity in enemy countries. *Repr.* Newspaper owners, journalists, &c. *Ref.* Cmd. 325, p. 35.

INFORMATION ADVISORY COMMITTEE.—*App.* by the Government, Dec. 1916. *Obj.* To advise Information Department and later M.I. *Repr.* Leading newspaper owners and journalists. *Ref.* H.C. No. 132, 1918, p. 59.

INFORMATION, HOME OFFICE, BUREAU.—*App.* by H.O. in 1916, or earlier, and absorbed into M.I. in 1917. *Obj.* To organize information and propaganda. *Repr.* Not stated. *Ref.* H.C. No. 132, 1918, p. 59.

PUBLICITY IN ENEMY COUNTRIES.—*See* Crewe House Committee.

WAR AIMS, NATIONAL, COMMITTEE.—*App.* privately in June 1917, taken over later in the year by War Cabinet and subsequently worked in close connexion with M.I. *Obj.* To organize propaganda relating to British War Aims in U.K. *Repr.* Prominent public men, the Press. *Ref.* H.C. No. 132, 1918, p. 36 ; Cmd. 325, p. 35.

WAR PROPAGANDA BUREAU.—*App.* by the Government apparently in 1916 or earlier. *Obj.* To organize propaganda. *Repr.* Not stated. *Ref.* H.C. No. 132, 1918, p. 59. *Diss.* Absorbed into general organization of M.I. in 1917.

IRISH OFFICE

BELFAST PRISONS, SPECIAL COMMISSION.—*App.* by C.S. under Special Commission (Belfast Prisons) Act, about Nov. 1918. *Obj.* To inquire into complaints of ill-treatment of Sinn Fein prisoners. *Repr.* Judges. *Ref.* Cmd. 83. *Diss.* Feb. 1919.

COMPENSATION (IRELAND) COMMISSION.—*App.* by L.L., May 1922. *Obj.* To fix, after investigation, fair compensation for destruction, &c. of property in Ireland between Jan. 1919 and July 1921 (including military destruction under martial law). *Repr.* Judges, Board of Inland Revenue, &c. *Ref.* Cmd. 1654. *Still in existence end 1922.*

FOOD CONTROL, IRELAND.—*See* M.F.

IRISH COAL INDUSTRY COMMITTEE.—*App.* by C.S., May 1919. *Obj.* To conduct general inquiry into Irish Coal Industry. *Repr.* Judge (Chairman), employers, workpeople. *Ref.* Cmd. 650. *Diss.* Feb. 1920.

IRISH REBELLION (VICTIMS) COMMITTEE.—*App.* in 1916. *See* Cd. 8741, p. 8. No details given.

MIDWIVES.—*See* L.G.B.(I.) and P.C.

NURSING.—*See* L.G.B.(I.).

POLICE FORCES FEDERATION, IRELAND.—*App.* by L.L. under Constabulary and Police (Ireland) Act, about end of 1919. *Obj. Repr.* Much as with English Police (*see* H.O.), both Royal Irish Constabulary, and Dublin Metropolitan Police being represented. *Ref.* P.G.A., 1919. *Permanent Body.*

POLICE FORCES, IRISH, VICE-REGAL COMMISSION.—*App.* by L.L., Oct. 1919. *Obj.* To report upon re-organization in connexion with proposals of Desborough Committee (*see* H.O.). *Repr.* I.O., Tre., Irish Judges, English and Irish Police. *Ref.* Cmd. 603. *Diss.* Dec. 1919.

PROPERTY LOSSES (IRELAND) COMMITTEE.—*App.* prior to Sept. 1917. *Ref.* without details, Cd. 8741, p. 9.

PUBLIC HEALTH COUNCIL, IRELAND.—*App.* by C.S., presumably attached to L.G.B.(I.). *See* L.G.B.(I.).

RAILWAY EXECUTIVE COMMITTEE, IRELAND.—*App.* by the Government, at beginning of 1917, on taking control of Irish railways. *Obj.* To exercise control of Irish railways on behalf of the Government. *Repr.* General managers of the railways. *Ref.* H.C. No. 136, 1918, p. 4. *Diss.* End of 1919.

RECRUITING, CENTRAL, COMMITTEE, IRELAND.—*App.* apparently by L.L. early in War. *Obj.* To organize and stimulate recruiting throughout

Ireland. *Repr.* Not stated. *Ref.* Cd. 8168. *Diss.* Organization of recruiting was taken over by Recruiting Department, Oct. 1915, but Committee continued in existence for other purposes.

RECRUITING LOCAL COMMITTEES.—*App.* under Central Committee, early in the War. *Obj.* To supervise and stimulate recruiting in their localities. *Repr.* Not stated. *Ref.* Cd. 8168.

REPRESENTATION.—*See* Parliament.

LABOUR, MINISTRY OF

The Ministry of Labour was established in Dec. 1916, under a Minister and Parliamentary Secretary, by the New Ministries and Secretaries Act, 1916 (6 and 7 Geo. V, c. 68), and definitely commenced the exercise of its duties on 11th Jan. 1917. The *object* of the Ministry was to create a department to deal specifically with labour problems and to concentrate as far as possible the work of government relating to labour. The Act transferred to the Ministry the former powers of the Board of Trade in regard to Conciliation, Labour (later Employment) Exchanges, Trade Boards, Unemployment Insurance, and subsequently Labour Statistics, and under Part I of the Munitions of War Act, 1915. The Act also provided for the exercise by the Ministry of such powers of other Departments as might be transferred by Order-in-Council. The Ministry is established ' during His Majesty's pleasure '. *Reference* Public General Acts, 1916. It is a Permanent Department.

ABBREVIATIONS

M.L.	= Ministry of Labour.
J.I.C.(s)	= Joint Industrial Council(s).
L.E.C.(s)	= Local Advisory and (later) Employment Committee(s).
E.E.	= Labour and (later) Employment Exchanges.

ABERCONWAY COMMITTEE.—*See* Out-of-work Donation.

ADVISORY, CENTRAL, COMMITTEE, EMPLOYMENT EXCHANGES. —*See* Labour Resettlement Committee.

ADVISORY, LOCAL, COMMITTEES, EMPLOYMENT EXCHANGES.— *See* Employment, Local, Committees.

APPOINTMENTS DEPARTMENT.—*App.* by M.L., Mar. 1918, absorbing Professional and Business Register (q.v.) and Officers' Technical Training Courses of M.M. *Obj.* To advise and assist ex-officers and men of similar education on future careers, bring them into touch with employers and organize professional and business training. *Repr.* M.L., the staff consisting mainly of officers and ex-officers, with expert assistance and advice (*see also* Officers' Resettlement Advisory Committee, and Officers' University and Technical Training Committee below). *Ref.* L.G., May 1918, p. 175.

See also Business Men, District Directorates, Officers, Travelling Advisory Boards.

APPRENTICESHIPS, INTERRUPTED, SUB-COMMITTEE.—*App.* by Labour Resettlement Committee in or after Mar. 1918. *Obj.* To consider proposals for financial assistance towards completion of apprenticeships interrupted by war service. *Repr.* Much as with main Committee (q.v.). *Ref.* Cmd. 325, p. 276. *Diss.* Later in 1918.

APPRENTICESHIPS, INTERRUPTED, TRADE DRAFTING, &c., COMMITTEES.—Certain industries appointed special Committees early in 1919 to negotiate schemes with M.L., or to prepare draft schemes for consideration by J.I.C.'s. Information as to these is given in A.T.S. forms of M.L.

ARBITRATION, INTERIM COURT OF.—*App.* by M.L., Nov. 1918, under Wages (Temporary Regulation) Act, 1918. *Obj.* To form a central court of arbitration for settlement of disputes, taking over much of the work of the Committee on Production (*see* B.T.). *Repr.* Independent chairmen (public men), employers, workpeople, forming panels from which the Courts were selected. *Ref.* H.C. No. 221, 1921, pp. 5, 29, 31. *Diss.* Replaced by Industrial Court (*see* below) Nov. 1919.

ARMY EDUCATION TECHNICAL COMMITTEE.—*App.* by M.L., at request of W.O., early in 1919. *Obj.* To advise G.H.Q. in France on training of men in Army. *Repr.* M.L. and others. *Ref.* Cmd. 568, p. 7.

BUILDING LABOUR COMMITTEE.—*See* M.M.

BUILDING LABOUR EXECUTIVE COMMITTEE.—*App.* by M.L. in 1918. *Obj.* To co-ordinate executive work in connexion with Building Labour Committee. *Repr.* M.L. and Government Departments concerned. *Ref.* Cmd. 325, p. 161.

BUILDING TRADES ADVISORY COMMITTEE OF WORKMEN'S REPRESENTATIVES.—*App.* by M.L., Mar. 1917. *Obj.* To advise and assist the Employment Department, M.L. in working E.E. in these trades. *Repr.* Building T.U.'s. *Ref.* B.T.J., 15th Mar. 1917. *Diss.* Presumably superseded in May 1918 by J.I.C. for Building Trades.

(A similar Committee was formed somewhat later of Building Trades employers. Similar bodies were established in other important industries.)

BUILDING TRADES CENTRAL ADVISORY COMMITTEE (EMPLOYMENT AND INSURANCE DEPARTMENT).—*App.* by M.L., Jan. 1917. *Obj.* To advise the Department on matters affecting the industry in administration of E.E., and Unemployment Insurance. *Repr.* Employers' and Workmen's Associations (equal numbers) in Building Industry. *Ref.* Cd. 8741, p. 3, details supplied by M.L. *Diss.* May 1918, superseded by J.I.C. for Building Industry.

BUILDING.—*See also* M.H.

BUSINESS MEN'S COMMITTEE (APPOINTMENTS DEPARTMENT). —*App.* in connexion with London Directorate of the Department, Nov. 1919. *Obj.* To assist in placing ex-officers in professional and business work, and deal through small Committees with complaints. *Repr.* Prominent business men of various types. Panels were formed for Stock Exchange, Baltic, Banking, &c., for interview, &c., of candidates. *Ref.* T., 14th Nov. 1919, p. 19. (*See also* Professional and Business Men.)

CIVIL LIABILITIES—ADVISORY COMMITTEE ; DEPARTMENT ; LOCAL COMMISSIONERS.—Transferred to M.L. *See* L.G.B.

CIVIL SERVICE SELECTION BOARDS.—*App.* by M.L. from Sept. 1919 for each Government Department, on transfer of work of selection from C.S.C. *Obj.* To select men for appointment as temporary clerks. *Repr.* M.L., presumably C.S.C., and Government Departments concerned. *Ref.* Cmd. 887, p. xxx. (*See also* Ex-Service Men.)

CASUAL LABOUR.—*See* Port of London.

CIVIL SERVICE.—*See also under* Cost of Living, Whitley Council, Report.

COST OF LIVING COMMITTEE OF CIVIL SERVICE NATIONAL WHITLEY COUNCIL.—*App.* by the Council, Oct. 1919. *Obj.* To report upon effect of increased cost of living on salaries of civil servants. *Repr.* The Council. *Ref.* Cmd. 1107. *Diss.* May 1920.

COST OF LIVING, IRISH FREE STATE, AND NORTHERN IRELAND DEPARTMENT, DEPARTMENTAL COMMITTEES.—*App.* by I.F.S. and Northern Governments in June and Sept. 1922, respectively. *Obj.* To determine increase between 1914 and 1922 (I.F.S.) ; to consider differences in cost of living compared with G.B. (Northern). *Repr.* Government Departments concerned. *Ref.* L.G., Sept. 1922, p. 364. *Diss.* About end 1922 (I.F.S.), Oct. 1923 (Northern).

COST OF LIVING JOINT (LABOUR) COMMITTEE.—*App.* jointly by chief Labour Organizations in the country. *See* L.G., 1920, p. 541, 1921, pp. 68–9, 392, 664.

DEMOBILIZATION AND RESETTLEMENT, CIVIL, DEPARTMENT. *App.* by the Government, Nov. 1918, and responsible to M.L., absorbing Labour Departments of Adm. and M.M. *Obj.* To deal with all questions of re-employment and resettlement of fighting forces and civil war workers. *Repr.* M.L., M.M., with official and expert staffs. *Ref.* L.G., Nov. 1918, Cmd. 325, pp. 278–9 (a good account). *Diss.* During 1919.
(*See also* Labour Resettlement Committee, and W.O.)

DISABLED AND OTHER EX-SERVICE MEN, EMPLOYMENT IN GOVERNMENT DEPARTMENTS, COMMITTEE.—*App.* by M.L. under instructions of War Cabinet, June 1919. *Obj.* To inquire into possibilities of increased employment of disabled men and of substituting ex-service men for temporary women clerks. *Repr.* Not stated. *Ref.* L.G., July 1919.

DISABLED MEN, JOINT EMPLOYMENT SUB-COMMITTEE.—*App.*, *Obj.* and *Repr.* in each L.E.C. district, as with Ex-Service Men, Joint Employment Sub-Committees, but limited to disabled men and set up by Mar. 1918. *Ref.* Cmd. 14, p. 54. *Diss.* They may have been absorbed later into Ex-Service Men, Joint Employment Sub-Committees (q.v.).
(*See also under* Labour Resettlement Committee, Wages Advisory Boards.)

DISTRICT DIRECTORATES' (APPOINTMENTS DEPARTMENT) ADVISORY PANELS.—*App.* by Appointments Department to each District Directorate in winter of 1918–19. *Obj.* To advise Directorate, and to interview and advise ex-officers requiring appointments. *Repr.* Prominent business men and other experts. *Ref.* Reconstruction Pamphlet, No. 12 (Resettlement of Officers) issued by M.R.

DISTRICT DIRECTORATES' (APPOINTMENTS DEPARTMENT) TECHNICAL SUB-COMMITTEES.—*App.* by Appointments Department for various professions and industries in each Directorate in winter of 1918–19, special naval advisers being also appointed to look after interests of naval men (*see* T., 8th Sept. 1919, p. 7). *Obj.* Much as with Advisory Panels (q.v.). *Repr.* Prominent men in profession or industry concerned. *Ref.* As with Advisory Panels.

DIVISIONAL COUNCILS, MINISTRY OF LABOUR.—*App.* by M.L., in 1918, for the nine administrative Divisions of U.K. *Obj.* To act as general advisory bodies and to co-ordinate work of L.E.C.'s in their areas. *Repr.* M.L., L.E.C.'s. *Ref.* Cmd. 325, p. 279. *Permanent Bodies.*

DOMESTIC SERVICE INQUIRY COMMITTEE.—*App.* by M.L., April 1923. *Obj.* To inquire into conditions (including Unemployment Insurance) affecting supply of domestic servants. *Repr.* Women of various experience, including politics, T.U.'s, social service, &c. *Ref.* H.M.S.O., 1923. *Diss.* Oct. 1923.

EMPLOYMENT.—*See under* Demobilization, Disabled, Ex-Service, Local Employment, &c.

EMPLOYMENT EXCHANGES, ACCOMMODATION, JOINT COMMITTEE.—Apparently appointed before establishment of M.L. *See* B.T.

EMPLOYMENT EXCHANGES INQUIRY COMMITTEE.—*App.* by M.L., June 1920. *Obj.* To examine working and administration and advise as to their future. *Repr.* Parliament, M.L., L.E.C.'s, employers, T.U.'s, economists, women. *Ref.* Cmd. 1040. *Diss.* Nov. 1920.

EMPLOYMENT EXCHANGES, NORTHERN IRELAND.—*See under* Unemployment Insurance.

EMPLOYMENT, LOCAL, COMMITTEES.—*App.* by M.L., in 1917, as Local Advisory Committees, the title being altered later. *Obj.* To advise and assist E.E.'s on demobilization and resettlement problems and on their general work. *Repr.* Local employers and T.U.'s with appointed members with special experience in labour matters. *Ref.* Cd. 9005, p. 104. *Permanent Bodies.*

(*See also under* Labour Resettlement Committee, Women.)

ENGINEERING AND SHIPBUILDING TRADES CENTRAL ADVISORY COMMITTEES (EMPLOYERS), (OPERATIVES).—*App.* July 1917. *Obj.*, *Repr.* As with similar Building Trades Committee (*see* above). *Ref.* T., 15th Aug. 1917, p. 3.

EX-SERVICE MEN'S BRANCH.—*App.* by M.L. in 1918. *Obj.* To look after interests of ex-service men in regard to employment. *Repr.* Largely staffed by ex-service men. *Ref.* Cmd. 325, p. 270.

EX-SERVICE MEN, CENTRAL SELECTION BOARD.—*App.* by M.L., apparently after Armistice. *Obj.* To select ex-service applicants for appointment in the Civil Service generally. *Repr.* Not stated. *Ref.* Lytton Committee 1st Interim Report, p. 5 (H.M.S.O. 1920).

(*See also* Civil Service Selection Boards.)

EX-SERVICE MEN'S EMPLOYMENT EXCHANGE.—Established at Catherine St., Strand, in 1918. *See* Cmd. 325, p. 270.

EX-SERVICE MEN, JOINT EMPLOYMENT SUB-COMMITTEES.—*App.* jointly by L.E.C.'s and W.P.C.'s in and after 1918. *Obj.* To deal jointly with all questions of employment of ex-service men in their areas. *Repr.* The appointing Committees. *Ref.* Cmd. 325, p. 270.

EX-SERVICE MEN, RE-EMPLOYMENT COMMITTEE.—*App.* by M.L., Mar. 1920. *Obj.* To report on best means of facilitating re-employment of ex-service men. *Repr.* M.L., employers, T.U.'s, Ex-service Men's Organizations. *Ref.* Cmd. 951.

EX-SERVICE MEN.—*See also under* Apprenticeships, Civil Service Selection Board, Disabled, Substitution.

EX-SERVICE STUDENTS (SCOTLAND) COMMITTEE.—*See* S.E.D.

HEALTH AND UNEMPLOYMENT INSURANCE DEPARTMENTAL COMMITTEE.—*App.* jointly by M.L. and M.H., Jan. 1922. *Obj.* To investigate relations of Health and Unemployment schemes, and possibility of economies in administration by modifications and amalgamation. *Repr.* M.L., M.H., S.B.H., Tre., Government Actuary's Department. *Ref.* Cmd. 1644. Still sitting at end of 1922.

HOURS.—*See* Production, Working Hours.

HOUSES.—*See* Steel Houses.

INCREASED PRODUCTION IN INDUSTRY COMMITTEE.—*App.* by the Government, in connexion with M.L., April 1920. *Obj.* To advise on means of securing maximum production, consistent with welfare of all concerned in industry. *Repr.* M.L., employers, T.U.'s, business Men. *Ref.* L.G., Apr. 1920, p. 168.

INDUSTRIAL COUNCILS, DISTRICT.—*App.* provided for in scheme for J.I.C.'s (*see* below), and established in some instances from mid. 1917. *Obj.* To form district organization for joint consideration by employers and workpeople of problems of their industries. *Repr.* Associations of Employers and Workpeople in the districts. *Ref.* Cd. 9002. *Intended to be Permanent.*

INDUSTRIAL COURT, STANDING.—*App.* by M.L., about end of 1919 under Industrial Courts Act, 1919, replacing Interim Court of Arbitration (q.v.). *Obj.* To deal with existing or apprehended disputes on reference by M.L., with consent of parties concerned. *Repr.* Employers, workpeople, women, with independent chairmen. *Ref.* H.C. No. 221, 1921, pp. 16–17, 30. *Intended to be Permanent.*

(The Court formed a Board of Arbitration, with three panels of Chairmen (independent), employers and workpeople, from whom Boards were chosen to deal with particular disputes. (For lists of panels *see* L.G., Mar. 1920, p. 154.)

INQUIRY, COURTS OF.—*App.* by M.L., as required, under Industrial Courts Act, 1919. *Obj.* To inquire into causes of existing or apprehended disputes, and report to M.L., to inform public opinion on questions at issue. *Repr.* Either Chairman and other persons appointed by M.L., or a single person, at discretion of M.L. *Ref.* P.G.A., 1919 (9 and 10 Geo. V, c. 69, Part II). *Diss.* On close of each inquiry.

(The Transport Workers' Court is dealt with below. Other Courts are dealt with in Cmd. 710 (Coal Tippers, &c.), Cmd. 790, Cmd. 1653 (Engineering Industry), and H.C. No. 37, 1921 (Tramways).)

INTERIM INDUSTRIAL RECONSTRUCTION COMMITTEES.—Transferred to M.L. *See* M.R.

INTERNATIONAL LABOUR ORGANIZATION STANDING INTER-DEPARTMENTAL COMMITTEE.—*App.* by M.L. early in 1921. *Obj.*

To deal under M.L. with international labour questions, and assist M.L. in organization of business connected with International Labour Organization at Geneva. *Repr.* M.L., B.T., H.O., C.O., F.O., S.O., Tre., International Labour Office (British representatives). *Ref.* L.G., Feb. 1921, p. 72. *Standing Body.*

IRISH DEPARTMENT.—*App.* by M.L. about Mar. 1919. *Obj.* To improve work of M.L. in Ireland, being responsible for branches which can be dealt with locally. *Repr.* Official and expert. *Ref.* L.G., Mar. 1919. *Diss.* Transferred to I.F.S., 1922.

JOINT INDUSTRIAL COUNCILS.—*App.* by industries concerned, on invitation of M.L., from middle of 1917. *Obj.* To establish a permanent organization for joint consideration by employers and workpeople of problems affecting their industries. *Repr.* Associations of Employers and Workpeople in the industry. *Ref.* Cd. 9231. *Diss.* Intended to be permanent bodies.

(Various Sub-Committees have been appointed for particular purposes or investigations : *see*, for instance, Cmd. 325, pp. 150–1, 941, pp. 108–10.)

JOINT INDUSTRIAL COUNCILS ; PROVISIONAL DRAFTING COMMITTEES.—These were appointed by the Employers and Workpeople's Associations concerned to draft constitutions for J.I.C.'s. *See* Cd. 9231.

KING'S ROLL LOCAL COMMITTEES.—*App.* by M.L., under Government decision, Jan. 1923, sometimes as Sub-Committees of L.E.C.'s. *Obj.* To carry out local efforts to secure through King's Roll employment of disabled men. *Repr.* L.E.C.'s, L.A.'s, and other local men. *Ref.* Cmd. 1919, p. 3. Apparently still in existence.

KING'S ROLL NATIONAL COUNCIL.—*App.* by the Government on recommendation of Select Committee on Disabled Men (*see* Parliament), Feb. 1923, to work under M.L. *Obj.* To co-ordinate work of Local Committees (q.v.) in connexion with King's Roll. *Repr.* Parliament, M.L., M.H., M.Pen., the Army, employers, Employers' Organizations, British Legion. *Ref.* Cmd. 1919. Apparently still in existence.

LABOUR ' EMBARGOES '.—*See* M.M.

LABOUR RESETTLEMENT COMMITTEE.—*App.* by M.L., Mar. 1918, having been under consideration during 1917. *Obj.* To advise generally on problems of demobilization and of discharge of civil war workers. *Repr.* Government Departments concerned, Associations of Employers and Workpeople in chief industries, including certain big general organizations of both, Women. *Ref.* Cmd. 325, p. 276 ; L.G., March 1918. *Diss.* After demobilization.

The main Committee appointed various Sub-Committees including Sub-Committees on Functions of Local Advisory (Employment) Committees in connexion with Demobilization, Apprenticeships interrupted by War Service, Unemployment Insurance, Employment of Disabled Men.

LONDON SHIPOWNERS AND TRANSPORT WORKERS' MILITARY SERVICE COMMITTEE.—*See* B.T., Port Labour Committees.

LYTTON COMMITTEE, LYTTON ENTRANTS COMMITTEE.—*See* Tre.

MINISTRY OF LABOUR COUNCIL.—*App.* by M.L. in 1918 or early 1919. *Obj.* To consider general questions of policy. *Repr.* Chief officials of Ministry. *Ref.* H.C. No. 238, 1919, p. 6. Presumably still in existence.

NAVAL ADVISERS.—*See under* District Directorates.

NIGHT WORK IN BAKERIES COMMITTEE.—*App.* by M.L., April 1919. *Obj.* To report upon the system in bread and flour confectionery trades, and on modification or abolition. *Repr.* Parliament, M.L., H.O., Legal Profession, Labour. *Ref.* Cmd. 246. *Diss.* July 1919.

OFFICERS' RESETTLEMENT LOCAL COMMITTEES.—*App.* by or through Appointments Department at provincial offices from April 1918. *Obj.* To advise locally in finding suitable employment for ex-officers and men of similar qualifications. *Repr.* Government Departments concerned, business and professional men, agriculturalists, ex-officers. *Ref.* L.G., May 1918, p. 175. *Diss.* Apparently absorbed into or replaced by organization of District Directorates early in 1919.

OFFICERS' RESETTLEMENT ADVISORY COMMITTEES, ENGLAND AND WALES, SCOTLAND.—*App.* by M.L. about April 1918. *Obj.* To advise M.L. on re-settlement of officers and men of similar standing during and after the War. *Repr.* Government Departments concerned, Employers' Associations, Chambers of Commerce, Professional Associations, Universities, Agriculture, Mercantile Marine, Ex-officers. *Ref.* Cd. 9231, p. 20 ; L.G., May 1918.

OFFICERS' UNIVERSITY AND TECHNICAL TRAINING INTER-DEPARTMENTAL COMMITTEES, ENGLAND AND WALES, SCOTLAND.—*App.* jointly by various Departments, July 1918, and absorbed later into Appointments Department, working in close touch with Officers' Resettlement Committees. *Obj.* To advise and assist in provision of education and training for ex-officers, &c. *Repr.* Government Departments concerned, Universities, Industrial, Commercial, Educational and Technical Organizations. *Ref.* L.G., May 1918; Cmd. 165, p. 35.

OFFICERS.—*See also* Professional and Business Men's Committees.

OUT-OF-WAR DONATION SCHEME COMMITTEE (ABERCONWAY COMMITTEE).—*App.* by M.L., May 1919. *Obj.* To inquire into working of scheme, including questions of abuse, &c., and suggest modifications. *Repr.* Parliament, M.L., N.H.I.C., Tre., Employers, Labour. *Ref.* Cmd. 196, 305. *Diss.* July 1919.

OVERSEAS EMPLOYMENT BRANCH.—*App.* by M.L. at end of 1919. *Obj.* To carry out work of M.L. in dealing with overseas employment, in co-operation with O.S.C. *Repr.* Official and expert. *Ref.* Cmd. 1134, p. 6. *Permanent.*

OVERSEAS EMPLOYMENT INTER-DEPARTMENTAL COMMITTEE. —*App.* jointly by M.L., O.S.C., and other Departments concerned, Oct. 1919. *Obj.* To direct and co-ordinate work of M.L. in connexion with overseas employment (imperial and foreign). *Repr.* M.L., O.S.C., In.O., O.T.D., *Ref.* Cmd. 573, p. 11 ; L.G., July 1920, p. 359. *Standing Body.*

OVERSEAS SETTLEMENT LOCAL INTERVIEWING COMMITTEES (MEN).—*App.* Rota Committees of L.E.C.'s were constituted for this purpose through M.L., in co-operation with C.O., about beginning of 1921. *Obj.* To interview male applicants who desire advice as to emigration. *Repr.* L.E.C.'s, with persons interested in emigration. *Ref.* Cmd. 1134, p. 6. Apparently *Permanent.*

OVERSEAS SETTLEMENT LOCAL INTERVIEWING COMMITTEES (WOMEN).—*App.* jointly by M.L. and O.S.C., in 266 provincial centres in 1920. *Obj.* As with Men's Committees. *Repr.* Women's Sub-Committees of L.E.C.'s, Women's Emigration Societies' Joint Council (*see* C.O.). *Ref.* Cmd. 1134, p. 11 ; L.G., July 1920, p. 259. Apparently *Permanent.*

OVERSEAS SETTLEMENT.—*See also* C.O.

PORT LABOUR CENTRAL ADVISORY (DEMOBILIZATION) COMMITTEE.—*App.* by M.L., Nov. 1918. *Obj.* To advise generally on Labour problems of demobilization at ports, allocate 'pivotal' men (released in advance from the Army) and co-ordinate work of local Port Labour Committees. *Repr.* M.L., M.S., Adm., B.T., Port and Transit Executive Committee, shipowners, port employers, Labour. *Ref.* T., 2nd Dec. 1918, p. 3 ; B.T.J., 5th Dec. 1918, p. 728.

PORT LABOUR COMMITTEES.—*See* B.T.

PORT OF LONDON CASUAL LABOUR (ROCHE) COMMITTEE.—*App.* by M.L., Jan. 1919. *Obj.* To report on best means of regulating and reducing casual labour in Port of London, and of preventing undue influx of unemployed, during demobilization. *Repr.* Legal Profession, Port of London Authorities, Port Employers, T.U.'s. *Ref.* B.T.J., 23rd Jan. 1919, p. 122.

PRE-WAR PRACTICES RESTORATION JOINT COMMITTEE.—*App.* jointly by Employers' Organizations and T.U.'s at Wages National Conference (q.v.), Nov. 1918. *Obj.* To consider draft of Bill to carry out Government pledges. *Repr.* Employers' Organizations, T.U.'s. *Ref.* H.C. No. 221, 1921, pp. 5, 23–4. *Diss.* Aug. 1919.

PRODUCTION AND WORKING HOURS, ENGINEERING AND SHIPBUILDING.—For Joint Investigating Committee appointed by the Industry *see* L.G., Nov. 1922, pp. 437–8.

PRODUCTION.—*See also* Increased Production, and B.T.

PROFESSIONAL AND BUSINESS MEN'S COMMITTEES.—*App.* by M.L. in the months following the Armistice, for chief professional and learned societies and in chief businesses. *Obj.* To assist in finding employment for ex-officers and men of like standard. *Repr.* The professions and businesses concerned. *Ref.* T., 4th April 1919, p. 12.

PROFESSIONAL AND BUSINESS REGISTER.—*App.* by B.T., May 1915 and subsequently transferred to M.L. *Obj.* Originally to secure professional engineers for munitions work, then to deal with all professional offers of service, including National Service Volunteers, and eventually took on duties connected with ex-officers. *Repr.* Official and expert. *Ref.* H.C. No. 132, 1918, p. 37. *Diss.* Apparently absorbed in Appointments Department. (*See also* Business Men.)

PROFESSIONAL WOMEN'S REGISTER.—*App.* as Women's War Register by B.T. in 1915, amalgamated in 1916 with Register of Federation of University Women and transferred to M.L. in 1917. *Obj.* To organize supply of educated women for war service. *Repr.* B.T., M.L. (later), The Federation, women generally. *Ref.* H.C. No. 132, 1918, p. 37.

PUBLIC ASSISTANCE COMMITTEE.—*App.* by P.M. early in 1923, and attached to M.L. *Obj.* To examine existing schemes of public assistance with view to fullest co-ordination. *Repr.* M.L., M.H., S.B.H., M.Pen. *Ref.* L.G., Feb. 1923, p. 42.

RAILWAY RECRUITING APPEAL COMMITTEE (1917).—*See* Cabinet.

RAILWAY WAGES BOARD, NATIONAL.—*See* M.T.

RE-ORGANIZATION, DEPARTMENTAL COMMITTEE.—*App.* by M.L. in 1919. *Obj.* To consider re-organization of M.L. on permanent basis. *Repr.* Chief Departments of M.L. *Ref.* H.C. No. 168, 1919, p. 8. *Diss.* Probably later in 1919.

RESETTLEMENT COMMITTEE, BUILDING TRADES JOINT INDUSTRIAL COUNCIL.—This Committee was appointed by the Council, presumably shortly before the Armistice, to take charge of the Council's work in post-war resettlement of Building Industry and represent it in negotiations with the Government. *See* L.G., especially Sept. 1920, p. 483.

RESETTLEMENT.—*See also* Demobilization and Resettlement, Labour Resettlement Committee.

SHAW AWARD.—*See* Transport Workers.

SHIPBUILDING, NATIONAL JOINT COMMITTEE.—*App.* by the industry in 1918 or earlier independently of Government action. *Obj.* To deal jointly with war and post-war problems. *Repr.* Employers, workpeople. *Ref.* Cmd. 325, p. 148.

STAFFS, SPECIAL INVESTIGATION COMMITTEE.—*See* Cabinet. *Ref.* Cmd. 1069.

STEEL HOUSES COURT OF INQUIRY.—*App.* by M.L., Mar. 1925. *Obj.* To report on causes and circumstances of threatened disputes. *Repr.* Independent Chairman and Representatives of Employers and Workpeople not directly affected. *Ref.* Cmd. 2392. *Diss.* April 1925.

SUBSTITUTION BOARD, JOINT.—*App.* jointly by M.L. and Tre., Sept. 1920, on recommendation of Lytton Committee (*see* Tre.). *Obj.* To act as Central Clearing House for substitution of ex-service men, who cannot be retained in their Departments, for non-service men and women. *Repr.* M.L., Tre., and others. *Ref.* Lytton Committee, 3rd Interim Report (H.M.S.O., 1921).

SUBSTITUTION, DEPARTMENTAL COMMITTEES.—*App.* for each Government Department from Sept. 1920, where not already in existence. *Obj.* To organize substitution of ex-service for non-service men in their Departments. *Repr.* The Department concerned, ex-service men. *Ref.* Lytton Committee, 1st and 3rd Interim Reports (H.M.S.O., 1920–1).
(For special organization of M.M., *see* M.M.)

SUBSTITUTION, WEST RIDING, COMMITTEES.—*App.* by M.L. with concurrence of M.M. and M.N.S., Jan. 1917. *Obj.* To advise and assist M.L. in connexion with substitution and reinforcement of labour in northern part of West Riding of Yorkshire, to release fit men for military service. *Repr.* Employers and workpeople, Military Service Tribunals. *Ref.* T., 26th Jan. 1917, p. 5.

TECHNICAL ADVISORY COMMITTEES, LOCAL.—*App.* jointly by M.L., M.Pen., and Trade Advisory Committees (q.v.), or by the Committees acting alone, in various trades and districts, from 1917. *Obj.* To organize training of disabled men in their trades and areas. *Repr.* Local employers and workpeople, L.E.A.'s, W.P.C.'s. *Ref.* Cmd. 14, pp. 48–9. *Still in existence end 1922.*

TEXTILE TRADES CENTRAL ADVISORY COMMITTEES.—Much as with Building Trades (q.v.). *See* T., 20th July 1917, p. 3.

TRADE ADVISORY COMMITTEES (DISABLED MEN), NATIONAL.— *App.* by M.L. in conjunction with M.Pen. and S.C. from about beginning of 1917. *Obj.* To advise on reinstatement of disabled men previously employed in the industry, and formulate and administer schemes for training and employment of disabled men not previously in the industry. *Repr.* Employers and workpeople in industry concerned. *Ref.* Cd. 8750, pp. 37–8. *Still in existence end 1922.*

TRADE ADVISORY SUB-COMMITTEES, NATIONAL.—*App.* in certain instances, notably in Building, for particular branches of an industry by the main Committee. *See* Cmd. 325, p. 271.

TRADE BOARDS ACTS INQUIRY COMMITTEE.—*App.* by M.L., Sept. 1921. *Obj.* To inquire into working and effects of Acts. *Repr.* Parliament, H.O., Legal Profession, Employers, Labour, Economists, Women. *Ref.* Cmd. 1645. *Diss.* April 1922.

(This Committee suggested establishment of District Boards in various industries. *See* L.G., July 1922, p. 286.)

TRAINING DEPARTMENT, MINISTRY OF LABOUR.—*App.* by M.L. as a separate Department early in 1919. *Obj.* To organize necessary industrial training for demobilized members of H.M. Forces and civil war workers. *Repr.* Official and expert. *Ref.* L.G., Feb. 1919. *Diss.* 1921 or 1922.

TRANSPORT WORKERS COURT OF INQUIRY (INDUSTRIAL COURTS ACT).—*App.* by M.L., Jan. 1920. *Obj.* To consider demands of National Transport Workers' Federation for improved wages and conditions, their finding being generally known as the Shaw Award. *Repr.* Legal Profession, Employers, T.U.'s. *Ref.* Cmd. 936; H.C. No. 195, 1920. *Diss.* Mar. 1920.

TRAVELLING ADVISORY BOARDS, APPOINTMENTS DEPARTMENT.—*App.* by the Department in winter of 1918–19. *Obj.* To visit armies abroad and advise officers on future careers. *Repr.* Official and expert. *Ref.* Reconstruction Pamphlets, No. 12 (Resettlement of Officers) issued by M.R. *Diss.* 1919 (presumably).

UNEMPLOYMENT DONATION.—*See* Out-of-Work Donation.

UNEMPLOYMENT INSURANCE ACTS CENTRAL AND LOCAL COMMITTEES.—*App.* by M.L. under Acts of 1920 and 1921, from Mar. 1921. *Obj.* To advise on questions of administration, including position of ex-service men. *Repr.* Employers, employed persons, and, on Local Committees, ex-service men, and women, where they are concerned. *Ref.* P.G.A., 1920, 1921 ; L.G., April 1921, p. 219. *Still in existence.*

UNEMPLOYMENT INSURANCE AND EMPLOYMENT EXCHANGES, NORTHERN IRELAND, ADVISORY COMMITTEE.—*App.* by Ministry of Labour for Northern Ireland in 1921 or early 1922. *Obj.* To report on their application to Northern Ireland. *Repr.* Parliament, The Ministry, and others. *Ref.* L.G., Jan. 1923. *Diss.* About end of 1922.

UNEMPLOYMENT INSURANCE, SPECIAL SCHEMES, JOINT BOARDS OF MANAGEMENT.—*App.* compulsory under Unemployment Insurance Act, 1920, by employers and workpeople concerned, in industries adopting special schemes for ' insurance by industry '. *Obj.* To collect funds, administer benefits, and generally carry out scheme. *Repr.* Employers and workpeople concerned. *Ref.* P.G.A., 1920 ; Cmd. 1613.

(By the end of 1922 only one such scheme, for the Insurance Industry, appears to have come into full operation. In 1919 a similar Joint Governing Body was appointed by B.T. to administer the Special Fund for Seamen, constituted under the National Health Insurance Act, 1918 : *see* L.G., April 1922, p. 158.)

UNEMPLOYMENT INSURANCE.—*See also under* Health, Labour Resettlement Committee.

UNEMPLOYMENT LOCAL COMMITTEES.—*App.* by L.A.'s concerned in important industrial centres, from autumn of 1920. *Obj.* To secure co-ordination of work of meeting unemployment in co-operation with M.L. *Repr.* L.A.'s concerned. *Ref.* L.G., Dec. 1920, p. 666.

(*See also* L.G., Feb. 1921, p. 61, for report on Special Committee of L.C.C.)

W.A.A.C.'s INQUIRY COMMISSION OF WOMEN.—*App.* by M.L., after consultation with W.O., Feb. 1918. *Obj.* To investigate in France rumours about conduct of members of Corps. *Repr.* Prominent public women, Women's T.U.'s and Friendly Societies, M.N.S., being accompanied by the Chief Controller of the Corps. *Ref.* T., 5th Mar. 1918, p. 6.

WAGES ADVISORY BOARDS (DISABLED MEN), LOCAL.—*App.* by M.L. early in 1917 in 20 large towns, the work being taken over from B.T. and subsequently extended. *Obj.* To advise on suitable wages for disabled men. *Repr.* Employers and workpeople with independent Chairmen, members of W.P.C.'s being present as assessors without power to vote. *Ref.* Cd. 8750, pp. 69, 70, 73.

WAGES ADVISORY COMMITTEES.—*App.* as separate Committees by Employers and T.U.'s respectively at National Conference (*see* next entry), Nov. 1918. *Obj.* To advise Government on legislation for stabilizing wages and restoring pre-war practices. *Repr.* Employers ; T.U.'s. *Ref.* Cmd. 325, p. 164. *Diss.* Presumably absorbed into Pre-War Practices Joint Committee (q.v.).

WAGES AND ARBITRATION DEPARTMENT.—*App.* by M.L. after passing of Wages (Temporary Regulation) Act, Nov. 1918. *Obj.* To deal with wage questions relating to wages under this and under the Conciliation Act, 1896. *Repr.* Official and expert, absorbing existing organization of M.L. dealing with work under Conciliation Acts. *Ref.* L.G., Dec. 1918. *Permanent.*

WAGES, NATIONAL CONFERENCE.—*App.* by M.L., Nov. 1918. *Obj.* To secure agreed arrangement as to wages during resettlement. *Repr.* Chief Employers' Organizations and T.U.'s. *Ref.* H.C. No. 221, 1921, p. 4.

This Conference resulted in the Wages (Temporary Regulation) Act 1918 and in setting up the Pre-War Practices Restoration Joint Committee (q.v.).

WHITLEY COUNCIL, CIVIL SERVICE, ARBITRATION BOARD.— *App.* jointly by the Official and Staff sides of the Civil Service National Whitley Council in 1919 or 1920. *Obj.* To adjudicate upon disputed claims regarding conditions of service in absence of agreement by Council. *Repr.* The Council. *Ref.* Cmd. 1181. *Intended to be Permanent.*

WHITLEY COUNCIL, CIVIL SERVICE, COST OF LIVING COMMITTEE.—*See* Cost of Living.

WHITLEY COUNCIL, CIVIL SERVICE, NATIONAL AND DEPARTMENTAL COUNCILS (ADMINISTRATIVE AND LEGAL DEPARTMENTS).—*App.* jointly by Officials and Staffs of Civil Service and of individual Departments in later part of 1919. *Obj.* To perform the functions of J.I.C.'s for Civil Service. *Repr.* Officials and Staffs of Civil Service. *Ref.* Cmd. 1181 ; L.G., May, July, &c., 1919. *Permanent Bodies.*

(The Councils were formed as a result of the work of a Provisional National Joint Committee on the Application of the Whitley Report to the Civil Service and Joint Drafting Committees for individual departments, *see* Cmd. 198.)

WHITLEY COUNCIL, CIVIL SERVICE, REORGANIZATION COMMITTEE.—*App.* by the Council in 1919. *Obj.* To report upon reorganization of Civil Service (Administrative and Legal Departments). *Repr.* The Council (Official and Staff sides). *Ref.* L.G., Mar. 1920, p. 120. *Diss.* Feb. 1920.

(A Sub-Committee dealt with the position of temporary staffs.)

WHITLEY REPORT, APPLICATION TO GOVERNMENT ESTABLISHMENTS, INTER-DEPARTMENTAL COMMITTEE.—*App.* jointly by Government Departments concerned probably late in 1918. *Obj.* To consider the application of Whitley Report to Government establishments generally. *Repr.* Government Departments concerned (Officials and Staff). *Ref.* Cmd. 9. *Diss.* Mar. 1919.

(This Committee worked largely through Sub-Committees, including one for application of report to Administrative Departments, *see* Cmd. 9.)

WHITLEY REPORT, IRISH JOINT COMMITTEE ON APPLICATION TO THE CIVIL SERVICE.—*App.* at Conference of Administrative Departments and Civil Servants, 3rd July 1919. *Obj.* To consider application of report to Civil Service in Ireland. *Repr.* Departments and Civil Servants concerned. *Ref.* L.G., July 1919. *Diss.* Later in 1919.

WOMEN'S AGRICULTURAL DISTRICT COMMITTEES (SCOTLAND); WOMEN'S TRAINING FOR AGRICULTURE IN SCOTLAND COMMITTEE.—Joint appointments. *See* B.A.(Sc.).

WOMEN'S (IRELAND) SELECTION COMMITTEE.—*App.* by M.L. in early summer of 1918. *Obj.* To select Irish women for agricultural work in England. *Repr.* M.L., agriculturalists, women. *Ref.* J.B.A., July 1918.

WOMEN'S SUB-COMMITTEES OF LOCAL EMPLOYMENT COM-MITTEES.—*App.* by L.E.C.'s, at suggestion of M.L., from early 1917. *Obj.* To deal with questions affecting women. *Repr.* Main Committees and women. *Ref.* Cmd. 14, pp. 51–2. *Permanent.*

WOMEN'S TRAINING AND EMPLOYMENT CENTRAL COMMITTEE. This was a reconstitution of the Women's Employment Central Committee of the war period in Jan. 1920. It was brought into close touch with, and received grants from, M.L., and was *still in existence at end of 1922.* Details much as with earlier Committee. *See* L.G.B.

WOMEN'S WAR REGISTER.—*See* Professional Women's Register.

WORKMEN'S COMPENSATION FOR DISABLED MEN.—*See* H.O.

WORKS COMMITTEES, JOINT.—*App.* by individual firms as part of scheme for J.I.C.'s from middle of 1917. *Obj.* Joint discussion of questions of trade, industrial conditions, &c., between firm and workpeople. *Repr.* Firm and workpeople. *Ref.* Cd. 8696, 9002. *Intended to be Permanent.*

LIQUOR CONTROL BOARD (CENTRAL CONTROL BOARD, LIQUOR TRAFFIC)

The *Central Control Board (Liquor Traffic)*, generally known as the *Liquor Control Board*, was constituted on 10th June 1915 by Order-in-Council (Liquor Control Regulations) under the Defence of the Realm (Amendment) (No. 3) Act, 1915.

The *object* was to secure such control of the sale and supply of intoxicating liquor as might be required for the prosecution of the War, and the Board's power did not cover the whole Kingdom, but applied to areas scheduled by Order-in-Council, where their exercise was found to be necessary for the successful prosecution of the War. The Board consisted of a Chairman and persons nominated by the Minister of Munitions, and represented Parliament, the Home Office, the War Departments, Employers, Trade Unions, the Catering Industry, the Clergy and the Medical Profession. The Board was brought to an end late in 1921, by the Licensing Act of that year, though the continuance of schemes of State Management under other Departments was provided for till Parliament should otherwise determine. *See* Cd. 8243 ; P.G.A., 1915, 1921.

ABBREVIATION
L.C.B. = Central Control Board (Liquor Traffic).

ALCOHOL, SCIENTIFIC ADVISORY COMMITTEE.—*App.* by L.C.B., Nov. 1916. *Obj.* To investigate physiological effects of alcohol on health and industrial efficiency. *Repr.* L.C.B., B.E., Medical Profession, scientific research, Asylums' work. *Ref.* Cd. 9055, pp. 7, 8.

CANTEEN COMMITTEE.—*App.* by L.C.B. in 1915 or early 1916. *Obj.* To assist in organizing canteens in munitions and other works. *Repr.* Not stated. *Ref.* Cd. 9005, p. 195 ; Cd. 9055, p. 12. *Diss.* Work transferred to special branch of M.M., Feb. 1918. For Canteens, *see also* M.M.

DRUNKENNESS AMONG WOMEN IN BIRMINGHAM COMMITTEE. —*App.* by L.C.B., July 1916, after preliminary investigation by earlier Committee. *Obj.* To investigate alleged drunkenness among women workers in Birmingham. *Repr.* L.C.B., H.O., M.M., Medical Health Service, Birmingham Women. *Ref.* Cd. 8558, App. II. *Diss.* Aug. 1916.

FINANCE, LIQUOR TRADE, ADVISORY COMMITTEE, ENGLAND AND WALES.—*App.* by the Government early in 1915. *Obj.* To report upon financial arrangements in case of decision for State purchase of liquor traffic or prohibition of retail trade in spirits. *Repr.* Parliament, L.G.B., Law Officers of the Crown, banking and finance, accountants, temperance reformers, Labour. *Ref.* Cd. 8283. *Diss.* April 1915.

FINANCE, LIQUOR TRAFFIC, ADVISORY COMMITTEE, SCOTLAND. —*App.*, *Obj.*, *Diss.* As with English Committee. *Repr.* Parliament, S.O., Scottish Law Officers and Lawyers, accountants, business men. *Ref.* Cd. 8319.

FINANCIAL ASPECTS OF CONTROL AND PURCHASE COMMITTEES.—*App.* following memorandum by L.C.B., by H.O., I.O., and S.O., Jan. 1917, for England and Wales, Ireland and Scotland, respectively. *Obj.* To report upon arrangements for direct State control and purchase. *Repr.* Parliament, N.H.I.C., Licensing Authorities, bankers, chartered accountants, business men, Legal Profession, Labour, temperance reformers. *Ref.* Cd. 8619. *Diss.* Oct. 1917 to Jan. 1918.

LIGHT BEERS COMMITTEE.—*App.* by L.C.B., May 1916. *Obj.* To consider what steps the Board could take to encourage production of light beers. *Repr.* Official and expert. *Ref.* T., 22nd May 1916.

LOCAL ADVISORY (DIRECT CONTROL) COMMITTEES.—*App.* by L.C.B., from late summer 1915, in areas taken under direct control. *Obj.* To advise L.C.B. in local application of control. *Repr.* (in case of Carlisle Committee) L.C.B., L.A.'s, Watch Committees, Labour, Women. *Ref.* Cd. 8558, p. 16, Cd. 9055, p. 14, Cmd. 137, p. 10. *Diss.* With cessation of control in the areas concerned.

STATE MANAGEMENT.—*See* H.O.

WOMEN'S ADVISORY COMMITTEE.—*App.* by L.C.B., Oct. 1915. *Obj.* To advise upon alleged excessive drinking among women and suggest necessary action in interests of national efficiency. *Repr.* Composed of women. *Ref.* Cd. 8243, p. 8. *Diss.* Reported before May 1916.

LOCAL GOVERNMENT BOARD (ENGLAND AND WALES) AND HEALTH (ENGLAND AND WALES), MINISTRY OF

The *Local Government Board* was established in 1871. The *Ministry of Health* was set up by the Ministry of Health Act, 1919, in June 1919, and a special Welsh Board of Health commenced to exercise various powers of the Ministry in Wales in October 1920. The Ministry was organized, under a Minister and Parliamentary Secretary, to exercise general powers with respect to Health and Local Government in England and Wales. It thus replaced the Local Government Board, absorbed the National Health Insurance Commission for England and Wales, and took over various powers from the Privy Council, the Board of Education and the Home Office. Other powers can be transferred to the Ministry by Order-in-Council. Most of the powers referred to were actually transferred to the Ministry from July to October 1919 (*see* Cmd. 923, p. 57), and the staffs of the various Departments were taken over at the same time. *Reference.* Public General Acts, 1919 (9 & 10 Geo. V, c. 21), and Cmd. 923.

ABBREVIATIONS

L.G.B. = Local Government Board for England and Wales.
M.H.   = Ministry of Health for England and Wales.

AGRICULTURAL RENTS.—*See under* Housing, Government Scheme.

ALIENS, MEDICAL INSPECTION, COMMITTEE.—*App.* by M.H., possibly in co-operation with H.O., in 1920. *Obj.* To advise on principles of medical inspection of aliens arriving in the country. *Repr.* Presumably M.H., H.O., and experts. *Ref.* Cmd. 923, p. 43. Possibly *Permanent.*

ALIENS (MILITARY SERVICE) SPECIAL LOCAL TRIBUNALS OR COMMITTEES.—*App.* by L.G.B. in 1917 under Conventions with Allies, dealing mainly, and outside London almost entirely, with Russians. *Obj.* To deal with claims to exemption by men concerned. *Repr.* As with ordinary Local Tribunals (*see* below) but with special representatives of aliens. *Ref.* Cd. 9155, p. 48. *Diss.* After close of War.

ALIENS.—*See also* Russian Dependants.

ALLOTMENTS COMMITTEES.—*App.* by L.A.'s made obligatory in large urban L.A.'s from Aug. 1922, by Allotments Act,1922,unless exempted by M.H. *Obj.* To exercise powers of L.A.'s under Allotment Acts. *Repr.* L.A.'s concerned, Allotment occupiers and experts. *Ref.* P.G.A., 1922. *Permanent.*

APPEAL, CENTRAL COMMITTEE (DERBY SCHEME).—Absorbed later into Tribunal, Military Service, Central (q.v.).

APPROVED SOCIETIES, ADMINISTRATION ALLOWANCE, DEPARTMENTAL COMMITTEE.—*App.* by M.H., through N.H.I.C., Jan. 1921. *Obj.* To report upon adequacy of administration allowance and provision of necessary increases. *Repr.* M.H., S.B.H., Tre., Irish Insurance Commission, Welsh Board of Health, Government Actuary. *Ref.* Cmd. 1291. *Diss.* May 1921.

APPROVED SOCIETY OFFICIALS JOINT ENLISTMENT COMMITTEES.—*App.* jointly by L.G.B., N.H.I.C., and S.B.H., shortly before Armistice, to sit at London and Liverpool. *Obj.* To consider claims by Approved Societies for exemption of officials from enlistment. *Repr.* Included members with special knowledge. *Ref.* Cmd. 913, p. 8. *Diss.* Nov. 1918.

ASSESSORS, MEDICAL.—*App.* jointly by L.G.B. and S.S. in 1918. *Obj.* To re-examine men appealing against grading by M.N.S. Medical Boards. *Repr.* Leading physicians and surgeons. *Ref.* Cmd. 325, p. 133.

BALFOUR SUB-COMMITTEE.—*See under* National Relief Fund.

BARLOW COMMITTEE.—*See* Tuberculosis.

BELGIAN OFFICIAL COMMITTEE FOR GREAT BRITAIN (COMITÉ OFFICIEL BELGE POUR L'ANGLETERRE).—*App.* by the King of the Belgians, 1st Nov. 1914. *Obj.* To advise and co-operate with the British Committees (*see* Refugees, War, Committee) and private organizations in relief of Belgian refugees, but with no power to administer relief or raise funds. *Repr.* Belgian Ministers and Parliament, and other prominent Belgians. *Ref.* Cmd. 7750. *Diss.* Presumably at close of War and repatriation.

BELGIAN REFUGEE COMMITTEES, LOCAL. —*App.* in various districts (over 1400 in all) sometimes as Sub-Committees of Local Relief of Distress Committee at request of L.G.B., and sometimes as voluntary bodies, in closing months of 1914. *Obj.* To find suitable accommodation for Belgian refugees. *Repr.* Various local interests. *Ref.* Cd. 7763.

BELGIAN REFUGEES, DUKE OF NORFOLK'S COMMITTEE.—This appears to have been a Voluntary Committee, appointed in first half of the War to look after refugees' welfare (*see* Cd. 8697, p. 16).

BELGIAN REFUGEES, RECEPTION AND EMPLOYMENT, DEPARTMENTAL COMMITTEE (HATCH COMMITTEE).—*App.* by L.G.B., Oct. 1914. *Obj.* To report on these matters, and on finding occupations which did not compete with British labour. *Repr.* Parliament, L.G.B., B.T., Labour, Roman Catholic Relief Organizations, other prominent men and women. *Ref.* Cd. 7750. *Diss.* Not clear ; 1st Report issued Dec. 1914, and no others apparently issued.

BELGIAN REFUGEES, SCOTTISH ADVISORY COMMITTEE.—*See* L.G.B.(Sc.).

BELGIAN REPATRIATION COMMITTEE.—*App.* before Sept. 1917. *Ref.* Cd. 8741, p. 2. No other details.

BLIND WELFARE ADVISORY COMMITTEE.—*App.* by L.G.B. in 1917. *Obj.* To advise newly established Department for treatment of the blind. *Repr.* Largely expert. *Ref.* Cd. 9005, p. 190. Apparently *Permanent.*

(To secure local interest in the work Regional Committees were appointed for seven areas in 1918 or 1919 (*see* Cmd. 420, p. 130), and the responsible L.A.'s were empowered to appoint Local Committees (*see* P.G.A., 1920, Blind Persons Act).)

BUILDING BYE-LAWS DEPARTMENTAL COMMITTEE.—*App.* by L.G.B., April 1917. *Obj.* To report upon effects of existing bye-laws and local regulations. *Repr.* Parliament, L.G.B., L.A.'s, landowners, architects, building industry, Housing Co-Partnership, Labour. *Ref.* Cd. 9213. *Diss.* Nov. 1918.

BUILDING CONSTRUCTION (TUDOR WALTERS) COMMITTEE.— *App.* by L.G.B., July 1917, for England and Wales, and extended to Scotland by arrangement with S.S., April 1918. *Obj.* To report on rapid and efficient construction of working-class dwellings. *Repr.* Parliament, L.G.B., O.W., architects, builders, engineers, estate agents, Labour. *Ref.* Cd. 9191. *Diss.* Oct. 1918.

BUILDING, HIGH COST OF, COMMITTEE.—*App.* by M.H., Feb. 1921. *Obj.* To report on causes and means of reducing high costs of building working-class dwellings in England and Wales [for Scotland, *see* L.G.B.(Sc.)]. *Repr.* Parliament, M.H., builders, building T.U.'s, architects, chartered accountants, engineers, surveyors. *Ref.* Cmd. 1447. *Diss.* July 1921.

BUILDING INDUSTRIES CONSULTATIVE BOARD.—*App.* by various professional and trade bodies in building industry, June 1919. *Obj.* To investigate nature, causes and remedies of existing unsatisfactory conditions in industry. *Repr.* Architects, surveyors, builders, T.U.'s. *Ref.* T., 1st July 1919, p. 9.

BUILDING INDUSTRY COMMITTEE.—*App.* by M.H., M.L., and representatives of the industry, March 1924. *Obj.* To inquire into means of carrying out a full housing problem. *Repr.* Employers and employed in all branches of the industry. *Ref.* Cmd. 2104. *Diss.* Later in 1924.

BUILDING MATERIALS, SURVEY OF PRICES, INTER-DEPARTMENTAL COMMITTEE.—*App.* jointly by M.H. and B.T., April 1923. *Obj.* To survey prices of materials, consider complaints, and report to the two Departments, especially in cases of unduly high prices caused by combines. *Repr.* Parliament, O.W., L.A.'s, engineers, mining experts, accountants, Labour, and other public men. *Ref.* Cmd. 1935.

BUILDING MATERIALS.—*See* M.M., M.R.

BUILDING.—*See also* Housing.

CANADIAN FUND LOCAL COMMITTEES.—*App.* in various districts of East Coast in 1915. *Obj.* Administration of the fund raised in Canada for relief of local distress. *Repr.* Local interests. *Ref.* Cd. 8697, p. 15. *Diss.* Early 1920.

CANAL BOAT CHILDREN COMMITTEE.—*App.* by M.H., after consultation with B.E., Aug. 1920. *Obj.* To report upon practice of living-in on canal boats as affecting children. *Repr.* M.H., B.E., M.L., B.T., L.A.'s, Labour, Women. *Ref.* Cmd. 1451, p. 18 ; L.G., Oct. 1920.

CHARITIES, WAR, CENTRAL COMMITTEE.—*App.* by voluntary effort early in the War and co-operating largely with Relief of Distress Committee. *See* Cd. 7763, p. 30 ; Cd. 8331.

CHILD WELFARE.—*See* Maternity.

CHOLERA.—Joint Appointment. *See* F.O., Pilgrimage Quarantine.

CIVIL LIABILITIES (MILITARY SERVICE) ADVISORY COM-MITTEE.—*App.* by L.G.B. late in 1916. *Obj.* To advise generally the Civil Liabilities Central Committee and Department in dealing with recommendations of Local Commissioners, Panels being constituted for preliminary consideration of cases. *Repr.* Parliament, L.A.'s, Stipendary Magistrates, Legal Profession, Accountants. *Ref.* Cd. 8331 ; Cmd. 39. *Diss.* As with Civil Liabilities Department (q.v.) or earlier.

CIVIL LIABILITIES (MILITARY SERVICE) CENTRAL COMMITTEE (EXECUTIVE).—*App.* by Cabinet, May 1916. *Obj.* To administer Government Scheme for meeting cases of hardship due to civil liabilities of men joining the Forces. *Repr.* Law Officers of the Crown, L.G.B., Civil Service. *Ref.* Cd. 8331. *Diss.* Absorbed into Civil Liabilities Department later in the year.

CIVIL LIABILITIES (MILITARY SERVICE) DEPARTMENT.—*App.* by L.G.B. late in 1916, replacing Civil Liabilities Central Committee (q.v.). *Obj.* To administer scheme of grants to meet civil liabilities. *Repr.* Constituted from staff of L.G.B. *Ref.* Cd. 8331. *Diss.* Transferred to M.L. by 1920 ; work practically completed by end of 1920 (*see* H.C. No. 231, 1920, p. viii), and Department wound up by end of 1921.

CIVIL LIABILITIES (MILITARY SERVICE) LOCAL COMMIS-SIONERS.—*App.* by L.G.B., April or May 1916. *Obj.* To make recommendations to Central Committee upon applications under Civil Liabilities Scheme. *Repr.* Legal Profession. *Ref.* Cd. 8249. *Diss.* As with Civil Liabilities Department (q.v.) or earlier.

CLERICAL WORKERS.—*See under* Women's Employment Central Committee.

CONSULTATIVE COUNCILS.—*App.* by Order-in-Council under Ministry of Health Act, 1919, in and after 1919. *Obj.* To advise and assist the Ministry of Health. *Repr.* Persons with practical experience (medical, &c.), including women. *Ref.* P.G.A., 1919 ; Cmd. 917, p. 5.

(The Councils appointed include the Consultative Councils on Medical and Allied Services for England (Cmd. 693), and Wales (Cmd. 703), and the National Insurance (Approved Societies Work) Consultative Council, which took over much of the work of the former Advisory Committee to N.H.I.C. (Cmd. 913, p. 5). The Councils have appointed Committees for branches of their work, e.g. in Wales to deal with typical industrial, rural, and mixed areas (Cmd. 703, p. 11).)

DENTAL BOARD.—Consulted in appointment. *See* P.C., and for subject generally W.O.

DENTAL SERVICE COMMITTEE.—*App.* by L.G.B., in agreement with A.C., July 1917. *Obj.* To secure best use of available dentists and advise Tribunals accordingly. *Repr.* Largely dentists. *Ref.* Cd. 9157, p. 51.

DENTAL SERVICE TRIBUNAL.—*App.* by L.G.B., later in July 1917. *Obj.* To deal with exemptions of registered dentists from military service. *Repr. Ref.* As with Dental Service Committee.

DISABLED SAILORS AND SOLDIERS COMMITTEE.—*App.* by L.G.B., Feb. 1915. *Obj.* To report upon methods of providing employment for disabled men. *Repr.* Parliament, L.G.B., Adm., B.E., B.T., Tre., W.O. *Ref.* Cd. 7915. *Diss.* May 1915.

DISEASE.—*See* Infectious Diseases, Influenza.

ENLISTMENTS, GOVERNMENT DEPARTMENTS' CLAIMS, COMMITTEE.—*App.* by L.G.B. late in 1915. *Obj.* To reconcile claims of different Departments, as to men to be enlisted or retained in civil life. *Repr.* The Departments concerned, with neutral Chairman. *Ref.* Cd. 8331. *Diss.* Apparently before end of 1915, work being continued by Reserved Occupations Committee (*see* B.T.). *See also under* National Register.

EX-SERVICE MEN.—*See* Disabled, Tuberculous.

HATCH COMMITTEE.—*See* Belgian Refugees.

HEALTH AND UNEMPLOYMENT.—*See* M.L.

HEALTH, INTERNATIONAL.—*See* Cabinet.

HEALTH SERVICE JOINT LOCAL COMMITTEES.—*See* B.E.

HOSPITALS.—*See* Voluntary Hospitals.

HOUSE CONSTRUCTION, NEW METHODS, COMMITTEE.—*App.* by M.H., April 1924, and enlarged Dec. 1924. *Obj.* To report on new methods of building working-class houses and securing adoption by L.A.'s and others. *Repr.* L.A.'s, Building Industry (Employers and Workpeople), Engineers, Architects. *Ref.* Cmd. 2310, 2334. *See also* M.L. *under* Steel Houses.

HOUSING, BUILDERS' CONSULTATIVE COMMITTEE.—*App.* by M.H. between June and Oct. 1919. *See* T., 24th Dec. 1919, p. 7.

HOUSING, BUILDING PROHIBITIONS, TRIBUNAL.—*App.* by M.H. in or after Dec. 1919, as Standing Tribunal under Housing (Additional Powers) Act. *Obj.* To deal with appeals against rules of L.A.'s restricting operations on buildings other than dwellings. *Repr.* Legal Profession and others. *Ref.* P.G.A., 1919.

HOUSING, CO-OPERATIVE AND COMMUNAL ARRANGEMENTS, SUB-COMMITTEE.—*App.* by Housing (Government Scheme) Advisory Council (q.v.) in 1920. *Obj.* To report upon utilization of co-operative organizations for state-aided schemes. *Repr.* Housing and Town Planning Associations, L.A.'s, Co-operators, Labour, Social Workers. *Ref.* H.M.S.O., 1921. *Diss.* May 1921.

HOUSING, FINANCIAL ASSISTANCE, COMMITTEE.—Joint Appointment. *See* M.R.

HOUSING, GOVERNMENT SCHEME, ADVISORY COUNCIL.—*App.* by M.H. in winter of 1919–20. *Obj.* To assist in consideration of special housing problems, working mainly through Sub-Committees (q.v.). *Repr.* Parliament, M.L., L.A.'s, architects, builders, chartered accountants, surveyors, Housing Associations and experts, Labour, women. *Ref.* Cmd. 917, p. 8.

HOUSING GOVERNMENT SCHEME ADVISORY SUB-COMMITTEES. —*App.* by M.H. in winter of 1919–20. *Obj.* To assist in consideration of detailed and technical questions of particular branches of housing problem, namely Agricultural Rents, Contracts, Finance, Specifications, Standardization and New Methods of Construction, Unhealthy Areas and Women's Sub-Committees. *Repr*. The Council, with additional members. *Ref*. Cmd. 917, pp. 8, 9, 19.

HOUSING LABOUR, EMPLOYMENT OF EX-SERVICE MEN, DISTRICT COMMITTEES.—The scheme eventually accepted by the Building Trades employers with the Government in first half of 1921 provided for District Committees to allocate men accepted under the scheme. *See* Cmd. 1697, p. 86.

HOUSING LABOUR SUPPLY CABINET COMMITTEE.—*App*. by Cabinet about April 1920. *Obj*. To review problem of labour supply for housing schemes and prepare proposals for National Agreement with the industry for augmenting the supply. *Repr*. Cabinet. *Ref*. Cmd. 1446, p. 59. *Diss*. Proposals adopted by Cabinet, July 1920.

HOUSING LABOUR SUPPLY OPERATIVES' COMMITTEE.—*App*. by Building Trades Operatives Federation about April 1920. *Obj*. To prepare and submit to Government proposals for increasing supplies of building labour for housing schemes. *Repr*. Building T.U.'s. *Ref*. Cd. 1446, p. 59.

(The negotiations on this problem (*see* Cmd. 1446, p. 56) were eventually carried out with the Building Resettlement Committee of the National Joint Industrial Council for the Building Industry (*see* M.L.).)

HOUSING, LOAN BANKS.—*See* M.R., Housing, Financial Assistance.

HOUSING PROPAGANDA COMMITTEE.—*App*. by M.H. in winter of 1919–20. *Obj*. To organize propaganda on the Government housing scheme. *Repr*. Housing including Rural Housing Associations and Experts, Publicity Experts, Labour, Women. *Ref*. Cmd. 917, p. 10.

HOUSING REGIONAL COMMISSIONERS.—*App*. by M.H. in winter of 1919–20 for eleven regions covering whole country. *Obj*. To organize regionally administration of Government housing scheme in their areas and secure decentralization. *Repr*. Official and expert. *Ref*. Cmd. 917, p. 8.

HOUSING, SOUTH WALES, REGIONAL SURVEY, COMMITTEE.— *App*. by M.H., Feb. 1920. *Obj*. To inquire into distribution and location of houses to be erected with State aid in South Wales Coalfield. *Ref*. Parliament, interests concerned, experts. *Ref*. T., 24th Aug. 1921. *Diss*. Aug. 1921.

HOUSING STANDING CONFERENCE (LOCAL GOVERNMENT BOARD).—*App*. by L.G.B., by 1917. *Obj*. To consider methods of ascertaining requirements of each district, including need of State assistance, amendments of law to assist building, and definition of working classes. *Repr*. L.G.B., Civil Service, housing, town-planning and social experts. *Ref*. Cd. 8916.

HOUSING.—*See also* Building, Town Planning, Unhealthy Areas, and under Relief of Distress.

INCREASE OF RENT AND MORTGAGE INTEREST (WAR RESTRICTIONS) ACTS COMMITTEE.—*App*. by M.H., Feb. 1920. *Obj*. To report on operation, continuance and amendment of Acts. *Repr*. Parliament,

M.H., Legal Profession, Labour. *Ref.* Cmd. 658. *Diss.* Mar. 1920. *See also* Rent Restriction.

INFECTIOUS DISEASES, INTRODUCTION DURING DEMOBILIZATION, DEPARTMENTAL COMMITTEE.—*App.* by L.G.B., Jan. 1919. *Obj.* To report on administrative action to deal with risks of infection. *Repr.* L.G.B., L.G.B.(Sc.), M.N.S., M.Pen., Army and Navy Medical Services. *Ref.* Cmd. 322, Cmd. 462, p. 135. *Diss.* After Aug. 1919.

INFLUENZA EPIDEMIC INVESTIGATIONS COMMITTEE.—*App.* by L.G.B., either alone or jointly with other Government Departments, in 1919. *Obj.* To organize investigations and collate results. *Repr.* Medical heads of Departments concerned. *Ref.* Cmd. 462, p. 13.

INSURANCE, HEALTH, JUDICIAL COMMITTEE.—*App.* by M.H. in 1919 under Ministry of Health Act. *Obj.* To exercise judicial powers under National Insurance (Health) Acts transferred to M.H. *Repr.* Presumably Legal. *Ref.* P.G.A., 1919 (the words of the Act are ' special body or bodies, constituted as prescribed '). *Permanent.*

INSURANCE MEDICAL RECORDS INTER-DEPARTMENTAL COMMITTEE.—*App.* jointly by M.H. and S.B.H., Mar. 1920. *Obj.* To advise on revision of medical records for new Medical Benefit Regulations. *Repr.* M.H., S.B.H., Medical Profession, Statisticians. *Ref.* Cmd. 836. *Diss.* June 1920.

INSURANCE MEDICAL SERVICE CONFERENCES.—*App.* (arranged) by L.G.B. in 1918 and 1919. *Obj.* To discuss extensions of Insurance Medical Service in connexion with revision of conditions of service necessitated by the War. *Repr.* L.G.B., Insurance Medical Practitioners, Medical Profession generally (men and women). *Ref.* Cmd. 978, p. 199. *Diss.* Summer of 1919.

INSURANCE POOL (PANEL DOCTORS' FEES) DISTRIBUTION COMMITTEE.—*App.* by M.H. in 1919 or 1920. *Obj.* To fix the distribution between different areas of national pool, under revised scheme of payments to panel doctors, including allowance for increased cost of living. *Repr.* M.H., doctors. *Ref.* Cmd. 923, p. 70. Possibly *Permanent.*

INTELLIGENCE DEPARTMENT ADVISORY COMMITTEE.—*App.* by L.G.B. late in 1914. *Obj.* To assist L.G.B. in collection of evidence regarding prevalence of special war conditions. *Repr.* Parliament, L.G.B., B.T., Registrar General, social experts, women. *Ref.* Cd. 7763.

INTELLIGENCE DEPARTMENT, LONDON ADVISORY COMMITTEE.—*App.* by L.G.B. late in 1914. *Obj.* As with preceding Committee, for London area. *Repr.* Parliament, L.C.C., Registrar-General, economists, social experts, relief work, charitable agencies. *Ref.* Cd. 7763.

JUVENILES.—*See under* Women's Employment Central Committee.

LABOUR ADVISORY COMMITTEE ON RECRUITING.—*App.* by or with consent of L.G.B., from or by chief Labour Organizations, in 1916. *Obj.* To watch recruiting in interests of labour, act as check on industrial compulsion, facilitate getting men for Army, and deal with changes in certified occupations. *Repr.* Parliamentary Labour Party. *Ref.* T., 10th June 1916, p. 3.

This may have been a continuance of Labour Recruiting Committee (q.v.).

LABOUR RECRUITING COMMITTEE.—*App.* jointly by Trade Union Congress, Labour Party and General Federation of Trade Unions, Sept. 1915. *Obj.* To secure increased voluntary enlistments and maintain voluntary system. *Repr.* Appointing bodies. *Ref.* L.Y.B. 1919, p. 124. *Diss.* On or before passing of M.S.A., Jan. 1916, but see previous entry.

LANSDOWNE COMMITTEE.—*See* National Register.

MATERNITY AND CHILD WELFARE LOCAL COMMITTEES.—*App.* originally by some L.A.'s under Notification of Births Act, 1915, and made compulsory by Maternity and Child Welfare Act, 1918, on all L.A.'s adopting either Act, with option of either appointing a special Committee or utilizing an existing one. *Obj.* To advise and assist L.A.'s concerned on exercise of powers under the Act. *Repr.* L.A.'s concerned and experts in health and maternity questions (at L.A.'s option). *Ref.* P.G.A., 1918. *Permanent.*

MAYORAL WORKROOMS.—*See under* Women's Employment.

MEAT INSPECTION COMMITTEE.—*App.* by M.H. in summer of 1920 after conferences with interests concerned. *Obj.* To report on measures necessary in interests of public health in this connexion and with a view to preserving good results of war-time measures. *Repr.* Government Departments concerned, L.A.'s, meat traders. *Ref.* Cmd. 1397, p. 130, 1713, p. 20. *Diss.* July 1921.

MENTAL HOSPITALS, PUBLIC ADMINISTRATION, COMMITTEE.— *App.* by M.H., Dec. 1921. *Obj.* To report on charges, alleged to be based on war-time experiences, against administration of these hospitals, and suggest improvements. *Repr.* Parliament, Medical Profession. *Ref.* Cmd. 1730. *Diss.* Reported during 1922.

MILITARY SERVICE.—*See* Civil Liabilities, Dental Service, Enlistments, Professional, Tribunals.

MILK, CONDENSED, REGULATIONS COMMITTEE.—*App.* by M.H. early in 1920. *Obj.* To report on steps required under Public Health (Regulations as to Food) Act 1907, to deal with condensed, &c., milk. *Repr.* Not stated. *Ref.* Cmd. 923, p. 58.

MILK DISTRIBUTION INTER-DEPARTMENTAL COMMITTEE.— *See* B.A.

MILK PRICES, BIRMINGHAM COMMITTEE.—*App.* by Lord Mayor of Birmingham in 1916. *Obj.* To inquire locally into price of milk and causes of rise. *Repr.* Local interests. *Ref.* T., 28th Dec. 1916, p. 8. *Diss.* Dec. 1916.

MILK PRICES, POWERS.—*See* M.F.

MORTGAGE INTEREST.—*See* Increase of Rent.

NATIONAL REGISTER COMMITTEE (LANSDOWNE COMMITTEE). —*App.* by L.G.B. about end of 1915. *Obj.* To co-ordinate claims of Army, Navy, Civil Departments, and industry on available labour. *Repr.* Interests affected. *Ref.* Cmd. 413, p. 116. *Diss.* Apparently absorbed eventually into Reserved Occupations Committee (*see* B.T.), but part of its duties seem to have been taken over earlier by Special Cabinet Committee on Recruiting (*see* T., 15th Feb. 1916, p. 9).

NATIONAL REGISTER, UTILIZATION COMMITTEE.—*App.* by L.G.B. in autumn of 1915. *Obj.* To consider best means of utilizing Register for best distribution of man power. *Repr.* Presumably interests affected. *Ref.* Cd. 8331, pp. 21–2. *Diss.* Absorbed into National Register Committee (q.v.).

NATIONAL REGISTRATION COMMITTEE.—*App.* by L.G.B. presumably in 1917. *Obj.* To consider questions of registration for national purposes and amendment of system of registration of births, &c. *Repr.* L.G.B., H.O., Registrar-General, Medical Profession, experts in social problems. *Ref.* Cd. 8916.

NATIONAL RELIEF FUND.—This was raised on the appeal of H.R.H. the Prince of Wales in Aug. 1914 to deal with distress due to the War. *Ref.* Cd. 7603. It and its Committees (q.v.) were not Government bodies, but worked in close connexion with the Relief of Distress Organization (*see* below) of L.G.B.

NATIONAL RELIEF FUND EXECUTIVE COMMITTEE.—*App.* by H.R.H. the Prince of Wales, after consultation with P.M., early in the War. *Obj.* To administer the fund raised at beginning of War on appeal of Prince of Wales, to meet distress due to the War. *Repr.* Parliament, L.G.B., public men and women. *Ref.* Cd. 7603. *Diss.* Decided to discontinue grants in respect of distress due to the War, June 1919 (Cmd. 923, p. 119), and work practically completed early in 1920 and work of dealing with any further cases was handed over in Aug. 1919 to the Relief, War, Trustees (q.v.).

NATIONAL RELIEF FUND, POSITION AFTER THE WAR, SUB-COMMITTEE.—*App.* by Executive Committee in 1919. *Obj.* To consider future of fund and allocation of its balances. *Repr.* The Executive Committee. *Ref.* Cmd. 356, p. 3 ; T., 1st Nov. 1919, p. 9. *Diss.* Later in 1919.
   (The Executive Committee also set up Finance and Methods of Relief (Balfour) Sub-Committees, the latter to report on forms of relief and suggest methods for adoption (Cd. 7756), and a Professional Classes Sub-Committee (*see* T., 1st Nov. 1919, p. 9).)

NATIONAL RELIEF FUND, SCOTTISH COMMITTEE.—*See* L.G.B. (Sc.).

NURSING COUNCIL, GENERAL (ENGLAND AND WALES).—*App.* in 1920 under Nurses Registration Act, 1919, in connexion with M.H. *Obj.* To keep register of nurses. *Repr.* B.E., Medical Profession, nursing experts, nurses, independent members, appointed by P.C. *Ref.* P.G.A., 1919.

PROFESSIONAL CLASSES SPECIAL AID SOCIETIES.—*App.* by or through the Professional Classes Sub-Committee (q.v.) in 1914. *Obj.* To deal with relief of cases unsuitable for Professional Benevolent Societies. *Repr.* Sub-Committee and others. *Ref.* Cd. 7756, p. 8.

PROFESSIONAL CLASSES SUB-COMMITTEE, RELIEF OF DISTRESS COMMITTEE.—*App.* by main Committee late in 1914. *Obj.* To assist in dealing with distress among professional classes. *Repr.* Main Committee, Parliament, Women. *Ref.* Cd. 7763. *See also under* N.R.F., above.

PROFESSIONAL CLASSES WAR RELIEF COUNCIL.—*See* Cd. 8169, p. 8, apparently a voluntary body, organized early in the War.

PROFESSIONAL COMMITTEE OF REFERENCE.—*App.* by Royal Colleges of Physicians and Surgeons, about June 1916. *Obj.* To advise Professional Central Military Service Committees (*see* above) on certain matters. *Repr.* The Colleges. *Ref.* Cmd. 413, p. 125.

PROFESSIONAL JOINT COMMITTEE.—*App.* jointly in 1919 by Royal Colleges of Physicians and Surgeons and Society of Medical Officers of Health. *Obj.* To confer with the Government on the organization of M.H. prior to its establishment and subsequently discuss medical organization problems. *Repr.* The three bodies. *Ref.* Cmd. 978, p. 199. *Diss.* 1920 or later.

PROFESSIONAL (MEDICAL) CENTRAL MILITARY SERVICE COMMITTEES.—*App.* by L.G.B., June 1916, for England and Wales, Scotland, Ireland. *Obj.* To deal with applications for exemption by medical profession. *Repr.* Medical Profession and Military Authorities. *Ref.* Cmd. 413, p. 125.

QUEEN'S WORK FOR WOMEN FUND.—*App.* by H.M. the Queen in Aug. 1914, being known at first as the Queen's Collecting Committee. *Obj.* To secure funds to provide work for women unemployed owing to the War, to be administered by Women's Employment Central Committee (q.v.). *Repr.* Public men and women. *Ref.* Cd. 7848, p. 4.

RECRUITING LOCAL ADVISORY COMMITTEES.—*App.* by L.A.'s at instance of L.G.B., Oct. 1915. *Obj.* To secure recruits under Derby Scheme and relieve Tribunals (*see* below) of preliminary work. *Repr.* Local residents. *Ref.* Cd. 8331. *Diss.* Probably early 1916, after passing of first M.S.A.

REFUGEES, WAR, CENTRAL COMMITTEE.—*App.* by voluntary effort in London on 24th Aug. 1914, subsequently co-operating with L.G.B. and practically a Government Committee. *Obj.* To arrange for reception and maintenance of refugees. *Repr.* Prominent men and women, including representatives of Labour. *Ref.* Cd. 7750, p. 4. *Diss.* Spring of 1919 (Final Report).

(The Committee's organization had Transport and Allocation Departments.)

REFUGEES, WAR, COUNTY AND LOCAL COMMITTEES.—*App.* in very large numbers by voluntary local effort from Aug. 1914. *Obj.* To collect offers of hospitality and to receive and distribute refugees. *Repr.* Prominent local representatives, the practice varying as to inclusion of Labour and Women. *Ref.* Cd. 7750, pp. 35–6.

REFUGEES, WAR, EMPLOYMENT COMMITTEE.—*App.* late in 1914 by voluntary effort. *Obj.* To assist refugees in finding employment, especially in agriculture. *Repr.* Prominent men and women, especially agricultural and other experts. *Ref.* Cd. 7750, p. 25.

REFUGEES, WAR, FOLKESTONE COMMITTEE.—*Obj.* To take charge of refugees on landing and forward to Central Committee those without resources. *Otherwise* much as with Central Committee. *Ref.* Cd. 7750, p. 4.

REFUGEES, WAR, JEWISH COMMITTEE.—*App.* presumably early in the War. *Obj.* To deal with Jewish refugees. *Repr.* Largely Jewish interests. *Ref.* Cd. 9157, p. 45.

REFUGEES, WAR, REGISTRATION, OSTEND COMMITTEE.—*App.* locally through organizing officer of L.G.B., Sept. 1914. *Obj.* To arrange for registration of refugees before departure from Ostend. *Repr.* Belgian interests. *Ref.* Cd. 7763.

REFUGEES, WAR, REPATRIATION COMMISSION.—*App.* by L.G.B., after consultation with Tre., about Nov. 1918. *Obj.* To organize repatriation of refugees. *Repr.* Commissioner and staff (official and expert). *Ref.* Cmd. 413, p. 107.

REFUGEES, WAR.—*See also* Belgian Refugees, Wounded Allies Relief.

REGISTRATION.—*See* National Registration, and Tre.

RELIEF OF DISTRESS, GOVERNMENT COMMITTEE.—*App.* by P.M. on 4th Aug. 1914. *Obj.* To advise on measures for prevention and relief of distress due to the War. *Repr.* Cabinet, Parliament, L.G.B., Labour Women. *Ref.* Cd. 7603. *Diss.* By end 1919, probably.

RELIEF OF DISTRESS, LOCAL REPRESENTATIVE COMMITTEES. —*App.* by L.A.'s concerned, at invitation of L.G.B., mostly in Aug. 1914. *Obj.* To deal locally with prevention and relief of distress due to the War. *Repr.* L.A.'s (including Boards of Guardians), Distress Committees, T.U.'s, Soldiers and Sailors Families' Association, and other philanthropic agencies. *Ref.* Cd. 7603. *Diss.* Nearly all by end of Sept. 1919 (Cmd. 923, p. 119).

(Some at least of these Committees appointed Sub-Committees on Grant of Relief, at suggestion of L.G.B., to organize relief. *See* Cd. 7603.)

RELIEF OF DISTRESS, SCOTTISH ADVISORY COMMITTEE.—*See* L.G.B.(Sc.).

RELIEF OF DISTRESS, SUB-COMMITTEE ON AGRICULTURAL DISTRICTS. *App.* by Government Committee early in the War. *Obj.* To assist in relief in agricultural districts. *Repr.* Main Committee, Parliament, L.G.B., agriculturalists, agricultural experts. *Ref.* Cd. 7603. *Diss.* Work in abeyance at end of 1914, owing to absence of distress.

RELIEF OF DISTRESS, SUB-COMMITTEES FOR LONDON.—*App.* by Government Committee early in the War. *Obj.* To assist in dealing with relief of distress in London. *Repr.* The main Committee, London M.P.'s, L.G.B., L.C.C., Port of London Authority, Central Unemployed Body for London, Labour, Women. *Ref.* Cd. 7603.

RELIEF OF DISTRESS, SUB-COMMITTEE FOR URBAN HOUSING. —*App.* by Government Committee early in the War. *Obj.* To assist in promoting urban housing work to relieve distress. *Repr.* Main Committee, L.G.B., Tre., Urban L.A.'s, Building Trades, Labour, Housing Experts. *Ref.* Cd. 7603. *Diss.* About end of 1914, with improvement in employment.

RELIEF OF DISTRESS, WELSH INSURANCE COMMISSION INTELLIGENCE BUREAU.—*App.* by Welsh Insurance Commission, at request of L.G.B., Aug. 1914, co-operating with Government Committee.

Obj. To deal with distress due to the War in Wales. *Repr.* Welsh Insurance Commission and others. Ref. Cd. 8890, pp. 193–4. *Diss.* Suspended in 1915, owing to good employment.

RELIEF OF DISTRESS.—*See also* Professional Classes, Women's Employment Central Committee.

RELIEF, WAR, TRUSTEES.—*App.* by N.R.F. Executive Committee (q.v.), Aug. 1919. *Obj.* To deal with any future cases for relief from N.R.F. *Repr.* Presumably much as with Executive Committee. *Ref.* Cmd. 923, p. 119.

RENT RESTRICTIONS ACTS INQUIRY COMMITTEE.—*App.* by M.H. in co-operation with S.O. in July 1922, and reappointed Nov. 1922. *Obj.* To consider operations of the Acts and advise on continuance or amendment. *Repr.* H.C., M.H., S.O., Labour, Legal Profession, Surveyors. *Ref.* Cmd. 1803. *Diss.* Feb. 1928.

RENT.—*See also* Increase of Rent.

RENTS TRIBUNAL.—*App.* by M.H. by 1921. *Obj.* To decide disputes with L.A.'s on rents charged for state-aided houses. *Repr.* M.H., L.A.'s. *Ref.* Cmd. 1944, p. 42. *Still in existence end 1922.*

RHEUMATISM AND ALLIED DISEASES COMMITTEE.—*App.* by M.H. in 1920 or 1921. *Obj.* To inquire, in co-operation with similar Committee of M.R.C., into nature, distribution and incidence. *Repr.* M.H. *Ref.* Cmd. 1397, p. 157.

ROAD LOCOMOTIVES AND HEAVY MOTOR CARS DEPART-MENTAL COMMITTEE.—*App.* by L.G.B., Mar. 1915. *Obj.* To consider amendment of existing laws, &c. affecting construction and use. *Repr.* Parliament, L.G.B., L.A.'s, Engineers, Legal Profession. *Ref.* Cmd. 5. *Diss.* Oct. 1918.

RUSSIAN DEPENDANTS COMMITTEE.—*App.* by M.H., with approval of Tre., early in 1920. *Obj.* To co-ordinate grant of assistance to dependants of Russians from different resources, after discontinuance of war-time relief. *Repr.* Jewish Board of Guardians, Lithuanian Colony in London and other bodies interested. *Ref.* Cmd. 923, p. 121.

SAILORS.—*See* Disabled, Tuberculous.

SALVAGE, NATIONAL COUNCIL.—Joint appointment. *See* W.O.

SANATORIA.—*See* Tuberculosis.

SANITARY COMMISSION, INTER-ALLIED.—*App.* by Allied Governments, at request of French Government, early in 1916. *Obj.* To exchange views upon application and co-ordination of sanitary, &c. measures, periodical conferences being held for the purpose. *Repr.* Governments concerned, L.G.B. being represented in British delegation. *Ref.* Cd. 8767, p. vi.

SHELLFISH JOINT STANDING COMMITTEE.—*App.* jointly by M.H. and B.A. in winter of 1919–20. *Obj.* To deal jointly with cases of shellfish pollution for protection of public health. *Repr.* M.H., B.A. *Ref.* Cmd. 923, p. 62. *Standing Committee.*

SOLDIERS.—*See* Disabled, Tuberculosis.

STANDARDIZATION AND NEW METHODS OF CONSTRUCTION.— *See* the Sub-Committee with this title *under* Housing, Government Scheme, Advisory Sub-Committees, to which the references in Cmd. 917 to a Committee (p. 19) and a Sub-Committee (p. 10) appear to relate.

STATISTICS, LOCAL FINANCIAL, ADVISORY COMMITTEE.—*App.* by M.H. probably in 1920. *Obj.* To secure simplification and economy in financial returns of L.A.'s. *Repr.* L.A.'s, Municipal Finance Officers' Associations and others. *Ref.* Cmd. 1446, p. 2. *Diss.* Not before Mar. 1922.

SUPERANNUATION, LOCAL AUTHORITIES' EMPLOYEES, COMMITTEE.—*App.* by L.G.B., Oct. 1918. *Obj.* To report as to desirability of superannuation scheme for such employees, and suggest definite arrangements. *Repr.* L.G.B., B.E., L.A.'s, Government Actuary, Accountants, Municipal Finance and Law. *Ref.* Cmd. 329. *Diss.* July 1919.

THERAPEUTIC SUBSTANCES DEPARTMENTAL COMMITTEE.— *App.* by M.H., April 1920. *Obj.* To advise measures to control quality and authenticity of substances offered for sale which cannot be adequately tested. *Repr.* Civil Service, Medical Profession, Public Health Service, Royal Society. *Ref.* Cmd. 1156. *Diss.* Dec. 1920.

TOWN PLANNING, JOINT REGIONAL COMMITTEES.—*App.* jointly from 1920, by urban L.A.'s in large urban regions. *Obj.* To plan out and co-ordinate in advance building plans for whole of regions. *Repr.* L.A.'s concerned. *Ref.* Cmd. 1446, p. 82. *Still sitting end 1922.*
(These Committees have appointed various Sub-Committees.)

TRAINING.—*See under* Women's Employment Central Committee.

TRIBUNALS (MILITARY SERVICE), APPEAL.—*App.* usually for county areas by the Crown, after local consultation, from Jan. 1916 under M.S.A. *Obj.* To hear appeals from decisions of Local Tribunals. *Repr.* Parliament, L.A.'s, Legal Profession, Employers, Labour. *Ref.* Cd. 8331, Cmd. 413, p. 117. *Diss.* After the close of the War.

TRIBUNAL (MILITARY SERVICE), CENTRAL.—*App.* by L.G.B., under Derby Recruiting Scheme as Appeal Central Committee, Nov. 1915, and reappointed by the Crown under M.S.A., Jan. 1916. *Obj.* To hear appeals from Local Tribunals, with certain special cases, under Derby Scheme, and from Appeal Tribunals under M.S.A.'s. *Repr.* Prominent public men. *Ref.* Cd. 8331. *Diss.* After the close of the War.

TRIBUNALS (MILITARY SERVICE), LOCAL.—*App.* by L.A.'s, at invitation of L.G.B., under Derby Scheme, Nov. 1915 (*see also* Recruiting Local Advisory Committees), and usually continued with increased membership under M.S.A., Jan. 1916. *Repr.* L.A.'s and others appointed by them. *Ref.* Cd. 8331. *Diss.* After the close of the War.

TRIBUNALS (MILITARY SERVICE) LOCAL, AGRICULTURE SUB-COMMITTEES.—*App.* suggested to Tribunals by L.G.B., April 1918. *Obj.* To make preliminary survey on claims for exemption under Royal Proclamation of April 1918 (Order 459), with a view to granting exemption by agreement with representative of B.A. and M.N.S. *Repr.* Local Tribunals. *Ref.* J.B.A., May 1918, p. 240. *Diss.* At or before Armistice.

TRIBUNALS (MILITARY SERVICE) VETERINARY.—*App.* by L.G.B., Aug. 1918. *Obj.* To deal with cases of veterinary surgeons. *Repr.* Special provision for the profession. *Ref.* Cmd. 413, p. 132.

(*See also* Dental Service and Professional above, and Russian Military Service Tribunal under W.O.)

TUBERCULOSIS CARE COMMITTEES.—Interim Committees were established in London boroughs during the War by L.C.C., to make arrangements for after-care of tuberculous persons, and under Tuberculosis Act, 1921, permanent Committees were organized to co-ordinate work of Tuberculosis Dispensaries. *See* Cmd. 1713, pp. 1, 5, 1944, p. 2.

TUBERCULOSIS, GRANTS.—*See* Tre.

TUBERCULOSIS, SANATORIA FOR SOLDIERS, INTER-DEPARTMENTAL (BARLOW) COMMITTEE.—*App.* jointly by L.G.B. and M.Pen., April 1919. *Obj.* To report on immediate practical steps for providing sanatoria, and restoring the men to employment. *Repr.* Parliament, L.G.B., L.G.B.(Sc.), M.L., M.Pen., N.H.I.C., The Army, Select Committee on Pensions, Medical Profession. *Ref.* Cmd. 317. *Diss.* Aug. 1919.

TUBERCULOUS EX-SERVICE MEN, TRAINING SECTIONS.—These were established in connexion with various sanatoria, over 500 places having been provided by Mar. 1923. *See* Cmd. 1944, p. 3.

TUBERCULOUS SEAMEN ADVISORY COMMITTEE.—*App.* by M.H., Sept. 1921, under Tuberculosis Act, 1921. *Obj.* To advise L.A.'s in making arrangements for tuberculous seamen. *Repr.* Not stated. *Ref.* Cmd. 1713, p. 1. Apparently a *Standing Body.*

UNEMPLOYMENT, ADVANCES TO GUARDIANS.—*See* Cabinet.

UNHEALTHY AREAS COMMITTEE.—*App.* by M.H. early in 1920. *Obj.* To advise upon principles of dealing with unhealthy areas. *Repr.* Parliament M.H., L.A.'s (including medical service), Master Builders, Town Planning Associations, Labour, Co-operators, Women. *Ref.* Cmd. 1446, p. 72 ; H.M.S.O., 1921. *Diss.* April 1921.

VENEREAL DISEASES INQUIRY COMMITTEE.—*App.* by M.H., and chosen by a selection of leading Medical Men (*see* p. 12 of Report), April 1923. *Obj.* To report upon best remedial measures for preventing the disease. *Repr.* Medical Profession, Legal Profession. *Ref.* Report H.M.S.O., 1923. *Diss.* Probably in 1923.

VENEREAL DISEASES, NATIONAL COUNCIL FOR COMBATING.— *App.* by private effort in 1915 and recognized later by Government on recommendation of Royal Commission on Venereal Diseases (pre-war body) as an authoritative body for distribution of information and advice. *Obj.* To concert and organize measures for combating the disease. *Repr.* Public men, medical and scientific experts, &c. *Ref.* Cmd. 923, p. 18. *Permanent Body.*

VETERINARY TRIBUNALS.—*See under* Tribunals.

VOLUNTARY HOSPITALS COMMISSION.—*App.* by M.H. about June 1920, on recommendation of Voluntary Hospitals Committee (q.v.). *Obj.* To administer State grant of £500,000 to meet immediate needs of voluntary hospitals. *Repr.* M.H., S.B.H., British Hospitals, British Medical Association, Royal Colleges of Physicians and Surgeons, King Edward's Hospital Fund, Joint Committee of Red Cross and Order of St. John of Jerusalem. *Ref.* Cmd. 1402, 1335, p. 11.

VOLUNTARY HOSPITALS COMMITTEE.—*App.* by M.H., Jan. 1921. *Obj.* To consider financial position of hospitals and suggest action for assisting them. *Repr.* Parliament, L.C.C., Legal Profession, Employers, Accountants, Labour. *Ref.* Cmd. 1206. *Diss.* May 1921 (Cmd. 1335).

VOLUNTARY HOSPITALS CONSULTATIVE COMMITTEE.—*App.* by Voluntary Hospitals Commission (q.v.) in 1922. *Obj.* To secure close touch with Local Committees (*see* next entry) and local opinion. *Repr.* Local Committees. *Ref.* Cmd. 1944, p. 30. *Still sitting end 1922.*

VOLUNTARY HOSPITALS LOCAL COMMITTEES.—*App.* by Voluntary Hospitals Commission (q.v.) late in 1921, for administrative counties and large county boroughs. *Obj.* To consider and submit to Commission applications for assistance from Government grant. *Repr.* L.A.'s, Hospitals, Medical Profession, Local Residents. *Ref.* Cmd. 1713, p. 28. *Still existing end 1922.*

WATER POWER CO-ORDINATION INTER-DEPARTMENTAL COMMITTEE.—*App.* early in 1922, on recommendation of Water Power Resources Committee (*see* B.T.), by Government Departments concerned and apparently sitting at M.H. *Obj.* To secure co-ordination by Departments interested in water problem. *Repr.* Government Departments concerned. *Ref.* Cmd. 1713, p. 32. *Possibly Permanent.*

WATER SUPPLY STANDING ADVISORY COMMITTEE.—*App.* by M.H. in 1922 or 1923. *Obj.* To formulate, in conference with M.H., proposals for national water policy. *Repr.* British Water Works Association, Institute of Water Engineers and other experts. *Ref.* Cmd. 1944, p. 33. *Standing Body.*

WHEAT CONSERVATION INTER-DEPARTMENTAL COMMITTEE.—*App.* by L.G.B., at request of B.T., late in 1916 and transferred later to M.F. *Obj.* To consider means of increasing yield of flour from wheat and desirability of altering law regarding mixing of wheat and other flours. *Repr.* L.G.B., other Departments concerned, millers, bakers. *Ref.* Cd. 8767, App. II.

WOMEN'S EMPLOYMENT CENTRAL (STANDING) COMMITTEE.—*App.* by L.G.B., Aug. 1914. *Obj.* To organize schemes of work and relief for women and girls unemployed owing to the War under Relief of Distress Committee. *Repr.* Prominent women of varied experience, with official and commercial advisers. *Ref.* Cd. 7848. *Diss.* This Committee appears to have ceased to exist by end of 1916, but was reconstituted in 1920 as Women's Training and Employment Central Committee (*see* M.L.).

(The Committee established Sub-Committees for Finance and General Purposes; Contracts, Purchase and Workrooms; Mayoral Workroom Schemes; Juvenile and Training Schemes (including Clerical Workers); New Trades.)

WOMEN'S EMPLOYMENT, DIVISIONAL COMMITTEES.—*App.* in certain big industrial districts through Central Committee in autumn of

1914. *Obj.* To control and supervise schemes in their areas. *Repr.* Prominent local women presumably. *Ref.* Cd. 8051, p. 32. *Diss.* Probably as with Central Committee.

WOMEN'S EMPLOYMENT, LOCAL SUB-COMMITTEES.—*App.* locally in autumn of 1914 by Local Representative Committees (*see under* Relief of Distress) on initiative of the Women's Employment Committee. *Obj.* To organize local (mayoral) workrooms for unemployed women over 16. *Repr.* Local women, business men, Labour. *Ref.* Cd. 7848. *Diss.* By Sept. 1915 (last of the workrooms closed).

WOMEN.— *See also under* Housing, Government Schemes, Advisory Sub-Committees.

WOUNDED ALLIES RELIEF COMMITTEE.—*App.* apparently by voluntary effort in autumn of 1915. *Obj.* To deal with wounded Belgians in co-operation with Belgian authorities, L.G.B., and W.O. *Repr.* Not stated. *Ref.* Cd. 7763.

LOCAL GOVERNMENT BOARD (IRELAND)

ABBREVIATION

L.G.B.(I.) = Local Government Board for Ireland.
L.G.B. alone refers to Local Government Board (England and Wales).

ALLOTMENTS, LOCAL COMMITTEES.—*App.* by District Councils allowed under order of L.G.B.(I.), under Local Government (Allotments and Land Cultivation) (Ireland) Act, of Aug. 1917. *Obj.* To organize provision of allotments in the district. *Repr.* Not stated. *Ref.* P.G.A., 1917–18.

BELGIAN REFUGEES COMMITTEE (SOMETIMES CALLED WAR REFUGEES (IRELAND) COMMITTEE).—*App.* by L.G.B.(I.), Oct. 1914. *Obj.* To arrange for reception, allocation, and despatch to destination of Belgian refugees in Ireland. *Repr.* Public men and women, L.G.B.(I.). *Ref.* Cd. 8016, p. xl ; Cmd. 578, p. xx. *Diss.* May 1919.

BELGIAN REFUGEES DEPARTMENT.—*App.* by L.G.B.(I.), Oct. 1914. *Obj.* To deal with correspondence concerning offers of hospitality, &c. *Repr.* L.G.B.(I.). *Ref.* Cd. 8016, p. xxxviii. *Diss.* Presumably winter of 1918–19.

BELGIAN REFUGEES LOCAL COMMITTEES.—*App.* locally, often at instigation of L.G.B.(I.), from Oct. 1914. *Obj.*, *Repr.* Much as in England (*see* L.G.B.). *Ref.* Cd. 8016, pp. xxxviii–xl. *Diss.* Many Committees by beginning of 1917, and all by May 1919.

BLIND, IRISH ADVISORY COMMITTEE.—*App.* by L.G.B.(I.), Jan. 1918. *Obj.* To advise on measures for dealing more systematically with the blind. *Repr.* Various experts. *Ref.* Cmd. 65, p. xviii. Apparently a *Standing Committee.*

HOUSING (IRELAND) COMMITTEE.—*App.* by L.G.B.(I.) in or after Aug. 1919, under Housing (Ireland) Act, 1919, along with a special Housing Department. *Obj.* To advise L.G.B.(I.) in housing policy and administration, assist L.A.'s and deal with preliminary stages of housing schemes. *Repr.* L.G.B.(I.), Congested Districts Board (Ireland), architects, engineers. *Ref.* Cmd. 1432, p. lii.

HOUSING SCHEMES, ARCHITECTS' PANEL SELECTION COMMITTEE.—*App.* by L.G.B.(I.) in winter of 1919–20. *Obj.* To select architects to form panel of architects from which choice could be made to supervise local housing schemes. *Repr.* L.G.B.(I.) through Housing (Ireland) Committee (q.v.), architects. *Ref.* Cmd. 1432, p. lxx.

IRISH REBELLION (VICTIMS) COMMITTEE.—*App.* by L.G.B.(I.), 1916. *Obj.* To maintain and allocate food supplies in Dublin during, and relieve those in distress owing to, the Rebellion. *Repr.* L.G.B.(I.), and other local interests. *Ref.* Cd. 8765, pp. xv, xvi. *Diss.* May 1916.

MIDWIVES BOARD FOR IRELAND, CENTRAL.—*App.* through P.C., under Midwives (Ireland) Act, 1918. *Obj.* To regulate training and practice of midwives in Ireland. *Repr.* L.G.B.(I.), L.A.'s, Medical Profession, Nursing Associations, Women. *Ref.* P.G.A., 1917–18. *Permanent.*

MIDWIVES COMMITTEES, LOCAL.—*App.* (optional) by L.A.'s under Midwives (Ireland) Act, 1918. *Obj.* To supervise, locally, practice and conduct of midwives. *Repr.* L.A.'s, Women. *Ref.* P.G.A., 1917–18. *Permanent.*

NURSING COUNCIL FOR IRELAND, GENERAL.—*App.* by C.S. in 1920 under Nurses Registration (Ireland) Act, 1919. *Obj.* To keep register of nurses in Ireland. *Repr.* Medical Profession, nurses, and experts. *Ref.* P.G.A., 1919. *Permanent.*

PRISONERS OF WAR, IRISH COMMITTEE.—Mentioned on p. xviii of Cd. 8365. No details given.

PUBLIC HEALTH COUNCIL, IRELAND.—*App.* by C.S. in 1919, under Ministry of Health Act. *Obj.* To investigate Irish Public Health Administration and formulate proposals for reorganization. *Repr.* L.G.B.(I.), N.H.I.C.(I.), Registrar-General for Ireland, L.A.'s, Medical Profession (including Public Health Services), Approved Societies, Women. *Ref.* Cmd. 761.

RELIEF OF DISTRESS, LOCAL REPRESENTATIVE COMMITTEES. —*App.* by various L.A.'s, at instigation of L.G.B.(I.) and at request of Government Committee for Relief of Distress, in and after Aug. 1914. *Obj., Repr.* Much as in England (*see* L.G.B.). *Ref.* Cd. 8016, pp. xxviii– xxxiii. *Diss.* Operations discontinued by close of 1915 in Belfast and Londonderry.

WAR REFUGEES.—*See* Belgian Refugees.

WOMENS' EMPLOYMENT, LEINSTER, MUNSTER AND CONNAUGHT CENTRAL COMMITTEE.—*App.* by L.G.B.(I.) in autumn of 1914. *Obj.* To consider principles of, and suitable schemes for, employment and relief of women workers in distress owing to the War. *Repr.* Public men and women, including experts in women's relief problems. *Ref.* Cd. 8016, p. xxxi. *Diss.* After close of 1915.

WOMEN'S EMPLOYMENT, ULSTER, CENTRAL COMMITTEE.— Separate Committee appointed owing to difference in industrial conditions. Conditions as in preceding entry. *Diss.* Meetings suspended, May 1915.

WOMEN'S EMPLOYMENT SUB-COMMITTEES.—*App.* in autumn of 1914, outside Ulster, where work appears to have been done by Local Representative Committees, as Sub-Committees of Local Representative Committees or of Women's Employment Committee. *Obj.* To prepare and manage employment schemes in their localities. *Repr.* Women's Industrial Organizations, other Women's Agencies concerned with relief of distress. *Ref.* Cd. 8016, p. 51. *Diss.* End June 1919.

LOCAL GOVERNMENT BOARD (SCOTLAND) AND HEALTH, SCOTTISH BOARD OF

The *Scottish Board of Health* was established on the 3rd June 1919 by the Scottish Board of Health Act, under a Parliamentary Under-Secretary responsible to the Secretary of State for Scotland. The *object* of the Board is to exercise powers in respect to health and local government in Scotland, thus superseding the Scottish Local Government Board and absorbing the National Health Insurance Commission for Scotland, and taking over various powers from other Departments. Other powers can be conferred on the Board by Order-in-Council. The Board, as originally appointed, included representatives of the Scottish Local Government Board and Health Insurance Commission, and must at all times include representatives of the Medical and Legal Professions and of Women. *Reference.* Public General Acts, 1919 (9 and 10 Geo. V, c. 20).

ABBREVIATIONS

L.G.B.(Sc.) = Local Government Board, Scotland (till June 1919).
S.B.H. = Scottish Board of Health (from June 1919).
S.S. = Secretary for Scotland.
The abbreviation L.G.B. used without qualification means the Local Government Board for England and Wales.

ASSESSORS, MEDICAL.—Joint Appointment, *see* L.G.B.

BELGIAN REFUGEES, GLASGOW CORPORATION COMMITTEE.— *App.* by the Corporation early in the War, subsequently undertaking wider duties at request of the Government. *Obj.* To find hospitality for Belgian Refugees in Scotland, with assistance from L.G.B.(Sc.) in dealing with lunatics and consumptives. *Repr.* Glasgow Corporation. *Ref.* Cd. 8273.

BLIND WELFARE ADVISORY COMMITTEE.—*App.* by L.G.B.(Sc.), Jan. 1918. *Obj.* To advise generally newly formed Department for the Blind. *Repr.* Persons (including women) with special knowledge and experience. *Ref.* Cmd. 230, pp. vii, viii. *Permanent.*

BUILDING CONSTRUCTION (TUDOR WALTERS) COMMITTEE.— Extended to Scotland April 1918, by agreement with S.S. *See* L.G.B.

BUILDING, HIGH COST OF, SCOTLAND, COMMITTEE.—*App.* by S.B.H., Feb. 1923. *Obj.* To report upon causes of, and means of reducing, high cost of building working-class dwellings. *Repr.* S.B.H., builders, building T.U.'s, Trade Councils, architects, surveyors, chartered accountants, engineers, Legal Profession, surveyors. *Ref.* Cmd. 1411. *Diss.* June 1921.

BUILDING MATERIALS ADVISORY COMMITTEE.—*App.* by S.B.H. early in 1921. *Obj.* To provide expert advice and assistance regarding production and distribution of materials required for state-aided housing schemes. *Repr.* L.A.'s, employers in industries concerned, quarry masters. *Ref.* Cmd. 1697, p. 82.

BUILDING.—*See also* Housing.

CONSULTATIVE COUNCILS.—*App.* by Order-in-Council under Scottish Board of Health Act, 1919, four Councils being established, Dec. 1919, for Medical and Allied services (*see also* Cmd. 1039), National Health Insurance (Approved Societies' Work), Local Health Administration, and General Health Questions (Highlands and Islands). *Obj.* To advise and assist S.B.H. on the matters referred to them. *Repr.* Persons with practical experience and interests specially concerned, including L.A.'s, Labour, Women. *Ref.* P.G.A., 1919 ; Cd. 825, pp. 82–3. Generally *Permanent.*

(The Councils have appointed Committees and Sub-Committees for particular problems.)

ECONOMY IN EXPENDITURE LOCAL COMMITTEES.—*App.* suggested to L.A.'s by L.G.B.(Sc.), where not already in existence, Aug. 1915. *Obj.* To report upon practicable savings in local expenditure. *Repr.* L.A.'s concerned. *Ref.* Cmd. 8273.

EXECUTIVE CENTRAL COMMITTEE FOR SCOTLAND.—For relief of war distress. *See under* National Relief Fund below.

HIGH COST OF BUILDING.—*See* Building.

HIGHLANDS.—*See under* Consultative Councils, Women's Relief.

HOUSE PLANNING, WOMEN'S COMMITTEE.—*App.* by S.S., June 1918. *Obj.* To advise on planning and arrangement of houses from housewife's standpoint. *Repr.* Representative women from various districts. *Ref.* Cmd. 230, p. xxxviii. *Diss.* Oct. 1918.

HOUSING, BUILDING PROHIBITIONS TRIBUNAL, SCOTLAND.— As with English Tribunal, except that by Housing (Scotland) Act, 1920, panels for selection of chairmen and ordinary members were substituted for Standing Tribunal.

HOUSING PLANS, COMMITTEE OF ARCHITECTS.—*App.* by L.G.B.(Sc.), Jan. 1919. *Obj.* To adjudicate upon plans submitted by architects in connexion with post-war housing schemes. *Repr.* Architects, Town-planning Experts. *Ref.* Cmd. 230, pp. xxxv–xxxvi. *Diss.* Close of competition.

HOUSING SPECIAL COMMITTEES.—*App.* by L.A.'s, at instigation of L.G.B.(Sc.), in 1918. *Obj.* To organize preparation of housing schemes for post-war operations. *Repr.* L.A.'s. *Ref.* Cmd. 230, p. xxvi.

INSURANCE, HEALTH, JUDICIAL COMMITTEE.—*App.* by S.B.H. late in 1919 under Scottish Board of Health Act, 1919. *Obj.* To exercise judicial powers under National Health Insurance Acts, transferred to S.B.H. *Repr.* Presumably Legal. *Ref.* P.G.A., 1919. Apparently *Permanent.*

INSURANCE MEDICAL RECORDS.—Joint Appointment. *See* M.H.

LOCAL TAXATION, SCOTLAND, COMMITTEE.—*App.* by L.G.B.(Sc.) in 1921. *Obj.* To investigate system of local taxation in Scotland and suggest alterations. *Repr.* Parliament, L.G.B.(Sc.), L.A.'s, Legal Profession, accountants and other prominent Scotsmen. *Ref.* Cmd. 1674. *Diss.* May 1922.

MATERNITY AND CHILD WELFARE LOCAL COMMITTEES.—As with England (*see* L.G.B.). Joint Committees for combined districts may be appointed in Scotland.

MIDWIVES, CENTRAL BOARD, SCOTLAND.—*App.* by S.S., under general control of L.G.B.(Sc.), under Midwives (Scotland) Act, 1915, Feb. 1916. *Obj.* To control and supervise conditions, training and practice of midwives in Scotland. *Repr.* L.A.'s, Medical Profession, Midwives, Nursing Associations. *Ref.* P.G.A., 1914–16. *Permanent Body.*

MILK INTER-DEPARTMENTAL COMMITTEE (SCOTLAND).—*App.* by S.B.H., April 1920. *Obj.* To report generally on laws, regulations, &c. for sale of milk and suggest necessary alterations. *Repr.* S.B.H., B.A.(Sc.), L.A.'s, Scottish Chamber of Agriculture, farmers, dairymen, milk dealers, scientific research, women. *Ref.* Cmd. 1749. *Diss.* April 1922.
(A Sub-Committee was appointed to deal with problem of buttermilk.)

NATIONAL RELIEF FUND, SCOTTISH ADVISORY COMMITTEE.—*App.* by a Conference convened by L.G.B.(Sc.) at Edinburgh, 7th Aug. 1914, and originally called the Executive Central Committee for Scotland. *Obj.* To distribute share of National Relief Fund (*see* L.G.B.) allocated to Scotland. *Repr.* Prominent men and women with expert knowledge of social problems. *Ref.* Cd. 8041, p. xii ; Cd. 8129.

NOURISHMENT FOR MOTHERS AND CHILDREN, SPECIAL COM-MITTEES.—*App.* by L.A.'s under order of S.B.H. from Aug. 1921 as Sub-Committees of Maternity and Child Welfare Committees (*see* above) or as independent bodies. *Obj.* To lay down and supervise procedure for dealing with applications for food and milk. *Repr.* Not stated. *Ref.* Cmd. 1697, p. 229. Apparently *still in existence end 1922.*

NURSING COUNCIL, GENERAL, FOR SCOTLAND.—*App.* in 1920 under Registration of Nurses (Scotland) Act, 1919, under general control of S.B.H. *Obj., Repr.* As with Council for England and Wales (*see* L.G.B.). *Ref.* P.G.A., 1919. *Permanent Body.*

PROFESSIONAL CENTRAL (MEDICAL) MILITARY SERVICE COM-MITTEE.—*See under* L.G.B.

RELIEF OF DISTRESS, ADVISORY, SCOTTISH, COMMITTEE.—*App.* by Government Committee on Relief of Distress (*see* L.G.B.) early in the War. *Obj.* To advise Scottish Local Committees for Relief of Distress. *Repr.* Much as with Government Committee. *Ref.* Cd. 9111, pp. 5, 19.

RELIEF OF DISTRESS, LOCAL COMMITTEES.—*App.* by L.A.'s through Scottish Advisory Committee of N.R.F. (*see* above) early in the War with parish and ward sub-committees in some cases. *Obj.* To deal locally with relief of distress due to the War. *Repr.* Official members, experts in charitable work, Labour. *Ref.* Cd. 8141.

RELIEF OF DISTRESS.—*See also* Women's Relief.

RENTS TRIBUNAL.—*App.* by S.B.H. in 1920. *Obj.* To decide disputes as to initial rents for houses erected by L.A.'s with State aid. *Repr.* S.B.H., L.A.'s, and presumably experts. *Ref.* Cmd. 1697, pp. 107, 261. *Still in existence end 1922.*

SALVAGE AND PUBLIC CLEANSING BRANCH.—*App.* by S.B.H. in 1920. *Obj.* To organize public cleansing and salvage of waste materials for health and economy, continuing war-time developments. *Repr.* Official and expert. *Ref.* Cmd. 1319, p. 73. *Permanent Organization.*

**SLAUGHTERHOUSES AND DISTRIBUTION OF MEAT COM-
MITTEES (Three).**—*App.* by S.B.H., Feb. 1920, for Administration,
Rural Areas and Standards. *Obj.* To assist in formulating definite pro-
posals for regulating these matters. *Repr.* Government Departments and
L.A.'s (sanitary, medical, &c.) concerned, meat traders, agriculturalists,
Sanitary Associations. *Ref.* Cmd. 1319, pp. 116–17. *Diss.* Nov. 1920.

(These Committees were largely due to resumption of work interrupted
by the War, but were presumably as with similar English Committee concerned with preserving good war-time developments.)

TINKERS DEPARTMENTAL COMMITTEE.—*App.* by L.G.B.(Sc.),
Sept. 1917. *Obj.* To investigate conditions of living, and suggest improve-
ments. *Repr.* L.G.B.(Sc.) and others. *Ref.* Cd. 9020, p. vi, Cmd. 824, p. liv.
Diss. Early in 1918.

TRADES, NEW.—*See under* Women's Relief.

TUBERCULOSIS, GRANTS.—*See* Tre.

WOMEN'S RELIEF, SCOTTISH COMMITTEE.—*App.* by Scottish Advisory Committee of N.R.F., Sept. 1914. *Obj.* To deal with relief of women
unemployed, owing to the War. *Repr.* Prominent public women with
experience of social problems. *Ref.* Cd. 8129.

The Main Committee appointed Sub-Committees for Education and
Training, Highland Industries (to deal with Distress in Highlands due to
change of herring-fishing season and lack of demand for home-spun, hand-
woven tweeds) and New Trades to investigate possibilities of employment,
owing to shortage of male labour, and secured appointment by Relief of
Distress Scottish Advisory Committee of Women's Sub-Committees of
Local Relief Committees to deal locally with relief of women.

WOMEN.—*See also* House Planning.

MUNITIONS OF WAR, MINISTRY OF

The Ministry of Munitions was established by the Ministry of Munitions Act, 1915 (5 & 6 Geo. V, c. 51) of 9th June 1915, under a Minister and Parliamentary Secretary and (later) Secretaries. It absorbed the Armaments Output Department of the War Office and various Committees. The *object* of the Ministry was to organize generally the output of munitions of war ; and the scope of its work was largely increased by transfers from other Departments and by the taking over of the Royal Arsenals. The Ministry was established for the period of the War, and not more than twelve months after its conclusion. *See* Public General Acts, 1915.

At the close of the War the Ministry had sixty or more Departments, divided into ten groups, namely : (1) *Secretariat,* including Priority, Requirements, Statistics, Demobilization and Resettlement, &c. ; (2) *Finance,* including Contracts, Factory Audit, Costs, &c. ; (3) *Design,* including Inspection ; (4) *Steel and Iron* ; (5) *Materials,* including Non-Ferrous Metals, Railway Materials, Optical Munitions, Potash, &c. ; (6) *Explosives,* including Oils and Chemical Warfare ; (7) *Ordnance* ; (8) *Warfare,* including Mechanical Warfare, Trench Warfare, Mechanical Transport, &c. ; (9) *Aircraft* ; (10) *Labour.*

After the Armistice proposals for reorganizing the Ministry as a Ministry of Supply were considered, but subsequently abandoned. It was decided by the Cabinet that the Ministry should cease as a purchasing department in Mar. 1920 (*see* H.C., Nos. 100 &c., 1920, p. xx). This decision does not appear to have been carried out ; but the Ministry was subsequently wound up by the end of Mar. 1921, when the Disposals and Liquidation Commission (*see* below) took over its remaining functions (*see* H.C., No. 102, 1921, p. 18).

ABBREVIATIONS

M.M. = Ministry of Munitions.
M.W.A.(s) = Munitions of War Act(s). The date after the letters M.W.A. indicates an Act of a particular year.

ACCOUNTANTS, JOINT COMMITTEE.—*App.* jointly by M.M., Adm., W.O., in 1917 or earlier. *Obj.* To assist the Departments in systematizing costs. *Repr.* Accountants. *Ref.* H.C., No. 132, 1918, p. 15.

ACCOUNTS LIQUIDATION COMMITTEE.—*App.* by M.M., under powers delegated by Tre., at end of 1919. *Obj.* To co-ordinate and expedite liquidation and settle disputes. *Repr.* Mainly Financial Officers of M.M. *Ref.* Cmd. 1055, p. 13 ; H.C., No. 97, 1919, p. 23. *Diss.* Not later than Mar. 1921.

(An Aircraft Production Sub-Committee was appointed by this Committee.)

ADVISORY COUNCIL, MUNITIONS.—*See under* Munitions.

AGRICULTURAL MACHINERY ADVISORY COMMITTEE.—*App.* jointly by M.M., B.A., and M.F., at instance of M.M., Jan. 1917. *Obj.* To advise Agricultural Machinery Branch upon control of manufacture of machinery and implements. *Repr.* M.M., B.A., B.A.(Sc.), D.A.T.I., M.F., agricultural machinery trade. *Ref.* J.B.A., Jan. 1917; B.T.J., 11th Jan. 1917.

AGRICULTURAL MACHINERY BRANCH.—*App.* by M.M. jointly with B.A., and M.F., Jan. 1917. *Obj.* To control manufacture of agricultural machinery and implements (control of distribution and use remaining with B.A.). *Repr.* Official and expert. *Ref.* B.T.J., 11th Jan. 1917.

AIRCRAFT COMMITTEE, INTER-ALLIED.—*See under* Munitions Council, Inter-Allied.

AIRCRAFT DISPOSALS COMPANY.—Formed to carry out disposal of surplus aircraft and aeronautical effects purchased from Disposals Board (*see* Cmd. 800, p. 11).

AIRCRAFT PRODUCTION.—*See under* Accounts Liquidation above.

AIRCRAFT.—*See also* Aviation.

ALCOHOL FOR MOTOR FUEL, INTER-DEPARTMENTAL COMMITTEE.—*App.* by Petroleum Executive (q.v.), Oct. 1918. *Obj.* To report generally upon manufacture and use of motor fuel from alcohol. *Repr.* Petroleum Executive, various Government Departments, motor users, oil companies, chemical research. *Ref.* Cmd. 218. *Diss.* June 1919.

ALCOHOL SUPPLIES COMMITTEE.—*App.* by M.M. at beginning of 1917. *Obj.* To advise M.M. on means of securing adequate supplies for war purposes and essential industries. *Repr.* M.M., B.A., B.T., Board of Customs and Excise, distilleries, rectifiers, methylators, blenders, merchants. *Ref.* B.T.J., 4th Jan. 1917.

ALLOY STEEL, SHEFFIELD, COMMITTEE.—*App.* by the Government in 1918 or earlier. *Obj.* To develop production of alloy steel for war purposes. *Repr.* Manufacturers, experts. *Ref.* Cmd. 325, p. 114.

AMMONIA EXECUTIVE COMMITTEE.—*App.* by M.M., after consultation with Nitrogen Products Committee (q.v.), Mar. 1917. *Obj.* To take necessary action to develop production of ammonia, &c., and provide plant, on lines laid down by Nitrogen Committee. *Repr.* M.M., W.O., technical engineers, explosives and other experts. *Ref.* Cmd. 482, p. 141. (*See also* Nitrogen, Synthetic Compounds.)

ARBITRATION TRIBUNAL, SPECIAL (MEN'S WAGES).—*App.* by M.M., Mar. 1916, under M.W.A., 1916. *Obj.* To advise M.M. on issue of directions as to wages of semi-skilled and unskilled men on munitions work, and deal with trade disputes referred to them under M.W.A.'s. *Repr.* Legal Profession, M.M., employers, T.U.'s of skilled and unskilled workers. *Ref.* P.G.A., 1914–16 ; Cole, p. 104 ; H.C., No. 185, 1918, pp. 19, 20. *Diss.* Had very few cases and appears soon to have fallen into abeyance.

ARBITRATION TRIBUNAL, SPECIAL (12½ PER CENT. WAR BONUS).—The Committee on Production (*see* B.T.) was appointed as the Special Tribunal for dealing with disputes relating to the bonus, at end of Dec. 1917 under M.W.A., 1917. *See* Cole, p. 171 ; B.T.J., 14th Feb. 1918, p. 192.

ARBITRATION TRIBUNAL, SPECIAL (WOMEN'S WAGES).—*App.* by M.M., Mar. 1916, under M.W.A., 1916, and reconstituted, in view of increased work, Oct. 1917. *Obj.* To advise M.M. on issue of directions as to women's wages on munitions work, and deal with trade disputes referred to them under M.W.A.'s. *Repr.* Legal Profession, B.T., employers and T.U.'s, women. *Ref.* P.G.A., 1914–16 ; L.G., July 1916, p. 265 ; Cole, pp. 84–5. *Diss.* Replaced after close of war by Interim Court of Arbitration (*see* M.L.).

ARMAMENTS OUTPUT COMMITTEE, (LATER) DEPARTMENT.— *See* W.O. This organization formed nucleus of M.M.

ARMAMENTS OUTPUT COMMITTEES, LOCAL.—*App.* under auspices of W.O. in April and May 1915, by local employers and T.U.'s, beginning with North-East Coast, 9th April, and taken over by M.M. *Obj.* To organize and develop generally by joint action munitions production in their areas. *Repr.* Employers and T.U.'s concerned. *Ref.* Cole, pp. 75–6, 124. *Diss.* Fell into abeyance by winter of 1915–16, being replaced sometimes by Boards of Management, District (q.v.).

ARMY RESERVE MUNITIONS WORKERS.—*App.* by, or by arrangement with, M.M. early in 1917. *Obj.* To secure necessary supplies of unskilled labour of military age for munitions work, subject to liability to recall to military service. *Repr.* Unskilled men of military age. *Ref.* Cole, pp. 136–7. *Diss.* Close of war.

AVIATION, BRITISH, COMMISSION.—*App.* either by M.M. or Adm. in 1917 or earlier, in Paris. *Obj.* To make contracts for aeroplanes and engines in France. *Repr.* Presumably expert. *Ref.* H.C., Nos. 83 &c., 1919, p. xv.

BALFOUR-MACASSEY COMMISSION.—*See* Clyde Munition Workers.

BILLETING BOARD, CENTRAL.—*App.* by M.M., under Billeting of Civilians Act, in summer of 1917. *Obj.* To organize provision of billets for persons engaged on work of national importance. *Repr.* Government Departments concerned, and other members appointed by M.M., including housing experts and women. *Ref.* P.G.A., 1917–18.

BILLETING COMMITTEES, LOCAL.—*App.* by Central Billeting Board (q.v.) from summer of 1917, in localities where civilian workers were billeted. *Obj.* To organize and supervise locally provision of billets. *Repr.* L.A.'s concerned and others chosen by Billeting Board. *Ref.* P.G.A., 1917–18.

BLEACHING POWDER USERS COMMITTEE.—*App.* by M.M., Nov.– Dec. 1916. *Obj.* To advise M.M. on needs of users of bleaching powder. *Repr.* Users of bleaching powder. *Ref.* B.T.J., 7th Dec. 1916.

BOARDS OF MANAGEMENT, MUNITIONS, DISTRICT.—*App.* in various districts, at instigation of M.M., from spring of 1915, forty-six being in existence at end of 1917. *Obj.* To develop and organize local munitions output. *Repr.* Employers in engineering and munitions trades, and, in a few cases, on their invitation, T.U.'s. *Ref.* H.C., No. 40, 1917, pp. 11, 12.

(These bodies were sometimes known as Local Munitions Committees, and appointed various local representatives on their work.)

BOARDS OF MANAGEMENT, MUNITIONS, EXECUTIVE COMMITTEE.—*App.* by M.M. in or after summer of 1915. *Obj.* Presumably to carry out central administration in connexion with work of District Boards. *Repr.* Not stated. *Ref.* Cd. 8741, p. 8.

BOY WELFARE.—*See* Health and Welfare Department.

BUILDING LABOUR COMMITTEE.—*App.* by M.M., Nov. 1915, and reorganized and attached to M.L. in 1918. *Obj.* To secure uniformity in application of Fair Wages Resolution to Government Building Contracts, and (later) co-ordinate use of building labour by Government Departments. *Repr.* Government Departments concerned. *Ref.* Cmd. 325, p. 161; L.G., July 1918, p. 300; H.C., Nos. 185, p. 29, 221, p. 15, 1919. *Still in existence* as Inter-Departmental Consultative body at M.L.

BUILDING MATERIALS SUPPLY DEPARTMENT.—*App.* by M.M. shortly after Armistice. *Obj.* To organize supply of building materials for housing schemes. *Repr.* Official and expert. *Ref.* Cmd. 824, p. xlii; Cmd. 1446, p. 121; H.C., No. 10, 1922, p. xxv. *Diss.* Transferred to M.H., June 1920, and in course of liquidation, Feb. 1922.

CANADIAN SHELL COMMITTEE.—*App.* by Canadian, in co-operation with British, Government early in the War. *Obj.* To develop Canadian output of shells. *Repr.* Canadian Government, business men, &c. *Ref.* H.C., No. 40, 1917, p. 15. *Diss.* Replaced by Imperial Munitions Board (q.v.), Nov. 1915.

CANTEENS, MUNITIONS, FINANCE COMMITTEE.—*App.* jointly by M.M. and L.C.B., Mar. 1917. *Obj.* To secure financial solvency of canteens. *Repr.* M.M., L.C.B. *Ref.* H.C., No. 100, &c., 1918, p. viii.

CHEMICAL COMMITTEE (MUNITIONS INVENTIONS DEPARTMENT).—*See* Cd. 9231, p. 29. Details lacking.

CHEMICALS, MUNITIONS, COMMITTEE INTER-ALLIED.—*See under* Munitions Council, Inter-Allied.

CHEMICAL WARFARE COMMITTEE.—Mentioned Cmd. 905, p. 70. No details.

CHEMICAL WARFARE, MEDICAL PROBLEMS.—*See* W.O.

CHINA WOOD OIL SALES DEPARTMENTAL COMMITTEE.—*App.* by M.M., probably in 1920. *Obj.* To inquire into contracts for sales of surplus oil. *Repr.* M.M. *Ref.* H.C., No. 102, 1921, p. 28. *Diss.* Before May 1921.

CIVIL INDUSTRIES COMMITTEE.—*App.* by M.M., originally in Feb. 1917, as Priorities Advisory Committee, and reconstituted under new title, Dec. 1917, as Sub-Committee of Priorities, War Committee (*see* Cabinet). *Obj.* To investigate needs of non-essential industries for raw materials, prevent undue restriction and arrange for supplies for them. *Repr.* Government Departments concerned and prominent business men. *Ref.* B.T.J., 1st Aug. 1917 and 9th Jan. 1919. *Diss.* Jan. 1919.

CLYDE MUNITION WORKERS' COMMISSION.—*App.* by M.M., Oct. 1915. *Obj.* To inquire into apprehended differences and discontent affecting munition workers in Clyde District. *Repr.* Composed of Lord Balfour of Burleigh and Mr. (now Sir) Lynden Macassey, K.C. *Ref.* Cd. 8136. *Diss.* Nov. 1915.

COAL GAS.—*See under* Gas Traction.

CONTRACTS, MUNITIONS, LIQUIDATION COMMITTEE.—*App.* by M.M., Sept. 1919. *Obj.* To expedite and be responsible for liquidation of contracts and co-ordinate work. *Repr.* M.M. (Financial Departments), business experts. *Ref.* T., 23rd Sept. 1919, p. 11.

CONTRACTS, READJUSTMENT, ADVISORY COMMITTEE.—*App.* jointly by Disposals and Liquidation Commission (q.v.) and Tre., early in 1921. *Obj.* To advise Commission upon readjustment of contracts, on grounds of trade and monetary stringency, during post-war liquidations. *Repr.* The Commission, Tre. and others presumably. *Ref.* H.C., No. 10, 1922, p. xxxiii, No. 102, 1921, p. 26.

CONTROLLED ESTABLISHMENTS, PROFITS.—*See* Limitation of Profits.

CO-ORDINATING, MINISTRY OF MUNITIONS, COMMITTEE.—*App.* by Munitions Council (q.v.) late in 1917. *Obj.* To co-ordinate work of various Departments of M.M. under the Council. *Repr.* The Council, various Departments. *Ref.* H.C., No. 132, 1918, p. 4.

COPPER, PURCHASE AND DISTRIBUTION, COMMITTEE.—*App.* by M.M., Dec. 1916. *Obj.* To advise M.M. on these matters. *Repr.* Merchants, importers, Metal Exchanges. *Ref.* B.T.J., 14th Dec. 1916; T., 12th Dec. 1916, p. 5.

COSTS OF PRODUCTION (NATIONAL FACTORIES) COMMITTEE.— *App.* by M.M. late in 1916 or in 1917. *Obj.* To control costing work of National Factories and secure improvements. *Repr.* Presumably largely expert. *Ref.* Cmd. 325, p. 111.

DEMOBILIZATION BOARD, MUNITIONS.—*App.* by M.M., early Nov. 1918, to co-operate with Demobilization and Resettlement Department (*see* M.L.). *Obj.* To secure speedy transition from munitions to normal production, and carry out liquidation of contracts, excluding questions assigned to M.L. *Repr.* M.M., the Military Services, &c., with financial and expert advisers. *Ref.* B.T.J., 14th Nov., p. 609 ; L.G., Nov. 1918.

(*See also* Reconstruction and Demobilization.)

DESTRUCTION OF DOCUMENTS TRIBUNAL.—*App.* by H.O., April 1921, under Tribunals of Inquiry (Evidence) Act, 1921. *Obj.* To report upon alleged instructions by officer of M.M. to destroy or conceal documents. *Repr.* H.L., Legal Profession, business men, chartered accountants. *Ref.* Cmd. 1340. *Diss.* May 1921.

DILUTION COMMISSIONS, CLYDE AND TYNE.—*App.* by M.M., Jan. 1916. *Obj.* To organize and supervise drawing up of schemes of dilution in individual establishments, in consultation with shop stewards and local T.U. officials. *Repr.* M.M., B.T., Employers, Legal Profession, Labour. *Ref.* Cole, pp. 108–9 ; Orton, Labour in Transition, p. 85. *Diss.* Tyne Commission, May 1916, work being taken over by Clyde Commission, which came to an end by 1st Sept. 1916.

(Provision was later made by appointment of Dilution Officers and otherwise for a similar development of dilution in other areas.)

DILUTION, SHOP COMMITTEES.—*App.* by workpeople concerned at suggestion of Dilution Commissions in Clyde and Tyne areas and of M.M.

elsewhere in individual establishments, from 1916. *Obj.* To discuss with management details and difficulties of schemes of dilution. *Repr.* Sometimes skilled workpeople only (shop stewards and T.U.'s), sometimes firm and skilled workpeople jointly, usually with provision for arbitration on disputed points. *Repr.* Cole, p. 109 ; Orton, Labour in Transition, p. 85.

DISPOSALS ADVISORY COMMITTEES.—*App.* by M.M. from Jan. 1919. *Obj.* To advise the Sectional Boards established to deal with individual classes of property. *Repr.* Not stated, presumably largely expert. *Ref.* H.C., No. 97, 1920, p. 26.

DISPOSALS ADVISORY COUNCIL.—This was a reconstitution of the Surplus Government Property Advisory Council (*see* M.R.), which was dissolved on constitution of Disposals Board (q.v.).

(This appears to be the Standing Advisory Committee of M.M. on Surplus War Munitions which in T. of 17th April 1919, p. 535, was referred to as having existed for some time.)

DISPOSALS AND LIQUIDATION COMMISSION.—*App.* apparently by Government on closing down of M.M., at end of Mar. 1921, absorbing Disposals Board. *Obj.* To wind up accounts of war-time Ministries and Departments, and to carry out disposal of surplus stores. *Repr.* Parliament, W.O., A.M., M.M., Prominent Business Men, Chartered Accountants. *Ref.* Cmd. 1412, No. 102, 1921, passim. *Still in existence at end of 1922.*

DISPOSALS BOARD.—*App.* by M.M., under Cabinet decision, Jan. 1919, in place of Surplus Government Property Disposals Board (*see* M.R.). *Obj.* To organize disposal of surplus government property. *Repr.* Parliament, M.M., W.O., prominent manufacturers and business men. *Ref.* Cmd. 850, pp. 3, 13. *Diss.* Absorbed into Disposals and Liquidation Commission (q.v.), Mar. 1921.

(The Board appointed Sectional Boards to deal with particular classes of property.)

DISPOSALS BOARD, AMALGAMATION COMMITTEE.—*App.* by the Board in 1920 or early 1921. *Obj.* To secure amalgamation of controls during disposal, with a view to economy. *Repr.* The Board. *Ref.* Cmd. 1412, p. 6.

DISPOSAL SECTIONAL BOARDS.—*See under* Disposals Board.

DISPOSALS.—*See also* Salvage, and M.R. under Surplus Government Property.

EMERGENCY (MUNITIONS' EXPENDITURE) COMMITTEE.—*See* Tre.

ENLISTMENTS.—*See* Labour Enlistments.

ESTABLISHMENT, BRANCH SUB-COMMITTEES.—*App.* by M.M. since Armistice. *Obj.* To expedite reduction of staffs of particular branches of M.M. *Repr.* Experienced officials. *Ref.* Cmd. 1055, p. 14.

ESTABLISHMENT COMMITTEE.—*App.* by M.M., Feb. 1919. *Obj.* To expedite reductions in head-quarters' staff. *Repr.* Business men with experience of Government Departments. *Ref.* Cmd. 1055, p. 14.

EXPENDITURE, MUNITIONS, STANDING AND EMERGENCY STANDING COMMITTEES.—Incidental reference on pp. 15, 16 of H.C.,

No. 102, 1921. The Emergency Standing Committee may be the Emergency Committee referred to above. *See also* Tre.

EXPLOSIONS (COMPENSATION) ADVISORY COMMITTEE.—*App.* by M.M. about end of 1916, under Munitions (Liability for Explosions) Act, 1916. *Obj.* To advise M.M. on rate of contributions to scheme of insurance against liability to injury, fix rates and decide disputes. *Repr.* Mainly Insurance Experts. *Ref.* P.G.A., 1916.

(This is presumably the Explosions at Government and Controlled Factories Committee of Cd. 8741, p. 5.)

EXPLOSIONS IN EXPLOSIVE FACTORIES, STANDING COMMITTEE.—*App.* by M.M. in 1917. *Obj.* To inquire into causes of explosions and fires in explosives factories. *Repr.* M.M., H.O., and others. *Ref.* Cd. 9050, p. 2.

EXPLOSIVES AND EXPLOSIVES' MATERIALS INTER-ALLIED ADVISORY COMMITTEE.—*App.* jointly by chief Allied Governments early in 1918. *Obj.* To advise as to purchase of these products by British Government for European Allies. *Repr.* Chief Allied Governments. *Ref.* Cd. 9005.

EXPLOSIVES, HANDLING AND STORAGE COMMITTEE (LOCAL).—*App.* by M.M. in 1917. *Obj.* To investigate this matter in a Northern Port. *Repr.* M.M., H.O., and others. *Ref.* Cd. 9050, p. 2. *Diss.* Presumably later in 1917.

FERROUS SCRAP BRANCH.—*App.* by M.M. by May 1918. *Obj.* To organize recovery of materials from ferrous scrap. *Repr.* Official and expert. *Ref.* Cmd. 325, p. 114.

FERTILIZERS COMMITTEES.—*See* M.F., *under* Fertilizers, Phosphates and Potash, Sulphate of Ammonia.

FINANCE, MUNITIONS, ADVISORY COMMITTEE.—*App.* by M.M. prior to Sept. 1917. *Ref.* without details, Cd. 8741, p. 8.

FINANCE MUNITIONS COMMITTEE.—*App.* prior to June 1916. *Ref.* without details, Cd. 8256, 8741, p. 8.

FLAX SUPPLIES COMMITTEE.—*App.* by M.M., about Aug. 1917, after requisitioning of flax crop. *Obj.* To assist organization of M.M. at Belfast in purchase, &c., of crop. *Repr.* M.M., the Linen Trade and, apparently, farmers. *Ref.* B.T.J., 27th June 1918, p. 802. *Diss.* Transferred to B.T., April 1919 and terminated by Mar. 1920.

FOOD SECTION, MINISTRY OF MUNITIONS.—*App.* by M.M. in winter of 1917–18. *Obj.* To secure, in co-operation with M.F., L.C.B., &c., adequate supplies of food for munition workers, and advise upon administration of canteens, taking over certain duties from L.C.B. *Repr.* M.M., L.C.B., M.F., W.O. and others. *Ref.* Cmd. 325, p. 291, 340, p. 30. *Diss.* Some duties transferred back later to L.C.B. For Food, *see also* S.I.R.

FOOD SUPPLY TO MUNITION WORKERS COMMITTEE (SOMETIMES CALLED MUNITIONS FOOD COMMITTEE).—*App.* by M.M. early in 1918. *Obj.* To advise on supply and distribution of food to munition workers. *Repr.* M.M., Adm., L.C.B., medical and canteen experts, Labour, women. *Ref.* B.T.J., 25th April 1918 ; Cd. 9005, p. 195.

FRENCH MUNITIONS OUTPUT, MISSION ON.—*App.* by M.M., with approval of French Minister of Munitions, Nov. 1915. *Obj.* To visit French industrial districts and report on causes of increased munitions output. *Repr.* M.M., engineering employers, Labour, experts in munitions engineering. *Ref.* Cd. 8187. *Diss.* Dec. 1915.

(*See also* H.O. *under* Munitions Manufacture.)

FUEL OIL.—*See under* Oil.

GAS FIRING.—*See under* Nitrogen Products.

GAS PLANT PRIORITY.—*See under* Priority, Munitions, Sub-Committees.

GAS TRACTION, INTER-DEPARTMENTAL COMMITTEE.—*App.* by Petroleum Executive, Nov. 1917. *Obj.* To investigate use of coal and other gas for power, especially in motor traction. *Repr.* The Executive, B.T., H.O., L.G.B., M.M., M.R., L.A.'s, gas producers and engineers, motor users. *Ref.* Cmd. 263. *Diss.* June 1919.

GAS TRACTION, EXPERT SUB-COMMITTEE.—*App.*, at request of Main Committee, May 1918. *Obj.* To carry out expert technical investigations required. *Repr.* Main Committee, engineering and scientific experts. *Ref.* Cmd. 263. *Diss.* June or July 1919.

GRAIN FOR YEAST AND ALCOHOL COMMITTEE.—*App.* by M.M., April 1917. *Obj.* To consider consumption of grain for yeast and munitions' alcohol. *Repr.* M.M. and others. *Ref.* B.T.J., Oct. 1918, p. 456. *Diss.* May 1917.

GRETNA AND WALTHAM ABBEY, COMMITTEE OF INQUIRY.—*App.* by M.M., Feb. 1919. *Obj.* To consider future of these factories. *Repr.* Parliament, M.M., B.T., W.O., manufacturers, contractors. *Ref.* Cmd. 667. *Diss.* June 1919.

HEALTH AND WELFARE DEPARTMENT, MINISTRY OF MUNITIONS.—*App.* by M.M., early in 1916, as Welfare Department and subsequently expanded. *Obj.* To promote and organize good welfare conditions in munitions' factories and subsequently outside the factories, e.g. provision for maternity, care of children, &c. *Repr.* Official and expert. *Ref.* Cd. 9005, pp. 192–3 ; Cmd. 340.

A Boy Welfare Section was also established. *See also* Welfare, Works Committees.

HEALTH OF MUNITION WORKERS ADVISORY COMMITTEE.—*App.* by M.M., May 1918. *Obj.* To advise on general principles of carrying out welfare and health work of M.M., and report on matters specially referred to them. *Repr.* M.M. and Health and Welfare Departments, H.O., M.R.C., Employers, Labour, Women. *Ref.* T., 20th May 1918.

HEALTH OF MUNITION WORKERS COMMITTEE.—*App.* by M.M., Sept. 1915. *Obj.* To advise upon industrial fatigue, hours and other matters affecting health and efficiency of munition workers. *Repr.* M.M., H.O., Medical Profession and Research, Manufacturers, Labour, Women. *Ref.* Cd. 8511, 9065. *Diss.* April 1918, work being continued permanently in Industrial Fatigue Research Board (*see* N.H.I.C.).

HIGH EXPLOSIVES DEPARTMENT.—*See* W.O.

HOLIDAYS, MUNITIONS, COMMITTEE.—*App.* by M.M., July 1916. *Obj.* To recommend arrangements for workmen to take holidays in relays to secure uninterrupted output. *Repr.* Parliament, M.M., H.O., Employers, Labour, women, social experts. *Ref.* T., 28th July 1926.

HORSE CHESTNUTS.—*See* M.F.

HOSTELS DEPARTMENT.—*App.* by M.M. in 1916. *Obj.* To organize hostel accommodation for female and other munition workers required to live away from home. *Repr.* Official and expert. *Ref.* Cmd. 340.

HOURS OF LABOUR, MUNITIONS, COMMITTEE.—*App.* by M.M. late in 1915, in co-operation with H.O. *Obj.* To secure joint consideration by two Departments of applications for Sunday work or long overtime during the week. *Repr.* M.M., H.O. *Ref.* Cd. 8276, p. 6.

IMPERIAL MINERAL RESOURCES BUREAU INTER-DEPARTMENTAL COMMITTEE.—*App.* by M.M., June 1917. *Obj.* To prepare scheme for Bureau in London. *Repr.* M.M., In.O., G.I., The Dominions, Geological Survey, Imperial Institute, mining experts. *Ref.* Cd. 8916. *Diss.* Late in 1917.

IMPERIAL MUNITIONS BOARD.—*App.* by Canadian Government, in co-operation with M.M., Nov. 1915, replacing Canadian Shell Committee. *Obj.* To develop Canadian munitions production, and act as purchasing agent for G.B. and (later) U.S.A. in Canada. *Repr.* Canadian Government, business men, &c. *Ref.* H.C., No. 40, 1917, p. 15 ; Cmd. 325, p. 118. *Diss.* Operations terminated by M.M. immediately after Armistice.

IRISH BRANCH, MINISTRY OF MUNITIONS.—*App.* by M.M. in second half of 1915. *Obj.* To organize munitions output in Ireland. *Repr.* Official and expert. *Ref.* Cd. 8393, p. xiii.

INDIA MUNITIONS BOARD.—*See* In.O.

INDUSTRIAL UNREST COMMISSION OF INQUIRY.—*See* Cabinet.

INTER-ALLIED MUNITIONS BUREAU.—*See* Munitions.

LABOUR ADVISORY BOARDS OR COMMITTEES ON WAR OUTPUT, LOCAL.—*App.* by M.M. and Labour Advisory Committee, National (*see* next entry), mainly in Oct. and Nov. 1915, but some earlier and later. *Obj.* To assist in enrolment of W.M.V.'s, and generally investigate employers' failure to observe M.W.A.'s, secure records of changes in workshop practice and watch dilution schemes. *Repr.* Munitions T.U.'s. *Ref.* L.Y.B., 1919, p. 112 ; Cole, p. 194.

LABOUR ADVISORY COMMITTEE ON WAR OUTPUT, NATIONAL. —*App.* by the Government after Treasury Conference (Mar. 1915), and subsequently absorbed in M.M. *Obj.* To advise generally in regard to securing and utilizing labour for munitions work. *Repr.* Munitions T.U.'s. *Ref.* L.Y.B., 1919 ; Cole, p. 74. *Diss.* Superseded by Trade Union Advisory Committee (q.v.) about end of 1917.

LABOUR EMBARGOES JOINT CONSULTATIVE COMMITTEE.— *App.* by the Government on recommendation of Labour Embargoes Inquiry Committee (q.v.), Oct. 1918. *Obj.* To advise M.M. and Adm. on means of securing best possible distribution of skilled labour in munitions trades. *Repr.* The Government, Employers and T.U.'s concerned. *Ref.* L.Y.B., 1919, p. 105 ; Cole, p. 156. *Diss.* Rendered nugatory by Armistice.

(The Trade Union Women's Advisory Committee were also invited to appoint members, but some difficulties arose over the representation to be accorded to them.)

LABOUR EMBARGOES INQUIRY COMMITTEE (MR. JUSTICE McCARDIE'S COMMITTEE).—*App.* by M.M., Aug. 1918. *Obj.* To investigate question of embargoes on employment of skilled labour and causes of strike over them. *Repr.* M.M., Adm., M.L., Employers, T.U.'s. *Ref.* H.M.S.O., 1918 ; Cole, p. 156. *Diss.* Sept. 1918.

LABOUR ENLISTMENTS COMPLAINTS COMMITTEE AND SECTION.—*App.* by M.M., April 1917. *Obj.* To deal with cases where Local Committees (q.v.) fail to agree. *Repr.* Presumably Departments concerned and Labour. *Ref.* L.Y.B., 1919, p. 147.

LABOUR ENLISTMENT COMPLAINTS, LOCAL COMMITTEES.—*App.* by M.M., April 1917, for each area, under Schedule of Protected Occupations. *Obj.* To deal with complaints of victimization and improper enlistment. *Repr.* M.M., W.O., Adm., Chief Dilution Officer for each area, Labour. *Ref.* L.Y.B., 1919, p. 147.

LABOUR PRIORITY MUNITIONS COMMITTEE.—*App.* by M.M. in 1915 or early 1916. *Obj.* To deal with questions of priority for available labour. *Repr.* Not stated. *Ref.* Cd. 8741, p. 8.

LABOUR SUPPLY, MUNITIONS, CENTRAL COMMITTEE.—*App.* by M.M., Sept. 1915. *Obj.* To promote and speed up dilution and preparation of definite schemes. *Repr.* M.M., National Labour Advisory Committee, engineering employers and T.U.'s. *Ref.* Orton, pp. 60, 72 ; Cole, p. 88. *Diss.* In 1917, its functions having been gradually taken over by Arbitration Tribunals, Special (*see* above).

LEAD, SPANISH, PURCHASES, INTER-ALLIED COMMITTEE.—*App.* jointly by the Chief Allied Governments early in 1918. *Obj.* To purchase supplies jointly. *Repr.* The Governments concerned. *Ref.* Cd. 9005.

LEAVING CERTIFICATES.—*See under* Rates of Skilled Time-workers.

LIMITATION OF PROFITS, ACCOUNTANTS ADVISORY COMMITTEE.—*App.* by M.M. before June 1917. *Obj.* To advise on questions of valuation, accountancy, &c., in this connexion. *Repr.* Consulting chartered accountants. *Ref.* Cd. 8623, pp. 3–5.

LIMITATION OF PROFITS, BOARD OF REFEREES.—*App.* by M.M. under M.W.A., 1915, by Munitions (Limitation of Profits) Rules, Sept. 1915. *Obj.* To decide disputed cases of assessment, &c. *Repr.* Largely expert. *Ref.* P.G.A., 1915 ; L.G., Oct. 1916 (Supplement, pp. 5–7) ; Cd. 8741, p. 4 (Controlled Establishments, Board of Referees on Profits).

LIQUIDATION BOARD.—*App.* by the Disposals and Liquidation Commission (q.v.), April 1921. *Obj.* To exercise certain of former powers of M.M. for liquidating accounts and contracts. *Repr.* The Commission, Civil Service, Chartered Accountants. *Ref.* Cmd. 1640, p. 15.

LOCAL MUNITIONS COMMITTEES.—*See* Armament Output Committees ; Boards of Management, District ; Metropolitan Munitions Committee.

LUBRICATING OILS ADVISORY COMMITTEE.—*App.* by M.M. prior to Sept. 1917. *Ref.*, without details, Cd. 8741, p. 7.

McCARDIE (MR. JUSTICE) COMMITTEE.—*See* Labour Embargoes.

MACHINE TOOLS CENTRAL CLEARING HOUSE.—*App.* by M.M. late in 1916. *Obj.* To secure most efficient distribution of existing machine tools and plant. *Repr.* Official and expert. *Ref.* Cd. 9005, p. 74.
(A Census of Machinery had already been carried out under W.O. and M.M. in 1915.)

MACHINE TOOLS COMMITTEE.—*App.* prior to Sept. 1917, either by M.M. or by Armaments Output Committee, and absorbed later in M.M. *Obj.* To organize and supervise output of machine tools. *Repr.* Machine tool makers and others. *Ref.* Cd. 8741, p. 7.

MAN POWER, TRADE UNION, COMMITTEE.—*App.* by Munitions Trade Unions (other than Amalgamated Society of Engineers) during negotiations with the Government, early in 1918. *Obj.* To discuss with Amalgamated Society of Engineers revision of schedule of Protected Occupations and demand for combing out of all dilutees before taking of skilled engineers for the Army. *Repr.* The T.U.'s concerned. *Ref.* T., 15th Feb. 1918, p. 7.

MATERIALS.—*See* Metals and Materials.

MECHANICAL TRANSPORT INTER-ALLIED COMMITTEE.—*See under* Munitions Council, Inter-Allied.

METALS AND MATERIALS ECONOMY COMMITTEE.—*App.* by M.M. Nov. 1916. *Obj.* To advise on most economical use of metals in manufacture of munitions. *Repr.* Not stated. *Ref.* B.T.J., 30th Nov. 1916.

METROPOLITAN MUNITIONS COMMITTEE.—*App.* by M.M. in summer of 1915. *Obj.* To organize production of munitions in London area for M.M. *Repr.* Manufacturers and others in London area. *Ref.* B.T.J., 23rd May 1918. *Diss.* Absorbed into central organization of M.M., Jan. 1918.

MILITARY SERVICE COMMITTEE.—*App.* by M.M. in autumn of 1916. *Obj.* To examine cases of fit men of military age on head-quarters' staff, to secure release for military service of all not indispensable to efficiency of M.M. *Repr.* M.M., London Ship-owners' and Transport Workers' Military Service Committee. *Ref.* Cd. 8411. *Diss.* Oct.–Nov. 1916.

MINERAL OIL.—*See under* Oil.

MINERAL RESOURCES ADVISORY COMMITTEE.—*App.* by M.M., Mar. 1917. *Obj.* To advise on development of home resources (other than coal and iron) for war purposes. *Repr.* M.M., B.T., D.A.T.I., Geological Survey, mining and metallurgical experts. *Ref.* B.T.J., 5th April 1917 ; Cd. 9184. *Diss.* Reported Mar. 1918, but seems to have continued in existence subsequently.

MINERAL RESOURCES DEVELOPMENT DEPARTMENT.—*App.* by M.M., Mar. 1917. *Obj.* To examine and develop home mineral properties (except coal and iron) for war purposes. *Repr.* Official and expert. *Ref.* B.T.J., 5th April 1917, p. 66; Cd. 9184.

MOTOR VEHICLES PRIORITY.—*See under* Priority, Munitions, Sub-Committees.

MOTORS, ARMY, SALES ADVISORY COMMITTEE.—*App.* by Disposals Board in winter of 1918–19. *Obj.* To advise and assist in disposal of surplus army motors. *Repr.* Motor manufacturers and users. *Ref.* T., 20th Mar. 1919, p. 7.

MUNITIONS ACT, 1915, AMENDMENT COMMITTEE.—*App.* by Munitions T.U.'s at a Conference with the Minister of Munitions, 30th Nov. 1915. *Obj.* To negotiate for amendments to M.W.A. *Repr.* Munitions T.U.'s. *Ref.* Cole, pp. 118–21. *Diss.* The Committee appears to have come to an end, Dec. 1915, and a further National Conference of Munitions T.U.'s appointed another Committee to negotiate with M.M.
  (*See also* Munitions of War Bill, 1917.)

MUNITIONS ADVISORY COMMITTEE.—*App.* prior to June 1916. *Ref.* without details, Cd. 8256, p. 6. This appears to be either the Advisory Council or the Cabinet Committee (*see* below).

MUNITIONS ADVISORY COUNCIL.—*App.* by M.M. in 1915 or early 1916. *Obj.* To advise and assist M.M. generally. *Repr.* Heads of important departments in M.M. *Ref.* H.C., No. 132, 1918, p. 3. *Diss.* Absorbed into Munitions Council (q.v.), Aug. 1917.

MUNITIONS BUREAU, INTER-ALLIED.—*App.* prior to Sept. 1917. *Ref.*, without details, Cd. 8741, p. 8.

MUNITIONS, CABINET COMMITTEE.—*See* Cabinet.

MUNITIONS COUNCIL.—*App.* by Minister of Munitions, in reorganization of M.M., Sept. 1917, and reconstructed shortly after the Armistice for purposes of disposal and liquidation. *Obj.* To co-ordinate and direct different branches of the work, and settle important questions of policy. *Repr.* Composed of the Minister, Parliamentary Secretaries and representatives of the ten Groups of Departments (*see* Heading to Section) in M.M. *Ref.* H.C., No. 151, 1917, p. xi; Cd. 9005, p. 68; Cmd. 325, p. 125. *Diss.* By end of Mar. 1921.

MUNITIONS COUNCIL, INTER-ALLIED.—*App.* by Chief Allied Governments, June 1918. *Obj.* To organize single control of purchase and distribution of munitions for allies, and co-ordinate work of Committees (similarly constituted) for important branches of munitions work. *Repr.* Chief Allied Governments. *Ref.* Cmd. 325, pp. 23, 108–9, 169. *Diss.* At or after Armistice.
  (Committees were constituted for Aircraft, Chemicals, Explosives, Mechanical Transport, Nitrates (*see* Nitrate of Soda Executive), Non-Ferrous Metals, and Steel.)

MUNITIONS FOOD COMMITTEE.—*See* Food Supply.

MUNITIONS INVENTIONS ADVISORY PANEL.—*App.* by M.M., Aug. 1915. *Obj.* To assist Munitions Inventions Branch in dealing with projects of inventions for munitions for land warfare. *Repr.* Scientific experts. *Ref.* B.T.J., Sept. 1915.

(The Panel appointed Committees of its members to investigate various projects.)

MUNITIONS INVENTIONS BRANCH, (LATER) DEPARTMENT.— *App.* by M.M. in summer of 1915. *Obj.* To examine and develop projects for inventions for land warfare, submitted to M.M. *Repr.* M.M. and experts. *Ref.* Cd. 9005, p. 62.

MUNITIONS LEVY.—*See* Limitation of Profits.

MUNITIONS OF WAR BILL, 1917, TRADE UNION COMMITTEE.— *App.* by 50 Munitions' Trade Unions after conference with Government, May 1917. *Obj.* To consider amendments to the Bill and confer with M.M. on its terms and on any grievances arising from it. *Repr.* The T.U.'s concerned. *Ref.* T., 11th May 1917, p. 3. *Diss.* Later in 1917.

MUNITIONS PARLIAMENTARY, PARLIAMENTARY EXECUTIVE, COMMITTEES.—The former referred to without details in Cd. 8256, p. 6, was probably appointed in 1915. The Executive Committee (*Ref.* Cd. 8741, p. 8) would appear to have come into existence in 1916 or the first half of 1917, and was probably a reorganization of the Parliamentary Committee. The purpose in each case was presumably to organize the work of Members of Parliament in expediting output of munitions and the Committees represented the chief parties in Parliament.

MUNITIONS WORK BUREAUX.—*See* War Munition Volunteers.

MUNITION WORKERS' COMB-OUT, AREA COUNCILS.—*App.* by M.M., May 1917. *Obj.* To carry out government scheme for comb-out of munitions works under new Trade Card Scheme. *Repr.* M.M., M.L., M.N.S., W.O., Labour, Enlistment Complaints Committee. *Ref.* T., 9th May 1917, p. 3.

NATIONAL FACTORIES COMMITTEE.—Referred to on pp. xvi, xvii, 126–7 of H.C., Nos. 100, &c., 1920. No details are given, but the Committee was apparently appointed by M.M., who were represented by the Chairman.

See also Costs of Production (National Factories).

NITRATE OF SODA EXECUTIVE.—*App.* after Inter-Allied Conference at Paris, Nov.–Dec. 1917, by chief Allied Governments, and attached to M.M. *Obj.* Joint purchase and supply of Chilian Nitrates for Allied Governments. *Repr.* Governments concerned, Commission Internationale de Ravitaillement. *Repr.* J.B.A., Feb. 1918. *Diss.* April or May 1919.

NITROGEN PRODUCTS COMMITTEE.—*App.* by M.M., June 1916. *Obj.* To advise upon problems of production, supply and distribution of nitrogen and its products in peace and war, and carry out experiments. *Repr.* M.M., B.A., B.T., Royal Scientific Societies, eminent scientists, engineers and business experts. *Ref.* Cmd. 4872. *Diss.* May 1919.

NITROGEN PRODUCTS SUB-COMMITTEES were appointed by the Main Committee, ' to utilize the special qualifications and experience of its members to the best advantage,' for Economics, Experiments, General Purposes, Power and Gas-Firing Processes (*see* Cmd. 482, p. 2). A Research Section was also organized by the Munitions Invention Department (q.v.) to conduct experiments.

NITROGEN, SYNTHETIC COMPOUNDS, COMMITTEE OF MUNITIONS COUNCIL.—*App.* by the Council, Oct. 1917. *Obj.* To examine proposals of Ammonia Executive Committee for factory and processes for synthetic nitrogen production. *Repr.* Munitions Council. *Ref.* Cmd. 482, pp. 141–2. *Diss.* About April 1918.

NON-FERROUS METALS DEPARTMENT.—*App.* by M.M., Mar. 1917. *Obj.* To assist in increasing home output. *Repr.* Official and expert. *Ref.* Cd. 9005, p. 71.

NON-FERROUS METALS, INTER-ALLIED, COMMITTEE.—*See* Munitions Council, Inter-Allied.

OIL FUEL, PRODUCTION FROM HOME SOURCES, COMMITTEE.—*App.* by M.M. in consultation with C.O. and Petroleum Executive, April 1918. *Obj.* To advise on proposals of Petroleum Executive, and measures taken by M.M., to increase home production. *Repr.* Parliament, M.M., Adm., Coal Controller, with technical adviser (Fuel Research Board). *Ref.* Cd. 9128. *Diss.* Later in 1918.

OIL, MINERAL, PRODUCTION DEPARTMENT.—*App.* by M.M. at instance of the Government, May or June 1917. *Obj.* To undertake production of oils from home sources. *Repr.* Official and expert. *Ref.* Cd. 9005, p. 135.

OILS AND FATS BRANCH.—*App.* by M.M. as Branch of Explosives Department, on assuming control of these products, Mar. 1917. *Obj.* To organize control of fats, oils, oil seeds and products (except mineral and essential oils, butter and lard). *Repr.* Official and expert. *Ref.* B.T.J., 15th Mar. 1917.

OILS AND FATS CONSULTATIVE COMMITTEE.—*App.* by M.M. by arrangement with B.A. and F.C., Mar. 1917. *Obj.* To assist in organizing control of fats, oil seeds and cake, &c. *Repr.* Government Departments concerned in control. *Ref.* J.B.A., Mar. 1917.

ORDNANCE FACTORIES COMMITTEE.—*See* Woolwich.

ORDNANCE, MUNITIONS, COMMITTEE.—*App.* by M.M. prior to Sept. 1917. *Obj.* To initiate and supervise research and, in advisory capacity, criticize and amend designs, submitted by Woolwich Arsenal and armament firms. *Repr.* 'Officers of high attainments and scientific ability.' *Ref.* Cd. 8741, p. 8; Cmd. 229, p. 12.
  (The Committee worked through a number of Sub-Committees.)

PARLIAMENTARY EXECUTIVE, MUNITIONS, COMMITTEE.—*See under* Munitions.

PETROLEUM ALLOCATION COMMITTEE.—*App.* by U.S.A. Fuel Administration about end of 1917. *Obj.* To avoid competition in placing orders in U.S.A. and (later) fix prices. *Repr.* The Fuel Administration. *Ref.* Cmd. 325, p. 204.

PETROLEUM DISTRIBUTION COMMITTEE.—*App.* as Committee of the Petroleum Supplies Pool Board (q.v.), about April 1917. *Obj.* To control and regulate distribution of supplies. *Repr.* The Pool Board. *Ref.* B.T.J., 3rd May 1917; J.B.A., Mar. 1918, p. 1481. *Diss.* Apparently absorbed into Petroleum Executive by end of 1917.

PETROLEUM EXECUTIVE.—*App.* at request of Cabinet, by Minister in charge of problem, to work in M.M., Aug. 1917. *Obj.* To settle questions of policy affecting petroleum oils and oil products and co-ordinate work of consuming Departments. *Repr.* Departments concerned, scientific and business experts. *Ref.* Cd. 9005, p. 136; B.T.J., 11th Oct. 1917.

PETROLEUM EXECUTIVE COMMITTEE.—Such a Committee, presumably advisory to the Executive, and appointed about the same time, is referred to (without details) in Cmd. 137.

PETROLEUM INTER-ALLIED COUNCIL.—*App.* jointly by American, British, French and Italian Governments, Nov. 1917. *Obj.* To advise Petroleum Executive on means of providing for Allied requirements and approve purchasing programmes. *Repr.* The four Governments. *Ref.* Cmd. 325, pp. 203–4. *Diss.* After close of War.

(The Council appointed Tank Storage and Specifications Commissions, which visited France and U.S.A. respectively, and co-operated with the Programmes Committee for Petroleum, *see* Cabinet.)

PETROLEUM, REGULATION OF SUPPLIES, INTER-DEPARTMENTAL COMMITTEE.—*App.* by the Government and housed with M.M., Feb. 1917. *Obj.* To co-ordinate work of different Departments in connexion with petroleum. *Repr.* The Departments concerned. *Ref.* Cd. 9005, p. 135. *Diss.* Superseded later in 1917 by the Oil, Mineral, Production Department and the Petroleum Supplies Pool Board (q.v.).

PETROLEUM SUPPLIES, MUNITIONS, BRANCH.—*App.* by M.M., Feb. 1917. *Obj.* To organize provision and distribution of petroleum and similar oils for munitions purposes. *Repr.* Official and expert. *Ref.* B.T.J., 18th Feb. 1917. *Diss.* Apparently absorbed into Petroleum Executive by end of 1917.

PETROLEUM SUPPLIES, MUNITIONS, BRANCH, RESEARCH SECTION.—*App.* by M.M., Feb. 1917 or later. *Obj.* To investigate and develop unproved home sources of supply of mineral oils. *Repr.* Petroleum technologists and experts. *Ref.* B.T.J., 25th Sept. 1917. *Diss.* Apparently absorbed into Petroleum Executive by end of 1917.

PETROLEUM SUPPLIES POOL BOARD.—*App.*, at instance of Government, by chief Petroleum Companies jointly with M.M., April 1917. *Obj.* To ensure adequate supplies for essential purposes by pooling tonnage and distributing facilities and make possible release of men for the Army. *Repr.* M.M., Petroleum Companies. *Ref.* B.T.J., 3rd May 1917.

PHOSPHATES AND POTASH DISTRIBUTION COMMITTEE.—*See under* Fertilizers.

POTASH PRODUCTION BRANCH.—*App.* by M.M., June 1917. *Obj.* To secure increased supplies of potash, to meet shortage due to cessation of German imports. *Repr.* Official and expert. *Ref.* B.T.J., 5th Sept. 1918.

POWER AND GAS FIRING.—*See under* Nitrogen Products Sub-Committees.

PRINTERS' METAL FOR BULLETS, TRADE COMMITTEE.—*App.* by M.M. about Jan. 1918. *Obj.* To prepare scheme for using printers' metal and plates for shrapnel bullets to save tonnage. *Repr.* Printing and publishing firms. *Ref.* B.T.J., 7th Feb. 1918.

PRIORITY AUTHORITIES IN BRITISH DOMINIONS.—*App.* in all British Overseas Dominions at instigation of M.M., apparently in first half of 1917. *Obj.* To secure uniformity in allocation of supplies throughout the Empire according to needs of Dominions. *Repr.* Not stated. *Ref.* Cd. 9005, p. 72.

PRIORITIES, MUNITIONS, ADVISORY COMMITTEE.—*See* Civil Industries Committee.

PRIORITY, MUNITIONS, COMMITTEE.—*App.* by M.M. in summer or autumn of 1915. *Obj.* To advise Priority, Munitions, Department (q.v.) in its work. *Repr.* Departments of M.M., and later other Government Departments concerned. *Ref.* B.T.J., 1st Aug. 1918.

PRIORITY, MUNITIONS, DEPARTMENT.—*App.* by M.M. in summer or autumn of 1915. *Obj.* To co-ordinate and adjust work of different departments and claims to priority. *Repr.* Official and expert. *Ref.* B.T.J., 1st Aug. 1918. *Diss.* April 1918.

PRIORITY, MUNITIONS, LABOUR.—*See under* Labour.

PRIORITY, MUNITIONS, SUB-COMMITTEES.—*App.* in 1916 and 1917 by M.M. for Gas Plant, Motor Vehicles, Railway Material and Textile Machinery. *Obj.* To perform functions of Priority Committee for those products. *Repr.* As with Priority Committee. *Ref.* B.T.J., 1st Aug. 1918.

PROGRAMME SUB-COMMITTEE.—*App.* by Munitions Council in 1917. *Obj.* To carry out continuous systematic review of munitions' programme. *Repr.* The Council and various Departments, and largely technical. *Ref.* H.C., No. 132, 1918, p. 6.

RAILWAYS MATERIALS.—*See* Priority, Munitions, Sub-Committees.

RATES OF SKILLED TIME-WORKERS DEPARTMENTAL COMMITTEE.—*App.* by M.M., Aug. 1917. *Obj.* To report upon these rates with special reference to relation to wages of less skilled men on payment by results, and to question of abolition of leaving certificates. *Repr.* Parliament, M.M., Adm., M.L., Employers, T.U.'s in Skilled Trades. *Ref.* Cole, pp. 160, 168–9. *Diss.* Sept. 1917.

RECONSTRUCTION AND DEMOBILIZATION COMMITTEE.—*App.* by M.M. about June 1917. *Obj.* To deal with these questions as affecting M.M. *Repr.* Various Departments of M.M. *Ref.* Cd. 8916 ; Cmd. 25, p. 125. *Diss.* Absorbed, Nov. 1918, into Demobilization Board (*see* above), and into Department of Civil Demobilization and Resettlement (*see* M.L.).

RESTORATION OF TRADE UNION CONDITIONS SPECIAL COMMITTEE.—This was appointed by the Joint Committee on Labour Problems after the War, representing principal national Labour bodies, to suggest measures for making guarantees effective and generally watch position. *See* Cole, pp. 190–5.

(For other Committees on this subject *see* Cabinet, M.L., M.R.)

RESTRICTIONS, TRADE UNION.—*See* Trade Union Negotiating Committee, below.

RHODESIA MUNITIONS, (LATER) MUNITIONS AND RESOURCES, COMMITTEE.—*App.* by Chartered Company, Nov. 1915. *Obj.* To assist M.M. in developing local munitions production, in co-operation with similar Committee for Union of South Africa, and (later) to carry out general survey of Rhodesian resources. *Repr.* Not stated. *Ref.* B.T.J., 24th Oct. 1918.

ROAD STONE CONTROL COMMITTEE.—*App.* by M.M., May 1917. *Obj.* To put into operation control of road stone quarries and supplies for M.M. *Repr.* M.M., L.G.B., W.O., quarry and road experts. *Ref.* B.T.J., 17th May 1918.

ROAD STONE LOCAL COMMITTEES.—*See* W.O.

ROYAL ORDNANCE FACTORIES, WOOLWICH.—*See* Woolwich.

RUBBER CONTROL COMMITTEE.—*App.* by M.M. by Oct. 1918. *Obj.* To advise M.M. on establishment of control, with view to economizing in ocean carriage. *Repr.* Business experts and others. *Ref.* B.T.J., 17th Oct. 1918, p. 487 ; T., 24th Aug., 11th Oct., 1918, p. 5.

SALVAGE, MUNITIONS, BRANCH.—*App.* by M.M., May 1918. *Obj.* To organize disposal of obsolete munitions, materials and scrap. *Repr.* Official and expert. *Ref.* Cmd. 325, p. 113.
   (For Ferrous Scrap Branch, *see* above.)

SALVAGE, SPECIAL COMMITTEE.—*App.* by Disposals Board, Feb. 1919. *Obj.* To deal with scientific utilization of scrap, possessing otherwise little or no value. *Repr.* Disposals Board. *Ref.* B.T.J., 6th Mar. 1919.

SCIENTIFIC ADVISORY COMMITTEE.—*App.* by M.M. in 1915. *Obj.* To investigate scientific problems of munitions supply and output of essential products. *Repr.* Presumably various experts. *Ref.* Cd. 8282, p. xlii.

SEMI-SKILLED MEN'S WAGES.—*See* Arbitration Tribunal.

SHALE INDUSTRY, SCOTTISH, COMMITTEES.—*App.* by M.M., after consultation with Adm. and H.O., Feb. 1917 as separate Committees of owners and men, with joint Chairman representing H.O. and M.M. *Obj.* To advise M.M. on the industry, and organize increased output. *Repr.* M.M., H.O., Owners' and Men's Associations, with technical expert adviser. *Ref.* B.T.J., 1st Mar. 1917 ; Cmd. 490, p. 96.

SHIPYARD TONNAGE OUTPUT COMMITTEES.—*App.* secured both by M.M. and H.O. *See* H.O.

SKILLED TIME-WORKERS.—*See* Rates of.

SLOUGH DEPOT, STANDING COMMITTEE.—*App.* by M.M. in 1920 or 1921. *Obj.* To deal with sale, &c., of depot. *Repr.* M.M. and experts, presumably. *Ref.* H.C., No. 102, 1921, p. 27.

SOCIAL STUDIES, JOINT COMMITTEES.—*App.* by Conference of representatives of University Departments held apparently at instigation of M.M. in 1916 or 1917. *Obj.* To consider means of training welfare workers. *Repr.* The Universities, social welfare workers, &c. *Ref.* Report on Selection and Training of Welfare Supervisors (P. S. King & Son), 1917. *Diss.* During 1917.

SOUTH AFRICA MUNITIONS COMMITTEE.—*See under* Rhodesia.

SPECIFICATIONS COMMITTEE.—*App.* by M.M. prior to 1918. *Obj.* To advise generally upon specifications for contracts. *Repr.* Presumably largely technical. *Ref.* H.C., No. 132, 1918, p. 56.

STAFF, DEPARTMENTAL, COMMITTEE.—*App.* by M.M. about Jan. 1918. *Obj.* To report on economies and improvements in organization of head-quarters' staff. *Repr.* Parliament, M.M., Tre. (Staffs Committee), business men, women. *Ref.* Cd. 9220. *Diss.* Nov. 1918. For later Committee on M.M. and Disposals Board (staffing and methods), *see* T., 12th Sept. 1922, pp. 10, 11.

STEEL, INTER-ALLIED, COMMITTEE.—*See under* Munitions Council, Inter-Allied.

STEEL ROLLING AREA COMMITTEES.—*App.* jointly by M.M. and Adm., early in 1918, in six areas, covering whole country. *Obj.* To advise Steel Superintendent for the area, in carrying out control of steel rollings and arranging rolling programmes. *Repr.* Principal steel manufacturers in area. *Ref.* B.T.J., 21st Feb. 1918, p. 209.

STORAGE OF FILLED GUN AMMUNITION COMMITTEE.—*App.* by M.M. in 1916. *Obj.* To investigate and advise upon methods of storage. *Repr.* M.M., H.O., and others. *Ref.* Cd. 8609, p. 4.

STORES CENTRAL COMMITTEE.—*App.* by Finance Department of M.M. in 1917. *Obj.* To take charge of custody and accounting for all munitions, except explosives. *Repr.* Official and expert. *Ref.* Cd. 9005, p. 79 ; Cmd. 325, p. 112.

STORES CONCENTRATION, INTER-DEPARTMENTAL COMMITTEE.—*App.* jointly by Disposals Board (q.v.) and other Government Departments concerned. *Obj.* To secure concentration of surplus stocks in a few depots. *Repr.* The Board, Departments concerned. *Ref.* Cmd. 1412, p. 7. *Still in existence early in 1922.*

SUBSTITUTION DEPARTMENTAL COMMITTEES (INVESTIGATING, PLACING, AND CENTRAL).—*App.* by M.M., apparently in 1919. *Obj.* To carry out substitution of ex-service for non-service men within Department by discovery of suitable posts (INVESTIGATING COMMITTEE), providing suitable candidates for them (PLACING COMMITTEE), and dealing with disagreements between the two other Committees (CENTRAL COMMITTEE). *Repr.* M.M. and others. *Ref.* Lytton Committee, 1st Interim Report, pp. 4, 5 (H.M.S.O., 1923). *Diss.* At or before termination of M.M. *See also* M.L.

SULPHUR COMMITTEE.—*App.* by M.M., May 1917. *Obj.* To carry out arrangements for purchase of supplies of Sicilian sulphur from Italian Government and distribution to consumers. *Repr.* M.M., B.A., B.T., C.O., F.O., In.O. *Ref.* B.T.J., 26th Sept. 1918, p. 413.

SULPHURIC ACID AND FERTILIZER TRADES, POST-WAR POSITION, DEPARTMENTAL COMMITTEE.—*App.* by M.M., Jan. 1917, after consultation with B.T. *Obj.* To consider post-war position of trades, and effects of war-time erections of plant. *Repr.* M.M., B.A., B.T., M.F., L.G.B., manufacturers. *Ref.* Cmd. 23. *Diss.* Reported Feb. 1918.

SULPHURIC ACID TRADE ADVISORY COMMITTEE.—*App.* by M.M. in 1917 or 1918. *Obj.* To assist M.M. in determining costs, prices, &c., under control. *Repr.* Sulphuric Acid Trade. *Ref.* B.T.J., 3rd Oct. 1918, p. 425.

SUPERPHOSPHATE ADVISORY COMMITTEE.—*App.* presumably by M.M. prior to 1918. *Obj.* To advise generally on production of superphosphate. *Repr.* Not stated. *Ref.* Cmd. 185, 1919, p. lvi.

TEXTILE MACHINERY.—*See under* Priority, Munitions, Sub-Committees.

TIME-WORKERS.—*See* Rates of.

TIN, INTER-ALLIED EXECUTIVE.—*App.* by Allied Governments, Sept. 1918, apparently to work in connexion with M.M. *Obj.* To distribute supplies equitably and prevent unnecessary competition. *Repr.* Allied Governments. *Ref.* Cmd. 325, p. 114.

T.N.T. POISONING COMMITTEE.—*App.* by M.M., Oct. 1916. *Obj.* To co-ordinate results of inquiries, advise on administrative action, and draw up rules for protection. *Repr.* M.R.C., medical and other experts. *Ref.* Cd. 8825, p. 85.

TRADE UNION ADVISORY COMMITTEE, MINISTRY OF MUNITIONS.—*App.* by M.M., Aug. 1917, superseding Labour Advisory Committee, National (q.v.). *Obj.* To advise M.M. on various questions affecting labour and T.U.'s in regard to munitions. *Repr.* Munitions T.U.'s, the Committee being divided into three panels for Engineering (skilled workers), Shipbuilding (skilled workers), and General Labour. *Ref.* Cole, p. 152 ; L.Y.B., 1919, p. 104.

(Following difficulties as to the position of women on the General Labour panel, a separate Committee (*see* below) was established for them.)

TRADE UNION NEGOTIATING COMMITTEE.—*App.* by T.U.'s represented at Treasury Conference, Mar. 1915. *Obj.* To prepare detailed proposals on suspension of T.U. restrictions for negotiation with the Government. *Repr.* T.U.'s concerned. *Ref.* Cole, p. 70. *Diss.* At close of Conference.

TRADE UNION WOMEN'S ADVISORY COMMITTEE.—*App.* by M.M., Nov. 1917, following difficulty as to the position of women on the General Labour Panel of the Trade Union Advisory Committee. *Obj.* To advise M.M. on all questions of women's work on munitions. *Repr.* Women's T.U.'s in munitions industries. *Ref.* Cole, p. 70 ; L.Y.B., 1919, p. 104.

TRAMWAYS COMMITTEE.—*See* B.T.

TRENCH WARFARE, CHEMICAL, COMMERCIAL, MINES, RESEARCH, ADVISORY COMMITTEES.—*App.* by M.M., probably in 1915 and 1916. *Obj.* To advise and assist Trench Warfare Department of

M.M. in these subjects. *Repr.* Presumably largely expert (scientists, business men, &c.). *Ref.* Cd. 8741, p. 11.

TRIBUNALS, APPEAL, MUNITIONS.—*App.* by Lord Chancellor and in Scotland Lord President of Court of Session, about Feb. 1916. *Obj.* To hear appeals from decisions of Munitions Tribunals on questions of law or mixed law and fact. *Repr.* To consist of Judges specially appointed. *Ref.* L.G., Mar. 1916 (Appendix). *Diss.* As with General and Local Tribunals or earlier.

TRIBUNALS, GENERAL MUNITIONS.—*App.* by M.M., under M.W.A., 1915, in summer of 1915, reorganized Feb. 1916, and transferred to M.L. under Restoration of Pre-War Practices Act, Aug. 1919. *Obj.* To deal with offences and other questions under M.W.A.'s, not dealt with by Local Munitions Tribunals, and matters referred to them by M.M. from Local Tribunals, and, after the War, with cases from Local Munitions Tribunals under Wages (Temporary Regulation) and Restoration of Pre-War Practices Acts. *Repr.* Independent Chairman, appointed by M.M., and two or four assessors representing employers and workpeople, the M.W.A., 1916 providing for creation of panels of assessors and for presence of woman assessor on workpeople's side in cases affecting women. *Ref.* P.G.A., 1915 and 1916 ; L.G., Mar. and April 1916 (Statutory Orders printed in Appendices). *Diss.* About Sept. 1920 on expiry of Wages (Temporary Regulation) Act and close of work under Restoration of Pre-War Practices Act.

TRIBUNALS, LOCAL MUNITIONS.—*App.* by M.M., as with General Munitions Tribunals. *Obj.* To deal with various offences under M.W.A.'s, applications for leaving certificates, and, after the War, with disputes under Wages (Temporary Regulation) and Restoration of Pre-War Practices Acts. *Repr., Ref., Diss.* As with Tribunals, General Munitions (q.v.). *See also* H.C., No. 185, 1921, p. 37.

(The Scottish and Irish General and Local Tribunals were appointed under separate Orders, but otherwise were the same as in England.)

VALUATIONS COMMITTEE.—*App.* by M.M. in winter of 1915–16 and subsequently retained by Board of Inland Revenue. *Obj.* To advise as Committee of experts in dealing with values of buildings, plant and machinery set up in Controlled Establishments. *Repr.* Auctioneers, civil engineers, estate agents, surveyors, and Receiver of Crown Lands. *Ref.* T., 18th Aug. 1917, p. 3.

WAGES OF SKILLED TIME-WORKERS.—*See* Rates of.

WALTHAM ABBEY.—*See* Gretna and Waltham Abbey.

WARBLE FLY COMMITTEE.—*App.* by M.M. in 1917. *Obj.* To circulate information regarding the warble fly, and conduct trials of dressings for their destruction. *Repr.* Apparently B.A., B.A.(Sc.), D.A.T.I., and others. *Ref.* Cmd. 929, p. 56. *Diss.* Presumably replaced by Warble Fly Pest Committee, July 1918 (*see* W.O.). *See also* B.A.

WAR BONUS 12%.—*See* Arbitration Tribunals.

WAR MUNITION VOLUNTEER SCHEME.—*App.* by M.M., June 1915. *Obj.* To secure voluntary enrolment of skilled workers, for munitions work in any controlled establishment at choice of M.M., two hundred Munitions

Work Bureaux being established temporarily for enrolment. *Repr.* Skilled workers. *Ref.* L.G., July 1915 ; Cole, pp. 80, 81. *Diss.* At or after close of war.

WELFARE DEPARTMENT.—*See* Health and Welfare.

WELFARE, WORKS' COMMITTEES.—*App.* in individual factories during the War, some as result of Welfare campaign, others being Workers' Committees initiated by the workpeople, independently of or in consultation with the management, to organize welfare work and raise funds (*see* Cmd. 8570, p. 10), representing both male and female workers in various departments (*see* Cmd. 8570, p. 10). *Obj.* To secure co-operation of management and workpeople in welfare work within the factory. *Repr.* Management (in many cases), workpeople (male and female). *Ref.* Cmd. 340, p. 34. The movement was probably not entirely new, but received a great impetus owing to the War and was introduced for the first time in many factories.

WOMEN'S SERVICE COMMITTEE.—*App.* by Health of Munition Workers' Committee in 1915 or 1916. Details lacking. *Ref.* Confidential Report (copy in Imperial War Services Museum Library, Women's Work Section). *Diss.* Reported before end of 1916.

WOMEN.—*See also* Arbitration, Trade Unions.

WOOL, BRITISH AUSTRALIAN, REALIZATION ASSOCIATION.—This was an independent company, formed in 1920, which took over from M.M. liquidation of remaining Government stocks of wool. It represented Australian wool growers who formed a directorate. An Australian Wool Council of 18 representing the growers of all the states of the Australian Commonwealth was formed to assist the Association. Similar organizations were contemplated for New Zealand and other wools. *See* Cmd. 1368, pp. xv, xvi ; B.T.J., 20th Jan. 1921, p. 69.

WOOLWICH, ROYAL ORDNANCE FACTORIES, COMMITTEE OF INQUIRY.—*App.* by M.M., July 1918. *Obj.* To report on work of factories, with special reference to efficiency, and suggest improvements. *Repr.* Parliament, M.M., Adm., W.O., engineers, National Shell Factories, accountants. *Ref.* Cmd. 229. *Diss.* Mar. 1919.

WORKS' BOARD, MUNITIONS.—*App.* by M.M., Feb. 1917. *Obj.* To examine proposals for, and supervise, extensions of Controlled Establishments. *Repr.* Official and expert. *Ref.* H.C., No. 132, 1918, p. 7. *Diss.* After the War, presumably.

ZIRCONIUM.—*See* S.I.R.

NATIONAL SERVICE, DEPARTMENT AND (LATER) MINISTRY OF

The Department of National Service was formed in Dec. 1916, the first Director-General being appointed on 19th Dec., and it was established as a Ministry on 28th Mar. 1917 under a Director-General by the Ministry of National Service Act, 1917 (7 Geo. V, c. 6). The *object* was ' to make the best use of all persons, whether men or women, able to work in any industry, occupation, or service '. The Ministry exercised powers transferred to it by Order-in-Council from other Departments and Authorities or conferred on it by regulations under the Defence of the Realm Consolidation Act 1915, with the proviso that the Ministry possessed no powers for compulsory employment or transfer of any person, or for imposing penalties for breaches of voluntary agreements entered into with it. By a decision of Aug. 1917 the Ministry was completely reconstructed by the War Cabinet, with greatly extended powers (*see* Cd. 9005, pp. 85–6), taking over, among other things, the work of recruiting for the Forces, from the War Office (formal transfer 1st Nov.). The work of the Ministry was divided among the following Departments—Finance, Labour Supply, Medical, Recruiting, Registration, Secretariat, Statistics, Trade Exemptions, Women's Recruiting (*see* below), each of them being assisted after Aug. 1917 by Advisory Boards. The country was divided into a number of districts (Regions) with a Regional Organization, under a Regional Director of National Service, assisted by a Deputy Director of Recruiting and representatives of other important branches of the Ministry. There was a special Department for Ireland (*see* below). The Ministry was brought to an end in the first part of 1919. *Reference* P.G.A., 1917 ; Cd. 9005, pp. 80–8.

ABBREVIATION

M.N.S. = Department, and subsequently Ministry, of National Service.

ADVISORY, CENTRAL COMMITTEE, DEPARTMENTAL BOARDS. —*See* below.

ADVISORY COMMITTEE, NATIONAL SERVICE.—*App.* by M.N.S., Mar. 1917. *Obj.* To act in advisory capacity in regard to exercise of Director's (Minister's) power of regulating and restricting labour in non-essential trades. *Repr.* Parliament, business experts and others. *Ref.* T., 13th Mar. 1917, p. 10. *Diss.* Aug. 1917 on appointment of Central Advisory Committee (*see* below).

AGRICULTURAL COMMISSIONERS AND SUB-COMMISSIONERS.— Commissioners were *appointed* by M.N.S., Mar. 1917, with honorary Sub-commissioners in the various districts. *Obj.* To carry out scheme for supply of civilian volunteer labour for agriculture. *Repr.* Official and expert. *Ref.* T., 31st Mar. 1917, p. 3.

AGRICULTURAL LABOUR, SELECTION FOR RELEASE, SCOTLAND, COMMITTEE.—*App.* jointly by M.N.S. and B.A.(Sc.), May 1918. *Obj.* To select men for release from agriculture in Scotland for military service. *Repr.* Scottish District Agricultural Executive Committees and local staff of M.N.S. *Ref.* Cmd. 325, p. 241.

APPEAL COURTS (NATIONAL SERVICE).—*App.* by M.N.S. about Jan. 1917. *Obj.* To hear appeals by National Service Volunteers against nature or conditions of work to which they were transferred. *Repr.* Not stated. *Ref.* L.G., May 1917. *Diss.* From about May 1917, the Substitution Volunteer Scheme giving the right to refuse transfer without appeal.

APPEAL TRIBUNALS.—*See* L.G.B. It was decided on transfer of recruiting to M.N.S. (Nov. 1917) to provide an appeal to an independent body. These Tribunals were constituted by and under L.G.B. and S.O., with medical assessors appointed by these Departments. *See* Cd. 9157, p. 41.

APPROVED SOCIETIES JOINT ENLISTMENT COMMITTEE.—*App.* jointly on initiative of N.H.I.C. *See* L.G.B.

ASSESSORS, MEDICAL (MILITARY SERVICE).—*See* L.G.B.

CENTRAL ADVISORY COMMITTEE, NATIONAL SERVICE.—*App.* by M.N.S. in or after Aug. 1917, following reports of Commission on Industrial Unrest (*see* Cabinet) and decision for transfer of recruiting to M.N.S. *Obj.* To advise M.N.S. generally, with special reference to recruiting questions. *Repr.* The former Labour Advisory Committee (*see* below) acted in this capacity. *Ref.* L.G., Oct. 1917.

COLLIERY RECRUITING.—*See* H.O.

DEPARTMENTAL ADVISORY BOARDS.—*App.* by M.N.S., after reorganization, Aug. 1917. *Obj.* To assist each administrative department in performance of its work. *Repr.* Professional and business men with expert knowledge of work of Department concerned. *Ref.* Cd. 9005, p. 87.

GOVERNMENT DEPARTMENTS, EXEMPTIONS, REVISION, PANEL AND COMMITTEES.—*App.* by M.N.S. in spring of 1918. *Obj.* To re-examine exemptions granted to employees by Government Departments under M.S.A.'s. *Repr.* Men with experience of Tribunal work, including Members of both Houses of Parliament, Judges, Business Men and Labour, a Committee being appointed from the Panel for each Department, to which a representative of the Department concerned was added. *Ref.* Cmd. 325, p. 131 ; T., 17th May 1918, p. 7. *Diss.* Later in 1918.

HARVEST, CENTRAL COMMITTEE.—*App.* by M.N.S. in early summer of 1917, in consultation with B.A. *Obj.* To organize supplies of voluntary labour for harvest work in 1917, being continued or re-appointed for 1918 harvest. *Repr.* Cavendish Associations who undertook work of organization. *Ref.* B.T.J., June 1917, 1918. *Diss.* Apparently after 1918 harvest.

HARVEST, COUNTY, TEMPORARY ADVISORY COMMITTEES.—*App.* by the bodies represented, at request of M.N.S., in early summer of 1917. *Obj.* To assist War Agricultural Committees (*see* B.A.) and representatives of M.N.S. in finding local employment for volunteer labour in 1917 harvest, the Committees being possibly continued for 1918 harvest. *Repr.* Cavendish Associations, Church of England Diocesan Organization, Free Church Federation, National Union of Teachers. *Ref.* J.B.A., June 1917. *Diss.* After 1917 or 1918 harvest.

IRISH NATIONAL SERVICE DEPARTMENT.—*App.* by M.N.S. prior to Sept. of 1917, with head-quarters in Dublin. *Obj.* To organize work of

M.N.S. in Ireland. *Repr.* Presumably much as with M.N.S. *Ref.* Cd. 8741, p. 8. *Diss.* On termination of M.N.S. or earlier.

LABOUR ADVISORY COMMITTEE (SOMETIMES CALLED LABOUR ADVISORY BOARD).—*App.* by M.N.S. early in 1917. *Obj.* To advise M.N.S. generally on Labour questions and secure improved relations between employers and employed. *Repr.* M.N.S., M.L., Employers in Industry and Agriculture, T.U.'s. *Ref.* L.G., April 1917 ; T., 26th Nov. 1917, p. 5. *Diss.* Became Central Advisory Committee (*see* above) after reorganization of M.N.S., Aug. 1917, though still sometimes known by former title.

LABOUR PRIORITY COMMITTEE, NATIONAL.—*App.* by M.N.S. in autumn of 1917. *Obj.* To secure carrying out, through E.E.'s and Trade Committees (*see* below), of instructions of War Cabinet Priority Committee (*see* Cabinet). *Repr.* Presumably Government Departments chiefly concerned, as with Regional Committees (q.v.). *Ref.* Cd. 9005, p. 90.

LABOUR PRIORITY REGIONAL COMMITTEES.—*App.* by M.N.S. late in 1917 or in 1918, for each National Service Region (*see* Heading to Section). *Obj.* To determine priority for, and transfer of, labour within their regions, stimulate substitution and advise Regional Officers. *Repr.* M.N.S., Adm., M.L., M.M. *Ref.* Cmd. 325, p. 141.

LOCAL NATIONAL SERVICE COMMITTEES.—*App.* by M.N.S., in every urban area, from May 1917. *Obj.* To carry out locally scheme for releasing suitable men from unorganized or less-organized trades for work of national importance. *Repr.* Employers and workpeople in these trades. *Ref.* L.G., May 1917.

LOCAL RECRUITING COMMITTEES.—*See* Recruiting.

LONDON SHIPOWNERS AND TRANSPORT WORKERS MILITARY SERVICE COMMITTEE.—*See* B.T., *under* Port Labour.

MAN POWER AND PRODUCTION, INDUSTRIAL ADVISORY COMMITTEE.—*See* W.O.

MEDICAL BOARD, ADVISORY.—*App.* by M.N.S., Oct.–Nov. 1917, on transfer of recruiting for Forces from W.O. *Obj.* To advise M.N.S. on choice of members of new National Service Medical Boards and on medical matters generally. *Repr.* Medical War Committees (*see* N.H.I.C.), other important Medical Bodies, doctors. *Ref.* L.G., Oct. 1917, p. 355.

MEDICAL BOARD (SCOTLAND), ADVISORY.—A similar Board was appointed for Scotland. *See* T., 3rd Nov. 1917, p. 7.

MEDICAL BOARDS, CIVILIAN.—*App.* by M.N.S. at request of M.Pen. and W.O., early in 1918, at all discharge centres. *Obj.* To consider whether health of men, released as physically unfit, had been impaired by military service, and grade them accordingly. *Repr.* Civilian medical men. *Ref.* H.C. No. 39, 1920, p. 26. *Diss.* Aug. 1918, being replaced by additional Medical Boards, National Service (q.v.).

MEDICAL BOARDS, NATIONAL SERVICE.—*App.* by M.N.S. on transfer of recruiting from W.O., about Nov. 1917, and reorganized later with creation of additional Boards (*see* preceding entry). *Obj.* To examine recruits for Army, perform other duties of W.O. Medical Boards, and after

Aug. 1918 deal with health of discharged men. *Repr.* Civilian medical men with military member of each Board. *Ref.* Cd. 9005, p. 88. *Diss.* Transferred to M.Pen., April 1919, and continued for Pensions purposes.

MEDICAL SERVICES INTER-DEPARTMENTAL COMMITTEE.— *App.* by M.N.S. in late summer of 1918, under authority from War Cabinet and Government Departments concerned. *Obj.* To regulate demobilization of medical practitioners and dental surgeons. *Repr.* Presumably M.N.S., Government Departments concerned, Medical Profession. *Ref.* Cmd. 325, p. 134. *Diss.* Close of general demobilization or earlier.

MEDICAL.—*See also under* Professional, Women.

MEETINGS, NATIONAL SERVICE, PARLIAMENTARY COMMITTEE. —*See* Publicity Campaign, below, and Parliament.

PART-TIME COMMITTEES.—*App.* under M.N.S. in many districts, in spring of 1918 or earlier. *Obj.* To organize supplies of part-time labour for farm work. *Repr.* Agriculturalists and other local interests presumably. *Ref.* J.B.A., July 1918. *Diss.* Probably later in 1918.

PORT LABOUR COMMITTEES.—*See* B.T.

PROFESSIONAL CENTRAL MEDICAL COMMITTEES.—*App.* by M.N.S., apparently late in 1917, for England and Wales, Scotland, and Ireland, presumably replacing Professional Central Military Service Committees (*see* L.G.B.). *Obj.* To deal with distribution of supply of doctors, claims of doctors to exemption from military service, &c. *Repr.* Central Medical War Committees (*see* N.H.I.C.) appear to have formed the Committees. *Ref.* Cmd. 325, p. 134 ; Cd. 9169, p. lxxvii.

PROFESSIONAL TRAVELLING MEDICAL BOARDS.—*App.* by M.N.S. in 1918. *Obj.* To carry out examination of doctors for military service in different districts under Central Committees. *Repr.* Medical Profession. *Ref.* Cmd. 325, p. 134. *Diss.* June–Aug. 1918.

PUBLICITY CAMPAIGN, NATIONAL SERVICE, PARLIAMENTARY COMMITTEES.—*App.* by War Cabinet, Feb. 1917. *Obj.* To organize publicity campaign to secure National Service Volunteers, there being apparently three Committees (for the General Campaign, Newspaper Publicity, and Public Meetings). *Repr.* Parliament (both Houses and chief parties). *Ref.* H.C. No. 151, 1917, p. x. *Diss.* About summer of 1917, on conclusion of campaign.

RECRUITING ADVISORY BOARD.—*App.* by M.N.S., on transfer of recruiting from W.O., Oct.–Nov. 1917. *Obj.* To advise and assist M.N.S. in dealing with recruiting. *Repr.* Parliament, M.N.S., Legal Profession, Employers, Labour. *Ref.* L.G., Oct. 1917, p. 355 ; T., 26th Nov. 1917, p. 5.

RECRUITING LOCAL COMMITTEES.—*App.* by M.N.S. in various districts from Oct. or Nov. 1917. *Obj.* To deal with local grievances in regard to recruiting. *Repr.* Not stated. *Ref.* L.G., Oct. 1917, p. 355.

RECRUITING STATISTICS COMMITTEE.—*App.* by M.N.S., Mar. 1918. *Obj.* To consider best methods of utilizing, in public interest, information obtained by recruiting Medical Boards. *Repr.* M.N.S., M.Pen., M.R.C., Registrar-General, Medical Profession, Research Workers. *Ref.* Cmd. 504. *Diss.* Dec. 1919.

RECRUITING, TRADE COMMITTEES.—*See under* Substitution.

REGISTRATION ADVISORY BOARD.—*App.* by M.N.S. by Nov. 1917. *Obj.* To advise on use of national register and similar problems. *Repr.* M.N.S., M.Pen., Registrar-General, the Army. *Ref.* T., 26th Nov. 1917, p. 5.

RESERVED OCCUPATIONS INTER-DEPARTMENTAL COMMITTEE.—Transferred to M.N.S., April 1917, and functions considerably extended (*see* B.T.).

SCHOOLBOY LAND-WORKERS' COMMITTEE.—*App.* by M.N.S., April 1917. *Obj.* To organize under M.N.S., in co-operation with Cavendish Association, scheme for holiday employment of schoolboys on land. *Repr.* Schools and School Masters. *Ref.* T., 24th April 1917, p. 3.

SUBSTITUTION CENTRAL JOINT (TRADE) COMMITTEES.—*App.* at request of M.N.S. by various inportant industries not mainly concerned in war work, after April 1917, apparently replacing in some cases previously existing Committees. *Obj.* To advise as to numbers of men to be taken and arrange for release of suitable men from their industries for work in trades of national importance, in connexion with scheme of National Service Volunteers. *Repr.* Employers and workpeople in industries concerned. *Ref.* L.G., May 1917 ; Cd. 9005, p. 84.

(Committees were established in the Building, Pottery, Printing and Book-binding, and Furniture and Woodworking Industries. For less well-organized trades, *see* Local National Service Committees.)

SUBSTITUTION, LOCAL JOINT (TRADE) COMMITTEES.—*App.* locally, at request of M.N.S., by industries in which Substitution, Central, Committees were established, from May 1917. *Obj., Repr., Ref.* As with Substitution, Central, Committees (q.v.), but for particular localities. *See also* M.L.

(These Committees must not be confused with earlier Substitution Committees, organized under H.O. (q.v.) to secure substitution of women and others for men in various industries, whilst the Substitution Local Committees under H.O. scheme of Sept. 1916 seem to have continued to do detailed work of substitution in some districts at least.)

TRADE CONSULTATIVE COMMITTEES.—*App.* by M.N.S. in 1917 or 1918 in a number of trades. *Obj.* To advise Regional Officers on cases before Military Service Tribunals and on issue of Protection Certificates. *Repr.* Employers and workmen in trades concerned. *Ref.* Cmd. 325, p. 138.

(The Substitution, Local, Committees under the Scheme of Sept. 1916 (*see* H.O.) seem to have continued to carry out the detailed local work of substitution.)

TRADE, SUBSTITUTION, COMMITTEES.—*See* Substitution.

TRIBUNAL, DENTAL SERVICE.—*See* L.G.B., under Dental Service but additional Tribunals appear to have been appointed by M.N.S. (*see* Cmd. 325, p. 134).

TRIBUNALS, MILITARY SERVICE.—Brought under M.N.S. on transfer of Recruiting, Oct.–Nov. 1917. *See* L.G.B.

VOLUNTEERS, NATIONAL SERVICE.—The scheme was inaugurated by M.N.S., Dec. 1916 or Jan. 1917. Volunteers were recruited with the undertaking to accept any work assigned to them by M.N.S. at standard rates of job, with right of appeal to an Appeal Court (*see* above). They were supplemented in April 1917 by the Substitution Volunteers (*see* next entry) and replaced in Oct. 1917 by the War Work Volunteers (*see* below). *See* L.G., Jan.–May 1917 ; Cole, p. 179.

VOLUNTEERS, SUBSTITUTION.—The scheme was started by M.N.S., in April and May 1917, in connexion with the Scheme of Substitution by transfer from non-essential to essential industries (*see* Substitution, Trade, Committees above). Volunteers were invited to enrol for specific classes of work and were paid subsistence allowance when working away from home. *See* L.G., May 1917 ; Cole, p. 179.

VOLUNTEERS, WAR WORK.—The scheme was established by M.N.S. in Oct. 1917, to replace the National Service Volunteers. Under it volunteers were only enrolled for specific types of work, and it appears to have been a more extended form of the Substitution Volunteers (*see* preceding entry). *See* Cole, p. 179.

WOMEN FOR THE LAND, SELECTION, WAGE COMMITTEES.— *See* B.A.

WOMEN'S SECTION, MINISTRY OF NATIONAL SERVICE.—This was set up in 1917 to establish a central control of the recruiting of women for National Service and generally organize their work. *See* Cd. 9005, p. 92 ; Cole, p. 180.

WOMEN'S SELECTION, MEDICAL, BOARDS.—*App.* under Women's Section of M.N.S. in winter of 1917–18. *Obj.* To carry out selection and medical examination of women for various forms of National Service. *Repr.* Government Departments concerned, Medical Profession, business men, &c. *Ref.* Cd. 9005, p. 93.

WOMEN, TRAINING FOR AGRICULTURE, SCOTLAND, COMMITTEE.—Joint Appointment. *See* B.A.(Sc.).

OVERSEAS TRADE (DEVELOPMENT AND INTELLIGENCE) DEPARTMENT

The Department was formed jointly by the Board of Trade and the Foreign Office in the autumn of 1917, under a Parliamentary Under-Secretary responsible to both Departments, under the Overseas Trade Department (Secretaries) Act, 1918. The Department comprised the former Commercial Intelligence Department of the Board of Trade, the War Trade Intelligence Department, and that part of the Foreign Trade Department of the Foreign Office which dealt with the promotion of trade abroad. It also undertook control of the Trade Commissioner and Commercial Attaché Services, and took over the Commercial and Consular departments of the Foreign Office. The *objects* were the organization of commercial intelligence, and the active promotion of overseas trade. The Department has three main Divisions—Overseas, United Kingdom, and Exhibitions. The Department was established as a Permanent Body. *References* : Public General Acts, 1918 (8 and 9 Geo. V, c. 3) ; B.T.J., 13th Dec. 1917, p. 568.

ABBREVIATION
O.T.D. = Overseas Trade Department.

BELGIAN TRADE COMMITTEE.—*See* B.T., the Belgian Section of the O.T.D. being constituted from its secretariat (*see* Cmd. 325, p. 221).

COMMERCIAL, DIPLOMATIC AND CONSULAR SELECTION COMMITTEE.—*App.* by O.T.D., Feb. 1918. *Obj.* To select candidates for reorganized and increased Service. *Repr.* O.T.D., F.O., C.S.C., manufacturers, commerce. *Ref.* Cmd. 1052. *Diss.* Nov. 1920.

INTELLIGENCE, WAR TRADE, DEPARTMENT.—Transferred to O.T.D., Sept. 1917. *See* W.T.D.

OVERSEAS EMPLOYMENT COMMITTEE.—Joint Appointment. *See* C.O.

OVERSEAS TRADE ADVISORY COMMITTEE.—*App.* as part of organization of O.T.D., April 1918. *Obj.* To advise O.T.D. generally. *Repr.* Parliament, Chambers of Commerce, British Trade and Hudson's Bay Corporations, manufacturers, merchants, shipping, banking, finance, Labour, The Press. *Ref.* B.T.J., 18th April 1918. *Presumably Permanent.*

OVERSEAS, TRADE, MISSIONS.—*App.* by O.T.D., sometimes in co-operation with Trade Associations, in and after 1918. *Obj.* To make expert investigations into markets for particular industries in foreign countries as part of policy of post-war development, or in certain cases into the prospects of trade generally in particular countries. *Repr.* Experts in trades concerned, &c. *Ref.* Cmd. 325, p. 220. *See also* B.T. *under* Serbia.

RUSSIA AND SIBERIA INTER-DEPARTMENTAL ECONOMIC CONFERENCE.—*App.* jointly by Government Departments concerned, with Secretariat from Russia Section of O.T.D. *Obj.* To consider economic questions affecting Russia, and form and operate a Government organization for supplying Eastern Siberia. *Repr.* The Departments concerned. *Ref.* Cmd. 325, p. 221.

STATISTICAL, WAR TRADE, DEPARTMENT.—Transferred to O.T.D., Sept. 1917. *See* W.T.D.

TRADE COMMISSIONER SERVICE, SELECTION COMMITTEE.— *App.* by O.T.D. in 1917. *Obj.* To select suitable persons for increased trade commissioner and commercial attaché service. *Repr.* O.T.D., B.T., industrial and business experts. *Ref.* B.T.J., 28th Feb. 1918, p. 240. *Diss.* Possibly absorbed into or replaced by Commercial, &c., Selection Committee (above).

TRADE DEPARTMENT, BRITISH, WASHINGTON.—*App.* presumably by B.T. or O.T.D., in later part of war. *Obj.* To undertake work connected with grant of licences to export from U.S.A. to Europe. *Repr.* Official and expert. *Ref.* H.C. Nos. 54, &c., 1920, p. 336. *Diss.* Remaining duties absorbed into general organization of O.T.D., at beginning of 1921.

PARLIAMENT : HOUSES OF LORDS AND COMMONS

ABBREVIATIONS

H.L. = House of Lords.
H.C. = House of Commons.

AGRICULTURAL PARLIAMENTARY COMMITTEE.—Referred to in T., 29th Oct. 1918, p. 7.

AIR, PARLIAMENTARY COMMITTEE.—*App.* jointly by H.C. and H.L., Aug. 1916. *Obj.* To secure parliamentary supervision and investigation of air affairs. *Repr.* Both Houses and chief parties. *Ref.* T., 10th Aug. 1916, p. 5.

(This Committee at first meeting appointed an Executive Committee of its own.)

ALIENS, ENEMY, PARLIAMENTARY INQUIRY.—*App.* by P.M. from H.C., July 1918. *Obj.* To investigate enemy alien problem, and advise on action to allay public anxiety. *Repr.* H.C. (chief parties). *Ref.* T., 29th July 1918. *Diss.* By end of July, being replaced by Aliens Watch Committee (*see* next entry).

ALIENS PARLIAMENTARY WATCH COMMITTEE.—*App.* Aug. 1918 by meeting of members especially interested in question. *Obj.* To watch action of the government and of Government Committees in dealing with the problem. *Repr.* Members of all parties specially interested. *Ref.* T., 17th Aug. 1918, p. 7.

ARMY COMMITTEE, PARLIAMENTARY.—With Executive and General Committees referred to in T., 10th May 1919, p. 13.

BETTING DUTY SELECT COMMITTEE.—*App.* by H.C., May 1923. *Obj.* To report whether duty on betting desirable and practicable. *Repr.* H.C. (chief parties). *Ref.* H.C. No. 139, 1923. *Diss.* Nov. 1923.

BOUNDARY COMMISSION.—*App.* by Parliament in 1917 or early 1918. *Obj.* To work out re-arrangement of Parliamentary Divisions, preparatory to passing Representation of the People Act, 1918. *Repr.* H.C. and H.L., with assistance of L.G.B. *Ref.* Cd. 9157, p. 55. *Diss.* 1918.

BOUNDARY COMMISSIONS.—*See* Representation of the People.

BUSINESS PREMISES SELECT COMMITTEE.—*App.* by H.C., June 1920. *Obj.* To inquire into position of tenants of business premises and changes in law required to remove obstacles to business development. *Repr.* H.C. (chief parties). *Ref.* H.C. No. 237, 1920. *Diss.* Dec. 1920.

CANALS, SELECT COMMITTEE.—*App.* by H.C. in 1920. *Obj.* To investigate position of canals. *Repr.* H.C. (chief parties). *Ref.* H.C. Nos. 100, 118, &c., 1920, p. xvi. *Diss.* 1921.

CANTEENS.—*See* Navy and Army below.

CIPPENHAM GOVERNMENT WORKS, JOINT SELECT COMMITTEE.—*App.* jointly by H.C. and H.L., April 1919. *Obj.* To inquire into conditions and costs of the work and responsibility for the Scheme.

Repr. H.C. and H.L. (chief parties). *Ref.* H.C. No. 131, 1919. *Diss.* July 1919.

COAL, PARLIAMENTARY COMMITTEE AND EMERGENCY SUB-COMMITTEE.—Referred to without details, T., 13th July 1919, p. 13.

COASTWISE TRADE, SPECIAL COMMITTEE OF MEMBERS OF PARLIAMENT.—*App.* apparently by Government, July 1919. *Obj.* To consider conditions of coastwise traffic, and submit results and recommendations to Departments concerned. *Repr.* Members of Parliament. *Ref.* T., 12th July 1919, p. 14.

COMMERCIAL GROUP OR COMMITTEE of H.C., referred to in T., 11th June 1917, p. 13.

CONSCIENTIOUS OBJECTORS, EMPLOYMENT IN CIVIL SERVICE, SELECT COMMITTEE.—*App.* by H.C., Feb. 1922. *Obj.* To report upon employment in Civil Service of conscientious objectors, granted exemption from combatant service. *Repr.* H.C. (chief parties). *Ref.* H.C. No. 69, 1922.

DEVOLUTION (PARLIAMENTARY) CONFERENCE.—*App.* by P.M. in Oct. 1919, under resolution of H.C. of June 1919. *Obj.* To report upon scheme of legislative and administrative devolution for U.K. *Repr.* H.L. and H.C. (chief parties). *Ref.* Cmd. 692. *Diss.* April 1920.

DISABLED EX-SERVICE MEN, TRAINING AND EMPLOYMENT, SELECT COMMITTEE.—*App.* by H.C., May 1922. *Obj.* To report on means adopted by foreign countries to provide employment for disabled men and recommend system for adoption in this country. *Repr.* H.C. (chief parties). *Ref.* H.C. No. 170, 1922. *Diss.* Aug. 1922.

DISABLED MEN.—*See also* Pensions.

EMERGENCY LEGISLATION SELECT COMMITTEE.—*See* Termination of the War.

EXPENDITURE, NATIONAL, SELECT COMMITTEE.—*App.* by H.C., July 1917, and subsequently re-appointed annually. *Obj.* To examine public expenditure and report on economies consistent with policy of Government and improved methods of public control. *Repr.* H.C. (chief parties). *Ref.* H.C. Nos. 151, &c., 1917 ; 132, &c., 1918. *Now a Regular Annual Appointment.*

(N.B. The Committee was a revival due to war needs of an earlier practice. No such Committee was apparently appointed in the years immediately preceding the War nor in 1915 and 1916.)

EXPENDITURE, NATIONAL, SUB-COMMITTEES.—*App.* by Select Committees. *Obj.* To investigate individual departments, each Sub-Committee dealing with a few departments. *Repr.* As above. *Ref.* As with Select Committee.

EXPENDITURE, SELECT COMMITTEE (1917).—*App.* by H.C., with Government consent, July 1917. *Obj.* To consider means of securing increased H.C. control as permanent thing, and examine methods and expenditure of individual departments. *Repr.* H.C. (chief parties) with power to co-opt additional members from outside. *Ref.* T., 7th July, p. 3, 19th July, p. 11, 1917.

EXPENSES, MEMBERS.—*See* Members' Expenses.

EX-RANKER OFFICERS COURT OF INQUIRY.—*App.* by P.M. in fulfilment of promise to H.C., Mar. 1924. *Obj.* To investigate complaints and claims of these officers in respect of pensions. *Repr.* The Cabinet, business men, Legal Profession, Labour. *Ref.* Daily Press, 1st April 1924.

FOOD ECONOMY PARLIAMENTARY COMMITTEE.—*App.* by Parliament in spring of 1917, and apparently revised at close of the year. *Obj.* To co-operate in dealing with the food crisis in spring of 1917, and later with M.F. in carrying out new measures of control, &c. *Repr.* Parliament (chief parties). *Ref.* T., 12th Dec. 1917, p. 9.

GAS UNDERTAKINGS (STATUTORY PRICES), SELECT COMMITTEE.—*App.* by H.C., April 1918. *Obj.* To report on expediency, &c., of modifying statutory requirements in case of gas undertakings injuriously affected by the War. *Repr.* H.C. (chief parties). *Ref.* H.C. No. 74, 1918. *Diss.* June 1918.

GOVERNMENT DISTRIBUTION AND OVERSEAS PURCHASE OF COMMODITIES, SPECIAL SUB-COMMITTEE OF COMMERCIAL COMMITTEE.—*App.* by H.C. in or before 1917. *Obj.* To investigate objections raised to Departmental methods. *Repr.* Presumably H.C. (chief parties). *Ref.* Timber and Woodworking Machinery, 8th Dec. 1917. *Diss.* Prior to Dec. 1917.

HIGH PRICES AND PROFITS, SELECT COMMITTEE.—*App.* by H.C., July 1919. *Obj.* To consider how far high prices of articles of general consumption are due to excessive profits and advise on necessary action. *Repr.* H.C. (chief parties). *Ref.* H.C. Nos. 166, 234, 1919. *Diss.* Dec. 1919.

INCREASE OF WEALTH (WAR) SELECT COMMITTEE.—*App.* by H.C., Feb. 1920. *Obj.* To report on practicability of taxing war-time increases of wealth. *Repr.* H.C. (chief parties). *Ref.* H.C. No. 102, 1920. *Diss.* May 1920.

INDIAN AFFAIRS, STANDING JOINT COMMITTEE.—*App.* by H.L. and H.C. jointly after passing of Government of India Act, 1919, apparently for first time. *Obj.* To report as required on Indian affairs. *Repr.* H.L. and H.C. (chief parties). *Ref.* H.C. Nos. 102, 136, 1922. *Standing Committee.*

INTER-ALLIED PARLIAMENTARY COMMITTEE.—*App.* in or after 1915 by British, French, and Italian Parliaments. *Obj.* To keep the different Parliaments in touch and hold periodical meetings in different capitals. *Repr.* The Parliaments concerned. *Ref.* T., 21st Oct. 1918, p. 5.

KITCHEN, HOUSE OF COMMONS, ADVISORY COMMITTEE.—*App.* by main Kitchen Committee (pre-war) of H.C., at request of Tre., Mar. 1916. *Obj.* To report on adaptation of kitchen arrangements to proposed withdrawal of Government grant. *Repr.* Main Kitchen Committee ; general catering trade (co-opted). *Ref.* H.C. No. 98, 1916. *Diss.* June 1916.

LAND VALUES, SELECT COMMITTEE.—*App.* by H.C., June 1919. *Obj.* To report upon present and future position of land values duties and land valuations. *Repr.* H.C. (chief parties). *Ref.* H.C. No. 243, 1919. *Diss.* Nov. 1919 (the Committee failing to agree).

LUXURY DUTY, SELECT COMMITTEE.—*App.* by H.C., April 1918. *Obj.* To prepare lists of articles and places of luxury for purpose of luxury duties in Budget of 1918. *Repr.* H.C. (chief parties), with power to co-opt from outside on to Sub-Committees. *Ref.* H.C. No. 101, 1918. *Diss.* Aug. 1918.

LUXURY DUTY, SUB-COMMITTEES (FOUR).—*App.* by Select Committee (q.v.) about end of April 1918. *Obj.* To deal on behalf of Main Committee with (No. 1) articles used chiefly by men, (No. 2) articles used chiefly by women, (No. 3) furniture and household articles, and (No. 4) objects of art, fancy goods and miscellaneous articles. *Repr.* Select Committee, prominent women (co-opted), except on Sub-Committee No. 1. *Ref.* B.T.J., 16th May 1918. *Diss.* By Aug. 1918.

MARRIED WOMEN, NATIONALITY, SELECT COMMITTEE.—*App.* jointly by H.L. and H.C., April–May 1923. *Obj.* To investigate British Law on nationality of married women, and results of husband and wife having different nationality. *Repr.* H.L., H.C. (chief parties). *Ref.* H.C. No. 115, 1923. *Diss.* July 1923.

MEDICAL BOARDS, RECRUITING, SELECT COMMITTEE.—*App.* by H.C. in 1917. *Obj.* To investigate character and methods of the Boards and suggest improvements. *Repr.* H.C. (chief parties). *Ref.* Cd. 9005, p. 87. *Diss.* About July 1917.

MEMBERS' EXPENSES, SELECT COMMITTEE.—*App.* by H.C. Nov. 1920. *Obj.* To report upon salaries of members of H.C. in connexion with expenses incurred on parliamentary duties. *Repr.* H.C. (chief parties). *Ref.* H.C. No. 255, 1920. *Diss.* Dec. 1920.

MERCANTILE MARINE.—*See* Pensions (1920).

MILITARY SERVICE (REVIEW OF EXCEPTIONS) ACT, 1917, SELECT COMMITTEE.—*App.* by H.C., June 1917. *Obj.* To report upon W.O. instructions on administration of the Act, and system of medical examination under the M.S.A.'s generally. *Repr.* H.C. (chief parties). *Ref.* H.C. Nos. 126 and 185, 1918 ; T., 22nd June 1917, p. 6, where it is referred to as a Government Committee. *Diss.* End Jan. 1918.

MINISTERS.—*See* Remuneration of Ministers.

NATIONAL SERVICE (MEETINGS) PARLIAMENTARY COMMITTEE. —*App.* by Parliament at request of P.M., Feb. 1917. *Obj.* To assist National Service recruiting scheme by arranging meetings and providing speakers, &c. *Repr.* Parliament (chief parties). *Ref.* T., 2nd Feb. 1917, p. 8.

NATIONAL EXPENDITURE.—*See* Expenditure, National.

NAVAL AND MILITARY SERVICES (PENSIONS AND GRANTS), SELECT COMMITTEE.—*App.* by H.C., Nov. 1914. *Obj.* To prepare scheme of pensions and grants for officers and men and their dependants, and to consider amendment of scheme of separation allowances. *Repr.* Leaders of chief political parties. *Ref.* H.C. Nos. 53, 328, 1915. *Diss.* Sept. 1915.

NAVY AND ARMY CANTEENS SELECT COMMITTEE.—*App.* by H.C., April 1920. *Obj.* To inquire into taking over by Navy and Army Canteens Boards of assets, &c. of Expeditionary Force Canteens and into

Board's subsequent administration. *Repr.* H.C. (chief parties). *Ref.* H.C. No. 117, 1923. *Diss.* July 1923.

OFFICERS.—*See* Ex-Ranker Officers.

PENSIONS, PARLIAMENTARY COMMITTEE.—*App.* by H.C. apparently early in the War, and in any case before Nov. 1916. *Obj.* To watch and supervise pensions matters in Parliament. *Repr.* H.C. (chief parties). *Ref.* T., 3rd Nov. 1916, p. 9.

PENSIONS, PARLIAMENTARY INFORMATION BUREAU, EXECUTIVE COMMITTEE.—*App.* by Parliamentary Pensions Committee, Nov. 1916. *Obj.* To organize information bureau for use of M.P.'s. *Repr.* The Pensions Committee. *Ref.* T., 3rd Nov. 1916, p. 9.

PENSIONS (1919), SELECT COMMITTEE.—*App.* by H.C., April 1919. *Obj.* To report upon administration of Pension Acts and Warrants and means of removing grievances of pensioners. *Repr.* H.C. (chief parties). *Ref.* H.C. No. 39, p. 46, and No. 247, 1919. *Diss.* Dec. 1919.

PENSIONS (1920), SELECT COMMITTEE.—*App.* by H.C., May 1920. *Obj.* To report upon employment and training of disabled ex-service men, grants by Civil Liabilities Department, and pensions of officers and other ranks of Mercantile Marine, engaged on War service. *Repr.* H.C. (chief parties). *Ref.* H.C. No. 185, 1920. *Diss.* Aug. 1920.

PENSIONS (WAR).—*See also* Naval and Military Services.

PREMIUM BONDS, SELECT COMMITTEE.—*App.* by H.C., Nov. 1917. *Obj.* To report upon desirability of raising money for the War by issue of Premium Bonds. *Repr.* H.C. (chief parties). *Ref.* H.C. No. 168, 1918. *Diss.* Jan. 1918.

PRISONERS OF WAR.—*See* W.O.

PROPORTIONAL REPRESENTATION, ROYAL COMMISSION.— *App.* by Royal Warrant, Feb. 1918, under Representation of the People Act, 1918. *Obj.* To prepare scheme for proportional representation as provided by the Act. *Repr.* H.C., L.G.B., Civil Service, Judges. *Ref.* Cd. 9044. *Diss.* April 1918.

RECRUITING, CENTRAL COMMITTEE.—*App.* through combination of Parliamentary Recruiting Committee (*see* next entry) and Joint Labour Recruiting Committee, about Sept. 1915. *Obj.* To advise and assist Director General of Recruiting in carrying out Derby Scheme. *Repr.* The two component Committees. *Ref.* Cd. 8149.

RECRUITING, PARLIAMENTARY, COMMITTEE.—*App.* jointly by H.L. and H.C., Sept. 1914. *Obj.* To stimulate recruiting and organize propaganda, with assistance of Local Committees. *Repr.* H.L. and H.C. (chief parties). *Ref.* Cd. 8149 ; Cmd. 1193. *Diss.* Absorbed into Recruiting Central Committee about Sept. 1915.

RECRUITING, PARLIAMENTARY, LOCAL COMMITTEES.—*App.* by Recruiting Committee (*see* above) from Sept. 1915. *Obj.* To stimulate recruiting in their localities. *Repr.* M.P.'s concerned. *Ref.* Cd. 8149.

(For Recruiting Local Advisory Committees, established by the Local Parliamentary Committees, *see* W.O.)

RECRUITING.—*See also* Medical Boards.

REMUNERATION OF MINISTERS, SELECT COMMITTEE.—*App.* by H.C., Nov. 1920. *Obj.* To consider what remuneration of ministers should be. *Repr.* H.C. (chief parties). *Ref.* H.C., No. 241, 1920. *Diss.* Dec. 1920.

REPRESENTATION OF THE PEOPLE BILL, 1917, BOUNDARY COMMISSIONS.—*App.* under Royal Warrant for England and Wales, Ireland, and Scotland, May 1917, by H.O., I.O., S.O., respectively. *Obj.* To determine membership and boundaries of counties and boroughs under the Bill. *Repr.* H.C., L.G.B., Ordnance Survey, other prominent persons. *Ref.* Cd. 8576, 8786, 8585. *Diss.* Later in 1917.

SEPARATION ALLOWANCES.—*See* Naval and Military Services Select Committee.

SLOUGH DEPOT.—*See* Cippenham.

STATUTORY REQUIREMENTS.—*See* Gas Undertakings, Tramways.

TEACHERS' SUPERANNUATION SELECT COMMITTEE.—*App.* by H.C., May 1922. *Obj.* To report whether in fixing existing scale of salaries in grant-aided schools any undertaking was given by the Government or Parliament that non-contributory pensions should continue to be paid. *Repr.* H.C. (chief parties). *Ref.* H.C., No. 106, 1922. *Diss.* May 1922.

TELEPHONE CHARGES SELECT COMMITTEE.—*App.* by H.C., June 1920. *Obj.* To report upon telephone charges and their revision. *Repr.* H.C. (chief parties). *Ref.* H.C., No. 247, 1920. *Diss.* Dec. 1920.

TELEPHONE SERVICE, SELECT COMMITTEE.—*App.* by H.C., Mar. 1921. *Obj.* To inquire into organization, administration, and methods of charging. *Repr.* H.C. (chief parties). *Ref.* H.C., No. 191, 1921.

TELEPHONE SERVICE, SELECT COMMITTEE (1922).—*App.* by H.C., Feb. 1922. *Obj.* To inquire into organization, administration, and methods of charging. *Repr.* H.C. (chief parties), with engineering expert as assessor. *Ref.* H.C., No. 54, 1922. *Diss.* Mar. 1922.

TERMINATION OF THE WAR, DEFINITION, SELECT COMMITTEE. —*App.* by H.C., July 1918, on recommendation of Conference convened by M.R. *Obj.* To consider, in light of report of the ' Period of the War ' Interpretation Committee (*see* M.R.), the provision to be made by Parliament for defining ' the end of the War ', and continuing emergency legislation. *Repr.* H.C. (chief parties). *Ref.* H.C., Nos. 108, 141, 1918. *Diss.* Nov. 1918.

TRAMWAYS (STATUTORY REQUIREMENTS) SELECT COMMITTEE.—*App.* by H.C., Feb. 1918. *Obj.* To consider expediency and best means of modifying statutory charges on tramways severely affected by the War. *Repr.* H.C. (chief parties). *Ref.* H.C., No. 72, 1918. *Diss.* June 1918.

TRANSPORT, METROPOLITAN AREA, SELECT COMMITTEE.—*App.* by H.C., May 1919. *Obj.* To investigate congestion of traffic and fares charged in Metropolitan area. *Repr.* H.C. (chief parties), largely London members. *Ref.* H.C., No. 147, 1919. *Diss.* July 1919.

TRANSPORT, SELECT COMMITTEE.—*App.* by H.C., Aug. 1918. *Obj.* To investigate need and methods of improving, developing, and co-ordinating internal transport facilities of U.K. *Repr.* H.C. (chief parties), with power to co-opt members of outside bodies on Sub-Committees. *Ref.* H.C., Nos. 130, 136, 1918. *Diss.* Nov. 1918.

TRANSPORT SUB-COMMITTEE, IRELAND.—*App.* by Select Committee on Transport (q.v.), Aug. 1918. *Obj.* To investigate transport facilities offered by Irish ports and canals, and suggest means of equipping and developing them. *Repr.* Select Committee, the right to co-opt not exercised. *Ref.* H.C., Nos. 130, 136, 1918. *Diss.* Nov. 1918.

VALUATION OFFICE.—*See under* Land Values.

WAR SAVINGS, PARLIAMENTARY COMMITTEE.—*App.* in 1915 or later to promote movement for war savings. Details lacking.

WAR-TIME INCREASES OF WEALTH.—*See* Increases of Wealth (War).

PENSIONS, WAR: STATUTORY COMMITTEE AND MINISTRY

The *Statutory Committee on War Pensions* (or, more fully, the *Statutory Committee of the Royal Patriotic Fund Corporation*) was appointed under the Naval and Military War Pensions Act (5 & 6 Geo. V, c. 83), 10th Nov. 1915. It was established for the general supervision and control of grants of pensions under Royal Warrants, the award of supplementary pensions and grants, the decision of disputed questions, the provision for, and care of, disabled men, &c. Its twenty-seven members were chosen as follows : 12 by the Crown, 7 by various Government Departments, 6 by the Corporation and 2 by the Soldiers' and Sailors' Families Association.

The *Ministry of Pensions* was established for similar purposes on 22nd Dec. 1916, under a Minister and Parliamentary Secretary, by the Ministry of Pensions Act, 1916 (6 & 7 Geo. V, c. 65). It took over the duties in respect of Pensions, previously performed by the Admiralty, the War Office, and the Commissioners of Chelsea Hospital, the functions of the Commissioners being transferred to them by the War Pensions Act, 1920 (10 & 11 Geo. V, c. 23). The powers of the Statutory Committee were now exercised under the control of the Minister, and the Committee advised and assisted the Ministry as required. By the Naval and Military War Pensions (Transfer of Powers) Act, 1917 (7 & 8 Geo. V, c. 37) of 21st Aug. 1917, the powers and duties of the Committee were definitely transferred to the Ministry, and the Committee was dissolved by Order-in-Council on 1st Dec. 1917. A Special Grants Committee (*see* below) was established to take over the Statutory Committee's duties in respect of supplementary pensions, &c. *References*. Report of the Statutory Committee for 1916 (Cd. 8750) and Public General Acts, 1914–16, 1916, and subsequent years.

ABBREVIATIONS

M.Pen. = Ministry of Pensions.
S.C. = Statutory Committee on War Pensions.
W.P.C.(s) = Local War Pensions Committee(s).

AFTER-CARE.—*See* Inter-Allied.

APPEAL BOARDS, MEDICAL.—*App.* by M.Pen. in 1919 or early 1920, in various regions, as quasi-judicial bodies. *Obj.* To give right of appeal against amount of pensions awarded to officers and men. *Repr.* M.Pen., Medical Profession. *Ref.* H.C., No. 35, 1921.

APPEAL BOARDS, OFFICERS.—*App.* by M.Pen., Feb. 1918, for various districts. *Obj.* To hear appeals by officers and their dependants against refusal of pensions. *Repr.* Parliament, Legal and Medical Professions, Disabled Officers, Labour. *Ref.* H.C., No. 39, 1920, p. 24. *Diss.* Superseded, 1st Nov. 1919, by new Appeal Tribunals, Ministry (q.v.).

APPEAL SUB-COMMITTEES, LOCAL WAR PENSIONS COMMITTEES.—*App.* by W.P.C.'s in 1917 or earlier. *Obj.* To make preliminary examination of appeals against refusal of pensions prior to reference to Appeal Tribunals. *Repr.* W.P.C.'s concerned. *Ref.* Cmd. 14, pp. 16–17.

APPEAL TRIBUNALS, MINISTRY.—*App.* by Lord Chancellor, in consultation with M.Pen., starting work on 1st Nov. 1919, for various districts, under War Pensions (Administrative Provisions) Act, 1919. *Obj.* To hear appeals from officers and men and their dependants against rejection of claims to pension or grant. *Repr.* Legal and Medical Professions, Disabled Officer or Man (according to the case under consideration). *Ref.* P.G.A., 1919. *Still in existence at end of 1922.*

(These were called Ministry Tribunals in the Act, but the older term, Pensions Appeal Tribunals, was sometimes used. They put an end to the system of separate Appeal Boards for Officers, and Appeal Tribunals for Men.)

APPEAL TRIBUNALS, PENSIONS.—*App.* by M.Pen. in 1917, at first a single tribunal, but the number had increased to seven by Mar. 1919. *Obj.* To hear appeals by men (not officers) and their dependants against rejection of claims to pension or grant. *Repr.* Legal and Medical Profession, Disabled Men. *Ref.* H.C., No. 39, 1920, p. 21. *Diss.* Superseded, 1st Nov. 1919, by Appeal Tribunals, Ministry (q.v.).

ARTIFICIAL LEGS, STANDARDIZATION (BACON) COMMITTEE.—*App.* by M.Pen., July 1919. *Obj.* To advise and report upon this matter. *Repr.* Presumably expert, the Fighting Services being also represented. *Ref.* H.C., No. 35, 1921, p. 20. *Diss.* about end of 1919.

ARTIFICIAL LIMBS, ADVISORY COUNCIL.—*App.* during the War by S.C. or M.Pen. *Obj.* To examine and approve new types of artificial limbs, and assist in arranging their production. *Repr.* Presumably largely expert. *Ref.* H.C., No. 39, 1920, p. 30.

ARTIFICIAL LIMBS COMMITTEE.—*App.* by M.Pen., Feb. 1919. *Obj.* To advise generally in regard to artificial limbs and surgical appliances. *Repr.* Parliament, M.Pen., Surgeons, Disabled Men, Labour. *Ref.* H.C., No. 39, 1920, p. 31.

ATTRIBUTABILITY ADVISORY BOARD.—*App.* by M.Pen. about beginning of 1917. *Obj.* To advise in difficult and doubtful cases of attributability of disablement to war service. *Repr.* Presumably largely medical. *Ref.* Cmd. 14, p. 16. *See also* Disability, Refusal of Pensions, below.

AURAL BOARD, SPECIAL.—*App.* by M.Pen. during 1917. *Obj.* To assist in organizing training for disabled men suffering from deafness and mutism. *Repr.* M.Pen., B.E., Aurists, Lip-reading Specialists. *Ref.* Cd. 9206, pp. 84–5.

BACON COMMITTEE.—*See* Artificial Legs.

CASE SECTIONS.—*App.* by Sub-Committees of S.C. in 1916. *Obj.* To deal with individual applications under the Acts. *Repr.* The Sub-Committee concerned. *Ref.* Cd. 8750, p. 3. Presumably absorbed permanently into M.Pen. in 1918.

CENTRAL ADVISORY COMMITTEE, WAR PENSIONS.—*App.* by M.Pen., under War Pensions Act, 1921, about Sept. 1921. *Obj.* To advise M.Pen. generally on administration of war pensions. *Repr.* M.Pen., W.P.C.'s, Ex-Officers, Ex-Service Men. *Ref.* P.G.A., 1921 ; H.C., No. 18, 1922, p. 5. *Permanent Body.*

CHILDREN'S SUB-COMMITTEES.—*App.* by W.P.C.'s, under regulations of M.Pen., early in 1923. *Obj.* To deal with care of children under W.P.C. *Repr.* W.P.C.'s, with co-opted members. *Ref.* H.C., No. 1, 1924, p. 16. Presumably *still in existence*.

DISABILITY COMMITTEE.—*App.* by M.Pen., Oct. 1919. *Obj.* To advise M.Pen. on attributability or aggravation of diseases and injuries by war service, and on assessment of pensions. *Repr.* M.Pen., M.R.C., Royal Colleges of Physicians and Surgeons, Medical and Surgical Specialists. *Ref.* H.C., No. 244, 1921, p. 14.

DISABLED MEN.—*See* M.L., Joint Employment Sub-Committees, and under Inter-Allied below.

DISABLEMENT JOINT COMMITTEES.—*App.* at instance of M.Pen., in 1917, by co-operation of W.P.C.'s, in less populous counties. *Obj.* To utilize efficiently available resources for treatment and training of disabled men. *Repr.* W.P.C.'s concerned, Medical Profession, employers, workpeople, technical institutions. *Ref.* Cmd. 14. *Diss.* In 1919 or early 1920.

DISABLEMENT, LOCAL SUB-COMMITTEES.—*App.* from 1916 by over 200 W.P.C.'s. *Obj.* To deal with employment, treatment and training of disabled men in their areas. *Repr.* W.P.C.'s, and presumably experts. *Ref.* Cd. 8750, p. 22.

DISABLEMENT SPECIAL COMMITTEE.—*See* Officers Sub-Committee.

DISABLEMENT SUB-COMMITTEE.—*App.* by S.C., Jan. 1916. *Obj.* To deal with questions affecting disablement, with separate sections for health and training and employment. *Repr.* S.C., various Government Departments, Employers, Labour, Technical Education, Soldiers and Sailors Help Society. *Ref.* Cd. 8750, p. 17 seq.

EX-SERVICE QUESTIONS STANDING JOINT COMMITTEE.—*App.*, presumably by M.Pen., apparently in 1921, with separate panels for Officers and Men. *Obj.* To discuss and advise upon questions affecting disabled men. *Repr.* Government Departments concerned, Ex-Officers, Ex-Service Men. *Ref.* H.C., No. 1, 1924, p. 18. *Standing Body.*

EX-SERVICE MEN.—*See* M.L.

FINANCE SUB-COMMITTEE.—*App.* by S.C., Jan. 1916. *Obj.* To deal with finance work of S.C., including framing of regulations for supplementary pensions, &c. *Repr.* S.C. *Ref.* Cd. 8750, pp. 3–7. *Diss.* Presumably absorbed into organization of M.Pen. by end of 1917.

GRANTS.—*See* Special Grants Committee.

HOSPITAL COMMITTEES.—*App.* from time to time at hospitals for the disabled (e.g. Roehampton). *Obj.* General supervision of work of hospitals. *Repr.* Not stated. *Ref.* Cd. 8750, p. 19.

INQUIRY, DEPARTMENTAL COMMITTEE.—*App.* by M.Pen., Nov. 1920. *Obj.* To inquire generally into administration of M.Pen. and local organizations. *Repr.* Parliament, M.Pen., W.P.C.'s, The Army, Ex-Service Organizations, Labour. *Ref.* H.C., No. 244, 1921, pp. 19–20.

INSANE EX-SERVICE MEN, MEDICAL COMMITTEE.—*App.* by M.Pen., in 1917, after conference on the subject. *Obj.* To devise standards for guidance of Medical Boards regarding attributability of insanity to war service. *Repr.* M.Pen., Board of Control (Lunacy) for England and Wales, Medical Profession. *Ref.* H.C., No. 102, 1918, pp. 30–1. *Diss.* Apparently at end of 1917.

INTER-ALLIED CONFERENCES ON AFTER-CARE OF DISABLED MEN.—*Held* at Paris, Jan. 1917, at suggestion of Belgian Government, in London, May 1918, and annually at various capitals. *Obj.* To pool experience in general pensions problems, medical and surgical treatment, training and re-education, &c. *Repr.* Chief Allied Governments and Pensions Authorities. *Ref.* Cmd. 14, p. 76 ; H.M.S.O., 1917 and 1918.

INTER-ALLIED PERMANENT COMMITTEE ON DISABLED MEN.— *App.* by Second Inter-Allied Conference (*see* preceding entry), July 1917. *Obj.* To form permanent body in Paris for joint consideration of problem of re-education. *Repr.* Chief Allied States, including British Dominions. *Ref.* Cmd. 14, pp. 76–7. *Permanent Body.*

INSTITUTIONAL JOINT COMMITTEE (ENGLAND).—*App.* by M.Pen., Feb. 1917. *Obj.* To consider provision of institutional treatment for illness, for which civil institutions are not normally available. *Repr.* M.Pen., S.C., L.G.B., W.O., British Red Cross Society, Medical Profession. *Ref.* Cmd. 14, pp. 3–8. *Diss.* Jan. 1918.

INSTITUTIONAL JOINT COMMITTEE (SCOTLAND).—*App.* by M.Pen., June 1917. *Obj.* As with English Committee. *Repr.* M.Pen., W.O., Scottish Joint Disablement Committees, Special Medical Board for Scotland, British Red Cross Society. *Ref.* Cmd. 14, p. 38. *Diss.* During 1918.

LOCAL AREAS, ORGANIZATION, COMMITTEE.—*App.* by M.Pen., late in 1921, as result of War Pensions Act, 1921. *Obj.* To consider organization of local areas and prepare new scheme of areas in accordance with the Act. *Repr.* M.Pen., M.H., W.P.C.'s. *Ref.* H.C., No. 10, 1922 (sess. 2), p. 2. *Diss.* During 1922. *See also* Regulations, Reorganization.

LOCAL WAR PENSIONS COMMITTEES.—*App.* Nov. 1915, under Naval and Military War Pensions Act, 1915, for every county and county borough, and for some other boroughs and urban districts, their functions being increased in Dec. 1916, under Ministry of Pensions Act. By Aug. 1917 there were 302 Committees. *Obj.* To assist S.C. and M.Pen. locally in carrying out duties under Pensions Acts and Royal Warrants. *Repr.* As decided by L.A.'s concerned, the majority of members being appointed by (but not necessarily members of) the L.A.'s, provision being also made for representation of Labour and Women, whilst in 1918 the M.Pen. was empowered to appoint additional members. *Ref.* P.G.A., 1914–16, 1916, 1918 ; Cd. 8750, pp. 51–5. *Still in existence at end of 1922.*

(In the Acts the Committees are called Local Committees in Boroughs, and District Committees in County Areas, but the term Local is commonly used to refer to either.)

LOCAL WAR PENSIONS COMMITTEES ASSOCIATION.—W.P.C.'s were authorized by War Pensions (Administrative Provisions) Act, 1918, to contribute, with consent of M.Pen., to such an Association and to expenses of members attending meetings.

LOCAL WAR PENSIONS COMMITTEES, DISTRICT AND LOCAL SUB-COMMITTEES.—*App.* provided for by Naval and Military War Pensions Act, 1915, whilst in 1918 M.Pen. was empowered to require appointment of District Sub-Committees in counties, and Local Sub-Committees for parts of other areas. *Obj.* To assist the main Committees in their areas. *Repr.* Similar to main Committees, apparently. *Ref.* P.G.A., 1915, 1918.

(The W.P.C.'s were also empowered to establish Sub-Committees for various purposes, some of which are referred to elsewhere.)

LOCAL WAR PENSIONS JOINT COMMITTEES.—*App.* by W.P.C.'s, probably in individual cases in 1917 or earlier, whilst in 1918 M.Pen. was empowered to require their formation, and to direct amalgamation of W.P.C.'s to provide single W.P.C. for two or more areas. *Obj.* To administer jointly, part, or with amalgamations all, of the work of the separate W.P.C.'s. *Repr.* The Committees concerned. *Ref.* P.G.A., 1918.

MEDICAL ADVISORY COMMITTEE.—This was already in existence at establishment of M.Pen. Its functions were to advise Pensions Authorities generally on medical matters. *Repr.* Medical Profession. *Ref.* Cmd. 14, p. 11.

MEDICAL BOARDS, PENSIONS, were appointed, in early stages of work, to examine disabled men for grant and renewal of pensions, &c. *See* Cmd. 14, pp. 14–15. Appeal Boards, &c., are dealt with above.

MEDICAL BOARDS, SPECIAL.—*App.* by M.Pen. in or before 1922. *Obj.* To decide questions of permanent basis of individual pensions. *Repr.* Medical Profession, with specialists in each case in particular disability from which the individual man is suffering. *Ref.* H.C., No. 1, 1924, p. 3. Presumably *still in existence.*

MEDICAL BOARDS.—*See also* Officers and Nurses, Overseas Contingents, Paris, and M.N.S.

MEDICAL REFEREES.—These were experienced medical men chosen by W.P.C.'s, but appointed by M.Pen., to give necessary medical advice and assistance to W.P.C.'s. Preference was given to men with experience of treatment of men injured in the War. *See* Cmd. 14, p. 11.

MEDICAL WAR, CENTRAL, COMMITTEE.—*See* N.H.I.C.

NURSES.—*See* Officers and Nurses.

OFFICERS AND NURSES, MEDICAL BOARDS.—*App.* originally by W.O., and taken over by M.Pen., Aug. 1919. *Obj.* To examine discharged officers and nurses, with separate divisions for wounds and other disabilities. *Repr.* M.Pen., R.A.M.C., Medical Profession. *Ref.* H.C., No. 35, 1921, p. 21.

OFFICERS AND NURSES REGULATIONS, DEPARTMENTAL COMMITTEE.—*App.* by M.Pen., Feb. 1919. *Obj.* To consider existing Officers' Warrant, and regulations of Special Grants Committee. *Repr.* Parliament, M.Pen., and possibly others. *Ref.* H.C., No. 247, 1919, p. 14 ; No. 39, 1920, p. 3. *Diss.* April 1919.

OFFICERS' FRIEND BRANCH.—*App.* by M.Pen., Feb. 1919, with local representatives. *Obj.* To give semi-official advice to invalided officers and dependants of deceased officers. *Repr.* Official and expert. *Ref.* H.C., No. 39, 1920, p. 6.

OFFICERS SUB-COMMITTEE.—*App.* by S.C., Oct. 1916, originally with title of Disablement Special Committee. *Obj.* To deal with pensions, &c., to officers and their dependants and care of disabled officers and men of similar education. *Repr.* S.C. and co-opted members, who included representatives of officers and their dependants, and of Imperial Civil Service. *Ref.* Cd. 8750, pp. 3–16 ; T., 3rd Nov. 1916, p. 5.

OVERSEAS CONTINGENTS MEDICAL BOARDS.—*App.* or taken over by M.Pen. in 1919. *Obj.* To deal with members of Overseas Contingents resident in U.K. *Repr.* Medical Profession and others. *Ref.* H.C., No. 35, 1920, p. 21.

OVERSEAS SETTLEMENT COMMITTEE AND NATIONAL RELIEF FUND JOINT COMMITTEE.—*App.* jointly in connexion with M.Pen., apparently in 1919. *Obj.* To arrange for special assistance to disabled officers and men desiring to emigrate. *Repr.* O.S.C., N.R.F. *Ref.* H.C., No. 35, 1921, p. 26 (footnote).

ORGANIZATION SUB-COMMITTEE.—*App.* by S.C., Jan. 1916. *Obj.* To prepare and supervise general organization of the work. *Repr.* S.C. *Ref.* Cd. 8750, p. 3.

PARIS MEDICAL BOARD.—*App.* by M.Pen. in 1919 or early 1920. *Obj.* To examine pensioners resident in or near Paris. *Repr.* Medical Profession and others. *Ref.* H.C., No. 35, 1921.

PENSION ADVANCES COMMITTEE OR COMMITTEES.—*App.* by M.Pen. in 1919. *Obj.* To advance to disabled men rates of pension, &c., recommended by Medical Referees, pending final settlement of pension. *Repr.* Not stated. *Ref.* H.C., No. 39, 1920, p. 20.

PENSIONS BOARD, SPECIAL SUB-COMMITTEE.—*App.* by S.C., Oct. 1916. *Obj.* To report on Government proposals for establishing Pensions Board (subsequently changed to Ministry) and suggest amendments. *Repr.* S.C. *Ref.* Cd. 8750, p. 24. *Diss.* Nov. or Dec. 1916.

PENSIONS GRANTS AND ALLOWANCES SUB-COMMITTEE.—*App.* by S.C., Jan. 1916. *Obj.* To deal with problems specially connected with these matters, including supplementary pensions and separation allowances, and to make special grants where no pension is payable. *Repr.* As with S.C., with one co-opted member, a woman. *Ref.* Cd. 8750. *Diss.* Apparently superseded, Aug. 1917, by Special Grants Committee (q.v.) under Pensions Act, 1917.

PENSIONS, NATIONAL, COMMITTEE.—*App.* by Select Committee on War Pensions (*see* Parliament) in or before Aug. 1916. *Obj.* To watch over interests of local authorities in the central administration. *Repr.* Various L.A.'s. *Ref.* T., 14th Aug. 1916, p. 3.

PENSIONS SELECT COMMITTEES.—*See* Parliament, *under* Naval and Military Services, Pensions.

PRISONERS OF WAR.—*See* Repatriated.

RED CROSS AND ST. JOHN'S AMBULANCE ASSOCIATION, JOINT COMMITTEE.—*App.* by the two Societies for war purposes co-operating with M.Pen. and other Government Departments. *See* H.C., No. 39, 1920, p. 31.

RE-EDUCATION.—*See under* Inter-Allied.

REFUSAL OF PENSIONS, SPECIAL (LOCAL) SUB-COMMITTEES.— *App.* by W.P.C.'s in autumn of 1917. *Obj.* To re-investigate previous refusals of pensions on grounds of non-attributability. *Repr.* W.P.C.'s, Medical Referees. *Ref.* Cd. 8826.

REGIONAL ADVISORY COUNCILS.—*App.* by M.Pen., in 1919 and 1920, for each region in the country under the decentralization scheme (*see* Reorganization). *Obj.* To advise Regional Director on policy, and make proposals on administrative matters. *Repr.* Local M.P.'s, W.P.C.'s, Ex-Service Organizations. *Ref.* H.C., No. 35, 1921, p. 11.

REGULATIONS (LOCAL WAR PENSIONS COMMITTEES) ADVISORY COMMITTEE.—*App.* by M.Pen. in 1919. *Obj.* To assist in framing general regulations for procedure of W.P.C.'s. *Repr.* Selected W.P.C.'s. *Ref.* H.C., No. 39, 1920, p. 9. *Diss.* Mar. 1920.

RE-ORGANIZATION COMMITTEE.—*App.* by M.Pen., Feb. 1919. *Obj.* To report upon scheme of decentralized organization. *Repr.* Parliament, M.Pen., Labour, Women. *Ref.* H.C., No. 39, 1920, p. 6. *Diss.* Mar. 1919. (*See also* Local Areas, Organization.)

REPATRIATED BRITISH PRISONERS OF WAR, ADVICE BUREAUX.—*App.* by M.Pen., Nov. 1918. *Obj.* To advise and assist disabled prisoners at discharge centres. *Repr.* Official. *Ref.* H.C., No. 39, 1920, p. 12. *Diss.* Presumably in 1919.

ROYAL WARRANT REVISION, COMMITTEE OF MINISTERS.— *App.* by Cabinet, at instance of M.Pen., early in 1917. *Obj.* To discuss revised scheme of war pensions. *Repr.* Cabinet, Tre. *Ref.* Cmd. 14, p. 12. *Diss.* Mar. 1917.

SPECIAL GRANTS COMMITTEE.—*App.* by M.Pen., in or after Aug. 1917, under Naval and Military War Pensions Act, 1917. *Obj.* To exercise, under M.Pen., former powers of S.C. for provision, regulation, payment and forfeiture of supplementary grants in aid of pensions and grants for training of dependants, and to make necessary inquiries concerning those grants. *Repr.* Not more than 12 (later 15) persons appointed by M.Pen., to include persons with special knowledge, as members of S.C. or W.P.C.'s, and representatives of Labour and disabled men. *Ref.* P.G.A., 1917–18 ; Cmd. 14, pp. 57 seq. *Still in existence at end of 1922.*

(The work was divided into various sections (e.g. Education, Officers) and delegated to sectional Sub-Committees. The Committee's functions were altered later (*see* H.C., No. 224, 1921, p. 15). It is possible that Special Grants Sub-Committees were set up locally in some cases by W.P.C.'s (*see* Cmd. 14, p. 62).)

STANDING JOINT COMMITTEE.—*App.* by Government or M.Pen. early in 1920. *Obj.* To assist ex-service organizations to secure full information and enjoyment of their legal rights, &c., for their members, and to provide for consultation between the Government and the ex-service men. *Repr.* M.Pen., Adm., A.M., M.L., W.O. *Ref.* H.C., No. 244, 1921, p. 19. *Presumably Permanent.*

STATUTORY COMMITTEE OF ROYAL PATRIOTIC SOCIETY: STATUTORY WAR PENSIONS COMMITTEE.—*See* Heading to Section.

SUBSTITUTION COMMITTEES.—*App.* by M.Pen., Sept. 1920, for different branches of M.Pen. *Obj.* To organize substitution of ex-service men for non-service men and women as recommended by Lytton Committee (*see* M.L.). *Repr.* M.Pen., ex-service men, women. *Ref.* H.C., No. 244, 1920, p. 3.

TECHNICAL, TRADE ADVISORY COMMITTEES.—*See* M.L.

TUBERCULOSIS (SANATORIA FOR SOLDIERS) INTER-DEPARTMENTAL COMMITTEE.—*See* L.G.B.

VILLAGE CENTRES COUNCIL FOR CURATIVE TREATMENT AND TRAINING OF DISABLED MEN.—For information *see* First Annual Report to 31st Oct. 1919 (*address*, 5 Lincoln's Inn Fields, London, W.C.), and article on Village Centres in Réveille, Feb. 1919.

WORKMEN'S COMPENSATION FOR DISABLED MEN.—*See* H.O.

POST OFFICE

ABBREVIATION

P.O. = Post Office.

TELEPHONE RATES, DEPARTMENTAL COMMITTEE.—*App.* by Postmaster-General, May 1919. *Obj.* To report upon changes in telephone tariffs. *Repr.* P.O. officials. *Ref.* Cmd. 804. *Diss.* June 1920.

PRIVY COUNCIL

ABBREVIATION

P.C. = Privy Council.

DENTAL BOARD.—*App.* by P.C., apparently with co-operation of Health Departments, under Dentists Act, 1921, in or after Aug. 1921. *Obj.* To administer Dentists Acts of 1878 and 1921, and be responsible for registration of dentists. *Repr.* P.C., M.H., S.B.H., L.G.B.(I.), Medical Profession, Dentists. *Ref.* P.G.A., 1921; Cmd. 1713, p. 29. *Permanent Body.*

DENTISTS ACT COMMITTEE.—*App.* by P.C., July 1917. *Obj.* To investigate shortage of qualified dentists and evils of practice by unregistered dentists, and consider legislation and modifications in training. *Repr.* P.C., Parliament, B.E., L.G.B., Medical Profession, including Public Health Service, Dentists, Hospitals. *Ref.* Cmd. 33. *Diss.* Feb. 1919.

DENTISTS.—*See also* L.G.B.

EXPORT LICENCE.—*See* W.T.D.

GAS CHARGES COMMITTEE.—*App.* by P.C., at instance of B.T., in 1915. *Obj.* To inquire into quality of gas and methods of charging and make recommendations. *Repr.* P.C., H.O., engineering, scientific research. *Ref.* Evening Standard, 25th Aug. 1922, p. 6. *Diss.* Prior to Aug. 1922.

IMPERIAL MINERAL RESOURCES BUREAU.—*App.* through M.R. and under P.C. after approval by Imperial War Conference, April 1918. *Obj.* To collect information and advise on resources and requirements of the Empire. *Repr.* Governments of U.K., India, the Dominions, &c., mineral, mining and metal industries. *Ref.* Cd. 9231, p. 9. *Permanent.* *See also* Cabinet.

INVENTIONS BY WORKERS INTER-DEPARTMENTAL COMMITTEE.—*App.* by P.C. in 1920 or 1921. *Obj.* To consider means of dealing with inventions made by workers, aided or maintained by public funds, in interests of State, inventor and industry generally. *Repr.* Adm., A.M., B.T., M.R.C., Patents Office, S.I.R., W.O., Awards to Inventors Commission, Legal Profession, manufacturers, scientific experts. *Ref.* Report (H.M.S.O., 1922). *Diss.* Oct. 1921. *See* Cabinet, *under* Awards.

MEDICAL RESEARCH COMMITTEE OF THE PRIVY COUNCIL.— *App.* by Order-in-Council of 25th Mar. 1920, under the Ministry of Health Act, 1919. *Obj.* To supervise work of newly incorporated Medical Research Council, formed out of Medical Research Committee of N.H.I.C. (q.v.). *Repr.* Presumably much as with Medical Research Committee. *Ref.* P.G.A., 1919.

MIDWIVES BOARD FOR IRELAND, CENTRAL.—*See* L.G.B.(I.).

PATENTS FOR STATE-AIDED RESEARCH INTER-DEPARTMENTAL COMMITTEE.—*See* S.I.R.

SCIENTIFIC AND INDUSTRIAL RESEARCH COMMITTEE AND (LATER) DEPARTMENT.—*See* separate section.

TITLES DEPRIVATION COMMITTEE.—*App.* as Committee of P.C. under Titles Deprivation Act of Nov. 1917. *Obj.* To report to H.C. on cases of enemy holders of British titles in arms against the Allies. *Repr.* P.C., including two members of Judicial Committee. *Ref.* P.G.A., 1917–18.

RECONSTRUCTION, COMMITTEES AND MINISTRY

The *First Committee on Reconstruction* was appointed by Mr. Asquith, as a Committee of the Cabinet, in Mar. 1916, and the *Second Committee* was reconstituted, as a body of men possessing special knowledge, including Members of Parliament, representatives of Business, Finance and Labour, and Experts in social questions, and entrusted with a general survey of the problem of reconstruction, by Mr. Lloyd George, in Mar. 1917. These two Committees are referred to below as the Reconstruction Committtee (R.C.), the dates of appointment indicating whether the First or Second Committee is intended. The *Ministry* was established in Aug. 1917, by the New Ministries and Secretaries Act, 1917 (7 & 8 Geo. V, c. 44), under a Minister and Parliamentary Secretary, to promote organization and development after the War, by consideration of problems likely to arise, and preparation of schemes for dealing with them. The Act fixed the *duration* of the Ministry at not more than two years after the close of the War, but it appears to have come to an end in June 1919, by transfer of its work to other departments (*see* Public General Acts, 1917). For the general organization and activities of the Ministry, *see also* the Report on the Work of the Ministry for the Period to 31st Dec. 1918 (Cd. 9231).

The Ministry had a *General Branch* for the organization of staff and work, including accounts and estimates, which had a Trade Organization Section, and in addition to this the work of the Ministry was divided into the following branches :

A. TRANSITIONAL ECONOMICS (or Finance, Transport and Common Services), dealing with measures of control during the immediate post-war period, to meet war shortages of supplies, materials, tonnage, capital, &c. :

B. COMMERCE AND PRODUCTION, to deal with problems of increased production in the light of probable resources during the transition period (*see* Cmd. 455, for report on Anti-Dumping Legislation) :

C. LABOUR AND INDUSTRIAL ORGANIZATION, to deal with any problems likely to arise in these matters :

D. RURAL DEVELOPMENT, to deal generally with agricultural and rural problems : and

E. SOCIAL DEVELOPMENT, to deal with general social problems, as distinct from industrial questions, during the transition period.

ABBREVIATIONS

R.A.C. = Advisory Council to Ministry of Reconstruction.
R.C.   = Reconstruction Committee.
M.R.   = Ministry of Reconstruction.

ACQUISITION OF LAND.—*See* Land.

ACQUISITION OF POWERS COMMITTEE.—*App.* by R.C., Dec. 1916. *Obj.* To consider means of cheapening and simplifying process of obtaining parliamentary powers for public works. *Repr.* Parliament, L.G.B., B.T., S.O., L.A.'s. *Ref.* Cd. 8982. *Diss.* Feb. 1918.

ADULT EDUCATION COMMITTEE.—*App.* as Sub-Committee of R.C., July 1917. *Obj.* To consider question of adult education (other than technical or vocational) in G.B., and to make recommendations. *Repr.*

Universities and Education generally, Labour, Women, Teachers, W.E.A., Tutorial Classes. *Ref.* Cd. 9107. *Diss.* July 1919.

ADVISORY COUNCIL.—*App.* by M.R., Jan. 1918. *Obj.* To advise M.R. generally on difficult and complex questions, working through five Sections and a Women's Advisory Committee (q.v.). *Repr.* A panel of men and women of experience and distinction in public affairs. *Ref.* Cd. 9195. *Diss.* June 1919. *See also* Chairmen, Committee of, and the Sections under Finance (I), Production (II), Labour (III), Rural Development (IV), Social Development (V), membership representing main interests on Council.

AGRICULTURAL MACHINERY.—*See* Engineering Trades.

AGRICULTURAL POLICY SUB-COMMITTEE.—*App.* by P.M., Aug. 1916. *Obj.* To report upon best means of increasing home-grown food supplies. *Repr.* B.A., British and Irish agriculturalists, Labour, agricultural research. *Ref.* Cd. 8506, 9079. *Diss.* June 1918.

AIRCRAFT.—*See* Engineering Trades.

ALIENS AFTER THE WAR COMMITTEE.—*App.* by P.M. in 1916, as Sub-Committee of R.C. and continued under M.R. *Obj.* To consider postwar and general policy as to enemy aliens, alien restriction, repatriation and naturalization laws. *Repr.* C.O., F.O., H.O., In.O., L.G.B., S.O., W.O. *Ref.* Cd. 8916.

ALUMINIUM, ANTIMONY, ASBESTOS.—*See* Raw Materials.

APPRENTICESHIPS.—*See under* ' Period of the War '.

BUILDING INDUSTRY AFTER THE WAR.—*See* next entry.

BUILDING MATERIALS SUPPLY (BUILDING INDUSTRY AFTER THE WAR) COMMITTEE.—*App.* by M.R., Nov. 1917, after consultation with L.G.B. *Obj.* To report upon probable post-war demand and supply, allocation and increase of supply and causes of high prices, and make recommendations as to control. *Repr.* M.R., builders, builders' merchants, architects, engineers, surveyors. *Ref.* Cd. 9197. *Diss.* Nov. 1918.

CARBONIZATION SUB-COMMITTEE (COAL CONSERVATION COMMITTEE).—*App.* by main Committee, July 1916, and absorbing Metallurgical Sub-Committee, Jan. 1917. *Obj.* To consider application of carbon in preparing fuel for industrial and domestic purposes. *Repr.* H.O. (Mines Department), S.I.R., chemical and mining research, engineering industry. *Ref.* Cd. 9084. *Diss.* Jan. 1918.

CHAIRMEN OF SECTIONS OF THE ADVISORY COUNCIL, COMMITTEE OF.—*App.* by M.R., Jan. 1918. *Obj.* To advise M.R. informally in difficulties in daily work, and generally on important questions, especially of transport and electrical generation. *Repr.* Chairmen and Vice-Chairmen of Sections of R.A.C. *Ref.* Cd. 9195. *Diss.* June 1919.

CHEMICAL TRADE COMMITTEE.—*App.* by M.R., Sept. 1917. *Obj.* To advise on procedure in dealing with the chemical trades after the War, and to consider formation of organizations for industry itself to handle its own problems. *Repr.* M.M., M.S., chemical manufacturers, scientists. *Ref.* Cd. 8882. *Diss.* Nov. 1917.

CIVIL WAR WORKERS COMMITTEE.—*App.* as Sub-Committee of R.C. about July 1917. *Obj.* To consider arrangements for demobilization of civilians engaged on munitions, or government work, or as substitutes. *Repr.* B.A., B.T., H.O., M.L., M.M., W.O., representative employers, work-people and women. *Ref.* Cd. 9117, 9228. *Diss.* Nov. 1918. Three Sub-Committees were appointed, one for Unemployment Insurance (q.v.), and two others.

CIVIL WAR WORKERS RE-SETTLEMENT CO-ORDINATION COM-MITTEE.—*App.* by M.R. in 1918. *Obj.* To co-ordinate proposals of different Government Departments for labour re-settlement with each other and with military demobilization, including provision for labour dismissed during the War. *Repr.* M.R., Adm., A.M., W.O., B.T., H.O., L.G.B., M.L., M.M., and other Departments. *Ref.* Cmd. 9231. *Diss.* Apparently replaced by War Cabinet (Smuts) Committee (*see* Cabinet), Nov. 1918.

COAL CONSERVATION COMMITTEE.—*App.* by P.M., July 1916, as Sub-Committee of R.C. *Obj.* To advise upon best methods of mining and using coal and bye-products, and upon developments of new or existing mines. *Repr.* B.T., H.O., S.I.R., Geological Survey, coal mining, engineering, industry generally, Labour, scientific and other experts. *Ref.* Cd. 9084. *Diss.* Jan. 1918.
   (*See also* Carbonization, Electric Power Supply, Geological, Metallurgical, Mining Sub-Committees.)

COASTAL RIGHTS.—*See* Land, Acquisition.

COMMERCIAL AND INDUSTRIAL POLICY COMMITTEE.—*App.* by P.M., July 1916, in connexion with R.C. *Obj.* To consider post-war commercial and industrial policy with special reference to Paris Economic Resolutions, maintenance of essential industries, recovery of trade lost during the War, development of imperial resources and prevention of foreign control. *Repr.* Various important industries, mining and metallurgy, commerce, shipping, railways, agriculture, Labour. *Ref.* Cd. 9035. *Diss.* Dec. 1917.

COMMERCIAL ORGANIZATION.—*See under* Production.

COMMON AND HIGHWAY RIGHTS.—*See under* Land, Acquisition.

COMMON SERVICES.—*See under* Finance.

COMPANY LAW COMMITTEE.—*See* B.T.

COPPER.—*See under* Raw Materials.

CURRENCY AND FOREIGN EXCHANGES.—Joint appointment. *See* Tre.

DEMOBILIZATION OF THE ARMY COMMITTEE.—*App.* as Sub-Committee of R.C. in summer of 1916. *Obj.* To report upon arrangements for return to civil employment of Army officers and men. *Repr.* W.O., B.A., B.T. (later M.L.), Tre., Commercial Intelligence Department, Employers, Labour. *Ref.* Cd. 9231, App. I. *Diss.* Replaced at Armistice by Cabinet (q.v.) Committee.
   (*See also* Officers' Re-settlement Committee, and W.O.)

DISPOSAL OF WAR STORES ADVISORY BOARD.—Alternative title. *See* Surplus Government Property.

DOMESTIC SERVICE, HOME HELPS, SUB-COMMITTEE.—*App.* by Women's Advisory Committee, Dec. 1918. *Obj.* To inquire into questions of provision for home helps. *Repr.* The Committee, and women with special knowledge. *Ref.* Cmd. 67, p. 3. *Diss.* Inquiry not proceeded with.

DOMESTIC SERVICE INQUIRY OF WOMEN'S ADVISORY COMMITTEE.—This inquiry was undertaken by the Committee, at request of R.A.C., Dec. 1918, and completed Feb. 1919. It covered general conditions of Domestic Service as affected by women's war work, and the best means of utilizing available labour. It was largely carried out through Sub-Committees (*see* below). *Ref.* Cmd. 67. *Diss.* Mar. 1919.

DOMESTIC SERVICE, MACHINERY OF DISTRIBUTION, SUB-COMMITTEE.—*App.* by Women's Advisory Committee, Dec. 1918. *Obj.* To consider means of co-ordinating and developing existing agencies, and bringing employers and employees into closer touch. *Repr.* Men and women specially qualified on this question. *Ref.* Cmd. 67. *Diss.* Feb. 1919.

DOMESTIC SERVICE, ORGANIZATION AND CONDITIONS, SUB-COMMITTEE.—*App.* by Women's Advisory Committee, Dec. 1918. *Obj.* To consider organization and conditions of domestic service to render it attractive and maintain supply of labour. *Repr.* Women specially qualified on this question. *Ref.* Cmd. 67. *Diss.* Feb. 1918.

DOMESTIC SERVICE, TRAINING, SUB-COMMITTEE.—*App.* by Women's Advisory Committee, Dec. 1918. *Obj.* To suggest improvements in training, to raise status of domestic service. *Repr.* Women specially qualified on this problem. *Ref.* Cmd. 67. *Diss.* Jan. 1919.

EDUCATION, REVIEWING COMMITTEE.—*App.* by P.M., as Sub-Committee of R.C., July 1916. *Obj.* To consider national system of education as a whole and suggest practical developments. *Repr.* The Cabinet, ex-Cabinet ministers and others. *Ref.* T., 11th Oct. 1916, p. 9.

EDUCATION.—*See* Adult Education, and *under* Social Development.

ELECTRICAL APPARATUS.—*See* Engineering Trades.

ELECTRIC POWER SUPPLY SUB-COMMITTEE.—*App.* by Coal Conservation Committee, July 1916. *Obj.* To investigate economies in use of coal as affected by supply of electricity, for power and other purposes. *Repr.* H.O. (Mines Department), engineering, railways, electrical industries, chemical research. *Ref.* Cd. 8880. *Diss.* April 1917.

EMPLOYERS AND EMPLOYED.—*See* Industrial Relations.

EMPLOYMENT ON THE LAND.—*See under* Land.

ENGINEERING TRADES (NEW INDUSTRIES) COMMITTEE.—*App.* by M.R., Dec. 1917. *Obj.* To prepare list of engineering products, not adequately produced in U.K. before the War, with special reference to labour required and to make recommendations for post-war establishment, &c. *Repr.* Employers in engineering and allied trades. *Ref.* Cd. 9226. *Diss.* Dec. 1918.

ENGINEERING TRADES (NEW INDUSTRIES) COMMITTEE, BRANCH COMMITTEES.—*App.* by main Committee early in 1918. *Obj.* To deal with individual branches of the industry. *Repr.* Employers in branches concerned. *Ref.* Cd. 9195, 9226. *Diss.* Late in 1918.

(The branches in question included Agricultural, Leather-manufacturing, Paper-making, Printing, Printers' General, Textile (Manchester), Textile (Nottingham), Wire, Miscellaneous Machinery, Aircraft, Electrical Apparatus, Hollow-ware, &c., Light Section Rolling and Drawing, Machine Tools, Motor Industry, Scientific Instruments.)

ENGINEERING TRADES (NEW INDUSTRIES) COMMITTEE, LABOUR PANEL.—*App.* by M.R. in 1917. *Obj.* To advise on all matters affecting labour interests arising out of Committee's work. *Repr.* Labour Organizations (men's and women's). *Ref.* Cd. 9195. *Diss.* Dec. 1918.

ESSENTIAL INDUSTRIES BOARD, CONSTITUTION SUB-COMMITTEE.—*App.* by Section III of R.A.C. in 1918. *Obj.* To report on appropriate constitution for the Board, as recommended by Commercial and Industrial Policy Committee. *Repr.* Not stated. *Ref.* Cmd. 325, p. 308. *Diss.* Reported during 1918.

ESSENTIAL INDUSTRIES COMMITTEE.—*App.* by Section II of R.A.C. early in 1918. *Obj.* To advise on machinery for dealing with essential industries, and directions to the authority constituted for the purpose. *Repr.* Parliament, B.T., Industry, Commerce, Finance, Labour. *Ref.* Cd. 9231. *Diss.* July 1918.

EXCESS PROFITS COMMITTEE.—*App.* by Section I of R.A.C. in 1918. *Obj.* To deal with questions of Excess Profits Duty in relation to commercial undertakings. *Repr.* H.C., banking, finance, merchants and other interests concerned. *Ref.* Cd. 9231. *Diss.* Before end of 1918.

FERRO-ALLOYS, TRADE, COMMITTEE.—*App.* by M.R. about Nov. 1918. *Obj.* To deal with allocation of ferro-alloys in transitional post-war period in conjunction with Priority after the War Standing Council (q.v.). *Repr.* Manufacturers of ferro-alloys. *Ref.* Cd. 9231, p. 11.

(*See also under* Raw Materials.)

FINANCE, TRANSPORT AND COMMON SERVICES, SECTION I OF ADVISORY COUNCIL.—*App.* by M.R., by arrangement with R.A.C., Jan. 1918. *Obj.* To advise M.R. on difficult and complex questions. *Repr.* Banking, finance, shipping, manufacture, contractors, Labour. *Ref.* Cd. 9195. *Diss.* June 1919.

FINANCIAL FACILITIES.—Joint Committee. *See* Tre.

FINANCIAL RISKS COMMITTEE.—*App.* by M.R., after consulting Tre. and B.T., Feb. 1918. *Obj.* To report on measures to enable manufacturers to hold stocks after the War and safeguards against serious loss due to depression following inflation. *Repr.* Government Departments concerned, Industry, Commerce, Banking, Accountancy, Labour, Economists. *Ref.* Cd. 9224. *Diss.* Dec. 1918.

FISHERIES, STANDING CONFERENCE.—*App.* by M.R. in 1917 or 1918. *Obj.* To consider measures for early reinstatement of industry after the War, and to make proposals for better administration of fishery harbours receiving Government assistance. *Repr.* D.C., English and Scottish Fishery Authorities (Irish Authorities unable to assist). *Ref.* Cd. 9231, p. 8. *Diss.* Presumably by June 1919.

FORESTRY COMMITTEE.—*App.* as Sub-Committee of R.C., July 1916. *Obj.* To report upon conservation and development of forests in light of war experience. *Repr.* B.A., B.A.(Sc.), D.C., Tre., Forestry Inspectorate and research, landowners (including Irish), mining, Labour. *Ref.* Cd. 8881. *Diss.* Jan. 1918. *See also* Cabinet.

GEOLOGICAL (COAL CONSERVATION) SUB-COMMITTEE.—*App.* by Coal Conservation Committee, July 1916. *Obj.* To advise upon steps for developing new or existing mines to maintain our industrial position. *Repr.* H.O. (Mines Department), Geological Survey (England and Scotland), coal-owners and miners, Royal Society. *Ref.* Cd. 9084. *Diss.* Feb. 1917.

HEALTH AND KINDRED SERVICES, SUBSIDIARY, COMMITTEE. —*App.* by Section V of R.A.C. in 1918. *Obj.* To consider provision for women workers in these services after the War and conditions of employment. *Repr.* Public women of various experience, women doctors, L.A.'s. *Ref.* Cd. 9231. *Diss.* First half of 1919.

HEALTH.—*See also under* Social Development.

HIDES AND SKINS.—*See under* Raw Materials.

HIGHWAY RIGHTS.—*See under* Land, Acquisition.

HOLLOW-WARE.—*See under* Engineering Trades, Raw Materials.

HOURS OF LABOUR, JUVENILES.—*See* Juvenile Employment.

HOUSING ADVISORY PANEL.—*App.* by M.R., about Aug. 1917. *Obj.* To review probable housing conditions at close of war. *Repr.* Prominent public persons, N.H.I.C., Legal Profession, housing and social experts. *Ref.* Cmd. 9087. *Diss.* June 1918.

HOUSING, ARCHITECTS' COMMITTEE.—*App.* by M.R. in 1917 or 1918. *Obj.* To prepare model plans, &c., as basis of housing policy. *Repr.* Architects. *Ref.* Cd. 9166, p. 3.

HOUSING (FINANCIAL ASSISTANCE) COMMITTEE.—*App.* by M.R., in consultation with L.G.B., May 1918. *Obj.* To advise on practicability and conditions of financial assistance to persons or bodies (other than L.A.'s) for building working-class houses immediately after the War, including State or Municipal Housing Banks. *Repr.* M.R., L.G.B., L.A.'s, accountants, L.C.C., County and Borough Councils, surveyors, Banks, Building Societies, housing and social experts. *Ref.* Cd. 9223, 9238 ; T., 16th May 1918. *Diss.* Feb. 1919.

HOUSING, WOMEN'S SUB-COMMITTEE OF THE ADVISORY COUNCIL.—*App.* by Section V of R.A.C. early in 1918. *Obj.* To investigate house-planning problem from housewife's point of view. *Repr.* Prominent Public Women, representing M.F., Women's Co-operative Guild, Housing Associations, National Women's Labour League, King's College for Women. *Ref.* Cd. 9166, 9232. *Diss.* Jan. 1919.

HOUSING.—*See also under* Social Development.

IMPERIAL MINERAL RESOURCES.—*See* P.C.

INCREASE OF RENT AND MORTGAGE INTEREST (WAR RE-STRICTIONS) ACTS COMMITTEE.—*App.* by M.R., April 1918. *Obj.* To consider Acts in reference to working-class housing after the War and recommend measures for removing difficulties. *Repr.* M.M. (Housing Department), Legal Profession, architects, builders, estate agents, Labour, social experts. *Ref.* Cd. 9235. *Diss.* 31st Dec. 1918.

(For other Committees on these Acts *see* Cabinet, M.H.)

INDUSTRIAL ORGANIZATION.—*See under* Labour.

INDUSTRIAL RELATIONS (WHITLEY) COMMITTEE.—*App.* by P.M., Oct. 1916. *Obj.* To report upon suggestions for permanently improving relations between employers and employed, and for systematic review of these relations. *Repr.* Parliament, employers, T.U.'s (including women), economists. *Ref.* Cd. 8616, 9135. *Diss.* July 1918.

INTERIM INDUSTRIAL RECONSTRUCTION COMMITTEES.—*App.* by M.R. from middle of 1917 and transferred to M.L., Mar. 1919. *Obj.* To deal with reconstruction problems in industries in which formation of J.I.C.'s is not immediately feasible, certain Committees continuing, after formation of J.I.C.'s, to deal with commercial and technical questions outside their scope. *Repr.* Associations of employers and workpeople in industries concerned. *Ref.* Cd. 9195.

JUVENILE EMPLOYMENT SUB-COMMITTEE.—*App.* by Section III of R.A.C. in later part of 1918. *Obj.* To advise on further restriction of hours of juvenile workers. *Repr.* Experts in juvenile problems, employers, Labour, women. *Ref.* Cd. 9231 ; Cmd. 325, p. 303.

LABOUR AND INDUSTRIAL ORGANIZATION, SECTION III OF THE ADVISORY COUNCIL.—*App.* by M.R., Jan. 1918. *Obj.* To advise M.R. on difficult and complex questions. *Repr.* Mine-owners, manufacturers, Labour, women, social experts. *Ref.* Cd. 9195. *Diss.* June 1919.

LAND, ACQUISITION FOR PUBLIC PURPOSES, COMMITTEE.—*App.* as Sub-Committee of R.C. in first half of 1917. *Obj.* To report upon law and practice of acquisition and valuation of land. *Repr.* Largely expert, including H.C., L.A.'s, Legal Profession, surveyors, experts in land valuation. *Ref.* Cd. 8998. *Diss.* In 1919.

LAND, ACQUISITION FOR PUBLIC PURPOSES, SUB-COMMITTEES.—*App.* by main Committee in 1917. *Obj.* To inquire into following branches of subject—Coastal Rights, Common and Highway Rights, Land Transfer (q.v.), Mining (q.v.), Registration of Titles (q.v.), Riparian Rights (q.v.). *Repr.* Main Committee, with experts in subjects dealt with. *Ref.* Cmd. 325, p. 308. *Diss.* In 1919.

LAND FOR RETURNING SOLDIERS AND SAILORS COMMITTEE.—*App.* by Section IV of R.A.C., Mar. 1918. *Obj.* To consider means, apart from provision of holdings, of attracting ex-service men to the land. *Repr.* Parliament, Public Men, L.A.'s, agriculture, Labour, women, social experts. *Ref.* Cd. 9231. *Diss.* Dec. 1918.

LAND TRANSFER SUB-COMMITTEE.—*App.* as Sub-Committee of Land Acquisition Committee in 1917 (July or earlier). *Obj.* To consider present position and means of facilitating land transfer. *Repr.* Parliament,

L.A.'s, Legal Profession, surveyors, conveyancers, industry, mining. *Ref.* Cd. 9231. *Diss.* In 1919.

LEAD.—*See under* Raw Materials.

LEATHER COUNCIL.—*App.* by M.R. about Nov. 1918. *Obj.* To deal with allocation of supplies of hides and skins during transitional post-war period. *Repr.* Existing Leather Controls, and industries using leather. *Ref.* Cd. 9231.

LEATHER-MANUFACTURING MACHINERY; LIGHT SECTION ROLLING AND DRAWING.—*See* Engineering Trades.

LEATHER, MATERIALS FOR, TRADE COMMITTEE.—*App.* by M.R., with the assistance of W.O., in 1917. *Obj.* To advise as to available supplies and control required after the War, in light of probable demands. *Repr.* Traders, manufacturers. *Ref.* Cd. 9231, p. 12. *Diss.* Before end of 1918.

LOAN BANKS FOR HOUSE BUILDING.—*See under* Housing (Financial Assistance).

LOCAL GOVERNMENT COMMITTEE.—*App.* as Sub-Committee of R.C., July 1917. *Obj.* To report upon means of securing better co-ordination of public assistance, and other matters referred to them. *Repr.* L.G.B., N.H.I.C., L.A.'s (including Poor Law), Labour, experts in public assistance and local government. *Ref.* Cd. 8917. *Diss.* Dec. 1917.

LOCAL ORGANIZATIONS, RECONSTRUCTION, COMMITTEE (SECTION V).—*App.* by Section V of R.A.C. in 1917–18. *Obj.* To report on means of stimulating local reconstruction organization, especially for social development. *Repr.* Parliament, The Army, L.A.'s, Labour, women, Ireland, social experts. *Ref.* Cd. 9231; Cmd. 136. *Diss.* Mar. 1919.

MACHINERY OF GOVERNMENT COMMITTEE.—*App.* as Sub-Committee of R.C., July 1917. *Obj.* To investigate position and responsibilities of departments of Central Government. *Repr.* Parliament, Tre., industry, Labour, industrial research, political experts. *Ref.* Cd. 9230. *Diss.* Dec. 1918.

MACHINERY, MISCELLANEOUS, MACHINE TOOLS.—*See* Engineering Trades.

METALLURGICAL SUB-COMMITTEE, COAL CONSERVATION COMMITTEE.—*App.* by main Committee, July 1916, and absorbed into Carbonization Sub-Committee (q.v.), Jan. 1917.

MINING COMMITTEE.—*App.* by P.M., as Sub-Committee of Land Acquisition Committee, by July 1917. *Obj.* To report upon principles of acquisition for public purposes and valuation of mines and mining rights, especially royalties and way-leaves, and consider action to prevent losses to the Nation by restrictive covenants, &c. *Repr.* Parliament, L.A.'s, Legal Profession, surveyors, experts in mining and land valuation. *Ref.* Cd. 9231. *Diss.* Early 1919.

MINING SUB-COMMITTEE (COAL CONSERVATION COMMITTEE). —*App.* by main Committee, July 1916. *Obj.* To advise upon improvements in mining to prevent loss of coal in working and minimize costs. *Repr.*

H.O. (Mines Department), Geological Survey, mining research and engineering, coal-owners, miners, industry. *Ref.* Cd. 9084. *Diss.* Jan. 1918.

MORTGAGE INTEREST.—*See* Increase of Rent.

MOTOR INDUSTRY.—*See* Engineering Trades.

NICKEL.—*See under* Raw Materials.

NON-FERROUS METALS, CENTRAL COMMITTEE.—*App.* by M.R. about Nov. 1918. *Obj.* To deal with their allocation during transitional post-war period, along with Priority after the War Standing Council (*see* below). *Repr.* Mainly traders. *Ref.* Cd. 9231. *Diss.* First half of 1919.
   (*See also under* Raw Materials.)

OFFICERS RE-SETTLEMENT SUB-COMMITTEE.—*App.* by Demobilization of the Army Committee (q.v.) in winter of 1916–17. *Obj.* To report upon arrangements for civil re-settlement of officers and men of like standing. *Repr.* Adm., A.M., W.O., M.L., M.M., S.C., experts in employment questions. *Ref.* Cd. 8916. *Diss.* Absorbed, about time of Armistice, into Appointments Department of M.L.

OFFICERS' UNIVERSITY AND TECHNICAL TRAINING COMMITTEES, ETC.—Original appointment by M.R. (*see* M.L.).

PAPER-MAKING MACHINERY.—*See* Engineering Trades.

' PERIOD OF THE WAR ' INTERPRETATION COMMITTEE.—*App.* by M.R. jointly with the Attorney-General, July 1917. *Obj.* To report upon legal questions depending upon this, and effects of the War on contracts, including apprenticeships. *Repr.* Judges, Legal Profession. *Ref.* Cd. 9100. *Diss.* May 1918.
   (For subsequent action *see* Parliament, Emergency Legislation, Termination of the War.)

PRE-WAR PRACTICES.—*See* Restoration of, *and* War Pledges.

PRINTERS, PRINTING, MACHINERY.—*See* Engineering Trades.

PRIORITY AFTER THE WAR, STANDING COUNCIL.—*App.* by M.R., in consultation with War Cabinet Committee on Post-War Priority, about late summer of 1918. *Obj.* To organize generally a system of post-war priority. *Repr.* M.R., War Priority Committee, B.T., M.L., M.M., M.S., W.O., employers in various industries, Labour. *Ref.* Cd. 9195.

PRIORITY, PRIORITIES.—*See also under* Cabinet.

PRODUCTION AND COMMERCIAL ORGANIZATION, SECTION II OF THE ADVISORY COUNCIL.—*App.* by M.R., Jan. 1918. *Obj.* To advise M.R. on difficult and complex problems in these connexions. *Repr.* Manufacture, Commerce, Labour, Persons experienced in public affairs. *Ref.* Cd. 9195. *Diss.* By June 1919.
   (Subjects referred to this Section included Anti-Dumping, Importation of Sweated Goods, and Allocation of Raw Materials after the War.)

RAW MATERIALS SUPPLY, CENTRAL COMMITTEE.—*App.* by M.R., Oct. 1917. *Obj.* To advise on supplies of materials and foodstuffs required during reconstruction by U.K., British Empire, belligerents and neutrals, sources of supply for U.K. and need for control. *Repr.* M.R.,

O.T.D., M.M., mining, industry, Imperial interests. *Ref.* Cd. 8916. *Diss.* By end of 1918.

RAW MATERIALS SUPPLY COMMITTEES.—*App.* by M.R. from Oct. 1917, for each of the following : Asbestos, Aluminium, Antimony, Copper, Ferro-Alloys, Lead, Nickel, Spelter, Tin. *Obj.* To advise M.R. as with Central Committee (q.v.) on particular materials. *Repr.* M.M., manufacturers, and in certain cases London Metal Exchange and importers. *Ref.* Cd. 9195. *Diss.* By end of 1918.

RAW MATERIALS.—*See also* Building Materials and *under* Production and Commercial Organization.

RECONSTRUCTION, LOCAL.—*See* Local Organizations.

REGISTRATION OF TITLES SUB-COMMITTEE.—*App.* by Land Acquisition Committee (q.v.) in 1918. *Obj.* To consider Registration of Titles in relation to rural development. *Repr.* Main Committee ; experts. *Ref.* Cd. 9231, p. 26. *Diss.* In 1919.

RENT.—*See* Increase of Rent.

RESTORATION OF PRE-WAR PRACTICES, INTER-DEPARTMENTAL CONFERENCE.—*App.* by M.R. in spring of 1918 (till summer), and re-appointed Oct. 1918. *Obj.* To consider question and prepare draft bill for purpose. *Repr.* M.R., M.M., M.L., H.O. *Ref.* Cd. 9231, p. 21. *Diss.* Early Nov. 1918, when draft bill referred to Joint Committee (*see* next entry).

RESTORATION OF PRE-WAR PRACTICES, JOINT COMMITTEE.— *App.* by Joint Conference of Employers and T.U.'s, summoned to consider problem, Nov. 1918. *Obj.* To deal with draft bill (*see* preceding entry) for securing restoration. *Repr.* Employers, T.U.'s. *Diss.* Early in 1919.
    (*See also* War Pledges, and Cabinet, M.M., M.L.)

RIPARIAN RIGHTS SUB-COMMITTEE.—*App.* by Land Acquisition Committee (q.v.) early in 1919. *Obj.* To report on riparian and similar rights, in connexion with industrial use of water-power. *Repr.* Main Committee ; experts. *Ref.* Cd. 9231, p. 16.

RURAL DEVELOPMENT, INCLUDING AGRICULTURE, SECTION IV OF THE ADVISORY COUNCIL.—*App.* by M.R., Jan. 1918. *Obj.* To advise M.R. on difficult and complex questions affecting agriculture and rural development. *Repr.* Parliament, L.A.'s, agriculture, Labour, women, persons with public experience. *Ref.* Cd. 9195. *Diss.* By June 1919.

SCIENTIFIC INSTRUMENTS.—*See* Engineering Trades.

SOCIAL DEVELOPMENT, INCLUDING EDUCATION, HEALTH AND HOUSING, SECTION V OF THE ADVISORY COUNCIL.—*App.* by M.R., Jan. 1918. *Obj.* To advise M.R. on difficult and complex questions affecting these problems. *Repr.* Employers, Labour, women, social experts. *Ref.* Cd. 9195. *Diss.* By June 1919.

SPELTER.—*See under* Raw Materials.

STORAGE AND TRANSIT COMMITTEE.—*App.* by M.R., June 1918. *Obj.* To prepare scheme for utilizing facilities available to avoid congestion during demobilization, and subsequently given executive powers, jointly with B.T., to allocate surplus storage. *Repr.* Government Departments occupying storage, manufacturers, shipowners, railways, docks. *Ref.* Cd. 9195. *Diss.* Reported in 1918, but continued in existence as executive body.

STORAGE EXECUTIVE.—*App.* by M.R. in 1917 or 1918. *Obj.* To collect information regarding storage and to allocate between Government Departments. *Repr.* Government Departments chiefly affected, R.E.C., Port and Transit Committee. *Ref.* Cd. 9195. *Diss.* Apparently replaced by Storage and Transit Committee (q.v.) in 1918.

SURPLUS GOVERNMENT PROPERTY, ADVISORY COUNCIL.— *App.* by M.R., Sept. 1917, being sometimes known as Disposal of War Stores Advisory Board. *Obj.* To prepare inventories of Government property (except shipping and factories) and advise on use or disposal of surplus after the War. *Repr.* Government Departments concerned, prominent men of affairs, Labour. *Ref.* Cd. 8916, p. 22 ; 9231, p. 17. *Diss.* Jan. 1919, when duties transferred to M.M., and Committee reconstituted.

SURPLUS GOVERNMENT PROPERTY DISPOSALS BOARD.—*App.* by Order-in-Council, after consultation between M.R., M.M., and other Government Departments, Mar. 1918. *Obj.* To carry out recommendations of Advisory Council. *Repr.* Government Departments concerned, prominent business men. *Ref.* Cd. 9231, p. 17 ; Cmd. 850, p. 3. *Diss.* Jan. 1919, on transfer of work to Disposals Board (*see* M.M.).

TERMINATION OF THE WAR.—*See* Period of the War.

TEXTILE MACHINERY.—*See* Engineering Trades.

TIN.—*See* Raw Materials.

TRADE UNION PRACTICES.—*See* Restoration of Pre-War Practices, War Pledges.

TRADING STOCKS.—*See* Financial Risks.

TRANSIT.—*See* Storage and Transit.

TRANSPORT.—*See under* Finance.

TRUSTS, COMMITTEE ON.—*App.* by M.R., Feb. 1918. *Obj.* To consider action necessary to safeguard public interest from extensions of trade organizations and combinations. *Repr.* Parliament, B.T., M.M., Industry, Co-operative Movement, Labour, accountants, costing, economic and social experts. *Ref.* Cd. 9236. *Diss.* April 1919.

UNEMPLOYMENT INSURANCE SUB-COMMITTEE.—*App.* by Civil War Workers' Committee (q.v.) about Aug. 1917. *Obj.* To consider possible extensions of insurance to meet post-war needs. *Repr.* M.L., employers, Labour, women, economists. *Ref.* Cd. 9192. *Diss.* Feb. 1918.

WAGES' AWARDS COMMITTEE.—*App.* by M.R., with concurrence of Government Departments concerned, Oct. 1918. *Obj.* To consider continuance of compulsory wage awards and orders after the War. *Repr.* Parliament, M.R., M.M., M.L., Employers' Associations, T.U.'s (including Women's T.U.'s). *Ref.* Cd. 9231. *Diss.* Nov. 1918.

WAR PLEDGES SUB-COMMITTEE.—*App.* by R.C. late in 1916. *Obj.* To advise on means of carrying out promise to restore T.U. practices after the War. *Repr.* Government Departments, Employers, T.U.'s. *Ref.* Cd. 9231, p. 21. *Diss.* Work taken over by Labour and Industrial Branch of M.R. late in 1917.

(*See also* Restoration of Pre-War Practices.)

WATER-POWER RESOURCES.—Joint Committee. *See* B.T.

WIRE MACHINERY.—*See* Engineering Trades.

WOMEN'S ADVISORY COMMITTEE OF THE ADVISORY COUNCIL.—*App.* by M.R., Jan. 1918. *Obj.* To advise generally on questions affecting women, including domestic service. *Repr.* Women members of Advisory Council. *Ref.* Cd. 9195, 9231. *Diss.* By June 1919.

WOMEN (AGRICULTURE).—*See under* Women's Employment.

WOMEN'S EMPLOYMENT COMMITTEE.—*App.*, as Sub-Committee of R.C., Aug. 1916. *Obj.* To advise, in light of war experience, on opportunities and conditions of women's employment. *Repr.* B.T., H.O., M.F., M.L., M.M., employers, agriculture, Labour, women and women's interests. *Ref.* Cd. 8916, 9239. *Diss.* Mar. 1919.

WOMEN'S EMPLOYMENT COMMITTEE, AGRICULTURAL GROUP.—*App.* by the Committee, probably in 1917. *Obj.* To consider opportunities for women's employment in agriculture. *Repr.* Members of the Committee with agricultural experience. *Ref.* Cd. 9239, p. 17. *Diss.* Nov. 1918 (*see also* next entries).

WOMEN'S EMPLOYMENT IN AGRICULTURE IN ENGLAND AND WALES SUB-COMMITTEE.—*App.* by Section IV of R.A.C., Nov. 1918, and transferred to B.A., Mar. 1919. *Obj.* To report upon economic place of women in post-war developments of agriculture. *Repr.* M.R., B.A., agriculture, agricultural research, women. *Ref.* Report, H.M.S.O., 1919. *Diss.* Dec. 1919.

WOMEN'S EMPLOYMENT IN AGRICULTURE IN SCOTLAND, SUB-COMMITTEE.—*App.* by Section IV of R.A.C., Nov. 1918. Much as with English Sub-Committee (q.v.). *Ref.* H.M.S.O., 1920. *Diss.* Late in 1919.

WOMEN'S EMPLOYMENT COMMITTEE, CLERICAL AND COMMERCIAL GROUP.—*App.* by the Committee, probably late in 1916. *Obj.* To report to main Committee on women's position in clerical and commercial employments. *Repr.* Members of the Committee with experience of such work. *Ref.* Cd. 8916. *Diss.* By Mar. 1919.

WOMEN'S EMPLOYMENT COMMITTEE, INDUSTRIAL GROUP.—*Obj.* To deal with the position of women in industry. Otherwise as with Clerical and Commercial Group.

WOMEN IN GOVERNMENT DEPARTMENTS SUB-COMMITTEE.—*App.* by Women's Advisory Committee (q.v.), Nov. 1918. *Obj.* To consider provision required for women temporarily employed in Government Departments during the War, with special reference to openings in the permanent Civil Service. *Repr.* Women Civil Servants, experienced public men and women, educational experts. *Ref.* Cmd. 199. *Diss.* Jan. 1919.

WOMEN, VOCATIONAL TRAINING, CO-ORDINATION, SUB-COM-MITTEE OF WOMEN'S EMPLOYMENT COMMITTEE.—*App.* jointly by Women's Advisory Committee and Social Development Section of R.A.C. in 1918. *Obj.* To investigate problem of co-ordinating authorities for such training. *Repr.* Prominent public women (including representatives of Labour), educational experts. *Ref.* Cd. 9231. *Diss.* Probably before end of 1918.

WOOL COUNCIL.—*See* W.O.

WORKS' COMMITTEES.—Under Whitley Scheme. *See* M.L.

SCIENTIFIC AND INDUSTRIAL RESEARCH COMMITTEE OF THE PRIVY COUNCIL FOR AFTERWARDS DEPARTMENT OF

The Committee of Council for Scientific and Industrial Research was established, with an Advisory Council, by Royal Warrant of 28th July 1915. The appointment, whilst forming part of a scheme of general educational development, was accelerated, and rendered urgent, by war needs. The Committee is responsible for expenditure of all new moneys granted by Parliament for Scientific and Industrial Research, and consists of members of the Government and non-official members. The Advisory Council is composed of eminent scientists and representatives of industries which depend largely on research, with assessors (not entitled to vote) representing the Government Departments concerned and the Canadian Research Council. The Advisory Council's *functions* are to make recommendations, on proposals referred to them by the Committee, for establishing research institutions, fellowships and scholarships, and for initiating schemes of research, and to advise the Committee generally on matters of research and the Education Departments on the supply of research workers. The Council have also power to take the initiative in matters of research. The Committee and Council were at first housed with the Board of Education.

On 23rd Nov. 1916, however, the existing members of the Committee were, by Royal Charter, constituted a body corporate under the title of ' The Imperial Trust for the Encouragement of Scientific and Industrial Research '. Following this, the *Department of Scientific and Industrial Research* was constituted in Dec. 1916. Various Standing Committees (*see* below) assist the Department, which is a *permanent* one. Early in 1918 the control of the National Physical Laboratory, and, in November 1919, of the Geological Survey were transferred to the Department, a Geological Survey Board being set up (*see* Cmd. 905, pp. 22, 94) to supervise this work, which was extended in 1921 by addition of representatives of the Government Departments mainly concerned (*see* Cmd. 1471, pp. 39, 40). *Reference*: 1st Annual Report of the Department (Cd. 8336) and later Annual Reports.

ABBREVIATIONS

S.I.R. = Committee and Department of Scientific and Industrial Research.
A.C(S). = Advisory Council to the Committee and Department.
N.P.L. = National Physical Laboratory.

ABRASIVES AND POLISHING POWDERS RESEARCH COMMITTEE. —*App.* by A.C(S), Mar. 1917, having existed as a Sub-Committee of the Standing Committee on Glass, after Aug. 1916. *Obj.* To investigate preparation and properties of abrasives and powders for use in accelerating output of lenses and prisms for optical instruments for peace and war purposes. *Repr.* N.P.L., chemical, metallurgical, optical and scientific instruments' research. *Ref.* Cd. 9144, pp. 32, 75. *Diss.* 1920 or earlier.

ACOUSTICAL RESEARCH DEPARTMENT ; ACCUMULATORS AND DRY CELLS.—*See under* Research Co-ordinating Boards.

ADHESIVES RESEARCH COMMITTEE.—*App.* by S.I.R., after Armistice, to carry on work of Committee of Conjoint Board of Scientific Societies for A.M. *Obj.* To carry out research to improve yield and quality of adhesives for industry (previously only for aircraft work). *Repr.* Scientists, &c. (including British Scientific Instruments Research Association), representatives of the Fighting Services being added later. *Ref.* Cmd. 905, pp. 65–6, 95 ; Cmd. 1471, p. 56. *Still in existence Aug. 1922.*

ADVICE, SPECIAL COMMITTEES.—*See under* Applications.

ADVISORY COUNCIL FOR SCIENTIFIC AND INDUSTRIAL RESEARCH.—*See* Heading to Section.

ADVISORY PANELS.—In Cd. 8336, p. 18, the A.C(S) was reported to be attempting with the help of its Standing Committees, H.O. and the Professional Societies, to construct panels of names enabling the best advice to be secured on the problems with which they had to deal, and the support of the business world to be obtained.

AERONAUTICAL RESEARCH COMMITTEE.—*See* A.M.

ALLOYS RESEARCH.—*See under* Research Committees.

ALUMINIUM CORROSION RESEARCH COMMITTEE.—*App.* by S.I.R., at request of A.M., about middle of 1920. *Obj.* To survey and direct research on aluminium and alloys. *Repr.* A.M., W.O., scientists. *Ref.* Cmd. 905, pp. 65, 95. *Diss.* Apparently in 1921, the work being transferred to Sub-Committee of Corrosion Research Committee of Institute of Metals, which contained representatives of the Fighting Services and received grant from S.I.R.

APPLICATIONS COMMITTEE (ADVISORY COUNCIL).—*App.* by A.C(S), Feb. 1917. *Obj.* To deal with applications for assistance to schemes of research. *Repr.* A.C(S). *Ref.* Cd. 8718, p. 9. *Apparently a Standing Body.*

(In the year ending 31st July 1917 the Council was assisted by 28 Special Committees in dealing with applications for grants, and similar Committees were appointed in later years as Special Committees of Advice (*see* Cd. 8718, pp. 9, 63 ; 9144, p. 10).)

ATMOSPHERICS.—*See under* Radio Research.

AUSTRALIA.—*See* Dominions.

BREWING, INSTITUTE OF, RESEARCH FUND COMMITTEE.—*App.* by Institute in 1918 or 1919, receiving grant from S.I.R. *Obj.* To perform functions of Research Association (*see* below) for Brewing Industry. *Repr.* Institute of Brewers, maltsters, distillers, barley and hop-growers, and other interests concerned. *Ref.* J.B.A., Nov. 1921, p. 750. *Permanent.*

(The Committee has appointed Advisory Committees for hops, timber, barley, &c., with power to initiate research.)

BUILDING MATERIALS RESEARCH COMMITTEE.—*App.* by A.C(S) about July 1917. *Obj.* To be responsible for research in building construction, instituted by A.C(S), and similar matters. *Repr.* L.G.B., Building Construction Committee (*see* L.G.B.), architects, Housing and Town Planning experts. *Ref.* Cd. 8916, p. 17. *Diss.* Absorbed into Building Research Board (*see* next entry).

BUILDING RESEARCH MATERIALS AND CONSTRUCTION BOARD.
—*App.* by S.I.R., at request of M.H., early in 1920. *Obj.* To consider and direct researches into building materials and methods of construction. *Repr.* S.I.R., M.H., W.O., O.W., architects. *Ref.* Cmd. 905, pp. 5, 91.

CANADA.—*See* Dominions.

CASTINGS, BRASS AND COPPER, RESEARCH COMMITTEE.— Referred to as having completed labours prior to Aug. 1920, in Cmd. 920, p. 28. Other details lacking.

CEMENTS FOR LENSES AND PRISMS.—*See* Vitreous Compounds.

CHEMISTRY.—*See* Research Co-ordinating Boards.

CHEMISTRY OF LUBRICANTS.—*See* Lubricants.

COAL RESOURCES, NATIONAL, PHYSICAL AND CHEMICAL SURVEY, LOCAL COMMITTEES.—*App.* by Fuel Research Board in and after 1922, for chief mining areas. *Obj.* To carry out locally Board's national survey of coal resources, which was continuance of work begun during the War by special reports. *Repr.* The Board, coal-owners, colliery managers, geologists. *Ref.* Cmd. 1735, pp. 51–2, 87. *Survey still in progress at end of 1922.*

COAL SAMPLING AND ANALYSIS COMMITTEE.—*App.* by Fuel Research Board in 1922. *Obj.* To recommend best accepted methods of sampling, &c., for use in connexion with National Survey (*see* preceding entry) and generally. *Repr.* Royal Society, chemists and other scientists and experts. *Ref.* Cmd. 1735, p. 52. *Diss.* After Aug. 1922.

COLD STORAGE.—*See* Food Investigation Board.

CONCRETE, FIRE-RESISTING PROPERTIES, COMMITTEE.—*App.* by British Fire Prevention Committee, at request of A.C(S), July 1917. *Obj.* To make exhaustive tests of fire-resisting properties of concretes. *Repr.* L.G.B., O.W., experts. *Ref.* Cd. 8718, p. 23.

COOKING RESEARCH.—*See* Food, Chemistry of.

COPPER.—*See* Zinc and Copper.

COTTON INDUSTRY, RESEARCH AND EDUCATION, PROVISIONAL COMMITTEE.—*App.* by industry, at instigation of S.I.R., Sept. 1916. *Obj.* To organize Research Association for Cotton Industry. *Repr.* Associations and firms in cotton, hosiery, dyeing and calico-printing industries ; Manchester, Leicester, and Nottingham Chambers of Commerce. *Ref.* Cd. 8916, p. 19.

COTTON JOINT SCHOLARSHIPS COMMITTEE.—*See* B.T.

DOMINIONS ORGANIZATIONS FOR SCIENTIFIC AND INDUSTRIAL RESEARCH.—The Governments of the chief Dominions established organizations similar to S.I.R. In Australia the Commonwealth Government appointed a Committee on Scientific and Industrial Research, late in 1915, to prepare a scheme (*see* Cd. 8336, p. 37), and subsequently established in 1916 an Advisory Council and Executive Committee in Science and Industry on lines similar to S.I.R. and A.C(S) (*see* Cd. 8718, pp. 31–2). In Canada the Governor-General established, in June 1916, a

Committee of Council for Scientific and Industrial Research with an Honorary Advisory Committee (*see* Cd. 8336, App. IV). In South Africa a Scientific and Technical Committee (Mar. 1917) and an Industries Advisory Board (Oct. 1916) were brought into existence and combined in 1918 as the Advisory Board of Industry and Science (*see* Cd. 8718, p. 32, and App. IV, Cmd. 357, p. 25). The establishment of the Industries Advisory Board was the result of a recommendation by a Committee on the Manufacture of Machinery Parts for the U.K.

EDIBLE TEST CONFERENCE.—*See under* Oils and Fats.

ELECTRICAL RESEARCH COMMITTEE.—*App.* by Institute of Electrical Engineers and Electrical Manufacturers' Association, with grant from S.I.R., in 1916 or 1917. *Obj.* To direct researches affecting their industry. *Repr.* The two bodies. *Ref.* Cd. 8916, p. 17 ; Cmd. 905, pp. 35, 80. *Diss.* Transferred to Research Association for the Industry about end of 1920.

ENGINEERING COMMITTEE, FOOD INVESTIGATION BOARD.— *App.* by Board in 1918. *Obj.* To prepare, initiate and supervise scheme of research into engineering problems of food preservation. *Repr.* S.I.R., N.P.L., Royal Society, Professional Societies, engineers, scientists. *Ref.* Cd. 9144, pp. 26, 74.

The Committee delegates particular problems to Sub-Committees, e.g., on Insulation, Literature, Refrigerating Cars and Barges (*see* Cmd. 320, p. 80).

ENGINEERING, STANDING COMMITTEE.—*App.* by S.I.R. in or shortly after July 1915. *Obj.* To advise A.C(S) on engineering research and cognate subjects. *Repr.* Adm., Dock Authorities, engineering, ship-building, railways, Professional Engineering Societies, engineering research. *Ref.* Cd. 8916, p. 15. *Diss.* Sept. 1918, owing to development of Research Associations.

ENGINEERING.—*See also* Research Co-ordinating Boards.

ESTIMATES REDUCTION SPECIAL COMMITTEE.—*App.* by A.C(S) in early summer of 1921. *Obj.* To examine most suitable means of obtaining reduction in estimates required by the Government. *Repr.* A.C(S). *Ref.* Cmd. 1471, p. 14. *Diss.* About July 1921.

FABRICS RESEARCH CO-ORDINATING COMMITTEE.—*App.* by S.I.R., in co-operation with War Departments, late in 1921. *Obj.* To co-ordinate researches by War Departments and the Textile Industry. *Repr.* Adm., A.M., W.O., N.P.L., Research Associations concerned. *Ref.* Cmd. 1471, p. 18, 1735, p. 81. *Still in existence Aug. 1922.*

FATS.—*See* Oils and Fats.

FISHERIES RESEARCH ADVISORY COMMITTEE.—*See* D.C. Questions of demarcation of function arose.

FISH PRESERVATION COMMITTEE.—*App.* by Food Investigation Board (q.v.) early in 1918. *Obj.* To inquire and experiment in methods of preserving, freezing and storing fish. *Repr.* S.I.R. (sec.), B.A., F.B.(Sc.), M.F., The Dominions, Research, Fish Preserving Trade. *Ref.* B.T.J., 13th June 1918. *Still in existence Aug. 1922.*

(This Committee delegated much work to Sub-Committees, *see* Cmd. 320, p. 8.)

FOOD, CANNED, COMMITTEE.—*App.* by S.I.R. in 1918. *Obj.* To deal with researches into canning of food. *Repr.* L.G.B., Medical Profession, scientists. *Ref.* Cmd. 320, p. 82. *Still in existence Aug. 1922.*

FOOD, CHEMISTRY OF, AND COOKING RESEARCH COMMITTEES. —*App.* by S.I.R., in consultation with M.M. and M.F., about Aug. 1917. *Obj.* To direct researches into bread-making and preservation of meat and vegetables. *Repr.* S.I.R., L.G.B., M.M., M.R.C., chemical and other research. *Ref.* Cd. 8916, p. 17. *Diss.* April 1919, work transferred to Food Investigation Board (q.v.).

FOOD INVESTIGATION BOARD.—*App.* by S.I.R., originally as Cold Storage Research Board, early in 1918. *Obj.* To organize and control research into preparation and preservation of food. *Repr.* A.C(S), D.C., M.R.C., Port of London Authority, The Dominions, Royal Society, with assessors from Government Departments concerned. *Ref.* Cd. 9144, p. 25. *Permanent Body.*
    (In addition to the Committees of the Board separately referred to, an Expert Committee of Management of the Low Temperature Station in Bio-Chemistry and Bio-Physics was appointed in 1921–2 (*see* Cmd. 1735, p. 86).)

FOREST PRODUCTS RESEARCH BOARD.—*App.* by S.I.R., under Government decision, in late summer of 1921, following resolution of British Empire Forestry Conference. *Obj.* To organize research into utilization of timber and forest products. *Repr.* Forestry, Royal Society, Scientists. *Ref.* Cmd. 1471, p. 50. *Still in existence at end of 1922.*
    (The Board appointed Committees for various branches of work, *see* Cmd. 1735, pp. 86–7.)

FRUIT AND VEGETABLES COMMITTEE.—*App.* by Food Investigation Board in first half of 1918. *Obj.* To organize investigations into problems affecting fruit and vegetables. *Repr.* Scientists, growers. *Ref.* Cd. 9144, pp. 26, 74.

FUEL RESEARCH BOARD.—*App.* by S.I.R., on advice of A.C(S), Feb. 1917. *Obj.* To investigate nature, preparation, and utilization of fuel of all kinds. *Repr.* H.O., Royal Society, engineering, chemical research. *Ref.* Cd. 8718, p. 5. *Permanent.*

FUEL RESEARCH (CONSTITUTION) SUB-COMMITTEE OF THE ADVISORY COUNCIL.—*App.* by A.C(S), Nov. 1916. *Obj.* To consider constitution and terms of reference of body to deal with fuel research. *Repr.* A.C(S). *Ref.* Cd. 8718, p. 18. *Diss.* Early 1917.

GAS CYLINDERS INQUIRY COMMITTEE.—*App.* by S.I.R. in 1918 or early 1919. *Obj.* To investigate manufacture and transport of cylinders for compressed gases. *Repr.* S.I.R., Adm., H.O., M.M., engineering, research. *Ref.* Cmd. 320, pp. 43, 84.

GLASS AND OPTICAL INSTRUMENTS STANDING COMMITTEE.— *App.* by A.C(S), Dec. 1916. *Obj.* To organize investigation of urgent problems in these industries, the Committee subsequently appointing various Sub-Committees for special problems (*see*, e.g., next entry). *Repr.* Adm., N.P.L., Professional Associations, industries concerned, scientists. *Ref.* Cd. 8718, pp. 31, 62. *Diss.* Mar. 1918, duties being transferred to

British Scientific Instruments Research Association, and various special Research Committees.

GLASS, ANTI-GLARE, COMMITTEE.—*App.* by Glass, &c., Standing Committee (*see* preceding entry) as Sub-Committee in 1917, and by A.C(S) as independent Committee, Mar. 1918. *Obj.* To organize and supervise investigations into this type of glass. *Repr.* Adm., W.O., N.P.L., scientists. *Ref.* Cd. 9144, pp. 32, 75. *Diss.* About June 1920.

GLASS RESEARCH COMMITTEE, INSTITUTE OF CHEMISTRY.— *App.* by the Institute in 1915 or early 1916, co-operating with S.I.R. *Obj.* To organize and supervise researches particularly into optical glass. *Repr.* The Institute ; experts. *Ref.* Cd. 8718, p. 24.

HUMAN NUTRITION.—*See* N.H.I.C.

ILLUMINATING ENGINEERING, JOINT STANDING COMMITTEE. —*App.* by S.I.R. in 1916 or 1917. *Obj.* To survey field for, and forms of, research. *Repr.* Standing Committees (*see* above) for Engineering and Glass, Society of Illuminating Engineers, research experts. *Ref.* Cd. 8718, pp. 31, 62. *Diss.* 1920.

INDUSTRIAL FATIGUE RESEARCH BOARD.—*See* N.H.I.C.

INTERNAL COMBUSTION ENGINE INDUSTRY, PROVISIONAL COMMITTEE.—*App.* by S.I.R., following negotiations with informal Committee of Manufacturers, in 1918. *Obj.* To organize Research Association for the industry. *Repr.* Adm., H.O., manufacturers and users of such engines, engineering experts, Royal Society, chemical and other research. *Ref.* Cd. 8916, p. 19 ; 9144, p. 18.

IRON AND METALLIFEROUS ORES, RESOURCES AND PRODUCTION, SUB-COMMITTEE.—*App.* by Standing Committee on Metallurgy (q.v.) late in 1916. *Obj.* To consider desirability of statistical survey of iron and steel industry. *Repr.* The appointing Committee. *Ref.* Cd. 8718, p. 28. *Diss.* In 1917.

LUBRICANTS AND LUBRICATION INQUIRY COMMITTEE.—*App.* as special Committee of Standing Committee on Engineering in 1916 or 1917. *Obj.* To prepare memorandum on fields and problems of research, and suggest suitable scheme. *Repr.* Standing Committee on Engineering, Professional Associations, scientists. *Ref.* Cd. 8718, pp. 28, 63. *Diss.* About July 1920.

LUBRICANTS, CHEMISTRY OF, SUB-COMMITTEE.—*App.* by Lubricants and Lubrication Inquiry Committee (q.v.), probably in first half of 1917. *Obj.* To collect and review information on the subject. *Repr.* Royal School of Mines, Royal College of Science, Chemical Society and other experts. *Ref.* Cd. 8916, p. 18. *Diss.* 1920 or earlier.

LUBRICATION RESEARCH COMMITTEE.—*App.* by S.I.R. about July 1920, and reconstituted later. *Obj.* To carry on work of Lubricants and Lubrication Inquiry Committee (q.v.) into theory and practice of lubrication. *Repr.* S.I.R., scientists. *Ref.* Cmd. 905, pp. 28, 63, 95 ; Cmd. 1471, pp. 37, 60. *Diss.* Work approaching completion at end of 1922.

MACHINERY PARTS COMMITTEE.—*See under* Dominions.

MEAT PRESERVATION COMMITTEE.—*App.* by Food Investigation Board in first half of 1918. *Obj.* To organize and supervise investigations into problems affecting meat. *Repr.* Royal Society, scientists, and others, including women. *Ref.* Cd. 9144, pp. 26, 74.

METALLURGY STANDING COMMITTEE.—*App.* by S.I.R. about Aug. 1915. *Obj.* To advise A.C(S) on metallurgical research and cognate matters. *Repr.* Iron, steel and non-ferrous metal industries, Professional Associations, metallurgical science. *Ref.* Cd. 8916, p. 15. *Diss.* 1920 or earlier.

MINES, ATMOSPHERIC CONDITIONS, RESEARCH COMMITTEE.— *App.* by S.I.R. late in 1918 or in 1919. *Obj.* To organize research into atmospheric conditions of deep and hot mines, developing work of Committee of Institute of Mining Engineers. *Repr.* H.O., mining research, with technical assessor. *Ref.* Cmd. 905, pp. 28, 95. *Diss.* Work transferred to Mines Department of B.T., April 1922 (Cmd. 1735, pp. 56–7).

MINES, RESCUE APPARATUS, RESEARCH COMMITTEE.—*App.* by A.C(S), at request of H.O., July 1917, and by W.O. as Committee to deal with Army mining problems, at request of Commander-in-Chief, in summer of 1918. *Obj.* To investigate, and experiment in existing types of apparatus, suggest improvements and consider standardization. *Repr.* H.O., Royal Society, mining research. *Ref.* Cd. 8718, p. 22 ; 9144, p. 24. *Diss.* Late in 1922.

MINING, STANDING COMMITTEE.—*App.* by S.I.R. about Aug. 1915. *Obj.* To advise on mining research and cognate matters. *Repr.* Coal and other mining, iron and steel industry, Royal Society, Professional Associations, mining and metallurgical science. *Ref.* Cd. 8916, p. 15. *Diss.* In 1921 or earlier (*see* Cmd. 1471), responsibility for research in mining being taken over by Special Committee of Mines Department of B.T.

MINOR METALS RESEARCH EXPERT COMMITTEE.—*App.* by Engineering Research Co-ordinating Board in 1922, after request by Imperial Mineral Resources Bureau. *Obj.* To organize investigation of commercial use of minor metals found in British Empire. *Repr.* Adm., A.M., W.O., N.P.L., Imperial Mineral Resources Bureau, engineers, scientists. *Ref.* Cmd. 1735, pp. 38, 82. *Still in existence end 1922.*

NATIONAL PHYSICAL LABORATORY, SALARIES COMMITTEE.— *App.* by S.I.R., April 1918. *Obj.* To consider scale of salaries at N.P.L. in consultation with its Executive Committee. *Repr.* S.I.R. *Ref.* Cd. 9144, p. 21. *Diss.* Summer of 1918.

OILS AND FATS COMMITTEE.—*App.* by Food Investigation Board, at request of M.F., in summer of 1918. *Obj.* To organize investigations concerning oils and fats. *Repr.* M.M., Royal Society, scientists. *Ref.* Cd. 9144, pp. 26, 27.

(The Committee delegated work to a Chemical Sub-Committee and to Edible Test, and Technical, Conferences.)

OPTICAL DESIGN, STANDARDIZATION, INQUIRY COMMITTEE.— *App.* by A.C(S), Mar. 1918, on termination of Glass and Optical Instruments Standing Committee. *Obj.* To complete inquiries needed for standardizing optical design. *Repr.* Adm., W.O., N.P.L., scientists, optical industries. *Ref.* Cd. 9144, pp. 32–3 ; Cmd. 905, p. 66. *Diss.* About June 1920.

OXYGEN.—*See* Cabinet.

PATENTS INTER-DEPARTMENTAL COMMITTEE.—*App.* by P.C., apparently under S.I.R., Nov. 1920. *Obj.* To consider and co-ordinate methods of dealing with inventions by workers aided or maintained from public funds, with reference to the interests of the nation, industry, and the inventor. *Repr.* Adm., A.M., B.T., M.R.C., P.O., S.I.R., W.O., Royal Commission on Awards to Inventors, Legal Profession, Royal Society, Scientists and other experts. *Ref.* Cmd. 1471, pp. 9, 77, 107–8. *Diss.* Feb. 1922.

(The Committee recommended establishment of Inter-Departmental Patents Board : *see* Cmd. 1735, p. 79.)

PEAT, IRISH, INQUIRY COMMITTEE.—*App.* by Fuel Research Board, with consent of S.I.R., and after consultation with D.A.T.I., July 1917. *Obj.* To inquire, in light of previous experience, into means of utilizing Irish peat supplies for fuel and other purposes. *Repr.* D.A.T.I., chemical research, engineering experts. *Ref.* Cd. 8916, p. 18 ; Cmd. 106, p. 11. *Diss.* Prior to Aug. 1920.

PHYSICS.—*See* Research Co-ordinating Boards.

POTTERY RESEARCH.—*See under* Research Committees.

RADIO RESEARCH CO-ORDINATING BOARD.—*App.* by S.I.R., at instance of Cabinet Committee on Imperial Communications, in 1919. *Obj.* To co-ordinate and develop research work for fighting services and other Government Departments. *Repr.* Adm., A.M., W.O., P.O., N.P.L., scientific experts. *Ref.* Cmd. 905, pp. 25–6, 90. *Apparently Permanent.*

(The Board appointed Sub-Committees for Atmospherics, Directional Wireless, Propagation of Wireless Waves, Thermionic Values, and later Radio-Telephony—*see also* Cmd. 1707.)

RESEARCH ASSOCIATIONS.—*App.* by various industries, at instigation of S.I.R., from end of 1917, when first Association established, whilst twenty-four had been recognized by S.I.R. by Aug. 1922. *Obj.* To carry out co-operative research in their industries, and act as vehicles for expenditure of funds of S.I.R. *Repr.* Firms in industries concerned. *Ref.* Cd. 8718, p. 4, and subsequent annual reports of S.I.R. *Intended to be Permanent.*

(In certain cases Provisional Committees were appointed to prepare schemes for Associations, *see* e.g. Cmd. 320.)

RESEARCH COMMITTEE.—*App.* by S.I.R., presumably about Aug. 1915. *Obj.* To advise generally on possibilities of research. *Repr.* Presumably largely scientific and expert. *Ref.* B.T.J., 14th Mar. 1918. *Possibly Permanent.*

RESEARCH COMMITTEES, JOINT COMMITTEES (INDUSTRIAL), ETC.—*App.* from time to time for various industries by Manufacturers' Associations and others interested, sometimes at instigation of S.I.R., e.g. Alloys Research Committee of Institute of Mechanical Engineers, Joint Pottery Research Committee by Staffordshire Pottery Manufacturers' Association and Stoke Central School of Science and Technology, from about autumn of 1915, and in other cases independently by Research Association for the Industry (e.g. Silk). *Obj.* To carry out definite schemes of research for particular industries. *Repr.* Manufacturers in the industry and others interested. *Ref.* Cd. 8336, pp. 20–2 and 49.

RESEARCH CO-ORDINATING BOARDS, CHEMISTRY, ENGINEERING AND PHYSICS.—*App.* by S.I.R., under Government decision, in first part of 1920. *Obj.* To co-ordinate and develop research for fighting services and other Government Departments, provide central finance fund for researches, promote researches inadequately provided for, and secure full circulation of available information. *Repr.* S.I.R., Adm., A.M., W.O., M.T., N.P.L., scientific experts. *Ref.* Cmd. 905, pp. 25–6, 89 ; Cmd. 1471, pp. 15–23, where there is a good account of their operations. *Permanent Bodies.*

A special Sub-Committee of the Chemistry Board was appointed in 1921, representing the three Fighting Services, to examine possibilities of research in development of accumulators and dry cells (*see* Cmd. 1471, p. 53). The work of the Acoustical Research establishment of the W.O. was similarly co-ordinated by a Committee representing the three Fighting Services and S.I.R. (*see* Cmd. 1735, p. 32).

(For Radio Research Co-ordinating Board, *see* above.)

RESEARCH CO-ORDINATION, GOVERNMENT COMMITTEE.—*See* Cabinet.

RESEARCH, DISTRICT, COMMITTEES.—*App.* from time to time in various industries in the course of establishing Research Associations (q.v.), from about summer of 1917. *Obj.* To assist locally in establishment of Research Associations. *Repr.* Local industrial and scientific interests concerned. *Ref.* Cd. 9144, p. 16.

RUBBER RESEARCH IMPERIAL ADVISORY COMMITTEE.—*App.* in 1920 or earlier, possibly by S.I.R. *Obj.* To co-ordinate rubber research throughout the Empire. *Repr.* Presumably scientists, &c. *Ref.* Cmd. 905, p. 74. *Probably Permanent.*

RUBBER RESEARCH, MALAYA, BOARD.—*App.* probably jointly by S.I.R., G.I., and C.O. in 1920. *Obj.* To co-ordinate and extend rubber growing in Malaya. *Repr.* Presumably the Departments concerned, rubber growers, scientists. *Ref.* Cmd. 905, p. 74.

SOUTH AFRICA.—*See under* Dominions.

STANDARDIZATION, OPTICAL INSTRUMENTS.—*See* Optical Instruments.

STEAM PLANT FOR HIGH PRESSURES AND TEMPERATURES SUB-COMMITTEE.—*App.*, as special Sub-Committee of Standing Committee on Engineering, in 1916 or 1917. *Obj.* To direct and supervise research into this subject. *Repr.* Standing Committee and others. *Ref.* Cd. 8718, p. 40.

TANK ADVISORY COMMITTEE.—Date of appointment and purpose doubtful, but work included investigation of resistance of merchant and (apparently) warships to waves. *See* Cmd. 1735, p. 47.

THERMIONIC VALUES.—*See under* Radio Research.

TIN AND TUNGSTEN RESEARCH BOARD.—*App.* by S.I.R. about end 1917, following Conference. *Obj.* To carry out extended research to secure increased recovery of metals from ores. *Repr.* S.I.R., A.C(S), M.M., Cornish Chamber of Mines, Institute of Mining and Metallurgy. *Ref.* Cd. 9144, p. 27. *Diss.* At end of 1920.

TIN AND TUNGSTEN RESEARCH COMMITTEE.—*App.* as Committee of Research Board (q.v.) early in 1918, having existed previously as Research Committee of Institution of Mining and Metallurgy. *Obj.* To supervise research workers and extended scheme of research. *Repr.* Research Board, the industries, scientists. *Ref.* Cd. 9144, pp. 27, 75. *Diss.* At or before dissolution of Research Board.

TIN, CORNISH, RESEARCH SUB-COMMITTEE.—*App.* as Sub-Committee by Tin and Tungsten Research Board, early in 1918, having previously existed as independent body. *Obj.* To supervise research workers and extended research scheme on behalf of the Board. *Repr.* Cornish tin mining industry, scientists. *Ref.* Cd. 9144, p. 27. *Diss.* At or before dissolution of Research Board.

TUNGSTEN SUB-COMMITTEE.—*App.* by Standing Committee on Metallurgy in 1916 or 1917. *Obj.* To prepare survey of field for research. *Repr.* Standing Committee, steel-makers and others. *Ref.* Cd. 8718, p. 28. *Diss.* Apparently by Nov. 1917.

TUNGSTEN.—*See also* Tin and Tungsten.

VEGETABLES.—*See* Fruits.

VITREOUS COMPOUNDS AND CEMENTS RESEARCH COMMITTEE. —*App.* by S.I.R. in 1917 or early 1918. *Obj.* To conduct researches into preparation, properties and employment of cements for lenses and prisms, and draw up classified list of vitreous compounds. *Repr.* Experts in chemical, scientific and other research. *Ref.* Cd. 8916, p. 17. *Diss.* 1920 or earlier.

WIRELESS.—*See under* Radio Research.

WOOL AND SHEEP BREEDING PROVISIONAL JOINT COMMITTEE.—*App.* jointly, at instance of Woollen Industries Research Association, by Government Departments and other interests concerned, Nov. 1919. *Obj.* To secure co-operation of classes concerned in investigating influence of sheep breeding in improving qualities of wools. *Repr.* B.A., B.A.(Sc.), D.A.T.I., The Research Association, Sheep Breeders' Associations. *Ref.* Cmd. 1471, p. 27.

WOOL AND WORSTED INDUSTRIES, PROVISIONAL COMMITTEE ON RESEARCH.—*App.* by the industries, at instigation of S.I.R., in 1916 or 1917. *Obj.* To organize Research Association for the industries. *Repr.* Various branches of the Industries, wool textile and other research. *Ref.* Cd. 8916, p. 19. *Diss.* By July 1918.

WOOL AND WORSTED INDUSTRIES, LOCAL COMMITTEES ON RESEARCH.—*App.* To assist main Committee in 1917 and 1918, owing to necessity of providing for needs of different areas. *Obj.*, *Repr.* Locally, as with main Committee. *Ref.* Cd. 9144, p. 15. *Diss.* By July 1918.

ZINC AND COPPER INQUIRY COMMITTEE.—*App.* by A.C(S), on advice of Standing Committee on Metallurgy, in 1916 or 1917. *Obj.* To survey existing knowledge and practice in these industries and direct research into best methods of producing brass and copper castings. *Repr.* The Standing Committee, Institutes of Metals and of Mining and Metallurgy, industries concerned, metallurgical research. *Ref.* Cd. 8718, p. 28. *Diss.* 1920 or earlier.

ZIRCONIUM INQUIRY COMMITTEE.—*App.* by S.I.R., at request of M.M., July 1918. *Obj.* To investigate preparation of ferro-zirconium, and zirconium-containing steels. *Repr.* M.M., metallurgical research, engineers. *Ref.* Cmd. 320, p. 85. *Diss.* About June 1920.

SCOTTISH OFFICE

(exclusive of Fishery Board for Scotland—*see* Separate Section).

ABBREVIATIONS

S.O. = Scottish Office.
S.S. = Secretary of State for Scotland.

ALIENS AFTER THE WAR.—*See* M.R.

ALIENS, SCOTTISH ADVISORY COMMITTEE.—*Ref.* without details, Cd. 8741, p. 2. *App., Obj.,* &c., presumably the same as Aliens, Enemy, Advisory Committee (*see* H.O.). Committee remained in existence till after the close of the War.

ALLOTMENTS, DEPARTMENTAL COMMITTEE.—Joint appointment.—*See* B.A.

BUILDING CONSTRUCTION COMMITTEE.—Joint appointment. *See* L.G.B.

COAL AND COKE SUPPLIES, SCOTLAND, DISTRICT COMMITTEE. —*App.* by Coal Controller or S.O., apparently in 1918. *Obj.* To organize distribution of available supplies. *Repr.* Departments and interests concerned. *Ref.* Cmd. 185, p. lii.

DISTRIBUTING TRADES, SCOTLAND, COMMITTEE.—*App.* by S.S., June 1915. *Obj.* To consider readjustment of employment in these trades to release men for military service or work of national importance. *Repr.* Parliament, S.O., B.T., wholesale and retail traders, women. *Ref.* Cd. 7987, 8220. *Diss.* Mar. 1916 (Second Report).

DISTRIBUTIVE TRADES, SCOTLAND, TRADE COMMITTEES.— *App.* suggested by Distributing Trades Committee (q.v.), July 1915 and again Mar. 1916. *Obj.* To reorganize arrangements, and secure release of men for military service in particular trades. *Repr.* Employers and work-people concerned. *Ref.* Cd. 7987, p. 3 ; Cd. 8220, p. 3.

EDINBURGH CASTLE, UTILIZATION AS SCOTTISH NATIONAL WAR MEMORIAL, COMMITTEE.—*App.* by S.S., Oct. 1918. *Obj.* To consider steps necessary for this purpose. *Repr.* Representative Scotsmen, including Parliament, Commanders of Military and Naval Forces in Scotland, the Army and Navy, Lord Provosts, &c. *Ref.* Cmd. 279. *Diss.* July 1919.

(The Committee appointed several Sub-Committees with co-opted members.)

FIARS PRICES COMMITTEE.—*App.* with head-quarters at Edinburgh prior to June 1917. Other details lacking. *See* Cd. 8741, p. 5.

GAME AND HEATHER BURNING (SCOTLAND) COMMITTEE.—*See* B.A.(Sc.).

JUVENILE ORGANIZATIONS, SCOTTISH NATIONAL COUNCIL.— *App.* by S.O. early in 1917, presumably about same time as similar body for England (*see* H.O.). *Obj.* To secure full co-ordination of work of official and voluntary organizations dealing with juvenile problems. *Repr.* S.O., S.E.D., M.L., W.O., Legal Profession, Local Juvenile Organizations' Committees, Organizations dealing with juveniles (boys and girls). *Ref.* Report of Council on Juvenile Delinquency, p. 2 (H.M.S.O., 1923). *Permanent.*

(Local Committees with similar purpose and constitution were likewise established.)

LABOUR SUBSTITUTIONARY (SCOTLAND) COMMITTEE.—*App.* by S.O., presumably in 1915 or 1916. *Ref.* without details, Cd. 8741, p. 7. This clearly dealt with problem of substitutes for men released for military service.

LOCAL TAXATION, SCOTLAND, DEPARTMENTAL COMMITTEE.— *App.* by S.O. in 1920 or 1921. *Obj.* To report on present system and suggested alterations. *Repr.* S.B.H., Scottish L.A.'s, agriculturalists, chartered accountants, land-owners, Legal Profession, manufacturers. *Ref.* Cmd. 1674. *Diss.* May 1922.

(Though not actually a War Committee, its work was definitely affected by war developments, e.g. Rent Restriction.)

POLICE FEDERATION (SCOTLAND).—*App.* under the Police Act, 1919, under S.O. *Obj.*, *Repr.*, *Ref.* as with Police Federation in England (*see* H.O., and for joint Police Service Committee).

RECRUITING, SCOTLAND, CENTRAL COMMITTEE.—Reference in Cd. 7897, p. 4, without details.

RENTS OF SMALL DWELLINGS IN SCOTLAND, INCREASES, COMMITTEE.—*App.* by S.O., Oct. 1915. *Obj.* To investigate recent increases in rentals in industrial districts. *Repr.* Legal Profession, Economists. *Ref.* Cd. 8111. *Diss.* Nov. 1915.

REPRESENTATION.—*See* Parliament.

RURAL TRANSPORT (SCOTLAND) COMMITTEE.—*App.* by S.O., Feb. 1918. *Obj.* To report upon needs of rural transport in Scotland and suggest improvements. *Repr.* S.O., B.A.(Sc.), F.B.(Sc.), agriculture, agricultural and engineering experts, economists. *Ref.* Cmd. 227, 987. *Diss.* Mar. 1920.

(A Sub-Committee was appointed to visit France and report upon permanent way material and rolling stock, used by the British Expeditionary Force.)

SCOTTISH NATIONAL WAR MEMORIAL.—*See* Edinburgh Castle.

STATE MANAGEMENT DISTRICTS.—Joint appointment. *See* H.O.

TRANSPORT, INLAND, SCOTLAND, STANDING CONFERENCE.— *App.* jointly by Departments concerned, July 1920. *Obj.* To consider proposals for new and improved inland transport facilities in Scotland and report through Development (Scotland) Committee to M.T. *Repr.* S.O., B.A.(Sc.), F.B.(Sc.), S.B.H., B.T. *Ref.* Cmd. 1393, p. 33. *Standing Body :* but practically in abeyance for considerable time after Mar. 1921, owing to need of economy (*see* Cmd. 1675, p. 30).

SHIPPING, MINISTRY OF

The Ministry of Shipping was developed out of the Transport Department of the Admiralty and was established on 22nd Dec. 1916, by the New Ministries and Secretaries Act, 1916 (6 & 7 Geo. V, c. 68), under a Shipping Controller (Minister of Shipping) and a Parliamentary Secretary. Its *object* was to control and organize the available shipping, so as to utilize it to the best advantage for the needs of the country, and to take such steps as were possible for providing and maintaining an efficient supply. The Ministry was established for the period of the War and for a year after this, unless terminated earlier by Order-in-Council. The control of merchant shipbuilding was only for a few months under the Ministry, as in May 1917 it was transferred to the Admiralty, but the work of dealing with repair and reconditioning was again transferred from the Admiralty after the Armistice. It was originally intended that the Ministry should be brought to an end in the winter of 1919–20, but, in view of services required in connexion with control of wheat and sugar, it was continued temporarily and does not appear to have been finally closed down till 1921. *References.* P.G.A., 1916, 1921 ; Cmd. 325, pp. 179–81 ; H.C., Nos. 100, &c., 1920, pp. xxviii, xxix, xxxii.

ABBREVIATIONS

M.S. = Ministry (or Minister) of Shipping.
N.M.B. = National Maritime Board.

BRISTOL.—*See* Tug Owners, West of England and Bristol Channel.

BRITISH SHIPPING MISSION TO U.S.A.—*App.* by M.S., May 1917. *Obj.* To act as link between U.S.A. and M.S., advise British Embassy on shipping matters and co-operate with U.S.A. in putting their shipping resources to best use for war purposes. *Repr.* Shipping Control Committee and Directorate of Ships' Requisitioning. *Ref.* T., 2nd June 1917, p. 6.

CANALS, LOCAL CONSULTATIVE COMMITTEES.—*App.* by Port and Transit Executive Committee, probably in 1917 or 1918. *Obj.* To deal with applications of Canal Companies, &c., for use of Transport Workers' Battalions. *Repr.* included representatives of National Transport Workers' Federation among others. *Ref.* L.Y.B., 1919, p. 167.

CARGOES, DELAY IN UNLOADING, COMMITTEE.—*App.* by M.S. in 1917 (prior to Sept.). *Obj.* To consider means of reducing delays in unloading and securing fuller use of available shipping. *Repr.* M.S., shipowners, dock, &c., authorities. *Ref.* Cd. 8741, p. 3.

COASTING TRADE BRANCH.—*App.* by M.S. in 1917. *Obj.* To watch and control movement of steamers in coasting trade of U.K. and in trade with France, south to Bordeaux. *Repr.* Official and expert. *Ref.* Cd. 9005, p. 109.

(*See also under* Port Facilities.)

CONVOY, OR CONVOY CO-ORDINATION, COMMITTEES.—*App.* locally in chief ports in later part of 1917. *Obj.* To assist in organizing convoy system. *Repr.* Presumably the various interests involved. *Ref.* Cmd. 325, p. 187.

EXPENDITURE, EMERGENCY, INTER-DEPARTMENTAL COM-MITTEE.—*See* Tre.

GRATUITY, MERCHANT SHIPS, COMMITTEE.—*App.* by M.S. (or Adm.), presumably late in the War. *Obj.* To deal with grants to officers and crews of merchant ships which rendered conspicuous service in resisting enemy attacks. *Repr.* Not stated. *Ref.* H.C., No. 97, 1921, p. 3.

HARBOUR CRAFT SUB-COMMITTEE.—*App.* jointly by the two Officers' Panels, with the Owners' Panel, of N.M.B. with consent of L.A.'s and officers concerned in winter of 1917–18. *Obj.* To deal with pay and conditions of officers on vessels belonging to various L.A.'s. *Repr.* Ship-owners' and Officers' Panels of N.M.B. *Ref.* Cmd. 545. *Diss.* Presumably by close of 1919.

LIQUIDATION CLAIMS COMMITTEE.—*App.* by M.S., Mar. 1920. *Obj.* To deal with claims in respect of cancelled and reduced orders of M.S., excluding concrete ship construction. *Repr.* Not stated. *Ref.* H.C., No. 55, 1921, p. 7.

MARITIME BOARD, NATIONAL.—*App.* by M.S., Nov. 1917, after consultation with ship-owners and seamen, with separate panels for Engineer Officers, Navigating Officers, Sailors and Firemen, and the Catering Departments. *Obj.* To introduce standard rates of pay and conditions and deal with disputes, secure greater co-operation between ship-owners and seamen, and advise upon personnel of industry. *Repr.* Equal numbers in each case of ship-owners and of the officers and men affected, with independent chairmen. *Ref.* Cmd. 545. *Diss.* 31st Dec. 1919, on constitution of Joint Industrial Council for Mercantile Marine.

(*See also* Harbour Craft Sub-Committee ; Mercantile Marine Conciliation Committee.)

MARITIME BOARD, NATIONAL, ESTABLISHMENT COMMITTEE.—*App.* by M.S., Aug. 1917. *Obj.* To prepare scheme for permanent Joint Board for settlement of differences in mercantile marine. *Repr.* M.S., ship-owners, officers, seamen. *Ref.* Cmd. 545, p. 3. *Diss.* Oct. or Nov. 1917.

MARITIME BOARDS, DISTRICT.—*App.* as part of organization of N.M.B. from Nov. 1917, in twenty-one ports. *Obj.* To deal with local difficulties (wages, supply of seamen, &c.). *Repr.* Local shipowners and branches of Sailors' and Firemen's Union. *Ref.* Cmd. 545. *Diss.* Presumably on dissolution of Board at end of 1919.

MERCANTILE MARINE CONCILIATION COMMITTEE.—*App.* by M.S., Sept. 1917, as Inter-Departmental Committee. *Obj.* To secure speedy settlement of differences between ship-owners and seamen. *Repr.* Govern-ment Departments concerned, ship-owners, seamen. *Ref.* B.T.J., 11th Oct. 1917. *Diss.* Nov. 1917 (constitution of N.M.B.).

MERCANTILE MARINE TRAINING SCHEME ORGANIZATION COMMITTEE.—*App.* by M.S. in co-operation with B.T., at conference of the two Departments, the Shipping Federation and the Seamen's and Fire-men's Union, in autumn of 1918. *Obj.* To initiate and supervise scheme for intensive training of youths for mercantile marine. *Repr.* M.S., B.T., Shipping Federation, Sailors' and Firemen's Union. *Ref.* Cmd. 524.

PORT AND TRANSIT EXECUTIVE COMMITTEE.—*App.* by Cabinet, Oct. 1915, and attached to Adm., and transferred later to M.S. *Obj.* To investigate congestion and regulate and co-ordinate traffic at ports and docks, and later advise on proposals of civil departments and requisition shipping for them. *Repr.* Government Departments concerned, Port Authorities, Ship-owners, Labour. *Ref.* H.C., No. 245, 1919, p. 45. *Diss.* Duties taken over by M.T. late in 1920.

(*See also* West of England and Bristol Channel Committee.)

PORT CONSULTANTS.—*App.* jointly at different ports by Ship-owners and Seamen's Union, in or after Nov. 1921, as part of organization of N.M.B. *Obj.* To deal jointly with disputes, grievances and labour supply, pending discussion by District Maritime Boards, and so avoid delays in sailings. *Repr.* Local ship-owners and branches of Seamen's Union. *Ref.* Cmd. 545.

PORT FACILITIES AND COASTAL TRADE DEPARTMENT.—*App.* by M.S. in 1917 (May or earlier). *Obj.* To be responsible for port work and developments, including those affecting coastal trade. *Repr.* Official and expert. *Ref.* B.T.J., 31st May 1917.

PORT LABOUR COMMITTEES.—*App.* by and under the Port and Transit Executive Committee in spring of 1916 in every important port, and presumably transferred to M.S. in 1917. *Obj.* To accelerate work at docks, control work of Transport Workers Battalions, and deal with exemption of dockers from military service in conjunction with B.T. *Repr.* Adm., W.O., Port Authorities, Labour. *Ref.* Cd. 9005, p. 115.

RIVER CRAFT, NORTH RUSSIA, COMMISSION.—*App.* by M.S. in 1919. *Obj.* To supervise use of river craft required by Allied Forces in North Russia. *Repr.* Owners of craft utilized. *Ref.* H.C., No. 10, 1922, p. xliii. *Diss.* 1919 or 1920.

SALES OF SHIPS, DELAYS IN PAYMENTS, COMMITTEE.—*App.* by M.S., with consent of Tre., in 1920. *Obj.* To deal with cases (including those of ex-enemy vessels) of failures to make payments at agreed dates and grant extensions of time. *Repr.* Not stated. *Ref.* H.C., No. 10, 1922, p. xliv.

SEAFARERS' JOINT COUNCIL DRAFTING COMMITTEE.—*App.* by N.M.B., Nov. 1919. *Obj.* To draw up a constitution for a Joint Industrial Council for mercantile marine. *Repr.* M.S., ship-owners, officers and men of mercantile marine. *Ref.* Cmd. 545. *Diss.* Dec. 1919.

SERVICE OF FOOD TO CREWS SUB-COMMITTEE.—*App.* by N.M.B. in spring of 1918. *Obj.* To consider introduction of arrangements for improved service of food to sailors and firemen, in connexion with proposed reduction in legal allowance of meat. *Repr.* Ship-owners', Seamen's and Firemen's, Panels. *Ref.* Cmd. 545. *Diss.* April 1918.

SHIPBUILDING CONSTRUCTION COMMITTEE.—*App.* by M.S. in 1917. *Ref.* without details, Cd. 8741, p. 10.

SHIPPING CONTROL ADVISORY COMMITTEE.—*App.* by Shipping Controller, Dec. 1916. *Obj.* To advise Shipping Controller on acceleration of merchant shipbuilding, on administration of merchant shipbuilding programme and on shipping control generally. *Repr.* B.T., Shipbuilding and Engineering Employers Federations, shipbuilders, marine engineers. *Ref.* T., 29th Dec. 1916, p. 7.

SHIPPING CONTROL COMMITTEE.—*App.* apparently in 1915 to advise Transport Department of Adm., becoming Committee of M.S. later. *Obj.* To advise as to control of shipping, act as link between various Shipping Committees, and, after Armistice, advise on sale of ships. *Repr.* Apparently an Advisory Committee of owners, builders and repairers. *Ref.* Cd. 8256 ; H.C., No. 245, 1919, p. 5. *Diss.* Apparently continued for some time after the Armistice.

SHIPPING CONTROL, INTERNATIONAL, COMMITTEE.—*App.* by the Government, Jan. 1916, and presumably brought later into M.S. *Obj.* To control distribution of available shipping between Allied powers. *Repr.* Cabinet and others. *Ref.* Cmd. 325, p. 167. *Diss.* Apparently replaced by, or absorbed into, Allied Maritime Transport Council about end 1917 (*see* Cabinet).

SHIP REPAIRS JOINT NEGOTIATING COMMITTEE.—*App.* jointly by M.S. and Adm., July 1919. *Obj.* To negotiate jointly an agreement with the Ship Repairers' Conference, on rates for repairs and re-conditioning of requisitioned ships. *Repr.* M.S., Adm. *Ref.* H.C., Nos. 100, &c., 1920, p. xxxii. *Diss.* Had apparently ceased to function by end of 1919.

SHIPS' LICENSING COMMITTEE.—*See* B.T.

TEXTILE EXPORTS.—*See* B.T.

TONNAGE PRIORITY COMMITTEE.—*App.* by or under M.S., about middle of 1917. *Obj.* To co-ordinate demands for tonnage in national interest and adjust them to supplies available. *Repr.* Various Government Departments affected. *Ref.* Cd. 9005, p. 108.

TRAMP OWNERS' COMMITTEE ; TRANSPORT ARBITRATION BOARD.—*See* Adm.

TRANSPORT CO-ORDINATION CENTRAL COMMITTEE.—*App.* by War Cabinet or M.S. in 1918. *Obj.* To co-ordinate railroad, canal and sea transport to secure maximum efficiency. *Repr.* Experts in different forms of transport apparently. *Ref.* Cmd. 325, p. 177.

TRANSPORT CO-ORDINATION PORT COMMITTEES.—*App.* by War Cabinet or M.S. in 1918, at principal outports of U.K. *Obj.*, *Repr.* as with Central Committee, for their particular localities. *Ref.* Cmd. 325, p. 177.

TRANSPORT WORKERS' BATTALIONS.—*App.* by the Government, Feb. 1916, and extended, early in 1917, under Port and Transit Executive, and Port Labour, Committees, thus apparently coming largely under M.S. *Obj.* To form mobile labour force under military conditions for transfer from port to port as required. *Repr.* Consisted of men in Home Army, transferred temporarily to dock work. *Ref.* Cd. 9005, p. 115.

TRANSPORT WORKERS' BATTALIONS LOCAL COMMITTEES.— *App.* locally from Feb. 1916. *Obj.* To supervise employment of the Battalions. *Repr.* Not stated. *Ref.* Cmd. 325, p. 187.

TUG OWNERS' COMMITTEE (BRISTOL).—Incidental reference in B.T.J., 14th March 1918, p. 303, where it appears to have been local committee of owners appointed to assist the shipping authorities. Similar Committees may have existed elsewhere.

WEST OF ENGLAND AND BRISTOL CHANNEL COMMITTEE.—*App.* by Port and Transit Executive Committee as Sub-Committee, Feb. 1918. *Obj.* To maintain flow of traffic through, and secure fuller use of sea-carrying power of, Bristol Channel Ports. *Repr.* District Coal Control and Coal Supplies Committees, Landed Grain Committee (M.F.), tug owners, coal owners and traders, railways, Associated China Clay Company, Dockers' Union. *Ref.* Cmd. 325 ; B.T.J., 14th Mar. 1918.

TRADE, BOARD OF, INCLUDING THE MINES DEPARTMENT

The *Board of Trade* was enlarged and reorganized for war and reconstruction purposes. The following special Departments and Authorities were added or attached to the Board during the War : Aircraft Insurance, Air Raid Compensation, and Canal Control, Committees ; Coal Control (*see* below); Cotton Control Board ; Dyes Commissioner ; Horse Transport, Import Restrictions, Insurance, Intelligence, Departments ; Industrial (War Inquiries) Branch ; Paper Supplies Royal Commission and later Paper Control ; Petrol Control Department, Petroleum Supplies Pool Board (*see also* Ministry of Munitions) ; Purchases Department ; Railway Executive Committee ; Timber Supplies Department ; Tobacco and Matches Control Board ; Tramways Committee ; War Risks Insurance Department ; Work of National Importance Committee.

In Feb. 1918 the Board was reorganized, and strengthened, with a view to the increased needs of trade after the War, into two main Divisions or Departments, for Commerce and Industry, and for Public Service Administration, concerned respectively with general trade developments and the statutory duties of the Board in respect of trade and commerce. A General Economic Department (for inquiries, &c.) was also established at this time. The Overseas Trade Department (*see* Separate Heading) had already been formed as a Joint Department with the Foreign Office (*see* Cd. 8912, where the reorganization is described and a list of special war organizations is given). In Sept. 1918 a provisional Advisory Council was appointed, pending formation of a permanent Council to advise generally the Department of Commerce and Industry. It included representatives of various Board of Trade Committees, of the Colonial, Foreign, and India Offices, of the Dominions Governments, of Chambers of Commerce and the Federation of British Industries, and of Labour. (*See* Board of Trade Journal, 10th Oct. 1918, p. 450.)

By the Mining Industry Act, 1920 (10 & 16 Geo. V, c. 50), a *Mines Department* of the Board was established under a Parliamentary Secretary of the Board, known as Secretary for Mines, ' for the purpose of securing the most effective development and utilization of the mineral resources of the United Kingdom and the safety and welfare of those engaged in the mining industry '. The Department, in regard to safety and health in the mines, took over the duties previously performed by the Mines Department of the Home Office. *See* Public General Acts, 1920.

ABBREVIATIONS

B.T. = Board of Trade.
C.M.D. = Coal Mines Department.
R.E.C. = Railway Executive Committee.
S.C.P. = Standing Committee on Prices (*see* below) under Profiteering Acts.
S.C.T. = Standing Committee on Trusts (*see* below) under Profiteering Acts.

ADMINISTRATIVE COUNCIL (INTERNAL).—*App.* by President of B.T., Sept. 1919. *Obj.* To meet regularly and frequently to deal with business involving questions of policy. *Repr.* The President, Parliamentary and Permanent Secretaries and heads of Chief Administrative Departments of B.T. *Ref.* B.T.J., 25th Sept. 1919, p. 386. *Permanent.*

ADVISORY COUNCIL, PROVISIONAL.—*See* Heading to Section.

AGRICULTURAL IMPLEMENTS AND MACHINERY SUB-COMMITTEE (PROFITEERING ACTS).—*App.* by S.C.P., Nov. 1919. *Obj.* To investigate profits, cost and prices of production and distribution. *Repr.* Agriculturalists, business men, &c. *Ref.* Cmd. 1315. *Diss.* April 1921.

AIRCRAFT INSURANCE COMMITTEE.—*App.* by B.T., June 1915. *Obj.* To consider possibilities of contributory scheme of insurance against aircraft and bombardment. *Repr.* Insurance Companies, Financial Interests. *Ref.* Cd. 7997. *Diss.* July 1915.

AIRCRAFT INSURANCE EXPERT COMMITTEE.—*App.* by B.T. Board on recommendation of Aircraft Insurance Committee (q.v.), July 1915. *Obj.* To control State Insurance Office established under proposed Aircraft Insurance Scheme. *Repr.* B.T., Lloyds, Fire Insurance Offices. *Ref.* Cd. 7997.

AIR RAID COMPENSATION COMMITTEE.—*App.* by B.T., Sept. 1917. *Obj.* To deal with claims under new compensation scheme for losses of property of £500 or less. *Repr.* Presumably much as with Aircraft Insurance Committee. *Ref.* B.T.J., 20th Dec. 1917 ; H.C., No. 132, 1918, p. 28. *Diss.* 1st Oct. 1919.

AIR RAID DAMAGES IN EASTERN COUNTIES COMMITTEE.— Appointment under Chairmanship of Lord Parmoor to investigate the damages in the Eastern Counties referred to in T., 14th April 1916, p. 5.

AIR RISKS INSURANCE SCHEME COMMITTEE.—*Ref.* without details, Cd. 8741, p. 2. Presumably the same as Aircraft Insurance Expert Committee above.

ALIENS, EX-ENEMY, RELEASE OF PROPERTY, COMMITTEE.— *App.* by B.T., Oct. 1920. *Obj.* To advise upon applications for release of property by ex-enemy aliens in necessitous circumstances, and, from Aug. 1923, on extensions of grounds of release. *Repr.* Parliament, Judges, Legal Profession. *Ref.* Cmd. 1687, 2046. *Still sitting end 1923.*

(Other Committees dealing with Aliens will be found under H.O., L.G.B., M.R., &c.)

ANTI-DUMPING.—*See* Safeguarding of Industries.

ASPIRIN.—*See* Drugs.

AUSTRIAN AND BULGARIAN PROPERTY COMMITTEE.—*App.* by B.T., Dec. 1920. *Obj.* To advise on administration of such property. *Repr.* B.T., Public Trustee, Accountants, Business Men. *Ref.* B.T.J., 30th Dec. 1920, p. 758.

BELGIAN TRADE COMMITTEE.—*App.* apparently by Government, as joint Committee of B.T. and F.O., by summer of 1917. *Obj.* To investigate means of promoting Anglo-Belgian trade and commerce. *Repr.* B.T., F.O., Chambers of Commerce and Shipping, British Trade Corporation, F.B.I., banks, railways, shipowners. *Ref.* B.T.J., 9th Aug. 1917 ; Cd. 8916, p. 15.

BISCUIT TRADE.—*See under* Prices, Investigation.

BOARD OF TRADE REORGANIZATION ADVISORY COMMITTEE. —*App.* informally in 1917. *Obj.* To advise B.T. in framing scheme of reorganization for affording increased assistance to business community after the War. *Repr.* Parliament, prominent men in industry and business. *Ref.* Cd. 8912. *Diss.* 1917 or 1918.

BOLTS.—*See* Iron and Steel Products.

BOOT AND SHOE STANDARD SCHEME JOINT SUB-COMMITTEE (PROFITEERING ACTS):—*App.* jointly by S.C.P. and S.C.T., Oct. 1920. *Obj.* To investigate position of scheme and relation to prevailing prices. *Repr.* M.L., S.C.P., S.C.T., Employers, Labour. *Ref.* Cmd. 1269. *Diss.* Feb. 1921.

(*See also* report by S.C.P. on subject, Cmd. 592.)

BOOTS, SHOES AND FOOTWEAR, REPAIRING, SUB-COMMITTEE (PROFITEERING ACTS).—*App.* by S.C.P., Sept. 1920. *Obj.* To investigate charges, costs and profits of all types of repairs. *Repr.* Business men, Labour, women, social experts. *Ref.* Cmd. 1345. *Diss.* May 1921.

BREWING ECONOMIES COMMITTEE.—*See* M.F.

BRICK TRADE.—*See under* Stone, &c.

BRITISH INDUSTRIES FAIRS.—*App.* (organized) by B.T., the first in London, May 1915, and being subsequently held annually. *Obj.* To provide display of British goods of types formerly imported from enemy countries, in connexion with Exhibitions of Samples (q.v.). *Ref.* B.T.J., 25th Feb. 1915, and later issues.

BRITISH INDUSTRIES FAIRS COMMITTEE.—*App.* by B.T., July 1920. *Obj.* To advise on future policy as to holding and organization of Fairs. *Repr.* B.T., O.T.D., manufacturers, and others. *Ref.* B.T.J., 22nd July 1920.

BRITISH TRADE AFTER THE WAR SUB-COMMITTEE.—*App.* by Advisory Committee on Commercial Intelligence (q.v.), July 1915. *Obj.* To report upon steps to secure after-war position of firms producing goods formerly imported from enemy countries. *Repr.* Prominent manufacturers and business men. *Ref.* Cd. 8181. *Diss.* Jan. 1916.

BRUSHES AND BROOMS SUB-COMMITTEE (PROFITEERING ACTS).—*App.* by S.C.P., May 1920. *Obj.* To investigate prices, costs and profits at all stages. *Repr.* Business men, women and others. *Diss.* April 1921.

BUCKMASTER COMMITTEE.—*See* Contracts, Pre-war.

BUILDING MATERIALS, JOINT SUB-COMMITTEE (PROFITEERING ACTS).—*App.* jointly by S.C.P. and S.C.T., Jan. 1920. *Obj.* To investigate prices, costs and profits at all stages of various building materials, and existence and effects of combinations, the Sub-Committee acting through Sectional Committees for Cement ; Light Castings ; Pipes and Castings ; Stone, Brick and Clayware (q.v.). *Repr.* Not stated, but presumably much as with other Sub-Committees and the Sectional Committees. *Ref.* Only incidentally in reports of Sectional Committees (q.v.). *Diss.* About middle of 1921. *See also* L.G.B.

BULGARIAN PROPERTY.—*See* Austrian, above.

CANADIAN MUNITION WORKERS, SPECIAL MISSION OF IN-QUIRY TO CANADA.—*App.* by B.T. in 1915. *Obj.* To investigate in Canada possibilities of securing skilled workmen for munitions' work in U.K. *Repr.* Parliament, B.T., Labour. *Ref.* B.T.J., 7th Oct. 1915. *Diss.* Later in 1915.

CANAL CONTROL COMMITTEE.—*App.* by B.T., about beginning of Mar. 1917. *Obj.* To operate control for B.T. and secure increased use of canals to relieve railways. *Repr.* Government Departments concerned, Railways, Canal Companies, Carriers, Chambers of Commerce, Engineering Experts. *Ref.* B.T.J., 1st Mar. 1917.

CANAL CONTROL, AREA SUB-COMMITTEES.—*App.* by Canal Control Committee, about Sept. 1917, for Northern, Midland, and Southern Areas. *Obj.* To control under main Committee, and secure fullest use of, canals in their Areas. *Repr.* W.O., M.M., Railways, Canal Companies, Carriers. *Ref.* B.T.J., 4th Oct. 1917.

CANAL CONTROL, IRISH SUB-COMMITTEE.—*App.* by Canal Control Committee, by Mar. 1918. *Obj.* To take charge of controlled canals in Ireland under main Committee. *Repr.* Irish Board of Works, Harbour and Canal Experts, Railways, Merchants. *Ref.* B.T.J., 14th Mar. 1918.

CARBON MONOXIDE DEPARTMENTAL COMMITTEE.—*App.* by B.T., Jan. 1921. *Obj.* To report upon limitation of carbon monoxide in gas for domestic purposes. *Repr.* H.C., M.H., chemical manufacturers, chemical, engineering and medical experts. *Ref.* Cmd. 1422. *Diss.* July 1921.

CARGOES, DIVERTED, COMMITTEE.—*App.* by B.T., Aug. 1914. *Obj.* To decide immediately on disposal of, and methods of dealing with, ships and cargoes diverted to British ports, because suspected of containing contraband. *Repr.* Parliament, Government Departments affected, Port of London Authority. *Ref.* B.T.J., 27th Aug. 1914; Cd. 7816, p. 30.

CARGOES, PRIZE, RELEASE COMMITTEE.—*App.* by B.T. early in the War. *Obj.* To deal, apart from Prize Courts, with cargoes, technically prizes, which it is desirable to release. *Repr.* Presumably somewhat similar to Cargoes, Diverted, Committee (q.v.). *Ref.* Cd. 7855. *Diss.* Apparently in 1916 or 1917.

CASTINGS.—*See* Light Castings, Pipes and Castings.

CATALOGUES, GERMAN, ETC., EXHIBITIONS.—A collection of German Trade Catalogues in languages and currencies of various countries was made and exhibited by B.T. from about April 1915, to assist manu-facturers in capture of German Trade and extension of foreign trade. *See* B.T.J., Aug.–Dec. 1914, 15th April 1915, and subsequent issues.

CEMENT AND MORTAR SECTIONAL COMMITTEE (PROFITEER-ING ACTS).—*App.* by Building Materials Sub-Committee (q.v.) about Feb. 1920. *Obj.* To investigate prices, costs and profits, and existence and effects of combines or trusts, in these trades. *Repr.* Engineers, architects, scientists, Labour and others. *Ref.* Cmd. 1091. *Diss.* Nov. 1920.

CHEMICAL PRODUCTS COMMITTEE.—*App.* by B.T., Aug. 1914. *Obj.* To advise on best means of securing adequate supplies of chemical products and dyestuffs, previously imported from enemy countries. *Repr.* B.T., Customs and Excise, manufacturers of these products, chemical research. *Ref.* B.T.J., 3rd Sept. 1914. *Diss.* Prior to Sept. 1917.

The Committee appointed various Sub-Committees (*see* Cd. 8336, p. 8), including Lord Moulton's Dye-Stuffs Sub-Committee (q.v.).

CLEARING OFFICE (GERMANY) AND DEPARTMENTS (AUSTRIA, HUNGARY AND BULGARIA).—*App.* by B.T., apparently in winter of 1919–20, except for Hungarian Department, appointed July 1921. *Obj.* To clear obligations between British Empire and enemy powers under Peace Treaties. *Repr.* Official and expert. *Ref.* Second Annual Report, H.M.S.O., 1922. *Still in existence end 1922. See also* Enemy Debts.

CLOGS COMMITTEE (PROFITEERING ACTS).—*App.* under the Acts in 1919. *Obj.* To investigate costs of production and prices. *Repr.* Parliament, S.C.P., M.L., Civil Service, Manufacturers, Labour, Women. *Ref.* Cmd. 541. *Diss.* Nov. 1919.

CLOTHING, STANDARD, VOLUNTARY SCHEME, SUB-COMMITTEE (PROFITEERING ACTS).—*App.* jointly by S.C.P. and S.C.T., Oct. 1920. *Obj.* To consider scheme put forward by Wool Textile and Clothing Trades. *Repr.* S.C.P., Civil Service, Employers, Labour. *Ref.* Cmd. 1314. *Diss.* April 1921.

CLOTHING, UNIFORM, SUB-COMMITTEE (PROFITEERING ACTS). —*App.* by S.C.T., Dec. 1919. *Obj.* To investigate existence and effects of trade combinations on supply and prices of uniform clothing. *Repr.* S.C.T., S.C.P., Civil Service, Business Men, Labour, Anti-Sweating League, Social Experts. *Ref.* Cmd. 1339. *Diss.* April 1921.

COAL AND COAL INDUSTRY ADVISORY COMMITTEE.—*See under* Mining Industry.

COAL AND COKE, INLAND SUPPLIES CO-ORDINATING COMMITTEE, LOCAL SUPPLIES COMMITTEES.—*See* B.T.J., 13th Jan. 1921, p. 30, where the former is described as charged with ensuring that inland supplies are fully sufficient to meet the needs, and the latter as dealing with local supplies subject to their control. Full details are lacking.

COAL AND COKE SUPPLIES DISTRIBUTION, CENTRAL COMMITTEE.—*App.* by B.T., Dec. 1915. *Obj.* To advise on distribution of available supplies. *Repr.* B.T., Adm., H.O., M.M., coal-owners, merchants, railways. *Ref.* B.T.J., 10th Feb. 1916. *Diss.* On establishment of Coal Control, Feb. 1917.

COAL AND COKE SUPPLIES, DISTRIBUTION, DISTRICT COMMITTEES.—*App.* by B.T., in chief mining areas, Jan. 1916, on nomination of Local Coal-owners' Associations, and continued under C.M.D. *Obj.* To regulate supply and distribution to ensure sufficiency for munitions and important national work. *Repr.* Local coal-owners. *Ref.* B.T.J., 6th July, T., 7th Feb., 1916. *Diss.* Apparently continued through 1919.

COAL, DISPUTES, JOINT COMMITTEES.—*App.* in some mines during war by agreement between owners and miners. *Obj.* To adjust disputes affecting working conditions. *Repr.* Employers and workpeople. *Ref.* Cd. 9093. *Diss.* Probably at or before close of war.

COAL EXPORTERS' COMMITTEE.—*App.* by exporters at request of B.T., May 1916. *Obj.* To assist B.T. to prepare and carry out scheme to limit prices of coal exported to France. *Repr.* Exporters in chief districts. *Ref.* T., 18th May 1916, p. 5.

COAL EXPORTS COMMITTEE.—*App.* by B.T., May 1915, on prohibition of coal exports, and continued under C.M.D. *Obj.* To advise on questions of exports of coal and coke, other than to British Empire, Allies and Portugal. *Repr.* B.T., H.O., shipping, commerce. *Ref.* B.T.J., 13th May 1915. *Diss.* Mar. 1919, duties merged in Coal Control.

COAL EXPORTS, LOCAL COMMITTEES.—*App.*, apparently by the interests concerned, in various mining districts, June 1916. *Obj.* To distribute and supervise orders for coal for France and (later) Italy and secure necessary shipping. *Repr.* Local interests concerned. *Ref.* B.T.J., 1st June and 14th Dec. 1916.

COAL, HOUSE, LOCAL DISTRIBUTION COMMITTEES.—*App.*, in larger towns, at instigation of Coal Controller, in autumn of 1917. *Obj.* To accumulate stocks of coal for winter distribution and allocate to consumers. *Repr.* Presumably L.A.'s concerned and others. *Ref.* B.T.J., 31st Jan. 1918.

COAL INDUSTRY, ROYAL COMMISSION.—*See* Cabinet.

COAL, LONDON, COMMITTEE.—*App.* in 1915, apparently as a County Committee of the Coal Merchants' Federation of G.B., co-operating with B.T. and (later) C.M.D. *Obj.* To regulate distributive charges and perform other duties in reference to coal in the London area, and, after June 1920, it practically took over the control of coal prices in London. *Repr.* The Coal Merchants' Federation of G.B. *Ref.* Cmd. 1161, pp. 3, 4.

COAL, LONDON, MAXIMUM RETAIL PRICES, JOINT COMMITTEE (PROFITEERING ACTS).—*App.* jointly by S.C.P. and S.C.T., Sept. 1920. *Obj.* To investigate suggested scheme of maximum coal prices for London. *Repr.* Parliament, S.C.P., S.C.T., Civil Service, business men, Labour. *Ref.* Cmd. 1161. *Diss.* Jan. 1921.

COAL, METROPOLITAN EMERGENCY COMMITTEE.—*App.* by C.M.D., Oct. 1920. *Obj.* To advise on questions arising out of Household Fuel and Lighting Order, 1919, deal with general distribution and co-ordinate administration. *Repr.* All interests affected by Order. *Ref.* B.T.J., 28th Aug. 1920.

COAL MINES ADVISORY COMMITTEE AND (LATER) BOARD.—*App.* by B.T., Mar. 1917, under Coal Mines Control Order of 22nd Feb., on lines similar to former Coal Mines Organization Committee (*see* H.O.). *Obj.* To advise and assist Coal Controller and C.M.D. (q.v.) in carrying out coal control. *Repr.* Coal-owners and miners in equal numbers. *Ref.* B.T.J., 8th Mar. 1917.

COAL MINES CONTROL BOARD OF FINANCIAL ADVISERS.—*App.* by B.T., Mar. 1917. *Obj.* To assist in financial administration of C.M.D. *Repr.* Institute of Chartered Accountants. *Ref.* B.T.J., 8th Mar. 1917.

COAL MINES (CONTROL IN SOUTH WALES) ADVISORY INTER-DEPARTMENTAL COMMITTEE.—*App.* by B.T., Nov. 1916. *Obj.* To advise Departments concerned in operation of new Control Order and settle outstanding wage questions in South Wales. *Repr.* B.T., Adm., H.O. *Ref.* B.T.J., 7th Dec. 1916. *Diss.* Apparently absorbed into, or replaced by, Coal Mines Advisory Committee (q.v.).

COAL MINES DEPARTMENT.—*App.* by B.T., Feb. 1917, under Coal Mines Control Order of 22nd Feb., under a Coal Controller. *Obj.* To carry out control of mines, as well as existing duties of B.T. in regard to coal. *Repr.* Official and expert. *Ref.* B.T.J., 23rd Feb. 1917. *Diss.* Presumably absorbed in 1920 into general Mining Department, under Mining Industry Act.

COAL MINES DISTRICT MOBILITY BUREAUX.—*App.* by Miners' Federation and their District Associations, at suggestion of Coal Controller, Jan. and Feb. 1918. *Obj.* To transfer miners from mines not working full time to mines (including fireclay and ganister mines) short of labour. *Repr.* District Associations. *Ref.* B.T.J., 31st Jan. 1918.

COAL MINES, ECONOMIES, SUB-COMMITTEE.—*App.* by Coal and Coal Industry Advisory Committee, about Aug. 1922. *Obj.* To suggest action for reviving prosperity in industry by securing economies in distribution, &c. *Repr.* The Advisory Committee. *Ref.* Mines Department Report, 1922 (H.M.S.O., 1923). *Diss.* Probably before end of 1922.

COAL MINES, FLOODED, COMMITTEE.—*App.* by C.M.D., in co-operation with Coal Mines Inspectorate (H.O.), April 1919. *Obj.* To inquire into and advise upon emergency caused by flooding of South Staffordshire Coal Mines. *Repr.* The appointing bodies and other experts, with legal assessor. *Ref.* T., 12th April 1919, p. 9.

COAL MINES, SHORT TIME, SPECIAL COMMISSIONS OF INQUIRY.—*App.* by Coal Controller in export districts, where short time was being worked, in 1917. *Obj.* To investigate working of short time and suggest improvement. *Repr.* Coal owners, miners' leaders and others. *Ref.* B.T.J., 31st Jan. 1918.

COAL MINING, CONCILIATION; BOARDS, AREA AND NATIONAL; COMMITTEES, DISTRICT AND PIT.—*App.* provided for by the Mining Industry Act, 1920, secs. 7–12, by owners and miners, for joint settlement of questions of wages, health, safety, output, &c. (*see* P.G.A., 1920). But they have never come into existence (*see* Cmd. 1583) and were largely replaced, as regards wages, by the Coal Mining, National and District (Wages) Boards (q.v.).

COAL MINING, NATIONAL AND DISTRICT (WAGES) BOARDS.—*App.* by voluntary agreement by coal-owners and miners under Agreement of 28th June 1921, for the whole country and the chief mining districts. *Obj.* To fix and adjust wages in accordance with the agreement. *Repr.* Coal owners and miners (equal numbers). *Ref.* Cmd. 1387. *Still in existence at end of 1922.*

COAL, OUTPUT AND WAGES, JOINT COMMITTEE.—*App.* by Joint Conference of Coal Industry, Nov. 1920. *Obj.* To consider output and wage question, along with general question of future of industry. *Repr.* Coal-owners, miners. *Ref.* L.G., Dec. 1920, p. 664. *Diss.* Prior to Mar. 1921 apparently (*see* L.G., Mar. 1921, p. 122).

COAL OUTPUT, JOINT COLLIERY COMMITTEES.—*App.* jointly, on initiative of Miners' Federation, by coal-owners and miners at various collieries in summer of 1918. *Obj.* To secure removal of hindrances to output. *Repr.* Coal-owners, miners. *Ref.* B.T.J., 15th Aug. 1918.

COAL-OWNERS' CONSULTATIVE COMMITTEE.—*App.* by Mining Association of Great Britain between Feb. and June 1917. *Obj.* To negotiate with Coal Controller in matters arising out of control. *Repr.* The Mining Association. *Ref.* P.G.A., 1917–18 (7 & 8 Geo. V, c. 56 (Schedule)).

COAL RATIONING, LACE INDUSTRY, COMMITTEE.—*App.* by B.T., Sept. 1918. *Obj.* To advise Coal Controller on means of mitigating effects of coal shortage on lace industry and, if necessary, prepare definite scheme. *Repr.* Employers and workpeople in the industry. *Ref.* B.T.J., 10th Oct. 1918, p. 450.

COAL, RETAIL PRICES, COMMITTEE.—*App.* by B.T., Feb. 1915. *Obj.* To investigate recent increases in price of domestic coal, especially to poorer consumers, in London and other industrial centres. *Repr.* B.T., D.C., Chambers of Commerce, Railways, Labour, Economists. *Ref.* Cd. 7866. *Diss.* Mar. 1915.

(*See also under* Coal, London.)

COAL SUPPLIES PRIORITY COMMITTEE.—*App.* by Coal Controller about June 1918. *Obj.* To determine distribution of coal for industry, in light of war requirements. *Repr.* Government Departments concerned. *Ref.* B.T.J., 1st Aug. 1918, p. 142.

COAL SUPPLIES, STRIKES, COMMITTEE.—*App.* by C.M.D., Oct. 1920, and reappointed by Mining Department, April 1921. *Obj.* To regulate supplies of coal on national basis during coal strikes of 1920 and 1921. *Repr.* C.M.D. and others. *Ref.* Cmd. 1393, p. 45, 1675, p. 39. *Diss.* After close of strikes.

COAL SUPPLIES, STRIKES, FISHERY LOCAL SUB-COMMITTEES. —*App.* at chief fishing ports in Oct. 1920 and April 1921. *Obj.* To regulate under Shipping Sub-Committee (next entry) distribution of bunker coal supplies to local fishing fleets during coal strikes. *Repr.* Local representatives of Government Departments concerned, local fishing trade. *Ref.* Cmd. 1393, p. 45, 1675, p. 39. *Diss.* At close of strikes.

COAL SUPPLIES, STRIKES, SHIPPING, SUB-COMMITTEE.—*App.* by main Committee, Oct. 1920, and reappointed, April 1921. *Obj.* To organize distribution of available supplies of bunker coal during coal strikes. *Repr.* C.M.D., B.A., F.B.(Sc.), D.A.T.I., and presumably others. *Ref.* Cmd. 1393, p. 45, 1675, p. 39. *Diss.* At close of strikes.

COAL TRADE AFTER THE WAR, DEPARTMENTAL COMMITTEE. —*App.* by B.T., June 1916. *Obj.* To consider position of, and safeguards for, the industry after the War. *Repr.* Mining Association, coal-owners, exporters. *Ref.* Cd. 9093. *Diss.* April 1917.

COAL, TRANSPORT COSTS, ADVISORY SUB-COMMITTEE.—*App.* by C.M.D. as Sub-Committee of Coal Mines Advisory Committee (Board) (q.v.), July 1922. *Obj.* To examine possibility of economies in transport costs, to assist revival of mining industry. *Repr.* Coal owners, miners, merchants, other employers, Labour. *Ref.* B.T.J., 3rd Aug. 1922, p. 118.

COAL.—*See also* Paper Mills, Pitwood, *and under* Cotton Manufacture and Kitchens.

COLOUR USERS' COMMITTEE.—*App.* by B.T. during the War. *Obj.* To advise generally on problems of dye industry as affecting colour users. *Repr.* Trades using dyes and colours. *Ref.* Cd. 9194, p. 5.

COMMERCIAL INTELLIGENCE ORGANIZATION COMMITTEE.— Joint appointment. *See* F.O.

COMMERCIAL RECONSTRUCTION BRANCH.—*App.* by B.T. in 1916. *Obj.* To provide secretariat for Committees on post-war industry and commerce. *Repr.* Official and expert. *Ref.* H.C., No. 132, 1918, p. 28. *Diss.* Absorbed into other departments on re-organization of B.T. in 1918.

COMMISSION INTERNATIONALE DE RAVITAILLEMENT, ETC.— *See* Cabinet.

COMPANY LAW AMENDMENT JOINT COMMITTEE.—*App.* jointly by B.T. and M.R., Feb. 1918. *Obj.* To report upon amendments required to Companies Acts, with special reference to war and post-war conditions. *Repr.* B.T., Legal Profession, chartered accountants, insurance, general business interests. *Ref.* Cd. 9138. *Diss.* Aug. 1918.

COMPLAINTS STANDING COMMITTEE (PROFITEERING ACTS).— *App.* by Profiteering Acts Central Committee (q.v.) about Oct. 1919. *Obj.* To hear and deal with complaints of profiteering other than in retail trading, Tribunals being formed from the Committee to deal with individual complaints. *Repr.* As with Central Committee. *Ref.* B.T.J., 28th Aug. 1919, p. 262 ; 4th Dec. 1919, p. 679. *Diss.* Termination of Acts.

CONSCIENTIOUS OBJECTORS (WORK OF NATIONAL IMPORTANCE) COMMITTEE.—*App.* by the Government to work in close touch with B.T., Mar. 1916. *Obj.* To assist in finding, and supervise, employment for men exempted from military service for work of national importance, and advise Military Service Tribunals as to suitable work. *Repr.* Parliament, Civil Service, Business Men, Labour. *Ref.* Cd. 8331.

CONSULAR SERVICE, RECRUITING.—*See* F.O.

CONTRACTS, PRE-WAR, COMMITTEE (BUCKMASTER COMMITTEE).—*App.* by B.T., April 1917. *Obj.* To report upon position of British manufacturers and merchants after the War in respect of fulfilment of pre-war contracts impeded by the War. *Repr.* Parliament, Legal Profession, business and other experts. *Ref.* Cd. 8975. *Diss.* Jan. 1918.

COSTINGS IN GOVERNMENT DEPARTMENTS COMMITTEE.—*App.* by S.C.P. in 1919. *Obj.* To advise in regard to investigations of Government costings. *Repr.* S.C.P., M.L., accountants, including Directors of Costings in M.F., M.M., and W.O. *Ref.* Cmd. 1047. *Diss.* Feb. 1920.

COSTINGS SUB-COMMITTEE, ADVISORY (PROFITEERING ACTS). —*App.* by S.C.P., Dec. 1919. *Obj.* To deal with various matters of costings in connexion with Acts. *Repr.* Not stated. *Ref.* B.T.J., 24th Dec. 1919, p. 783.

COTTON CONTROL BOARD.—*App.* by B.T., June 1917, after consultation with the industry. *Obj.* To carry out control of cotton supplies under the Order of 28th June. *Repr.* B.T., cotton spinners, manufacturers, merchants and T.U.'s. *Ref.* B.T.J., 5th July 1917. *Diss.* Came to an end as Control Board, Feb. 1919 (except for winding up Unemployment Scheme), but continued as Cotton Reconstruction Board (q.v.).

COTTON EXPORTS COMMITTEE.—*See* W.T.D.

COTTON, FINE, SPINNING.—*See under* Fabric Gloves.

COTTON-GROWING, EMPIRE, COMMITTEE.—*App.* by B.T., July 1917. *Obj.* To investigate, and advise upon, encouragement of cotton-growing within the Empire. *Repr.* B.T., C.O., F.O., In.O., M.R., Dominions and Egyptian Governments, Cotton Industry in England (employers, workpeople) and India, Liverpool Cotton and British Cotton-Growing Associations, Scientific Experts. *Ref.* Cmd. 523. *Diss.* Oct. 1919.

(In Sept. 1918 a scheme for expanding the Committee's work was put forward, and under this Sub-Committees, with co-opted members for interests specially concerned, were established for Collection and Dissemination of Information ; Commerce ; Development, Research and Education ; and Finance. *See* B.T.J., 3rd Oct. 1918, p. 419.)

COTTON-GROWING, EMPIRE, CORPORATION.—*App.* by Royal Warrant, after recommendation by Cotton Growing, Empire, Committee, Nov. 1921. *Obj.* To carry out Cotton Growing, Empire, Committee's recommendations, with power to assist Agricultural Departments in Empire and provide facilities for training under them. *Repr.* Largely interests concerned. *Ref.* Cmd. 1735, pp. 69–70. *Permanent.* The Corporation appointed a Committee in 1922, largely of expert traders, on research and training.

COTTON INQUIRY TRIBUNAL.—*App.* by the Government, Sept. 1918. *Obj.* To report immediately on causes of recent dispute in the industry over abolition of rota system of unemployment pay and payment for short time. *Repr.* Prominent business men. *Ref.* B.T.J., 31st Oct. 1918, pp. 543–4 ; H. D. Henderson, Cotton Control Board, pp. 62–3. *Diss.* Oct. 1918.

COTTON JOINT SCHOLARSHIPS COMMITTEE.—*App.* jointly by Cotton Growing, Empire, Committee (q.v.) and British Cotton Industry Research Association in 1918 or 1919. *Obj.* To consider training of research workers for the industry. *Repr.* The appointing Bodies. *Ref.* Cmd. 320, p. 17.

COTTON MANUFACTURE, ECONOMY IN COAL AND GAS, COMMITTEE.—*App.* by Cotton Control Board, Aug. or Sept. 1918. *Obj.* To consider best method of running 45½-hour week, with view to economy in coal and gas. *Repr.* Not stated. *Ref.* B.T.J., 11th Sept. 1918, p. 333.

COTTON, RAW, OFFICIAL VALUES COMMITTEES.—*App.* as Committees of Liverpool Cotton Exchange, to act under B.T., Sept. 1917, under

Raw Cotton (Prices) Order, 1917, and later Orders, one Committee dealing with American and the other with Egyptian cotton. *Obj.* To fix and notify, daily or otherwise, official values of different classes of cotton. *Repr.* Existing Official Values Committees of Liverpool Cotton Association appointed to act as these Committees. *Ref.* B.T.J., 27th Sept. 1917.

COTTON RECONSTRUCTION BOARD.—*App.* by the Government, and consisting of the Cotton Control Board (q.v.), Feb. 1919. *Obj.* To advise the Government during ' reconstruction ' period. *Repr.* As with Cotton Control Board. *Ref.* H. D. Henderson, Cotton Control Board, pp. 8, 66.

COTTON, SEWING.—*See* Sewing Cotton.

COTTON TRADE WAR MEMORIAL FUND TRUSTEES.—*App.* by B.T., Dec. 1920, in consultation with Cotton Reconstruction Board. *Obj.* To apply jointly with B.T. the War Memorial Fund, consisting of balances of unemployment levies under Control Scheme. *Repr.* Employers and workpeople (equal numbers). *Ref.* As with Cotton Reconstruction Board.

COTTON UNEMPLOYMENT LOCAL JOINT COMMITTEES.—*App.* by Cotton Control Board in various districts, from Sept. 1917, in connexion with scheme of unemployment pay during output restriction. *Obj.* To deal equitably with necessary displacement of labour in their areas, and to settle details of scheme. *Repr.* Employers, workpeople. *Ref.* L.G., Oct. 1917.

(Mr. H. D. Henderson, Cotton Control Board, p. 30, says : ' In the spinning districts the Joint Committees were never formed. In most manufacturing districts a Joint Committee was set up; but the degree of its activity varied enormously.')

COTTON UNEMPLOYMENT SCHEME.—*See* Cotton Inquiry Tribunal.

CUSTOMS, IMPERIAL CONFERENCE.—*App.* by B.T. at suggestion of High Commissioner for South Africa, and held Feb.–Mar. 1917. *Obj.* To discuss means of securing uniformity in customs procedure and administration. *Repr.* B.T., O.T.D., G.I., Board of Customs and Excise, the Dominions and Dependencies. *Ref.* Cmd. 1231.

(Certain questions of special post-war legislation came up for consideration. A Sub-Committee of the Conference dealt with the question of a Customs' Investigating Service.)

DIAMOND EXPORT COMMITTEE.—*App.* by B.T. *See* W.T.D. *Obj.* To issue certificates for exports of varieties of diamonds (not suitable for industrial use), where export is prohibited. *Repr.* Diamond merchants and traders. *Ref.* B.T.J., 5th Aug. 1915.

DISABLED SAILORS AND SOLDIERS.—*See under* Soldiers.

DRUGS AND MEDICINAL TABLETS (INCLUDING ASPIRIN) SUB-COMMITTEE (PROFITEERING ACTS).—*App.* by S.C.P., late 1919 or early 1920. *Obj.* To investigate prices, costs and profits at all stages, with special reference to aspirin. *Repr.* Included Medical Profession and others. *Ref.* Cmd. 633. *Diss.* Mar. 1920.

DYE COLOURS DISTRIBUTION COMMITTEE.—*App.*, apparently early in the War, by B.T. *Obj.* To arrange for best allocation and distribution of available supplies. *Repr.* Government Departments and manufacturing and business interests concerned. *Ref.* Cd. 8741, p. 4. *Diss.* Prior to Sept. 1917. *See also under* Colour Users.

DYEING AND CLEANING SUB-COMMITTEE (PROFITEERING ACTS).—*App.* jointly by S.C.P. and S.C.T., Oct. 1921. *Obj.* To report upon memorandum of National Federation of Dyers and Cleaners to B.T. *Repr.* S.C.P., W.O., business men, Labour, women. *Ref.* Cmd. 1361. *Diss.* May 1921.

DYEING, FINISHING, BLEACHING AND PRINTING, SUB-COMMITTEE (PROFITEERING ACTS).—*App.* by S.C.P., Nov. 1919, and incorporated in Dyes and Dye-stuffs Sub-Committee (q.v.), Dec. 1919. *Obj., Repr.* As with latter Committee. *Ref.* Cmd. 1371. *Diss.* May 1921.

DYES AND DYE-STUFFS SUB-COMMITTEE (PROFITEERING ACTS).—*App.* by S.C.T., Dec. 1919 (*see also* preceding entry). *Obj.* To investigate effect of trade combinations on prices, costs and supplies of drugs and on processes of textile bleaching, printing, &c. *Repr.* Parliament, B.T., S.C.P., S.C.T., W.O., employers, business men, Labour, technical and social experts. *Ref.* Cmd. 1370. *Diss.* May 1921.

DYES COMMISSIONER AND DEPARTMENT.—*App.* by B.T., June 1917, first as temporary, and then apparently as permanent, department. *Obj.* To deal with development and regulation of dye industry in co-operation with interests concerned, and, from Nov. 1918, to administer scheme of State assistance. *Repr.* Presumably official and expert. *Ref.* B.T.J., 21st June 1917 ; Cd. 9194, p. 5. *Still in existence at end of 1922.*

DYES, IMPORT LICENSING, SUB-COMMITTEE.—*App.* by Dyes Trade and Licensing Committee (q.v.) in 1918. *Obj.* To licence import of colours after the War, under scheme of post-war control. *Repr.* B.T. ; dye manufacturers and users (equal numbers). *Ref.* Cd. 9194, p. 5.

DYES, LOANS AND GRANTS ALLOCATION, COMMITTEE.—*App.* by the dye-making and using industries, at invitation of the B.T., in summer of 1918. *Obj.* To assist Dyes Department in allocation of State aid to dyemaking industry. *Repr.* B.T. ; persons of business and financial experience acceptable to, but not directly connected with, dyemaking and using industries. *Ref.* B.T.J., 20th June 1918, p. 760 ; Cd. 9194, p. 5. *Still in existence apparently at end of 1922.*

DYE-STUFFS, IMPORT LICENCES, COMMITTEE.—*App.* by B.T., about beginning of 1921, under Dye-stuffs (Import Regulation) Act, 1920. *Obj.* To advise B.T. on grant of licences to import prohibited dye-stuffs. *Repr.* Dye-stuff manufacturers and users, persons not concerned with dye-stuffs. *Ref.* P.G.A., 1920. *Apparently still in existence at end of 1922.* A Dye-Industries Development Committee similarly constituted was appointed under this Act to advise B.T.

DYE-STUFFS (MOULTON) SUB-COMMITTEE OF CHEMICAL PRODUCTS COMMITTEE.—*App.* by main Committee in autumn of 1914. *Obj.* To advise as to securing supplies of dye-stuffs, formerly imported from enemy countries. *Repr., Diss.* Presumably much as with main Committee (q.v.). *Ref.* Cd. 8336.

DYE-STUFFS, REPARATIONS, DISTRIBUTION, ADVISORY SUB-COMMITTEE.—*App.* by Colour Users' Association, with approval of B.T., about beginning of 1920. *Obj.* To advise Trade and Licensing Committee (q.v.) on distribution and other matters of interest to consumers of dye-stuffs. *Repr.* Colour users. *Ref.* B.T.J., 15th Jan. 1920, p. 71.

DYES, TRADE AND LICENSING, COMMITTEE.—*App.* by B.T. about end of 1918. *Obj.* To recommend colours, &c., of which production should be encouraged and (through Sub-Committee) decide upon and license imports after the War. *Repr.* B.T., dye, paint, &c., manufacturers, colour users. *Ref.* Cd. 9194, p. 5. *Still in existence at end of 1922.*

DYE USERS' PROVISIONAL COMMITTEE.—*App.* originally by representatives of dye and colour-using industries at Conference with B.T., Nov. 1914, and enlarged, Jan. 1915. *Obj.* To confer with B.T. as to scheme for establishing national dye-making industry on large scale. *Repr.* Industries using dyes, dye-stuffs and colours. *Ref.* B.T.J., 28th Jan., 4th Feb. 1915. *Diss.* Scheme adopted in 1915.

ECONOMISTS, COMMITTEE OF.—*App.* by B.T. in 1916. *Obj.* To consider probable state of industry after the War. *Repr.* Well-known economists. *Ref.* Cd. 9117, p. 3. *Diss.* About mid 1917.

ECONOMY.—*See* Cotton Manufacture.

ELECTRICAL CABLE INDUSTRY SUB-COMMITTEE (PROFITEERING ACTS).—*App.* by S.C.T., Sept. 1920. *Obj.* To investigate existence, and effects on supplies and prices, of combinations in making, or dealing in, electrical cables and materials. *Repr.* Parliament, S.C.P., Civil Service, business men, civil, electrical and mechanical engineers. *Ref.* Cmd. 1332. *Diss.* May 1921.

ELECTRICAL LAMP INDUSTRY SUB-COMMITTEE (PROFITEERING ACTS).—*App.* by S.C.T. in winter of 1919–20. *Obj.* To inquire into existence and effect on prices of combinations in the industry. *Repr.* S.C.T., S.C.P., M.L., employers, business men and others. *Ref.* Cmd. 622. *Diss.* Mar. 1920.

ELECTRICAL POWER SUPPLY COMMITTEE.—*App.* by B.T., Mar. 1917. *Obj.* To report on steps required to ensure adequate and economical supplies, especially for industries dependent on cheap power. *Repr.* Parliament, B.T., L.G.B., L.A.'s, electrical manufacture and supply, consumers, experts, Legal Profession. *Ref.* Cd. 9062. *Diss.* April 1918.

ELECTRICAL TRADES AFTER THE WAR, DEPARTMENTAL COMMITTEE.—*App.* by B.T., April 1916. *Obj.* To report upon position and necessary safeguards for the trades after the War. *Repr.* Various branches of these trades. *Ref.* Cd. 9072. *Diss.* April 1917.

ELECTRICITY ADVISORY COMMITTEE.—*App.* by Electricity Commissioners allowed under Electricity (Supply) Act, 1919. *Obj.* To advise and assist Commissioners in improvement and development of electricity supply. *Repr.* Joint Electricity Authorities (q.v.), Electricity Supply Undertakings, experts. *Ref.* P.G.A., 1919.

ELECTRICITY AUTHORITIES, JOINT.—*App.* by Electricity Commissioners provided for in Electricity (Supply) Act, 1919. *Obj.* To organize abundant and cheap supply of electricity in districts established under the Act. *Repr.* L.A.'s, Electricity Undertakings, large consumers of electricity and other interests. *Ref.* P.G.A., 1919.

ELECTRICITY COMMISSIONERS.—*App.* by B.T. under Electricity (Supply) Act, 1919. *Obj.* To carry out reorganization of supply of electricity, under general supervision of B.T. *Repr.* Persons of practical, commercial and scientific knowledge and business experience, including electrical supply. *Ref.* P.G.A., 1919.

EMPIRE COTTON, FLAX, GROWING.—*See* Cotton, Flax.

EMPLOYMENT EXCHANGES, ACCOMMODATION, JOINT COMMITTEE.—*App.* by B.T. and O.W. jointly, probably early in the War. *Obj.* To arrange extensions, &c. of premises. *Repr.* B.T., M.M., O.W. *Ref.* H.C., No. 132, 1918, p. 43.

ENEMY DEBTS CLEARING OFFICE AND ADVISORY COMMITTEE. —*App.* by B.T. in London, with branch in Germany, under Peace Treaties, about end of 1919. *Obj.* To deal generally with mutual obligations between British and ex-enemy nationals, and advise on such matters. *Repr.* Official and expert (Office), B.T., Public Trustee, Accountants, and others (Committee). *Ref.* B.T.J., 20th Nov. 1919, p. 614, 15th Jan. 1920, p. 70. For different enemy powers, *see under* Clearing.

ENEMY EXPORTS COMMITTEE.—*See* F.O.

ENEMY GOODS: EXHIBITION OF SAMPLES OF GERMAN AND AUSTRIAN GOODS FROM ABROAD; EXCHANGE MEETINGS OF BUYERS AND MANUFACTURERS.—These were organized by B.T. early in the War, the first meeting being held late in Sept. 1914 and the Exhibition opened about the beginning of that month. It was extended to cover many articles. The object of the Exhibition and Meetings was to assist British manufacturers to establish themselves in British and Imperial markets for goods formerly obtained from Germany and Austria. *See* B.T.J., 3rd Sept., 1st Oct. 1914, and subsequent issues.

ENEMY GOODS.—*See also* Catalogues, German.

ENEMY SUPPLIES RESTRICTION DEPARTMENT.—*App.*, in connexion with B.T. and W.T.D., probably between spring of 1915 and summer of 1917. *Obj.* To restrict, by purchase or otherwise, supplies reaching enemy countries from Holland, Scandinavia, and elsewhere. *Repr.* Official and expert. *Ref.* Cmd. 1368, p. 106; Cd. 8741, p. 9. *Diss.* By Mar. 1920.

ENGINEERING TRADES AFTER THE WAR DEPARTMENTAL COMMITTEE.—*App.* by B.T., Mar. 1916, as Joint Committee for Iron, Steel and Engineering, and reconstituted for Engineering only, July 1916. *Obj.* To consider position and necessary safeguards of trades after the War. *Repr.* Prominent engineering and other employers. *Ref.* Cd. 9073. *Diss.* Mar. 1917.

ENLISTMENTS.—*See* Railwaymen.

EXCHANGE MEETINGS.—*See* Enemy Goods.

EXHIBITIONS.—*See* Catalogues, German; Enemy Goods.

EXPLOSIVES, HIGH, COMMITTEE (LORD MOULTON'S COMMITTEE).—*App.* by B.T. late in 1914. *Obj.* To consider methods of securing adequate supplies of high explosives. *Repr.* Parliament, B.T., W.O., H.O., M.M. (later). *Ref.* Cd. 8029, p. 4. *Diss.* Transferred to M.M. in summer of 1915, becoming eventually Explosives Department.

EXPLOSIVES, STORAGE ON COAL SHIPS, COMMITTEE.—*App.* by B.T. in 1918. *Obj.* To inquire into storage of explosives on ships carrying coal. *Repr.* Not stated. *Ref.* Cmd. 278, p. 2.

EXPLOSIVES SUB-COMMITTEE (PROFITEERING ACTS).—*App.* by S.C.T., Sept. 1920. *Obj.* To inquire into existence and effects on supplies and prices of combinations of ammunition and explosives' makers. *Repr.* Parliament, Adm., W.O., M.M., Civil Service, S.C.T., business men, scientific and social experts. *Ref.* Cmd. 1347. *Diss.* May 1921.

EXPORT CREDITS ADVISORY COMMITTEE.—*App.* by B.T., in or after Aug. 1920, under Overseas Trade (Credit and Insurance) Act. *Obj.* To advise B.T. in granting credits and insurances under the Act. *Repr.* Presumably business, financial and insurance experts. *Ref.* P.G.A., 1920. *Still in existence at end of 1922.*

EXPORT CREDITS DEPARTMENT.—*App.* by B.T., with office in City of London, Sept. 1919. *Obj.* To carry out actual administration of Government export credits scheme. *Repr.* Business and other experts. *Ref.* T., 8th Sept. 1919, p. 17.

EXPORT SUB-COMMITTEE.—*App.* by Advisory Committee on Commercial Intelligence (pre-war), Jan. 1917. *Obj.* To report upon desirability of, and possible action by B.T. in encouraging, associations of manufacturers for pushing industries in export markets and appointing travelling investigators. *Repr.* The Advisory Committee. *Ref.* Cd. 8815, pp. 7–8. *Diss.* By early 1918.

EXPORTS ASSOCIATIONS, MANUFACTURERS.—*App.* by manufacturers in various industries, from winter of 1917. *Obj.* To develop industries concerned in various export markets on lines suggested by Export Sub-Committee (q.v.), in co-operation with B.T. and possibly with Government assistance. *Repr.* Manufacturers and experts in industries concerned. *Ref.* B.T.J., 21st Feb. 1918.

EXPORTS COMMITTEE.—*App.* by B.T. about Mar. 1917. *Obj.* To prepare scheme for reorganizing export trade, in relation to changes due to import restrictions and shortage of tonnage. *Repr.* Government Departments chiefly concerned. *Ref.* Cd. 8741, p. 5. *Diss.* About June 1917 (work not proceeded with, as scheme proved unnecessary).

EXPORTS CONSULTATIVE COUNCIL.—Reference without details in B.T.J., 3rd April 1919, the council to be known henceforth as Exports Restriction Department.

FABRIC GLOVES AND FINE COTTON SPINNING INDUSTRY COMMITTEE.—*App.* by B.T., July 1922. *Obj.* To investigate influence of import of German gloves and fabrics on fine cotton spinning industry of U.K. *Repr.* Membership as with following Committee. *Ref.* H.M.S.O., 1922. *Diss.* July 1922.

FABRIC GLOVES AND GLOVE FABRICS COMMITTEE.—*App.* by B.T., under Part II of Safeguarding of Industries Act, Nov. 1921. *Obj.* To hear complaints as to import and sale of German gloves and fabrics, in connexion with conditions of Exchanges. *Repr.* Civil Service, commercial and business men. *Ref.* H.M.S.O., 1922. *Diss.* Jan. 1922.

FARRIERY TRADE COMBINATIONS SUB-COMMITTEE (PROFIT-EERING ACTS).—*App.* by S.C.T., Oct. 1919. *Obj.* To inquire into alleged combine. *Repr.* B.T., S.C.T., S.C.P., M.L., employers, Labour. *Ref.* Cmd. 540. *Diss.* Dec. 1919.

FERTILIZERS.—*See* Sulphuric Acid.

FINANCIAL FACILITIES FOR BRITISH TRADE, COMMITTEE.— *App.* by B.T., July 1916. *Obj.* To prepare scheme for providing financial facilities after the War for British trade, especially for large overseas contracts. *Repr.* B.T., bankers, industry, commerce. *Ref.* Cd. 8346. *Diss.* Aug. 1916.

FINANCIAL RISKS COMMITTEE.—*See* M.R.

FIRE IN PASSENGER SHIPS.—*See* Oil Fuel.

FISH AND OIL, NORWEGIAN AND ICELANDIC PURCHASE COM-MITTEE.—*App.* by B.T. about end of 1915. *Obj.* To purchase Norwegian and Icelandic fish and oil and prevent sale to Germany. *Repr.* B.T., B.A., trawler owners. *Ref.* Cmd. 585, p. 110. *Diss.* Work taken over in 1917 by Restriction of Enemy Supplies Department of M.B.

FISHERY.—*See* Coal Supplies.

FISH, PRESERVED, IMPORT RESTRICTION, COMMITTEE.—*App.* by B.T. in consultation with F.C., Mar. 1917, being sometimes called Fish Trade Committee. *Obj.* To advise Imports Restrictions Department in regard to prohibited classes of fish. *Repr.* Not stated. *Ref.* B.T.J., 15th Mar. 1917.

FISH TRADE COMMITTEE (PROFITEERING ACTS).—*App.* by S.C.T. in autumn of 1919. *Obj.* To inquire into alleged increase of prices by rings and combinations. *Repr.* S.C.T., employers, Labour, social experts. *Ref.* Cmd. 514.

FIXED RETAIL PRICES SUB-COMMITTEE (PROFITEERING ACTS). —*App.* by S.C.T., late in winter of 1919–20. *Obj.* To report upon extent and results of fixing minimum retail prices by manufacturers. *Repr.* S.C.T., S.C.P., M.H., M.L., manufacturers, business men, Labour, social experts. *Ref.* Cmd. 662. *Diss.* End Mar. 1920.

FLAX GROWING, EMPIRE, COMMITTEE.—*App.* by B.T., Feb. 1919. *Obj.* To investigate question of increasing flax supplies in Empire. *Ref.* B.T., B.A., Flax Control Board, Imperial Institute, Dominions, India, Linen Industry. *Ref.* Cmd. 281. For Flax, *see also* M.M., W.O.

FOOD SUPPLY OF THE UNITED KINGDOM, PHYSIOLOGY (WAR) COMMITTEE, USUALLY CALLED THE FOOD (WAR) COMMITTEE, OF THE ROYAL SOCIETY.—*App.* by the Society, at request of B.T., in 1916. *Obj.* To report upon food supply of U.K. before and during the

War and suggest economies. *Repr.* The Society, B.T., B.A., D.C., L.G.B., industrial, scientific and economic research. *Ref.* Cd. 8421. *Diss.* Dec. 1916.

FORESTRY CORPS.—Sent from Dominions and U.S.A. to assist in felling, &c., British timber : *see* Cmd. 325, p. 205.

FRUIT, IMPORT LICENCES, COMMITTEE.—*App.* by B.T., Mar. 1916. *Obj.* To grant licences for imports of dried, &c., fruits, from outside British Empire. *Repr.* B.T., importers, traders.

FRUIT PRICES SUB-COMMITTEE (PROFITEERING ACTS).—*App.* by S.C.T., Feb. 1920. *Obj.* To inquire into existence of combine and effects on fruit prices. *Repr.* S.C.T., M.H., employers and others. *Ref.* Cmd. 878. *Diss.* July 1920.

FUEL AND LIGHTING COMMITTEES, LOCAL.—*App.* by L.A.'s, from July 1918, under Household Fuel and Lighting Order, 1918. *Obj.* To decide appeals by householders, from Local Fuel Overseers, for allowances of coal, gas and electricity. *Repr.* L.A.'s concerned, coal merchants and dealers, gas and electricity undertakings and, at option of L.A.'s or Coal Controller, Railway, Canal and Harbour Companies.

FURNITURE SUB-COMMITTEE (PROFITEERING ACTS).—*App.* by S.C.P., Nov. 1919. *Obj.* To investigate prices and profits of furniture at all stages. *Repr.* Furniture manufacturers, builders, Labour, women. *Ref.* Cmd. 983. *Diss.* Sept. 1920.

GAS APPARATUS SUB-COMMITTEE (PROFITEERING ACTS).— *App.* by S.C.P., June 1920. *Obj.* To investigate charges for sale and hire of apparatus. *Repr.* Business men, technical engineers, Labour, women, S.C.P. *Ref.* Cmd. 1381. *Diss.* May 1921.

GAS INCOMBUSTIBLES COMMITTEE.—*App.* by B.T., Jan. 1921. *Obj.* To inquire into limitation of incombustible constituents in gas. *Repr.* Legal Profession, chemical and engineering experts. *Ref.* Cmd. 1492. *Diss.* Aug. 1921.

GAS.—*See under* Cotton Manufacture, and Cabinet (Traction), P.C. (Charges).

GATTIE COMMITTEE.—*See* M.T.

GERMAN REPARATIONS RECOVERY COMMITTEE (OR COM-MITTEES).—*App.* by B.T., under German Reparations Recovery Act, Mar. 1921. *Obj.* To recommend relaxations of Act for appropriating part of purchase price of imported German goods towards reparations. *Repr.* Persons of commercial, financial and industrial experience. *Ref.* P.G.A., 1921.

GLASS BOTTLES, JARS, AND SCIENTIFIC GLASSWARE SUB-COMMITTEE (PROFITEERING ACTS).—*App.* by S.C.T., April 1920. *Obj.* To inquire into existence and effects of combinations in these trades. *Repr.* S.C.T., Employers, Labour. *Ref.* Cmd. 1066, 1385. *Diss.* May 1921.

GLOVES.—*See* Fabric Gloves.

HARDWARE (IMPORT PRICES) COMMITTEE.—*App.* by Import Restrictions Department in winter of 1917–18. *Obj.* To draw up scales of maximum prices for imported articles. *Repr.* Members of hardware trade. *Ref.* B.T.J., 21st Mar. 1918.

HIGH EXPLOSIVES.—*See* Explosives.

HOME TRADE DISTRICT TRANSPORT COMMITTEES.—*App.* by B.T. during or shortly after the War in various districts. *Obj.* To organize attempt to relieve congestion on railways resulting from diversion to them of coastwise traffic, and in 1919 to administer Government Scheme to revive coasting trade. *Repr.* B.T., Railway Companies, other interests concerned. *Ref.* B.T.J., 21st Aug. 1919, p. 226. *Diss.* End 1920.

HORSE TRANSPORT ADVISORY INTER-DEPARTMENTAL COMMITTEE.—*App.* by B.T., June 1917. *Obj.* To assist Controller of Horse Transport in controlling use and feeding of horses for urban use, and take census of horses. *Repr.* Government Departments concerned, horse-owners. *Ref.* B.T.J., 21st Mar. 1918. *Diss.* April 1919.

HORSES, UTILIZATION AND FEEDING, COMMITTEE.—*App.* by B.T., in consultation with other Departments concerned, Mar. 1917. *Obj.* To advise on utilization of horses, in U.K., especially for the Army, and means of securing economy in feeding. *Repr.* B.A., B.T., W.O. and other Departments concerned, Railway Companies. *Ref.* B.T.J., 29th Mar. 1917.

HORSES, UTILIZATION, LOCAL COMMITTEES.—*App.* by B.T., from Mar. 1917, in forty large towns. *Obj.* To supervise utilization, &c. of local horses. *Repr.* Not stated. *Ref.* H.C., No. 132, 1918, p. 27.

HOTEL MEALS.—*See* M.F.

ICELANDIC FISH, ETC.—*See* Fish and Oil.

IMPORTS CONSULTATIVE COUNCIL.—*App.* by B.T., Mar. 1919. *Obj.* To examine revision of lists of import prohibitions, and arrange transitional imports policy for period of change-over from war to peace. *Repr.* Parliament, B.T., Tre., manufacturers, merchants, retail distributers, Chambers of Commerce, F.B.I., and similar bodies, J.I.C.'s, Co-operative Societies, T.U.'s. *Ref.* B.T.J., 27th Mar. 1919, p. 402. *Diss.* June 1919.

IMPORT RESTRICTION DEPARTMENT.—*App.* by B.T., Mar. 1916. *Obj.* To carry out Government policy of prohibition and restriction for all goods except sugar and paper, specially for saving of tonnage, and, after Armistice, protection of home industries. *Repr.* Official, assisted by Advisory Trade Committees (*see* Fruit, Oranges, Tobacco, Woods and Stones (Import Licences Committees). *Ref.* B.T.J., 23rd Mar. 1916 ; 13th Nov. 1919, p. 609. *Diss.* Amalgamated with Export Licence Department as single Department under Industries and Manufactures Department of B.T., Oct. or Nov. 1919.

IMPORT RESTRICTION INTER-DEPARTMENTAL COMMITTEE.— *App.* in 1917 or earlier (appointing body not stated, but possibly B.T.). *Obj.* To decide questions affecting import restrictions. *Repr.* Government Departments concerned. *Ref.* H.C., No. 132, 1918, p. 25.

INDUSTRIAL ASSURANCE COMMITTEE.—*App.* by B.T. in summer of 1919. *Obj.* To report upon business of Industrial Assurance Societies and Collecting Companies and changes in law. *Repr.* Parliament, B.T.,

Legal Profession, Chief Registrar of Friendly Societies, Government Actuary, Government Controller of Companies, Business Men, Labour. *Ref.* Cmd. 614. *Diss.* Feb. 1920.

INDUSTRIAL (WAR INQUIRIES) BRANCH.—*App.* by B.T., Aug. 1914. *Obj.* To watch and report upon state of industry during the War. *Repr.* Largely expert (economists and others). *Ref.* Cd. 8912. *Diss.* Absorbed into General Economic Department early in 1918, on reorganization of B.T.

INDUSTRY AFTER THE WAR.—*See* Economists.

INSURANCE INTELLIGENCE OFFICE, DEPARTMENT.—*App.* by B.T., prior to June 1917. *Ref.* without details, Cd. 8741, p. 6 (Department), 8912 (Office).

INSURANCE OF BRITISH SHIPS' CARGOES COMMITTEE.—*See* War Risks. More commonly known as War Risks Insurance Committee (q.v.).

INSURANCE.—*See also under* Aircraft, Air Risks, Industrial Assurance, Under-writing, War Risks.

IRON AND STEEL PRODUCTS SUB-COMMITTEE (PROFITEERING ACTS).—*App.* by S.C.T., Feb. 1920. *Obj.* To report on existence and effects on prices of combines in cut-nail, horse-nail, and bolt and nut, trades. *Repr.* S.C.T., Civil Service, business men, technical engineers, Labour. *Ref.* Cmd. 1268. *Diss.* Mar. 1921.

IRON AND STEEL TRADES AFTER THE WAR, DEPARTMENTAL COMMITTEE.—*App.* by B.T., Mar. 1916, as combined Committee with Engineering, and reappointed as above, July 1916. *Obj.* To consider position of industry, and safeguards necessary, after the War. *Repr.* Employers and workpeople in the industry, iron and steel users. *Ref.* Cd. 9071. *Diss.* June 1917.

(In Aug. 1916 a Conference of firms in the Iron, Steel and Allied (Engineering, &c.) Trades appointed an Iron and Allied Trades Post-war Committee to prepare scheme for a strong central organization of these industries to deal with post-war problems, with special reference to the Empire. *See* T., Dec. 1916.)

IRON MINERS.—*See* H.O.

KEY INDUSTRIES.—*See* Safeguarding of Industries.

KITCHENS, EMERGENCY, COMMITTEE.—*App.* by B.T., April–May, 1921. *Obj.* To deal with emergency caused by coal strike, where small householders are or may be unable to secure coal for cooking food. *Repr.* Official and expert. *Ref.* L.G., May 1921, p. 230. *Diss.* Later in 1921.

LACE INDUSTRY.—*See* Coal Rationing.

LAUNDERERS' COMBINES, SUB-COMMITTEE (PROFITEERING ACTS).—*App.* by S.C.T. in winter of 1919–20. *Obj.* To investigate existence of combines and effect upon prices. *Repr.* Employers, Labour, Anti-Sweating League, women, social experts. *Ref.* Cmd. 903. *Diss.* July 1920.

LIGHT CASTINGS SECTIONAL COMMITTEE (PROFITEERING ACTS).—*App.* by Building Materials Sub-Committee (q.v.), Feb. 1920.

Obj. To investigate prices, costs and profits, and existence and effects of trusts and combines, in Light Castings Industry. *Repr.* S.C.P., business men, architects, surveyors, Labour, social experts. *Ref.* Cmd. 1200. *Diss.* Feb. 1921.

LONDON SHIP-OWNERS AND TRANSPORT WORKERS MILITARY SERVICE COMMITTEE.—*See under* Port Labour.

MARGARINE.—*See* Oils.

MATCH CONTROL ADMINISTRATIVE COMMITTEE.—*App.* by Tobacco and Matches Control Board, Sept. 1917. *Obj.* To carry out scheme for pooling output and regulating distribution. *Repr.* Match manufacturers and possibly others. *Ref.* B.T.J., 13th Sept. 1917. *See also under* Tobacco.

MATCH PRICES ADVISORY COMMITTEE.—*App.* by Tobacco and Matches Control Board, Sept. 1917. *Obj.* To advise on fixing of wholesale and retail prices. *Repr.* Match manufacturers, wholesale and retail tobacconists, provincial grocers, oil and colour trade, London Chamber of Commerce. *Ref.* B.T.J., 27th Sept. 1917. *Diss.* Apparently in same month on completion of schedule of prices.

MATCH PRICES SUB-COMMITTEE (PROFITEERING ACTS).—*App.* by S.C.P., Nov. 1919. *Obj.* To inquire into conditions and remedies for present prices. *Repr.* Manufacturers, retailers, social experts and others. *Repr.* Cmd. 924. *Diss.* June 1920.

MEAT SUB-COMMITTEE (PROFITEERING ACTS).—*App.* by S.C.T., Jan. 1920. *Obj.* To investigate trusts, combines and price agreements in meat trades as affecting British consumers. *Repr.* S.C.T., B.T., M.H., Public Health Service, business men, Labour and others. *Ref.* Cmd. 1057, 1556. *Diss.* Mar. 1921.

MEAT SUPPLIES INTER-DEPARTMENTAL COMMITTEE.—*App.* by B.T., April 1919. *Obj.* To report on means of securing adequate supplies at reasonable prices for U.K., with due regard to British and Imperial markets, and protection from foreign domination. *Repr.* B.T., B.A., C.O., M.F., the Dominions, meat traders. *Ref.* Cmd. 456. *Diss.* Sept. 1919.

MEAT TRADERS' ASSOCIATION, FEDERATION OF, ADVISORY COMMITTEE.—*App.*, at instigation of B.T., at outbreak of war. *Obj.* To recommend to B.T. reasonable maximum prices for meat under conditions produced by outbreak of war. *Repr.* Associations of Meat Traders. *Ref.* L.G., Sept., 1914.

MERCANTILE MARINE RATIONING.—*See* M.F.

MERCANTILE MARINE (SEAMEN'S EFFECTS) COMMITTEE.—*App.* by B.T., April 1915. *Obj.* To consider claims, and make grants, for loss by hostile operations of effects of mercantile seamen and fishermen who cannot otherwise obtain compensation or help. *Repr.* Government, B.T., Legal Profession, Marine and War Risks Insurance. *Ref.* B.T.J., 29th April 1915.

MERCANTILE MARINE, STANDARD UNIFORM, COMMITTEE.—*App.* by B.T., Mar. 1917. *Obj.* To advise on adoption of standard uniform for mercantile marine (made desirable by events of war and recommended by Adm.). *Repr.* B.T., Adm., Chamber of Shipping, ship-owners, officers of mercantile marine. *Ref.* Cd. 9030. *Diss.* Dec. 1917.

MERCANTILE MARINE TRAINING SCHEME.—*See* M.S.

MERCHANDIZE MARKS COMMITTEE.—*App.* by B.T., Nov. 1919. *Obj.* To report upon amendment of Acts as to indications of origin, value of National Trade Marks and need for international action to prevent false marking. *Repr.* Parliament, B.T., Board of Customs and Excise, Legal Profession, agricultural, manufacturing and commercial interests, with special Irish representative, Co-operative Societies. *Ref.* Cmd. 760. *Diss.* June 1920.

METAL BEDSTEADS.—*See under* Prices, Investigation.

MILK SUB-COMMITTEE (PROFITEERING ACTS).—*App.* by S.C.T., Jan. 1920. *Obj.* To investigate effects of trusts and combines on prices of milk and milk products. *Repr.* Parliament, S.C.T., B.A.(Sc.), M.H., L.A.'s, agriculture, business men, Labour. *Ref.* Cmd. 1102. *Diss.* Later in 1920.

MINERS' WELFARE CENTRAL COMMITTEE.—*App.* by Secretary of Mines in 1921 under Mining Industry Act, 1920. *Obj.* To allocate funds for miners' welfare provided under the Act. *Repr.* Parliament, Mines Department, coal-owners, miners, medical experts, with assessors representing B.E., M.H., S.B.H. *Ref.* Mines Department Report for 1921 (H.M.S.O., 1922), p. 19. Presumably *Permanent.*

MINERS' WELFARE, DISTRICT COMMITTEES.—*App.* jointly by coal-owners and miners in various districts at invitation of Mines Department, Oct.–Dec. 1921. *Obj.* To advise Central Committee on local allocation of funds. *Repr.* Coal-owners and miners in districts. *Ref.* As in preceding entry. Possibly *Permanent.*

MINING EDUCATION AT UNIVERSITIES SUB-COMMITTEE.—*App.* by University Grants Committee (*see* Tre.), after consultation with Miners' Welfare Central Committee, in 1922. *Obj.* To advise on available facilities and means of giving financial assistance. *Repr.* University Grants Committee. *Ref.* Mines Department Report, 1922 (H.M.S.O., 1923), p. 15. *Diss.* About end 1922.

MINING INDUSTRY, COAL AND COAL INDUSTRY ADVISORY COMMITTEE.—*App.* by B.T. about June 1921, under Mining Industry Act, 1920 (sec. 4). *Obj.* To advise and assist B.T. in exercising powers relating to coal mines under the Act. *Repr.* Employers and workpeople in coal mining and in industry generally, mining engineers and agents, coal exporters and merchants, general commerce, Co-operators, medical and scientific experts. *Ref.* P.G.A., 1920. *Permanent.*

MINING INDUSTRY, METALLIFEROUS MINING ADVISORY COMMITTEE.—*App., Obj.,* &c. as with Coal Industry (q.v.).

MINING INDUSTRY, OTHER ADVISORY COMMITTEES.—The Act empowers B.T. to appoint Committees, after consultation with interests concerned, in respect of ' other ' powers of B.T. under the Act.

MOTOR FUEL, SUB-COMMITTEE (PROFITEERING ACTS).—*App.* by S.C.P., Nov. 1919. *Obj.* To investigate costs, prices and profits of motor fuels. *Repr.* B.T., Petroleum Executive, manufacturing and technical engineers, traders, business men generally, Legal Profession, Labour. *Ref.* Cmd. 597, 1119. *Diss.* Nov. 1920.

MOTOR SPIRIT (IRELAND) CONTROL COMMITTEE.—*App.* by B.T., Aug. 1917. *Obj.* To advise Petrol Controller on distribution of spirit in Ireland for civil and industrial needs. *Repr.* L.G.B.(I.), D.A.T.I., Royal Irish Constabulary, Dublin Metropolitan Police, Irish Command (Army). *Ref.* B.T.J., 23rd Aug. 1917.

MOULTON COMMITTEE.—*See* Explosives, High.

MOULTON SUB-COMMITTEE.—*See* Dye-stuffs Sub-Committee.

NAILS (CUT AND HORSE).—*See* Iron and Steel Products.

NON-FERROUS METALS (APPLICATIONS) COMMITTEE.—*App.* by B.T. about July 1918. *Obj.* To hear applications under Rule 6 under Non-Ferrous Metals Industry Act, 1918. *Repr.* Parliament, Legal Profession, Chambers of Commerce, F.B.I. *Ref.* B.T.J., 4th July 1918.

NON-FERROUS METALS (LICENCES) COMMITTEE.—*App.* by B.T. in 1918. *Obj.* To examine and report to B.T. on all applications for licences under Non-Ferrous Metals Industry Act, 1918. *Repr.* Parliament, Legal Profession. *Ref.* P.G.A., 1918. Presumably *Permanent.*

NON-FERROUS METAL TRADES AFTER THE WAR, DEPARTMENTAL COMMITTEE.—*App.* by B.T. in 1916 or 1917. *Obj.* To consider position and safeguards for these trades after the War. *Repr.* London Metal Exchange ; manufacturers in the various trades. *Ref.* Cd. 8916. *Diss.* Presumably in 1917 or 1918.

NON-FERROUS MINING INDUSTRY, DEPARTMENTAL COMMITTEE.—*App.* by B.T., Aug. 1919. *Obj.* To report upon condition and economic possibilities of industry in U.K. *Repr.* Parliament, Legal Profession, mine-owners, mining experts, Transvaal Gold Mining Industry, Labour. *Ref.* Cmd. 652. *Diss.* Mar. 1920.

NORWEGIAN FISH, ETC.—*See* Fish and Oil.

NUTS.—*See* Iron and Steel Products.

OIL FUEL COMMITTEE.—*App.* by B.T., Jan. 1920. *Obj.* To advise on means of preventing danger of fires on passenger ships burning oil fuel. *Repr.* H.O., shipbuilders, naval architects, scientific experts. *Ref.* Cmd. 944. *Diss.* Aug. 1920.

OILS, FATS AND MARGARINE TRADES SUB-COMMITTEE (PROFITEERING ACTS).—*App.* by S.C.T., Feb. 1920. *Obj.* To inquire into existence, and effects on prices and supplies, of combines and agreements in these trades. *Repr.* S.C.T., Civil Service, business men, medical profession and others. *Ref.* Cmd. 982.

OILS.—*See also* Fish and Oil.

ORANGES (IMPORT LICENCES) ADVISORY TRADE COMMITTEE. —*App.* by B.T., July 1916. *Obj.* To assist in organizing scheme for import of oranges from foreign countries in specially licensed ships. *Repr.* Importers and others interested. *Ref.* B.T.J., 3rd Aug. 1916. *Diss.* Oct. 1916, on withdrawal of restrictions on import of oranges.

PAPER CONTROL.—The Paper Controller was appointed by B.T. on 9th Mar. 1918, with necessary staff and Advisory Committee (q.v.), to take over general control of paper production and distribution from Royal Commission on Paper Supplies (q.v.). The Control was abolished in 1919. *See* B.T.J., 11th April 1918, p. 430.

PAPER CONTROL ADVISORY COMMITTEE.—*App.* by B.T., on appointment of Paper Controller, Mar. 1918. *Obj.* To advise generally on control of paper. *Repr.* Consisted of members of dissolved Royal Commission on Paper Supplies (q.v.). *Ref.* B.T.J., 11th April 1918, p. 430. *Diss.* In 1919.

PAPER IMPORT RESTRICTION DEPARTMENT.—*App.* by B.T. during the War. *Obj.* To carry out the administration work of import restriction. *Repr.* Official and expert. *Ref.* B.T.J., 4th Sept. 1919, p. 298. *Diss.* Sept. 1919.

PAPER INDUSTRY COMMITTEE.—*App.* by B.T., April 1919. *Obj.* To report on condition of industry, with special reference to restriction of manufacture in Britain and unemployment owing to competition of imported paper. *Repr.* Government, B.T., paper trade, newspaper proprietors, printing industry and others interested. *Ref.* B.T.J., 10th April 1919, p. 466. *Diss.* May 1919.

PAPER MILLS, COAL AND TRANSPORT ECONOMIES, COMMITTEE. —*App.* by Paper Controller, April 1918. *Obj.* To report upon coal consumption in mills and economies in coal and transport. *Repr.* Paper Control, paper manufacturers, coal trade, transport trades. *Ref.* B.T.J., 25th April 1918.

PAPER SUPPLIES, ROYAL COMMISSION.—*App.* by Royal Warrant, Feb. 1916, and reconstituted June 1917. *Obj.* Originally to arrange and grant licences for imports of paper and materials as determined by B.T. and, later, to carry out restriction of imports and equitable distribution of supplies. *Repr.* Parliament, Stationery Office, paper manufacturers and users. *Ref.* B.T.J., 21st Feb. 1916. *Diss.* 8th Mar. 1918, members forming Paper Control Advisory Committee (q.v.).

PATENTS, DESIGNS AND TRADE MARKS, AVOIDANCE OF ENEMY ALIEN, TRIBUNAL.—*App.* by B.T. under Patents (Temporary) Rules Order of 21st Aug. 1914. *Obj.* To inquire into claims for avoidance and suspension of patents, referred to them by B.T. *Repr.* Not stated. *Ref.* Statutory Rules and Orders, 1914, vol. iii, No. 1256; B.T.J., 24th Sept. 1914.

PETROL CONTROL COMMITTEE.—*App.* by B.T., April 1916. *Obj.* To organize adequate supplies for essential needs and control use for other purposes. *Repr.* B.T., M.M., business interests, prominent public men. *Ref.* B.T.J., 27th April 1916. *Diss.* By July 1917, being absorbed into Petrol Control Department.

PETROL CONTROL COMMITTEE (IRELAND).—*App.* by Petrol Control Committee in first half of 1917. *Obj.* To deal with Irish applications for petrol and issue of licences. *Repr.* Presumably as with Petrol Control Committee (q.v.). *Ref.* B.T.J., 8th Feb. 1918. *Diss.* Apparently replaced by Motor Spirit (Ireland) Control Committee (q.v.), Aug. 1917.

PETROL CONTROL DEPARTMENT.—*App.* by B.T., Aug. 1916. *Obj.* To control distribution of petrol for industrial and other civil purposes. *Repr.* Official and expert. *Ref.* B.T.J., 5th July 1917. *Diss.* Nov. 1919.

PETROL SUPPLIES PRIORITY SUB-COMMITTEE.—*App.* by Petrol Control Committee, May or June 1916. *Obj.* To regulate distribution of petrol according to classifications of priority. *Repr.* Chief petrol distributing organizations. *Ref.* B.T.J., 8th June 1916.

PETROL.—*See also* Motor Spirit (Ireland).

PHOSPHATES AND POTASH.—*See* Potash.

PIPES AND CASTINGS SUB-COMMITTEE (PROFITEERING ACTS). —*App.* by S.C.T., Oct. 1920. *Obj.* To inquire into existence, and effects on supplies and prices of combine in these trades (except light castings), and in production of materials for them. *Repr.* S.C.T., M.M., business men, technical engineers and others. *Ref.* Cmd. 1217. *Diss.* Mar. 1921.

PIT TIMBER.—*See* H.O.

PITWOOD DISTRICT ASSOCIATIONS.—*App.* locally at instigation of District Committees in or after 1917, seven being appointed by end of year. *Obj.* To develop supplies of home-grown timber to counteract reduced imports. *Repr.* Colliery owners, and possibly others interested. *Ref.* B.T.J., 31st Jan. 1918.

PITWOOD, DISTRICT, COMMITTEES.—*App.* by Coal Controller in 1917 in eight districts. *Obj.* To organize supplies of home pitwood and secure formation of District Pitwood Associations. *Repr.* C.M.D., H.O., coal-owners and others. *Ref.* B.T.J., 31st Jan. 1918.

PORT LABOUR COMMITTEES.—*App.* by B.T. in 1915 or 1916 for chief ports in U.K. and transferred to M.L. in 1917. *Obj.* To conduct survey of port labour and issue of certificates of exemption from military service. *Repr.* B.T., M.L. (later), Port Authorities and Employers, T.U.'s. *Ref.* B.T.J., 13th June 1918, p. 749.

(In London the work was apparently carried out by the London Ship-owners and Transport Workers Military Service Committee, presumably a joint body appointed at request of B.T. or M.L.)

PORTS CONGESTION COMMITTEE.—*App.* by B.T., Feb. 1915. *Obj.* To recommend to Dock Authorities measures for dealing with congestion at ports and securing efficient handling of traffic. *Repr.* Dock and Railway Authorities, shipping industry. *Ref.* B.T.J., 11th Feb. 1915. *Diss.* May 1915.

(For Committee appointed by P.M., *see* Cabinet.)

POTASH DISTRIBUTION COMMITTEE.—*App.* by B.T., in conjunction with B.A., Aug. 1919. *Obj.* To direct sales by British Potash Company of recent supplies of German potash salts suitable for agriculture. *Repr.* B.T., B.A., B.A.(Sc.), D.A.T.I., trade interests involved. *Ref.* J.B.A., Sept. 1919 ; Cmd. 773, pp. lxix–lxx. *Diss.* April 1920.

(Sometimes called Phosphates and Potash Distribution Committee.)

POTATOES SUB-COMMITTEE OF THE FOOD (WAR) COMMITTEE OF THE ROYAL SOCIETY.—*App.* by Committee in 1918 or late in

1917. *Obj.* To investigate the composition of potatoes grown in U.K. *Repr.* The Committee and others. *Ref.* J.B.A., Oct. 1918.

POTTERY SUB-COMMITTEE (PROFITEERING ACTS).—*App.* by S.C.P., Nov. 1919. *Obj.* To investigate prices, costs and profits in production and distribution of pottery. *Repr.* Parliament, S.C.P., business men, pottery trade employers, Labour, women, consumers. *Ref.* Cmd. 1360. *Diss.* May 1921.

PRICES, INVESTIGATION OF, STANDING COMMITTEE.—*App.* by Profiteering Acts Central Committee (q.v.), about Oct. 1919. *Obj.* To investigate prices, costs and profits at all stages. *Repr.* Parliament, B.T., M.F., M.L., manufacturers, accountants, Labour, women, consumers, economic experts. *Ref.* P.G.A., 1919 ; Cmd. 607, 1047. *Diss.* Termination of Acts.

(The Committee usually delegated investigation of prices in particular trades to Sub-Committees, which are dealt with elsewhere. Certain trades were, however, dealt with by the Committee as a whole, e.g. Biscuit Trade (Cmd. 856), Boot and Shoe, Standard, Scheme (Cmd. 592), Metal Bedsteads (Cmd. 607).)

PRICES OF COMMODITIES, WAR INCREASES, DEPARTMENTAL COMMITTEE.—*App.* by B.T., June 1916. *Obj.* To investigate causes of increase in articles of common consumption during the War and suggest remedies. *Repr.* Parliament, Industry, Agriculture, Railways, Labour, Women, Economists. *Ref.* Cd. 8358, 8483. *Diss.* Dec. 1916.

PRIZE CLAIMS COMMITTEE.—*See* Cabinet.

PRODUCTION, COMMITTEE ON.—*See* next entry.

PRODUCTION IN ENGINEERING AND SHIPBUILDING ESTAB-LISHMENTS COMMITTEE (COMMONLY KNOWN AS COMMITTEE ON PRODUCTION).—*App.* by the Government, 4th Feb. 1915, originally as Tre. Committee, but subsequently attached to B.T. and then to M.L., being reorganized and reappointed, May 1917. *Obj.* Originally to report on best means of making labour power in engineering and ship-building most available, and, from end of Feb. 1915, to act as tribunal to deal with disputes on Government work. *Repr.* Prominent men of business and others, with representatives of employers, workpeople and other ' important ' persons from May 1917. *Ref.* L.G., Mar. 1915 ; Cmd. 70, p. 2 ; Cole, pp. 61–6, 162. *Diss.* Absorbed into Wages and Arbitration Department of M.L., Dec. 1918, and reappointed as the Interim Court of Arbitration (*see* M.L.) under Wages (Temporary Regulation) Act, 1918.

PROFITEERING ACTS, CENTRAL COMMITTEE.—*App.* by B.T., with power to appoint Sub-Committees, under Profiteering Act, 1919, Sept. 1919, and subsequently divided into three Standing Committees on Complaints, Prices and Trusts (*see* under these heads). *Obj.* To organize and supervise inquiries under the Act, and investigate profiteering by persons other than retail traders. *Repr.* Parliament, B.T., B.A., M.F., M.L., Chambers of Commerce, business men, Labour, Co-operative Societies, consumers, social experts, women. *Ref.* P.G.A., 1919 ; B.T.J., 28th Aug. 1919, p. 262. *Diss.* Termination of Acts.

PROFITEERING ACTS DEPARTMENT.—*App.* by B.T., under Profiteering Act, 1919, in or after Aug. 1919. *Obj.* To organize administration of Acts. *Repr.* Parliament ; official and expert. *Ref.* Generally in reports of Sub-Committees of S.C.P. and S.C.T. under the Act. *Diss.* Termination of Acts.

PROFITEERING APPEAL TRIBUNALS.—*App.* under Profiteering Act, 1919, from Aug. 1919 by B.T. (with assistance of L.A.'s) in England and Wales, by I.O. and S.O. *Obj.* To hear appeals from decisions of Profiteering Committees Local (q.v.), except those going before Court of Summary Jurisdiction. *Repr.* L.A.'s, Employers' Associations, T.U.'s. *Ref.* P.G.A., 1919 ; Cmd. 1384 which describes constitution and working of London Tribunal ; B.T.J., 28th Aug. 1919, p. 262. *Diss.* Termination of Acts.

PROFITEERING COMMITTEES, LOCAL.—*App.* by L.A.'s, under authority of B.T., after passing of Profiteering Act of Aug. 1919. *Obj.* To exercise locally powers delegated to them by B.T., other than fixing of prices, and in particular deal with profiteering by retail traders. *Repr.* Presumably local industries, consumers, Labour, women, &c., but members of any trade subject to inquiry definitely excluded. *Ref.* P.G.A., 1919 ; B.T.J., 28th Aug. 1919, p. 262. *Diss.* Termination of Acts.

PURCHASES DEPARTMENT.—*App.* by B.T. early in 1915. *Obj.* To do necessary accountancy for purchasing Committees and agents of B.T. *Repr.* Expert accountants. *Ref.* H.C., No. 132, 1918, p. 28.

QUININE SULPHATE, PRICES AND SUPPLY, COMMITTEE.—*App.* by B.T. in 1919. *Obj.* To investigate prices and supply of quinine sulphate. Other details lacking.

RAILWAY ACCOUNTS COMMITTEE.—*App.* by the Government during the War, and sometimes called Railways Financial Control Committee. *Obj.* To deal with disputed questions in audit of Railway Companies' accounts. *Repr.* Railway managers, with appeal to independent arbitrators. *Ref.* H.C., Nos. 100, &c., 1920, p. v. *Diss.* Replaced after the War by Railway Advisory Committee (*see* M.T.).

RAILWAYS AFTER THE WAR, ADVISORY PANEL.—*App.* by B.T. about April 1918. *Obj.* To advise B.T. on future position of railways, and preparation of post-war policy. *Repr.* Not stated. *Ref.* B.T.J., 23rd May 1918.

RAILWAYS AND CONGESTION AT PORTS COMMITTEE.—*App.* to inquire into facilities offered by railways for clearing goods from docks in U.K. reported in T., 10th Feb. 1917, p. 7. Other details lacking.

RAILWAY EXECUTIVE COMMITTEE.—*App.* originally by the Government under an Act of 1871, prior to the War, to act in advisory capacity, but, on taking over of the railways at outbreak of war, appointed by B.T. as executive body. *Obj.* To administer the railways for the Government. *Repr.* General managers of chief railways (with President of B.T. as Chairman). *Ref.* H.C., No. 118, 1920, p. v. *Diss.* On removal of control, 15th Aug. 1921.

RAILWAY FINANCIAL CONTROL.—*See* Railway Accounts.

RAILWAY MANAGEMENT COMMITTEE.—*App.* under National Agreement of Mar. 1919, between Government, R.E.C., and Railway T.U.'s. *Obj.* To consider appointment of Joint Committee to deal temporarily with pay and conditions of railway servants and consider future of Conciliation Boards. *Repr.* R.E.C., Railway T.U.'s.

RAILWAYMEN, RELEASE FOR MILITARY SERVICE, COMMITTEE. —*App.* by B.T., Aug. or Sept. 1916. *Obj.* To inquire into cases in which instructions of R.E.C. in regard to release for military service are alleged not to have been observed, and advise on necessary action. *Repr.* Legal Profession, Labour, and possibly employers. *Ref.* T., Sept. 1916 ; Cd. 8741, p. 9. *Diss.* Apparently replaced by Railway Recruiting Appeals Committee, Sept. 1917 (*see* M.N.S.).

RAILWAY RECRUITING APPEALS.—*See* M.N.S.

RAILWAY ROLLING STOCK SHORTAGE COMMITTEE.—*App.* by R.E.C. in 1916 or 1917. *Obj.* To examine causes of shortage and suggest remedies. *Repr.* Government Departments concerned, Railways. *Ref.* B.T.J., 4th April 1918, p. 398. *Diss.* Late summer of 1917 (apparently).

RAILWAY WAGONS, POOLING, COMMITTEE.—*App.* by R.E.C., Jan. 1918. *Obj.* To organize distribution of pooled railway-owned wagons between different companies. *Repr.* Railway Companies. *Ref.* B.T.J., 11th April 1918, p. 430.

RAILWAY WAR MANUFACTURES COMMITTEE.—*App.* by R.E.C., as Sub-Committee, early in the War. *Obj.* To consolidate work of railway workshops for production of munitions. *Repr.* W.O., chief Railways, and later M.M. and Adm. *Ref.* B.T.J., 18th April 1918, p. 462.

RAILWAY WAR MANUFACTURES COMMITTEE, DISTRICT (GEOGRAPHICAL) SUB-COMMITTEES.—*App.* by main Committee early in the War. *Obj.* To keep in touch locally with firms engaged on war work, and arrange to assist and co-operate with them. *Repr.* Presumably as with main Committee. *Ref.* B.T.J., 18th April 1918, p. 462.

RAILWAYS, EMPLOYMENT OF DISABLED.—*See* Soldiers.

REGISTRY OF BUSINESS NAMES COMMITTEE.—*App.* by B.T., about beginning of 1917, under Registry of Business Names Act, 1916, and situated at Dublin. *Obj.* To advise Dublin Registration Office on application of the Act to Ireland. *Repr.* Official and expert. *Ref.* P.G.A., 1916 ; Cd. 8741, p. 10.

REQUISITIONING.—*See* Ships.

RESERVED OCCUPATIONS INTER-DEPARTMENTAL COMMITTEE. —*App.* by the Government, Nov. 1915, and attached to B.T., being transferred to M.N.S., April 1917. *Obj.* To prepare lists of occupations whose enlistment should be restricted in interests of trade, and, under M.N.S., adjust claims for man-power of recruiting, munitions, foreign trade, and general civilian needs. *Repr.* Under B.T., mainly chief man-power using Departments, but, on reorganization by M.N.S., these members were replaced by representatives of employers and T.U.'s. *Ref.* Cd. 9005, p. 89.

RETAIL PRICES.—*See* Fixed Retail Prices.

RETAIL TRADERS ADVISORY COMMITTEE.—*App.* by B.T. at outbreak of war. *Obj.* To recommend reasonable maximum prices for articles of food specially affected by outbreak of war. *Repr.* Various branches of retail trade. *Ref.* L.G., Aug. 1914.

ROAD TRANSPORT AREA COMMITTEES.—*App.* by Divisional Boards (q.v.), April 1918, for 100 Road Control Areas in G.B. *Obj.* To administer control locally under the Boards. *Repr.* B.T., M.M., F.C.C.'s, local interests. *Ref.* B.T.J., 18th April 1918.

ROAD TRANSPORT CONTROL BOARD.—*App.* by B.T., with concurrence of War Cabinet, Feb. 1918. *Obj.* To co-ordinate road transport work of existing departments and secure further economy in and proper allocation of road vehicles. *Repr.* Government Departments concerned, and possibly others. *Ref.* B.T.J., 31st Jan., 21st Feb. 1918.

ROAD TRANSPORT CONTROL BOARD ADVISORY COMMITTEE.—*App.* by B.T., April 1918. *Obj.* To advise Control Board in organizing road transport. *Repr.* Commercial Motor Users and Road Transport Associations, Cartage Firms, Associated Chambers of Commerce, London Distributing Firms. *Ref.* B.T.J., 11th April 1918.

ROAD TRANSPORT CONTROL BOARD, CO-ORDINATION SUB-COMMITTEE.—*App.* by the Board, about Mar. 1918. *Obj.* To consider co-ordination of work of Government Departments in connexion with road transport. *Repr.* The Board. *Ref.* B.T.J., 18th April 1918.

ROAD TRANSPORT DIVISIONAL ADVISORY COMMITTEES.—*App.* by Divisional Boards (q.v.) about April 1918. *Obj.* To keep Boards in touch with trade interests. *Repr.* Trade interests concerned. *Ref.* B.T.J., 31st Jan., 18th April 1918.

ROAD TRANSPORT DIVISIONAL (CONTROL) BOARDS.—*App.* by B.T., April 1918, under scheme of control, for thirteen districts of G.B. *Obj.* To organize control in their districts. *Repr.* B.T., M.F., M.M., Chambers of Commerce. *Ref.* B.T.J., 18th April 1918.

ROAD TRANSPORT RATES, SUB-COMMITTEE (PROFITEERING ACTS).—*App.* by S.C.T. in autumn of 1919. *Obj.* To inquire into effect on rates of alleged combine. *Repr.* S.C.T., S.C.P., M.L., business men, Labour, social experts. *Ref.* Cmd. 549. *Diss.* Dec. 1919.

RUBBER AND TIN EXPORTS COMMITTEE.—*App.* by B.T. for rubber, Jan. 1915, and extended to tin, Mar. 1915. *Obj.* To deal with applications for licences to export from U.K. and Empire, and advise generally on these matters. *Repr.* Prominent public men, with expert knowledge of British and Imperial trade. *Ref.* B.T.J., 28th Jan., 25th Mar. 1915.

RUSSIAN CLAIMS DEPARTMENT.—*See* B.T.J., 1st June 1922, p. 600. Full details lacking.

RUSSIAN LIQUIDATION COMMITTEE.—*See* Cabinet.

SAFEGUARDING OF INDUSTRIES ACT (PART II) COMMITTEES.—*App.* by B.T. from Sept. 1921, under Part II (Prevention of Dumping) of Act. *Obj.* To inquire into demands for application of Act to particular trades, and make recommendations. *Repr.* Chosen from panel composed mainly of persons with commercial and industrial experience, but not directly connected with goods affected. *Ref.* P.G.A., 1921. *Act still in operation at end of 1922.* (Disputed points under Part I of the Act (Safeguarding of Key Industries) were to be dealt with by arbitration through Referees—*see* sec. 1 (5).)

(By the end of 1922 Committees had been appointed for Aluminium Hollowware, Baths (Plain and Enamelled), Fabric Gloves and Glove Fabrics, Fabric Gloves and Fine Cotton Spinning Industry, Gas Mantles, Glass Bottles, Glassware (Domestic, Illuminating and Mounting), Gold and Aluminium Bronze Powders, Gold Leaf, Hollowware (Wrought, Enamelled), Optical, &c. Instruments, Snap Fasteners and Hooks and Eyes, Toys, Vulcanized Fibre, Wire Nails. Some of these are dealt with elsewhere in Section.)

SALT TRADE SUB-COMMITTEE (PROFITEERING ACTS).—*App.* by S.C.T. about end 1919. *Obj.* To inquire into existence, and effect on prices, of a ring in the trade. *Repr.* Traders, Labour, and others. *Ref.* Cmd. 832. *Diss.* May 1920.

SAMPLES.—*See* Enemy Goods.

SERBIA, SOUTH RUSSIA, BRITISH ECONOMIC MISSIONS.—*App.* by B.T. or O.T.D. in 1919. *Obj.* To investigate economic requirements of countries with view to development of British trade with them. *Repr.* Expert, with official members. *Ref.* B.T.J., 1919, 19th June, 21st Aug., p. 238, 4th Sept., p. 302. *Diss.* Later in 1919 after return. For Overseas Missions, *see also* O.T.D.

SEWING COTTON SUB-COMMITTEE (PROFITEERING ACTS).— *App.* by S.C.T. late in 1919. *Obj.* To inquire into existence, and effects on prices, of manufacturers' combine. *Repr.* S.C.T., business men, Labour, social experts and others. *Ref.* Cmd. 563. *Diss.* Feb. 1920.

SEWING COTTON (NO. 2) SUB-COMMITTEE (PROFITEERING ACTS).—*App.* by S.C.T., Feb. 1920. *Obj.* To inquire further into existence and effects of combine. *Repr.* As with Sub-Committee, No. 1. *Ref.* Cmd. 930. *Diss.* May 1920.

SEWING COTTON (NO. 3) SUB-COMMITTEE (PROFITEERING ACTS).—*App.* by S.C.T., Oct. 1920. *Obj.* To investigate further position of industry, with special reference to one firm. *Repr.* S.C.T., business men, Labour. *Ref.* Cmd. 1173. *Diss.* Feb. 1921.

SHIP LICENSING COMMITTEE.—*App.* by B.T., Nov. 1915, and transferred to M.S. early in 1917. *Obj.* To grant licences to British ships for carrying goods between two foreign ports and, after Mar. 1916, for any foreign voyage. *Repr.* Shipping interests, Legal Profession. *Ref.* B.T.J., 11th Nov. 1915.

SHIPPING AND SHIPBUILDING AFTER THE WAR DEPARTMENTAL COMMITTEE.—*App.* by B.T., Mar. 1916. *Obj.* To report on position and safeguards for these industries after the War. *Repr.* Lloyd's Register, ship-owners, ship-builders, iron and steel industry, mercantile marine, naval architecture. *Ref.* Cd. 9092. *Diss.* Mar. 1918.

(About the same time as this Committee's appointment a joint Committee was established by the Chamber of Shipping and the Liverpool Ship-owners' Association to consider shipping policy after the War (*see* T., 20th Mar. 1916.)

SHIPPING BOARD.—*App.* by the Government, and attached to B.T., early in the War. *Obj.* To consider and fix rates payable for requisitioned ships. *Repr.* Legal Profession, ship-owners. *Ref.* L.Y.B., 1919, p. 165.

SHIPPING.—*See* Coal Supplies.

SHIPS INSURANCE.—*See* Underwriting, War Risks.

SHIPS, NEUTRAL.—*See* F.O.

SHIPS REQUISITIONING (CARRIAGE OF FOODSTUFFS) COMMITTEE.—*App.* by B.T., Nov. 1915. *Obj.* To exercise requisitioning powers of B.T. to secure tonnage for food and necessaries and prevent prohibitive rise in freights. *Repr.* Parliament, shipping experts. *Ref.* B.T.J., 11th and 18th Nov. 1915.

SLATES SUB-COMMITTEE (PROFITEERING ACTS).—*App.* jointly by S.C.P. and S.C.T., Nov. 1920. *Obj.* To investigate prices, costs and profits of slates and roofing materials, and existence and effects of combinations. *Repr.* Business men generally, builders, architects, surveyors. *Ref.* Cmd. 1338. *Diss.* April 1921.

SOAP SUB-COMMITTEE (PROFITEERING ACTS).—*App.* by S.C.T., Oct. 1919. *Obj.* To inquire into effects on industry of manufacturers' combines. *Repr.* S.C.T., S.C.P., M.L., Civil Service, business men, traders and others. *Ref.* Cmd. 1126. *Diss.* Dec. 1920.

SOFT WOODS.—*See under* Timber.

SOLDIERS AND SAILORS, DISABLED, EMPLOYMENT ON BRITISH RAILWAYS, COMMITTEE.—*App.* presumably by B.T. or R.E.C., prior to Sept. 1917. *Ref.* without details, Cd. 8741, p. 10.

STAFFS INVESTIGATION.—*See* Cabinet and Cmd. 1461 for operations of Committee at B.T.

STANDARD SCHEMES.—*See* Boot and Shoe, Clothing.

STONE, BRICK AND CLAYWARE TRADES, SECTIONAL COMMITTEE (PROFITEERING ACTS).—*App.* by Building Materials Sub-Committee of S.C.P. and S.C.T., Feb. 1920. *Obj.* To investigate prices, costs and profits of trades, and existence and effects of combinations. *Repr.* Parliament, S.C.P., business men generally, builders, architects, surveyors, Labour. *Ref.* Cmd. 959, 1208. *Diss.* Feb. 1921.

STORAGE.—*See* M.R.

SULPHURIC ACID AND FERTILIZERS.—*See* M.M.

TEXTILE EXPORTS SHIPPING COMMITTEE.—*App.* jointly by B.T. and M.S., Feb. 1918. *Obj.* To consult with these Departments as to tonnage requirements and supply and distribute available tonnage. *Repr.* Chambers of Commerce in chief textile towns, Manchester Ship Canal Company. *Ref.* B.T.J., 28th Feb., 28th Mar. 1918.

(The Committee was apparently limited at first to Cotton and Woollen (including Lace and Hosiery) exports, but subsequently extended to all textiles.)

TEXTILE TRADES AFTER THE WAR DEPARTMENTAL COMMITTEE.—*App.* by B.T., April 1916. *Obj.* To consider position after the War and safeguards against foreign competition. *Repr.* Manufacturers and merchants in various textile trades. *Ref.* Cd. 9070. *Diss.* May 1917.

TIMBER CONTROL (IMPORTED SOFT WOODS) COMMITTEE.—*App.* under auspices of Timber Trades Federation, and in conjunction with Timber Controller, about Feb. 1918. *Obj.* To prepare scheme for control of imported soft woods in consultation with Timber Controller. *Repr.* Timber merchants and importers. *Ref.* B.T.J., 7th Mar., 27th June 1918. *Diss.* June 1918.

TIMBER, IRISH, RATIONING COMMITTEE.—*App.* by Timber Controller, Oct. 1918. *Obj.* To assist in distribution among importers of Ireland's ration of timber. *Repr.* Irish timber importers. *Ref.* B.T.J., 24th Oct. 1918, p. 510.

TIMBER MERCHANTS (HOME GROWN) (IMPORTERS') ADVISORY COMMITTEES.—*Ref.* without details, B.T.J., 7th Mar. 1918, p. 273.

TIMBER, PIT (CANADA AND NEWFOUNDLAND), COMMISSION OF INQUIRY.—*App.* by B.T., Sept. 1914. *Obj.* To investigate on the spot available supplies and possibility of marketing at commercial rates. *Repr.* B.T., timber trade, Mining Association. *Ref.* Cd. 7728. *Diss.* Oct. 1914.

TIMBER, PIT.—*See* H.O. under Pit Timber.

TIMBER PURCHASING (IMPORTED SOFTWOODS) TRADE COMMITTEE.—*App.* by Timber Controller in first half of 1918. *Obj.* To assist Timber Supply Department in purchase of imported softwoods under control scheme (*see* Control Committee above). *Repr.* Timber importers and merchants. *Ref.* B.T.J., 27th June 1918.

(Possibly this is the same as the Timber Merchants' (Importers') Advisory Committee, above.)

TIMBER SECTIONAL COMMITTEE (PROFITEERING ACTS).—*App.* by Building Materials Sub-Committee of S.C.P. and S.C.T., about Mar. 1920. *Obj.* To investigate prices, costs and profits of timber at all stages, and existence and effects of trusts and combines. *Repr.* Parliament, S.C.T., architects and others. *Ref.* Cmd. 985. *Diss.* Sept. 1920.

TIMBER SUPPLIES DEPARTMENT.—Transferred along with Timber Advisory Committee to B.T. from W.O. (q.v.) in May 1917, and finally wound up apparently in 1919 or 1920. The Department included various sections, e.g. Home Supplies, Imported Timber, Disposals, &c. (*see* Cmd. 1368, pp. xvii, xviii, 122).

TIMBER SUPPLIES, INTER-DEPARTMENTAL CONSULTATIVE COMMITTEE.—*App.* by Timber Supplies Department in 1917 or early 1918. *Obj.* To co-ordinate demands of various Government Departments for timber. *Repr.* Government Departments concerned. *Ref.* B.T.J., 7th Mar. 1918, p. 272.

TIMBER.—*See also* Forestry Corps ; Wood, Economies in Packing.

TOBACCO AND MATCHES CONTROL BOARD.—*App.* by B.T., for tobacco only, June 1917, and extended to matches, Sept. 1917. *Obj.* To administer control of tobacco and matches. *Repr.* W.O., tobacco trades, and subsequently match trades and Labour. *Ref.* B.T.J., 7th June, 13th Sept. 1917. *See also under* Matches.

TOBACCO CONTROL ADVISORY COMMITTEE.—*App.* by B.T., May 1917. *Obj.* To advise Tobacco Control Board in carrying out control. *Repr.* Tobacco trades. *Ref.* B.T.J., 7th June 1917.

TOBACCO CONTROL.—*See also under* Matches.

TOBACCO (IMPORT LICENCES) COMMITTEE.—*App.* by B.T., Feb. 1916. *Obj.* To grant licences to import, under general Prohibition of Feb. 1916. *Repr.* Parliament, importers, manufacturers, B.T. *Ref.* B.T.J., Mar. 1916.

TOBACCO SUB-COMMITTEE (PROFITEERING ACTS).—*App.* by S.C.T., Oct. 1919. *Obj.* To investigate existence of combinations and effects on prices and trade. *Repr.* S.C.T., B.T., Tobacco Control Board, manufacturers, business men, social experts. *Ref.* Cmd. 558. *Diss.* Dec. 1919.

TOPS.—*See* Wool.

TRADE RELATIONS AFTER THE WAR COMMITTEE.—*App.* by B.T. in 1916 or 1917. *Obj.* To investigate probable trade relations after the War, with a view to developing British trade and preventing peaceful penetration by Germany. *Repr.* Industry, shipping, banking, finance, economists. *Ref.* Cd. 8916. *Diss.* By summer of 1917.

TRADE.—*See* Financial Facilities, and O.T.D.

TRADING WITH THE ENEMY AMENDMENT ACT, 1916, ADVISORY COMMITTEE.—*App.* by B.T., Feb. 1916. *Obj.* To investigate cases and advise B.T. on exercise of powers of winding up enemy businesses under the Act. *Repr.* Parliament, Legal Profession, industry, commerce. *Ref.* Cd. 8308, 9059. *Diss.* April 1918.

TRADING WITH THE ENEMY DEPARTMENT.—*App.* as special department of the Public Trustee Office, 1914. *Obj.* To carry out duties of Custodian of Enemy Property and other duties under the Trading with the Enemy Acts. *Repr.* Official and expert. *Ref.* T., 8th April 1915, p. 5.

TRADING WITH THE ENEMY, INTER-DEPARTMENTAL COM-MITTEE.—*App.* by B.T. at beginning of the War. *Obj.* To deal with applications for import and export licences and movement of funds and similar matters under Trading with the Enemy Acts. *Repr.* Presumably similar to later Advisory Committee. *Ref.* B.T.J., 10th Dec. 1914, p. 692. *Diss.* Feb. 1915, when import and export licences transferred to W.T.D. and rest of work to Parliamentary Counsel to Treasury.

TRAFFIC DIVERSION COMMITTEE.—*App.* by B.T. in 1917. *Obj.* To report upon provision of facilities needed to allow diversion of traffic from East to West Coast Ports. *Repr.* B.T. and presumably other Departments, Port Authorities, and presumably port and dock users. *Ref.* H.C., No. 184, 1919, p. 4.

TRAMWAYS, AREA SUB-COMMITTEES.—*App.* by Tramways Committee (q.v.) early in 1918, four Sub-Committees being established to cover nine areas of G.B. *Obj.* To investigate position, and allocate supplies, in their areas. *Repr.* Main Committee, tramway undertakings. *Ref.* B.T.J., 7th Feb. 1918. *Diss.* Feb. 1919.

(Conferences consisting of two representatives of each undertaking in the area were to be summoned periodically by Sub-Committees, *see* B.T.J., 1st Mar. 1918, p. 266.)

TRAMWAYS COMMITTEE.—*App.* jointly by B.T. and M.M., Dec. 1917, with some compulsory powers, after consultation with chief Tramways' Associations. *Obj.* To consider means of securing necessary materials and labour for repairs and maintenance, allocate and transfer supplies, and facilitate travelling of munition workers. *Repr.* Experts chosen by L.C.C. and chief Tramways' Associations, with representatives of B.T. and M.M. in advisory capacity. *Ref.* B.T.J., 3rd Jan. 1917. *Diss.* Feb. 1919.

TRAMWAYS LOCAL ADVISORY COMMITTEES.—*App.* by Tramways Committee (q.v.), for nine areas of G.B., early in 1918. *Obj.* To advise Area Sub-Committees (q.v.) on position in their areas. *Repr.* Tramway undertakings in the area. *Ref.* B.T.J., 7th Feb. 1918. *Diss.* Feb. 1919.

TRANSPORT.—*See* Paper Mills and S.O.

TRUSTS, STANDING COMMITTEE (PROFITEERING ACTS).—*App.* by Profiteering Acts Central Committee (q.v.), about Oct. 1919, by reconstitution of former Committee on Trusts (*see* M.R.). *Obj.* To inquire into existence, and effects on prices, in various industries, of trusts, rings and combines. *Repr.* Parliament, B.T., M.L., Manufacturers and Business Men, Labour, Women, Consumers, Economic and Social Experts. *Ref.* P.G.A., 1919; Cmd. 1047; T., 4th Sept. 1919, p. 7; B.T.J., 25th Sept. 1919, p. 386. *Diss.* Termination of Acts.

UNDERWRITING COMMITTEE (WAR RISKS INSURANCE).—*App.* by B.T., Feb. 1918. *Obj.* To carry out new scheme of ship cargoes' insurance at rates graded according to risks. *Repr.* Marine Insurance Market. *Ref.* B.T.J., 28th Feb. 1918.

UNEMPLOYMENT, LACE, SILK AND EMBROIDERY INDUSTRIES COMMITTEE.—*App.* by B.T., about July 1923. *Obj.* To inquire into causes of existing unemployment and possible means of improving position. *Repr.* B.T., employers, T.U.'s, women. *Ref.* L.G. 1923, p. 311, 434. *Diss.* About end 1923.

VINEGAR SUB-COMMITTEE (PROFITEERING ACTS).—*App.* by S.C.T., Feb. 1921. *Obj.* To investigate existence, and effects on prices, of manufacturers' combinations. *Repr.* S.C.T., business men, Medical Profession, Public Health Service. *Ref.* Cmd. 1355. *Diss.* May 1921.

WAGES (DISABLED MEN) ADVISORY BOARDS.—*See* M.L.

WAR DAMAGE COMPENSATION COMMITTEE.—*App.* by Municipalities of the U.K. by April 1916. *Obj.* To secure payment of compensation for damage by enemy attacks from national funds in place of existing War Risks Insurance Scheme. *Repr.* 370 Municipalities. *Ref.* T., 14th April 1916, p. 5.

WAR RISKS INSURANCE COMMITTEE.—*App.* by B.T., Aug. 1914, and sometimes known as Insurance of British Ships' Cargoes Committee.

Obj. To administer for B.T. Government scheme for insurance of ships' cargoes and advise in connexion with it. *Repr.* B.T., Adm., Tre., ship-owners, shipping interests, underwriters, insurance brokers, legal experts. *Ref.* B.T.J., 27th Aug. 1914.

WAR RISKS INSURANCE OFFICE.—*App.* by B.T., Aug. 1914. *Obj.* To form department to carry out Government scheme of insurance for ships' cargoes and later for other risks. *Repr.* Official and expert. *Ref.* B.T.J., 28th Feb. 1918.

WAR RISKS MUTUAL ASSOCIATIONS.—These were Associations formed at instigation of the Government, prior to the War, to undertake insurance of part of war risks in event of war. *See* Cd. 7660, p. 4, 7997 ; H.C., No. 132, 1918, p. 27.

WATER-POWER RESOURCES INTER-DEPARTMENTAL COM-MITTEE.—*App.* jointly by B.T. and M.R., June 1918. *Obj.* To report on resources of U.K., utilization for industrial purposes, and measures for proper conservation and use. *Repr.* B.T., M.R., M.H. (later), engineering and electrical experts, research, Legal Profession, Labour. *Ref.* Cmd. 79, 776, 1079. *Diss.* End 1920, or 1921.

(An Irish Sub-Committee was appointed in Nov. or Dec. 1918, to report upon the problem as affecting Ireland, the representation including engineers, scientists, land-owners and other Irish interests ; *see* B.T.J., 12th Dec. 1918, p. 734 ; T., 6th Dec. 1918.)

WHEAT CONSERVATION.—*See* L.G.B.

WOMEN'S EMPLOYMENT AFTER THE WAR, SUB-COMMITTEE.— *App.* by the Women's War Employment (Industrial) Committee (q.v.), in 1916. *Obj.* To advise upon questions of post-war employment of women. *Repr.* As with main Committee. *Ref.* Cd. 8570, p. 2.

WOMEN'S WAR EMPLOYMENT (INDUSTRIAL) CENTRAL COM-MITTEE.—*App.* by B.T. and H.O. by Mar. 1916. *Obj.* To advise those Departments on means of promotion of employment of women in industry. *Repr.* Parliament, B.T., H.O., employers, Labour, women, social experts. *Ref.* B.T.J., 9th Mar. 1916.

WOMEN'S WAR EMPLOYMENT (INDUSTRIAL) LOCAL ADVISORY COMMITTEES.—*App.* by B.T. in consultation with H.O. and Central Committee (q.v.), being strictly Advisory Committees to E.E.'s in various districts, in 1916, thirty-seven being in operation by Nov. *Obj.* To promote locally women's employment in industry and organize conditions, including lodgings and welfare work. *Repr.* Employers, workpeople, societies interested in women's employment, with representatives of B.T. and H.O. in consultative capacity. *Ref.* L.G., Nov. 1916. *Diss.* Eventually absorbed in part at least into L.E.C.'s (*see* M.L.).

WOOD, ECONOMIES IN PACKING, COMMITTEES.—*App.* by Chambers of Commerce in districts mainly affected, with consent of Timber Supplies Department, May 1917. *Obj.* To administer regulations dealing with packing for export. *Repr.* Business interests affected. *Ref.* B.T.J., 3rd May 1917.

WOODS AND STONES (IMPORT LICENCES) COMMITTEE.—*App.* by B.T., Feb. 1915. *Obj.* To grant licences for import of furniture woods, hard woods, veneers, stones and slates, under import prohibitions. *Repr.* Importers and users of these commodities, B.T. *Ref.* B.T.J., 2nd Mar. 1916.

WOOL, PRIORITY, EXPORT COMMITTEE.—*See* W.O.

WOOL, TOPS AND YARN, SUB-COMMITTEE (PROFITEERING ACTS).—*App.* jointly by S.C.P. and B.T., Dec. 1919. *Obj.* To investigate cost of production and distribution and profits at all stages. *Repr.* Parliament, Central Profiteering Acts Committee, S.C.P., B.T., W.O. (Contracts Department), manufacturers, merchants, consumers, Labour, social experts. *Ref.* Cmd. 535, 1192. *Diss.* Feb. 1921.

WORSTED YARNS SUB-COMMITTEE (PROFITEERING ACTS).— *App.* by S.C.P. late in 1919. *Obj.* To investigate prices of worsted yarns. *Repr.* Parliament, S.C.P., B.T., M.L., W.O. (Contracts' Department), manufacturers, Labour, women, social experts. *Ref.* Cmd. 550. *Diss.* Jan. 1920.

(*See also* Yorkshire Tweed Cloths, below.)

YARNS.—*See* Wool, Worsted.

YEAST SUB-COMMITTEE (PROFITEERING ACTS).—*App.* by S.C.T., July 1920. *Obj.* To investigate existence, and effects on prices, of combinations. *Repr.* S.C.T., business men, chemists and other scientists. *Ref.* Cmd. 1216. *Diss.* Mar. 1921.

YORKSHIRE TWEED CLOTHS SUB-COMMITTEE (PROFITEERING ACTS).—*App.* by S.C.P. in winter of 1919–20. *Obj.* To investigate prices, costs and profits. *Repr.* B.T., W.O., S.C.P., business men. *Ref.* Cmd. 838. *Diss.* July 1920.

TRANSPORT, MINISTRY OF

The *Ministry of Transport* was established on 15th Aug. 1919 by the Ministry of Transport Act, 1919, under a Minister and Parliamentary Secretary. The *object* of the Ministry was to organize the improvement of means and facilities for transport and locomotion. For this purpose the various powers of other Government Departments, in respect of different forms and instruments of transport, were with certain exceptions transferred to the Ministry, and it was also given temporary powers of control, to allow time for the formation of future policy. The Ministry was also given power to establish transport services. Advisory Committees of experts could be set up to assist in its work. *Reference.* Public General Acts, 1919 (9 & 10 Geo. V, c. 50).

ABBREVIATION

M.T. = Ministry of Transport.

CANALS COMMITTEE.—*App.* by M.T., Sept. 1919. *Obj.* To deal with information and assist generally regarding canals. *Repr.* M.T., C.M.D., Canal Control Committee. *Ref.* T., 3rd Oct. 1919, p. 9.

FISHERY HARBOURS STANDING COMMITTEE.—*See* D.C.

FISH TRANSPORT FACILITIES COMMITTEE.—*App.* by Conference of interests concerned at M.F., June 1920. *Obj.* To investigate general problem of fish transport and suggest improvements. *Repr.* Government Departments concerned, fishing interests, Railway Companies. *Ref.* Cmd. 1393, pp. 31–2. *Diss.* Outstanding points delegated later to Standing Sub-Committee composed of representatives of M.T., M.F., M.A., and F.B.(Sc.), with power to summon main Committee, if necessary.

GATTIE SCHEME DEPARTMENTAL COMMITTEE.—*App.* by B.T., July 1919, but transferred to M.T., Nov. 1919. *Obj.* To investigate Mr. A.W. Gattie's proposals for improved handling of goods and traffic. *Repr.* B.T., M.T. (later), engineering and transport experts, National Union of Railwaymen. *Ref.* Cmd. 492. *Diss.* Dec. 1919.

HARBOURS, DOCKS AND PIERS ACT SUB-COMMITTEE.—*App.* as Sub-Committee of Rates Advisory Committee, Oct. 1920, under Harbours, &c. (Temporary Increases of Charges) Act. *Obj.* To advise M.T. on proposed revision of charges under the Act. *Repr.* Rates Advisory Committee, Port of London Authority, manufacturers, traders, Labour. *Ref.* Railway Rates Tribunal Report, 1922, p. 8 (H.M.S.O., 1923). *Still in existence at end of 1922.*

HARBOURS, STANDING INTER-DEPARTMENTAL CONFERENCE. —*App.* jointly by various Government Departments concerned in 1920. *Obj.* To secure co-ordination between Departments concerned with harbours. *Repr.* M.T., B.A., F.B.(Sc.), D.A.T.I., D.C. *Ref.* Cmd. 1393, p. 49. *Standing Body.*

HOME TRADE DISTRICT TRANSPORT COMMITTEES.—*See* B.T.

INLAND WATERWAYS.—*App.* by M.T., apparently late in 1920. *Obj.* To report upon policy of M.T. in acquiring parts of inland waterways for improvement and upon improvements to be carried out. *Repr.* Parliament, M.H., canal companies, railway experts, Legal Profession, Labour. *Ref.* Cmd. 1410.

IRISH BRANCH.—*App.* by M.T., Nov. 1919. *Obj.* To deal with Irish work of M.T. *Repr.* Official and expert. *Ref.* B.T.J., 13th Nov. 1919, p. 593.

IRISH RAILWAYS, SETTLEMENT OF CLAIMS, TRIBUNAL.—*App.* by Irish Railways, Settlement of Claims, Act of Aug. 1921. *Obj.* To decide disputes between the railways as to distribution of compensation under war-time agreements with the Government. *Repr.* Arbitration experts, Legal Profession, business men. *Ref.* P.G.A., 1921.

LIGHTS ON VEHICLES, DEPARTMENTAL COMMITTEE.—*App.* by M.T., Nov. 1919. *Obj.* To report on questions affecting lights on vehicles. *Repr.* M.T., H.O., S.O., Police, agriculture, motor manufacturers and users, omnibus owners, cyclists. *Ref.* Cmd. 659.

LONDON TRAFFIC ADVISORY COMMITTEE.—*App.* by M.T., on nomination of bodies interested, Nov. 1919. *Obj.* To advise and assist M.T. in regard to London Traffic. *Repr.* Parliament, Adm., L.C.C., Metropolitan Police, Railways, Architects, Labour. *Ref.* Cmd. 636. *Diss.* Mar. 1920.

(The Committee did much of its work through a Technical Committee representing all interests concerned.)

LORRY COMMITTEES.—*App.* locally in autumn of 1919, under auspices of Departments concerned. *Obj.* To promote use of motor lorries to relieve congestion at docks. *Repr.* M.T., M.M., M.F., Port Authorities, Railways. *Ref.* T., 24th Oct. 1919, p. 9.

PANEL, ADVISORY.—*App.* by M.T. in or after Aug. 1919, under Ministry of Transport Act, sec. 23. *Obj.* To form panel for choice of members of Advisory Committees to be established to assist M.T. in exercise of powers. *Repr.* Men of commercial and business experience and other experts. *Ref.* P.G.A., 1919. *Still in existence at end of 1922.*

RAILWAY ADVISORY COMMITTEE.—*App.* by M.T. late in 1919. *Obj.* To advise and assist M.T. in exercise of general control over railways. *Repr.* Railway managers and T.U.'s. *Ref.* H.C., Nos. 100, &c., 1920, p. v.

RAILWAY AGREEMENTS DEPARTMENTAL COMMITTEE.—*App.* by M.T., Sept. 1920. *Obj.* To report upon agreements between Government and Railway Companies regarding Government possession of railways and liability of State under them and steps for safeguarding State's interests. *Repr.* Parliament, Tre., F.B.I., business men, Labour. *Ref.* Cmd. 1132. *Diss.* Feb. 1921. *See also* Tre.

RAILWAYS AMALGAMATION TRIBUNAL.—*App.* by Railways Act, 1921, Sec. 9, Aug. 1921. *Obj.* To hear and determine objections to amalgamations and absorptions of railways under the Act. *Repr.* Prominent public men, with experience of arbitration, chartered accountants, Legal Profession. *Ref.* P.G.A., 1921. *Still in existence at end of 1922.*

(In dealing with local questions, a single Commissioner may act, or appoint a single person for the purpose.)

RAILWAY COUNCILS.—*App.*, one or more, for each railway or group of railways, from Aug. 1921, under Railways Act, 1921, sec. 63. *Obj.* To secure joint action by companies and employees in dealing with wages, hours and conditions. *Repr.* Railway Companies, railwaymen. *Ref.* P.G.A., 1921. *Apparently still in existence.*

(Drafting Committees were also to be appointed to prepare schemes for constitution of Councils, &c., *see* sec. 65 of the Act.)

RAILWAY POLICE FORCE CONFERENCE.—*App.* from Aug. 1921, under Railways Act, sec. 67, one Conference being established for each Company or after amalgamation for each amalgamated company, and a central conference for all railways of G.B. *Obj.* To secure joint action in dealing with pay, hours and conditions of railway police. *Repr.* Railway Companies, Railway Police. *Ref.* P.G.A., 1921. *Still in existence.*

RAILWAY RATES, LOCAL COMMITTEES.—*See* next entry and Rates Advisory Committee, below.

RAILWAY RATES TRIBUNAL.—*App.* under Railways Act, 1921, secs. 20–8, Aug. 1921, consisting of permanent officers, appointed by H.M. the King, on nomination of Lord Chancellor, B.T. and M.T., and two panels, a General Panel nominated by B.T., M.A. and M.L., and a Railway Panel by M.T. *Obj.* To hear and determine questions affecting railway rates and their administration. *Repr. Permanent Officers*—Law, Commerce, Railways : *General Panel*—Trading Interests, Labour, Agriculture : *Railway Panel*—Railways Association ; Non-Associated Railways. *Ref.* P.G.A., 1921. *Permanent.*

(The Tribunal was empowered by Sec. 28 of the Act to determine appointment and functions of Local Joint Committees for dealing with questions locally.)

RAILWAY TECHNICAL SUB-COMMITTEES.—*App.* by M.T. in winter of 1919–20. *Obj.* To advise M.T. on technical matters connected with railways. *Repr.* Technical experts. *Ref.* H.C., Nos. 100, &c., 1920, p. v.

RAILWAY WAGES BOARD, CENTRAL.—*App.* (reconstituted) under Railways Act, 1921, sec. 64, by Railway Companies and Railway T.U.'s. *Obj.* To deal on national basis with wages, hours and conditions of service. *Repr.* Railway Companies and T.U.'s. *Ref.* P.G.A., 1921. *Still in existence.*

RAILWAY WAGES BOARD, NATIONAL.—As with Central Board (previous entry), with additional appointment of four representatives of railway users by M.L. on nomination (one each) of Association of British Chambers of Commerce, Co-operative Union, F.B.I., and Parliamentary Committee of T.U.C. *Still in existence.*

RAILWAYS.—*See also* Irish Railways, Road Conveyance.

RATES ADVISORY COMMITTEE.—*App.* under Ministry of Transport Act, Oct. 1919. *Obj.* To advise and assist M.T. in fixing rates and fares and safeguarding interests involved. *Repr.* Legal Profession, agriculture, industry, transport, Labour. *Ref.* P.G.A., 1919 ; Cmd. 525, 1098. *Permanent.*

RATES.—*See also* Railway Rates.

ROADS ADVISORY COMMITTEE.—*App.* by M.T., under the Ministry of Transport Act, in Dec. 1919. *Obj.* To advise and assist B.T. in dealing with roads, bridges and road traffic, and safeguarding interests involved. *Repr.* Parliament, M.T. S.B.H., L.A.'s, Highway Authorities, users of horse and mechanical road transport, agriculture, engineers, Legal Profession, Labour. *Ref.* P.G.A., 1919 ; H.C., No. 10, 1921, pp. 6–7. *Permanent.*

ROAD CONVEYANCE OF GOODS BY RAILWAYS COMMITTEE.— *App.* by M.T. from Panel, Advisory (q.v.), Jan. 1921. *Obj.* To report upon questions of granting railway companies powers for such conveyance. *Repr.* Legal Profession, Railways, Road Transport Association, Motor Users, Chambers of Commerce, F.B.I., Transport Labour, with Technical Adviser. *Ref.* Cmd. 1228. *Diss.* Mar. 1921.

ROADS JOINT COMMITTEE.—Functions transferred to M.T. *See* W.O.

ROAD VEHICLES TAXATION AND REGULATION COMMITTEE.— *App.* by M.T., Nov. 1919. *Obj.* To report generally upon these matters. *Repr.* M.T., Tre., Board of Customs and Excise, L.A.'s, Police, agriculture, motor users, traders, manufacturers, omnibus owners. *Ref.* Cmd. 660.

(An Advisory Committee was established in 1920 to advise on administrative procedure for putting into operation proposals of this Committee's Interim Report (Cmd. 660), *see* H.C., No. 245, 1921, p. 4.)

STANDARDIZATION COMMITTEE.—*App.* by Railway Companies in 1919, receiving advice and assistance from M.T. *Obj.* To promote standardization of railway rolling stock, &c. *Repr.* Railway engineers. *Ref.* H.C., No. 100, &c., 1920, p. xii.

STORAGE, GOVERNMENT DEPARTMENTS, COMMITTEE.—*App.* by M.T. in 1920. *Obj.* To secure more economical use of storage by Government Departments and expedite release for trading purposes. *Repr.* Government Department using storage. *Ref.* H.C., No. 100, &c., 1920, p. ix.

TRADERS' CO-ORDINATING COMMITTEE.—Referred to in Report of Railway Rates Tribunal for 1922, as body representing traders in objections to proposed rates, &c. *See* pp. 19, 20 of Report (H.M.S.O., 1923) ; and B.T.J., 22nd Dec. 1922, p. 724.

TRAMWAYS ADVISORY COMMITTEE.—*App.* by M.T., about June 1920, under Tramways (Temporary Increase of Charges) Act, 1920. *Obj.* To advise (where necessary after public inquiry) and assist M.T. in making Tramway Orders and safeguarding interests of tramway users. *Repr.* Light Railways' Commissioners, men of commercial and business experience, experts. *Ref.* P.G.A., 1920.

TRANSPORT EXTENSIONS DEPARTMENTAL COMMITTEE.—*App.* by M.T., apparently in 1920. *Obj.* To report to M.T. on proposals for extending transport system. *Repr.* Not stated. *Ref.* H.C., Nos. 100, &c., 1920, p. xi. Possibly *Standing Committee.*

TREASURY, THE

(INCLUDING CIVIL SERVICE COMMISSION)

ABBREVIATIONS

Tre. = Treasury.
C.E. = Chancellor of the Exchequer.
C.S.C. = Civil Service Commission.

ACCOUNTS.—*See also* **M.M.**

AERODROME CONSTRUCTION ACCOUNTS COMMITTEE.—*App.* by Tre., May 1919. *Obj.* To report upon nature, extent and responsibilities for irregularities in A.M. accounts and suggest remedies and better methods. *Repr.* Tre., business men, accountants. *Ref.* H.C., Nos. 83, &c., 1919.

AIRCRAFT ACCOUNTS EXPERT COMMITTEE.—*App.* by Tre., Aug. 1918. *Obj.* To investigate alleged defects in system of control and accounting at A.M. *Repr.* Tre., chartered accountants, engineers (all experts). *Ref.* H.C., Nos. 83, &c., 1919, p. xix. *Diss.* Prior to Dec. 1919.

AMERICAN DOLLAR SECURITIES COMMITTEE.—*App.* by C.E. at end of 1915. *Obj.* To control operations of Tre. under scheme for deposit and sale of American Dollar Securities. *Repr.* Bank of England, Bankers' Clearing House, London Stock Exchange. *Ref.* H.C., No. 212, 1919. *Diss.* June 1919.

ANDERSON COMMITTEE.—*See* Pay, &c., of State Servants.

APPROVED SOCIETY FINANCE DEPARTMENTAL COMMITTEE.— *App.* by Tre., Jan. 1916. *Obj.* To suggest amendments and simplifications to financial scheme of National Health Insurance and means of reducing costs, with special reference to Approved Societies. *Repr.* N.H.I.C., Approved Societies, including T.U.'s and Women's Societies, Institute of Actuaries. *Ref.* Cd. 8251, 8396, 8451. *Diss.* Dec. 1916 (Cd. 8451).

AWARDS TO INVENTORS, INVESTIGATING COMMITTEE.—*See* Cabinet.

BANK AMALGAMATIONS COMMITTEE.—*App.* by Tre., March 1918. *Obj.* To report upon effects of bank amalgamations on industrial and mercantile interests, and upon need of legislation for dealing with them. *Repr.* Bank of England, Banks, Industry, Railways, Merchants. *Ref.* Cd. 9052. *Diss.* May 1918.

BRITISH CELLULOSE INQUIRY COMMITTEE.—*App.* by Tre., Aug. 1918. *Obj.* To inquire into formation, financial arrangements and relations with Government Departments of Cellulose Company and associated companies. *Repr.* Judges, prominent business men. *Ref.* Cmd. 306. *Diss.* July 1919.

CAPITAL ISSUES COMMITTEE.—*App.* by Tre., prior to April 1915. *Obj.* To deal with applications for issues of capital, subject to Tre. control, to conserve capital for war purposes—for duties after reappointment, *see* next entry. *Repr.* Presumably Tre., bankers and other experts. *Ref.* Cd. 7855 ; Cmd. 99. *Diss.* Reconstructed in 1919, *see* next entry.

CAPITAL ISSUES COMMITTEE (1919).—*App.* by Tre., Mar. 1919. *Obj.* To deal with applications for fresh issues of capital under revised Treasury control, with view of preserving capital for domestic use during reconstruction and preventing avoidable drain on foreign exchanges by export of capital. *Repr.* Parliament, Tre., Royal Mint, the Dominions, the Stock Exchange, big manufacturing and business interests in home and foreign trade, including certain concerns operating abroad and specially interested. *Ref.* B.T.J., 10th April 1919, p. 494.

CIVIL SERVICE, CLASS I EXAMINATION, COMMITTEE.—*App.* by Tre., Nov. 1916. *Obj.* To report upon existing scheme of examinations for Class I of Civil Service, and submit revised scheme to secure type of officer required and be advantageous to higher education. *Repr.* C.S.C., Universities of G.B. *Ref.* Cd. 8657. *Diss.* June 1917.

CIVIL SERVICE, RECRUITMENT AFTER THE WAR, COMMITTEE. —*App.* by Tre., Jan. 1918. *Obj.* To report upon various problems of post-war recruitment. *Repr.* Parliament, Tre., M.L., B.E., C.S.C., P.O. *Ref.* Cd. 34, 164. *Diss.* April 1919.

CIVIL SERVICE, SALARIES OF PRINCIPAL POSTS, COMMITTEE.— *App.* by C.E., in 1920. *Obj.* To report upon remuneration of principal posts in Civil Service. *Repr.* Parliament, business men. *Ref.* Cmd. 1188. *Diss.* July 1920.

CIVIL SERVICE STAFFS COMMITTEE.—*App.* by Tre., Feb. 1918. *Obj.* To inquire generally into clerical staffs of Departments, created or expanded by the War. *Repr.* Tre., other Government Departments, women. *Ref.* Cd. 9074. *Diss.* Feb. 1919.

CIVIL SERVICE STAFFS INSPECTING SUB-COMMITTEES.—*App.* by main Committee about April 1918 in London and big towns. *Obj.* To investigate individual departments or offices on the spot. *Repr.* Professional and commercial men, Civil Servants, women. *Ref.* Cd. 9220, pp. 3, 4. *Diss.* By Feb. 1919.

CIVIL SERVICE STAFFS, STANDING ESTABLISHMENT COMMITTEE.—*App.* by Tre. about Mar. 1919, on suggestion of Staffs Committee (q.v.). *Obj.* To advise and assist Tre. generally in staffing questions. *Repr.* Tre., Establishment Officers of Chief Government Departments. *Ref.* Cmd. 62, p. 5. *Permanent.*

CIVIL SERVICE.—*See also* Ex-Service Men.

CLAIMS ACCELERATION COMMITTEE.—*See* Adm.

COASTGUARD, CIVIL DUTIES, INTER-DEPARTMENTAL COMMITTEE.—*App.* by Tre., Mar. 1922. *Obj.* To report on establishment for civil duties of coastguards and possible economies. *Repr.* Tre., Adm., B.T., Customs and Excise. *Ref.* Cmd. 1753. *Diss.* July 1922.

COLWYN COMMITTEE.—*See* Contracts, Departmental.

COMMERCIAL AND BANKING TRANSACTIONS WITH ENEMY SUBJECTS COMMITTEE.—*App.* presumably by Tre., early in 1917. *Obj.* To suggest arrangements for liquidation of commercial and financial transactions between British and enemy subjects, not completed owing to outbreak of war. *Repr.* Largely business men apparently. *Ref.* Cd. 8575.

CONTRACTS, CANCELLED, STANDING (TREASURY) COMMITTEE. —*Ref.* without details in H.C., Nos. 83, &c., 1919, p. ix ; but reference is not clear as to exact character of the Committee.

CONTRACTS, DEPARTMENTAL, CO-ORDINATION COMMITTEE (COLWYN COMMITTEE).—*App.* by Tre. in 1918. *Obj.* To investigate and co-ordinate contracting methods of Departments, becoming subsequently Standing Committee. *Repr.* Government Contracts' Departments, bankers, manufacturers, accountants. *Ref.* Cd. 979.

CONTRACTS, SPECIAL TREASURY COMMITTEE.—*App.* by Tre. in 1915 or 1916. *Obj.* To consider with Departments concerned cases of allowance, on grounds of hardship, for special war conditions in non-fulfilled contracts. *Repr.* Tre. and Departments concerned, a Sub-Committee acting apparently for each Department. *Ref.* H.C., No. 113, 1917, pp. 117–18, No. 238, 1919, p. 5.

CONTRACTS.—*See also* M.M.

CORNHILL COMMITTEE.—*App.* by Tre. in winter of 1914–15. *Obj.* To keep general touch between the Government and the City over questions of trade and finance, including Blockade. *Repr.* City Interests (mainly) : the Government. *Ref.* Cd. 8741 (details privately communicated). *Diss.* Before end of 1916, being gradually superseded by later and more specialized organizations.

COST OF LIVING, WORKING CLASSES, (SUMNER) COMMITTEE.— *App.* by Tre., Mar. 1918. *Obj.* To report upon increases since July 1914, and counterbalancing factors due to the War. *Repr.* M.F., W.O., Legal Profession, Economists and Statisticians, Co-operative Societies, Employers, Labour, Women. *Ref.* Cd. 8980. *Diss.* Oct. 1918.

CROWN AND GOVERNMENT LANDS COMMITTEE.—*App.* by Tre., Oct. 1921. *Obj.* To examine question of single Department for all Government purchases and sales of land and buildings and for management of Crown and Government property. *Repr.* Tre., W.O., Royal Household, land-owners, land agents, surveyors. *Ref.* Cmd. 1689. *Diss.* May 1922.

CURRENCY AND FOREIGN EXCHANGES, JOINT COMMITTEE.— *App.* jointly by Tre. and M.R., Jan. 1918. *Obj.* To report on problems of currency and foreign exchanges likely to arise during reconstruction period, on functions of Bank of England and on Bank Charter Act, 1844. *Repr.* Tre., M.R., Bank of England, British and foreign Banks, Finance Houses, foreign merchants, Legal Profession, Economists. *Ref.* Cd. 9182 ; Cmd. 464. *Diss.* Dec. 1919.

CUSTODIAN OF ENEMY PROPERTY.—*App.* under Trading with the Enemy Acts early in the War, the Public Trustee being appointed to the position. *Obj.* To have control over enemy property or claims vested in him. *Ref.* Cd. 8575, p. 8.

DEFENCE, ECONOMY, COMMITTEES (TWO).—*App.* by Tre. in spring of 1922, following Geddes Reports. *Obj.* To consider practicability and possible economies in (i) establishment of Ministry of Defence, (ii) amalgamation and co-ordination of services common to Army, Navy, and Air Force. *Repr.* Official and expert. *Ref.* T., 16th May 1922, p. 10.

ECONOMY.—*See* Defence, Expenditure, Staffs, &c.

ELECTORAL EXPENSES.—*See* Registration.

ENEMY BANKS, TREASURY CONTROLLER AND SUPERVISERS. —*App.* by Tre. under H.O. Order, Aug. 1914. *Obj.* To supervise and control operations permitted to banks under the Order, with power to forbid payments and transactions. *Repr.* Prominent chartered accountants. *Ref.* Cd. 8430.

ESTIMATES AND EXPENDITURE OF PUBLIC SERVICES COMMITTEE.—*App.* by Tre., apparently in 1918. *Obj.* To consider suggestions of Select Committee on National Expenditure for improving form of estimates. *Repr.* Tre. and others. *Ref.* H.C., Nos. 83, &c., 1919.

EXCESS PROFITS DUTY, BOARDS OF REFEREES.—*App.* by Tre., under Finance (No. 2) Act, 1915, entering on duties, Feb. 1916. *Obj.* To determine disputed questions regarding excess profits and (later) certain income tax questions (wear and tear). *Repr.* Representative Bankers, Chartered Accountants, Manufacturers and Business Men. *Ref.* P.G.A., 1914–16 ; Cd. 9134.

EXCESS PROFITS DUTY COMMITTEE.—*App.* prior to June 1917. *See* Cd. 8741, p. 5. Details lacking.

EXCHEQUER AND AUDIT DEPARTMENTS ACT, 1866, AMENDMENT COMMITTEE.—*App.* by Tre., Oct. 1920. *Obj.* To report upon amendment of Act. *Repr.* Parliament, Tre., Comptroller and Auditor-General. *Ref.* Cmd. 1383. *Diss.* June 1921.

EXCHEQUER GRANTS, LOCAL SERVICES, COMMITTEE.—*App.* by the Government, Feb. or Mar. 1922, following reports of Geddes Committee. *Obj.* To report upon suitable system of Exchequer Grants for locally administered services to replace percentage grant system. *Repr.* Parliament and others. *Ref.* Cmd. 1713, p. xii. *Still sitting at end of 1922.*

EXPENDITURE EMERGENCY INTER-DEPARTMENTAL COMMITTEES.—*App.* jointly by Tre. and Adm. (1914), M.M. (Oct. 1915), and M.S. (1917). *Obj.* To deal jointly with urgent expenditure by Department concerned and secure immediate sanction of Tre. *Repr.* Tre. and Department concerned. *Ref.* H.C., Nos. 325, 1915 ; 40, 123, 167, 1917 ; 100, 1918.

EXPENDITURE NATIONAL (GEDDES) COMMITTEE.—*App.* by C.E. in 1921. *Obj.* To examine national expenditure on supply sources, with view to all reductions immediately possible. *Repr.* Prominent Business Men (Sir E. Geddes, Lord Inchcape, Lord Faringdon, Lord Mackay, Sir G. Granet). *Ref.* Cd. 1581. *Diss.* Feb. 1922.

EX-SERVICE CANDIDATES SELECTION BOARD.—*App.* by C.S.C., probably in 1919. *Obj.* To select qualified candidates for permanent posts in higher division of Civil Service. *Repr.* Not stated.

EX-SERVICE MEN APPOINTMENTS IN CIVIL SERVICE (LYTTON) COMMITTEE.—*App.* by Tre., July 1920. *Obj.* To advise on modifications of existing arrangements for appointment of ex-service men to permanent and temporary posts in Civil Service. *Repr.* H.L., H.C., Tre., M.L., ex-service men, women. *Ref.* Reports of Committee (H.M.S.O., 1920, 1921). *Diss.* June 1921.

EX-SERVICE MEN IN CIVIL SERVICE SALARIES (SOUTH-BOROUGH) COMMITTEE.—*App.* by C.E., May 1923. *Obj.* To consider how far recommendations of Lytton Committee (preceding entry) have been carried out and to report upon the modified initial rates proposed by the Committee. *Repr.* H.L., H.C. (chief parties), Labour, Women. *Ref.* Report of Committee (H.M.S.O., 1923). *Diss.* End of 1923.

FACILITIES FOR SAVING AFTER THE WAR COMMITTEE.—*App.* by Savings, War, National Committee (q.v.), June 1917. *Obj.* To consider provision of facilities for small investors after the War. *Repr.* Parliament, Tre., War Savings Committee, Bankers, Labour. *Ref.* Cd. 7112, p. 8. *Diss.* During 1918.

FINANCIAL OFFICERS, COUNCIL OF.—*App.* by Tre., Nov. 1919. *Obj.* To consider position of accounting officers of Government Departments. *Repr.* Tre. and Financial Officers of various Departments. *Ref.* H.C., No. 231, 1919, p. xix. *Diss.* Dec. 1919.

FINANCIAL FACILITIES, JOINT COMMITTEE.—*App.* by Tre. and M.R., Nov. 1917. *Obj.* To consider adequacy of normal financial facilities to needs of industry during reconstruction and suggest emergency arrangements. *Repr.* Tre., M.R., bankers, finance, industry, railways, commerce, Controlled Establishments' Association. *Ref.* Cd. 9227. *Diss.* Nov. 1918.

FINANCIAL RISKS.—*See* M.R.

FISHING VESSELS, IRISH WAR RISKS.—*See* D.A.T.I.

FOREIGN EXCHANGES.—*See* Currency and Foreign Exchanges.

FOREIGN TRADE DEBTS COMMITTEE.—*App.* by Tre., Nov. 1914. *Obj.* To approve advances to British exporters under scheme of State assistance in respect of outstanding foreign and colonial debts. *Repr.* Tre., Bank of England, Joint Stock Banks, Chambers of Commerce. *Ref.* B.T.J., 5th and 12th Nov. 1914.

GEDDES COMMITTEE.—*See* Expenditure, National.

GOLD PRODUCERS' COMMITTEE.—*App.* by representative meeting of Gold Mining Industry of the Empire, July 1918. *Obj.* To prepare producers' case for presentation to Government in relation to war difficulties of industry. *Repr.* Gold Mining Industry of the Empire. *Ref.* T., 4th July 1918, p. 11. *Diss.* Presumably later in 1918.

GOLD PRODUCTION (INCHCAPE) COMMITTEE.—*App.* by Tre., Sept. 1918. *Obj.* To report upon effects of war on gold production of British Empire, with special reference to low-grade ores. *Repr.* Tre., Banking, Finance, Commerce. *Ref.* Cmd. 11; H.M.S.O., 1918. *Diss.* Nov. 1918.

GOVERNMENT LANDS.—*See* Crown and Government.

GOVERNMENT LOANS.—*See* Overseas.

GOVERNMENT OFFICES, ORGANIZATION.—*See* Civil Service Staffs.

HOUSING FINANCE COMMITTEE.—*App.* by Tre., Oct. 1919. *Obj.* To consider means of raising capital for local housing schemes, and prepare model long-term security. *Repr.* Tre., M.H., L.A.'s, National War Savings

Committee, Banking, Finance, with special representatives for Scotland and Ireland. *Ref.* Cmd. 444.

KITCHEN.—*See* Parliament.

INCHCAPE COMMITTEE.—*See* Gold Production.

INSURANCE, IRISH FISHING.—*See* D.A.T.I., *under* Fishing.

INSURANCE, NATIONAL, AUDIT COMMITTEE.—*App.* by Tre., July 1916. *Obj.* To investigate question of audit of certain claims for repayment, following report of Public Accounts Committee. *Repr.* Parliament, Tre., B.T., Accountants, Auditors under National Insurance Acts, Labour. *Ref.* T., 7th July 1916, p. 5.

LAND PURCHASE, NORTHERN IRELAND, COMMITTEE.—*App.* by Tre., after consultation with H.O., June 1923. *Obj.* To report upon terms of future land purchase in Northern Ireland. *Repr.* Parliament, Tre., I.O. (former), Legal Profession, Government of Northern Ireland. *Ref.* Cmd. 1967. *Diss.* July 1923.

LOCAL LOANS, SERVICES.—*See* Exchequer Grants, Savings Certificates.

LONDON EXCHANGE COMMITTEE.—Mentioned in H.C., No. 116, 1920, p. 47. No details.

LONDON.—*See also* Savings, War.

LYTTON COMMITTEE.—*See* Ex-Service Men.

MERCANTILE MARINE.—*See* Savings, National.

NATIONAL EXPENDITURE.—*See* Expenditure.

OLD AGE PENSIONS, DEPARTMENTAL COMMITTEE.—*App.* by C.E., April 1919. *Obj.* To report upon alterations in rates of Old Age Pensions and conditions of qualification. *Repr.* Parliament, L.G.B., L.G.B.(Sc.), N.H.I.C., Board of Customs and Excise, Friendly Societies, National War Savings Committee, Labour, Actuaries, Surveyors, Women. *Ref.* Cmd. 410. *Diss.* Nov. 1919.

OVERSEAS AND GOVERNMENT LOANS COMMITTEE.—*App.* by Tre. prior to June 1917. Details lacking. *See* Cd. 8741, p. 8.

PAY, ETC., OF STATE SERVANTS (ANDERSON) COMMITTEE.—*App.* by Tre. early in 1923. *Obj.* To investigate remuneration and conditions of service of Civil and Fighting Services, and report on increases in numbers employed and duties since 1914. *Repr.* Civil and Fighting Services, Business Men. *Ref.* Report (H.M.S.O., 1923). *Diss.* July 1923.

PRISON OFFICERS SUPERANNUATION COMMITTEE.—*App.* by Tre., Dec. 1918. *Obj.* To report upon conditions of service of prison officers, with reference to grant of special pensions' benefits. *Repr.* Tre., H.O., S.O., Actuaries. *Ref.* Cmd. 313.

PRIZE (OVERSEA) DISPOSAL COMMITTEE.—*App.* by Tre., Dec. 1914. *Obj.* To report on sale, disposal and chartering of prizes captured or detained in overseas ports, and deal with cases remitted to them by authorities of overseas territories. *Repr.* Tre., B.T., C.O., F.O., In.O.,

Crown Agents for the Colonies. *Ref.* B.T.J., 3rd Dec. 1914 ; H.C., No. 24 1916.

PROCURATOR-GENERAL'S ADVISORY COMMITTEE.—*App.* by Tre., presumably early in war. *Obj.* To advise on procedure in conduct of Adm. business in Prize Courts. *Repr.* Not stated. *Ref.* Cd. 8741, p. 9 (full details lacking).

PRODUCTION.—*See* B.T.

PROFITS, FIXING OF RATES, COMMITTEE.—*App.* by Tre., on recommendation of Select Committee on National Expenditure (*see* Parliament), in 1917 or earlier. *Obj.* To co-ordinate rates of profit on various forms of war work. *Repr.* Not stated. *Ref.* H.C., No. 132, 1918, p. 16.

PUBLIC DEPARTMENTS, WAR EXPANSION, COMMITTEE.—*App.* by Tre., prior to Sept. 1917. Details lacking. *See* Cd. 8741, p. 11, *under* War Expansion.

RAILWAY AGREEMENTS, SETTLEMENTS, JOINT COMMITTEE.— *App.* jointly by Tre. and M.T., about April 1922. *Obj.* To deal informally with proposals for settlements under Railways Agreements and decide questions of principle. *Repr.* Tre., M.T. *Ref.* H.C., No. 7, 1923, p. xlvi. *See also* M.T.

REGISTRATION, ELECTORAL EXPENSES, DEPARTMENTAL COMMITTEE.—*App.* by Tre., at suggestion of M.H., late in 1919. *Obj.* To inquire into remuneration, &c., of registration officers and others under Representation of the People Act, 1918. *Repr.* Tre., M.H. and others. *Ref.* Cmd. 923, p. 115. *Diss.* Winter of 1919–20.

RETRENCHMENT IN PUBLIC EXPENDITURE COMMITTEE.— *App.* by C.E., July 1915. *Obj.* To report upon possible savings in civil departments, without detriment to national interests. *Repr.* Parliament, Business Experts, Labour. *Ref.* Cd. 8068, 8200. *Diss.* Feb. 1916.

RETRENCHMENT IN PUBLIC EXPENDITURE, OFFICE COM-MITTEES.—*App.* in certain Government Departments in 1915. *Obj.* To prepare schemes for securing economy in expenditure of Department concerned. *Rep.* The Department concerned. *Ref.* Cd. 8180.

SALES OF SHIPS.—*See* M.S.

SAVINGS CERTIFICATES AND LOCAL LOANS COMMITTEE OF INQUIRY.—*App.* by Tre., Nov. 1922. *Obj.* To report on future of arrangements for paying part of proceeds of certificates into Local Loans Fund, and of future relations of Savings Committees, P.O., and P.O. and Trustee, Savings' Banks. *Repr.* H.C., Tre., P.O., National Debt Office, L.A.'s, National and Scottish Savings Committees, Finance, Labour. *Ref.* Cmd. 1865. *Diss.* April 1923.

    (Relations with Trustee Savings Banks were dealt with by a Sub-Committee.)

SAVINGS, NATIONAL, ASSEMBLY.—*App.* July 1919 and subsequent years, by Local (*formerly* War) Savings Associations to meet twice yearly. *Obj.* To form consultative body for expression of views and experience of voluntary workers in savings campaign, and for electing representatives to National Savings Committee. *Repr.* Voluntary workers, through Savings Associations. *Ref.* Cmd. 775, p. 2.

SAVINGS, NATIONAL, ASSOCIATIONS, AUDIT AND INSPECTION, STANDING COMMITTEE.—*App.* by National Savings Committee about end of 1921. *Obj.* To consider means of systematizing and supervising audit and inspection. *Repr.* National Committee. *Ref.* 7th Annual Report of Committee, p. 2 (H.M.S.O., 1923). *Diss.* Prior to April 1923.

SAVINGS, NATIONAL, ASSOCIATIONS, COMMITTEE, LOCAL COM-MITTEES.—*See under* Savings, War.

SAVINGS, NATIONAL, CO-OPERATION WITH TRUSTEE SAVINGS BANKS, JOINT CONFERENCE.—*App.* jointly by National and Scottish Savings Committees and Trustee Savings Banks Association in 1923. *Obj.* To consider methods of co-operation on lines recommended by Savings Certificates and Local Loans Committee (q.v.). *Repr.* The appointing bodies. *Ref.* National Savings Committee, 7th Annual Report, p. 3 (H.M.S.O., 1923).

SAVINGS, NATIONAL, MERCANTILE MARINE SUB-COMMITTEE. —*App.* by National Committee, apparently in 1919 or earlier. *Obj.* To organize savings' propaganda in mercantile marine. *Repr.* The Com-mittee, B.T., ship-owners, Sailors' Societies. *Ref.* Cmd. 775, p. 3. *Per-manent.*

SAVINGS, NATIONAL, SCHOOLS ADVISORY COMMITTEE.—*App.* by National Committee in 1920, on recommendation of National Assembly (q.v.). *Obj.* To advise on best means of stimulating saving in schools. *Repr.* Teachers and others. *Ref.* Cmd. 1427. *Permanent.*

SAVINGS, NATIONAL, WOMEN'S ADVISORY COMMITTEE.— Presumably developed out of, or absorbed, Women's Auxiliary Committee (*see under* Savings, War) in 1919 or earlier, as *permanent part of organization.*

SAVINGS, WAR, ARMY.—*See* next entry.

SAVINGS, WAR, ASSOCIATIONS, LOCAL.—*App.* locally in many districts from 1916, becoming in 1919 changed to National Savings Associa-tions. *Obj.* To encourage and facilitate savings by persons of small means for purchase of war savings certificates. *Repr.* Prominent local persons. *Ref.* Cd. 8376, pp. 6, 7. *Still in existence.*

(Associations were also formed in various units of the Army during the War, and in June 1920 their formation in all units at home and abroad was made compulsory by A.C.)

SAVINGS, WAR, CENTRAL ADVISORY COMMITTEE.—*See* Savings, War, National Committee below.

SAVINGS, WAR, COMMITTEES, COUNTY, LOCAL CENTRAL, AND LOCAL.—*App.* locally at instigation of National and Scottish Committees, from spring 1916, each large borough and urban district having a Local Central Committee and the rest of each county being under a County Committee, with Local Committees in each district. *Obj.* To promote local organization of war savings. *Repr.* L.A.'s, local interests, and (from 1919) National Savings Associations. *Ref.* Cd. 8516, p. 6. *Diss.* County Com-mittees disbanded at close of war, Local still in existence.

SAVINGS, WAR, IRELAND, COMMITTEE.—A Committee was established presumably on similar lines to National and Scottish Committees (q.v.), but may have come to an end by May 1917, when the Scottish Committee was extended to Northern Ireland, or earlier. *See* Cd. 8741, p. 11, *under* War Savings.

SAVINGS, WAR, IRELAND, PROVINCIAL COMMITTEES.—*App.* for each of four provinces of Ireland, Mar. 1918. *Obj.* To promote war savings campaign in Ireland. *Repr.* Presumably as with other similar Committees. *Ref.* Cmd. 194, p. 4.

SAVINGS, WAR, LOCAL COMMITTEES.—*See under* County Committees.

SAVINGS, WAR, LONDON SCHOOLS COMMITTEE.—*App.* by National Committee, with consent of L.C.C., Oct. 1917. *Obj.* To increase number of War Savings Associations in London Schools. *Repr.* Associated teachers in London. *Ref.* Cd. 9112, p. 7.

SAVINGS, WAR, MERCANTILE MARINE.—*See under* Savings, National.

SAVINGS, WAR, METROPOLITAN COMMITTEE.—*App.* by National Committee, Jan. 1917, with Women's Sub-Committee. *Obj.* To assist in War Loan Campaign and later in extending general war savings. *Repr.* Lord Mayor and others, with chief National Women's Societies on Sub-Committee. *Ref.* Cd. 9112, p. 8. *Possibly still in existence.*

SAVINGS, WAR, NATIONAL COMMITTEE.—*App.* by Tre., Feb. 1916, originally as separate National Organizing, and Central Advisory, Committees, which were amalgamated in April 1916. *Obj.* To promote formation of agencies and societies for war savings, and advise upon, approve and supervise actual schemes. *Repr.* Parliament, Tre., P.O., Bank of England, insurance, business and financial experts, Labour, Friendly Societies, teachers, women. *Ref.* Cd. 8516. *Made permanent* in 1919 as the National Savings Committee.

SAVINGS, WAR, SCOTTISH COMMITTEE.—*App.* by Tre. in spring of 1916, and extended to cover Northern Ireland, May 1917. *Obj.* As with National Committee. *Repr.* L.A.'s, Bank of Scotland, Clergy, Actuaries, Legal Profession, Friendly Societies, Women. *Ref.* Cd. 8799. Presumably *Permanent*, as with National Committee.

SAVINGS, WAR, WOMEN'S AUXILIARY COMMITTEE.—*App.* by National Committee (presumably) in 1916. *Obj.* To utilize and develop women's side of war savings campaign. *Repr.* Representative women. *Ref.* Cmd. 194, p. 4. *Diss.* Presumably developed into, or absorbed by, Women's Advisory Committee (*see under* Savings, National) as permanent part of organization.

SAVINGS, WAR, WOMEN.—*See also* Savings, War, Metropolitan, and *under* Savings, National.

SCHOOLS.—*See under* Savings above.

SHIPPING LIQUIDATION COMMISSION.—*App.* apparently by Tre. in 1919 or 1920. *Obj.* To carry out final liquidation of accounts and claims of Government Departments in respect of shipping. *Repr.* Official and expert. *Ref.* H.C., Nos. 7, p. xliii, 32, p. 234, 1923.

SOUTHBOROUGH COMMITTEE.—*See under* Ex-Service Men.

SPIRITS AND WINE, DELIVERY FROM BOND, ADVISORY COMMITTEE.—*App.* by C.E., Mar. or April 1917. *Obj.* To advise the Board of Customs and Excise on issue of authorities for delivery from bond, under restrictions on issue. *Repr.* Board of Customs and Excise, Wine and Spirits Association, importers, wharfingers. *Ref.* B.T.J., 5th April 1917.

STAFFS.—*See* Civil Service, and under various Departments, Adm., M.M., &c.

SUBSTITUTION BOARD, JOINT.—*See* M.L.

SUMNER COMMITTEE.—*See* Cost of Living.

SUPERANNUATION OF SCHOOL TEACHERS DEPARTMENTAL COMMITTEE.—*App.* by Tre., Aug. 1922. *Obj.* To report upon modification of existing system of superannuation to secure economy and an adequate system. *Repr.* H.L., H.C., Tre., B.E., B.E.(Sc.), Government Actuary, educational experts, employers, teachers, women. *Ref.* Cmd. 1962. *Diss.* July 1923.

SUPERANNUATION.—*See also* Prison Officers.

TEACHERS.—*See* Superannuation.

TOBACCO GROWING IN GREAT BRITAIN INQUIRY COMMITTEE. —*App.* by Tre., Mar. 1923. *Obj.* To inquire into position and prospects of industry and question of granting Government assistance. *Repr.* H.C., Tre., B.A., B.A.(Sc.), B.A. (Northern Ireland), C.E., D.C. *Ref.* Cmd. 1983. *Diss.* Nov. 1923.

TRADE FACILITIES ACT ADVISORY COMMITTEE.—*App.* by Tre., about end of Nov. 1921, under Trade Facilities Act. *Obj.* To advise Tre., in exercise of powers under the Act of guaranteeing loans raised to finance capital undertakings. *Repr.* Presumably business and financial experts. *Ref.* P.G.A., 1921. *Still in existence at end of 1922.*

TRUSTEE SAVINGS BANKS.—*See under* Savings Certificates.

TUBERCULOSIS, GRANTS, SPECIAL COMMITTEE.—*App.* by C.E., Sept. 1919. *Obj.* To consider alterations in amount or conditions of grants from public funds for treatment of tuberculosis in civil population in light of experience and provision recommended for ex-service men. *Repr.* Tre., M.H., S.B.H., Welsh Board of Health, L.G.B.(I.), N.H.I.C. *Ref.* Cmd. 923, pp. 61–2. *Diss.* By Aug. 1920.

UNIVERSITY GRANTS STANDING COMMITTEE.—*App.* by Tre., in consultation with B.E., B.E.(Sc.), and Irish Education Authorities, June 1919. *Obj.* To inquire into needs of university education and advise on application of Parliamentary grants. *Repr.* B.E., C.S.C., Universities, including Women's Colleges, Scientists, &c. *Ref.* Cmd. 1163.

VALUATIONS.—*See* M.M.

WAR LOAN (1917) ADVERTISING COMMITTEE.—*App.* by C.E., Jan. 1917. *Obj.* To advise on advertising of Loan. *Repr.* Chartered accountants. *Ref.* T., 11th Jan. 1917, p. 9. *Diss.* Later in 1917.

WAR LOAN FOR SMALL INVESTORS COMMITTEE.—*App.* by C.E. in autumn of 1915. *Obj.* To suggest means for promoting investments in War Loan by small investors. *Repr.* Parliament, Tre., banking, business, insurance and educational experts, Labour. *Ref.* Cd. 8146, 8179. *Diss.* Jan. 1916.

WAR LOAN INFORMATION BUREAUX.—*App.* locally, with a Headquarters Bureau, in Jan. 1917. *Obj.* To give information as to 1917 War Loan. *See* Cd. 9112, p. 3.

WAR SAVINGS.—*See* Savings.

WAR TRADE DEPARTMENT.—*See* Separate Section.

WINES.—*See* Spirits and Wine.

WOMEN'S EMIGRATION, MISSIONS.—*See* C.O.

WOMEN.—*See also* Savings, National ; Savings, War.

WORKMEN'S COMPENSATION FOR DISABLED MEN.—*See* H.O.

WAR OFFICE, INCLUDING ARMY COUNCIL

ACCOUTREMENTS.—*See* Harness.

AFRICAN COLONIES.—*See* Cameroons.

AGRICULTURAL, ARMY, COMMITTEE.—*App.* by A.C., Jan. 1918. *Obj.* To co-ordinate and develop work of cultivation of land by Army units at home and abroad. *Repr.* A.C., Tre., F.P.D., Quartermaster-General, Directorate of Lands (W.O.), R.A.F. *Ref.* Cmd. 308. *Diss.* July 1919.

AGRICULTURAL, COMMAND, COMMITTEES.—*App.* by Commanders-in-Chief of each command in U.K., probably early in 1918. *Obj.* To co-ordinate and develop land cultivation in their commands. *Repr.* Not stated. *Ref.* J.B.A., Nov. 1918, p. 929.

AGRICULTURAL LABOUR.—*See* Census of.

AIR BOARD (FIRST).—*App.* in advisory capacity by Cabinet, May 1916. *Obj.* To discuss air policy, make recommendations to War Departments, with power of appeal to War Committee of Cabinet and consider amalgamation of supply and design for military and naval services. *Repr.* Cabinet, W.O., Adm. *Ref.* Cd. 9005. *Diss.* Dec. 1916, on formation of Second Air Board (*see* A.M., heading).

AIR, JOINT, COMMITTEE.—*App.* by Cabinet, Feb. 1916. *Obj.* To act in advisory, not executive, capacity for preventing competition between military and naval air services, and improve output of machines by co-ordinating design and placing of orders. *Repr.* W.O., Adm., Naval and Military Forces and other experts. *Ref.* Cd. 9005. *Diss.* April 1916.

ALIENS AFTER THE WAR.—*See* M.R.

AMMUNITION, ORDNANCE DEPOTS, COMMITTEE.—*App.* by W.O. in 1920 or earlier. *Obj.* To report upon existing depots. *Repr.* W.O., H.O. (Explosives Department) and others. *Ref.* Cmd. 1324, p. 2.

ANTI-AIRCRAFT EQUIPMENT COMMITTEE.—*App.* prior to Sept. 1917. *Ref.* without details, Cd. 8741, p. 2.

ARMAMENTS OUTPUT COMMITTEE.—*App.* by Lord Kitchener on 31st Mar. 1915. *Obj.* To supervise and facilitate diversion of labour to war work, and generally stimulate output of munitions. *Repr.* Expert business men and others. *Ref.* Cd. 9005, p. 68 ; Orton, p. 31. *Diss.* Developed into Armaments Output Department of W.O., May 1915, and formed nucleus of M.M., June 1915.

ARMY SANITARY COMMITTEE.—*See under* Sanitary.

ARMY TRUSTEE.—This official, with the appropriate organization, was appointed by A.C., July 1918, to provide for safe custody of funds (other than public money) existing for benefit of Army, and act as trustee, agent or custodian, executing provisions of trusts, A.C. orders or instructions of persons or bodies providing the funds. *See* T., 1st Aug. 1918, p. 3.

(*See also under* Funds.)

BATTLES NOMENCLATURE COMMITTEE.—*App.* by A.C. after the War. *Obj.* To classify the actions fought by British military forces during the War. *Repr.* Officers of British and Imperial Armies. *Ref.* T., 10th May 1921, pp. 10, 11. *Diss.* May 1921.

BELTING.—*See* Harness.

BOOT PRICES COMMITTEE.—*App.* to act under Leather Supplies Central Committee (q.v.) in spring of 1917. *Obj.* To advise on prices for various manufactures of Army Boots. *Repr.* W.O., manufacturers. *Ref.* Cd. 8447, pp. 9, 25.

BOOT PRICES LOCAL COMMITTEES were similarly constituted in chief centres of the industry, to undertake preliminary discussion of prices for submission to Boot Prices Committee. *See* Cd. 8447, pp. 9, 26.

BOOT PRODUCTION COMMITTEES, LOCAL.—*App.* by W.O. in sixteen areas early in 1918. *Obj.* To secure samples and costings for local production of standard boots. *Repr.* Manufacturers in various branches of the industry. *Ref.* B.T.J., 8th Aug. 1918.

BOOT PRODUCTION SUB-COMMITTEE.—*App.* under Leather Supplies Central Committee (q.v.) in spring of 1917. *Obj.* To advise on measures for securing adequate production of boots. *Repr.* W.O., manufacturers, T.U.'s. *Ref.* Cd. 8447, p. 25.

BRADFORD WAR DEPARTMENT CLOTH OFFICE.—*App.* by W.O. in 1916. *Obj.* To secure decentralization in work of wool control. *Repr.* Official, with business experts. *Ref.* Cd. 8447, pp. 15–16.

BRIDGEMAN COMMITTEE.—*See* Nurses, Supply.

BUILDING RECONSTRUCTION.—*See* Land and Building.

CAMEROONS AND GERMAN AFRICAN COLONIES, COMMITTEE.—*App.* presumably by W.O. immediately after the outbreak of war. *Obj.* To consider advisability of expeditions to these colonies, special importance being attached to wireless stations. *Repr.* Presumably W.O., Adm., and others. *Ref.* Daily Telegraph, 5th Oct. 1922 (details incomplete).

CANTEEN, ARMY, COMMITTEE.—*App.* by W.O. in 1915 or early 1916. *Obj.* To organize and supervise working of Army Canteens. *Repr.* Not stated. *Ref.* Cd. 8905, p. 10. *Diss.* Probably on establishment of Canteen Board.

CANTEEN BOARD, NAVY AND ARMY.—*App.* by W.O., April 1916, to replace the Institutes, Regimental, Board of Control (q.v.), and formed subsequently into trading company, Jan. 1917. *Obj.* To supervise, and, from Jan. 1917, conduct as trading body, canteens in U.K. and to purchase supplies for, but not conduct, Expeditionary Forces Canteens (q.v.). *Repr.* Mainly, if not entirely, naval and military. *Ref.* Cmd. 1280, pp. 3, 4 ; H.C., No. 139, 1918, p. 47. *Diss.* Replaced by Institutes, Navy, Army and Air Force (*see* below), 1st Jan. 1921.

CANTEENS, EXPEDITIONARY FORCES, COMMITTEE.—*App.* by W.O., apparently in Jan. 1915. *Obj.* To supervise conduct of canteens with overseas forces. *Repr.* Not stated. *Ref.* Cd. 8741, p. 3, under Expeditionary; Cmd. 1280, p. 3; P.G.A., 1922 (War Service Canteens Act).

CANTEENS INTER-DEPARTMENTAL COMMITTEE.—*See* Cmd. 1280, p. 4, 1717, p. 4. Details are lacking, but the Committee, which reported before the end of 1920, was apparently appointed to advise on future organization of Navy, Army and Air Force Canteens. It resulted in establishment of Navy, Army and Air Force Institutes under a Council equally representative of three Services, which replaced the Canteen Board (q.v.) at beginning of 1921.

CANTEEN PROFITS COMMITTEE.—*App.* by W.O. in 1920. *Obj.* To report upon apportionments of available profits of Canteen Board and Expeditionary Forces Canteens. *Repr.* Parliament, Employers, Labour. *Ref.* Cmd. 1280. *Diss.* May 1921.

CANTEENS.—*See also* United Services Fund.

CARPET TRADE.—*See* Jute Yarn, Wool.

CENSORSHIP (PRIVATE AND COMMERCIAL COMMUNICATIONS). —*App.* by the Government, under direct control of A.C., at outbreak of war. *Obj.* To control communications to prevent information reaching the enemy and acquire information for our own use. *Repr.* Military, Naval and Civilian Censors, with clerical and administrative staff. *Ref.* Cd. 7679.
   (This is distinct from Press Censorship, *see* Press Bureau.)

CENSUS OF AGRICULTURAL LABOUR, AREA COMMITTEES OF SCRUTINY.—*App.* by W.O. in winter of 1916–17, containing representatives of War Agricultural Committees, and agricultural representatives on County Appeal Tribunals. *Obj.* To scrutinize returns to Census of Agricultural Labour, and report upon local labour supplies. *Repr.* W.O., L.G.B., agriculture (as above). *Ref.* J.B.A., Dec. 1916.

CHAPLAINS (ARMY) ADVISORY BOARD OF SELECTION.—*App.* by W.O., Aug. 1916. *Obj.* To deal with selection of Chaplains of the Forces. *Repr.* W.O. and chief religious bodies. *Ref.* T., 1st Aug. 1916, p. 5. *Diss.* Presumably after Armistice.

CHAPLAINS (ARMY) INTER-DENOMINATIONAL COMMITTEE.— *App.* presumably by W.O. prior to Sept. 1917. *See* Cd. 8741, p. 3. Details lacking.

CHEMICAL FACTORIES, ENEMY, BRITISH MISSION.—*App.* by A.C., Jan. 1919. *Obj.* To visit German chemical munitions' factories in Allied Zone. *Repr.* W.O., M.M., The Army, engineers, chemical manufacturers, with delegates of Allied Governments. *Ref.* Cmd. 1137. *Diss.* Feb. or Mar. 1919.

CHEMICAL WARFARE, MEDICAL PROBLEMS, COMMITTEE.—*App.* by W.O., with concurrence of M.M., Jan. 1918. *Obj.* To advise generally on scientific medical aspects of chemical warfare, circulate information and co-ordinate research. *Repr.* W.O., M.R.C., R.A.M.C., Medical Profession, Scientific Research, with corresponding members abroad. *Ref.* Cd. 8981, p. 76. *Diss.* During 1919.

CIVIL ENGINEERS COMMITTEE.—*App.* by Institute of Civil Engineers early in the War, at request of W.O. *Obj.* To give technical advice on military works of construction. *Repr.* The Institute. *Ref.* H.C., No. 132, 1918, p. 33.

CLOTHING, ARMY, PATTERNS AND SPECIFICATIONS, COM-MITTEE.—*App.* by W.O. in 1918. *Obj.* To review patterns and specifications with view to securing economy by using cheaper materials or manufacturing articles requiring less labour. *Repr.* Clothing trades and others. *Ref.* Cmd. 325, p. 215.

CLOTHING, ECONOMY, COMMITTEE.—*App.* by W.O. early in 1916. *Obj.* To report on issue, condemnation and disposal of military clothing, with view to more effective control. *Repr.* Departmental Committee. *Ref.* H.C., No. 123, 1917, p. 11. *Diss.* Later in 1917.

CLOTHING, STANDARD, COMMITTEE.—*App.* by W.O., under Wool Control, late in the War. *Obj.* To administer scheme for provision of standard clothing. *Repr.* W.C.B., manufacturers and others. *Ref.* H.C., No. 102, 1921, p. 24. *Diss.* Winter of 1919–20.

CLOTHING, STANDARD, WOOL COUNCIL, COMMITTEE.—*App.* by W.C.B., Sept. 1919. *Obj.* To approach Central Profiteering Acts Committee (*see* B.T.), to expedite adoption of the scheme (*see* next entry). *Repr.* Employers, Labour and official members of the Council. *Ref.* B.T.J., 11th Sept. 1919, p. 331.

CLOTHING, STANDARD, SPECIAL COMMITTEE.—*App.* by W.C.B. in first half of 1919. *Obj.* To consider revival of standard clothing scheme. *Repr.* Employers and workpeople in wool textile industry. *Ref.* T., 15th July, p. 9, 18th, p. 11, 1919. *Diss.* July 1919.

CLOTHING, TECHNICAL.—*See* Stores and Supplies.

COMMUNICATIONS, BOARD OF.—*App.* originally before the War (about 1912–13) by W.O., but given increased functions during the War. *Obj.* To work out in peace, and put in operation in war, a scheme for adapting communications to mobilization and other war needs. *Repr.* W.O., Adm., B.T., H.O., Railways and presumably other transport agencies. *Ref.* B.T.J., 28th Mar. 1918.

CONTRACTS, ARMY, ADVISORY COMMITTEE.—*App.* by W.O., Dec. 1915. *Obj.* To advise W.O. on difficulties and important questions of policy. *Repr.* W.O., prominent manufacturers and business men, chartered accountants. *Ref.* Cd. 8447.

CONTRACTS CO-ORDINATING COMMITTEE.—*App.* jointly by W.O., Adm., and A.M. in 1920. *Obj.* To act as advisory body to secure economy, elimination of competition and uniformity in contracting. *Repr.* Contract Departments of W.O., Adm., and A.M. with addition, where necessary, of members of other Government Buying Departments. *Ref.* H.C., No. 47, 1922, p. 197. Apparently *Permanent*.

COURTS MARTIAL, MILITARY, COMMITTEE.—*App.* by A.C., April 1919. *Obj.* To inquire into law and procedure of Courts Martial in peace and war. *Repr.* Parliament, Legal Professions, W.O., the Army, R.A.F., Labour. *Ref.* Cmd. 428 ; T., 1st April 1919, p. 6. *Diss.* July 1919.

CUTTING.—*See* Government Cutting.

DEFENCE OF THE REALM REGULATIONS AMENDMENT COM-MITTEE.—*App.* prior to Sept. 1917, apparently by W.O. *Ref.* without details, Cd. 8741, p. 4.

DEMOBILIZATION CO-ORDINATION COMMITTEE.—*App.* jointly by W.O., Adm., M.L. and other Government Departments affected, Aug. 1917. *Obj.* To co-ordinate in detail plans of War Departments and M.L. for speedy demobilization and resettlement of the Forces, consider early release of ' pivotal ' men, and issue instructions as to priority for demobilization. *Repr.* W.O., Adm., M.L. and other Departments concerned. *Ref.* Cd. 8916 ; Cmd. 325, p. 277. *Diss.* On appointment of Cabinet Committee (q.v.), Nov. 1918.

DEMOBILIZATION, HORSE, COMMITTEE.—*App.* by W.O., probably late in 1917, or in 1918. *Obj.* To frame proposals for demobilization of horses and mules. *Repr.* Branches of W.O. concerned. *Ref.* Cd. 8916.

DEMOBILIZATION, WAR OFFICE, COMMITTEE.—*App.* by W.O. in 1916. *Obj.* To consider demobilization as affecting W.O., prepare scheme and act as link with Committee of R.C. *Repr.* Various Branches of W.O. *Ref.* Cd. 8916.

DEMOBILIZATION.—*See also* Emergency Legislation.

DENTAL SERVICE.—*See* L.G.B., P.C.

DYSENTERY COMMITTEE.—*App.* by W.O., May 1918. *Obj.* To collect information and investigate incidence and segregation of dysentery. *Repr.* W.O., L.G.B., M.R.C., Scientific Research. *Ref.* Cd. 8981, p. 77. *Diss.* By autumn of 1919.

EDUCATION AND TRAINING, OFFICERS, COMMITTEE.—*App.* by W.O. late in 1922. *Obj.* To consider system of training Officers prior to entering Army, and suggest means of economy and efficiency. *Repr.* Parliament, W.O., educational experts. *Ref.* Cmd. 2031. *Diss.* June 1923.

EDUCATION, ARMY, BRANCH.—*App.* as new branch by W.O., Aug. 1918. *Obj.* To direct and co-ordinate educational scheme for the Army. *Repr.* Official and expert. *Ref.* Cmd. 325, p. 298. *Permanent.*

EDUCATIONAL, ARMY, CORPS.—*App.* under Royal Warrant, June 1920, to carry out improved scheme of Army Education, and composed partly of pre-war educational units, and partly of the new organizations set up to deal with the men of the New Armies during demobilization. *See* Cmd. 568, pp. 11–14.

EDUCATION, ARMY, EGYPTIAN ADVISORY COMMITTEE.—*App.* jointly by W.O. and Y.M.C.A. at close of 1918. *Obj.* To advise General Head-quarters in Egypt on educational matters. *Repr.* The Army, Y.M.C.A. *Ref.* Cmd. 321, p. 340.

EDUCATION, ARMY, IMPERIAL, COMMITTEE.—*App.* by W.O. during or shortly after the War. *Obj.* To secure co-operation and co-ordination among Imperial Army Educational Organizations. *Repr.* W.O., Adm., A.M., the Dominions. *Ref.* Cmd. 321, p. 350.

(A Conference was held in London, June 1919, to discuss proposals before this Committee, arising out of experiences of education schemes of British Army and Imperial Forces. *See* T., 12th June 1919, p. 12.)

EDUCATION, ARMY, IMPERIAL FORCES.—Schemes were established in the Forces of the various Dominions, and an Overseas Sailor and Soldier Scholarships Scheme was established in England. *See* Cd. 9225, pp. 8, 9.

EDUCATION, ARMY, INTER-DEPARTMENTAL COMMITTEE.— *App.* by A.C. in 1917 or 1918. *Obj.* To assist W.O. in preparing and administering scheme of Army Education. *Repr.* W.O., Education Departments, and others. *Ref.* Cd. 165, p. 35.

EDUCATION, ARMY, LECTURES COMMITTEE.—*App.* jointly by W.O. and others during the War. *Obj.* To administer scheme of lectures for the Forces at home and overseas, and secure lecturers. *Repr.* W.O., Adm., A.M., The Dominions' Forces, Universities, Victoria League, British and American Y.M.C.A. *Ref.* Cmd. 321, pp. 346, 355. *Diss.* By close of demobilization.

EDUCATION, ARMY, TECHNICAL COMMITTEE.—*See* M.L., *under* Army.

EDUCATION, ARMY, Y.M.C.A., UNIVERSITIES COMMITTEE.—*App.* by the Y.M.C.A., in close touch with B.E., in spring of 1918. *Obj.* To administer Y.M.C.A.'s educational work, including that in the Armies. *Repr.* Universities, Y.M.C.A., working class educational bodies, educational experts. *Ref.* Cmd. 321, p. 339.

EDUCATION, ARMY.—*See also* Musical Training.

EMERGENCY LEGISLATION, WAR OFFICE, COMMITTEE.—*App.* by A.C., July 1917. *Obj.* To consider continuance of emergency powers to facilitate demobilization and resettlement. *Repr.* Various branches of W.O. *Ref.* Cd. 8916.

EXPEDITIONARY FORCES SANITARY COMMITTEE.—*See* Sanitary, Army.

EXPENDITURE, ARMY, ADMINISTRATION AND ACCOUNTING, COMMITTEE.—*App.* by W.O., July 1922. *Obj.* To report on existing system of accounts and suggest changes for economy and efficiency. *Repr.* W.O., Tre., the Army, accountants. *Ref.* Cmd. 2073. *Diss.* Oct. 1923.

(A Sub-Committee was appointed to deal with technical processes of accounting in the Army.)

EXPENDITURE, WAR OFFICE, COMMITTEE.—*App.* by the Government in 1916. *Obj.* To investigate W.O. expenditure and make recommendations. *Repr.* Apparently Cabinet Committee. *Ref.* H.C., No. 151, 1917, p. iv. *Diss.* Before end of 1916.

EXPENDITURE.—*See also* Finance.

EXPLOSIVES, MAGAZINES ON SHIPS, COMMITTEE.—*App.* by W.O., apparently towards close of war. *Obj.* To recommend measures for improving construction, &c. *Repr.* Various Government Departments and possibly others. *Ref.* H.C., No. 184, 1919, p. 20 ; Cmd. 278, p. 2. *Diss.* Apparently reported in 1918.

FARM PRODUCE FOR H.M. FORCES, ORGANIZING COMMITTEE.— *App.* by W.O. about Aug. 1914. *Obj.* To secure sufficient supplies for use of Forces. *Repr.* W.O., Military Authorities, and agriculturalists presumably. *Ref.* Cd. 7855. *Diss.* By Sept. 1917.

FARM PRODUCE COUNTY COMMITTEES.— *App.* by A.C. in 1914. *Obj.* To decide disputes and questions of allocation, price, &c., of forage requisitioned by Military Authorities, and (*see* T., 24th Aug. 1918, p. 11) deal with appeals from Hay Allotment (Traders') Committees (q.v.). *Repr.* Farmers. *Ref.* J.B.A., Sept. 1918. *Diss.* Probably in 1919.

FINANCE, WAR, COMMITTEE.— *App.* apparently by Lord Kitchener in 1914 or 1915. *Obj.* To review financial operations of different departments of W.O. and suggest economies. *Repr.* A.C., W.O., mainly composed of chief Financial Officers. *Ref.* H.C., No. 151, 1917, p. iv. *Diss.* About June 1916. (*See also* Expenditure.)

FLANNEL.—*See under* Man Power and Production.

FLAX CONTROL BOARD.— *App.* by W.O., with approval of the Government, Oct. 1917, and transferred to B.T., April 1919, with amended reference. *Obj.* To secure sufficient supplies of seed, flax, and flax goods for war purposes, and, after satisfying aeroplane requirements, for other purposes; and from April 1919, to promote and co-ordinate arrangement for supply and distribution of sufficient amounts for Government and civilian use. *Repr.* W.O., Adm., M.M., D.A.T.I., Scottish and Irish spinners and manufacturers, T.U.'s in the industry. *Ref.* B.T.J., 1st Nov. 1917; T., 8th May 1919, p. 9.

FLAX CONTROL BOARD, IRISH SUB-COMMITTEE.— *App.* by the Board, Dec. 1917. *Obj.* To issue permits in Ireland to manufacture flax and tow yarn under Flax (Restriction of Consumption) Order, 1917. *Repr.* Government Departments concerned, flax spinners, linen manufacturers, merchants, Labour (later). *Ref.* B.T.J., 3rd Jan. 1918.

FLAX CONTROL BOARD, LABOUR ADVISORY COMMITTEES.— *App.* by the Board, Dec.–Jan. 1917–18. *Obj.* To sit with Irish and Scottish Sub-Committees (q.v.) (*see* preceding and following entries) when considering labour questions. *Repr.* Workpeople in linen trades. *Ref.* B.T.J., 3rd Jan. 1918. *Diss.* By June 1918, when Labour representatives were included in the Sub-Committees.

FLAX CONTROL BOARD, SCOTTISH ADVISORY COMMITTEE.— *App.* by the Board, Dec. 1917. *Obj., Repr.* Similar to Irish Sub-Committee (q.v.). *Ref.* B.T.J., 3rd Jan. 1918.

FLAX EXPORTERS' COMMITTEE (PETROGRAD).— *App.* by W.O. in 1916 and stationed at Petrograd. *Obj.* To organize centralized purchase of Russian flax and arrange for transport. *Repr.* Firms with business organizations in Russia incorporated into single organization for this purpose. *Ref.* B.T.J., 27th June 1918, p. 802.

FLAX OFFICE, WAR DEPARTMENT.— *App.* by W.O. and stationed at Dundee, with branch at Belfast, on or after April 1916. *Obj.* To act as selling organization for Government purchases of Russian flax. *Repr.* W.O., the linen trade. *Ref.* B.T.J., 27th June 1918, p. 802.

FLAX PRODUCTION SCHEME EXAMINATION COMMITTEE.—*App.* by Flax Control Board early in 1919. *Obj.* To advise on position and future of Scheme and of Government flax factories. *Repr.* Flax experts. *Ref.* Cmd. 1205, pp. 3, 4. *Diss.* Later in 1919.

FORAGE, CENTRAL COMMITTEE.—*App.* by W.O. early in the War, and reconstitution recommended by F.P.D. in summer of 1918. *Obj.* To advise in central administration of forage matters, reporting to A.C. and, from June 1918, make better arrangements to assist farmers to dispose profitably of any surplus hay. *Repr.* W.O., B.A., B.A.(Sc.), D.A.T.I., hay producers, traders, users. *Ref.* B.T.J., 14th Sept. and 16th Oct. 1916; T., 15th June 1918, p. 3.

FORAGE COUNTY DISTRIBUTING COMMITTEES.—*See* next entry. *The Times* gives same duties as Hay Allotment County Committees (q.v.). *Repr.* Producers, traders, users. *Ref.* T., 24th Aug. 1918, p. 11.

FORAGE, COUNTY DISTRIBUTION COMMITTEES.—*App.* by A.C., probably early in the War. *Obj.* To organize distribution of requisitioned forage, allocate surplus forage to civilians, and (later) issue licences to use hay and straw. *Repr.* Apparently Traders, as with Hay Allotment Committees (q.v.), and Military Authorities. *Ref.* J.B.A., Oct. 1916, p. 705. *Diss.* Replaced by reformed Committees, Aug. 1918.

FORAGE DEPARTMENT, ARMY.—This Department was responsible for the organization of forage supplies under war conditions, till replaced by Central Council. *See* next entry.

FORAGE DEPARTMENT, CIVIL SUPPLIES, CENTRAL COUNCIL.—*App.* by W.O., Aug. 1918. *Obj.* To act as central authority in place of previous Forage Department, Army. *Repr.* Forage Distributing County Committees. *Ref.* T., 24th Aug. 1918, p. 11 ; J.B.A., Oct. 1918.

FORAGE, IRISH ADVISORY COMMITTEE.—*See* J.B.A., 14th Sept. 1916 ; B.T.J., 22nd Aug. 1918, p. 269.

FORAGE REFERENCE COMMITTEE, SCOTLAND.—*See* J.B.A., 14th Sept. 1916. Possibly came to an end during 1917, as not mentioned with other Forage Committees in J.B.A., Aug. 1917, p. 586.

FUNDS, CENTRAL, REPRESENTATIVE COMMITTEE.—*App.* by A.C., in connexion with Army Trustee (q.v.), July 1918, with power to appoint Committees for special objects. *Obj.* To assist administration of funds (other than public money) for benefit of army under control of A.C., assure contributors to these funds a voice in their distribution, and advise on their custody and disposal. *Repr.* A.C., Overseas, Garrison and Home Forces, London and other district Commands in U.K., with provision for including representation of non-commissioned ranks and co-optation of additional members for other interests concerned, with consent of A.C. *Ref.* T., 1st Aug. 1918, p. 3. Presumably *Permanent.*

GERMAN AFRICAN COLONIES.—*See* Cameroons.

GOVERNMENT CUTTING FACTORY.—*App.* in 1918, to secure economy in cutting. *See* Cmd. 325, p. 215.

GRAVES, ADVISORY COMMITTEE FOR THE UNITED KINGDOM. —*App.* by Imperial War Graves Commission, before June 1918. *Obj.* To consider erection of memorial upon military graves in U.K. *Repr.* The Commission. *Ref.* Cd. 9177, p. 228 ; Cmd. 1076. *Diss.* In 1920.

GRAVES, ANGLO-FRENCH.—*See under* Graves, Mixed.

GRAVES, EGYPTIAN EXECUTIVE COMMITTEE.—*App.* by Egyptian Government, at Imperial War Graves Commission's suggestion, in 1917 or 1918. *Obj.* To organize constructional work on British graves in Egypt. *Repr.* Egyptian Government, British, Indian and Dominions' Forces. *Ref.* Cd. 9177, p. 28 ; Cmd. 1076.

GRAVES, EGYPTIAN LABOUR, AND CAMEL TRANSPORT, CORPS, ADVISORY COMMITTEE.—*App.* by Imperial War Graves Commission in 1920 or early 1921. *Obj.* To consider memorial for members of these Corps. *Repr.* Prominent Egyptians. *Ref.* Commission's Report, 1920–1, p. 8 (H.M.S.O., 1921).

GRAVES, EMPIRE COUNTRIES, COMMITTEES, ETC.—Committees were appointed for various parts of the Empire and Mandated Territories which were theatres of war. Some, like the Anglo-Egyptian and Anglo-Palestine War Cemetery Committees, were appointed by the Imperial War Graves Commission with civilian and military members. South Africa and Ceylon appointed Agencies, representing their Governments and Military Authorities, to act for the Commission. *See* Report of Commission, 1921–2, pp. 6, 7, 13 (H.M.S.O., 1922).

GRAVES, GREECE.—*See under* Graves, Mixed.

GRAVES, HEADSTONES' SELECTION, ADVISERS.—*App.* by Imperial War Graves Commission in summer of 1918. *Obj.* To act as artistic advisers to select regimental headstones. *Repr.* Prominent artists. *Ref.* Cd. 9177.

GRAVES, IMPERIAL WAR, COMMISSION.—*App.* by Royal Warrant in May 1917, after discussion by Imperial War Conference, as separate body but connected with W.O. for parliamentary purposes, and working through various Sub-Committees, some of which are dealt with above and below. *Obj.* To take permanent charge after the War of graves of British and Imperial soldiers in all theatres, duties being extended in 1923 to cover charge of graves in Crimean and certain other previous wars. *Repr.* British and Dominions' Governments, India and Crown Colonies (through In.O. and C.O.), and other persons specially nominated, with Prince of Wales as Chairman. *Ref.* Cd. 8566, pp. 132–5, 145–50 ; Cmd. 1076. *Permanent.*

GRAVES, INDIAN, ADVISORY COMMITTEE.—*App.* by G.I., in co-operation with Imperial War Graves Commission, in 1920 or early 1921. *Obj.* To advise in dealing with graves and memorials in India. *Repr.* G.I., Indian Army and others. *Ref.* Imperial War Graves Commission's Report, 1920–1, p. 9 (H.M.S.O., 1921).

GRAVES, INDIAN, COMMITTEE.—*App.* by Imperial War Graves Commission in 1917 or early 1918. *Obj.* To consider special treatment for Indian graves in Western theatres of war. *Repr.* The Commission ; Hindu and Mohammedan Faiths. *Ref.* Cd. 9177, p. 228. *Diss.* Before June 1918.

GRAVES, INFORMAL COMMITTEE.—*App.* by Imperial War Graves Commission in 1917. *Obj.* To visit cemeteries and advise on methods. *Repr.* Artists, architects. *Ref.* Cd. 9177, pp. 226–7. *Diss.* Oct. 1917.

GRAVES, MISSING DEAD, COMMITTEE.—*App.* by Imperial War Graves Commission, Jan. 1921. *Obj.* To examine difficulties of providing memorials for missing dead and suggest plans. *Repr.* Not stated. *Ref.* Report of Imperial War Graves Commission, 1920–1, p. 5 (H.M.S.O., 1921). *Diss.* During 1921.

GRAVES, MIXED COMMITTEES.—*App.* jointly by Imperial War Graves Commission, bodies previously responsible, and Foreign Governments, for each country where there are British Graves, from May 1915 (formation of Anglo-French Committee). *Obj.* To ensure smooth working in acquiring land and constructing cemeteries in countries concerned. *Repr.* British and foreign members in equal numbers (in some cases, e.g. Greece, partly honorary and partly official members). *Ref.* Cmd. 1076, pp. 11–12.

GRAVES, REGISTRATION AND INQUIRIES DIRECTORATE.—*App.* by W.O., May 1915. *Obj.* To undertake care and supervision of soldiers graves during the War, with assistance of Graves Registration Units in different theatres of war, and deal with inquiries as to those whose fate was not known from the Casualty Lists. *Repr.* Official and expert. *Ref.* Cd. 8566, p. 133 ; Cmd. 1076. *Diss.* Close of war, work taken over by Imperial War Graves Commission.

GRAVES REGISTRATION UNITS.—*See* preceding entry.

GRAVES, SITES IN GERMANY, COMMITTEE.—*App.* by Imperial War Graves Commission by 1921. *Obj.* To select suitable sites in Germany for concentrating British soldiers' graves. *Repr.* The Commission. *Ref.* Report of the Commission for 1921–2, p. 14 (H.M.S.O., 1922).

GRAVES, SOLDIERS, NATIONAL (PRINCE OF WALES) COMMITTEE.—*App.*, at suggestion of Army by P.M., under Prince's Chairmanship, Jan. 1916. *Obj.* To take over care of soldiers' graves from Registration Directorate at close of war, and make necessary preparations for this. *Repr.* Representative men and women, the Dominions, India. *Ref.* Cd. 8566, pp. 133–5 ; Cmd. 1076. *Diss.* Replaced in 1917 by Imperial War Graves Commission.

GRAVES.—*See also* War Memorials.

GRAVEYARDS, ALLIED IN FRANCE, FRENCH COMMISSION.—*App.* by French Government early in 1917. *Obj.* To carry out French legislation to provide in perpetuity land for allied graveyards in France. *Repr.* French Army, British Graves Directorate. *Ref.* Cd. 8566, p. 133.

HALAKITE INQUIRY COMMISSION.—*App.* by A.C., Feb. 1917. *Obj.* To inquire into refusal of Departments concerned to utilize the substance halakite. *Repr.* Judge of the High Court, with expert assessor. *Ref.* Cd. 8446. *Diss.* May 1917.

HARNESS, ACCOUTREMENT, AND BELTING PRODUCTION SUB-COMMITTEE.—*App.* under Leather Supplies Central Advisory Committee in spring of 1917. *Obj.* To advise W.O. on means of securing adequate supplies, with due regard to transport and exchange. *Repr.* W.O., Manufacturers, T.U.'s. *Ref.* Cd. 8447, p. 25.

HATS.—*See* Wool Noils.

HAY ALLOTMENT CENTRAL COUNCIL.—*App.* recommended to W.O. by F.P.D., June 1918. *Obj.* To survey whole problem of hay and forage, and work out scheme for 1918 crop. *Repr.* W.O. and five areas into which England and Wales divided under Army Forage Department. *Ref.* T., 15th June 1918, p. 3.

HAY, ALLOTMENT, COUNTY COMMITTEES.—*App.* by W.O., on advice of F.P.D., Aug. 1918. *Obj.* To dispose of all hay, surplus to requirements of military authorities and farmers. *Repr.* Producers, traders, users. *Ref.* J.B.A., Aug. 1918 ; T., 15th June 1918, p. 3.
(Sometimes called Forage County Distributing Committees (q.v.).)

HAY ALLOTMENT (TRADERS') COMMITTEES.—*App.* by W.O. early in the War. *Obj.* To allot hay and straw after W.O. requirements satisfied, secure equitable distribution for civilian use and sufficient for needs of horse owners and others, with appeal from the Committees to Army Forage Department and Farm Produce County Committees. *Repr.* Hay traders. *Ref.* T., 15th June, p. 3, 24th Aug., p. 11, 1918. *Diss.* Replaced, Aug. 1918, by Hay Allotment County Committees (q.v.).

HAY, REQUISITIONING, AREA COMMITTEES.—*App.* by W.O., July–Aug. 1915, for Northern and Southern areas of England. *Obj.* To adjudicate on disputes as to price of requisitioned hay, with appeal to County Courts. *Repr.* W.O., farmers, hay merchants. *Ref.* J.B.A., Aug. 1915.

HIDES AND SKINS, REGULATION AND DISTRIBUTION, SUB-COMMITTEE.—*App.* under Leather Supplies Central Advisory Committee in spring of 1917. *Obj.* To advise on adequacy of supplies, problems of importation, possibility of inter-allied purchase and distribution of British and imported hides. *Repr.* W.O., tanners, importers, distributors, Labour. *Ref.* Cd. 8447, p. 25.

HIDES, BRITISH MARKET, DISTRIBUTION SUB-COMMITTEE.—*App.* under Leather Supplies Central Advisory Committee in spring of 1917. *Obj.* To advise on distribution of hides in British markets. *Repr.* W.O., tanners, distributors. *Ref.* Cd. 8447, p. 25.

HIGH EXPLOSIVES DEPARTMENT.—*App.* by W.O. near end of 1914 and subsequently transferred to M.M. *Obj.* To develop output of explosives and propellants. *Repr.* Official and expert. *Ref.* H.C., No. 40, 1917, p. 10.

HOSIERY ALLOCATION COMMITTEES.—*App.* by W.O. in four chief centres of the industry, late in 1916. *Obj.* To advise on production of hosiery and allocation of contracts. *Repr.* Manufacturers in different sections of the industry. *Ref.* Cd. 8447, p. 24.

HOSIERY NEEDLE COMMITTEE.—*App.* by W.O. at Leicester, by Sept. 1917. *Obj.* To grant licences and authorize contracts for manufacture and dealings in hosiery latch needles. *Repr.* W.O., Leicester Chamber of

Commerce, needle makers, machine builders, hosiery manufacturers. *Ref.* B.T.J., 4th Oct., 8th Nov. 1917.

HOSIERY NEEDLE SUB-COMMITTEES.—*App.* by main Committee (q.v.), from Sept. 1917. *Obj.* To assist Committee in various branches of its work. *Repr.* Presumably as with main Committee. *Ref.* B.T.J., 8th Nov. 1917.

HOSIERY.—*See also under* Man Power and Production.

HUTTED CAMPS, CIVIL ENGINEERS' COMMITTEE.—*App.* by President of the Institute of Civil Engineers, at request of A.C., in spring of 1915. *Obj.* To visit large hutted camps and report upon work, materials, provision for sanitation and financial arrangements. *Repr.* Institute of Civil Engineers. *Ref.* H.C., No. 115, 1916, App. ix of Evidence. *Diss.* May 1915.

IMPERIAL WAR GRAVES.—*See* Graves.

INFLUENZA EPIDEMIC, COMMITTEES OF EXPERTS.—*App.* by W.O. in 1918. *Obj.* To investigate causes of epidemic and means of prevention among troops. *Repr.* Various experts. *Ref.* Cmd. 325, p. 90.

INSTITUTES, NAVY, ARMY AND AIR FORCE, COUNCIL.—*App.* at beginning of 1921, presumably by W.O., Adm., and A.M., to replace Canteen Board (q.v.). *Obj.* To control institutes established, on recommendation of Canteens Inter-Departmental Committee (q.v.), to replace the Navy and Army Canteens. *Repr.* The Navy, Army and Air Service equally. *Ref.* Cmd. 1280, p. 4, 1717, p. 4. *Permanent.*

INSTITUTES, REGIMENTAL BOARD OF CONTROL.—*App.* by W.O. early in 1915. *Obj.* To control, inspect, and fix prices for, regimental institutes at home. *Repr.* Parliament, the Army, including each Military Command in U.K., prominent business men. *Ref.* T., 2nd Mar. 1916, p. 5. *Diss.* Replaced by Canteen Board, Navy and Army (q.v.), April 1916.

JUTE PRIORITY ADVISORY COMMITTEE.—*App.* by W.O. about April 1917. *Obj.* To advise W.O. representatives at Dundee Jute Goods Depot on grant of priority certificates. *Repr.* Jute spinners and manufacturers. *Ref.* B.T.J., 18th July 1918.

JUTE TRADE, UNEMPLOYMENT, JOINT COMMITTEE.—*App.* by the trade at Dundee about Mar. 1918. *Obj.* To deal with unemployment caused by stoppage of machinery and to consider labour questions in the industry. *Repr.* Employers and workpeople (equal numbers). *Ref.* B.T.J., 18th July 1918.

JUTE YARN, SUPPLIES FOR CARPET MANUFACTURE, COMMITTEE.—*App.* by W.O., or by the trade at its request, late in 1917. *Obj.* To distribute available supplies of jute yarn among carpet manufacturers. *Repr.* Carpet trade. *Ref.* B.T.J., 18th July 1918.

KIPS, INDIAN, AND EAST AFRICAN HIDES SUB-COMMITTEE.—*App.* under Leather Supplies Central Advisory Committee, in spring of 1917. *Obj.* To advise on steps for securing adequate supplies of upper leather, with special reference to Indian and East African hides. *Repr.* W.O., British and Indian Farmers, Labour. *Ref.* Cd. 8447, p. 26.

KIPS, RAW, EAST INDIAN, SUB-COMMITTEE.—*App*. under Leather Supplies Central Advisory Committee in spring of 1917. *Obj*. To advise on measures to secure tanning of these hides in U.K. *Repr*. W.O., Tanners, Labour. *Ref*. Cd. 8447, p. 26.

LAND AND BUILDING RECONSTRUCTION COMMITTEE.—*App*. by W.O. in 1918. *Obj*. To deal with lands, &c., in temporary occupation of War Departments after close of war. *Repr*. Not stated. *Ref*. Cmd. 420, p. 115.

LEATHER CONTROL BOARD.—*App*. by W.O. (or Cabinet) in 1917 or 1918. *Obj*. To ensure sufficient supplies for military and essential civilian needs. *Repr*. Members of leather trades mainly. *Ref*. Cmd. 325, p. 216.

LEATHER, DRESSED AND SOLE, PRICES COMMITTEE.—*App*. under Leather Supplies Central Advisory Committee in spring of 1917. *Obj*. To advise on prices for various tannages of these leathers. *Repr*. W.O., Employers, T.U.'s. *Ref*. Cd. 8447, p. 25.

LEATHER, LIMITATION OF PRICES, SUB-COMMITTEE.—*App*. under Leather Supplies Central Advisory Committee in spring of 1917. *Obj*. To advise on limitation of price of leather manufactured for non-Government purposes from controlled hides. *Repr*. W.O., B.T., Employers, Labour. *Ref*. Cd. 8447, p. 25.

LEATHER SUPPLIES CENTRAL ADVISORY COMMITTEE.—*App*. by W.O., Feb. 1917. *Obj*. To advise on production, &c., of sufficient supplies for military and other needs, with due regard to transport, labour and exchange. *Repr*. Government Departments concerned, manufacturers and T.U.'s in leather and leather-using trades. *Ref*. Cd. 8447, pp. 20, 24 ; B.T.J., 25th Feb. 1917.

(This Committee absorbed some previously constituted Advisory Committees dealing with leather—*see* Cd. 9005, p. 145.)

LEATHER SUPPLIES SUB-COMMITTEES, ADVISORY.—*App*. by W.O. or main Committee from Feb. 1917, eighteen in all being appointed, some of which are described elsewhere. *Obj*. To advise on particular aspects of the trade of which their members have special knowledge. *Repr*. W.O., Employers, T.U.'s. *Ref*. B.T.J., 8th Aug. 1918.

LEATHER, TANNING AND DRESSING MATERIALS, SUB-COMMITTEE.—*App*. under Leather Supplies Central Advisory Committee in spring of 1917. *Obj*. To advise on measures to secure production and import of adequate supplies for military purposes. *Repr*. W.O., tanners, curriers, importers. *Ref*. Cd. 8447, p. 26.

LEATHER.—*See also* Boots, Harness, Hides, Kips.

MACHINE TOOLS.—*See* M.M.

MAGAZINES AND CARE OF WAR MATERIAL COMMITTEE.—*App*. by W.O. in 1918 or 1919. *Obj*. To revise regulations for magazines, &c. *Repr*. W.O., H.O., and probably others. *Ref*. Cmd. 841, p. 2.

MALARIA, PREVENTION, COMMITTEE.—*App*. by W.O. in 1917. *Obj*. To investigate methods of preventing malaria. *Repr*. W.O., L.G.B., Medical Profession. *Ref*. Cd. 9169, p. 64.

MAN POWER AND PRODUCTION, INDUSTRIAL ADVISORY COM-MITTEE.—*App.* by W.O. about end of 1916. *Obj.* To advise W.O. on best means of releasing men for forces and maintaining production in wool and allied trades, and later to act in regard to substitution and other matters for M.N.S., the Committee dividing itself into five separate committees for flannel, hosiery, wool, worsted and Scottish wool textiles. *Repr.* W.O., including Recruiting Department, Employers, T.U.'s. *Ref.* Cd. 8447, pp. 26–7.

MECHANICAL TRANSPORT TECHNICAL INTELLIGENCE BU-REAU.—*App.* by W.O. in 1918. *Obj.* To collect and classify technical information on mechanical transport under war conditions. *Repr.* Presumably experts. *Ref.* Cmd. 325, p. 92.

MEDICAL BOARDS.—*See* M.N.S.

MEDICAL SERVICES, WAR EMERGENCY, SCOTTISH, COM-MITTEE : MEDICAL WAR, CENTRAL COMMITTEE, LOCAL COM-MITTEES, ENGLAND AND WALES.—*App.* by Medical Profession to represent them in co-operation with Government Departments in war matters, and recognized by W.O. *See* N.H.I.C.; Cd. 8338 ; Cd. 9005, p. 189.

MEDITERRANEAN EXPEDITIONARY FORCE, MEDICAL AD-VISORY COMMITTEE.—*App.* by W.O. in 1915. *Obj.* To advise on measures to prevent and deal with disease in armies on Eastern fronts. *Repr.* Medical Profession, including Public Health Medical Service. *Ref.* Cd. 8767, p. xxxix.

MILITARY HEAD-QUARTERS' STAFF (MONEY) COMMITTEE.—*See* Staff.

MINES.—*See* S.I.R.

MOTOR TRANSPORT.—*See* Voluntary Motor Transport.

MUSICAL TRAINING IN THE ARMY, SUB-COMMITTEE.—*App.* by Education, Army, Y.M.C.A., Universities Committee (q.v.) in 1918. *Obj.* To supervise musical training in the Army. *Repr.* Musical experts. *Ref.* Cmd. 321, p. 339.

NEWTON COMMITTEE.—*See* Prisoners of War Inter-Departmental Committee.

NURSES, SUPPLY, COMMITTEE.—*App.* by W.O., Sept. 1916. *Obj.* To review existing methods of obtaining nurses for war hospitals, and suggest means of augmenting supply. *Repr.* Parliament, Medical Profession, Hospitals, Nurses (civil and military), Nurses' Institutes, Women. *Ref.* T., 17th Dec. 1917, p. 9. *Diss.* Before end of 1917.

OFFICERS.—*See* Promotion.

ORDNANCE, AMMUNITION DEPOTS, COMMITTEE.—*App.* by W.O. in or before 1921. *Obj.* To report on existing depots. *Repr.* W.O., H.O., and others. *Ref.* Cmd. 1632, p. 3.

ORDNANCE FACTORIES VALUATION COMMITTEES.—*App.* by W.O., with approval of Tre., in 1920 or 1921. *Obj.* To report upon and carry out ' financial reconstruction ' of factories for post-war needs. *Repr.* W.O., Tre., and others. *Ref.* H.C., Nos. 110, p. 10, 111, p. 26, 1921. *Diss.* 1921 or 1922.

PASSPORT OFFICE.—*App.* under W.O. early in the War. *Obj.* To regulate issue of passports. *Repr.* Official and expert. *Ref.* Cd. 9220, p. 13. *Still in existence at end of 1922.*

PAY.—*See* Cabinet *under* Army and Navy Pay.

PRESS BUREAU (PRESS CENSORSHIP).—*App.* by the Government, as separate Department, taking instructions from W.O. and Adm., Aug. 1914, and attached for administrative purposes to H.O. (*see* Hall, p. 74). *Obj.* To supervise, largely on voluntary basis, issue of news to and by Press, and to prevent information of value from reaching the enemy. *Repr.* W.O., Adm., the Press, through military, naval and civilian censors. *Ref.* Cd. 7680.

PRESS CENSORSHIP COMMITTEE.—*App.* jointly by W.O., Adm., and the Press, about a year before the War. *Obj.* To supervise voluntary agreement with the Press for withholding information whose publication is undesirable in national interest. *Repr.* W.O., Adm., The Press. *Ref.* Cd. 7679. *Diss.* Found adequate in peace time, but, owing to increased volume of war work replaced by Press Bureau, Aug. 1914.

(*See also* Censorship for Private Communications.)

PRICES.—*See* Leather, Woollen Goods.

PRINCE OF WALES' COMMITTEE.—*See under* Graves.

PRIORITY.—*See* Jute, Wool.

PRISONERS OF WAR, BRITISH RED CROSS AND ORDER OF ST. JOHN OF JERUSALEM, JOINT WAR COMMITTEE.—*App.* by the two bodies concerned early in the War. *Obj.* To advise and supervise their work. *Repr.* The two bodies. *Ref.* Cd. 8615, 8741.

PRISONERS OF WAR CENTRAL COMMITTEE.—*App.* by W.O., in co-operation with F.O., British Red Cross and Order of St. John of Jerusalem, Sept. 1916, to supersede existing voluntary organization (*see* Prisoners of War Help Committee). *Obj.* To organize and supervise dispatch of parcels and provision of bread for military and civilian prisoners, deal generally with prisoners' welfare, and regulate supplies likely to be useful to the enemy; and, from Aug. 1917, undertake scheme (*see* T., 7th July, p. 7) for limiting, and subjecting to uniform censorship, parcels to secure sufficient, but not excessive, supplies. *Repr.* Parliament, the Dominions, Civil Service, Prisoners of War Help Committee, British Red Cross, Order of St. John of Jerusalem, Indian Soldiers Fund. *Ref.* Cd. 8615.

(The organization was provided with a Records Department for registering prisoners' addresses in Germany and Austria : *see* Hall, p. 84.)

PRISONERS OF WAR, COMMITTEE ON ORGANIZATION AND METHODS OF CENTRAL COMMITTEE.—*App.* by two Houses of Parliament, in pursuance of Government promise, early in 1917. *Obj.* To inquire into organization and methods of Central Committee and secure improvements. *Repr.* The two Houses. *Ref.* Cd. 8615. *Diss.* June 1917.

PRISONERS OF WAR DEPARTMENT.—Established by W.O. early in war to deal generally with questions of prisoners of war. *See* Cd. 8741, p. 9 (no details given).

PRISONERS OF WAR EMPLOYMENT COMMITTEE.—*App.* by W.O. early in 1917. *Obj.* To deal with proposals for employment of enemy prisoners of war and decide applications for prisoners on national grounds. *Repr.* Parliament, W.O., M.M., B.A. *Ref.* Cd. 8741, p. 9 (no details) ; *T.,* Jan. 1917.

PRISONERS OF WAR HELP COMMITTEE.—*App.* by voluntary effort in 1914, and became W.O. Committee, Mar. 1915. *Obj.* To organize supply of food, &c., for British prisoners of war, and co-ordinate work of regimental and local bodies, having this purpose. *Repr.* Prominent public persons, including business men, British Red Cross and Order of St. John. *Ref.* Cd. 8615. *Diss.* Superseded, Sept. 1916, by Central Prisoners of War Committee (q.v.).
   (This Committee established a smaller Executive Committee.)

PRISONERS OF WAR INTER-DEPARTMENTAL (NEWTON) COMMITTEE.—*App.* by W.O. prior to June 1916. *Obj.* To advise the Government generally on questions concerning prisoners of war, and secure unity and control in administration. *Repr.* Adm., W.O., F.O., H.O. *Ref.* B.T.J., 7th Sept. 1916.

PRISONERS OF WAR REGIMENTAL CARE COMMITTEES AND LOCAL ASSOCIATIONS.—*App.* by voluntary effort from winter of 1914–15. *Obj.* To organize regimental and local provision for prisoners of war. *Repr.* Men and women interested. *Ref.* Cd. 8615.

PROMOTION OF OFFICERS COMMITTEE.—*App.* by W.O. early in 1917. *Obj.* To report generally on promotion and pay of officers of New Armies, Territorials and Special Reserve. *Repr.* Parliament, W.O., Army, Territorials. *Ref.* Cd. 8642, 8978. *Diss.* Jan. 1918.

QUARTERING COMMITTEES, LOCAL.—*Ref.* J.B.A., Aug. 1918, p. 562. Details lacking.

RAW MATERIALS FINANCE BRANCH.—*App.* by W.O. about end of April 1917. *Obj.* To organize financial side of W.O. dealings in home and imported materials. *Repr.* Presumably financial experts. *Ref.* Privately communicated.

RECRUITING, LOCAL ADVISORY COMMITTEES.—*App.* by Parliamentary Local Recruiting Committees (*see under* Parliament) for their areas, Dec. 1915. *Obj.* To advise W.O. representatives on Local Tribunals (*see* L.G.B.) in regard to appeals. *Repr.* Not stated. *Ref.* Cd. 8149. *Diss.* Transferred to M.N.S., Aug. 1917.

RECRUITING MEDICAL ADVISORY COMMITTEE.—*App.* by W.O. during the War. *Obj.* To advise Recruiting Officers and Medical Boards on medical questions. *Repr.* Doctors, &c. *Ref.* Cd. 8617, p. 5.

REGIMENTAL INSTITUTES.—*See* Institutes.

RELIEF, BRITISH RUSSIAN, COMMITTEE.—*App.* apparently by private action, Sept. 1918. *Obj.* To assist British and Russian units of British Societies providing relief in Russia for British, Russian, and Allied troops, and to relieve urgent distress among Russians in and outside Russia. *Repr.* Prominent public men and women, M.I., British Red Cross, Order of St. John of Jerusalem. *Ref.* T., 27th Sept. 1918, p. 6.

REPATRIATION STAFF.—*App.* by W.O. in 1918, with centre at Winchester. *Obj.* To administer scheme for free repatriation of men who returned from overseas to enlist. *Repr.* Official and expert. *Ref.* Cmd. 325, p. 94.

ROAD STONE CONTROL COMMITTEE.—*App.* by W.O., Aug. 1917. *Obj.* To limit supplies to roads required for military purposes and carry out scheme for reorganizing transport of stone. *Repr.* Not stated. *Ref.* Hall, pp. 89–90.

ROAD STONE LOCAL COMMITTEES.—*App.* apparently by W.O., Aug. 1917, under Road Stone Transportation Order, 1917. *Obj.* To assist locally in scheme for reorganizing transport of road material from quarries to users. *Repr.* Not stated. *Ref.* B.T.J., 6th Sept. 1917.

ROADS, JOINT COMMITTEE.—*App.* by A.C., Oct. 1918. *Obj.* To supervise and co-ordinate road works carried out for Government Departments, taking over war work of the Road Board ; and put into effect powers (control, &c.) of A.C. over roads and carry out duties of construction, &c., for war purposes. *Repr.* Not stated, but presumably Government Departments concerned and road users. *Ref.* H.C., Nos. 100, &c., 1920, p. x ; T., 14th Oct. 1918, p. 5. *Diss.* Work transferred to M.T. after Mar. 1920.

ROYAL AIRCRAFT FACTORY COMMITTEE.—*App.* by A.C., Mar. 1916, and terms of reference extended in April. *Obj.* To report upon organization and management of factory and suggest improvements. *Repr.* Commerce, engineers, W.O. (apparently). *Ref.* Cd. 8191. *Diss.* May 1916.

ROYAL FLYING CORPS, ADMINISTRATION AND COMMAND, COMMITTEE.—*App.* by W.O., May 1916. *Obj.* To inquire into administration and command of Corps, with special reference to charges against Higher Command. *Repr.* H.C., Judges, Legal Profession, Army, Engineers. *Ref.* Cd. 8192, 8194. *Diss.* Nov. 1916.

RUSSIAN COMMITTEE.—*See* F.O.

RUSSIAN MILITARY SERVICE APPEAL TRIBUNAL.—*App.* by W.O., in co-operation with Russian representatives in U.K., Sept. 1916. *Obj.* To deal with claims for exemption for Russian citizens resident in London and liable to military service in British Army under arrangements between British and Russian Governments. *Repr.* L.G.B., L.C.C., prominent public men, Legal Profession, Justices of the Peace, Local Clergy, representatives of Russians and Jews, employers. *Ref.* T., 1917, 6th Aug. p. 3, and 26th Sept., p. 7.

RUSSIA.—*See also* Relief.

SANITARY, ARMY, COMMITTEE.—*App.* by W.O., Oct. 1914, being sometimes called Expeditionary Forces Sanitary Committee. *Obj.* To advise on all matters affecting health of Expeditionary Forces at home and abroad. *Repr.* W.O., L.G.B., and others. *Ref.* Cd. 7763, p. 31.

SANITARY, ARMY, COMMITTEE OF THE GENERAL MEDICAL COUNCIL.—*See* Cd. 9157, p. 54. This appears to have been a representative medical body, appointed to advise the previous Committee.

SALVAGE, MILITARY.—Cd. 9005, pp. 146–7, reports a military salvage organization in course of formation for whole Army before end of 1917, incorporating Salvage Depots, established early in 1917 to deal with woollen goods. Hall, p. 91, refers to an Army Salvage Branch.

SALVAGE, NATIONAL, COUNCIL.—*App.* by W.O. early in 1918, with consent of the War Cabinet. *Obj.* To assist in promoting civil salvage, recovery of waste products, and prevention of waste. *Repr.* Principal Government Departments concerned. *Ref.* B.T.J., 7th Mar. 1918.

SALVAGE, NATIONAL, DEPARTMENT.—*App.* under direction of the National Salvage Council (q.v.) as part of Department of Surveyor-General of Supply, Mar. 1918. *Obj.* To carry out administrative work of Council, keep public informed and indicate openings for salvage. *Repr.* Government Departments concerned with salvage, and others. *Ref.* B.T.J., 7th Mar. 1918.

SALVAGE, NATIONAL, EXECUTIVE BOARD.—*App.* by and from National Salvage Council, Mar. 1918. *Obj.* To exercise general executive control on behalf of Council. *Repr.* As with Council. *Ref.* B.T.J., 14th Mar. 1918.

SHELL-SHOCK INQUIRY (SOUTHBOROUGH) COMMITTEE.—*App.* by A.C., Aug. 1921. *Obj.* To investigate types of shell-shock, collate expert knowledge of it acquired during the War, and advise on scientific methods of guarding against occurrence. *Repr.* Parliament, medical representatives of W.O., Adm., A.M., and M.Pen., Boards of Control for England and Scotland, the Army, independent medical men, Legal Profession, Labour. *Ref.* Cmd. 1734. *Diss.* June 1922.

SIR JOHN JACKSON LTD., ROYAL COMMISSION.—*See* Cabinet.

SOLDIERS' DEPENDANTS' APPEALS ASSESSMENT COMMITTEE. —*App.* by W.O. prior to May 1917. *Obj.* To deal with separation allowance appeals by dependants of unmarried soldiers. *Repr.* Not stated. *Ref.* Cd. 9020, p. xii.

SOLDIERS' HEART DISEASES, ADVISORY COMMITTEE.—*App.* by Army Medical Service early in 1916. *Obj.* To investigate complaint known as ' irritable heart of soldiers ' and supervise special hospital treatment for it. *Repr.* Prominent medical men. *Ref.* Cd. 8399, p. 58. *Diss.* In autumn of 1917 (*see* Cd. 8825, p. 74) or later.

SOUTHBOROUGH COMMITTEE.—*See* Shell-shock.

SPHAGNUM MOSS JOINT COMMITTEE.—*App.* in Scotland by Voluntary Organizations' Department of W.O. in 1918. *Obj.* To reorganize collection of sphagnum moss and secure adequate supplies. *Repr.* The Department, Red Cross Society, prominent Scottish residents and voluntary workers. *Ref.* Cmd. 173, p. 7.

STAFF, WAR OFFICE, REVISION COMMITTEE.—*App.* by A.C., by Jan. 1918. *Obj.* To examine systematically and supervise military head-quarters staff of W.O. with view to economies. *Repr.* A.C., and others. *Ref.* Cd. 9220, p. 5 ; H.C., No. 132, 1918, pp. 31, 109.

STAFF, WAR OFFICE, REVISION SUB-COMMITTEE (MONEY COMMITTEE).—*App.* by main Revision Committee, Jan. or Feb. 1918. *Obj.* To inquire into staff of each Department of W.O. *Repr.* W.O., including Finance Department and Secretariat. *Ref.* H.C., No. 132, 1918, p. 109. *Diss.* Work practically discontinued, April 1918.

STAFF, WAR OFFICE, SPECIAL COMMITTEE.—*App.* by A.C., about Aug. 1918. *Obj.* To inquire into present strength of departments of W.O., and report whether in excess of requirements. *Repr.* The Army, men with experience of business and of official administration, with representatives of each department, when under consideration. *Ref.* T., 3rd Sept. 1918, p. 6.

STANDARD ARTICLES.—*See* Wool, Standard Articles.

STORES AND SUPPLIES COMMITTEE.—*App.* by W.O. in 1917. *Obj.* To investigate expenditure on stores and supplies, and organization of Woolwich Ordnance Depot. *Repr.* Parliament, W.O. and others. *Ref.* H.C., No. 132, 1918, p. 47.
   (This Committee appointed six Technical Committees of experts to deal with particular branches of supply.)

SUPPLIES.—*See* preceding entry.

TANKS.—*See* Cabinet under Aviation and Tanks.

TEA PURCHASES COMMITTEE.—*App.* by W.O. before June 1917. *Obj.* To advise on methods of contract and purchase of tea for the Army. *Repr.* Expert buyers and others. *Ref.* Cd. 8447, p. 6.

TETANUS COMMITTEE.—*App.* by W.O. early in the War. *Obj.* To secure adequate supplies of anti-toxin and deal with other problems of tetanus. *Repr.* Presumably largely medical. *Ref.* Westminster Gazette, 27th Feb. 1923 (Letter of Dr. Stephen Paget).

TIMBER ADVISORY COMMITTEE.—*App.* by W.O., Feb. 1917. *Obj.* To assist Timber Supplies Department (q.v.) in organizing timber supplies for the Army, and general control of home-grown timber. *Repr.* Timber Federation and non-federated merchants. *Ref.* B.T.J., 25th Feb. 1917. *Diss.* Transferred to B.T., May 1917.

TIMBER SUPPLIES DEPARTMENT.—*App.* by War Cabinet, under W.O., early in 1917, taking over functions of O.W. and of Home-Grown Timber Committee (*see* B.A.). *Obj.* To secure supplies of timber for the Army, purchase imported, and control home-grown, timber, and stimulate felling. *Repr.* Official, with large expert element. *Ref.* B.T.J., 25th Feb. 1917. *Diss.* Transferred to B.T., May 1917.

TRAINING, OFFICERS.—*See under* Education.

TRANSPORT LIQUIDATION, FRANCE, COMMITTEE.—*App.* apparently by W.O. in winter of 1918–19. Incidental reference in H.C., No. 102, 1921, p. 21.

TROOPS, WELCOME TO LONDON, COMMITTEE.—*App.* at Conference of Common Council of City of London and officers of the Army, Dec. 1918. *Obj.* To arrange, and raise funds for, reception of City regiments on return from war, and permanent commemoration of services. *Repr.* Common Council, G.O.C., London District, Commanding Officers of City Regiments, Bank of England, Stock Exchange, Lloyds, Baltic and other City interests. *Ref.* T., 11th Dec. 1918, p. 5.

UNEMPLOYMENT.—*See* Jute Trades.

UNITED SERVICES FUND ADVISORY COMMITTEE.—*App.* when the Fund was established by or through W.O. in 1919. *Obj.* To deal with application for benefit of men in the Services and ex-Service men of realized war profits of military and naval canteens. *Repr.* The interests concerned, both service and ex-service. *Ref.* T., 22nd Aug. 1919, p. 13 ; H.C., No. 173, 1922, p. xiii. *Permanent.*

UNITED SERVICES FUND SUB-COMMITTEES OF ADVISORY COMMITTEE.—The Committee appointed various Sub-Committees, including both service and ex-service members, to deal with various subjects, such as, Help ; Wives ; Widows and Families ; Welfare ; Serving Officers and Men ; Women. Of these the first, third, and fourth received special attention and Sub-Committees started work at once. The Welfare Sub-Committee, with representatives of chief ex-service organizations and of Tre., set out to obtain views of ex-service men on provision of clubs, &c.

VOLUNTARY ORGANIZATIONS DEPARTMENT.—*App.* by W.O., Sept. 1915. *Obj.* To co-ordinate voluntary efforts on behalf of troops. *Repr.* Official, &c. *Ref.* Cmd. 173. *Diss.* By May 1919.

(The local work was co-ordinated through the Joint Committee of British Red Cross and Order of St. John of Jerusalem (*see under* Prisoners of War), the Queen Mary's Needlework Guild and various County, Borough and District Associations. *See* Cmd. 173, p. 4.)

VOLUNTARY ORGANIZATIONS, LOCAL COMMITTEES.—*App.* for various localities, in and after 1915. *Obj.* To co-ordinate local efforts on behalf of troops and allied populations. *Repr.* L.A.'s, local residents. *Ref.* Cmd. 173, p. 6. *Diss.* By May 1919.

VOLUNTEER MOTOR TRANSPORT COMMITTEE.—*App.* authorized by W.O., Sept. 1916. *Obj.* To deal with voluntary organization of motor transport in connexion with National Volunteers. *Repr.* Parliament, W.O., Territorial Forces, Motor Users and Associations. *Ref.* T., 29th Sept. 1916, p. 3.

W.A.A.C.'s.—*See* M.L.

WARBLE FLY PEST COMMITTEE.—*App.* July 1918 by Conference of Government Departments, traders and scientists and other experts, summoned by the W.O. *Obj.* To report upon means of extermination. *Repr.* As with Conference. *Ref.* J.B.A., Mar. 1919. *See also*—B.A., M.M.

WARBLE FLY PEST SCIENTIFIC SUB-COMMITTEE.—*App.* by main Committee in 1918. *Obj.* To supervise and control experiments into means for removal of pest. *Repr.* Presumably largely scientific, presided over by Chief Veterinary Officer of B.A. *Ref.* J.B.A., Mar. 1919.

WAR, HISTORY OF, COMMITTEE.—*App.* by W.O. before April 1915. *Obj.* To consider and advise upon collation of materials for history of war. *Repr.* Presumably W.O., Adm., The Services, Historians. *Ref.* Cd. 7855.

WAR MEMORIALS, MILITARY ADVISORY COMMITTEE.—*App.* by Imperial War Graves Commission in 1919 or early 1920. *Obj.* To advise upon requests by Governments and individuals in the Empire for permission to erect memorials on battle-fields. *Repr.* The Expeditionary Forces, the Dominions, India. *Ref.* Cmd. 1076, p. 13.

WAR RESERVES COMMITTEE.—*App.* by W.O. in 1919 or 1920. *Obj.* To consider what are proper reserves of stores for war. *Repr.* Not stated. *Ref.* H.C., No. 47, 1922, p. 214.

WAR TROPHIES, DISTRIBUTION, COMMITTEE.—*App.* by W.O. prior to Sept. 1917, to carry out the distribution. *Ref.* without details, Cd. 8741, p. 12 ; Hall, p. 102.

WOOD, ECONOMIES IN PACKING.—*See* B.T.

WOOL ADVISORY PANEL.—*App.* by W.O. in first two years of war. *Obj.* To advise W.O. generally on questions concerning wool. *Repr.* Presumably expert. *Ref.* T., 14th Mar. 1917, p. 3. *Diss.* Replaced by Wool Central Advisory Committee, April 1917.

WOOL, AUSTRALIA, CENTRAL EXECUTIVE AND STATE COMMITTEES.—*App.* by Conference of the industry called by P.M. of Australia, Nov. 1917. *Obj.* To organize purchase of wool clip on behalf of the Imperial Government. *Repr.* Growers, brokers, buyers, manufacturers, scourers. *Ref.* Cd. 9130, p. 8. *Diss.* Not before later part of 1918.

WOOL, AUSTRALIA.—*See also* Wool Realization, Valuation.

WOOL, BRITISH, CENTRAL, COMMITTEE.—*App.* by W.O. in 1914 or 1915. *Obj.* To advise on purchases of British wool. *Repr.* Trade interests involved. *Ref.* Cd. 8447, p. 15. *Diss.* Absorbed into Wool Purchase Committees in 1916.

(This Committee co-operated with various district and sectional Committees, the W.O. being assisted at each stage by trade and district Committees.)

WOOL CENTRAL ADVISORY COMMITTEE.—*App.* by W.O., April 1917, by amalgamation of smaller sectional Distribution Committees. *Obj.* To advise generally on problems of wool supply, and (later) distribution of wool. *See* Wool Purchase, Central Advisory Committees. *Repr.* W.O., other Government Departments, manufacturers and merchants (all sections from wool importers to cloth exporters), Labour. *Ref.* Cd. 8447, pp. 15, 23 ; B.T.J., 31st May 1917. *Diss.* Taken over by W.C.B., Sept. 1917.

WOOL, CONTRACT ALLOCATION, CENTRAL ADVISORY COMMITTEE.—*App.* by W.O. late in 1916. *Obj.* To advise on allocation of contracts to districts and manufacturers. *Repr.* Composed of Chairmen of Group Committees (q.v.). *Ref.* Cd. 8447, pp. 15, 24.

WOOL, CONTRACT ALLOCATION, GROUP ADVISORY COMMITTEES.—*App.* by W.O. in various manufacturing districts, in latter part of 1916. *Obj.* To allocate orders for cloth in their districts. *Repr.* Manufacturers in different sections of the industry. *Ref.* B.T.J., 4th July 1918.

(There appear also to have been Committees of trade representatives in each manufacturing town to co-operate with W.O. representative in securing fair distribution of Government orders. *See* Cmd. 788, p. 12.)

WOOL CONTROL.—*See* Wool Textile.

WOOL COUNCIL.—*App.* by A.C., Nov. 1918, following Trade Conference held at suggestion of M.R. *Obj.* To advise as to control during reconstruction and change-over from war to peace, and work out reconstruction scheme. *Repr.* Government Departments concerned, wool trade and commercial interests, Labour. *Ref.* Cmd. 325, p. 214 ; B.T.J., 28th Nov. 1918, pp. 672, 678.

(The Council at first meeting established Standing and Statistical Committees. The establishment of Sectional and Regional Committees was referred to Standing Committee. *See* B.T.J., 28th Nov. 1918, p. 672.)

WOOL DISTRIBUTION, SECTIONAL COMMITTEES.—*App.* by W.O., Dec. 1916. *Obj.* To advise on various aspects of distribution (top-making, imports, exports, &c.). *Repr.* Chosen from Wool Trade Advisory Panel (q.v.). *Ref.* Cd. 8447, p. 15. *Diss.* Merged into Wool Central Advisory Committee, April 1917. *See also* Wool Rationing.

WOOL, ECONOMIES, ADVISORY COMMITTEES.—*App.* by W.O. before June 1917. *Obj.* To advise on working of scheme for economies in transport and handling of wool and products, and in labour and materials. *Repr.* Farmers, Manufacturers, T.U.'s. *Ref.* Cd. 8447, p. 4.

WOOL EMERGENCY COMMITTEE OF CENTRAL WOOL ADVISORY COMMITTEE.—*App.* by Central Committee, May 1917. *Obj.* To act expeditiously in emergencies as required. *Repr.* Central Committee. *Ref.* T., 5th May 1917, p. 3.

WOOL, EXPORT OF SEMI-MANUFACTURED COMMODITIES, COMMITTEE.—*App.* by Wool Council in winter of 1918–19. *Obj.* To report upon classes of such commodities of which the export should be encouraged. *Repr.* Wool Council. *Ref.* B.T.J., 27th Mar. 1919, p. 409.

WOOL EXPORT, YARN RATIONING, COMMITTEE.—*App.* by W.C.B. about Oct. 1917. *Obj.* To allocate yarn available for civil purposes allotted to export trade. *Repr.* Not stated. *Ref.* B.T.J., 29th Nov. 1917.

WOOL EXPORT.—*See also* Wool Priority.

WOOLLEN AND WORSTED INDUSTRY LOCAL MAN POWER BOARDS.—*App.* by W.O. in chief centres of industry, Nov. 1916. *Obj.* To carry out policy of providing substitutes for men of military age in the industry. *Repr.* W.O., Employers and T.U.'s in the industry. *Ref.* T., 3rd Nov. 1916, p. 9. *Diss.* Apparently absorbed during 1917 in Trade Substitution Committees (*see* M.N.S.).

WOOLLEN GOODS, PRICES, COMMITTEE.—*App.* by various branches of the industry, at request of W.O., early in 1916. *Obj.* To negotiate with W.O. the price basis for purchase of goods at fixed ' conversion costs '. *Repr.* Manufacturers in branches concerned. *Ref.* L.Y.B., 1919, p. 171.

Diss. Presumably taken over by Wool Purchase Advisory Committee (q.v.), Aug. 1916.

WOOL, MANUFACTURERS' COMMITTEE.—*App.* under W.C.B., and attached to Wool Control at Bradford, in autumn of 1917. *Obj.* To allocate yarn to manufacturers and assist in dealing with questions affecting them. *Repr.* Trade interests concerned. *Ref.* B.T.J., 10th Jan. 1918.

WOOL NOILS FOR HAT MANUFACTURE, RATIONING COMMITTEE.—*App.* by W.O., in conjunction with W.C.B., Aug. 1918. *Obj.* To ration noils to hat manufacturers. *Repr.* Interests concerned. *Ref.* B.T.J., 29th Aug. 1918, p. 297.

WOOL PRIORITY, DISTRICT, COMMITTEES.—*App.* by W.O., May 1917, in six districts, covering whole woollen industry. *Obj.* To issue priority certificates under, and supervise, wool restriction scheme in their districts. *Repr.* Manufacturers and merchants (apparently). *Ref.* B.T.J., June 1917.

WOOL PRIORITY, EXPORT, COMMITTEE.—*App.* jointly by W.O. and B.T., by Mar. 1917. *Obj.* To consider whole problem and later distribute wool not required for military use for export work. *Repr.* Various sections of the industry, particularly those specially concerned. *Ref.* Cd. 8447 ; T., 14th Mar. 1917, p. 3.

WOOL PRIORITY, JOINT, COMMITTEE.—*App.* by A.C. by April 1917. *Obj.* To prepare, in consultation with W.O. and B.T., and operate wool priority scheme for U.K. *Repr.* Manufacturers and merchants. *Ref.* B.T.J., 26th April 1917.

WOOL PURCHASES, CENTRAL ADVISORY COMMITTEE, ENGLAND AND WALES.—*App.* by W.O., April 1916. *Obj.* To advise on purchase and (later) distribution of home wool, distribution being transferred to Wool Central Advisory Committee (q.v.), May 1917. *Repr.* Parliament, W.O., B.A., farmers, merchants, spinners, manufacturers, fellmongers, including special Welsh representatives. *Ref.* Cd. 8447, pp. 15, 23.

WOOL PURCHASES, ENGLAND AND WALES, LOCAL ADVISORY COMMITTEES.—*App.* by W.O. in thirteen districts, Aug. 1916. *Obj.* To assist W.O. representatives in purchases of wool. *Repr.* Farmers, merchants. *Ref.* B.T.J., 24th Aug. 1916.

WOOL PURCHASES, INTER-ALLIED, COMMITTEE.—*App.* jointly by chief Allied Governments, about end of 1917. *Obj.* To co-ordinate supply of wool and products (except cloth) for Allies. *Repr.* Governments concerned and Commission Internationale de Ravitaillement (*see* B.T.). *Ref.* Cd. 9005.

WOOL PURCHASES, IRELAND, ADVISORY COMMITTEE.—*App.* by W.O., in consultation with D.A.T.I., July 1916. *Obj.* To advise on purchases of wools in Ireland. *Repr.* Irish farmers, stock-owners, cattle traders, wool brokers, dealers, merchants, manufacturers. *Ref.* B.T.J., 27th July 1916 ; Cd. 8447, p. 23.

WOOL PURCHASES, SCOTTISH ADVISORY COMMITTEE.—*App.* by W.O. in or after Aug. 1916. *Obj.* To advise on purchase of Scottish wools. *Repr.* W.O., farmers, merchants, manufacturers. *Ref.* B.T.J., 14th June 1917 ; Cd. 8447, p. 23.

WOOL RATIONING, CARPET AND FELT TRADES, COMMITTEE.— *App.* under W.C.B. late in 1917. *Obj.* To consider questions affecting these trades, and allocate wool allotted to them. *Repr.* Carpet and felt trades. *Ref.* B.T.J., 10th Jan. 1918.

WOOL RATIONING COMMITTEE.—*App.* by W.O., apparently in spring of 1917. *Obj.* To allocate supplies of wool under, and carry out, rationing scheme. *Repr.* Presumably W.O. and trade interests concerned. *Ref.* B.T.J., 11th Oct. 1917. *Diss.* Apparently absorbed into Rationing Joint Committee (q.v.) about Oct. 1917.

WOOL RATIONING, DISTRICT, COMMITTEES.—*App.* by W.O., by Sept. 1917, probably under Wool Rationing Committee, for six Wool Textile districts, being sometimes called at first Wool Distribution Committees. *Obj.* To distribute fairly supplies of wool allocated to their districts. *Repr.* Trade interests involved. *Ref.* B.T.J., 10th Jan. 1918.

(The appointment of Sub-Committees, to deal with hard and special cases, was contemplated, *see* B.T.J., 10th Jan. 1918.)

WOOL RATIONING, JOINT COMMITTEE.—*App.* by W.C.B. about Oct. 1917, and apparently reconstituted early 1918. *Obj.* To ascertain supplies of wool available for civilian consumption and allocate them between different districts and between home and export trade. *Repr.* District, Carpet and Felt Trades', and Yarn Merchants', Rationing Committees ; Labour. *Ref.* B.T.J., 29th Nov. 1917 ; 10th Jan. 1918.

WOOL RATIONING.—*See also* Wool Export, Wool Noils.

WOOL, RAW, ADVISORY COMMITTEE.—Referred to incidentally, without details, in B.T.J., 17th Jan. 1918.

WOOL REALIZATION.—*See* M.M.

WOOL REGIONAL COMMITTEES.—*See under* Wool Council.

WOOL (REVIEW) SUB-COMMITTEE OF WOOL PURCHASE CENTRAL ADVISORY COMMITTEE.—*App.* by Central Committee, April 1917. *Obj.* To review whole wool position in light of recent wool census and need of building up reserve for military purposes. *Repr.* Various wool interests concerned. *Ref.* B.T.J., 26th April 1917 ; T., 5th May 1917, p. 3. *Diss.* May 1917.

WOOL SECTIONAL COMMITTEES.—*See under* Wool Council.

WOOL SPINNERS SECTIONAL COMMITTEE.—*App.* under W.C.B. late in 1917. *Obj.* To act for and under W.C.B. in rationing wool and tops to spinners. *Repr.* Trade interests concerned. *Ref.* B.T.J., 10th Jan. 1918.

WOOL, STANDARD ARTICLES, REPRESENTATIVE COMMITTEES. —Proposed scheme for limiting production to a number of standard products, with representative Committees of each branch of industry to work out details, referred to in T., 5th May 1917, p. 3.

WOOL STATISTICAL COMMITTEE.—*Ref.* without details, B.T.J., 7th July 1918. *See also under* Wool Council.

WOOL, SUGGESTIONS SUB-COMMITTEE.—*App.* by Wool, British, Central Committee, Jan. 1917. *Obj.* To consider suggestions from Local

Advisory Committees and other interested parties for dealing with British wool clip of 1917. *Repr.* The Committee, &c. *Ref.* T., 13th Jan. 1917, p. 3.

WOOL TEXTILE (CIVIL CONTRACTS) ARBITRATION PANEL.— *App.* by W.C.B., July 1918. *Obj.* To arbitrate in disputed questions respecting Government interference in civil contracts, and deal with applications for certificates under Courts (Emergency Powers) Act, 1917. *Repr.* W.O., top-makers, spinners, manufacturers, yarn merchants, hosiery and shoddy manufacturers. *Ref.* B.T.J., 4th July 1918.

WOOL TEXTILE MAN POWER COMMITTEE.—*App.* by W.C.B. in autumn of 1917. *Obj.* To advise upon, and deal with, release of men from the industry for military service. *Repr.* W.C.B., employers and workpeople. *Ref.* B.T.J., 4th July 1918.

WOOL TEXTILE PRODUCTION CONTROL BOARD.—*App.* by A.C., Sept. 1917, and sometimes known as Wool Control Board. *Obj.* To control production, allocation, &c., of wool, tops and bye-products, subsequently to the making of the tops, taking over existing Priority and various other Committees of the industry, and reviewing A.C. Orders affecting it. *Repr.* (equal numbers) W.O., employers, workpeople. *Ref.* B.T.J., 20th Sept. 1917.

WOOL TEXTILES, LOCAL CONTROL COMMITTEES.—*App.* by or through W.C.B., from Sept. 1917, in various districts. *Obj.* To assist W.C.B. locally in carrying out control, and distribute wool allotted to the district. *Repr.* W.O., employers, workpeople. *Ref.* B.T.J., 4th July 1918. Cd. 9005, p. 143 (where called Rationing Committees).

WOOL TEXTILES, SUBSTITUTION COMMITTEE.—*App.* by W.C.B. in autumn of 1917. *Obj.* To organize provision of substitutes for men joining the Forces. *Repr.* Generally as with W.C.B. *Ref.* B.T.J., 4th July 1918.

WOOL TRADE ADVISORY PANEL.—*App.* by A.C. in autumn of 1916. *Obj.* To form panel for selection of Sub-Committees to advise on various problems arising out of control and requisitioning of wool. *Repr.* Prominent members of industry. *Ref.* B.T.J., 4th Jan., 26th April 1917. *Diss.* Replaced by Wool, Central Advisory Committee, April 1917.

WOOL VALUATION, DOMINIONS, COMMITTEES.—*App.* by the Australian and New Zealand Governments, at request of W.O., about Nov. 1916. *Obj.* To organize purchase and valuation of local wool clips for British Government. *Repr.* Trade experts. *Ref.* Cd. 9005, p. 142. *Diss.* Apparently at close of 1916–17 season (*see* Wool, Australia, above).

WOOL, WORSTED.—*See under* Bradford, and Man Power and Production.

WOOL, YARN MERCHANTS, COMMITTEE.—*App.* under W.C.B. in autumn of 1917. *Obj.* To deal with questions affecting merchants under Wool Control. *Repr.* Merchants and mercantile interests. *Ref.* B.T.J., 10th Jan. 1918.

WOOL YARN.—*See also* Wool Export, Wool Manufacturers.

WAR TRADE DEPARTMENT

The *War Trade Department* was established by the Treasury under a minute of 17th Feb. 1915, under a Director and Secretary, owing to the growing complexity of the work of dealing with import and export licences. The *object* in the first place was to take over this branch of the work of the Trading with the Enemy Committee (*see* Board of Trade), and other duties were subsequently added. The remainder of the work of the Committee was transferred to the staff of the Parliamentary Counsel to the Treasury. The Department originally included the War Trade Intelligence and Statistical Departments (*see* below), which were transferred to the Overseas Trade Department in the autumn of 1917. The staff of the Department included a secretariat, and eventually thirteen Licensing Divisions for various classes of exports (*see* B.T.J., 25th Feb. 1915 and 29th Aug. 1918, for a full account of the work). The Department was transferred to the Board of Trade as the Export Licence Department in March 1919, and absorbed into the Industries and Manufactures Department of the Board in October 1919.

ABBREVIATION
W.T.D. = War Trade Department.

ADVISORY BOARD, WAR TRADE INTELLIGENCE DEPARTMENT. —*See* Intelligence.

BLACK LIST COMMITTEE.—*App.* by W.T.D. in 1915 or 1916. *Obj.* To deal with all cases of inclusion of firms in the Black Lists (trading prohibited). *Repr.* Official and expert. *Ref.* Cd. 9220, pp. 14–15.

BRUSHES AND BRUSHES FIBRE.—*See* Licensing Committees.

CONTRABAND COMMITTEE.—*See* F.O.

COTTON EXPORTS COMMITTEE.—*App.* by B.T., June 1915, on restriction of exports of cotton yarn and thread. *Obj.* To advise W.T.D. on grant of licences for export of raw cotton, cotton waste, yarns and thread under prohibitions in force. *Repr.* Cotton industry and interests, W.T.D. *Ref.* B.T.J., 1st July 1915. *Diss.* Absorbed into Export Licence Department of B.T., Mar. 1919.

DIAMOND EXPORT COMMITTEE.—*App.* by B.T., Aug. 1915, to work under W.T.D. *Obj.* To issue certificates for export of diamonds, not suitable for industrial use. *Repr.* Diamond merchants, traders. *Ref.* B.T.J., 5th Aug. 1915 ; 7th Nov. 1918, p. 581.

EAST INDIAN WOOL JOINT COMMITTEE.—*App.* by, or in co-operation with, W.T.D., by Dec. 1915. *Obj.* To deal with restrictions on export of such wool and grant certificates for export. *Repr.* Associations of importers, buyers and brokers concerned. *Ref.* B.T.J., 23rd Dec. 1919.

ENEMY SUPPLIES.—*See* B.T.

EXPORT LICENCE DEPARTMENT.—*App.* by P.C. early in the War and transferred to W.T.D., Feb. 1915. *Obj.* To issue export licences first for B.T. (Trading with the Enemy Committee) and then for W.T.D. *Repr.* Official and expert. *Ref.* B.T.J., 25th Feb. 1915, p. 528.

EXPORT LICENCE (SPECIAL DEPARTMENTS) SUB-COMMITTEES (THREE).—*App.* by W.T.D. in summer of 1915. *Obj.* To deal with applications for export licences specially affecting Adm., B.A., B.T., and (for certain goods only) W.O. *Ref.* B.T.J., 2nd Sept. 1915.

See also Licensing, below.

INTELLIGENCE, WAR TRADE, DEPARTMENT.—*App.* in connexion with W.T.D. in spring of 1915, and transferred to O.T.D. in 1917, though being also for a time partly under M.B. *Obj.* To advise, and collect information, on neutral and enemy trade generally. *Repr.* Official and expert. *Ref.* Cd. 8469, 9220 ; B.T.J., 29th Aug. 1918.

(The Department had an Advisory Board which was presumably comprised largely of business and other experts.)

LICENSING COMMITTEE (EXPORTS).—*App.* as part of organization of W.T.D. in Feb. or Mar. 1915. *Obj.* Originally to consider general questions involved in grant of licences, but, as work increased, much of it was delegated to Committees and Sub-Committees (*see* below), and the main Committee confined itself to questions of general policy or special importance. *Repr.* Government Departments concerned, trade experts. *Ref.* B.T.J., 29th Aug. 1918.

LICENSING (IMPORTS AND EXPORTS) COMMITTEE.—*Ref.* without details, Cd. 8741, p. 7. Possibly the same as the preceding Committee.

LICENSING, TRADE, COMMITTEES AND SUB-COMMITTEES.—*App.* by W.T.D. as required during the War (e.g. Wool Licensing Committee (q.v.), Brushes and Brush Fibre Sub-Committee), a total of twenty having been appointed up to Aug. 1918. *Obj.* To advise upon grant of licences and deal with details for particular exports. *Repr.* Government Departments concerned, trade experts. *Ref.* B.T.J., 29th Aug. 1918.

STATISTICAL, WAR TRADE, DEPARTMENT.—*See* M.B.

TRADE LICENSING.—*See* Licensing.

WAR TRADE ADVISORY COMMITTEE.—*App.* by, or in connexion with, W.T.D. in first half of 1916. *Obj.* To supervise, and assist W.T.D. in dealing with, work of Trade Licensing Committees and settle questions involving difficulty or general principles. *Repr.* Government Departments mainly concerned. *Ref.* Cd. 8741, p. 11.

WAR TRADE COMMITTEE.—*Ref.* without details, B.T.J., 25th Feb. 1915, p. 528.

WOOL LICENSING COMMITTEE.—*App.* by W.T.D., originally as Wool and Hair Licences Sub-Committee, April 1916. *Obj.* To consider applications to export wool, animal hair, and their products. *Repr.* Apparently trade experts and Government Departments concerned. *Ref.* B.T.J., 13th April 1916.

WOOL.—*See also* East Indian Wool.

WORKS, THE OFFICE OF

ABBREVIATION

O.W. = Works, Office of.

ACCOMMODATION, WAR DEPARTMENTS, INTER-DEPART-MENTAL COMMITTEE.—*App.* sanctioned by P.M., Jan. 1917. *Obj.* To determine allocation of accommodation during war, between war departments and departments not concerned directly with the War. *Repr.* Parliament, O.W., Adm., M.M., W.O. *Ref.* T., 25th Jan. 1917, p. 9.

EMPLOYMENT EXCHANGES, ACCOMMODATION.—*See* B.T.

IMPERIAL WAR MUSEUM.—*See* Cabinet.

TIMBER DEPARTMENTAL COMMITTEE.—*App.* by O.W. in 1914. *Obj.* To assist in dealing with work in connexion with timber. *Repr.* Apparently Departmental. *Ref.* H.C., No. 167, 1917, p. 2. *Diss.* Mar. 1917 (absorbed into Timber Supplies Department—*see* W.O., B.T.).

PRINTED IN ENGLAND AT THE UNIVERSITY PRESS, OXFORD
BY JOHN JOHNSON, PRINTER TO THE UNIVERSITY